HUNGARY

Szeged • •Arad

•Temesvar

RUMANIA

Dakovo

•Novi Sad •Deta
•Krusedol
Ruma
Zemun• •Pancevo
•Bjeljina Sabac• BELGRADE

•Ljesnica

Smed. Palanka• •Petrovac
Lazarevac

Knic •Kragujevac• •Cuprija
•Cacak
Kraljevo •Paracin

SERBIA
GOSLAVIA

•Nis
•Bela Palanka

ITENEGRO
•Niksic
•Botevgrad

Danilovgrad
•Kotor Podgorica
•Pristina
Scutari

•Urosevac
•Kumanovo

ALBANIA Tetovo •Skoplje
•Petrovac
Durazzo TIRANA Veles •Stip
•Elbasan MACEDONIA •Prilep
•Lushnje Pogradec Okhrid Strumica•
Monastir
•Fier •Berat (Bitolj)
Corovode Koritza• •Florina
Valona Biishte
Trebeshinj Kastoria MACEDONIA
•Dukati Kelcyre Leskoviku Neapolis
Himara •Premet

•Delvine Argyrokastron
grande Delvinakion

BULGARIA

SOFIA

•Kjustendil

Kriva
Palanka •Blagovgrad
•Kocani

Petrich
Rupel
Pass

R. Struma

•Edessa THESSALONIKI
•Perdika Verria •Salonika
•Ptolemais
•Kozani
Servia Katerini
Grevena Mt.
Olympus

Kassandra
Pen.

Lemnos

BLACK

SEA

•Edirne

ISTANBUL

SEA OF
MARMARA

THRACE

E Metsovon Pass
P Yanina
I Paramythia
R Arta
U Parga
S Prevesa

Corfu

GREECE

Paxoi

Levkas

Cephalonia

Zante

Kalambaka •Elasson
•Tirnavos
Larissa
•Trikkala Niamata
Volos

•Domokos
Almyros

•Lamia

Amphiklia •Molos
Mt. Thermopylae
Agrinion Parnassus •Dadion
Missolonghi Lepanto• Topolia
Patras Gulf of Corinth •Khalkis
Megara
Corinth Eleusis Tatoi
Argos Piraeus ATHENS
Mylol Nauplia Raphtis
Lavrion
•Sparta
Kythos
Molaoi
MIRTOAN Melos
•Monemvasia SEA
•Neapolis
C. Matapan
Kythera

PELOPONNESE

AEGEAN

SEA

TURKEY

Khios

CYCLADES

Leros

Kos

D
O
D
E
C
A
N
E
S
E

Rhodes

Antikythera
Antikythera Channel
Kissamos Bay C. Spada
Kastelli Galatas Suda Bay
Sphakia Retimo
Stilnos CRETE

SEA OF CRETE

Kasos Str.

Scarpanto

Kaso

C. Plaka

0 25 50 75   100 miles
0 25 50 75 100 kilometres

AIR WAR FOR YUGOSLAVIA GREECE AND CRETE 1940-41

Christopher Shores and Brian Cull
with Nicola Malizia

AIR WAR FOR YUGOSLAVIA GREECE AND CRETE 1940-41

Christopher Shores and Brian Cull
with Nicola Malizia

Published by
Grub Street
Golden House
28–31 Great Pulteney St
London W1

Copyright © 1987 Grub Street, London
Text copyright © 1987 Christopher Shores, Brian Cull, Nicola Malizia

Maps by Graham Andrews

Shores, Christopher
    Air war for Yugoslavia, Greece and Crete:
    1940–41.
    1. World War, 1939–1945—Aerial operations
    2. World War, 1939–1945—Campaigns—
    Yugoslavia 3. World War, 1939–1945—
    Campaigns—Greece 4. World War, 1939–1945
    —Campaigns—Greece—Crete
    I. Title II. Cull, Brian III. Malizia,
    Nicola
    940.54′21   D792.Y8

    ISBN 0-948817-07-0

Photoset and printed in Malta by Interprint Limited

CONTENTS

Tables

Acknowledgements

The authors wish to express their grateful thanks to a large number of persons who have assisted with their research, and without whose contribution this book would not have been possible. They also wish to acknowledge permission to quote from "Wings Over Olympus" by T H Wisdom (Allen & Unwin) and "Operation Mercury" by M G Comeau (William Kimber).

Contributors (Royal Air Force)

Wg Cdr E A Howell, OBE, DFC (33 Sqn); Wg Cdr V C Woodward, DFC (33 Sqn); Flt Lt D S F 'Bill' Winsland, DFC (33 Sqn) for use of much original material; Air Vice Marshal E G Jones, DSO, DFC (80 Sqn); Gen Paul Jacquier (274 Sqn); Flt Lt R I Laing, DFC (73 Sqn); Air Comm D F Rixson, OBE, DFC, AFC (113 Sqn); Eric Bevington-Smith (211 Sqn); Tom Henderson (211 Sqn); Albert Marteau (att'd 24(SAAF)Sqn; S W Lee (113 Sqn).

Next of kin

Mrs Kay Vale (widow of Sqn Ldr W Vale, DFC, 80 Sqn) including photocopied pages of logbook; Mrs Angela Acworth (widow of Sqn Ldr R A Acworth, DFC, 112 Sqn); Mrs Katharine Noel-Johnson (widow) and Mr Clive Noel-Johnson (son) of Flt Lt G D Noel-Johnson, 33 Sqn; Mrs Joan Hubbold (widow of Flg Off A F Butterick, 33 Sqn); Mr Geoffrey Hill (brother) and Mr Clifford Davis (cousin) of Sgt Vernon Hill, 33 Sqn.

Contributors (Fleet Air Arm)

Capt A F Black, DSC (805 Sqn); Maj L A Harris, DSC (805 Sqn); Lt Cdr J A Shuttleworth (805 Sqn); Lt Cdr D H Coates (805 Sqn); Lt Cdr R W M Walsh (805 Sqn); Lt R V Hinton (805 Sqn); W J Newman (805 Sqn); Vice Adm Sir Donald Gibson, KCB, DSC, JP (803 Sqn); Cdr D J Godden (803 Sqn); Lt Cdr F J L de Frias, DSM (803 Sqn); F P Dooley (803 Sqn); T S Melling (803 Sqn); Capt D Vincent-Jones, DSC (806 Sqn);Lt Cdr R MacDonald-Hall (806 Sqn); Cdr R S Henley, OBE, DSC (806 Sqn); Lt Cdr H Phillips (806 Sqn); Capt F M A Torrens-Spence, DSO, DSC, AFC (815 Sqn); Lt Cdr P N Beagley (815 Sqn); Lt K Sims, DSM (815 Sqn) (including kind permission to use extracts from unpublished m/s); N Hollis (HMS *Glasgow*).

Other Contributors

Andrew Stamatopoulos of Corfu, Greece (contributor of material re EVA and in checking m/s for spellings of Greek locations); Hellenic Air Force Historical Section, Athens; Zoran Jerin of Ljubljana, Yugoslavia (contributor of material re JKRV); Winfried Bock, München, Germany (contributor of material re Luftwaffe); Staff of Public Record Office, Kew, London; Staff of RAF Museum Archives, Hendon, London; Staff of Imperial War Museum, London; Air Cdr H Probert and Staff of Air Historical Branch (RAF 5), Ministry of Defence; Fleet Air Arm Officers Association, London; TAG Association (via Ken Sims); Royal Marines Museum, Southsea, Hants; WASt, Berlin; Amicale Des Forces Aeriennes Francaises Libres (the late G E Durand).

Bruce Lander of Oldham (and Eddie Pearson) for much appreciated assistance and encouragement; Paul Sortehaug of Dunedin, New Zealand and Ian Primmer of Thornton, NSW, Australia for varied contributions; FAA historians David Brown and Ray Sturtivant; Chris Ehrengardt re Free French aircrew. Our Maltese friends Philip Vella and Louis Tortell offered much help, the latter in reproducing many of the photographs used in the book.

Nicola Malizia offers personal thanks to Ufficio Storico dello Stato Maggiore Aeronautica, Ufficio Propaganda e Fotografico dello SMAM, Ufficio Storico Marina Militare Italiana, Ambasciata di Grecia in Italia. Prof Nicola Pignato, Carlo Lucchini, Giorgio Di Giorgio.

Brian Cull offers personal thanks to his good friend and neighbour Dick Rees, and to Mr Jack Lee (in the beginning ... !). And to staff of Bury St. Edmunds Library for obtaining many 'hard-to-find' relevant books.

Christopher Shores, Hendon
Brian Cull, Bury St. Edmunds
Nicola Malizia, San Arcangelo di Romagna
March 1987

COMPARATIVE RANKS OF THE CONTESTING AIR FORCES

Royal Air Force & Commonwealth	Fleet Air Arm	Royal Hellenic Air Force (EVA)
Sergeant (Sgt)	Petty Officer (Pty Off)	Episminias (Sgt)
Flight Sergeant (F/Sgt)	Chief Petty Officer (C/Pty Off)	Archisminias (F/Sgt)
Warrant Officer (Wt Off)	Warrant Officer (Wt Off)	Anthypaspistes (Wt Off)
Pilot Officer (Plt Off)	Midshipman (Midspmn)	Anthyposminagos (2/Lt)
Flying Officer (Flg Off)	Sub Lieutenant (Sub Lt)	Hiposminagos (1/Lt)
Flight Lieutenant (Flt Lt)	Lieutenant (Lt)	Sminagos (Capt)
Squadron Leader (Sqn Ldr)	Lieutenant Commander (Lt Cdr)	Epismingos (Maj)
Wing Commander (Wg Cdr)	Commander (Cdr)	Antisminarchos (Lt Col)
Group Captain (Grp Capt)	Captain (Capt)	Sminarchos (Col)
Air Commodore (Air Comdr)	Commodore (Comdr)	Taxiarchos

Royal Yugoslav Air Force (*JRKV*)	*Luftwaffe*	*Regia Aeronautica*
Podnarednik (Sgt)	Unteroffizier (Uffz)	Sergente (Serg)
Narednik (F/Sgt)	Feldwebel (Fw)	Sergente Maggiore (Serg Magg)
Narednik Vodnik (Wt Off)	Oberfeldwebel (Obfw)	Maresciallo (Mar)
Potporucnik (2/Lt)	Leutnant (Lt)	Sottotenente (Sottoten)
Porucnik (1/Lt)	Oberleutnant (Oblt)	Tenente (Ten)
Kapetan (Capt)	Hauptman (Hpt)	Capitano (Cap)
Major (Maj)	Major (Maj)	Maggiore (Magg)
Potpukovnik (Lt Col)	Oberstleutnant (Obstlt)	Tenente Colonello (Ten Col)
Pukovnik (Col)	Oberst (Obst)	Colonello (Col)
Brigadni General	Generalmajor	Generale di Brigata Aerea

Chapter One

THE ITALIAN ATTACK ON GREECE

The PZL P.24 formed the backbone of the Greek fighter force in 1940. A newly-built example is seen here shortly after delivery to the Elleniki Vassiliki Aeroporia (EVA). (*Greek Embassy via N Malizia*)

Early on 28 October 1940, Joannis Metaxas, Prime Minister of Greece, issued a Proclamation to the people of his nation:

'The moment has come for us to fight for independence, for the integrity, and for the honour of Greece. Although we have observed the strictest neutrality, with absolute impartiality towards all, Italy, denying to us the right to live the life of free Hellenes, demanded from me at 3 o'clock this morning the surrender of portions of the national territory, to be chosen by herself, and informed me that

1

her troops would move forward at 6 a.m. in order to take possession. I replied to the Italian Minister that I considered both the demand itself and the manner of its delivery as a declaration of war on the part of Italy against Greece. It is now for us to show whether we are indeed worthy of our ancestors and of the freedom won for us by our forefathers. Let the entire nation rise as one man. Fight for your country, for your wives, for your children, and for our sacred traditions. Now the struggle is for very existence.'

The Prime Minister's Proclamation was followed by one from George II, King of the Hellenes:

'The Prime Minister announced to you a short while ago the circumstances which have compelled us to go to war in reply to Italy's threat to suppress the independence of Greece. At this solemn moment I am confident that every Greek man and woman will do their duty to the last and will show themselves worthy of our glorious past. With faith in God and in the destiny of the Race, the Nation, united and disciplined as one man, will fight in defence of hearth and home until final victory. Given at the Palace of Athens, October 28th 1940.'

Before long the General Staff had issued their First War Communique:

'Since 5.30 this morning Italian military forces have been attacking our advanced units on the Greco-Albanian frontier. Our forces are defending the soil of the country.'

Indeed Greece was under attack, and from the Ionian coast to Koritza more than 100 000 men began moving over the frontier from Albania. Seven of the best divisions of the Italian army, with support forces, were faced by three ill-equipped Greek divisions; the result seemed a foregone conclusion. Overhead patrolled fighters from the 160° Gruppo Autonomo CT of the Regia Aeronautica, operating from their base at the forward airfields at Koritza. Soon after 1000 hours a trio of Fiat CR 42 biplanes from this unit's 393ª Squadriglia began their patrol from the area of Drenowa, during which they spotted their first Greek aircraft. It was a Henschel Hs126, a high-wing army co-operation machine from 3 Mira Stratiotikis Synergassias (Ground Support Squadron) of the Elleniki Vassiliki Aeroporia (Royal Hellenic Air Force). Tenente Mario Gaetano Carancini, leader of the Italian formation, attacked at once and shot the Henschel down east of Darda. Although the crew survived unhurt, the Elleniki Vassiliki Aeroporia (EVA) had suffered its first combat loss as Greece was dragged unwillingly into the morass of World War II. A new Balkan war had erupted which was to have critical effects on the course of military operations throughout Europe and North Africa thereafter.

But why had inoffensive Greece been subjected to this onslaught? Few of the normal economical, political and military considerations usually associated with such actions appear to fit Italy's action in opening up a third war front; the cause appears to have been almost entirely connected with the ego of the Italian Fascist Dictator, Benito Mussolini – 'Il Duce'.

There was however a historical background. Following the end of the Balkan

Wars of the early 20th Century, the Great Powers had used their influence to bring about the creation of an independent Kingdom of Albania. Poor, backward, and with few natural resources, this infant state was still in a condition of confusion and internal strife when events elsewhere in the Balkans precipitated the outbreak of the First World War. The Italians at once took the opportunity to occupy the port and capital city of Valona, while Greek troops moved back into the Northern Epirus district, which they had but recently evacuated at the insistence of Italy and Austria.

During May 1916 Fort Rupel in Eastern Macedonia was surrendered to the Bulgarians, providing the Italians, who were then allies of France and Great Britain, the opportunity to oust the Greek troops from Northern Epirus once more, extending their own line up to Koritza, which had been occupied by the French. Allied machinations to bring Greece formally into the war led in June 1917 to demands by the French and British for the abdication of King Constantine of the Greeks, and the independence of Albania as an Italian protectorate was declared. The Italians then advanced into Southern Epirus, occupying Yanina, but this new move upset their more powerful allies, and following pressure at the Allied Conference in Paris, they withdrew a month later. Their interest in the Epirus as a whole was now well established however, and was seen by them as an Italian sphere of influence.

By 1923 the delineation of the Greco-Albanian frontier was still in dispute. While motoring through Greek territory at this time the Italian President of the International Commission, Generale Tellini and four of his staff were killed by unknown assassins, creating a 'cause celebre'. In the following year Mussolini came to power and one of his first acts was to demand official apologies; the

Most numerous type in service with the Greek naval air service in 1940 was the Dornier Do.22G reconnaissance-bomber, used by 12 Mira. A pre-delivery example is seen here with its alternative wheeled undercarriage fitted in place of floats. In this modified form some of these aircraft would subsequently supplement Breguet XIXs on army co-operation duties. (*via A Stamatopoulos*)

3

rendering of military honours to the Italian flag by the Greek fleet; the holding of an enquiry by an Italian officer at the scene of the murders with capital punishment for all found guilty, and an indemnity of 50 000 000 Italian lire (£500 000) to be paid within five days. Not surprisingly, the Greek Government agreed only to the first two of the demands, and in consequence on 31 August, 1924 Mussolini ordered the Italian fleet to bombard Corfu, prior to occupation of the island by his troops. Sixteen inhabitants were killed and others wounded, but the International Commission of Enquiry demanded immediate Italian withdrawal, to which Mussolini acceded. Responsibility for the killings of Tellini and his staff was never ascertained; the Greek press blamed the Albanian Government of Ahmed Zogu (later to become King Zog at the instigation of the Italians), whilst Albania blamed Greece.

Italian designs on Albania developed into wholesale annexation in 1939. On Good Friday five warships bombarded Durazzo, while aircraft of the Regia Aeronautica dropped leaflets on Tirana, inviting the population to offer no resistance to occupying Italian forces. On 16 April, King Victor Emmanuel of Italy accepted the Crown of Albania.

A little over a year later Mussolini led his nation into World War II, just in time to move over the north-western frontier into France before the cessation of hostilities between that demoralized nation and Hitler's victorious Germany. By then Germany's great military success and unquestioned power had altered the balance between the two states; no longer was Mussolini the senior partner of the fascist alliance, and that rankled. He now desired to improve the standing of his regime in Europe, but how to do this was the problem. Virtually cut off from home by the presence of the British in Egypt, the Sudan and Kenya, his Empire in East Africa was under dire threat. Malta had not been subdued, despite frequent bombing attacks; the Italian fleet hardly risked leaving harbour due to the presence of the powerful British Mediterranean Fleet, while in Libya the first halting offensive into Egypt launched by Generale Graziani's army swiftly ground to a stop.

With so many fronts unresolved it would appear to most observers that another active area of military operations was most undesirable. However Mussolini wanted a decisive result, and preferably something with which he could present Berlin with a 'fait accompli', as he felt Hitler had done with him on too many occasions. Already in July 1940 the High Command had been ordered to plan operations necessary to deal with any hostile moves by Yugoslavia, and for this the occupation of certain of the Ionian Islands (Corfu, Levkas, Cephalonia and Zante) and a portion of north-eastern Epirus was greatly to be desired. These plans were developed into two distinct operations: Esigenza (Exigency) 'E' dealt with actions against Yugoslavia, and Esigenza 'G' with operations against Greece. The justification for these plans was given as the hostile attitude to Italy perceived in public opinion in these countries, and their increasing sympathy towards the British cause.

At the same time a number of provocations towards Greeks occurred, some of which were clearly accidental, but others of which were quite the reverse. On 8 July, 1940 a Savoia S.79 bomber from the 41° Gruppo BT at Brindisi force-landed on Crete, the crew being interned. Four days later three Italian aircraft bombed and machine-gunned the Greek lighthouse-tender *Orion*, and then attacked the destroyer *Ydra* when it came to the former's assistance. General Metaxas protested strongly to the Italian Legation, but ironically three days later the Legation contacted him to express thanks to the Greek authorities for aid rendered to the crew of an Italian seaplane forced to ditch near Cephalonia.

One of four British-built aircraft types employed by the EVA in 1940 was the Avro Anson I maritime reconnaissance-bomber of 13 Mira. (*A Stamatopoulos*)

British warships were of course in action against Italian vessels by this time, and on occasion mistaken identity could occur. This however could not have been the case early in August when the Greek destroyers *King George* and *Queen Olga* were bombed in the Gulf of Corinth, and two Greek submarines lying in the port of Lepanto were also attacked. On 15 August the Greek light cruiser *Helle* was torpedoed by an unidentified submarine whilst in harbour at Tenos for the Festival of Assumption. One torpedo struck amidships, killing one member of the crew and wounding 29 others, the vessel sinking at 0945. Two further torpedoes missed the ship and exploded against the pier where one Armenian woman died from a heart attack and several other people were slightly injured. At 1820 that same day two Italian aircraft machine-gunned the old Brindisi packet-boat *Frinton* two miles off the coast of Crete. All responsibility for these actions was flatly denied by the Italian authorities, but after the war records disclosed that the vessel responsible was indeed their submarine *Delfino*.

Convinced by flatterers and manipulators in his entourage, Mussolini was by now firmly resolved to move against the Greeks, fully believing that victory would be swift and cheap. His slogan 'We'll break Greece's ribs!' (Spezzeremo le reni alla Grecia) epitomized this view, as he prepared for a 'coup de main', planned for 26 October. In readiness for this, between 10 and 20 September, an Expeditionary Corps was despatched from Brindisi to reinforce the existing garrison, totalling 40 310 troops, 7728 horses, 701 vehicles and 33 535 tons of supplies.

Although surprised by the order to prepare for war with Greece, the local commanders did nothing to dissaude him. The prospects of easy victories with resulting promotions, honours and glories proved too strong in appeal to them. Yet Albania was far from being an ideal place from which to launch such a venture. Due to Italy's own economic situation, little had been done to develop the military facilities of the country, where communications were poor, ports and airfields inadequate. The long-term plan had indeed been to transform the country, but little success in this had yet been achieved due both to the hostility of the environment and of the populace. Much money was now poured in at the last moment to improve the situation, particularly that of the airfields, but most of the expenditure proved ill-founded and of little real effect.

The arrival of three additional infantry divisions — 29th, 49th and 51st — in Albania during 1940 greatly alarmed the Greek Government following the other provocations. In consequence the garrisons on the Albanian frontier were

The uneven, muddy airfields of Albania frequently required that the neat wheel fairings fitted to the Regia Aeronautica's Fiat CR 42 fighters be removed for operations. Aircraft 7 of 363ª Squadriglia, 150° Gruppo Autonomo CT is seen here so modified at Tirana in late 1940. (*N. Malizia*)

strengthened with additional infantry units. The Italians were also seeking to strengthen their air force element in the country, the Comando Aeronautica Albania, from its base of 61 operational aircraft at the start of the year. The main constraint, as stated above, was the availability of airfields, six of which had been constructed, or were being completed, at Tirana, Valona, Durazzo, Argyrokastron, Koritza and Berat. A few emergency landing grounds and poor grass strips were available at Shjac, Scutari, Devoli and Drenowa, but these lacked nearly all facilities and had few buildings. Close to the frontier Argyrokastron and two other strips at Delvine and Pogradec were suitable only for the operation of the light reconnaissance aircraft of the Osservazione Aerea.

At the outbreak of hostilities 394ª Squadriglia of the 160° Gruppo Autonomo CT at Koritza was still equipped with elderly Fiat CR32 fighters of Spanish Civil War vintage, one of which is seen here. (*G Bagnari via N Malizia*)

As plans progressed into October, the Comando still possessed only a single under-strength fighter unit, the 160° Gruppo Autonomo CT based at Tirana, equipped with five CR42 and twelve CR32 – all biplanes, plus three Fiat G.50bis monoplane fighters. At Tirana the 393ª and 394ª Squadriglia of this Gruppo flew the CR32s, while the 395ª Squadriglia operated the CR42s from Berat. More CR42s and G.50bis were due to arrive to replace the elderly CR32s however, and on 17 October the unit was reorganized, 393ª Squadriglia taking over the CR42s, while the 395ª took over the monoplanes. Two days later the two biplane-equipped squadriglie were ordered forward to Drenowa, near Koritza, while towards the end of the month three more squadriglie of CR42s were ordered to Albania from Italy; they would arrive on 1 November.

7

For the invasion the Italians divided the frontier, some 90 miles in length, into three sectors. The first of these – the Epirus – ran from the sea to Yanina, and was to be the zone of operations of the 23rd 'Ferrara' Division of Mountain Infantry, the 51st 'Siena' Division, the 'Centauro' Armoured Division, the 6th, 7th and 19th Regiments of Cavalry and the 3rd Regiment of Grenadiers, backed by eighteen batteries of heavy artillery. This powerful force was faced by the Greek 8th Division. The Central Sector – the Pindus – encompassed the peaks of the Pindus Mountains which ran from Albania right through Northern Greece from north-west to south-east. Here the 3rd 'Julia' Division of Italy's 'crack' Alpini troops were backed by a machine-gun battalion and a large contingent of mountain artillery. They were faced by a single regiment of Evzones – Greece's famous kilted mountain troops – with a single battery of artillery. The third, Eastern Sector, ran to the Yugoslav frontier, encompassing the area bordered by Koritza on the Albanian side of the frontier and Florina on the Greek side. Here, in less mountainous terrain, was the 16th army Corps of the 9th Army, comprised of the 19th 'Venezia', 29th 'Piedmonte' and 49th 'Parma' Divisions, three battalions of Albanian troops, the 101st Machine-Gun Battalion, fourteen batteries of heavy artillery and a regiment of tanks. To face the 16th Corps was the Greek 9th Division, reinforced by one additional brigade of infantry. The Greeks had no tanks, were low on machine-guns, mortars and other support weapons, including anti-tank and anti-aircraft guns, and were supplied almost entirely by mule over poor roads and mountain tracks from railroads further south.

The Greeks were backed by an air force of some 150 operational aircraft, but this was virtually without reserves, and had to guard the whole country, so could not operate in its entirety on the Albanian frontier. Equipment was heterogeneous in the variety and nationality of types used, so that maintenance and

Ready for action! Fully-camouflaged PZL P.24 fighters are lined up in front of the Henschel Hs126A army co-operation aircraft of 3 Mira. (*via A Stamatopoulos*)

supply during sustained operations would produce major problems. Aircraft purchased in recent years included:

  6 Avia B-534 fighters acquired in 1937 from Czechoslovakia
30 PZL P.24F and 6 P.24G fighters acquired in 1938 from Poland
  2 Gloster Gladiator I fighters acquired in 1938 from Great Britain
16 Henschel Hs126 army co-operation aircraft acquired from Germany
12 Dornier Do22G floatplanes acquired from Germany
12 Avro Anson I maritime patrol bombers acquired from Great Britain
11 Potez 63 light bombers acquired from France (24 ordered but 13 taken over by the Armee de l'Air on the outbreak of war in September 1939)
12 Fairey Battle I light bombers acquired from Great Britain
12 Bristol Blenheim IV bombers acquired from Great Britain
  9 Bloch MB151 fighters acquired from France

These were backed by a number of older biplane reconnaissance-bomber types, principally Breguet XIX and Potez 25 machines, and by a number of training types. As will be seen from the Order of Battle (Table 2) nearly all available aircraft were in use.

Within a few days of the commencement of hostilities the Comando Aeronautica Albania would have 187 relatively modern aircraft available to undertake three main duties:

(a) To provide support to the ground forces and to take part in the proposed occupation of Corfu;
(b) To maintain air offensive against airfields in the Epirus, Thessalonika and Macedonia, against military ports at Preveza and in Thessalonika, and against the main lines of communication; and
(c) To provide air defence of Albanian territory, particularly the fleet bases at Valona and Durazzo.

This disparity of strengths does not appear great at first sight, but the Italians could look to a ready supply of replacement aircraft and spare parts, coupled with reinforcement when necessary. More importantly, the Comando was backed up by the Comando 4ª Zona Aerea Territoriale based at airfields in south-east Italy from which the powerful bomber forces of this Commando could maintain attacks on the airfields and naval bases of Western Greece and the Ionian islands. It could also provide direct support to the ground forces in the Epirus when necessary, could contribute to operations against any British occupation of Crete, and could join in any operations on Corfu. Additionally, its fighters provided a secure defence of the ports of embarkation to the war zone at Taranto, Bari and Brindisi. Finally in the Dodecanese Islands to the south-east of Greece, was the Aeronautica Dell'Egeo which could also intrude over Crete and disrupt any supply lines set up through the Aegean from the British bases in Egypt to Southern Greece. And of course the 5ª Squadra Aerea in Libya could also interfere with any support offered by the British. The Regia Aeronautica's Order of Battle (Table 1) demonstrates well the power of the forces immediately ready for action over Greek territory.

The Regia Aeronautica had had a narrow escape nonetheless. On 26 October, two days before the outbreak of hostilities, three ships loaded with vital air force equipment had sailed from Bari for Valona. Just short of the destination, a British submarine put a torpedo into the SS *Chisone*, and the vessel came to a halt. At once the other ships, *Hermada* and *Olympus*, were ordered to return to base, but in the event the damaged *Chisone* was subsequently towed into Valona harbour without any loss of her precious cargo.

The initial Italian advance was in such strength that it sent the Greek forces on the frontier reeling back, particularly in the Epirus sector. Here the Italians claimed to have advanced up to 30 miles inside the country by 30 October, after the Greeks had retreated behind the Kalamas river. In the Pindus Mountains the Alpine of the 3rd 'Julia' Division were to get within 12 miles of the vital Metsovon Pass, but across the whole front the first four days of fighting were marked by foul weather conditions which slowed down the Italian supply convoys over the poor Albanian mountain tracks, and above all, restricted air support. This was particularly so in respect to the units of 4ª ZAT in south-eastern Italy, which hardly appeared at all during these opening days.

Immediately on the outbreak of war the former Chief of Staff of the Greek Army, 57 year-old Athenian General Alexander Papagos, was appointed Commander-in-Chief. A hero of past Balkan wars, and a regular adviser of the King, Papagos was quick to rush reinforcements to the front and to prepare counter-attacks. The first of these was launched in the Central Sector as early as 31 October, to regain a hill to the north of Yanina.

A formation of Savoia S.79 bombers from the 104º Gruppo Autonomo **BT**'s 253ª Squadriglia over the Epirus mountains, displaying a variety of camouflage patterns. (*N Malizia*)

After the initial clash in the air on 28 October, between the CR42s and the lone Hs126, eight Savoia S.81 bombers from the 38° Stormo BT carried out their first raids on the Doliana-Kalibaki road during the early afternoon, led by Col Ludovico, the commanding officer. The first foray for 4ª ZAT units followed, as 13 Cant Z.1007bis bombers of the 47° Stormo approached, joined by Fiat BR20s and S.81s of the 37° Stormo, and by some S.79s of the Albanian-based 105° Gruppo Autonomo BT. Over Patras AA fire hit one of the slow S.81s, and it subsequently force-landed near Otranto, being written-off in doing so.

Weather put a stop to all activity in the air on 29 October, but next day aircraft of both sides were in the air over the front again. Greek Hs126s of 3 Mira carried out repeated sorties over the Kastoria area of north-west Greece in the Epirus sector, where Italian fighters on patrol hunted for them. Early in the day a trio of CR32s of 394ª Squadriglia were scrambled from Koritza, intercepting a pair of Henschels, but Ten Mario Frascadore, the formation leader, suffered a guns stoppage, and the reconnaissance aircraft escaped into cloud. Somewhat later Ten Col Zanni, commander of the 160° Gruppo, led off five CR42s of 393ª Squadriglia, and these also encountered a pair of Henschels as they were making for the lines. Serg Magg Walter Ratticchieri at once attacked and shot down one, while Ten Col Zanni gained hits on the other before it escaped into cloud, obviously heavily damaged; the Henschel gunners had put up a spirited defence, several of the Fiats suffering damage from return fire. However both Greek aircraft were lost; one, flown by 1/Lt Evangelos Yiannaris, crashed near the village of Vassiliada, where the pilot was killed – the EVA's first official casualty of the war; the other failed to return, but its fate was not discovered, 2/Lt Lazaros Papamichael and Cpl Constantinos Gemenetris being posted missing.

Another older type used by the Italians over Greece in 1940 was the Savoia S.81 bomber of the Valona-based 38° Stormo BT. (*N Malizia*)

11

Continued bad weather on the last day of the month again restricted operations considerably. During the morning ten S.81s of the 38° Stormo BT set out to bomb targets at the front, but the crews could see nothing through the dense cloud and returned. A repeat attempt by three of the bombers during the afternoon met similar conditions. CR 32 and CR 42 fighters of the 160° Gruppo CT did get through to strafe the airfields at Florina and Kastoria, but a late afternoon operation ended badly for the unit. Scrambled at 1730 after Greek aircraft reported over Bilishte, two CR 32s of 394ª Squadriglia became lost in bad weather and gathering dusk, and both pilots were obliged to bale out, Ten Dino Ciarlo becoming a prisoner, although Mar Marcello Lui managed to return to Koritza on foot.

At last on 1 November the weather cleared sufficiently to allow a more active role to be played by the Regia Aeronautica. On an early patrol three CR 32s of 394ª Squadriglia encountered two slow-flying Greek reconnaissance aircraft over the frontier. Led by Frascadore, the Italian pilots attacked repeatedly, claiming many hits, and believed that they had probably shot down both aircraft within Greek territory. It appears that on this occasion their opponents were Breguet XIXs of 2 Mira, both of which were apparently lost, although the crews survived unhurt.

Breguet XIX army co-operation biplane of the EVA – the oldest type in use over the front in 1940. (*S W Lee*)

It was to be a day for famous names, for at 0835 ten S.79s of the 105° Gruppo Autonomo BT set off to attack Salonika, led by the gruppo commander, Ten Col Galeazzo Ciano, Mussolini's son-in-law and Italian Foreign Minister. Escort was provided by five 160° Gruppo CR 42s from 393ª Squadriglia, these led by Magg Angelo Mastragostino. Four more of this unit's fighters provided escort for ten Italy-based Z.1007bis of the 47° Stormo, which also headed for Salonika but also

12

bombing Larissa airfield en route. One of these bombers was piloted by Mussolini's eldest son, Cap Bruno Mussolini, who was commander of the Stormo's 260ª Squadriglia, while it is believed that a second son, Vittorio, was also involved in this attack. (Ciano and the Mussolini brothers had all flown previously on operations in both Ethiopia and Spain.)

A line of PZL P.24s of 22 Mira await another scramble in defence of the northern port-city of Salonika. (*Greek Embassy via N Malizia*)

The initial attack by the 105° Gruppo was aimed at the docks at Salonika, but seven PZL P.24 fighters from 22 Mira at the city's Sedes airfield intercepted. The escorting fighters claimed one of the Greek interceptors shot down and one probable, gunners in the S.79s claiming one more and a second probable also, one CR 42 sustaining damage during the fight. Any losses suffered by the defenders are unknown although no pilots were killed or wounded. The second raid was also engaged by PZLs, this time from 21 Mira, the pilots of which claimed one Z.1007bis shot down north of Yanina. They had in fact damaged an aircraft of 263ª Squadriglia, which managed to regain its base. Salonika suffered 35 of its citizens killed during these two attacks.

Towards evening three Blenheims from 32 Mira made their first raid, an attack on the two airfields at Koritza. Drenowa escaped damage, but Koritza itself was hard hit, 15 personnel being killed and 20 wounded. The Greeks believed that they had destroyed many aircraft, but none in fact suffered damage during the

13

Ground crew prepare a blenheim IV bomber of the EVA's 32 Mira for a raid. This is B261. (*Greek Embassy via N Malizia*)

bombing. However soon after the attacks a CR 42 and a CR 32, arriving from Tirana, crashed into bomb craters whilst landing, and both were damaged. During the return flight one of the Blenheims became lost in the dark, but soon fires were spotted on the ground, which the pilot assumed to be an improvised flare path at his base at Larissa, set up to aid his landing. In fact he landed in a field where peasants had been burning old grass! The bomber was undamaged, but the crew were confronted by the peasants who believed them to be Greek-speaking Italians! At first nothing would persuade them otherwise, not even the national markings on the Blenheim. The peasants stated repeatedly that the Italians were carrying duplicates on their own aircraft. This fallacy stemmed from the fact that at a distance the white cross displayed on rudders of Italian aircraft did indeed look like a Greek flag. Laymen were not aware at this time that Greek military aircraft carried no national markings on fin or rudder, or that they did carry blue-white-blue stripes on the rudder. The press and official communiques had stated on the radio that Italian bombers displaying the Greek flag on their tails had bombed Patras, Salonika and Corfu. Finally one of the crew, Lt K Maravelias, sang and danced a Greek folk dance, which at last convinced the peasants, who soon joined in!

1 November also noted the arrival in Albania of the 150° Gruppo CT from Turin, with 36 CR 42s. 363ª Squadriglia at once flew to Tirana, 364ª to Valona, while the Comando, led by Ten Col Rolando Pratelli, and 365ª Squadriglia went to Argyrokastron. No sooner arrived than 364ª and 365ª Squadriglia were back in the air to escort bombers over Corfu. Another arrival was Col Arrigo Tessari,

14

Bombs from ten 105° Gruppo BT S.79s explode in Salonika harbour on 1 November, 1940.
(*N Malizia*)

who was posted to Albania from the 53° Stormo CT as commander of fighters in the area. Next day the 24° Gruppo CT flew in from Pisa with its G.50bis monoplanes.

Preparing heavy bombs for the EVA's other twin-engined bomber type, the Potez 63, which was operated by 31 Mira.

The heaviest air fighting so far occurred on 2 November, as Italian bombers took the opportunity of better weather to attack Greek targets in strength. The engagements became confused, possibly overlapping, while both sides appear to have overclaimed somewhat. Four Albanian-based S.81s of the 38° Stormo's 39° Gruppo raided Doliana during the morning, but on a later sortie an aircraft from this Stormo's 40° Gruppo was apparently hit by AA fire and then attacked by a fighter; it blew up at 3000 feet, Sottoten Francesco Ruggero and his 202ª Squadriglia crew being killed.

Bombers of 4ª ZAT were very active, 37° Stormo S.81s bombing Corfu, which was also attacked by six Ju87B dive-bombers from the 96° Gruppo Ba'T, making their first raid, escorted across the Straits of Otranto by 35° Stormo BM Cant Z.506B floatplanes. Five more of the dive-bombers, this time Ju87R versions which enjoyed a longer range, attacked Yanina. This town was also raided by ten Z.1007bis trimotors of the 47° Stormo, while nine more raided Larissa, and ten 37° Stormo BR20s hit Patras. Yanina was the main base from which the Greek forces were now launching their counter-attacks, and three PZLs of 21 Mira had been detached here for defence. These were scrambled after the attack on Larissa, led by 1/Lt John Sakellariou. The interception took place over Mitsikeli mountain, close to Yanina, but during the fight Sakellariou was shot down and killed as he attacked one bomber; he was credited with having shot down two others before he fell. The formation of Z.1007bis due to attack Larissa itself arrived somewhat behind the Larissa raid, and by this time only one PZL was available for take-off. Cpl Christos Papadopoulos scrambled alone, and was seen to attack two aircraft, which it was believed he had shot down, before fire from a third apparently hit his fighter, setting fire to the fuel tank whereupon he crashed to his death in flames.

Three bomber squadrons – three bomber types! A Fairey Battle I single-engined bomber of 33 Mira, B282, seen at its base at Kouklaina early in the war. (*A Stamatopoulos*)

Somewhat later, in the early afternoon, a further ten Z.1007bis, this time from the 50° Gruppo Autonomo BT, approached Salonika. Here 22 Mira PZLs attacked, causing the bombers to jettison their bombs and turn for home. 1/Lt Marinos Mitralexes expended all his ammunition on one bomber, which he claimed to have shot down, and then deliberately rammed the tail of another with his propeller. This would seem to have been Sottoten Beniamino Pasqualotto's aircraft (MM22381) which crashed in the area of Langada, the pilot being killed, but the other four members of the crew managing to bale out. With his propeller smashed, Mitralexes force-landed nearby and with the aid of peasants who rushed to the scene, rounded up the Italian survivors. Meanwhile Sgt Epaminindas Dagoulas had claimed the destruction of a third bomber, then landed near the town of Verria with his fuel tanks empty. One further Cant (MM22152), piloted by Ten Omero Matteuzzi, force-landed in the area, and it was reported that another also came down here, although this is not confirmed in Italian records. One aircraft of the 211ª Squadriglia was hit however, and one gunner was seriously wounded, dying on his return to Brindisi. It seems that one of the PZLs was hit and damaged during the engagement, or perhaps force-landed, Capt John Kyriazes being wounded.

1/Lt Marinos Mitralexes, the 22 Mira PZL P.24 pilot who became a Greek national hero when he deliberately rammed a 50° Gruppo Cant Z.1007bis bomber over Salonika. (*EVA via D Chalif*)

Cant Z.1007bis No.3 of 210ª Squadriglia, 50° Gruppo BT, which crash-landed near Nauussa on 2 November, 1940 after being hit by 22 Mira PZL P.24s during a raid on Salonika. Sottoten Omero Matteuzzi and his crew were captured.

Although not mentioned in the Greek account of these raids, escorting CR 42s were present over both Salonika and Yanina. Over the former city Cap Mariotti's nine 363ª Squadriglia fighters engaged eight PZLs, claiming four shot down, while two CR 42s were damaged. It seems that over Yanina Cap Giorgio Graffer's 365ª Squadriglia was engaged, Graffer himself being credited with three PZLs shot down. Magg Angelo Mastragostino of the 160° Gruppo also claimed a PZL on this day, and may possibly have been flying with Mariotti's unit on this occasion. Gunners aboard the various bombers optimistically claimed six attacking fighters shot down, so that total claims against PZLs amounted to 13 or 14 whereas actual losses were perhaps three. It would seem that one of the 21 Mira pilots may have shot down the 38° Stormo S.81, but that otherwise the claims made on behalf of the two dead pilots at Yanina for four victories was wishful thinking. This day's raids had however cost the Greeks some 200 civilian casualties, mainly in Salonika itself.

Bombing-up a 32 Mira Blenheim IV (B252) at Trikkala. (*A Stamatopoulos*)

During the afternoon three 32 Mira Blenheims again raided the Koritza airfields. As they attacked Serg Pippo Ardesio of 393ª Squadriglia attempted to take-off in a CR 42, but his aircraft was caught by the blast of the bombs and was destroyed, the pilot being killed.

Breguet XIXs of 2 Mira were ordered to reconnoitre the front area along the route Samarina–Romios–Kerassovon–Fourka in the Pindus region, since the Greek HQ at Kozani had lost all contact with the Alpini, who were infiltrating along the paths and ravines. At 0700 one Breguet searched carefully over the area, spotting the troops of the 'Julia' Division moving towards Distraton, from

Samarina, accompanied by many laden mules. The report of this situation allowed aircraft to be sent out to bomb these columns repeatedly to delay their advance towards the Metsovon Pass, the loss of which could cause a very critical situation for the Greeks. During the next few days reinforcements were sent to this area and a counter-attack was launched which nearly cut off the 'Julia' Division after its 45-mile forced march to the area. By 7 November they would be in full retreat. While the Italians continued to make progress in the west, occupying Paramythia and Margarition on 3 November, to the east the Greeks had already struck back hard. As early as 2 November they had crossed more than three miles into Albanian territory, capturing nine officers and 153 men, together with mules and equipment. On the 4th they would launch their main counter-attack in the west on the Epirus Front.

Main Regia Aeronautica army co-operation aircraft throughout the campaign in Greece was to be the Meridionali Ro.37bis. This aircraft, No.9 of the 39ª Squadriglia OA is being flown over the front by Capitano Mario Crotti. (*G Tardivo via N Malizia*)

Meanwhile on 3 November, 4ª ZAT's offensive against Salonika was resumed, nine 47° Stormo Z.1007bis again attacking this city. One 262ª Squadriglia aircraft (MM21673) flown by Sottoten Vincenzo Pallara was reported shot down by AA fire, but probably fell to a 22 Mira PZL piloted by Sgt Panayotes Argyropoulos. Other fighters from this unit also engaged bombers. 1/Lt Constantinos Yianikostas chasing one over the frontier into Yugoslav airspace, where he claimed it shot down. It seems that on this occasion the bombers were escorted by the newly-arrived G.50bis monoplanes of the 24° Gruppo. One fighter – identified as a Macchi 200 – was claimed shot down by Sgt Dagoulas, and two others were claimed damaged, as were two more of the bombers. However two of the PZLs were hard hit, Sgt Constantine Lambropoulos baling out of his fighter after being wounded, while Sgt Demetrios Philes, also wounded, landed safely at Sedes airfield. On this occasion the Greek AA also claimed three bombers shot down, but the aircraft reported as falling were probably the bomber and two fighters (one Greek) which had actually been shot down during the combat. It was however the last raid that would be made on Salonika before the New Year; an indication of the EVA's fierce and determined defence of that city.

19

The Regia Aeronautica was again active on 4 November, fighters making several strafing attacks on Greek troops at the front, while the 96° Gruppo despatched four Ju87Rs and the prototype Savoia S.86 dive bomber – the latter flown by Savoia Marchetti test pilot Mar Elio Scarpini – to attack targets in the line at Yanina. (This aircraft had been similarly tested over Malta, but reports were unfavourable, and it would not be employed again.) Many raids were flown by Albanian-based S.79s and S.81s, and it appears that one S.81 of 38° Stormo was lost, Magg Mosca being amongst those killed. From 4ª ZAT eight 50° Gruppo Z.1007bis raided Volos harbour, where one was hit by AA fire, one member of the crew being mortally wounded. Three Italian bombers were claimed shot down by Greek fighters during the day, two by 2/Lt John Katsaros of 21 Mira and one by a pilot of 23 Mira. It was reported that one came down on the Plain of Thessaly, one crashed on a bridge over the river Arachthos, and the third at Kapetista. Information on such losses from Italian records is not available.

The 2 Mira Breguet XIXs continued their attacks on the Alpini in a ravine near Distraton, but here three of them were intercepted by a pair of 365ª Squadriglia CR42s flown by Sottoten Lorenzo Clerici and Serg Domenico Facchini. The Fiats concentrated their fire on the leading Breguet, the observer of which was unable to return fire due to a stoppage. The aircraft was hit and the observer wounded, but by skilful flying the pilot managed to evade the attackers and force-landed at Xyrolimni. The second aircraft, flown by the unit commander, Maj Fridericos Katassos, was shot down in flames, Katassos and 2/Lt Alexandros Sarvanis, the observer, being killed; the third aircraft escaped, unseen by the Italian pilots.

Float-fitted Dornier Do.22G N29 of 12 Mira in flight over a Greek coast shortly before the outbreak of war. (*A Stamatopoulos*)

This engagement brought the first week of fighting to an end. For the Greek Army the situation was changed greatly for the better. Counter-attacks had been made all along the front, and by 8 November the Italian offensive would collapse altogether. Many reasons could be offered for this incredible reverse; the unexpectedly bad weather, the lack of administrative arrangements and the shortage of transport, coupled with the low capacity of the supply ports of Valona and Durazzo. Doubt must however be cast upon the resolve of the Italian troops, thrown by their political and military leaders into an ill-prepared venture where great sacrifices were suddenly required for no easily discernible reasons. Fascist propaganda had depicted Greece as a poor and divided country, easily influenced by Italy's power. The reality was very different; the Greeks proved to be tenacious, fierce and indomitable in defence of their homeland, the stubborness of their defence and ferocity of their counter-attacks coming as a profound and unwelcome shock. In consequence Generale Soddu was sent from Italy to take over actual direction of the campaign, although for publicity purposes Generale Visconti Prasca remained in titular overall command.

The situation in the air was not so good for the Greeks however. Northern Greek towns had suffered heavy air raids, while the troops at the front were virtually without fighter defence. The Greek bomber force was still intact, but seven of the available army co-operation aircraft had been destroyed or seriously damaged*, while the precious small force of interceptors had been reduced by at least three total losses, two more aircraft requiring substantial repair. Attrition was the great problem for the Greeks until help could arrive from outside – but this was on the way.

*Two Yugoslav pilots and their JKRV Breguet XIXs had arrived in Greece earlier in the month on secondment to the EVA; one pilot however, Lt Dragan Djuric, would be attached to a PZL unit and would see much action during the next few months. It is not known if he gained any successes.

TABLE 1

Regia Aeronautica, Order of Battle 28 October 1940

Comando Aeronautica Albania: Generale S A Ferruccio Ranza (Tirana)

Fighters:		*BASE*	*COMMANDER*
160° Gruppo Autonomo CT		Drenowa	Ten Col Fernando Zanni
393ª Squadriglia	Fiat CR 42	Koritza	Cap Torquato Testerini
394ª Squadriglia	Fiat CR 32	Koritza	Cap Luigi Morelli
395ª Squadriglia*	Fiat G.50bis	Berat	Cap Giuseppe Scarpetta

Bombers:		
38° Stormo BT (Savoia S.81)	Valona	Col Domenico Ludovico
39° Gruppo BT	Valona	Magg Guido Simini
51ª Squadriglia	Valona	Cap Guglielmo Falcone
69ª Squadriglia	Valona	Cap Giulio Beccia
40° Gruppo BT	Valona	Ten Col Amato Panunzi
202ª Squadriglia	Valona	Cap Ettore Valenti
203ª Squadriglia	Valona	Cap Francesco Giordano
105° Gruppo Autonomo BT		
(Savoia S.79)	Tirana	Ten Col Galeazzo Ciano
254ª Squadriglia	Tirana	Cap Aldo Vitali
255ª Squadriglia	Tirana	Cap Carlo Susino

Reconnaissance:		
72° Gruppo Autonomo OA		
(Meridionali Ro37bis)	Argyrokastron	Ten Col Renzo Cozzi
25ª Squadriglia	Koritza	Cap G Piero Pratesi
42ª Squadriglia	Valona	Cap Renzo Mencaraglia
120ª Squadriglia	Tirana	Cap Francesco Criscioni

Between 1–5 November Comando Aeronautica Albania was reinforced with several additional units:

Fighters:		
24° Gruppo Autonomo CT		
(Fiat G.50bis)	Tirana	Ten Col Eugenio Leotta
354ª Squadriglia	Tirana	Cap Paolo Arcangeletti
355ª Squadriglia	Tirana	Cap Ettore Foschini
361ª Squadriglia*	Tirana	Cap Giuseppe Scarpetta
150° Gruppo Autonomo CT		
(Fiat CR 42)	Argyrokastron	Ten Col Rolando Pratelli
363ª Squadriglia	Tirana	Cap Luigi Mariotti
364ª Squadriglia	Valona	Cap Nicola Magaldi
365ª Squadriglia	Argyrokastron	Cap Giorgio Graffer

(*On arrival of the 24° Gruppo Autonomo CT at Tirana, the 361ª Squadriglia was detached, and together with the 395ª Squadriglia from the 160° Gruppo Autonomo CT, formed a new 154° Gruppo Autonomo CT at Beraf under Magg Angelo Mastragostino.)

Bombers:

104° Gruppo Autonomo BT		
(Savoia S.79)	Tirana	Ten Col Giorgio Porta
252ª Squadriglia	Tirana	Cap Gabriele Casini
253ª Squadriglia	Tirana	Cap Ernesto Carboni

(On arrival this gruppo formed the 46° Stormo BT with the resident 105° Gruppo Aut BT).
Together, these units brought strength in Albania to:

Savoia S.81	24
Savoia S.79	31
Fiat CR 32	14
Fiat CR 42	46
Fiat G.50bis	47
Meridionali Ro37bis	25
	187

Based in south-east Italy was Comando 4ª Zona Aerea Territoriale, which would also operate over Greece. This comando's strength was:

Comando 4ª *ZAT*: Generale S A Augusto Bonola (Bari)

Bombers:

35° Stormo BM (Cant Z.506B)	Brindisi	Col Enrico Grande
86° Gruppo	Brindisi	Magg Luigi Marini
190ª Squadriglia	Brindisi	Cap Domenico Senatore
191ª Squadriglia	Brindisi	Cap Dario Ceccacci
95° Gruppo	Brindisi	Magg Giovanni Morbidelli
230ª Squadriglia	Brindisi	Cap Ezio Rignani
231ª Squadriglia	Brindisi	Cap Severo Pritoni
37° Stormo BT (Savoia S.81/Fiat BR20)	Lecce	Ten Col Angelo Bancheri
55° Gruppo	Lecce	Ten Col Erminio Ermo
220ª Squadriglia	Lecce	Cap Ferruccio Scaroni
221ª Squadriglia	Lecce	Cap Giacomo Carnicelli
116° Gruppo	Lecce	Ten Col Giuseppe Scarlata
276ª Squadriglia	Lecce	Cap Pietro Gioia
277ª Squadriglia	Lecce	Cap Carlo Sandon
47° Stormo BT (Cant Z.1007bis)	Grottaglie	Col Scipione Tadé
106° Gruppo	Grottaglie	Magg Gori Castellani
260ª Squadriglia	Grottaglie	Cap Bruno Mussolini
261ª Squadriglia	Grottaglie	Cap Aldo Maggi
107° Gruppo	Grottaglie	Ten Col Amedeo Paradisi
262ª Squadriglia	Grottaglie	Cap Salvatore Balletta
263ª Squadriglia	Grottaglie	Cap Bernardo Quattrociocchi
50° Gruppo Autonomo BT**		
(Cant Z.1007bis)	Brindisi	Ten Col Raffaele Ortolan
210ª Squadriglia	Brindisi	Cap Ubaldo Cuomo
211ª Squadriglia	Brindisi	Cap Giuseppe La Cava

23

(**50° Gruppo BT withdrawn from
the 16° Stormo BT at Vicenza)
96° Gruppo B.a'T

(Junkers Ju87B2 & R5)	Lecce	Cap Ercolano Ercolani
236ª Squadriglia	Lecce	Ten Ferdinando Malvezzi
237ª Squadriglia	Lecce	Ten Giovanni Santinoni

Fighters: (for the defence of Puglie only)
2° Gruppo Autonomo CT

(Fiat CR 32/Fiat G.50bis)	Brindisi	Magg Giuseppe Baylon
150ª Squadriglia	Grottaglie	Cap Tullio De Prato
151ª Squadriglia	Grottaglie	Cap Elio Fiacchino
152ª Squadriglia	Grottaglie	Cap Edmondo Travaglini

Between 3 and 11 November, 4ª ZAT was reinforced by:

Bombers:

41° Gruppo Autonomo BT

(Cant Z.100Zbis)	Brindisi	Ten Col Ettore Muti
204ª Squadriglia	Brindisi	
205ª Squadriglia	Brindisi	

Fighters:

372ª Squadriglia Autonomo CT

(Macchi C.200)	Brindisi	Magg Armando Farina

These units brought strength of the Comando to:

Cant Z.1007bis 60; Fiat BR20 19; Savoia S.81 18; Junkers Ju87 20; Cant Z.506B 23; Fiat G.50bis 33; Macchi C.200 12; Fiat Cr 32 9.

Aeronautica Dell'Egeo: Generale D A Ulisse Longo

Fighters:

161ª Squadriglia Autonomo CM	Meridionali Ro43/Ro44
162ª Squadriglia Autonomo CT	Fiat CR42
163ª Squadriglia Autonomo CT	Fiat CR32

Bombers:

39° Stormo BT

56° Gruppo	Savoia S.81
222ª Squadriglia	Savoia S.81
223ª Squadriglia	Savoia S.81

92° Gruppo	Savoia S.79
200ª Squadriglia	Savoia S.79
201ª Squadriglia	Savoia S.79
34° Gruppo Autonomo BT	Savoia S.79
67ª Squadriglia	Savoia S.79
68ª Squadriglia	Savoia S.79

Reconnaissance:

147ª Squadriglia RM	Cant Z.501
185ª Squadriglia RM	Cant Z.501
Sezione Soccorso	Cant Z.506B

Total: 82 aircraft

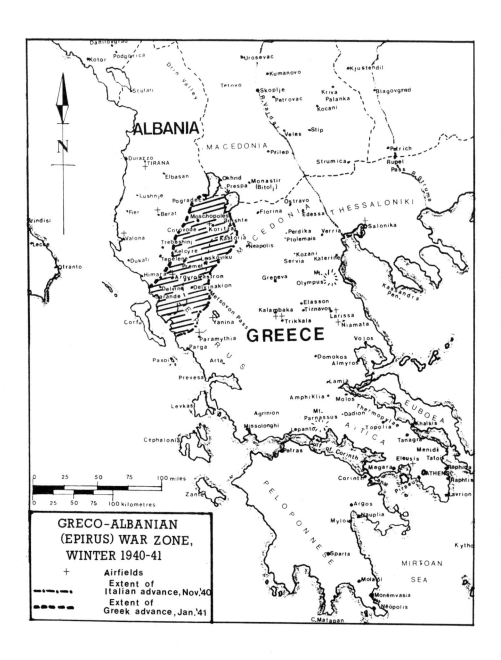

GRECO-ALBANIAN
(EPIRUS) WAR ZONE,
WINTER 1940-41

+   Airfields
━·━·━·   Extent of
           Italian advance, Nov.'40
━ ━ ━   Extent of
           Greek advance, Jan.'41

TABLE 2

Elleniki Vassiliki Aeroporia (Royal Hellenic Air Force) Order of Battle, 28 October 1940

Structure:

(a) Army Higher Air Force Command under General Commanding Land Forces, comprising the combat and army co-operation squadrons.
(b) Navy Higher Air Force Command under the Navy Commander-in-Chief, comprising the naval co-operation squadrons.

Mire Dioxes (Fighter Squadrons) Lt Col Emanuel Kelaides, o/c Fighter Command

21 Mira	12 PZL P.24s	Kalambaka, under Capt J Kellas (detachment of three aircraft at Yanina under 1/Lt J Sakellariou)
22 Mira	12 PZL P.24s	Salonika/Sedes, under Capt A Andoniou
23 Mira	12 PZL P.24s	Larissa, under Maj G Theodoropoulos

(NB: only 24 of the 36 PZL P.24s were serviceable)

24 Mira	9 Bloch MB.151s	Eleusis, under Capt A Anagnostopoulos and under control of Anti-Aircraft Command for defence of Athens.

(NB: only 6 of the 9 Bloch MB.151s were serviceable)

Mire Vomvardismou (Bomber Squadrons)

31 Mira	11 Potez 63 (8 serviceable)	Niamata, under Lt Col J Papadakis
32 Mira	12 Blenheim IVs (11 serviceable)	Larissa, under Maj M Anastasakis
33 Mira	12 Battles (10 serviceable)	Kouklaina, under Lt Col D Stathakis

Mire Stratiotkis Synergassias (Ground Support Squadrons)

1 Mira } 2 Mira }	18 Breguet XIXs	(only about half were serviceable) under Maj F Katassos
3 Mira	15 Henschel Hs126s,	under Maj D Paliatseas
4 Mira	17 Potez 25As	

Mire Naftikis Synergassias (Naval Co-operation Squadrons)

11 Mira	9 Fairey IIIFs	Valtoudi, Gulf of Pagassetikos (near Volos) under Lt Col Alexandros
12 Mira	12 Dornier Do22Gs	Peloukia, under Capt Christopoulos
13 Mira	9 Ansons	

27

Additionally a number of trainers and secondline aircraft were on strength, including:

6	Hawker Horsley II torpedo-bomber biplanes
6	Avia B-534 biplane fighters
2	Gloster Gladiator biplane fighters
20	Avro 621 Tutor biplane trainers
22	Avro 626 biplane trainers

Some of the latter would later be used operationally in the observation role.

Chapter Two

FORWARD THE ROYAL AIR FORCE!

Commander of the new RAF Contingent in Greece, Air Vice-Marshal J H D'Albiac, DSO.

While the British had been quick to secure Crete when the Italians declared war on Greece, initial reaction had not brought a similar despatch of aid to the mainland. On 30 October the British Minister in Athens sent a telegram to General Wavell indicating that, while Greek morale remained high, the need for direct, observable, aid was critical if their resistance was to be sustained. Wavell turned to the Air Officer Commanding in the Mediterranean, Air Chief Marshal

Sir Arthur Longmore, the latter at once allocating 30 Squadron for immediate movement to Greece. This unit, which operated one flight of Blenheim IF fighters and one of standard Blenheim I bombers, was to be followed as swiftly as possible by two more squadrons of Blenheim bombers and one of Gladiator fighters – the latter to be reinforced with Hurricanes as soon as these became available. At the same time Air Commodore J H D'Albiac, DSO, the AOC Palestine and Transjordan, was ordered to Greece to command the new air contingent there.

Greek fighter pilots lost in action during the campaign; 1 Capt John Kellas, 21 Mira; 2 Cpl Christos Papadopoulos and 3 1/Lt John Sakellariou, both 21 Mira, killed 2 November, 1940; 4 1/Lt Costantinos Yianikostas, 22 Mira, killed 18 November, 1940; 5 2/Lt Constantine Tsitsas, 23 Mira, killed 3 December, 1940; 6 2/Lt Anastassios Bardivilias, 21 Mira, killed 10 February, 1941; 7 and 8 Sgt Constantinos Chrizopoulos, 21 Mira, and Capt Nicholaos Scroubelos, 23 Mira, both killed 23 February, 1941; 9 and 10 Sgt Pericles Koutroumbas, 23 Mira, and Cpl George Mokkas, 24 Mira, both killed 15 April, 1941. (*A Stamatopoulos*)

Study of the situation in Greece had already demonstrated that the main problem associated with any sustained air effort would be the lack of suitable all-weather airfields. Only Athens-Eleusis and Menidi (Tatoi) could be considered moderately suitable, while both were situated an uncomfortably long way from the front line, and from the targets to be attacked in Albania. The mountainous nature of much of Greece left few suitable sites for the construction of other large fields, which would permanently constrain the number of units which might effectively be operated in the country. However, the matter could be eased at least partially if the heavier, longer-ranging Vickers Wellington bombers were retained in Egypt, using Eleusis as a forward refuelling and re-arming base. The Blenheims were to be based at Eleusis and Menidi as their home airfields, but the Gladiators would need to be situated at the less-than adequate fields at Trikkala and Yanina, from where they might reach the forward areas with some margin of fuel remaining for patrol, and combat.

The Greek anti-aircraft artillery available for the defence of these bases was extremely limited, so that Wavell was obliged to earmark one heavy and one light AA battery to accompany the engineer, signals and administrative detachments which the Army was to provide as back-up for the RAF units under D'Albiac's overall command. Meanwhile, the weakening of the air force in Egypt by this dispersion of strength was to be made good with all speed by the despatch of further units and aircraft to Egypt from the United Kingdom.

Thus it was that on 3 November, 1940 the first eight Blenheim IFs of 30 Squadron, led by Sqn Ldr U Y Shannon, flew into Eleusis, accompanied by four Bristol Bombay transports of 216 Squadron, which carried the initial servicing party. The rest of the unit's ground crew, equipment, bombs and ammunition followed by sea, reaching Athens three days later — the day on which Air Commodore D'Albiac and his staff also arrived in a 216 Squadron Bombay to take up his new command; promotion to Air Vice-Marshal followed immediately.

These arrivals, coming just as the unexpectedly strong Greek resistance brought the Italian advance to a halt, raised morale in the capital sky-high, and the British personnel soon found themselves fêted as saviours and conquering heroes. In fact the limited strength available to D'Albiac offered him only a relatively small number of options as to what he could usefully achieve. He already knew that Italian fighter strength in Albania was quite substantial, and that to use his small forces in direct support of the ground troops would dissipate what little he had, while inviting heavy losses to fighters where his own force of Gladiators would be too small in numbers to provide adequate escort or patrol capabilities. He therefore chose the strategic role for his bombers — at least initially. Although the route to strike at the Albanian ports of Durazzo and Valona would be long and difficult, he decided that these were the only targets truly worthy of the Blenheims' efforts.

The bombers would have to navigate their way through vile weather over ranges of high mountains, and with inadequate maps. They would then have to attack without the benefit of fighter escort, prior to making their way home through similar conditions. It was not a scenario designed to bring gladness to the heart of any airman! To support this effort, Wellingtons from Malta and

Egypt would also hit the Italian ports of despatch at Bari and Brindisi in the south-east of that country. The Greek troops at the front would have to be left to the depredations of the Regia Aeronautica, save where the remaining elements of the Greek air force and the few RAF Gladiators could offer some succour. Their main defence for the time being would have to be the cover so often afforded by the heavy clouds, rain and snow of the Balkan winter.

The newly-arrived Blenheim fighters of 30 Squadron flew their first patrol from Eleusis on 4 November, seeing a single Cant Z.501 flyingboat, but observing no results before it escaped their interception and disappeared into cloud. Next day Flg Off D R Walker arrived from Egypt at the head of four of the unit's bomber Blenheims, and a day later six Wellingtons of 70 Squadron also reached Eleusis on detachment from Kabrit, led by Sqn Ldr T U Rolfe. It was on this date that the first offensive action by the RAF occurred in the new war zone, when at 1120 in the morning Sqn Ldr Shannon led off three of the bomber Blenheims to undertake an offensive reconnaissance over Sarande, Tepelene, Valona and Argyrokastron. After refuelling at Trikkala, the bombers headed on to Sarande, where two ships were seen and bombed – without observed results. Valona was next to be visited, and here some 50 aircraft were counted on the ground at the port's airfield. These were identified as CR42s, Bredas and S.79s, and were bombed, one of the latter bombers being seen to receive a direct hit; in fact three S.81s of 38° Stormo BT were damaged, and the runway was holed in several places.

Following the initial bombing, Shannon led his formation down to strafe, but as he did so, he spotted a CR42 taking off and giving chase. Three of these fighters from 394ª Squadriglia had scrambled, and these pressed their attack on the bombers as they departed, all three Blenheims being considerably holed, while Sgt John Merifield, the gunner in the No 3 aircraft (pilot Sgt G W Ratlidge), was hit and killed. Cap Nicola Magaldi, the leader of the interceptors, believed that he had succeeded in shooting down one of the bombers, but in fact all three managed to limp back to Eleusis.

Next day it was the turn of the Wellingtons, all six 70 Squadron machines leaving at daybreak for Valona. Arriving over the port, the big bombers were attacked by a number of 154° Gruppo CR42s, the crews identifying their attackers as CR42s and Breda 65s. Wellington T2734 exploded in mid air, Sgt G N Brooks and his crew being killed, while T2731 went down in flames with the loss of Flt Lt A E Brian's crew; two more Wellingtons were hit and damaged, although returning crews claimed that they had shot down one CR42 and probably a Ba65. Three of the bombers were claimed shot down by the Italians, one each by fighter pilots Ten Walter Franchino and Serg Magg Adrio Gismondi, and one by AA. No losses were suffered, but Franchino's CR42 was apparently hit. That afternoon when he took off again, one wing broke off and he crashed to his death – unobserved combat damage during the morning's fight was considered to have been responsible.

Meanwhile the returning bombers encountered three Z.506B floatplane bombers of the 35° Stormo BM over the Otranto Channel. These aircraft had set out from Italy to make a raid south of Kalibaki but had been forced to abort by bad

32

Cant Z.506B reconnaissance-bomber floatplane of 146ª Squadriglia RM. (*AMI via N Malizia*)

weather. Flg Off Hubbard in T2816 and Plt Off R J K Hogg in T2813 (one of the damaged Wellingtons) attacked one floatplane jointly, but were driven off by a CR 42 which appeared on the scene, though they believed that their initial opponent had gone down. Indeed it had, force-landing on the sea about 20 miles from the coast. The other pair of floatplanes landed alongside and took off the crew, but the damaged aircraft was found to be a total loss, and was abandoned.

Following their return to Eleusis, the four remaining Wellingtons flew back to Egypt next day (8 November), but were replaced later in the day by a further six aircraft from Kabrit. The Wellingtons would not, however, fly any further daylight raids over Albania. Another arrival on this date was 'A' Flight of 84 Squadron, whose five Blenheim Is flew in to Eleusis, led by Sqn Ldr D G Lewis, before moving on to their allotted base at Menidi; three Bombays brought in ground crews and stores. The new bombers would carry out their first attack on Valona on 10 November, although the results were much restricted by adverse weather conditions. This day also saw action by Greek Blenheims, which left Larissa briefed to attack targets at Kalpaki, north of Yanina. On returning to base after darkness had fallen, they were prevented from landing at Larissa by fire from the airfield AA defences, and were obliged to divert to Menidi, where local gunners again gave them a hostile reception.

By now fuel was low as they continued to orbit the airfield until identification was established and they were given clearance to land. As a result one aircraft crashed and Capt Lambros Kousigiannes broke his back, although he was to survive this accident. Another Greek Blenheim was lost next day, failing to return from a reconnaissance to the north-west of Kelcyre on behalf of the 8th Division; Capt Photius Maravelias and his crew were killed. This aircraft was encountered by CR42s of 150° Gruppo Aut CT near Poligrade, and was shot down by Cap Giuseppe Scarpetta. While landing after this mission however, Serg Italo Ritegni crashed and was killed; during another landing on this date Ten Livio Bassi ran into a groundcrewman, who was killed outright, while the CR42 turned over and was damaged. The Italians had also lost another CR42 on 8 November when Sottoten Pietro Jannello of 363ᵃ Squadriglia was shot down by AA during a strafing attack over the front.

The new detachment of Wellingtons at Menidi were very active by night during this period. During the hours of darkness of 11/12 November, Flt Lt R J Wells led two bombers to Valona, reporting that an ammunition dump and some motor transport had been hit, while four other bombers led by Sqn Ldr Rolfe raided Durazzo, seeing hits near a jetty. Next night Valona was again the target for three Wellingtons, while Rolfe flew a lone sortie to Bari on the Italian east coast to bomb an oil refinery. The detachment was strengthened by the arrival of two more aircraft on 13 November, which also saw 84 Squadron's 'A' Flight out again, Valona and Argyrokastron being attacked on this occasion during the early morning. At the latter target a Meridionali Ro 37 and a Caproni 311 were destroyed, while one CR42 was damaged. Sottoten Ernesto Trevisi and Serg Mario Scagliarini of the 160° Gruppo Aut CT attacked, each claiming one Blenheim shot down; in fact only one suffered damage, and this made it back to Menidi.

By now the Allies had been greatly heartened by news of the successful attack on the Italian Fleet at Taranto by Fleet Air Arm Fairey Swordfish torpedo-bombers during the night of 11/12 November. On 14 November the Greeks launched an offensive along the whole front which quickly began to crumble the Italian defences. To support this the EVA made a maximum effort, and during

Bristol Blenheim I bomber of 84 Squadron, RAF, after arrival in Greece in November 1940. (*IWM*)

the two opening days of the new fighting there was much activity in the air. Blenheims, Potez 63s and Battles from all three bomber Mire made frequent attacks on 14 November on the northern and southern airfields at Koritza, and on Argyrokastron. As the bombers could not be given the luxury of fighter escorts, they had to fly deep into the ravines between the mountains for some protection. However, the raids were considered very important in support of the army's main drive on Koritza.

Six Battles and three Blenheims were formed into two flights, four of the former attacking the northern airfield at Koritza at 0800, destroying one Caproni Ca133 and damaging three CR42s and a CR32. Two Blenheims – the third having become stuck in the mud and failed to take off – and the other two Battles then raided the southern airfield at 0945, where the Italian defences claimed two Blenheims shot down, one by AA and one by a 393ª Squadriglia CR42 flown by Ten Torquato Testerini. Capt Demetrios Papageorgiou's Blenheim disintegrated in mid-air as the result of a direct AA hit, but the other Blenheim, damaged by the same explosion and attacked by a reported three CR42s, managed to release its bombs on target and get back to Larissa with a shattered tailplane and more than 100 bullet holes in the airframe; the gunner claimed one of the attackers shot down. Other 393ª Squadriglia pilots then saw the two Battles taking off from a nearby Greek forward airfield, and one of these was claimed shot down by Serg Walter Ratticchieri. In fact the bomber regained its base at Kouklaina, having suffered severe damage. During these operations the Greeks claimed to have destroyed ten Italian aircraft on the ground and damaged many others; the actuality was more prosaic. A Potez 25A of 4 Mira was also shot down by AA while on a reconnaissance sortie over the frontier during the morning, 1/Lt Demetrius Yiakas being killed.

As the morning wore on the biggest air superiority battle yet to be seen over Greece developed. Nine PZLs from 23 Mira at Larissa undertook a patrol during which they were surprised by a pair of 393ª Squadriglia CR42s, led by Ten Enea Atti. Although the Italians claimed one probable, the Greek fighters were able to scatter and evade their assault. The two Fiat pilots then spotted two Blenheims – aircraft of 32 Mira on their way to attack Koritza again – and claimed one of these as a probable also. Other 393ª Squadriglia fighters then appeared on the scene and engaged the 23 Mira formation in a fierce, whirling dogfight. Sottoten Ugo Drago claimed one PZL shot down, while Sottoten Romeo Della Costanza claimed one of three with which he was engaged; Ten Carancini claimed a third. Both formations then regrouped and attacked once again. This time Drago and his flight (Sottoten Ernesto Trevisi, Serg Augusto Manetti and Serg Vittorio Pirchio) claimed three more PZLs shot down between them, with a fourth probably so. The Greeks fought back tenaciously, shooting down Trevisi, who was killed, and Manetti, who baled out over Italian-held territory, while Pirchio's aircraft was badly shot-up and he was wounded in the left foot; his fighter overturned on landing. Maj Theodoropoulos and his pilots submitted claims for eight CR42s; while a number of PZLs may have been damaged, and some possibly shot down, no Greek pilots were killed or wounded during this engagement.

A section of three of the unit's PZLs led by 1/Lt G Laskaris also intercepted a lone S.79 of 254ª Squadriglia which was carrying out a reconnaissance sortie over the Koritza-Bilishte area. They attacked determinedly and the Savoia was seriously damaged, force-landing at Koritza with the pilot, Ten Calogero Mazza, wounded in the right leg and the radio operator, Mar Attilio Grassini, dead; the gunners claimed to have shot down one of the attackers.

Early in the afternoon three of 84 Squadron's Blenheims were over Koritza to attack troop concentrations and a bridge. The latter was destroyed, effectively preventing reinforcements reaching the battle area. CR 42s attacked, Flt Lt A F Mudie's L1389 and Sgt W F Sidaway's L1387 being shot down, while the third aircraft (L1536; Sgt L Nuthall) was damaged. The identity of the Italian unit responsible for these successes has not been identified. The Regia Aeronautica's 96º Gruppo B a'T's Ju 87s from Lecce in eastern Italy had also been active during the day, attacking a bridge near the isthmus of Lake Prespa during the morning and also Greek artillery batteries. A single dive-bomber also attacked a Greek landing ground north-east of Florina, claiming one PZL destroyed on the ground here, with hits on two more of these aircraft and a bomber. Four more PZLs scrambled after the intrepid aircraft, but failed to catch it. 22 Mira now moved with its PZLs from Salonika to join 21 Mira at Kalambaka/Vassiliki airfield, to add further strength to the forces operating in support of the drive on Koritza, against which the Italians were now making heavy raids.

There was little let-up in the fighting on 15 November, the day seeing a fight between Fiat G-50bis monoplane fighters of the 24º Gruppo Aut CT and the PZLs of the newly-arrived 22 Mira, as the Italian unit escorted five S.79s of the

Fiat G.50bis fighter of 355ª Squadriglia, 24º Gruppo Autonomo CT at Tirana. (*N Malizia*)

36

105° Gruppo **BT** to attack the line near Bilishte. Four or five Greek fighters attacked the bombers, Sgt Argyropoulos hitting one which force-landed near the landing ground at Koritza with one dead and one wounded aboard. The gunners in the bomber formation claimed two PZLs shot down in return, while five G-50bis led by Cap Ettore Foschini came to the rescue, claiming one and one probable without loss.

Soon after 1400 three Blenheim bombers from 30 Squadron set off to attack positions north-east of Koritza, and while the bomber crews reported being attacked by three CR42s and three G-50bis, no mention of the latter types is made in Italian accounts. Serg Walter Ratticchieri and Serg Domenico Tufano of 393ª Squadriglia claimed two of the Blenheims shot down; actual loss was one – Sgt E B Child's L1120 going down in flames. Another CR42, flown by a nobleman, Sottoten Maurizio Nicolis di Robilant, was sent off to escort a Ro37 reconnaissance aircraft of the 72° Gruppo Aut OA; while so engaged he encountered four Battles of 33 Mira which were attacking a target in the Koritza area, and at once attacked these, claiming three of them shot down. Sgt Frangoulis Arnidis and his crew were killed when their Battle crashed as a result of Robilant's attack, while a second regained its base in damaged condition, the observer, 2/Lt Aristofanes Papas, dying as a result of a severe leg wound. A Potez 63 also returned from a sortie badly shot-up, with the observer (2/Lt Spyridon Kovatzis) dead – the crew reported having been hit by Greek AA near Missolonghi.

Jimmie Newstead of 113 Squadron, RAF, tries the gunner's position in a Greek Fairey Battle of 33 Mira. (*S W Lee*)

Night activities by 70 Squadron's Wellingtons were continuing apace, two of these returning to the Bari oil refinery during the night of 14/15 November, while four raided oil tanks at Brindisi on 16/17 November and three hit Valona on 17/18 November. Here for the first time Sqn Ldr Rolfe encountered fighter opposition by night, but all bombers escaped unscathed. Three more Wellingtons raided Durazzo on this latter date, but severe weather conditions were encountered, and only one reached its target. However, during this night T2827, flown by Sgt J Palmer-Sambourne, which was carrying an American war correspondent, Ralph Barnes of the New York Herald Tribune, crashed into a mountain near Danilovgrad, Yugoslavia, everybody aboard being killed. After one further raid on Durazzo on 19/20 November, the detachment returned to Kabrit on 24 November.

Meanwhile, over the front by day weather prevented the continuation of sustained activity during 16 and 17 November, as the Greek offensive pressed the Italians back in growing confusion. Italian aircraft continued to appear over the front in strength whenever possible, and during 17 November the 35° Stormo BM lost one Z.506B from its 86° Gruppo to AA, two more being damaged from a force of 14.

Better weather on 18 November allowed the Greek fighters to get back into the air again and the three Mire were to make 20 sorties over Western Macedonia during the day. S.79s of the 105° Gruppo, 46° Stormo BT were in action over the Korciano area where an aircraft of 255ª Squadriglia was attacked by three PZLs of 23 Mira, and was shot down. All the crew baled out, but the parachute of the first pilot, Sottoten Alessandro Caselli, failed to open; the surviving members claimed to have shot down one of the attackers. Later that morning 18 Z.1007 bombers from 47° Stormo BT operated over the Bozigrad-Slinarisa-Ariza area, and these were also attacked by three PZLs; the gunners claimed one fighter shot down. An hour later six more Z.1007s, this time from 16° Stormo BT, appeared in the Koritza area and these were engaged by 23 Mira, whose pilots claimed three shot down. In fact only one bomber was lost – an aircraft of the 211ª Squadriglia captained by Sottoten Mario Longo. Again claims were made by the bombers' gunners, this time for two Greek fighters shot down.

Many patrols and escort sorties were undertaken by Italian fighters – 160° Gruppo alone carried out six patrols, three escorts and four scrambles during the day; both 24° and 154° Gruppo each flew five patrols and 150° Gruppo one more. Only one engagement ensued however, when CR42s of 160° Gruppo engaged PZLs from all three Mire and claimed six shot down and one probable. These claims were submitted by Serg Magg Arturo Bonato (two), Ten Torquato Testerini, Ten Carancini, Serg Luca Minella and Serg Teofila Biolcati. On this occasion at least three Greek fighters were lost, both 1/Lt Yianikostas of 22 Mira and Sgt Gregory Valcanas of 23 Mira being killed, while 1/Lt Corneleus Kotrones of 22 Mira was wounded in one leg, but managed to force-land his shot-up aircraft at an emergency airfield. In return the Greeks claimed two CR42s shot down, one each by 1/Lt Laskaris of 23 Mira and 2/Lt Katsaros of 21 Mira, but no Italian aircraft was actually lost.

During the heavy fighting on 14 and 18 November, 23 Mira had been credited with shooting down a total of nine CR 42s and five bombers. The following pilots are believed to have been those who shared the credit for these claims:

Maj G Theodoropoulos	1/Lt A Apladas	1/Lt N Scroubelos
1/Lt P Bousios	2/Lt C Tsitsas	Sgt Maj C Kabounis
1/Lt G Laskaris	Sgt N Stasinopoulos	Sgt K Sioris
Sgt G Nomikos	Sgt J Kouyioumzoglou	Sgt G Valcanas
Sgt S Depountis	Sgt P Koutroubas	

It was at this point, with the Greek fighters now much reduced in strength by attrition and unserviceability, that they were reinforced by the arrival at Eleusis from Egypt – via Crete – of 'B' Flight, 80 Squadron, RAF, with Gloster Gladiator biplanes. 'A' Flight would soon follow, while the ground party travelled aboard the cruisers HMS *Gloucester* and *Edinburgh*. 'B' Flight, which was led by the squadron commanding officer, Sqn Ldr W J Hickey, was an experienced unit in which several of the pilots already had a number of victories to their credit – notably Flt Lt M T St J Pattle with four, Plt Off Vincent Stuckey with three and Flg Off Sydney Linnard with two.

On 19 November the flight flew up to Trikkala during the morning. After refuelling, nine Gladiators took off, led by three Greek PZLs, for an offensive patrol over the Koritza area. CR 42s of 160° Gruppo were patrolling over this area, while G-50bis from 24° Gruppo were escorting bombers when the Allied fighters appeared. Due to their short range, the PZLs were obliged to turn back, but the Gladiators dived to attack the Italian fighters, which believed their new opponents to be 20 strong. Many individual dogfights developed over the mountainous terrain, the British pilots subsequently claiming nine shot down plus two probables:

Flt Lt Pattle	two CR 42s in flames	Plt Off Stuckey	one G.50 crashed one CR 42
Flg Off G F Graham	one G.50 one CR 42	Plt Off W Vale	one CR 42 share one CR 42
Plt Off S G Cooper	share one CR 42	Flg Off Linnard	two CR 42s probable
Sgt C E Casbolt	one G.50		

Stuckey was hit and wounded in the right shoulder and leg, but managed to get back to Trikkala from where he would be despatched to hospital in Athens. Three CR 42s and one G.50bis were actually lost; in 160° Gruppo Serg Magg Natale Viola and Mar Giuseppe Salvadori of 363ª Squadriglia and Serg Magg Arturo Bonato of 393ª Squadriglia all failed to return, as did Ten Attilio Meneghel of 355ª Squadriglia, 24° Gruppo. A fourth CR 42 flown by Serg Magg Ratticchieri was hit and the pilot was wounded in both legs. One CR 42 pilot, Serg Magg Luciano Tarantini, claimed a Gladiator shot down, two more being claimed as probables, one by Cap Paolo Arcangeletti, the other by a G.50bis pilot.

Activity reduced again thereafter. On 20 November, a Ro37 of 72° Gruppo OA was shot down by AA, the crew baling out over Italian lines, while a Z.1007bis bomber was claimed shot down by Capt John Kellas, commander of 21 Mira. Next day Blenheim L1166 of 30 Squadron became lost in bad weather during a reconnaissance sortie, Flg Off C W Richardson carrying out a successful crash-landing. On this same date three Hs126s from 3 Mira strafed a four and a half mile-long column of retreating Italians on the Pogradec road, causing great confusion, while Serg Dorva Bellucci of the 154° Gruppo CT reported being attacked by two Gladiators and claimed one probably shot down – no report of combat by 80 Squadron was noted, but it is possible that his opponents may have been Greek aircraft of some sort. Another engagement occurred on 22 November when 160° Gruppo CR42s were escorting S.79s over Koritza, one unidentified aircraft being claimed shot down. This was probably one of 3 Mira's Hs126s which was shot down in flames while flying over Kapetista, the pilot (1/Lt Demetrius Sideris) being killed.

Savoia S.73 transport 606-7 (ex I-LODI) which crashed on take off from Koritza on 19 November, 1940 and was still lying on the airfield when the Greeks captured the base.

By this time the Greeks had captured Koritza and Leskoviku, and in the south had re-crossed the Kalamas River. With a foothold secured on Albanian soil, and with the valuable lateral road south from Koritza in their hands, they now stopped to consolidate. Included amongst the equipment abandoned by the Italians was found a civil S.73 airliner in unserviceable condition; this aircraft, formerly I-LODI, had been given the military number 606-7 on the fuselage, indicating that it had served with the 606ª Squadriglia of the transport force. On 19 November while taking off from Koritza, the port engine had cut; Sottoten Francesco Martinelli had to abandon the take-off, and had collided with three parked CR42s; the Savoia was subsequently abandoned as beyond repair.

Italian morale was now in terrible shape, and only in the air could they still hit back effectively. The loss of Koritza and the closeness of Greek forces to Argyrokastron had precipitated a withdrawal of Regia Aeronautica units to the

40

Savoia S.79 of 254ᵃ Squadriglia, 105° Gruppo Autonomo BT, captured by the Greeks. (*E. Bevington-Smith*)

main Albanian airfields, which were now becoming very crowded as a result. From Koritza the headquarters and 393ᵃ Squadriglia of the 160° Gruppo CT had moved the Devoli, while the 394ᵃ Squadriglia had gone to share Berat airfield with the units of the 154° Gruppo CT. From the same base the 25ᵃ Squadriglia OA had moved to Tirana. From this base 363ᵃ Squadriglia had moved to join 364ᵃ Squadriglia at Valona, as had the headquarters and 365ᵃ Squadriglia of the 150° Gruppo CT from Argyrokastron, the whole Gruppo reuniting at this airfield. Only 120ᵃ Squadriglia OA remained at the front at Argyrokastron, having flown up from Tirana to this landing ground. This unit would withdraw to Valona during the following month. The airfield at Scutari was available for use now however, the bombers of the 38° Stormo and 104° Gruppo BT having moved here from Valona and Tirana.

On 23 November 'A' Flight of 80 Squadron reached Greece, led by Flt Lt E G 'Tap' Jones, and moved up to join the rest of the unit at Trikkala. The day also saw the beginning of the arrival from Egypt of 211 Squadron, which was led by Sqn Ldr J R Gordon-Finlayson, to join 84 Squadron at Menidi; for the time being the RAF Component was now at full strength.

Next day G.50bis fighters from 24° Gruppo reported engaging lone Blenheims on several occasions. One was claimed shot down by four pilots led by Ten Domenico Pancera, while another trio reported that one more Blenheim had been shot down by Ten Divo Bartaletti, and a second claimed probably destroyed by all three pilots in collaboration. No RAF operations were reported, and these would seem to have been Greek Blenheim IVs, although no losses seem to have been recorded by 32 Mira either. One Blenheim from this unit was lost in

41

Flt Lt E G 'Tap' Jones with his Gloster Gladiator, flanked by 80 Squadron's Warrant Officers. (*E G Jones*)

a raid in the vicinity of Pogradec on 27 November, presumably shot down by ground fire; 1/Lt Alexandros Malakes and his crew perished. British Blenheims were out in some strength on the day before, however, six 84 Squadron aircraft attacking Valona where three 154° Gruppo G.50bis intercepted, being identified by the British airmen as Macchi 200s or Messerschmitt 109s! Flg Off J F Evans escaped at low level, which allowed him to spot an Italian bomber on the ground which he bombed. Flt Lt R A Towgood also escaped three fighters, his gunner claiming one shot down. The Fiat pilots claimed one Blenheim probably destroyed.

Meanwhile three 211 Squadron Blenheims made their first attack, Durazzo being the target. AA fire was intense and Flt Lt G B Doudney's aircraft was hit, although he managed to get back; Sqn Ldr Gordon-Finlayson's L8511 was less fortunate, being badly damaged. He later recalled:

'Just as we released our bombs we received direct hits from AA. One tore a large hole in the port engine cowling, but the motor continued to function, despite the fact that oil was pouring out. The other engine was hit and stopped almost immediately.... We flew on, though slowly, and unable to gain height on our one engine. The cockpit was full of petrol fumes, and I was afraid we should either pass out or that the aircraft would catch fire.... We flew on for nearly two hours, and then we spotted an island just off the coast – Corfu. We had a look at it and decided there was only one place to attempt a landing – a strip of beach about 20 yards wide ... we put the aircraft down all right, although we could not

Officers of 211 Squadron, RAF, shortly before departing North Africa for Greece. Left to right, front row: Plt Off L S Delaney, Flg Off Farringdon ('A' Flight commander), Flt Lt G D 'Potato' Jones ('B' Flight commander), Sqn Ldr J R Gordon-Finlayson, Flt Lt G B Doudney ('C' Flight commander), Flt Lt Kelly (Engineer Officer), Flt Lt Squires (Medical Officer); middle row: Plt Offs Williams (Intelligence Officer), Barnes, Wingate-Grey (Cypher Officer), Ritchie, D C Barrett (Equipment Officer), G J Jerdien, L B Buchanan, R D Campbell, Chapman (Cypher Officer), R W Pearson; back row: Plt Offs K Dundas, E Bevington-Smith, G Davis, Bright (Adjutant) and A. Geary. (*E Bevington-Smith*)

get the wheels out and had to make a belly-landing. Some of our bombs were still on board, and they bounced along the beach behind us as we ploughed through the sand.'

Local fishermen would take them to the mainland where, after travelling by mule, car and train they would arrive back at Menidi some days later, none the worse for their adventure.

On 26 November a dozen 80 Squadron fighters had been detached to Yanina, this detachment being repeated next day. On this latter date Sqn Ldr Hickey led nine Gladiators off from Trikkala, these patrolling to the north of Yanina on arrival. Here they spotted a trio of S.79s escorted by some dozen 150° Gruppo CR42s, led by Cap Nicola Magaldi, commander of 364ª Squadriglia. The British pilots attacked at once, Flt Lt Jones in N5861 and Sgt D S Gregory in N5776, each claiming one Fiat shot down; Magaldi was killed in this combat and Serg Negri returned to base unhurt, but with his aircraft very badly shot-up. Meanwhile a dozen 24° Gruppo G.50bis, led by Magg Oscar Molinari, and covered by 15 160° Gruppo CR42s, strafed the Greek airfield at Kozani, home of 2 Mira, while returning from a bomber escort mission. The Italian pilots claimed five aircraft destroyed on the ground and three more damaged, and indeed 2 Mira did lose virtually all its Breguet XIXs in this attack, while one of the

Sqn Ldr Gordon-Finlayson and Plt Off Arthur Geary, DFC, his WOP/air gunner, who would be killed on 13 April 1941, with their 211 Squadron Blenheim.

pilots, 1/Lt Panayiotis Maroulakos was also hit and killed by a stray bullet; other personnel were wounded.

Six Gladiators from 80 Squadron's 'A' Flight were off again next day (28 November), led on this occasion by Flt Lt Jones. Over Delvinakion they reported meeting 20 CR42s – in fact ten aircraft of 150° Gruppo, led by Cap Giorgio Graffer, 365ᵃ Squadriglia commander. In the whirling dogfight which followed Flg Off H U Sykes in N5812 and Serg Corrado Mignani collided, both pilots being killed. Flt Lt Jones, after claiming two CR42s shot down off the tails of fellow pilots, had N5816 badly shot-up, his instrument panel smashed, and a bullet wound in his neck. He was escorted back to Yanina by Sgt D S Gregory, where he managed to land safely. Flg Off H D Wanklyn Flower was also shot-up in N5854, but believed he had shot down one CR42 first, while two more Gladiators – N5788 (Flg Off W B Price-Owen) and N5786 (Flg Off F W Hosken) were also both damaged. Claims totalled seven confirmed and two probables:

Sgt Gregory	three	Flt Lt Jones	two
Flg Off Wanklyn Flower	one	Flg Off Sykes	one (by collision)
Flg Off Hosken	one probable	Flg Off Price-Owen	one probable

Apart from Mignani, two more CR42s were actually lost, Giorgio Graffer – one of the most successful Italian fighter pilots of the war thus far, with five victories credited to him – being killed, while Serg Achille Pacini baled out. Two more

44

were damaged, Mar Guglielmo Bacci and Serg Arrigo Zotti both returning with wounds. Four Gladiators were claimed shot down in return, plus one probable. Graffer was subsequently awarded Italy's highest medal for valour, the Medaglio d'Oro 'alla memoria'; 150° Gruppo had now lost two squadriglie commanders to the RAF in as many days!

Dornier Do.22G of 12 Mira taking off from its base at Athens/Scaramanga. (*A Stamatopoulos*)

During the day nine Blenheims of 84 Squadron raided Durazzo, reporting interception by MC200s and CR42s. G.50bis from 24° Gruppo had been scrambled, two pilots spotting three of the Blenheims, Ten Bartaletti claiming one shot down and Serg Savino one probable; L1385 was forced down during the fight, Plt Off D R Bird and his crew being captured. CR42s of 150° Gruppo returning from an escort to S.79s over Koritza also reported claiming a Blenheim probably shot down – possibly from the same formation.

84 Squadron again had nine Blenheims up on 29 November, but this time an escort of six Gladiators from 80 Squadron was provided to see the bombers to their target at Tepelene. Four of the fighters then flew low over the mountains searching for Flg Off Sykes' aircraft, lost the day before, while Flt Lt Pattle and Plt Off Vale remained above as cover. A number of trimotor aircraft were then spotted, which were identified as S.79s – they were in fact part of a formation of 28 Z.1007bis of the 47° Stormo BT from Grottaglie on a raid. Both Pattle and Vale attacked, but though the pilots were able to see their fire striking home, they observed no results other than thin trails of black smoke from two aircraft, which they claimed damaged. The defending air gunners reported the Gladiators as nine strong (!), claiming one probably shot down – presumably Pattle's aircraft, which spun down after his attack.

The search for Sykes' aircraft was resumed on 30 November, when three of the squadron's aircraft escorted a Greek Breguet XIX over the area. No sign was found, but that evening a message came through from the Greek Army that he had been found in the burnt-out wreck of his aircraft, and had been buried nearby.

Greek mountain forces in pursuit of the Italians had by now almost run out of food. Heavy snow prevented supplies reaching them overland, so a Wellington of 70 Squadron was loaded with sacks of bread and bully-beef, which were dropped to them. Although dropped through heavy cloud, the food reached the hungry troops successfully – a new and unusual use of British air power.

December began quietly as the weather in the mountains started to enforce a period of stalemate. In the air conditions at times became extremely difficult. On 1 December three Blenheims of 30 Squadron, which were returning from a raid on Valona, ran into a severe front which caused ice to begin forming on the wings, badly affecting control of the aircraft. Flt Lt A L Bocking, a Canadian, was leading, and as conditions deteriorated further it became necessary to consider whether or not the crews should all bale out. At that point however, a gap in the snow clouds was sighted and two of the pilots were able to dive through and set course for base in clearer air. The third (K7103) had become detached during this manoeuvre, and Sgt Ratlidge attempted to climb to 20 000 feet in an endeavour to get above the cloud layer. Bocking recalled:

'... but at that altitude the machine was wallowing, and now and then slipped back into the cloud, whereupon ice immediately formed. The pilot struggled again and again to bring his aircraft into clear air above the cloud. Suddenly, probably owing to the formation of ice in the air intake, one engine cut out. The Blenheim went into a spin at once. The pilot ordered the crew to jump, but it was discovered the observer's parachute pack had been thrown out by the whirling machine into the well, and was out of reach. The pilot and the air gunner stayed with the observer. Still spinning, the aircraft came down into clear air at 7000 feet, and they found themselves in a narrow valley with mountains rising sheer on either side of them. The pilot, righting his aircraft, made a "dead-stick" landing in a tiny field, the only possible landing ground for miles around.'

First action in the air in December came on the 2nd when Flt Lt Pattle of 80 Squadron took off from Yanina on a morning weather reconnaissance. In the Argyrokastron area he spotted another lone biplane which he quickly saw to be a Ro37bis reconnaissance aircraft – from 42ᵃ Squadriglia, 72° Gruppo OA. He attacked and shot it down in flames five miles to the south, Serg Luigi Del Manno and his observer, Ten Michele Milano, being killed. Early in the afternoon Pattle was off again, this time at the head of 12 Gladiators to undertake an offensive patrol over the front lines in support of the Greek Army. Near Premet two more 72° Gruppo Ro37bis were seen 1000 feet below; Pattle and Plt Off Cooper dived on these and sent down both in flames. One man was seen to bale out of Cooper's victim, but both members of each crew were reported lost by the Italians (Cap Gardella/Cap Fuchs; Serg Leoni/Serg Vescia).

Nine Blenheims from 211 Squadron led by Sqn Ldr Gordon-Finlayson raided Valona, their bombs causing little damage of note. The leading flight was attacked by 150° Gruppo CR42s which saw little result of their fire and returned without loss or claim. Recalled Gordon-Finlayson:

We had to go in rather low because of cloud, and the fighters were waiting for us. They were completely out of luck however – while they were chasing one

A trio of 39ª Squadriglia OA Ro.37bis army co-operation aircraft over the front. (*G Tardive via N Malizia*)

flight another went in and dropped its bombs. We saw a big blaze with a tall column of black smoke above it, and it looked as if we had hit something quite important. One of the fighters caught the concentrated fire from one flight and it came down in a vertical dive with smoke pouring from the fuselage. My aerial was shot away and George Doudney got a bullet through his helmet, but that was all the damage they did to us.'

Personnel of 211 Squadron; l to r: 'Imbros', the Greek interpreter, Plt Off Gerry Davis, the commanding officer's observer, who would be killed on 13 April 1941, Sqn Ldr Gordon-Finlayson, Flg Off A J M 'Curly' Fabian of the Operations Staff (a W W I pilot) and Flg Off Alan Godfrey.

47

Reinforcements for the hard-pressed Greek fighters arrived during the day when eight RAF Gladiators from Sidi Haneish in Egypt were flown over by pilots of 112 Squadron and handed over to the EVA; the British pilots were flown back in a Bombay. To these aircraft (K8013, 8018, 8031, 8047, 8054, L7609, 7611 and 7623) were added five ex-80 Squadron machines (K7892, 7923, 7973, 8017 and L8011) and one from 112 Squadron (K6135). 21 Mira was withdrawn to Eleusis to re-equip, the remaining serviceable PZLs being distributed between 22 and 23 Mire, which were both now in the northern sector, supporting the army. The Gladiators were not the first to be employed by the Greeks; in 1938 a businessman had purchased two privately from Glosters at a cost of £9200, and had presented them to the EVA!

Greek troops with a PZL P.24 on a landing ground on the Albanian frontier. (*A Stamatopoulos*)

Greek fighters were in action again on 3 December when six 23 Mira PZLs engaged 18 CR42s of 160° Gruppo led by Magg Oscar Molinari, south-west of Moschopoles. Three of the Greek fighters were claimed shot down by Molinari, Sottoten Giorgio Moretti (a 24° Gruppo pilot flying with the unit temporarily) and Serg Luciano Tarantini, while a fourth and two probables were claimed shared by several pilots. Greek aircraft losses are not known in detail, but one pilot − 1/Lt Constantine Tsitsas − was killed in this combat; one CR42 was claimed by 23 Mira pilots. During the day the 80 Squadron detachment at Yanina was flown back to Larissa, the ground party being carried in a Greek Ju52/3m. In bad visibility Italian fighters shot down one of their own S.81s over the front, the crew managing to bale out of the stricken bomber.

The arrival of more British aircraft in Greece came on 4 December when a

48

Hudson (N7364) landed at Eleusis. This was in fact an ex-Imperial Airways Lockheed 14 (G-AGAR), serving with 267 Squadron on transport duties, but which had been modified to carry an aerial camera, although no turret or front gun armament had been fitted. Attached to 2 Photographic Reconnaissance Unit (2 PRU), it was to operate clandestinely during the rest of the month, carrying out sorties over Albania, Yugoslavia and Rumania in the hands of Flt Lt R G M Walker and Sqn Ldr H C MacPhail. It would return to Heliopolis on 30 December. Also on 4 December, four more Gladiators arrived from Egypt, but these were aircraft of 112 Squadron, led by Flt Lt C H Fry, to join 80 Squadron on detachment. At once these and 11 of the resident Gladiators were flown up to Yanina for further operations, from where Sqn Ldr Hickey led 14 aircraft on an offensive patrol over the Tepelane area. Here an estimated 27 CR42s were seen – actually 12 aircraft of 150° Gruppo led by Ten Col Rolando Pratelli, and ten G.50bis of the 154° Gruppo. Flt Lt Pattle claimed three CR42s shot down, one onto a hillside north of Delvinakion, one in flames from which the pilot baled out, and after his own aircraft had been hit in the main fuel tank and a wing strut, a third from which the pilot was also seen to bale out. A fourth was claimed by him as a probable when it poured black smoke; he then attacked a fighter which he identified as CR32, which stalled into cloud, claiming this as a probable also. Sgt E W F Hewett claimed two CR42s and a G.50, whilst Plt Off Vale, Sgt Gregory and Sgt G Barker each claimed one CR42 for a total of nine victories and two probables. In return the G.50bis pilots claimed two Gladiators shot down, but 150° Gruppo lost two CR42s, Ten Alberto Triolo and Sottoten Paolo Penna being killed; these were the only Italian losses. 80 Squadron returned to Larissa next day.

80 Squadron groundcrew inspect the wreckage of a Fiat CR42 shot down by one of the unit's Gladiators. (*A T Phillips*)

During 4 December, two Blenheims from 30 Squadron made a low-level attack on an Italian destroyer shelling Greek positions at Sarande. Next day three of this unit's fighter Blenheims returned to the same area to strafe the Sarande-Valona coast road. CR42s of 364ª Squadriglia attempted to intercept them without success, but despite this one Blenheim was forced to return early with engine trouble and the other two were both obliged to force-land during their return flight; both had been damaged by AA fire and were out of fuel. Flg Off H P G Blackmore came down at Korousades on the island of Corfu in K7100, while Plt Off J A F Attwell landed well to the south-west of Agrinion; both crews were unhurt.

At 1220 on 7 December six Blenheims from 84 Squadron took off to raid Valona, followed at 1300 by nine more from 211 Squadron. Extremely severe weather was encountered and 84 Squadron's leading trio were forced to return early due to heavy icing. The second three were intercepted over the target by 150° Gruppo CR42s, Flt Lt L P Cattell's L8455 and Sgt M P Cazalet's L8457 being shot down at once, while Flg Off Ken Linton force-landed L1381 near Sarande after his aircraft had been badly damaged by a single long burst of fire from one fighter. From the two former aircraft only Cazalet's gunner, Sgt C R Foster, survived. Two of 211 Squadron's sections were also obliged to turn back by ice, and two of these aircraft – L1535 (Flg Off P B Pickersgill) and L4926 (Plt Off G J Jerdein) – crashed in the hills around Lamia, both crews being killed.

The remaining three Blenheims, led by Flt Lt G D Jones, continued to Valona, meeting severe opposition from the defending CR42s over the target. All three bombed accurately and returned, believing that they had shot down one of the attacking fighters. 150° Gruppo, which claimed two Blenheims and a third probable during these actions, did not record any losses on this occasion.

Blenheim I of 211 Squadron heading out on a raid on Albania. (*E Bevington-Smith*)

It was at this stage that the first aid for the Italians from their German allies appeared. Desperately short of air transport to aid with the urgent reinforcement of the Albanian front, Mussolini appealed to Adolf Hitler for help in this respect, and on 10 December the first of 53 Junkers Ju52/3m troop carriers of III/KGzbV 1, commanded by Oberst Rudolf Starke, began arriving in the Foggia area from Wessendorf to undertake this function. In Greece by comparison, the RAF was also reinforced on this date when three new Blenheim IF fighters and two standard Blenheim I bombers joined 30 Squadron!

Reinforcement of the Regia Aeronautica's 4ª ZAT in Puglie had also occurred at this time. Late in November the 373ª and 374ª Squadriglia Autonomo CT, each equipped with a dozen MC200s, had moved from Treviso to this zone, going to Bari and Grottaglie respectively, followed on 7 December by the 370ª Squadriglia Aut CT with a further eight Macchi fighters, which arrived at Foggia. On 27 November the 14 S.79s of the 42º Gruppo BT had also arrived at Grottaglie from Naples, but on 14 December this unit would move to Libya, where a British offensive had begun; a week later the S.79s were followed by the Fiat G.50bis fighters of 4ª ZAT's resident 2º Gruppo Autonomo CT. The final reinforcement of the winter was a second dive-bomber gruppo, the 97º, which arrived on 6 December from Sicily's Trapani Milo airfield to join the 96º at Lecce. This unit's Ju87s made their first sorties over the Epirus front on 14 December.

With no Wellingtons operating from Greece since the departure of the 70 Squadron detachment, night raids had been much reduced. However, late on 13 December, four such aircraft from 148 Squadron on Malta made the long flight to attack Valona. Bad weather conditions forced the leader to turn back, but two of the remaining trio reached their target, the third bombing the secondary objective, Crotone. All returned safely to Malta before midnight. Next day however, a new detachment of four Wellingtons from 70 Squadron reached Menidi, and on the night of 15/16 December these raided Durazzo. Again weather was bad and Sqn Ldr Rolfe, the leader, was forced to turn back, flying direct to the unit's home base at Kabrit. The other three attacked and returned to Menidi, reporting seeing a large fire in the harbour area as a result of their bombing.

Ex-airline Junkers G-24 taken over by the EVA, at Menidi airfield. (*E Bevington-Smith*)

Meanwhile, 14 December saw a resumption of British day raids when Blenheims twice bombed Valona without effect. Four days later three Blenheim IFs of 30 Squadron flew a morning offensive reconnaissance up to Valona harbour. Here they bombed seaplane hangars, but were then intercepted by six CR42s and three G.50bis from the 150° and 154° Gruppo. Flg Off S Paget's aircraft (L8462) was hit in the port engine and caught fire, crashing into the sea eight miles west of Sarande. Flg Off R T P Davidson had fought a G.50bis briefly (believing that he had probably destroyed it) but then had to turn his attention to his colleague, flying over the spot where the Blenheim had ditched and dropping his dinghy; the aircraft had sunk like a stone with the loss of all the crew however. It seems that Davidson's fire had indeed struck home on the Fiat, which was damaged and as a result somersaulted and crashed while attempting to land back at Valona. While the G.50bis pilots claimed only one damaged, those in the CR42s believed that they had probably shot down all three Blenheims. That night however, the British battleships *Warspite* and *Valiant* shelled Valona, damaging 13 of the 150° Gruppo's CR42s on the airfield. The Royal Navy was not to escape its current round of operations without loss on this occasion, for the submarine HMS *Triton*, which had recently sunk a 6000 ton freighter off Durazzo, was itself intercepted in the Strait of Otranto, and sunk by the Italian torpedo-boat *Confienza*. While Valona was being bombarded, three Wellingtons from Menidi were raiding Brindisi railway station and oil storage tanks, large fires being started. On this occasion AA was heavy and Flt Lt J Barnard's T2829 was hit in the port engine, the airscrew breaking loose and flying off. By skilful handling while the crew jettisoned all moveable equipment, Barnard was able to fly back to Greece at 1000 feet and land safely at base.

At last with dawn on 19 December the weather cleared over the Larissa Plain, and in fine conditions nine Blenheims from 84 Squadron were off early to bomb Valona and Krionero. Once again, G.50bis were in the air to intercept and three of the bombers sustained damage, Serg Arrigo Zoli of the 154° Gruppo claiming one probably destroyed; the gunners claimed damage to one Fiat in return. Ju87 dive-bombers of the Regia Aeronautica were also out from Italy, 24 aircraft from the 96ª Gruppo attacking shipping in Port Edda harbour, claiming one small vessel sunk.

Shortly before midday Sqn Ldr Hickey led 14 of 80 Squadron's Gladiators up to Yanina, followed by the ground party in a Ju52/3m. After refuelling, 13 of these fighters were off to patrol over the Tepelene area where five S.79s of the 46° Stormo were seen, escorted by CR42s and G.50bis. The British pilots at once engaged the bombers, believing that they had shot one down (no loss was actually suffered), but return fire struck N5785 and it went down in flames, Plt Off Cooper being seen to bale out. Sqn Ldr Hickey thought that he had shot down one of the escorting CR42s, which now attempted to intervene, but he then went down to land on a waterlogged field near Argyrokastron to look for his missing pilot. With the aid of some Greek soldiers, the badly wounded Cooper was located, and was transferred to hospital in Argyrokastron, where he died that evening. Meanwhile Sgt Hewett's N5827 had been hit and badly damaged by AA fire, and he was obliged to force-land 20 miles north of Yanina during the return

EVA Junkers Ju52/3m transport at Menidi. (*S W Lee*)

flight; this Gladiator was later salvaged. The only Italian loss of the day occurred when Magg Angelo Mastragostino force-landed his CR42 near Bilishte while providing escort for a Ro.37bis – reason unspecified.

20 December dawned fine, and at 1000 Flt Lt Pattle was off at the head of nine Gladiators to meet Blenheims of 211 Squadron returning from a raid, and to carry out an offensive patrol over the Tepelene-Kelcyre area. Here a reported nine S.79s were seen – actually six aircraft of the 104° Gruppo BT, drawn equally from the 252ª and 253ª Squadriglia. Pattle at once attacked one of the latter, flown by Ten Andrea Berlingieri, and shot it down in flames, the crew of four being seen to bale out before it crashed into the mountainside and blew up; they did not return, and were reported missing. A second 253ª Squadriglia machine was badly damaged, returning to Tirana where the crew reported that a Gladiator had collided with them and had been seen to crash, minus its propeller. In another S.79 Ten Vivarelli's crew claimed a second Gladiator shot down. Two Gladiators were in fact damaged during this engagement and returned to Yanina.

Savoia S.79s of 253ª Squadriglia, 104° Gruppo Autonomo BT over Greece. (*N Malizia*)

53

The rest of the 80 Squadron formation continued their patrol, soon spotting another formation of trimotors – this time six S.81s from the 38° Stormo **BT**, escorted by 24° Gruppo G.50bis. These monoplanes had no chance to intervene as Pattle bored in to attack the middle aircraft of the leading section, and this was soon streaming fuel from the area of the starboard engine. He fired all his remaining ammunition into it and reported that it slowly lost height and force-landed some 15 miles north of Kelcyre, tipping onto its nose and losing its starboard wing. Plt Off Vale in N5784 claimed a second S.81 shot down. In fact one aircraft, carrying the Stormo commander, Col Domenico Ludovico, was badly damaged and landed at Berat with three dead, including Cap Giulio Beccia, the pilot, and three wounded. The survivors just managed to get out before the aircraft with all its bombs still aboard, blew up. A second S.81 returned with all its crew wounded. The British pilots reported that throughout the engagement the G.50bis patrolled overhead without attacking the Gladiators.

Savoia S.81 over Greece. (*N Malizia*)

The Gladiators were engaged in their third major combat in three days on 21 December, when the squadron was off again at 1030, ten strong, led by Sqn Ldr Hickey. They soon found action and a confused dogfight began which resulted in considerable over-claiming by both sides. As the British fighters headed for the front in three sections – the first comprised of four aircraft led by Hickey, the second of three led by Pattle and the final trio led by Flg Off Sidney Linnard –

three trimotor bombers were seen near Argyrokastron, which were identified as S.79s, and then three more aircraft with twin tails were seen, recognised in this case as Fiat BR20s. All six were in fact Cant Z.1007bis aircraft from the 47° Stormo BT from Grottaglie, and these were attacked by the Gladiators, Pattle believing that he had hit one. At that moment however 15 CR42s of the 160° Gruppo appeared on the scene; these were being led on an offensive reconnaissance over Yanina, Paramythia and Zitsa by Magg Oscar Molinari, the Gruppo commander. Seeing the bombers under attack by an estimated 20 Gladiators (!), the Italians piled in, joined by other aircraft from the 150° Gruppo, so that 80 Squadron pilots assessed the number of their opponents at 54!

After 25 minutes the air battle broke up and eight of the British pilots returned to claim eight confirmed and three probables. Plt Off Bill Vale claimed three, one of them in flames; Sgt Casbolt claimed one which blew up and another which spun down, shedding pieces; Sgt Gregory claimed another two, again one in flames, but his own aircraft was badly shot-up and he was wounded in the right eye. He managed to return to Yanina, as did Flg Off Linnard, whose N5834 was badly hit; he suffered several bullet wounds in his left leg. Pattle and F/Sgt S A Richens claimed one Fiat apiece, Pattle also reporting that his victim fell in flames, whilst Flg Offs Price-Owen and Hosken both claimed probables. However Flg Off A D Ripley in N5854 was seen to be shot down in flames and was killed, while Sqn Ldr Hickey was spotted baling out of N5816; sadly his parachute caught fire, and he died from his injuries soon after reaching the ground. Greek troops recovered the bodies of both pilots.

Fiat CR42 No.7 flown by Ten Edoardo Crainz of 394ª Squadriglia, displaying damage inflicted by a British Gladiator during a combat with 80 Squadron on 21 December, 1940. The bullet holes have been patched with small red, white and green discs, similar to those used in World War I. (*N Malizia*)

In return the 160° Gruppo pilots claimed six Gladiators, two each by Magg Molinari and Ten Edoardo Crainz, and one apiece by Ten Eber Giudici and Cap Paolo Arcangeletti. Probables were claimed by Ten Torquato Testerini, Serg Magg Francesco Penna and Serg Magg Domenico Tufano. The 150° Gruppo pilots claimed two more Gladiators in collaboration, while 47° Stormo gunners claimed one more and a probable. As in the case of the British fighters, actual Italian losses totalled just two aircraft, Serg Magg Mario Gaetano Carancini and Ten Mario Frascadore of the 160° Gruppo being lost, while Magg Molinari was wounded in the right foot and force-landed near Tepelene with a damaged engine. Following these three days of intensive action, the 80 Squadron detachment would return to Larissa on 23 December, their place at Yanina being taken by the Greek 21 Mira, now operational again with 11 Gladiator IIs.

Meanwhile, on the same day the Italians remained very active, three high-flying bombers raiding Larissa during the morning and hitting the town with eight or nine bombs, four of which fell in or near the central square; one fell within 50 yards of the RAF Officers' Mess, breaking many windows, while considerable numbers of the local Greek populace were killed or injured. Over the front during the afternoon three patrolling fighters from the 154° Gruppo encountered a Potez 63 of 31 Mira, between Devoli and Valona. This was piloted by the unit's commanding officer, Lt Col John Papadakis, who was carrying out a reconnaissance over Southern Albania at the request of the army. His aircraft was shot down by Ten Livio Bassi, Serg Emilio Piva and Serg Guido Pecile, Papadakis and his gunner baling out; apparently both landed in the sea, and they were lost. Ju87s from the 96° Gruppo were out twice; during the morning an attack on Doliana resulted in the loss of one aircraft crewed by Mar Elio Scarpini, the Savoia Marchetti test pilot, and his gunner 1e Av R T Catamaro, to AA fire. A second machine went down to similar causes during a repeat attack that afternoon with the loss of Ten Brezzi/1° Av Mot Stevanato.

Greek soldiers and a British officer with the wreckage of one of two Junkers Ju87B dive-bombers of the Regia Aeronautica's 96° Gruppo B a'T shot down by ground fire on 21 December, 1940.

56

Further success was claimed by 154° Gruppo G.50bis on 22 December when five of these aircraft intercepted nine 84 Squadron Blenheims raiding the Kucera oilfields, Serg Manfredo Bianchi claiming three of the bombers shot down in flames, while Serg Arrigo Zoli claimed a fourth; a fifth was believed to have been probably shot down. Two of the Blenheims were actually lost, L8471 going down with Flg Off P F Miles and his crew, while Flg Off John Evans managed to bale out of L8374 near Koritza. Five other Blenheims were damaged, some of them by AA fire; L4818 flown by F/Sgt A Gordon was badly damaged during attacks by several fighters, the observer – Sgt G Furney – receiving a severe head wound. Despite this, Gordon was able to fly the 200 miles back to base.

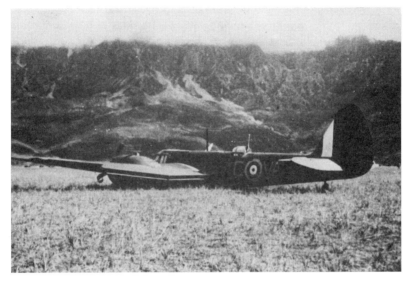

84 Squadron Blenheim is crash-landed at Greek airfields on return from operations. (*S W Lee*)

Flg Off Evans later returned, reporting that the cockpit of his aircraft had suddenly become a mass of flames. The observer had made an immediate and successful evacuation of the aircraft, but Evans, who had been hit in one arm, got caught up in the shroud-lines of his parachute so that the jerk as this opened broke one of his thigh bones. He landed in Greek lines where he was found by the observer, and with the aid of some Greek soldiers was carried to a nearby village. After emergency treatment, four soldiers were detailed to carry him by stretcher over mountain tracks to the nearest town – a nightmare journey which took three days. On arrival he was put on a train to Athens and safety.

On Christmas Day five Blenheims from 84 Squadron were despatched to Corfu in foul weather to drop sacks of gifts on the esplanade for the children of this island. During the afternoon more aircraft appeared overhead – but this time they were three Italian bombers which dropped a number of bombs on buildings near Corfu harbour, several of which were hit. One bomb went through a window of the National Bank of Greece building, piercing the concrete floor and exploding in the basement which was in use as an air raid shelter, and where on this festive day a dance was in progress. Eighteen people were killed and 25 others injured. Elsewhere in the town three others were killed and five hurt.

Fiat BR20M of 3ª Squadriglia, 43° gruppo, 13° Stormo BT over the mountains between Argyrokastron and Yanina. The underside gun position has been lowered. (*Guglielmetti via Lucchini/Malizia*)

When news of this attack reached Athens, an immediate raid on Valona was ordered, and 211 Squadron was detailed to undertake this mission. Unfortunately, the unit had already been officially stood down for the Christmas holiday, and it was only with difficulty that sufficient crews could be found. One of the observers, Plt Off Eric Bevington-Smith recalled:

'We assembled five crews and set off for Valona. The weather was appalling, with a cloud base below 2,000 feet and we flew along the Gulf of Corinth and up to Valona, where the cloud base was 1,700 feet ... we just managed to slip through in line astern, went up into cloud again, and by good luck came out of cloud over Valona and dropped our bombs. The AA had not yet woken up, so we put our noses down and went flat out for the harbour entrance. When we were at about 500 feet we met an Italian cruiser and destroyer coming in for Christmas. We turned our front machine guns on and dived on the ships, and as we passed our rear gunners sprayed the decks. It worked; we were at least two miles away before shellfire started bursting round us, and a quick change of course to the south got us away. If only those Italian gunners had not assumed that at the entrance to the harbour of their home port, they were safe!'

On Valona airfield one CR42 was destroyed by the bombs and two more were damaged. The AA defenders claimed one Blenheim probably shot down.

RAF Blenheim I shot down near Devoli by Italian fighters.

The rest of the holiday passed quietly enough as far as the RAF was concerned, although on 26 December five CR42 pilots of 150° Gruppo, led by Cap Luigi Corsini, reported intercepting eight Blenheims over Dukati, claiming two shot down and two probables. No engagements appear to have been recorded by the British units in Greece, and no aircrew losses were reported by the EVA either, so the identity of the possible victims has not been ascertained. Indeed it was to be 29 December before a further encounter between British and Italian machines was next recorded. On that day three of 30 Squadron's Blenheims were off on an early morning offensive reconnaissance over Valona, where Italian reinforcements were known to be disembarking. The bomb-aimers had just released their missiles on the port when three CR 42s and a single G.50bis attacked, Serg Arrigo Zoli of the 154° Gruppo in the latter fighter hitting K7104, the port engine of which burst into flames.

The bomber, in the hands of Flt Lt H D Card, a Canadian, crashed into the sea; while two parachutes were seen, only one member of the crew survived. Zoli also attacked both the other Blenheims, claiming one more shot down and the third probably so; Plt Off A G Crockett's L6677 was seriously hit but made it back to Eleusis, where it belly-landed; although hit in fuel tanks, wings and fuselage, Sgt L A Ovens' aircraft also returned. A little later in the morning 28 Z.1007bis bombers from the 47° Stormo BT made a raid over the front line area, where one formation was intercepted by nine Gladiators from the Greek 21 Mira; the bomber gunners claimed one of the fighters probably shot down.

These Gladiators were the only fighters available at the time. Earlier in December, 22 and 23 Mire had moved their PZLs to Ptolemais to be closer to the 3rd Army Corps, the Command Post of the Fighter Command under Lt Col Emanuel Kelaides also being established here. This airfield quickly proved to be quite unsuitable and the aircraft could barely be operated from here. After 15 December rain had intermittently flooded the field, but the snow began to fall and the temperature fell abruptly, the whole area freezing over. There was now a great danger that the aircraft, imprisoned on the ground by these conditions, might fall victim to Italian air attack, and since there was no let-up in the unfavourable weather, the machines were dismantled and taken by lorry to Amyndeon station, from where they were transported by rail to Salonika. The whole operation took just four days – 26–30 December – all aircraft being ready for operations again by the latter date! Similar conditions had flooded out Niamata airfield, the home of 31 Mira between Volos and Almyros, but from here the Potez 63s had been able to take off and fly down to Larissa.

Early on the morning of 30 December, five fighter Blenheims of 30 Squadron set off to patrol over the Preveza–Levkas area. On arrival the formation split into two patrols of three and two, and after about an hour Sgt Fred Goulding, gunner in Sqn Ldr Shannon's aircraft in the latter pair, spotted a Cant Z.506B floatplane of the 190ª Squadriglia, 86° Gruppo, 35° Stormo BM, below, as this was carrying out an offensive reconnaissance along the Greek coast in the hands of Ten Domenico Bazzi. Shannon dived to attack, firing with his front guns and making several passes, closing to 25 yards, until all his ammunition was exhausted. Flg Off Richardson, another of 30 Squadron's Canadians, then took up the attack from above and below, allowing his gunner to get in several bursts. Shannon also closed to allow Goulding a shot, but the latter was hit in the knee by an explosive bullet fired from the floatplane's dorsal gun position. Shannon broke off and headed for home, but quickly realising how badly hit his gunner was, he put down at Agrinion for help. Although a doctor arrived within minutes, Goulding was already unconscious and died shortly afterwards from loss of blood. Meanwhile Richardson had watched the stricken Cant crash into the sea. Two members of the crew could be seen waving a handkerchief, while three or four others were lying on the wing. Richardson's crew dropped their dinghy close by and returned to base, where they were later informed that the Greek Navy had picked up the Italians.

Meantime at 0935 Larissa had been under an air raid alert, but no hostile aircraft had been seen. The all-clear was sounded at 1020, but 20 minutes later a raid did take place. Three 80 Squadron Gladiators were scrambled, but one had to return early due to a lack of oil pressure. At 1115 another hostile was reported approaching from the north-east, and at that point ten Gladiators from the unit's detachment at Athens passed overhead, and were signalled to continue to search for the enemy aircraft. Flg Off R N Cullen then spotted a trimotor out to sea west of the Kassandra peninsula, which he identified as an S.81. He attacked and one engine caught fire, the aircraft diving into the sea and disintegrating; this is believed to have been a bomber from the 38° Stormo BT. Over the front on this day a Fiat BR 20 of the 37° Stormo BT was reported in action with Gladiators, suffering damage and having one member of the crew wounded; this was probably engaged by Greek Gladiators, rather than by Flg Off Cullen.

Fiat BR20M bomber of 276ᵃ Squadriglia, 116° Gruppo, 37° Stormo BT. (*AMI via N Malizia*)

By this date two Potez 25 army co-operation aircraft from 4 Mira were reported operating from Koritza airfield, carrying out reconnaissance, bombing and strafing sorties. During one such mission one failed to return, reportedly shot down over Elbasan by Italian 'Macchi fighters', but no Italian claim has been found. Two Blenheim IVs from 32 Mira were also lost on this date, one failing to return from a sortie over the 2nd Army sector where it was intercepted by two CR42s from 363ᵃ Squadriglia flown by Sottoten di Robilant and Serg Enrico Micheli, who reported that it fell near Valona; Capt Cleanthes Hatziioannou and his crew were reported killed. The second, flown by Lt Col Panayhiotis Orphanidis, the commanding officer of the unit, crashed near the Mira's airfield at Kazaklar, all aboard perishing; it was presumed that the crash was accidental in this case. Other fighter pilots from the 154° Gruppo CT reported sighting nine Blenheims during the day, but no engagements resulted.

On the last day of 1940 the RAF Blenheims were out again, nine 211 Squadron aircraft attacking storage dumps to the south of Valona, but once more interception was made by three CR 42s and a lone G.50bis of 154° Gruppo. Again it was the monoplane which managed to reach the bombers, and Sottoten Guiliano Fissore attacked Sgt S L Bennett's L1540. The port engine was hit and set on fire when the formation was at 7000 feet, 20 miles south of the target, and the aircraft dived into the sea with the loss of the whole crew. Thus ended 1940, and with it two months of fairly intense and difficult operations for the small RAF Contingent and their Greek allies.

By the end of 1940 Italian fighters had inflicted heavy losses on the RAF's Blenheim Is. Here the burnt-out wreckage of one such aircraft lies on Albanian soil. (*N Malizia*)

Chapter Three

THE BATTLES OF SPRING

The New Year of 1941 found a situation of stalemate fast developing along the front line. The weather had clamped down hard, making movement on the ground difficult, and in the air on many days, well nigh impossible. The Greeks were practically exhausted by the tremendous exertions of their autumn counter-attacks, and were still desperately short of transport, clothing and anti-tank and anti-aircraft artillery. The major part of their armed forces and most of their air power were involved at the front, leaving only four weak divisions on the frontier with Bulgaria. Should any threat from this area develop it was considered that nine more divisions and associated air support would be required to defend Eastern Macedonia and Salonika. Nothing however was to be allowed to alarm the Germans, and still no British land forces were to be accepted for service in Greece unless the Germans crossed the Danube and entered Bulgaria. RAF units should also operate only in the west and south, no squadrons being based in the Salonika area. Further reinforcements of air units within these parameters would however be accepted gratefully, allowing the EVA to withdraw to Salonika to reform. During January therefore the British High Command was to resolve to send two more squadrons to Greece, one of fighters and one of bombers, while planning at the same time to capture the Italian Dodecanese Islands – particularly Rhodes – to secure the Aegean and Eastern Mediterranean.

The threat of German intervention was a real one, for early in the month of January Adolf Hitler would decide to send a strong contingent to Albania to bolster the Italians, planning for this move beginning under the codename Operation *Alpenweilchen*. The end of the Greek counter-offensive and reinforcement of the Italian forces brought a halt to these preparations in mid February however, when it became clear that, with 21 divisions in Albania, the Italians should be able to secure their hold on Valona.

The early part of January was marked by continuous rain, airfields becoming seriously water-logged and operations rare. The opening days of the month did however see a number of moves and changes, coupled with events that were to affect a number of units to one extent or another. On 1 January the EVA's 23 Mira moved to Salonika from where it was proposed that its PZLs should operate over the 3rd Army front in the eastern sector, using the Koritza airfields as forward landing grounds for refuelling. Meanwhile 22 Mira moved to Yanina. For the RAF's 211 Squadron the new year was marked by a tragic accident.

63

Advice had just been received that Sqn Ldr Gordon-Finlayson had been awarded a DFC, while New Year's Eve was also Flt Lt G D Jones' birthday. With a triple reason to celebrate the squadron wined and dined at Maxim's in Athens, but while returning to the Mess, one car containing several officers crashed into a tree, the Equipment Officer, Flt Lt D C Barrett, dying of the injuries he received, whilst Gordon-Finlayson, Jones and Plt Off R W Pearson were also hurt – though fortunately none of them seriously. The squadron was one of the few active at this time, eight Blenheims raiding Elbasan and 2 January, and nine more going out over the front two days later.

A veteran of the early defence of Malta, Flt Lt W J 'Timber' Woods, DFC (centre) arrived to take over one of 80 Squadron's flights in March 1941. On his left is Flg Off G F 'Shorty' Graham. (*E G Jones*)

At this time a number of additional Gladiators were ferried to Greece, and four of these were supplied to 80 Squadron at Larissa as replacements. One was flown in by Flt Lt W J 'Timber' Woods, DFC, who remained with the unit as a flight commander. One of the original Malta Gladiator pilots of summer 1940, Woods had already some five victories to his credit. The unit was also joined by Plt Off Eldon Trollip, a Rhodesian, who had been in hospital in Athens, suffering from jaundice. A few days later nine Wellingtons from 70 Squadron would arrive on detachment at Menidi and Eleusis, led by Wg Cdr E B Webb. Two officers of the United States Army Air Force, Col G C Bower and Maj A T Craw, also arrived in Greece at this time as military observers. Both would fly as passengers in Blenheims and Wellingtons on a number of raids during the coming months.

The first real action of 1941 occurred on 6 January as weather permitted some more sustained operational flying. On their third raid of the month, nine

Plt Off E W C Trollip, 80 Squadron. (*M M Stephens*)

Blenheims from 211 Squadron appeared over Valona at 0940, bombing the foreshore from 4000 feet. CR42s of 150° Gruppo and G.50bis from 154° Gruppo were scrambled, intercepting as the bombers left the target. Ten Livio Bassi and two other 154° pilots claimed one Blenheim shot down between them, Bassi then attacking and shooting down a second Blenheim which appears to have been Flg Off R D Campbell's L1487. With the aircraft riddled, and the gunner, Sgt R Appleyard, having been wounded in the head twice, Campbell crashed into the sea south-west of Valona, breaking his leg as a result. Despite their wounds and injuries, all three members of the crew managed to extricate themselves, although they then became separated in the sea. Bassi, rather than pursue the remaining Blenheims, guided a destroyer to the area where the observer, Sgt J H Beharrell, was rescued. The pilot and gunner eventually managed to swim to the coast, but here they had great difficulty getting ashore due to perpendicular cliffs at the land's edge. They eventually managed it, and were finally found and made prisoners around midnight.

Meanwhile the CR42 pilots had kept up the pursuit, returning to claim four more Blenheims shot down, three of them by Serg Osvaldo Bartolaccini and one by Sottoten Pasquale Faltoni. Sgt J R Marshall's L1542 had been slightly damaged in the tail by AA when a CR42 attacked, but the gunner, Sgt Bill Baird, drove this off, reporting that smoke poured from its engine as it broke away. L8536, flown by Flg Off L S Delaney was badly hit, although Sgt T A McCord in the turret claimed that he believed he had shot down a 'Macchi' in flames. As the

65

A 211 Squadron Blenheim I bomber comes in to land at a Greek airfield. (*IWM*)

bomber headed away, the port engine stopped, but it headed on, accompanied by the formation leader, Flt Lt Doudney, whose Blenheim had also been heavily damaged. Near the frontier Delaney indicated that he was going down to land. As he attempted to bring the aircraft down on its belly, it struck some boulders and cartwheeled; the crew were killed outright. Doudney almost reached Menidi, but he too was obliged to crash-land short of this base. Two more Blenheims also received damage, Flg Off L B Buchanan reaching Menidi, while Plt Off J C Cox put down at Eleusis for temporary repairs. Losses were thus one Blenheim over the target and two crash-landed, one of them totally destroyed as a result, plus two more damaged against Italian claims for six destroyed and one damaged.

During the past month Hs 126 E33 of 3 Mira, crewed by Maj Demetrius Daliatseas and Capt Spyridon Nanopoulos, had undertaken daily patrols over the front lines in the Pogradec area whenever weather permitted. On this date the aircraft was hit and shot down by AA fire, the crew losing their lives.

Two days later on 8 January, a formation of Z.1007bis bombers appeared over the front, being attacked in the Ostravo area by 22 Mira PZLs. Capt G Phanourgakis is believed to have been the pilot credited with one bomber shot down, although it appears that on this occasion none were lost, the Italian gunners claiming one PZL in return, from an attacking force of PZLs, Gladiators and 'Hurricanes' (sic). Later in the day nine CR42s, apparently flown by pilots of the 154° Gruppo, escorted a 72° Gruppo Ro.37bis over the Kelcyre area, engaging 21 Mira Gladiators and 22 Mira PZLs. Each Greek unit claimed one Fiat shot down, one of these being credited to Capt Andrew Andoniou, the 22 Mira commander, while the Italians claimed five Gladiators, one of which was seen to force-land at Argyrokastron. So far as can be ascertained, neither side in fact suffered any loss.

Greek personnel dismantle two captured Meridionali Ro.37bis aircraft for shipment south from recently-captured Koritza airfield in January 1941. In the background is the crash-landed S.73, 606-7 (ex I-LODI).

Weather again reduced activity until 12 January, when 24 CR42s from the 150° and 160° Gruppo appeared over the front to strafe targets of opportunity such as mule trains. AA fire struck one 150° Gruppo aircraft, and Ten Francesco Gatti was shot down. Over Larissa the weather cleared and 80 Squadron was ordered to fly up to Yanina during the afternoon. Bad visibility prevented them from finding their way through the mountains, but in any event Yanina airfield was unserviceable. Indeed Larissa too would be so the next day, for during the night heavy snow fell. This was to continue, interspersed with rain, for the next five or six days, culminating on 17 and 18 January with continuous rain and thunderstorms which curtailed all flying.

However, pending the arrival of a further RAF fighter squadron, 80 Squadron was required to leave Larissa and get to Yanina as soon as possible. The ground personnel set out in a convoy of trucks on the direct route, but experienced great difficulty and hardships. Roads were virtually impassable, and at night temperatures dropped to 32°F below freezing! Eventually they had to give up and return to Larissa, setting out again via the long southerly route through Larissa,

Agrinion and Arta. Meanwhile on 14 January Sgt Gregory managed to fly one Gladiator up to the new base, followed by nine more two days later, and a further trio on 19 January.

Pilots of 21 Mira at Yanina following their re-equipment late in 1940 with ex-RAF Gladiators, one of which forms the background to their group. (*A Stamatopoulos*)

One of the worst-hit airfields had been Kalambaka in Central Greece, where the Gladiators of 21 Mira were based. When ordered to fly down to Eleusis to cover an incoming convoy, the base personnel were defeated by the task of trying to clear the runway. Capt John Kellas, the commanding officer, made a plea for help to the local villagers, and about 200 old men, women and children turned up, equipped with a variety of agricultural implements. Working with a will, they cleared the ground sufficiently to allow the squadron to get off next day. Subsequent to this, the Greek fighters began assembling at airfields in Macedonia. 21 Mira returned from Eleusis to Ptolemais, while 22 Mira moved to Salonika to replace 23 Mira, this latter unit withdrawing to Larissa to reorganise. 24 Mira, released from the control of AA Command, had moved with its Bloch MB151s to Salonika also, where it now joined the other Mire under the control of EVA Fighter Command.

The Regia Aeronautica also undertook some changes at this time. On 15 January the 5° Gruppo OA (31ª and 39ª Squadriglia) arrived at Devoli from Italy, equipped with Ro.37bis tactical reconnaissance aircraft, while next day the 154° Gruppo Autonomo CT and 394ª Squadriglia CT moved their fighters from Berat to Devoli. However on 20 January, the S.79s of the 105° Gruppo BT left Albania, flying back to Italy to become a part of the 4ª Squadra Aerea − as 4ª ZAT had been renamed on 1 January. This Comando had relinquished its 41°

Personnel of 24 Mira with one of their Bloch MB151 fighters at an advanced airfield early in 1941. (*A Stamatopoulos*)

Bloch MB151 fighter of 24 Mira with Greek groundcrew personnel. (*A Stamatopoulos*)

Gruppo BT on this same date (20 January), when it withdrew to Littoria without aircraft to remuster as a torpedo-bomber unit. In the 35° Stormo BM, the 95° Gruppo was now exchanging its Z.506Bs for Z.1007bis bombers, but the 86° Gruppo retained its bomber floatplanes for the time being. On 30 January the Comando would lose one of its dive-bomber units when the 96° Gruppo B a'T took its Ju87s over to Libya to support Graziani's hard-pressed army there.

On 20 January, 211 Squadron again despatched five Blenheims to bomb Valona during the morning. Four 150° Gruppo CR42s attacked just as they had finished their bombing, and two were slightly damaged, Sottoten Ernani Loddo claiming one shot down. Escaping the fighters, all five were heading back to base when ten miles south of Corfu a Z.506B from 35° Stormo BM was sighted, and was attacked by Flg Off Buchanan in L1490. Closing to 75 yards, Buchanan inflicted severe damage and silenced the turret gunner, but return fire had struck the Blenheim in one engine nacelle; on return the Italian gunner claimed to have shot down one Blenheim and possibly a second!

80 Squadron was still maintaining a detachment at Eleusis for the defence of Athens and at 1220 on this date three Gladiators were ordered off to patrol over Piraeus, as Italian bombers were reported approaching from the west. Two minutes later two more Gladiators were ordered off to patrol 15 miles to the south-west, and two of 30 Squadron's Blenheim fighters were also scrambled. At 1330 four Z.1007bis from 47° Stormo BT appeared over Athens and bombed from 13 000 feet, escaping interception, as the trio of Gladiators were patrolling at 10 000 feet and had no chance of reaching the bombers, although they did chase them out to sea. When a second formation of bombers approached however, the Gladiators had climbed to 15 000 feet and were well-placed to intercept, making a head-on attack as the bombers turned east for their target. Plt Off Stuckey then broke away and made an individual quarter attack closing to very short range; his Gladiator was struck by return fire and he broke away, diving to sea level and going in to land at a newly-constructed airfield at Hassani, just south of Athens. As he approached another aircraft was in his way, and he was forced to circuit again. However, as he glided in over the hangars, flames were see coming from the underside fuel tank of K7902, and next moment the Gladiator was engulfed, crashing into the ground; Stuckey was killed instantly.

Meanwhile Flt Lt Woods attacked the same bomber at which Stuckey had been firing, joined by one of the Blenheim IFs flown by F/Sgt D J Innes-Smith. Suddenly the big Cant trimotor also burst into flames and four members of the crew baled out just before it crashed into the sea ten miles south of Athens, exploding on impact. The other four bombers in the formation all suffered damage from the fighters' attacks, one of them having also been hit by Innes-Smith.

211 Squadron was active again on 22 January, Sqn Ldr Gordon-Finlayson leading six Blenheims on an offensive reconnaissance over the Kelcyre-Berat road. At Berat buildings were bombed from 6500 feet, but two G.50bis from 154° Gruppo then intercepted. These chased the Blenheims for ten minutes, claiming one shot down. Their fire had indeed struck four of the bombers, and in Flg Off A C Godfrey's aircraft one bullet set a Very cartridge on fire, starting a blaze which

Fiat G.50bis of 154° Gruppo Autonomo CT. (*F Pedriali via N Malizia*)

must have looked as though it spelled 'finis' for the machine; although preparing to bale out, the crew were able to extinguish the fire and return to base.

In Plt Off Cox's L1528, Plt Off Bevington-Smith, the observer, recalled: 'We were attacked over the target and escaped into cloud, becoming separated in the process. Flying alone, down the Ionian Sea and once we were south of Corfu, Cox let me fly, and I was stoodging along with Cox dozing in the observer's seat. Casting my eye over the instruments, I thought something might be wrong and I shook him awake (the oil pressure was nil and the oil temperature very high). I had never seen Cox move so quickly in his life! As he took control, our starboard engine started emitting copious volumes of smoke, and had to be shut down. Cox decided to force-land at Araxos, on the north-west corner of the Peloponnese. ... We fired off red Very lights and the people on the ground fired them back, warning us not to land, but we had no option. We touched down alright on the partly constructed runway; as we did so the starboard engine burst into flames and Cox yelled to open the exit hatches and be prepared to get out. To do this I undid my seat belt, and as the aircraft slowed down the main wheels sunk into the ground, pitching the aircraft up on its nose. I was precipitated into the nose, hitting my mouth on the bomb sight, and losing four of my front teeth.'

The three airmen obtained a lift in a farm cart to Patras where they contacted the US Consul. He advised them that there was no train to Athens for four or five days, so they walked to the harbour, and there hitched a lift on a boat to Piraeus that night.

The further reinforcements now began to arrive in Greece, the air party of 11 Squadron arriving at Eleusis on 23 January. This comprised six Blenheim Is and six Mark IVs, led by Sqn Ldr P Stevens; the ground party would follow five days later, the unit moving forward to Larissa to begin operations on 28th. On the same day 'A' Flight of 112 Squadron flew in – nine Gladiators, led by Sqn Ldr H L T Brown, and a Bombay of 216 Squadron carrying supplies. The ground party was on its way by sea, while 'B' Flight would follow in a few days, commanded by Flt Lt Charles Fry, an Australian. 'A' Flight commander was Canadian Flt Lt Lloyd G 'Algy' Schwab, who had gained four victories in the Desert to date.

Regular visitors to Greece were the supply-carrying Bristol Bombays of 216 Squadron, one of which approaches Athens. (*S W Lee*)

It was the turn of the Greek fighters again on 25 January when during the afternoon 4ª Squadra Aerea launched a resumption of their air attacks on Salonika. Ten Cant Z.1007bis from the 50° Gruppo Autonomo BT appeared over the city, being intercepted by 21 and 22 Mire, one bomber being claimed shot down by Capt Andoniou of the latter unit, and a second by one of the Gladiator pilots. The Italians reported that one Z.1007bis had been shot down, apparently by AA fire, while a second suffered damage to attacking Gladiators. Fiat BR20s from the 37° Stormo BT were also over Greece, reporting interception over Kelcyre by both Gladiators and PZLs, gunners claiming one of the latter shot down. Two BR20s were claimed in return, one by a pilot of 23 Mira and one by 22 Mira, the victor in the latter case being believed to be Capt G Doukas. Two BR20s were indeed hit, one force-landing near Berat, severely damaged, while a second regained its base at Lecce with three members of the crew wounded.

During the afternoon three of 30 Squadron's Blenheim bombers set off to raid Boultsov in Albania, but over the target area at 1505 six G.50bis were seen – part of a force of 14 of these aircraft and 20 CR 42s which were patrolling over all the main Albanian centres. L8443 (Sgt L W Stammers) was attacked several times, the gunner, Sgt W S Akeroyd, being wounded in the hand, arm and stomach. Despite his wounds, he continued to man his gun until the attacking fighters broke away. He then crawled forward to report the extent of his wounds, and of the damage to the aircraft, and to his pilot; the observer had also been hit in the leg. The G.50bis pilots claimed one Blenheim probably destroyed, but although one of the other bombers had also been badly damaged, all three got back to Eleusis. This unit had now been taken over by Sqn Ldr R A Milward, who had previously commanded a flight of Blenheims in 39 Squadron, based in Aden.

Very poor weather continued to limit flying on most days in the period 21–26 January, but on 27 January, the nine Gladiators of 80 Squadron's Eleusis detachment flew up to Yanina to rejoin the rest of the unit. Their role in the south was taken over by 112 Squadron, which undertook its first patrol over Athens on this date; the squadron would be fully operational by 1 February.

A formation of Cant Z.1007bis (twin tailed versions) of 191ᵃ Squadriglia, 86° Gruppo, 35° Stormo BT head for Greece. (*Fam Salvadori via N Malizia*)

The strengthened 80 Squadron was able to operate on 28 January, Sqn Ldr Jones leading 15 Gladiators on an offensive patrol between Kelcyre and Premet on this date. At 1420 four 37° Stormo BR20s and five 35° Stormo Z.1007bis were sighted, and Flt Lt Pattle's section of three (Pattle, Sgt Casbolt and Plt Off Trollip) engaged one of the latter unit's new aircraft, which fell in flames, only two members of the crew managing to bale out. Casbolt then attacked a second Cant, while Pattle and Trollip went after one of the BR20s; the latter was seen to go down gushing smoke from its starboard engine and was claimed as a probable. Flg Off Cullen also reported shooting down a Z.1007bis, which exploded in mid-air, but as only one was actually lost it is presumed that he also fired at the aircraft shot down by Pattle's section. One other Cant in another formation was damaged and returned with three wounded aboard – presumably the second bomber attacked and claimed damaged by Casbolt. Later in the afternoon the Greek authorities notified the squadron that a second Italian aircraft had crashed in the area and this was presumed to have fallen as a result of the earlier action. However this would in fact seem to have been a G.50bis of the 355ª Squadriglia CT (Serg Tommaso Pacini) which failed to return from a bomber escort sortie over the Koritza area, and was presumed shot down by AA fire.

Flg Off R N Cullen DFC (rt) of 80 Squadron with a visiting Army Officer. (*E G Jones*)

Thereafter the weather closed in again over Central and Southern Greece, preventing any worthwhile operations until 5 February. Flt Lt Pattle did lead six Gladiators up to patrol over Corfu on 31 January, but nothing was seen and on return Flt Lt Kettlewell's aircraft overturned after hitting a soft patch on landing, suffering severe damage. During the closing days of January, 211 Squadron learned that Flt Lt Graham Jones had been awarded a DFC, whilst 80 Squadron was advised of a posthumous award of this medal to their former commanding officer, Sqn Ldr Hickey.

February's bad weather led to an inauspicious start to the month. On 2 February one of 11 Squadron's newly-arrived Blenheims, N3580, force-landed near Salonika whilst on a non-operational flight, while a second, T2235, was lost on a flight from Eleusis to Abu Sueir, Sgt D G Strachan and his crew being posted missing. Sunderland 'U', L2166, patrolling over the coastal area from the detachment base at Scaramanga, was intercepted by a pair of Z.506B floatplanes which attacked for six minutes. The flyingboat was not hit, but its gunners believed that they had scored strikes on the attackers.

Two sergeants touch the bald head of a groundcrew NCO for luck before getting into their Blenheim for a raid.

84 Squadron tried on 5 February, three Blenheims going out at 0715, to bomb supply depots on the Valona-Tepelene road. They became separated in low cloud on the way to the target, attacking individually. As they returned the port engine of Flt Lt Towgood's L1392 failed and the Blenheim crashed near the boundary fence of Menidi airfield, the pilot being killed instantly, although the other

75

members of the crew survived unhurt. Next day Flg Off A N N Nicholson of this unit was off in L1393 on a solo midday sortie to the Tepelene area. The weather again deteriorated, and in very poor visibility he was obliged to ditch in the sea near a small island in the eastern end of the Gulf of Corinth. Sgt A J Hollist, the gunner, was killed in the crash, whilst the observer, Plt Off R G C Day, was drowned. Nicholson alone managed to inflate the dinghy and reached the island from where he was evacuated to hospital.

Italian bombers were again over Greece on 8 February according to Regia Aeronautica records. Cant Z.1007bis of 37° Stormo BT raided Cajazza and Suka, being engaged by Greek fighters. One Gladiator and one PZL were claimed shot down with a second PZL as a probable, but one bomber was badly hit and was destroyed in a force-landing on return to Lecce with three men being hurt. Another formation was attacked by PZLs and returned with one airman badly wounded, while an S.79 was damaged by AA. There are no Greek claims or losses recorded for this date and it is possible that these engagements were amongst those reported by EVA units on 9 February. During 8 February, 22 and 23 Mire moved with their PZLs to the forward landing ground at Paramythia, a valley in north-western Greece, close to the Epirus sector of the front line.

Next day the skies erupted with action. From Yanina at 1030 Sqn Ldr Jones led off 14 of 80 Squadron's Gladiators on an offensive patrol over the Tepelene area, although one Gladiator's engine stopped as it became airborne and Flg Off Price-Owen was forced to glide back to the airfield. Near Tepelene a trio of S.79s were seen, but lost in cloud, following which Sqn Ldr Jones and Flg Off Wanklyn Flower both experienced engine trouble and were obliged to turn back. Flt Lt Pattle took over the lead, and just before midday five CR 42s were seen, followed by many more, 30–40 being reported. In fact there were just 16 fighters of the 150° Gruppo, led by Cap Edmondo Travaglini, and the Italian pilots also overestimated the opposition, identifying the 11 Gladiators as 20 strong!

Many individual dogfights developed between Tepelene and Argyrokastron. Pattle shot down one Fiat which crashed into the ground at speed on the outskirts of Tepelene, while Flg Off Cullen put four bursts into another and reported seeing it crash into a hillside and burst into flames. The squadron returned to claim four definitely shot down and three probables, but the Greek authorities provided confirmation next day that all seven had crashed, and victories were credited to Flt Lt Kettlewell, Plt Off Vale, Plt Off C H Tulloch, Sgt Gregory and Sgt Casbolt, as well as the Pattle and Cullen. The initial claims had been nearer the truth, for four CR 42s were in fact hit; Serg Romano Maionica and Serg Barolo both failed to return, the latter being believed to have baled out, while Ten Rovetta was wounded and crashed while attempting to land at base, and Cap Travaglini force-landed near Tirana. In return the Italians claimed four Gladiators shot down and nine damaged. Flg Off Hosken baled out of N5811, wounded in one leg, when his controls were shot away; he came down near Tepelene. Flt Lt Kettlewell force-landed N5858 some 50 miles north of Yanina due to lack of oil pressure, but with his aircraft undamaged. Both returned to Yanina aided by the Greek army.

Whilst the Gladiators were away, Yanina was bombed at 1100 by five bombers

Flg Off P T 'Keg' Dowding, Lt Col Alex Melas, Greek Liaison Officer, Wt Off Casey and Flt Lt G W V 'Jimmie' Kettlewell of 80 Squadron. (*E G Jones*)

identified as BR20s, but these were in fact 104° Gruppo BT S.79s. Their bombs missed the target and the only damage was to the southern outskirts of the town. At 1600 a further raid was made, this time reported as comprising 15 bombers with an escort of six fighters; again there was no damage. 18 more 104° Gruppo S.79s were out to bomb in the Kelcyre-Tepelene area during the day, escorted by 12 G.50bis fighters from 24° Gruppo led by Magg Eugenio Leotta, and 12 CR42s of 160° Gruppo, led by Ten Edoardo Crainz. This formation was intercepted by four Gladiators of 21 Mira and eight PZLs from 22 and 23 Mire.

In a series of hectic dogfights the G.50bis pilots claimed one Gladiator and three PZLs shot down, while the CR42 pilots submitted claims for three Gladiators (one each by Ten Crainz, Serg Magg Luciano Tarantini and Serg Magg Aurelio Munich) and two PZLs (Sottoten Raoul Francinetti and Serg Antonio Crabbia). Against these nine claims it seems that three Greek fighters were actually hit; 1/Lt Antonis Papaioannou was wounded seriously in both legs and force-landed his Gladiator near Kakavia, damaged beyond repair; one PZL was hit in the engine and came down in a field, being totally destroyed in the crash-landing, although the pilot was unhurt; a second PZL was shot up by three fighters and Sgt John Michopoulos was wounded in the thigh, but he managed to get back to Salonika/Sedes and land.

In return the Greeks claimed six victories, Capt Kellas, commander of 21 Mira, claiming two bombers and Sgt Dagoulas of 22 Mira claiming one, while 2/Lt Anastassios Bardivilias of 21 Mira claimed two fighters and 1/Lt Mitralexes of 22 Mira one more over Berat. No Italian fighters were lost on this occasion, but some of the bombers claimed may have been Ju87s of 238ª Squadriglia, which were operating over the front on this date. Six of these dive-bombers were reportedly attacked by 20 Greek fighters, Sottoten Luigi de Regis's aircraft being seriously damaged and force-landing near Valona, while a second aircraft was damaged, although reportedly by AA fire. Other aircraft claimed may have been the bombers reported attacked by Greek fighters on the previous day.

Cant Z.1007bis bombers from the 47° Stormo and 50° Gruppo Autonomo BT were also in action during the day, raiding Salonika once again. Here they reported being attacked by 'Blenheim fighters and Hurricanes', one bomber being damaged by one of the latter. No RAF Blenheims were involved, but it is possible that 32 Mira bombers became engaged whilst on a sortie to the front. However the 'Hurricanes' were undoubtedly the Bloch MB151 fighters of 24 Mira from Sedes airfield, Sgt E Smyrniotopoulos of this unit claiming one bomber shot down.

During early February Italian submarines had been sighted several times in the South Aegean, Ansons of 13 Mira being ordered to patrol between the Saronic Gulf and Crete as a result. On 9 February, Anson N57 was ordered off on such a sortie in bad weather, but as it carried out its lonely duty a storm developed, and the crew became lost. Eventually, running low on fuel, they attempted a force-landing on the Plain of Messara in the centre of Southern Crete. As they approached, they released the bombload for safety, but one bomb hung-up and exploded as they touched down, destroying the aircraft and killing 1/Lt Nicholaous Toubakaris and his navigator, the gunner being injured.

Following the heavy fighting on this date, 80 Squadron received reinforcement during the evening by five Gladiators from 112 Squadron on attachment with their pilots. The squadron also celebrated the award of a DFC to Flt Lt Pattle, whose personal score now stood at over 15. Sqn Ldr Milward, commanding 30 Squadron at Eleusis, also received a DFC for his work in Aden earlier in the year. The day also saw the move of six of 211 Squadron's Blenheims to join the Greek PZLs at Paramythia. The 'Valley of Fairy Tales' as it became known to the RAF, was to become of increasing importance in the weeks which followed. Ten miles long, 3000 feet above sea level, and surrounded by mountains reaching 6000 feet to the dominating Mount Kovillas, the valley was accessible only by the air, or by foot and mule. It was approached by following a dried-up river bed which meandered for many miles until a break in the mountains appeared. This was wide enough to allow an aircraft the size of a Wellington to fly through – with caution – to reach the airfield, which was a mere 30 minutes flying time from the front. There were no buildings, only tented accommodation, but despite many reconnaissances, the Italians had not been able to locate the base. The Blenheims would use it as an advanced landing ground, and the crews light-heartedly discussed the use of their secret weapons on further raids – empty beer bottles and full latrine buckets!

Sustained attacks on Yanina were made on 10 February by Italian bombers of all types. Fighters of both the EVA and the RAF patrolled and intercepted in a series of rather confused engagements. During the morning three formations of 47° Stormo Z.1007bis and five S.79s from the 104° Gruppo attacked, the latter escorted by 154° Gruppo CT G.50bis fighters, led by Magg Leotta. The second formation was intercepted by a trio of 21 Mira Gladiators, but the escort were on them like a shot, Leotta claiming one shot down and his pilots a second in collaboration; 2/Lt Bardivilias of the Greek unit was shot down and killed. Five of the Z.1007bis crews reported being attacked by ten Gladiators and a 'Curtiss' (possibly a Bloch MB151 from Sedes), the gunners claiming one fighter shot down, but three of the Cants being damaged by fighters and AA. A second formation of nine bombers met five Gladiators, while a third formation encountered eight Gladiators and PZLs, claiming three PZLs shot down. Thirteen BR20s of 37° Stormo BT also met PZLs, claiming one shot down but suffering damage to one BR20 which force-landed at Valona. It would seem that this was claimed by a pilot of 23 Mira as shot down.

Three Gladiators of 80 Squadron had chased five Z.1007bis bombers during mid morning (probably the initial 47° Stormo formation), but could not gain sufficient height to make an effective attack. Nevertheless they saw their fire strike two of the bombers, Flt Lt Pattle claiming one damaged. During these morning raids bombs fell on the west and north sides of the airfield, but little damage was caused other than to one staff car.

The afternoon was practically a continual air raid alarm. Four S.79s of 104° Gruppo again attacked under escort by a dozen 154° Gruppo G50bis, the escort claiming a further Gladiator shot down when a single Allied fighter of this type intercepted. Ten more 47° Stormo Z.1007bis crews reported attack by ten Gladiators and seven PZLs, claiming four Gladiators shot down. However seven of the bombers were hit, one of them badly, and a number of aircrew were wounded. Fourteen RAF Gladiators, 12 from 80 Squadron and two from 112, undertook defensive patrols, during one of which Flg Off Cullen chased away one formation of five trimotors, then attacked five more, identified as S.79s, and chased these out to sea, claiming to have shot one down into the sea south of Corfu. Another formation identified as BR20s, but almost certainly the 47° Stormo Z.1007bis, was intercepted by Flt Lt Pattle, Flt Lt Woods and Sgt Casbolt, each of these pilots claiming one damaged, while Plt Off Vale caught another which he reported crashed some 15 miles south-west of Yanina. At least five formations raided the airfield during the afternoon, an estimated 150 heavy bombs falling on or near the base. Three 80 Squadron Gladiators were damaged and one 21 Mira fighter was destroyed. In the nearby town much damage was caused and many civilians killed or injured. While returning to Berat from one of their escort missions, 154° Gruppo G.50bis pilots came across a lone Potez 63 of 31 Mira and shot this down at Voskopoulia Therapeli, 1/Lt George Stavraetos, the pilot, being killed.

At 0745 next morning, 11 February, 17 CR42s of 150° Gruppo CT, led by Cap Luigi Mariotti, and covered by 15 G.50bis from 154° Gruppo, swept in over Yanina without warning, and carried out a strafe, shooting down a Greek Gladiator as it attempted to scramble (they claimed two), and slightly damaged three more Gladiators on the ground (they claimed three more destroyed on the ground and 15 damaged!). It was believed that AA fire had struck one CR 42 and that it had crashed some miles to the south, but all in fact returned. Standing patrols were maintained by four or five RAF Gladiators through the rest of the morning, but no more hostile aircraft appeared.

Junkers Ju87B dive-bombers of 209ª Squadriglia, 97° Gruppo Autonomo B a'T taking off from Lecce airfield to cross the Adriatic for a raid on targets in Greece. (*AMI via N Malizia*)

The AA gunners did gain one success on this date, shooting down a 97° Gruppo B a'T Ju87R over the front, Serg Magg DiCarlo and 1° Av Arm Bincelli of 238° Squadriglia baling out into Italian-held territory; a second aircraft from 239ª Squadriglia was damaged. At 2245 in conditions of perfect moonlight six of 150° Gruppo's CR42s again swept in over Yanina, three of these strafing once more for 20 minutes. They claimed to have damaged six more Gladiators and destroyed a lorry; they actually damaged one more fighter.

Flg Off C W 'Bud' Richardson and his WOP/air gunner, Plt Off D Kirkman of 30 Squadron pose for the official Air Ministry photographer in their Blenheim IF.

80 Squadron was now verbally promised eight Hawker Hurricane fighters and Flt Lt Kettlewell flew down to Athens to be ready to test fly these when they arrived. Next day nine Blenheims of 84 Squadron, led by Sqn Ldr Lewis, and three from 30 Squadron, led by Flt Lt T M Horgan, arrived at Paramythia on detachment, joined before the end of the day by four 37 Squadron Wellingtons, six of which had arrived at Menidi earlier in the day, led by Wg Cdr R C M Collard.

The Greek AA enjoyed a good day on 12 February; 15 Z.1007bis of 47° Stormo raided Argyrokastron, where one was shot down by the guns, only two members of the crew managing to bale out. Twelve more Cants were hit and damaged. Six more of these aircraft from the 35° Stormo raided Preveza, where three suffered damage, while one of five attacking Ju87s of the 97° Gruppo was also hit. The Greek gunners claimed four shot down during these actions. G.50bis fighters of the 24° Gruppo reported intercepting and shooting down an aircraft near the Tobari-Mali Kaloja mountains. This was tentatively identified as a Hudson from which apparently one man baled out; no clue as to the identity of this aircraft has been found.

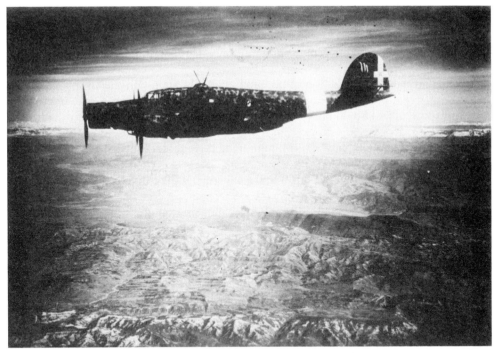

Lone Cant Z.1007bis (single fin and rudder) of 231ª Squadriglia, 95° Gruppo, 35° Stormo BT over the Epirus mountains. Note the stylised 'M' for Mussolini on the fin. (*Fam Salvadori via N Malizia*)

With darkness one of the Wellingtons at Paramythia (T2822 'D') was off to attack Tirana airfield, where Sgt A T H Gillanders and his crew reported setting fire to four aircraft although the bomber was hit by shrapnel twice. They had destroyed an S.81 and damaged two more, together with four Breda Ba44s. The other three Wellingtons attacked Durazzo, seeing fires but actually causing no material damage.

Next morning however the RAF hit back hard in return for the attacks of the last two days. At 1000 12 Blenheims from 84 and 211 Squadrons were led by the respective commanding officers to attack targets north of Tepelene, escorted by 14 Gladiators of both squadrons. 154° Gruppo G.50bis which had been escorting a reconnaissance Ro.37 over the front, sighted the Blenheims and attacked, claiming one shot down. They had hit Flg Off Buchanan's L8541, which was damaged in fuselage, wings and undercarriage, landing back at Paramythia on one wheel. The gunner, Sgt G Pattison, believed that he had shot down one of the fighters into a hillside, but none were reported lost. Sqn Ldr Tom Wisdom, the RAF Press Officer, was present in Sqn Ldr Gordon-Finlayson's aircraft and he recorded:

'Our bombs were on their way. It was most exciting. I peered out and saw below me, a number of fleecy white puffs followed by great spurts of earth and moving specks that must have been running men. We turned and retraced our course with AA bursting all round us. Then young Gerry (Plt Off G Davis, the observer) turned to me and shouted: "Fighters!" They were on to Buck's (Flg Off Buchanan) flight, but I did not see them. Then they came and had a look at us, judging from the way Arthur Geary (Plt Off A C Geary, the gunner), in the tunnel behind me, was operating his gun.'

The Gladiator escort had become separated when the Blenheims had dived through cloud near Tepelene to sight their target, and these did not encounter the G.50bis, returning to Yanina where they landed at 1135.

The squadrons were off again at 1500, 12 Gladiators rendezvousing with six 211 Squadron Blenheims bound for Bousi and six of 11 Squadron from Larissa heading for Berat. The latter formation was intercepted by six G.50bis scrambled by 154° Gruppo and led by Cap Giuseppe Scarpetta. The bombers were attacked over Berat, several being forced to jettison their bombs, and T2166 was seen to go down in flames, only Sgt L Williams, the pilot, managing to bale out. Sqn Ldr Stevens' aircraft came under attack but his gunner, Sgt H Bowen, believed that he had shot down one attacker, identified as an MC200, in flames, and caused a second to go down smoking. As the Blenheims turned for home, two lagged behind and the fighters pursued these, catching Plt Off J Hutchinson's L3581, which fell in flames, only one man baling out before it hit a mountainside. Flg Off J V Berggren's aircraft force-landed in a field with one engine shot out, while two of the survivors got back to Larissa without further incident, followed 30 minutes later by Plt Off A D P Hewison's badly damaged aircraft. The victorious Fiat pilots claimed two shot down and a third subsequently crashed in the mountains.

The 211 Squadron formation did not escape attack, one Blenheim – again flown by Flg Off Buchanan – was damaged, while Flg Off Alan Godfrey's aircraft was attacked by a fighter and sustained damage to the port engine nacelle. The gunner, Sgt J Wainhouse, believed he had hit the attacker in an exchange of fire; he also identified the interceptor as a Macchi. This time Sqn Ldr Wisdom was acting as bomb-aimer – a task for which he had received earlier instruction – and he wrote:

'We were quite alone with the Macchi attempting a beam attack. I looked back once – the Macchi was so close that you could see the pilot's hooded head. Tracer came past the cockpit window, there was a tinkling, tinny sound, accompanied by an unpleasant burning smell, as an explosive bullet struck the port engine nacelle. We took avoiding action – sudden banking and tight turns as the enemy positioned himself for the "coup de grace". The air gunner, blasting away with his single gun the while, was directing the pilot in this exciting game of aerial tag. We've made it! The Blenheim and her crew sink into the kindly cloud. We fly blind for a minute – the hidden mountains are the menace now – and then pop out. The fighters have lost us – the sky is ours again. Phew!'

Although the Gladiator pilots had seen four G.50bis, they did not manage to engage them, and unaware of the Blenheims' plight, carried out their allotted task of strafing Italian positions in the Tepelene area. AA was intense and several Gladiators were hit by shrapnel. Sgt Barker's N5761 was hit in the engine, and he was obliged to try and force-land 40 miles north of Yanina, the Gladiator somersaulting and being completely wrecked. He was unhurt and returned in a Greek army truck. That evening five more of 112 Squadron's Gladiators arrived at Paramythia from Athens. Meanwhile during the day a pair of 150° Gruppo CR42s on a weather reconnaissance had spotted a lone Greek Fairey Battle over Trebeshinj, Sottoten Ugo Drago and his wingman claiming to have shot this down.

A quieter period ensued, and while Gladiators and Blenheims were in the air over the front every day during the next four days, no Italian formations were encountered. On 14 February, 80 Squadron despatched five more pilots led by Flt Lt Woods, and including Flg Off R A Acworth, one of the attached 112 Squadron pilots, in a Bombay to Athens to collect the promised Hurricanes; only six of these were now available, two having been redirected elsewhere. A signal was received from Headquarters, British Forces in Greece at this time, which stated:

'General Papagos has asked me to thank all RAF units on behalf of the Greek Army for their magnificent support in today's field operations. The Greek Army have reached all their intended objectives. D'Albiac, 13 February 1941.'

During the night of 15/16 February, Wg Cdr Collard led his detachment of 37 Squadron Wellingtons from Menidi for an attack on Brindisi. Four of five bombers got off, bombing the airfield where it was believed a floatplane hangar was set on fire, together with one aircraft on the ground. Intense AA was encountered and T2822 'D' (Sgt Gillanders) was shot down, two members of the crew being taken prisoners, although the pilot and three others were killed. A trio of Blenheim IFs of 30 Squadron searched for the missing aircraft next morning, one crew spotting five 47° Stormo Z.1007bis which they chased to the Italian coast. Three G.50bis then appeared, which they managed to evade. 47° Stormo reported that one of their Cants was damaged by AA over Preveza, while from 37° Stormo 31 BR20s raided targets in the Trebeshinj mountains. Again much

AA was met, and one pilot was killed. During the afternoon a reported 20 Gladiators and PZLs attacked aircraft from this unit, one crewman being wounded while gunners claimed one PZL shot down; one bomber was claimed shot down by 23 Mira.

Evocative study of a 211 Squadron Blenheim I (L1434) being serviced at Paramythia early in 1941. (*T D Henderson via A Thomas*)

While 80 Squadron's Gladiators continued to operate from Yanina, those of 21 Mira moved up to Paramythia at this time, and here on 17 February they were joined by the six new Hurricanes, led by Flt Lt Kettlewell, and by four 30 Squadron Blenheims. One aircraft was lost here during the day when an 84 Squadron Blenheim (L6662) crashed on take-off; the crew survived. Two days later Wg Cdr P B 'Paddy' Coote and Maj Sevastopulo arrived to set up an Advanced Operations Wing at the base, to be known as 'W' (Western) Wing. This comprised initially the Blenheim detachment of 30 Squadron, the whole of 84 and 211 Squadrons, and a detachment of 11 Squadron which was due to arrive in a few days; the Wellingtons of the 37 Squadron detachment were also to return, while the six 80 Squadron Hurricanes would shortly be joined by six more from 33 Squadron, which was just arriving that day.

The Wing Headquarters were to be based at Yanina, where the Gladiators of 80 and 112 Squadrons would remain. The PZLs were also attached temporarily to the Wing. Flying in that evening at dusk, two of these little fighters collided in the middle of the airfield. Overnight one good machine was rebuilt from the two

84

Sqn Ldr Charles Ryley at the head of 'B' Flight, 33 Squadron as the unit prepared to move from Egypt to Greece in February 1941. L to r: unidentified, Flg Off C H Dyson, DFC, Flg Off P R St Quintin, Plt Off H J Starrett, Flt Lt G E Hawkins, Sgt J Craig (probably), Flg Off J F Mackie and Flg Off V C Woodward.

damaged airframes. A Greek Ju52/3m also flew in loaded with food and supplies to be dropped to isolated forces in the Kelcyre area.

During these days of reinforcement heavy rain fell almost continuously, preventing nearly all activities over the front line or the Albanian bases. The new arrival from Egypt, 33 Squadron, was already a well-experienced unit, having played an important part in Wavell's December 1940 offensive in Libya. The air party of 16 Hurricanes flew in via Crete, led by Sqn Ldr Charles Ryley, who had until recently been temporary commander of 230 Sunderland Squadron; one Hurricane force-landed at Buq Buq as the unit set out, but would follow later. The unit's 'A' Flight was led by Flt Lt John Littler and 'B' Flight by Flt Lt Alfred Young. Already credited with some 80 victories, the unit included amongst its experienced pilots Flg Off Charles Dyson, DFC, who was credited with nine victories, while Canadians Flg Off Vernon Woodward and Flg Off John Mackie had eight and six respectively. F/Sgt Len Cottingham and Rhodesian Flg Off Frank Holman had also each claimed six victories, as had Flg Off Peter Wickham; Flg Off 'Dixie' Dean was credited with five and Flg Off Harry Starrett a South African, with three. The ground party, under Plt Off D S F 'Bill' Winsland, and including most of the NCO pilots would arrive by sea within a day or so. Winsland, together with Plt Offs Ray Dunscombe, Charles Chetham and Sgt G E C Genders, had reached Egypt the previous month after flying Hurricanes from Takoradi, West Africa, which they had flown off the carrier *Furious*. All three officers had served in Hurricane units in England prior to this; Winsland had flown with 601 Squadron, but had no combat experience; Dunscombe had claimed one victory with 213 Squadron, but had been shot down and burned, receiving treatment at the experimental plastic surgery unit at East Grinstead, as one of the first RAF 'Guinea Pigs'. Chetham had flown with 1 Squadron during the Battle of Britain, and had a couple of victories to his credit.

Some slight improvement in the weather on 20 February allowed a resumption of activity, and at 0900 15 G.50bis of 154° Gruppo took off led by Magg Mastrogostino to escort four Ro.37bis on reconnaissance over the Kelcyre-Tepelene area. At 0930 they reported encountering 30 Greek Gladiators and PZLs which were also apparently escorting bombers and reconnaissance aircraft. There were in fact 19 such fighters present, and the pilots reported meeting a far greater force of Italian aircraft. Pilots of 22 Mira claimed three G.50bis and two probables, while Sgt Dagoulas claimed a reconnaissance aircraft – presumably one of the Ro.37bis, none of which were in fact lost, although one suffered slight damage, reportedly to AA fire. Two G.50bis were in fact hit, Ten Franchini and Ten Fusco both carrying out force-landings at Berat, where one of the fighters was destroyed. In return the Italian pilots claimed ten shot down and eight damaged; Greek losses are not recorded, but none of their pilots were reported killed or wounded.

Eight Blenheims of 84 Squadron and three from 30 Squadron were off next to bomb in the Tepelene area, escorted by six of 80 Squadron's new Hurricanes on their first sorties over the front. Over the target at 1025 the bombers split into two formations to attack, at which point six CR42s appeared. These did not interfere, having apparently spotted the Hurricanes.

Early in the afternoon eight Gladiators of 80 Squadron and nine of 112 Squadron flew up to Paramythia from Yanina. At 1445, 15 of these took off in five sections of three, led by Sqn Ldr Brown, to escort two Wellingtons of 37 Squadron, flown by Flt Lt M J Baird-Smith and Sgt R T Spiller, each carrying about one and a half tons of supplies; they were accompanied by the Greek Ju52/3m to drop these supplies to the troops near Kelcyre. Low cloud and rain made the flight difficult, and near Korouode five hostile aircraft were seen, but these did not approach. The supplies were dropped successfully, and the three aircraft were escorted back to Paramythia; the fighters then returned to the frontline to patrol.

Soon after the supply-droppers had gone, 17 Blenheims – eight of 84 Squadron, six of 211 Squadron and three of 30 Squadron – commenced taking off for a bombing attack on Berat. One of the 84 Squadron aircraft suffered an engine failure and belly-landed, but the remaining 16 (with an escort of six Hurricanes led by Flt Lt Pattle), arrived over the target, their bombs falling on the town, supply dumps, and demolishing a bridge carrying the main road over the River Osem. AA fire was experienced and 154° Gruppo G.50bis from the 361ª and 395ª Squadriglia were scrambled from Berat airfield. Pattle's section took on four of the attackers as they climbed up, Pattle firing on one which exploded in flames. Flt Lt Woods claimed another and Sgt Casbolt considered that he had shot

A group of 80 Squadron's 'noteables' in early 1941; l to r Sgt E W F Hewett, Plt Off W Vale, Flg Off P T Dowding, Flg Off F W Hosken, Flg Off Trevor-Roper (84 Sqn), Flt Lt M T StJ Pattle, Flg Off H D W Flower, Plt Off J Lancaster. (*J McGaw*)

down two. These claims were verified by the crews of the Blenheims under attack; Plt Off Cox's L8542 of 211 Squadron was badly shot-up, but their attacker was seen to be shot down by two Hurricanes. Plt Off Geary, gunner in Sqn Ldr Gordon-Finlayson's aircraft, reported:
'A G 50 came for us and in a flash a Hurricane just shot it off our wingtip. It simply rolled over, went on fire, and dived into the mountain. It was wizard.'

Other Fiats followed the Blenheims as they withdrew; one of the 30 Squadron machines had its starboard engine shot out, but Sgt Ratlidge managed to get it back to Paramythia. As the formation neared the front, the patrolling Gladiators of 80 and 112 Squadrons spotted the pursuing Italian fighters and engaged them. Flg Off Cullen reported:
'The leader came into close range and then flicked over on its back and dived down. I did a half-roll and got into position dead astern. Four long bursts and the enemy caught fire and crashed into a snow-covered hill. Then engaged another G.50 and got in some good deflection shots. Saw two formations of biplanes, thought they were Glads and went to take a look at them. They were CR 42s. Got on the tail of one, gave him a burst, and he went over on his back, and the pilot baled out. The others made off at once. Just as well – I hadn't any ammo left.'

Cullen's Gladiator received some damage during these combats and one bullet furrowed the knuckles of his right hand, but he returned to Yanina without further incident. Flt Lt Schwab of 112 Squadron also claimed one G.50 shot down, and three others were claimed damaged by 112 Squadron pilots Flt Lt R J Abrahams, Flg Off E T Banks and Plt Off J L Groves. Flt Lt Kettlewell of 80 Squadron also claimed a G.50, but did not see it crash whilst Plt Off Trollip claimed another probably destroyed.

The Italian fighters had claimed one Blenheim shot down and one fighter – identified as a 'Spitfire'. Despite the many RAF claims, it seems that only two Fiats were actually lost. Ten Alfredo Fusco of the 361ª Squadriglia was shot down and killed, while Ten Livio Bassi of 395ª Squadriglia was wounded; attempting to force-land his damaged aircraft at Berat, the Fiat flipped over and caught fire. Bassi, credited at this time with seven victories, was to linger for 43 days before dying in hospital in Rome. A third G.50bis, flown by Serg Gambetta, was damaged. Both Bassi and Fusco were subsequently awarded posthumous Medaglia d'Oro.

Tenente Livio Bassi of 395ª Squadriglia, 154° Gruppo Autonomo CT with his Fiat G.50bis, showing well the unit marking, a chicken in British colours, transfixed by an arrow. Bassi was wounded in combat with Hurricanes on 20 February 1941, and crashed while attempting to force-land; he died on 2 April 1941, receiving a posthumous award of the Medaglia d'Oro. (*AMI via N Malizia*)

Poor weather again put a stop to most flying on 21 February; the two detached 37 Squadron Wellingtons prepared to return to Menidi, but on take-off the undercarriage of Sgt Spiller's T2607 'P' collapsed, and the big bomber was damaged beyond repair. 80 Squadron's Hurricane detachment at Paramythia was joined by Flg Off Acworth from 112 Squadron to gain further experience on the type. On 22 February the four remaining Wellingtons of 37 Squadron at Menidi left to return to Shallufa.

On this latter date continuing rain rendered Yanina unserviceable, although Hurricanes and Blenheims from Paramythia were able to attack the Bousi-Glara road. Further south however, the defenders of Athens were in action for the first time in some weeks. From Eleusis six of 30 Squadron's Blenheim IFs were sent off in pairs at hourly intervals to patrol. The first pair, Sqn Ldr Milward and Flg Off Davidson, were off at 1015 and sighted a Cant Z.506B floatplane of the 86° Gruppo BM near Zante Island at 7000 feet. The Blenheims dived out of the sun to make successive attacks which drove it down to sea level. Finally it came down on the water with all engines dead, the crew waving a white cloth. Davidson dropped a dinghy nearby, while Sqn Ldr Milward dropped a message on Agrinion airfield, indicating the plight of the crew. For Milward's gunner, Sgt Herbert 'Lofty' Lord, it had been the fourth successful combat in which he had participated.

Leading pilots of 30 Squadron's fighter-Blenheims outside the Mess. L to r: Flg Off R T P Davidson, Flg Off A J Smith and Flt Lt D R Walker.

At 1235 another pair of Blenheims flown by Flt Lt Derek Walker and Flg Off 'Bud' Richardson encountered five 47° Stormo Z.1007bis bombers 12 miles west of Preveza. Walker attacked in a dive from the beam and the aircraft in the 'box' formed by the other four dropped out of control, reportedly crashing into the sea south of Levkas. He then attacked the trailing aircraft, seeing oil and smoke pour from the starboard engine whereupon it slowed down. At this point Walker's guns jammed, but Richardson took up the attack, making several passes, and the Cant glided down and crash-landed in the sea. Circling, he saw two members of the crew climb onto the fuselage; a few bullets had struck his Blenheim, but no serious damage had been caused. According to Italian records one Z.1007bis actually came down – obviously the second aircraft – but they recorded that it had been hit by AA.

Next morning (23 February) at 1030, Flg Off Cullen of 80 Squadron was sent off to search for the Z.506B forced down by the Blenheims during the previous morning, which was believed to be on the sea ten miles south of Parga with engine trouble. Obviously the crew had been able to repair the damage inflicted by Milward and Davidson, for as Cullen flew south he saw it at the southern end of Antipaxoi Island, trying to take off. Diving down, he fired a burst and it came to a halt, a white cloth again being waved. As he circled overhead it attempted to take off again and he attacked, his fire being returned even though the white cloth was still flying. The stricken aircraft then began to sink, and he flew to Paramythia to report. Later a second Gladiator confirmed that the aircraft was ashore on Akra Novare Island, where the Greek hospital ship *Andros* later rescued four survivors and collected two bodies. Subsequently one of 30 Squadron's Blenheims reported that the aircraft was half submerged, its floats sticking up out of the water.

Cant Z. 506B of 191ª Squadriglia RM capsized in the sea; this floatplane was forced to ditch off Prevaza by 30 Squadron Blenheim IFs on 22 February 1941, and was then shot-up by Flg Off R N Cullen of 80 Squadron as it attempted to take off after repair next day. (*A. Stamatopoulos*)

Over the front little was seen, but Paramythia was further reinforced. Ten Blenheims of 11 Squadron flew up from Larissa in very bad weather, but four were forced to return, and a fifth crashed while attempting a force-landing in a valley, Plt Off Hewison and his gunner being killed while the observer survived with leg injuries. The remaining five aircraft were attached to 211 Squadron. Six

Hurricanes of 33 Squadron's 'B' Flight also flew in, but as they approached Plt Off Winsland suffered an engine seizure in P3970:

'I was left with insufficient time to complete the necessary emergency hand pumping operation of the hydraulic systems controlling the rather vital bits of equipment for a landing – flaps and the lowering of wheels. I got the former about half down and frantically changed over then to the wheel pumping which I was still doing even during hold-off and actually touching down knowingly with only one green light (instead of two) showing. The result was a wide ground loop on one wheel and one wingtip, a smashed propeller, and coming to rest only some 40 yards short of a small outside bomb dump – small (perhaps 30 250 lb bombs) but big enough to have made an even worse mess of the machine and anyone else unlucky enough to have been around.'

While the RAF saw no action over the frontline on 23 February, this was not the case for the Greeks. Here 12 G.50bis of the 154° Gruppo on a patrol over the Kelcyre-Devoli area met a formation of fighters estimated to include ten PZLs and 15 Gladiators. The Italian pilots claimed four PZLs shot down and three probables, together with one Gladiator and three probables. Gladiator pilot Sgt Constantinos Chrizopoulos of 21 Mira was shot down and killed, as was Capt Nicholaos Scroubelos of 23 Mira; the latter unit claimed three fighters shot down in return, although the Italians appear to have suffered no losses on this occasion.

Rain continued to disturb the flying programme, particularly at Yanina, which remained unserviceable. Paramythia could be used however, Hurricanes and Blenheims continuing to make raids over the Kelcyre-Tepelene road on 24 and 25 February. So bad was the weather however, that on the latter date. Sunderland L5804 of 230 Squadron was sunk in a gale at Scaramanga. On 26 February, 33 Squadron's detachment at Paramythia, brought back up to six following the crash of Winsland's aircraft, joined 80 Squadron's six aircraft to escort Blenheims from 11 and 211 Squadrons to raid Buzat, near Tepelene; the new unit flew a further escort mission during the afternoon, this time to within a few miles of Valona. That day was also marked by a visit to Paramythia by Air Chief Marshal Longmore, Mr Anthony Eden (the Foreign Secretary), General Sir John Dill and General Sir Archibald Wavell.

More rather heavy overclaiming was to occur on 27 February, when at 1500 nine Blenheims, six from 211 Squadron and three from 11 Squadron, set off to bomb Valona, escorted by five 80 Squadron Hurricanes and four more from 33 Squadron. An hour later, as the formation arrived over Valona, 13 CR 42s of the 150° Gruppo attacked as the Blenheims were bombing. Although the Hurricane escort engaged them at once, some got through to the bombers and damaged five of them, including all three of the 11 Squadron machines. Two of these would crash-land on return to Paramythia, both having suffered heavy damage to their hydraulic systems; N3579 would be written off. The Hurricanes meanwhile had become involved in a heavy battle with the Fiats during which seven of the Italian fighters were claimed shot down, and two more were reported to have collided with each other and crashed. Claims were made by Flt Lt Pattle, Flg Off Cullen, Sgt Hewett (two), Flg Off Acworth, and Flg Off Wanklyn Flower, who shared one with a 33 Squadron pilot, believed to have been Flg Off Starrett. The seventh claim was believed to have been made by 33's F/Sgt Len Cottingham.

In the event it seems that only two CR42s were lost, Sottoten Egidio Faltoni, the formation leader, baling out after suffering wounds, as did Serg Osvaldo Bartolaccini, who was almost dead when he hit the ground. The Italians made no claims and believed that their attackers had been Spitfires. 'Pat' Pattle's Hurricane suffered a single bullet through the petrol tank – the only damage recorded to the British fighters. A further CR42 of the Gruppo's 364ª Squadriglia was destroyed on the ground by the Blenheims' bombs, and several others were damaged. A dozen drums of fuel went up in flames, and two airmen were wounded.

Again Plt Off Geary, gunner in L1481, recorded his impressions of the raid: 'I had a grandstand view of the whole affair. It was lovely bombing – direct hits all over the aerodrome and on buildings. A large formation of CR42s took off to intercept us. One got on my tail, so I put a burst into him, and he fell away. Then two Hurricanes appeared in a flash, and well, he just fell to pieces. The Hurricanes wheeled and proceeded to deal with the others. The sky was full of crashing aircraft – and they were all enemy. We had a most pleasant tour home, and the scenery looked more lovely than ever.'

On coming back from this raid, the remains of the 11 Squadron detachment returned to Larissa.

So it was that 28 February arrived – a day which was to be recorded as the RAF's most successful of the campaign, but which was to give rise to much controversy as to the true results achieved. HQ 'W' Wing ordered that all available aircraft should patrol between Tepelene and the coast between 1530 and 1630, since Intelligence sources indicated the operation of large numbers of Italian aircraft in that area at that time. Hence during the morning all available Gladiators of 80 and 112 Squadrons were flown up to Paramythia in preparation for this action. Patrols were flown during the morning by flights of Hurricanes but nothing was seen.

At about 1500 Sqn Ldr Brown and Sqn Ldr Jones led off 11 Gladiators of 112 Squadron and seven of 80 Squadron to patrol over the designated area; they were accompanied by the 'W' Wing leader, Wg Cdr 'Paddy' Coote, flying an 80 Squadron Gladiator. Fifteen minutes later Flt Lt Pattle in Hurricane V7589 led Flg Off Cullen (V7138), Flg Off Wanklyn Flower (V6749) and Flg Off Acworth (V7288) to the same area, while Flt Lt Young led four 33 Squadron Hurricanes to patrol near the coast. Here some S.79s were seen and chased over Corfu, two being claimed damaged, one of them by Plt Off Winsland. These were probably 105° Gruppo BT aircraft, which reported being attacked by Spitfires, one Savoia landing at Tirana with one member of the crew dead.

Meanwhile Pattle's section spotted BR20s of 37° Stormo BT flying south from Valona; they identified the ten-strong formation as comprising 15 aircraft, while the bomber crews reported being attacked by 18 'Spitfires'! Pattle selected one on the starboard flank of the formation, and after three short bursts it broke into

Two-Gun Cullen! Flg Off R N 'Ape' Cullen of 80 Squadron plays it tough for the camera. (*E G Jones*)

flames and went down; a second bomber likewise burst into flames following a further attack by Pattle, and his windscreen was covered in oil from this doomed aircraft. Reducing speed, Pattle attempted to clean the screen with his scarf, but he was then attacked by five G.50bis which dived on him. After a brief skirmish he managed to get away and returned to Paramythia. Both Wanklyn Flower and Acworth also claimed BR20s, although the latter thought his victim may have been a Z.1007bis. Flg Off Cullen reported considerable success in the run of claims which was to bring him the award of an immediate DFC. He later recalled:

'The battle extended right across Albania. First I found four Breda 20s (sic). I got one, which went down in flames. Then we found three formations of S.79s. I took on one and aimed at the starboard engine. It caught fire, and crashed in flames. I climbed and dived on the next – and he too crashed in flames. Then we attacked ten CR 42s, climbing to get above them. I got behind one, and he caught fire and went down in flames. Up again immediately, dived, fired into the cockpit, and another took fire, rolled over and crashed. I had to come home then – no more ammo.'

Three BR20s were in fact shot down during this combat and a fourth force-landed near Otranto; others returned with wounded crew members aboard, plus one dead.

By now the Gladiators had joined the fighting, as had CR42s of 160° Gruppo and G.50bis of 24° Gruppo. A single Hurricane of 33 Squadron arrived late on the scene, Flg Off Newton having scrambled from Paramythia when news of the heavy fighting came through. On arrival over the battle area he promptly attacked a CR42, only to find that it was an 80 Squadron Gladiator! A 112 Squadron biplane then got on his tail, obviously taking the Hurricane for a G.50bis, and inflicted damage on his aircraft, chasing him back towards Paramythia. A few of the Gladiators made contact with the bombers, Plt Off Vale claiming an S.79 shot down, whilst Flg Off Banks and Plt Off R H McDonald of 112 Squadron each claimed damage to a BR20. The Gladiators' main claims were for nine CR42s and two probables, plus six G.50bis:

80 Squadron		*112 Squadron*	
Sqn Ldr Jones	2 CR42s	Sqn Ldr Brown	G.50bis
Wg Cdr Coote	CR42	Flt Lt Fraser	CR42; G.50bis
Wt Off Richens	CR42	Flt Lt Fry	CR42; G.50bis
Plt Off Vale	S.79; G.50bis	Flt Lt Abrahams	G.50bis
Flt Lt Kettlewell	CR42 probable	Flg Off Cochrane	CR42
	G.50bis probable	Flg Off Banks	CR42; CR42
Plt Off Trollip	CR42 probable		damaged
Flg Off Dowding	G.50bis probable	Plt Off Groves	CR42
		Sgt Donaldson	G.50bis;
			G.50bis probable

Sqn Ldr Brown recorded that the G.50bis he attacked turned sharply to starboard on its back and fell away in an inverted spin; he thought he had hit the pilot. Flt Lt Fraser claimed that his victim flew into a mountainside, while the pilot of the CR42 he claimed baled out, but his parachute failed to open; Sgt G M Donaldson's victim was seen to crash on the seashore. Flt Lt 'Dicky' Abrahams, after his victory, was attacked by another G.50bis – believed to have been flown by Ten Mario Bellagambi – and was shot down near Sarande. He recalled:

'The old Glad suddenly went all soft. Nothing would work. I sat there and then decided I had better get out. I couldn't, so I sat there with my hands on my lap, the aircraft spinning like mad. Then, eventually, I did manage to get out. It was so pleasant sitting there in the air than I damn nearly forgot to pull the ripcord. I reckon I did the record delayed drop for all Albania and Greece. I landed, and no sooner had I fallen sprawling on the ground than I was picked up by Greek soldiers who cheered and patted me on the back. I thought I was a hell of a hero until one soldier asked me. "Milano, Roma?" and I realized that they thought I was an Iti. They didn't realize it was possible for an Englishman to be shot down. So I said "Inglese", and then the party began. I was hoisted on their shoulders, and the "here the conquering hero comes" procession started. We wined and had fun. Jolly good chaps.'

Following his initial combats, Pattle had returned to Paramythia, landed, and

Officers of 80 Squadron indulge in a little pistol practice, watched by Greek soldiers. The marksman is one of the squadron's leading personalities, Plt Off Bill Vale. (*E G Jones*)

taken off again ten minutes later in another Hurricane, V7724. Returning to the battle area, he spotted three CR42s in formation, heading back towards Valona: 'I got behind them and put a long burst into all three. One went down vertically at once, but in case it was a trick I followed him. He was in difficulties, that was most obvious, and when it looked as if he was going straight into the sea I decided to go and see what the other two were up to. As I climbed again I was most surprised to see two parachutes float down past me.'

On his return, Pattle claimed two destroyed, those from which he had seen the pilots come down by parachute, and one probable for that which he had followed down. Just before he got back to Paramythia for the second time at 1740, Flg Off Wanklyn Flower, who had returned an hour earlier, also took off for a second patrol over the area after his Hurricane had been refuelled and rearmed. There was nothing to be seen – the battle was over. ...

On the Italian side, the CR42s of 160° Gruppo had been escorting four S.79s of 104° Gruppo in the Kuc area, between Tepelene and Himara, when 'British fighters identified as Spitfires, Hurricanes and Gladiators, were encountered. Two Gladiators were claimed shot down and one as a probable, a 'Spitfire' also being claimed. Sottoten Francinetti was wounded in the leg, and Sottoten Italo Traini was shot down. Gunners in the S.79s also claimed two Gladiators shot down, as did the G.50bis pilots of the 24° Gruppo, the latter also claiming two more as probables. Ten Bellagambi, following his combat with Flt Lt Abrahams, was then shot down and wounded in one arm; he force-landed near Tirana airfield. Cap Ettore Foschini's aircraft was also hit and he was wounded, also coming down at Tirana.

Fiat CR42 of Sottotenente Raoul Francinetti of 394ª Squadriglia, 160º Gruppo CT which was damaged in combat over Kuc on 28 February 1941, the pilot being wounded. (*N Malizia*)

When Pattle's late claims were added, the total for the day appeared to amount to 27 Italian aircraft, with six more probables. Claims and actual losses are summarized below:

Royal Air Force claims		*Actual Casualties Recorded*
Fiat BR20	5 destroyed, 2 damaged	4 lost and several damaged
Savoia S.79	3 destroyed, 2 damaged	0 lost, 1 damaged
Fiat CR42	13 destroyed, 3 probable, 1 damaged	2 lost
Fiat G.50bis	6 destroyed, 3 probables	2 lost

Regia Aeronautica claims		*Actual Casualties*
CR42 pilots	2 Gladiators and 1 probable;	0 lost
	1 'Spitfire'	0 lost
G.50bis pilots	2 Gladiators, 2 probables	1 lost
S.79 gunners	2 Gladiators	0 lost

Immediately following this apparent triumph, the Greeks were hard hit from a different source. During the night of 28 February/1 March Larissa was devastated by the most severe earthquake that Greece had suffered in a century. Great rifts

Pilots of 80 Squadron on the wing of a Hurricane, early March 1941; 1 to r; Flg Off P T Dowding, Plt Off J 'Ginger' Still, Sgt C E Casbolt, Wt Off S A 'Mick' Richens, Sgt E W F Hewett, Flg Off H D 'Twinstead' Flower. (*C E Casbolt*)

opened up on the airfield, where buildings and hangars collapsed, many personnel being buried under the rubble. After salvaging what they could, RAF personnel worked all through the rest of the night rescuing people trapped in the debris of the stricken town. Street after street of poorly-constructed houses had collapsed, and many of those dug out were already dead. One of the main features of the town had been a number of mosques, but the minarets of these had all tumbled. Next morning with the arrival of March, 30 Squadron Blenheims flew in carrying first aid equipment, RAMC doctors and orderlies.

There was no let-up in the war however, and on this first day of the new month the Hurricanes of 33 and 80 Squadrons were out three times to escort Blenheims of 30 and 211 Squadrons to attack Paraboa (to the north of Bousi), Berat and Valona harbour. At the latter target Flt Lt Pattle with 33 Squadron's Flg Off Newton as his wingman, went below cloud to see what activity there might be in the harbour itself. They spotted a large merchant vessel which was strafed, Pattle going in for a second attack at very close range. As the Hurricanes had set out on one of their sorties, Sgt Ted Hewett of 80 Squadron realized that he was having trouble with the undercarriage retraction of V7589 and returned to Paramythia. Here the problem was rectified, and he set out again alone. He returned to report that near the target area he had encountered five CR42s, claiming to have shot down three of them in flames, at which the others fled. No Italian account of this engagement has been found.

Next day six of 80 Squadron's Hurricanes escorted nine Blenheims drawn from 84 and 211 Squadrons to raid Berat and Devoli in the early afternoon. Bombs were seen bursting amongst parked aircraft of the 72° Gruppo OA, one Ro.37bis

97

Sgt E W F Hewett, DFM, of 80 Squadron with a Hurricane. (*IWM*)

being destroyed and three damaged; two of the unit's pilots were wounded, Serg Magg Giovanni Mencarelli fatally so. CR 42s of 160° Gruppo were scrambled in pursuit, claiming one Hurricane probably destroyed and two damaged, but no damage of any sort was actually occasioned.

On 3 March two Hurricanes from 80 Squadron were ordered up on patrol at 1025, flown by Flg Off Cullen and Plt Off Vale, while a third, flown by the attached 112 Squadron pilot, Flg Off Acworth, was sent up on an air test. As these got into the air ten Cant Z.1007bis bombers of 50° Gruppo Autonomo BT from Brindisi approached the area in two formations of five each, while other such aircraft from 47° Stormo BT were also over Greece at this time. The 50° Gruppo aircraft bombed the earthquake-shattered town of Larissa, and were on their way home by the time the Hurricanes were vectored onto them. Flg Off Acworth was first on the scene, soon joined by the other pair, and he reported: 'Took off to test aircraft – before leaving heard that ten enemy aircraft heading towards Preveza. I flew in that direction and saw bombing in progress, and although I had not enough speed to catch the first section of bombers, I finally got near enough to second section – attacked No 5 and shot it down in flames – witnessed by Flg Off Cullen, who shot down No 4. I saw one crew member leaving No 5 but afterwards, apart from an empty chute floating down, no trace of him was found. Both mine and Flg Off Cullen's first bomber crashed into the sea five miles south-west of Corfu.'

Cullen continued to attack and returned to claim a total of four Cants shot down, although his Hurricane was badly damaged by return fire, one bullet passing through his flying boot and grazing his shin; he reported seeing 18 parachutes in the air at one time. Plt Off Vale also claimed a bomber shot down, but identified his victim as an S.81. It seems however that the 50° Gruppo formation lost only the first two bombers shot down; the crews reported that they were pursued initially by two Greek PZLs, both of which the gunners claimed to have shot down. They were then attacked south of Corfu by 'seven Spitfires', claiming two of these shot down also. The second formation reported encountering intense AA fire over Preveza and returned with three aircraft damaged, while a 47° Stormo Z.1007bis was also hit and one member of the crew wounded. Sqn Ldr Gordon-Finlayson of 211 Squadron went out to drop a dinghy to any survivors who might be found, but none were seen.

First RAF Blenheim IVs to reach Greece were those of 113 Squadron's special photographic detachment, one of which is seen on Menidi airfield, carrying the unit code letters AD. (*S W Lee*)

At this time several more aircrew decorations were notified. DFCs were awarded to Sqn Ldr 'Tap' Jones and Flg Off Cullen of 80 Squadron – both of these being 'immediate awards' – while Sqn Ldrs Peter Stevens of 11 Squadron and Dudley Lewis of 84 Squadron also received these medals; a DFM went to Sgt W S Akeroyd, the 30 Squadron gunner, for his action on 25 January. Sqn Ldr Lewis was at the same time posted to Air Headquarters, his place at the head of 84 Squadron being taken by H D 'Jonah' Jones, formerly an instructor on attachment to the Royal Egyptian Air Force. While the main body of this unit was still operating from Paramythia with a mixed establishment of Blenheim Is and IVs, the HQ was still at Menidi, where a secret flight of three photo-reconnaissance Blenheim IVs from 113 Squadron from Egypt had recently arrived on attachment to the squadron. A number of clandestine reconnaissances were flown over Bulgaria by these aircraft. To maintain security, the flight was attached for servicing and administration only, the crews being billetted else-where. At Scaramanga, the detachment of 230 Squadron Sunderlands were now co-operating with 13 Mira Ansons and Greek destroyers on anti-submarine duties.

Five Italian warships identified as two cruisers and three destroyers, sortied down the Albanian coast during the morning of 4 March and commenced shelling the coastal road near Himara and Port Palermo, under cover of a strong

Sqn Ldr H D Jones (left), commanding officer of 84 Squadron with the war correspondent, Sqn Ldr T H Wisdom in front of one of the unit's Blenheims.

fighter escort of G.50bis and CR42s from the 24° Gruppo CT. The flotilla actually comprised the cruiser *Riboty*, the torpedo-destroyer *Andromeda* and three MAS boats. An immediate strike was ordered by RAF units, 15 Blenheims being ordered off. Nine 211 Squadron aircraft and five from 84 Squadron (a sixth failed to start) were led to the area by Sqn Ldrs Gordon-Finlayson and Jones, escorted by ten Hurricanes, followed by 17 Gladiators, 14 from 112 Squadron and three from 80 Squadron. Four 80 Squadron Hurricanes led by Flt Lt Pattle flew on the starboard flank of the bombers, with four from 33 Squadron to port, and two more above as 'weavers'. At 1500 the warships were seen ten miles south of Valona, and the Blenheims went in to bomb in line astern; several near misses were seen, but no hits were recorded.

At this point six G.50bis dived on the Hurricanes, shooting down V7801 in flames; Wt Off Harry Goodchild, DFM, was killed. It seems that the Italian fighters did not see the bombers, for they reported only single-engined types – ten 'Spitfires', three 'Battles' (obviously Hurricanes) and 20 Gladiators. Once the Blenheims had completed their run and were on their return flight, Pattle ordered the Hurricanes to hunt in pairs over the warships, where a number of Italian fighters were seen. At once a lone G.50bis attacked Pattle and his No 2 – on this occasion Flg Off Cullen – but Pattle promptly shot this down and watched it spiral into a mountainside just north of Himara. At this moment a second Fiat 'jumped' Cullen's V7288, and he was not seen again; his aircraft crashed near Himara, and the Australian 'ace' was killed.

Pattle flew on towards Valona, and was attacked by another lone G.50bis which he reported went into the sea after a brief combat. He then became

100

involved with a third such fighter over Valona harbour and claimed to have shot this down into the sea in flames. Nine CR42s were then seen below and he dived on these, reporting that one went into a spin with smoke pouring from its engine; he claimed this as a probable. Sgt Hewett was also heavily engaged, claiming one G.50bis shot down near Himara and three of eight CR42s near Valona. The only other claim by a Hurricane pilot was made by Plt Off Vale, who claimed another G.50bis.

Flg Off R N Cullen with one of 80 Squadron's first Hawker Hurricane I fighters (V7288), seen on 4 March, 1941 about to take off on the sortie from which he failed to return.

Meanwhile the Gladiators, led by Sqn Ldr Brown, tangled with a reported ten G.50bis and five CR42s. Flt Lt Fraser led the third section after some G.50bis which entered clouds, but he claimed one shot down and a second shared with the CO and two other pilots. Flg Off Acworth was about to attack another when he came under fire himself and was driven down to 2000 feet. He got in a few deflection shots, saw smoke issue from his opponent's engine, and claimed a probable. Flg Off Banks attacked a G.50bis which went into a spin; as he saw a parachute in the vicinity he also claimed a probable, and two more such claims were made by Flt Lt Fry and Sgt Donaldson, while four more aircraft damaged were also claimed.

In return the 24° Gruppo pilots claimed four Gladiators, one 'Spitfire' and one 'Battle' shot down. Sottoten Nicolo Cobolli Gigli of 355ª Squadriglia, who was flying a CR42 on this occasion, and Serg Marcello De Salvia of 354ª Squadriglia were both shot down and killed, while Ten Francesco Rocca of the latter unit was

Fiat G.50bis of 354ª Squadriglia, 24° Gruppo Autonomo CT in flight over Greece. (*N Malizia*)

wounded. No losses by other CR 42 equipped units have been discovered. Cobolli Gigli and De Salvia were both awarded posthumous Medaglia d'Oro.

Six leading pilots of 80 Squadron in February 1941; l to r: Sgt C E Casbolt, Sgt G Barker, Sgt D S Gregory, Plt Off W Vale, Flt Ot M T StJ Pattle, Flg Off R N Cullen. (*G F Graham*)

This was virtually the last operation over the Albanian front for 80 Squadron, for on 6 March the pilots at Yanina withdrew to Eleusis to complete re-equipment with Hurricanes; most of the remaining Gladiators were handed to 112 Squadron. They were followed next day by four Hurricanes from Paramythia led by Flt Lt Pattle. On arrival at Eleusis a number of pilots were despatched to Egypt to fly-in the new aircraft. Consequently on 8 March, 112 Squadron flew forward to Paramythia to take over 80 Squadron's role, joined there by the 33 Squadron detachment.

Gladiators of 112 Squadron, which replaced 80 Squadron at the front in March 1941, are seen here at Yanina; nearest aircraft is RT-K.

112 Squadron at Yanina, Gladiator RT-Y in the background. Amongst the group of pilots is Flt Lt L G 'Algy' Schwab, wearing sun glasses. (*IWM*)

They were just in time for renewed action, for the Italian Army was about to launch a new offensive, following a visit to Albania by Benito Mussolini at the start of the month. Twenty-eight divisions were now available in Albania, supported by 26 bombers and 105 fighters of the Comando Aeronautica Albania, plus 134 more bombers and 54 fighters of 4ª Squadra Aerea. During the period 5–7 March, the locally-based fighters had been reinforced with the latest types, the

36 Macchi C.200 fighters of the 22° Gruppo Autonomo CT (359ᵃ, 362ᵃ and 369ᵃ Squadriglia) moving to Tirana from Ciampino, while the similarly-equipped 371ᵃ Squadriglia took its ten Macchis to Valona on attachment to the 150° Gruppo CT. 4ᵃ Squadra also received 12 more of these fighters with the arrival of 73ᵃ Squadriglia CT at Brindisi from Gorizia. Comando Albania also received 114ᵃ Squadriglia OA at Tirana with eight Ro.37bis, while 238ᵃ Squadriglia from 101° Gruppo Autonomo B a'T moved over from 4ᵃ Squadra command, reaching Tirana from Lecce. Meanwhile the 150° Gruppo CT now began a gradual re-equipment with MC200s, and the 38° Stormo BT started to receive a few Cant Z.1007bis bombers to replace its elderly S.81s. The only additional RAF reinforcement at this time was the arrival of seven of 37 Squadron's Wellingtons at Menidi on a further detachment from their base at Shallufa. On arrival one of them crashed while in the landing circuit, six of the ten personnel aboard dying. These bombers made their first raid during the night of 8/9 March, attacking Durazzo.

Eleusis, 2 March 1941; the British Foreign Secretary, Anthony Eden, visits 30 Squadron while in Greece for talks with the Greek government. In the background is the unit commander, Sqn Ldr R A Milward, DFC.

The new Italian offensive began on 9 March, at once putting the overstretched defenders under great pressure. The Greek Commander-in-Chief at once requested that the RAF bombers operate in direct support of his hard-pressed ground forces instead of their usual strategic targets. Although still reluctant to agree to what many in the RAF still considered a misuse of air power, D'Albiac now had little option but to agree in the circumstances, and for the next four days the RAF at least gave the Greeks the support they really desired, all attacks being directed on tactical targets. During the afternoon of this first day Sqn Ldr Brown led 15 Gladiators of 112 Squadron on an offensive patrol over Kelcyre and Tepelene, where at 1400 an estimated 30 G.50bis were reported, escorting BR.20s which were bombing forward troops. Flt Lt Fraser led his section in an attack on the bombers, claiming one shot down, which he reported fell near Garneo. Flg Off Banks attacked another without obvious results, but was then engaged by one of the escorts before being forced to withdraw when his engine blew a sparking plug. Flt Lt Fry's section also went after the low-flying bombers, one of which was seen to jettison its bombs, and one of these aircraft was claimed probably destroyed by Plt Off Groves.

Sqn Ldr H L I Brown, commanding officer of 112 Squadron, with Sgt G N Donaldson and one of the unit's Gladiators. (*IWM*)

105

At this point the escort, which in fact comprised 25 MC200s from the newly-arrived 22° Gruppo, attacked and became involved in a dogfight with Fry's flight. Fry claimed one shot down, which dived vertically and crashed, while Sqn Ldr Brown also saw one crash into a hillside after he had fired a long burst into its tail. Six more were claimed by Sgt Donaldson (two), Flt Lt Fraser, Flg Off Acworth, Flg Off Cochrane and Plt Groves, while Flg Off R J Bennett claimed a probable. Despite all these claims, it seems that only one Macchi was actually lost, Serg Magg Marino Vannini failing to return; Mar Guido LaFerla landed at Lushnje and was taken to hospital – reportedly due to illness, rather than wounds. The Italian fighters were unable to submit any claims. The bombers attacked had been BR.20s of 37° Stormo and S.79s of 105° Gruppo, the former reporting that two of their aircraft were damaged, apparently by AA fire, while one or two Savoias were hit by fire from Gladiators, one man being wounded. The 105° Gruppo's gunners claimed three Gladiators shot down, while the crew of a Z.1007bis of 50° Gruppo, reportedly attacked by a lone Gladiator (possibly a Greek machine), also claimed shot down. One Gladiator was in fact shot down, Plt Off McDonald baling out of his blazing N5823, while four more of these fighters were damaged. Flg Off Cochrane landed on a village green to organise a search for McDonald, who would die of the burns and other injuries he had sustained two months later.

This was to be only the first of a number of dogfights between 112 Squadron and the Italian fighters during the next two weeks in which, in conditions of heavy cloud and rain over the mountainous terrain, some fairly substantial overclaiming was to result. Weather prevented operations on 10 March, but one day later 15 of the unit's aircraft were again over the front, this time to escort 211 Squadron Blenheims on a raid in the Bousi area. An estimated 40–50 G.50bis were reported patrolling in the area, and nine of these fighters from the 24° Gruppo (led by Magg Cesare Valente) engaged the formation, claiming a Blenheim and one Gladiator shot down. The British fighters turned on the attackers and claimed six shot down, one probable and seven damaged without loss. Two G.50bis went down at once, Magg Valente and Serg Luigi Spallacci both being killed, while Serg Bruno Fava and Serg Magg Ermes Lucchetta were both wounded and crash-landed their Fiats on their bellies. MC200s of the 22° Gruppo may also have become involved, for Serg Anselmo Andraghetti of 369ª Squadriglia was lost, the cause not being ascertained. 112 Squadron's claims were:

Flt Lt Fraser one and one damaged	Plt Off N Bowker one
Flg Off Banks one and two damaged	Plt Off D F Westerna one
Flg Off Acworth one	Flt Lt Fry one probable and one damaged
Flg Off Cochrane one	Sqn Ldr Brown one damaged
Flg Off E H Brown one damaged	Flg Off R H Smith one damaged

Neville Bowker, a Rhodesian, and Derek 'Jerry' Westenra, a New Zealander, were both involved in only their second engagements since joining the unit from Flying Training School.

A trio of 112 Squadron pilots with a Gladiator at Yanina. The pilot on the left is believed to be Flt Lt J F Fraser, while Flg Off R A Acworth sits on the wing, with Plt Off P L C Brunton on his left. (*Mrs Angela Acworth*)

During the next two days there were few operations, although EVA bombers were in action. 32 Mira had been brought up to strength with six ex-RAF Blenheim Is (L6658 and 6670 from 211 Squadron; L8384 and 8385, both ex-39 Squadron, amongst them). The Mark I was not favoured by the Greek crews as there were no floor hatches for emergency bale-outs, the aircraft requiring to be inverted, fighter-fashion, to allow personnel to drop free. On this date one of the Blenheim Is was hit by Italian AA fire, but when the pilot rolled the bomber onto its back he was the only member of the crew to escape as it fell to crash at Koukouvaounes, north of Athens. A Battle from 33 Mira, crewed by Lt Col Demetrius Stathakis and Maj Demetrius Pitsikas, was shot down in flames by Italian fighters over Nivitsa, but the identity of the unit responsible has not been found. 21 Mira at Paramythia was reinforced with two more Gladiators from the RAF, K7932 and 7984. Two Bücker Jungmann trainers and a Fi156 of the JKRV also arrived on secondment to the EVA; the Yugoslav pilots were briefly attached to the Po.63 unit (31 Mira) but not in an operational capacity.

On 12 March, the six Hurricanes of 33 Squadron's 'B' Flight again moved up to Paramythia on detachment, where they joined 30 Squadron's 'A' Flight of Blenheim I bombers. 'B' and 'C' Flights of this unit, both equipped with Mark IFs, remained at Eleusis for the defence of Athens, joined now in this duty by two of 80 Squadron's Hurricanes. The latter squadron received two more decorations at this time, a Bar to Flt Lt Pattle's DFC, this pilot's credited score now having reached 23, while the citation to Sgt Ted Hewett's DFM recorded 13 victories. Pattle was advised that he was to take over command of 33 Squadron forthwith, Sqn Ldr Ryley also being awarded a DFC (mainly for his activities earlier in the war as a flyingboat pilot) and being promoted to Wing Commander, with a posting to Air H.Q. Immediately on taking over his new squadron, Pattle also assumed the duty of Station Commander at Larissa. He decided at once that a satellite airfield should be established, and requested the assistance of the local Army Liaison Officer, Capt M E H Churton, RAOC. A small grass field was eventually located by Capt Churton, some six-seven miles south-west of Larissa, where some of the Hurricanes could be dispersed to guard against all being destroyed during a sudden surprise strafing attack on Larissa. On acceptance of this field by Pattle, it became known unofficially as 'Churton's Bottom' in recognition of the ALO's endeavours!

Junkers Ju87B of 208ª Squadriglia, 101º Gruppo Autonomo B a'T. (*N Malizia*)

British air striking power in Greece was about to be reinforced by a small but important addition. At the end of February the detachment of 53 Ju52/3ms of III/KGzbV 1 to the Regia Aeronautica had ended, after the German aircraft had made 1665 troop-carrying and 2363 supply sorties from Foggia to Albania, carrying across 30 000 men and 4700 tons of supplies, whilst bringing back 10 000 sick and wounded. Now however with their departure, the shipping routes between the Italian ports and those in Albania had become busier again and this had soon been noted by RAF reconnaissance aircraft. Hence six of 815 Squadron's Fairey Swordfish torpedo-bombers which were based in Crete (see Chapter 4) were to be despatched to Paramythia for nocturnal anti-shipping activities. Led by Lt Cdr Jago, the aircraft flew initially to Eleusis, since it would be here that torpedoes would be fitted as facilities were not available at the forward airfield. Jago's aircraft ('A'; P4083) carried the normal crew of three, but each of the other five were fitted with long-range fuel tanks in the centre cockpits. These increased range to over 1000 miles, and endurance to nine hours, but the tanks were not self-sealing, and represented a major fire hazard if punctured at all. The main fuel tanks were located in the upper wings, but there was also a 'last-gasp' gravity tank which held a few extra gallons. Gunner Leading Airman Ken Sims recalls:

'The few gallons had to be hand pumped up. The pilot could use this – the handle was under his seat on the starboard side – but so could the observer, by crawling under the pilot's seat. In "last-gasp" conditions obviously the pilot wanted control so the observer was called upon. With the long-range tank if we got the call this meant crawling under the tank and under the seat. Not much chance of getting out then!'

Loading a torpedo under an 815 Squadron Swordfish.

On arrival at Eleusis the aircrews were reunited with some of the unit's ground crews who had travelled on HMS *Protector* with the torpedoes, but learned that there had already been some trouble. German Consular officers from the Legation in Athens wore their uniforms in public, and the sight of these incensed the newly-arrived Naval airmen, particularly when fortified with local beer.

Consequently the odd scuffle had broken out, ending when one German was pushed through a shop window. Arrested by the Greek police, the culprits had been handed over to the shore patrol, who promptly released them. Next day a senior Greek naval officer appeared to request the detachment's personnel to be more tolerant under the circumstances, since Greece was not at that stage at war with Germany.

Capt (then Lt) F M A Torrens-Spence, commander of 815 Squadron, Fleet Air Arm, photographed after the war.

On 12 March the six Swordfish, now armed with torpedoes, flew on up to Paramythia, their arrival coinciding with the full moon period. That same night Lt Cdr Jago led five off over the mountains to attack the ten-mile long harbour at Valona. Four Blenheims of 211 Squadron went off first at 20-minute intervals from 0300 onwards, each aircraft spending 15 minutes over the target area to create a diversion and draw off the AA. At 0415 the initial Swordfish flight went off as follows:

'A' P4083 Lt Cdr Jago; Lt Caldecott-Smith; L/A P N Beagley
'B' P4080 Lt C Lamb; L/A K Sims
'F' L9774 Sub Lt A J B Forde; L/A L W Smith
'K' P4025 Lt Torrens-Spence; Sub Lt P Winter
'M' P4071 Lt O A G Oxley; L/A S L Boosey

Having climbed with difficulty to some 8000 feet out to sea off Corfu, the torpedo-bombers went into a controlled glide between the 2750 feet peak of

Mount St Basilios and its neighbour, and arrived over the harbour at about 60 feet. The diffused moonlight made the surface of the water difficult to see, and as the aircraft swept in, their engines throttled right back, the AA defences opened up a heavy barrage. At once Jago's Swordfish was hit and flew into the water, Charles Lamb taking over the lead. As he headed for a large vessel, his undercarriage struck the water, and the aircraft lurched violently, but he was able to keep it airborne, and to arm and launch his torpedo.

Of the following Swordfish, only Lt Torrens-Spence was able to attack successfully, claiming to have gained a hit on a large passenger vessel. As the ship was in complete darkness he had not been able to observe that it carried Red Cross markings, and was in fact the 7289-ton hospital ship *Po*. Reportedly, this ship was hit by two torpedoes and was beached, sinking later. Italian radio claimed that the vessel had been 'fully-illuminated' and condemned the attack, adding that Mussolini's daughter, the Countess Ciano was aboard and was one of the last to leave the sinking vessel. It seems unlikely that the *Po* was hit by two torpedoes since only two were launched, the other pair of crews returning to Paramythia with their missiles still beneath their aircraft since no worthwhile targets had been seen. It is possible that Lamb's torpedo also struck this ship, but since the 3539-ton *Santa Maria* was also sunk, this seems unlikely.

Personnel of 815 Squadron in Greece with an Evzone. Third from left is Leading Airman Ken Sims, while second from right is L/A Laurie Smith, and on the far right L/A Sid Boosey.

Jago and his crew had survived their crash and were able to get into their dinghy, from which they were rescued by an Italian MAS boat (motor gunboat) after seven hours. Initially well-treated, they were later interrogated by Blackshirts who – angry over the sinking of the hospital ship – threatened them with shooting. Fully convinced that his collision with the water had ripped the undercarriage off P4080 meanwhile, Charles Lamb returned to Paramythia ready to belly-land. In the dawn light however, Ken Sims was able to lean out and confirm that the wheels were still attached. A gentle landing was made, the undercarriage showing no signs of any damage! Command of 815 Squadron now passed to Lt Torrens-Spence; Lt A W F Sutton, who had been acting as Fleet Air Arm Liaison Officer in Greece, was sent forward to act as Senior Observer. Next day Lamb and Sub Lt Forde flew back to Eleusis to collect further torpedoes.

From Paramythia during the afternoon of 13 March Sqn Ldr Brown led 14 Gladiators from his squadron and six of 33 Squadron's Hurricanes off for an offensive patrol over the Kelcyre area. Here an estimated 14 S.79s were seen – aircraft from 104° Gruppo BT – with an escort identified as 20 G.50bis and 20 plus CR 42s. Three of the Hurricanes attacked the mass of fighters, followed by the Gladiators, and again many individual dogfights ensued. Sqn Ldr Brown attacked the leading fighter of a flight of three, but broke off to get on the tail of another, which he saw crash; he claimed a G.50 and another damaged. Flt Lt Fraser attacked a CR 42 which he reported burst into flames and crashed near Bousi; two more were claimed destroyed by Flg Off Cochrane and Plt Off Groves, while another pair were claimed as probable.

The Gladiators reformed, then spotted about 30 more CR 42s with 38° Stormo BR 20s. Seven of Flt Lt Fry's 'C' Flight pilots went after the bombers, while Flt Lt Fraser's 'A' Flight tackled the fighters, claiming seven more shot down. Two of these were credited to Fraser, one reportedly diving into the ground north of Corovode with the pilot slumped in his cockpit, while the second went down in flames; Fraser's own aircraft was badly shot up, as was that of Plt Off Groves, but both managed to get back to base.

Again the 'G.50bis' seem to have been 22° Gruppo Macchis, 11 of which accompanied 18 CR 42s from the 160° Gruppo over the front. The Italian pilots claimed four Gladiators and one Hurricane shot down, losing just two CR 42s flown by Ten Gualtiero Bacchi and Sottoten Enzo Torroni, but no MC200s. However although no claims were made against the bombers on this occasion, several were in fact hit and damaged, a number of crewmen being wounded. 112 Squadron's claims were:

Sqn Ldr Brown	G.50bis and one damaged	Plt Off P L C Brunton	CR 42
Flt Lt Fraser	3 CR 42s	Flg Off Brown	CR 42
Flg Off Cochrane	3 CR 42s	Plt Off Bowker	CR 42 probable
Plt Off Groves	2 CR 42s and one damaged	Plt Off D G MacDonald	CR 42 probable

During the day however Flg Off Edwin Banks from this unit took off to test the guns of N5913 over Lake Yanina, but while doing so suddenly dived into the water for no apparent reason, and was killed.

Next day three of 33's Hurricanes were again off with 12 Gladiators to escort 211 Squadron Blenheims to the Tepelene-Kelcyre area, where a large formation of Italian fighters was again reported, variously identified by the Hurricane pilots as 12 CR42s, 12 G.50bis and 12 MC200s, and by the Gladiator pilots as 40–50 CR42s and G.50bis. In addition ten Z.1007bis and five BR20s were seen – aircraft from 47° and 38° Stormo respectively. The opposing fighters were from the same units as the day before – 16 Macchis of the 22° Gruppo and 12 CR42s of the 160° Gruppo reported meeting 20 Gladiators and eight Hurricanes, escorting five Blenheims.

While Flt Lt Fry and his flight attacked the bombers, Fry himself claiming a BR20 shot down north of Kelcyre and Flg Off Smith a damaged, 'C' Flight once again became involved in a swirling dogfight with the Italian monoplane fighters, claiming four shot down, four probables and a damaged. Sgt Donaldson claimed two, both of which dived away pouring smoke, while Flt Lt Fraser was attacked head-on by one, but managed to evade this and get on its tail, his fire causing the pilot to bale out. One Macchi shot the tail off N5916 and Sqn Ldr Brown managed to bale out only with the greatest difficulty; Plt Off Bowker's Gladiator was also damaged. The Hurricanes also engaged the Macchis, 33 Squadron claiming two shot down and two probables, but after believing that he had got one of these, Flg Off Holman was himself shot down and had to bale out. The Italian pilots claimed two Hurricanes and two Gladiators shot down on this occasion, their own losses being Ten Luigi Locatelli, who was killed, and Serg Ferruccio Miazzo, who baled out, while Sottoten Edgardo Vaghi's fighter was damaged. The British claims were:

112 Squadron		33 Squadron	
Flt Lt Fry	one BR20	Flg Off Holman	one monoplane
Flt Lt Fraser	one 'G.50'	F/Sgt	
		Cottingham	one monoplane and
Sgt Donaldson	two 'G.50s'		one probable
Flg Off Bennett	one 'G.50'	Plt Off Starrett	one monoplane
Flg Off Cochrane	one 'G.50' probable		probable
Plt Off Groves	one 'G.50' probable		
Plt Off Bowker	one 'G.50' probable		
Flg Off Smith	one 'G.50' probable,		
	one BR20 damaged		
Plt Off Brunton	one 'G.50' damaged		

Gunners in one Cant Z.1007bis claimed one Gladiator shot down, and one bomber was damaged – reportedly by AA – returning with some of the crew wounded.

Meanwhile one of 815 Squadron's Swordfish was flying back to Paramythia after being re-armed with its torpedo at Eleusis. Flying over Corfu at 5000 feet, P4080, flown by Lt Lamb with Sub Lt Bowker in the rear seat, was intercepted by two 160° Gruppo CR42s. Lamb at once jettisoned the torpedo, stood the aircraft on its tail just as the fighters opened fire, and both stalled and spun away as they attempted to keep their sights on the almost stationary Swordfish.

Recovering, they came in again side by side, but this time Lamb threw his aircraft into a dive beyond the vertical in which his speed rose to well over 200 mph. Again the Fiats attempted to keep after him, but in doing so collided with each other and crashed into the sea. Ten Ettore Campinoti being killed, while Serg Magg Maurizio Mandolesi managed to take to his parachute. On landing at Paramythia, Lamb found a jagged hole in the back of his seat and an unexploded 12.7mm shell lodged in his parachute.

That night at 2115 three of 815's Swordfish were out again after shipping in Valona harbour, again supported by 211 Squadron Blenheims making a diversionary attack on the town. Attacks were made on two vessels, hits being reported on one 10 000-ton liner by Lt Oxley and Sub Lt Macaulay, but no ships were recorded lost on this occasion.

From Paramythia 211 Squadron's Sqn Ldr Gordon-Finlayson had flown to Eleusis on 13 March to report to Air HQ on the unit's recent experiences at the forward field, where 30 operations had been flown in 25 days. On his arrival he was advised of his promotion to Wg Cdr and the award of a DSO. He was to be posted to set up a new 'E' (Eastern) Wing to command units to be established on the Thessalonikan Plain, following the success of 'W' Wing in the Yanina/Paramythia area. His Wing would comprise 11 Squadron at Almyros; the 113 Squadron detachment at Menidi, soon to be joined by the rest of the unit; the Wellingtons of 37 Squadron at Menidi; 'B' and 'C' Flights of 30 Squadron at Eleusis; the balance of 33 Squadron not at Paramythia; and two new squadrons which were due to be despatched from Egypt shortly (73 and 208).

His place in 211 Squadron was taken by Sqn Ldr R J C Nedwill AFC, a New Zealander who had been a fighter instructor at the Habbaniya flying school in Iraq. 33 Squadron was meanwhile reinforced by two new pilots, both of whom had been working as instructors at 70 OTU, Ismailia; Flt Lt A B Mitchell had flown with 430 Flight in East Africa, where he had shot down a Caproni Ca133 while flying a Gloster Gauntlet. He and the other pilot, Flg Off D T Moir, had formed an impromptu fighter defence flight while with 70 OTU to provide some defence for the Suez Canal.

Soon after midday on 15 March, ten Z.1007bis of 47° Stormo appeared over Yanina and commenced bombing just as a 112 Squadron Gladiator flown by Flg Off Bennett was approaching to land. Bomb blast flicked the fighter over on its back, but the pilot was able to right it, and land the damaged machine safely. On the ground another Gladiator was set on fire, but two of 112 Squadron's airmen, LACs Reed and Walter, rushed from their shelter although bombs were still falling, and managed to extinguish the flames and save the aircraft. A Greek Ju52/3m was also damaged, but was swiftly repaired and was soon back in service.

At 1325 seven Blenheims from 84 and 211 Squadrons were off from Paramythia to raid Devoli airfield where three Ro.37bis of 72° Gruppo OA were destroyed and three 395ª Squadriglia G.50bis damaged; three airmen were wounded. The units sent out another eight Blenheims at 1730 to attack Valona airfield, and here a 364ª Squadriglia CR42 was destroyed in flames. During the day, eight 37 Squadron Wellingtons and five 30 Squadron Blenheim IFs flew up to Paramythia to undertake night attacks on Tirana and Valona.

The night's activities were opened by three 815 Squadron Swordfish which went out at 2030 to attack Valona harbour again, Blenheims of 211 Squadron once more providing the diversion. As on the previous occasion it was found that the vessels in harbour had been moved around, and the torpedo-bombers had to fly about looking for targets. A small AA vessel opened fire on Lt Lamb's aircraft suddenly, but no damage was done. In Sub Lt Macaulay's 'P' was gunner Ken Sims: 'We were still at 1,000 feet but the fire was sporadic and not particularly close. We soon got underneath it. And judging the height was easy. For there in the middle of the harbour, lit up like some glittering crown, was a hospital ship. We skirted by it, picked out the dark shape of a merchant ship and closed in. Mac didn't go for long shots. He seemed to know just how much he needed to get the fish running and primed, and that was the range it was dropped. The shape was looking pretty big when he let go. We banked away and watched. I was expecting something spectacular but the flash, when it came, was quite subdued. It could even have been a reflection from the gun flashes which were spraying around, mostly above us. But we believed we had gained a hit. We skirted the hospital ship again and headed for the harbour entrance, still at no more than 100 feet.'

It seems that they hit the destroyer *Andromeda* with this attack. Lt Lamb also spotted the hospital ship, but finding nothing else worth attacking, he released his torpedo at the small AA vessel, which he believed he had sunk. Sub Lt Forde saw nothing warranting an attack, and returned with his torpedo, but could not find Paramythia, force-landing in a field where the aircraft ran into a ditch and overturned.

At 0330 the five Blenheim IFs followed, armed with 20 lb and 30 lb fragmentation bombs, attacking Valona airfield at ten-minute intervals. Although one Blenheim was hit in both wings by AA fire, four more of 72° Gruppo's Ro.37bis were hit and damaged. Behind the Blenheims came 37 Squadron's Wellingtons, their target being Tirana airfield. In the moonlight a number of CR42s from 160° Gruppo had scrambled, and these attacked Sgt D C Murrell's 'D', R1387, which was seen to be shot down in flames; three of the crew were killed, including the pilot, and three became prisoners. Two more Wellingtons were hit by the fighters, Flt Lt P C Lemon's 'C', T2580, having its port wheel punctured, the aileron controls shot away and the rear turret damaged by an explosive shell. 'J', T2895 (Sgt D J Paul) was badly damaged down the starboard side of the fuselage, but both this and Lemon's bomber got back to Menidi to land.

By now the Italian offensive had been brought to a halt after a week of bitter fighting which had inflicted heavy losses on each side. The Greeks, though victorious again, were now exhausted, and were short of ammunition and supplies. In the air activity continued, particularly by night for the duration of the moonlit period. During 16 March, a Blenheim of 211 Squadron was despatched on a special reconnaissance of Durazzo harbour to check on the amount of shipping present, pending an attack on this target by the Swordfish. A number of good-sized ships were seen, but during the return flight a Z.506B floatplane of the 86° Gruppo BM was met near Valona. Plt Off Ron Pearson, the Blenheim pilot, later recalled:

'We were evenly matched – the Blenheim had two guns and the Cant had three, two in the rear turret and one front. We tackled first the stings in the tail, and with my second burst I got the rear gunner. Just in time, too, for the tracer from the top turret was fairly sizzling past the cockpit – most unpleasant. Then, the rear guns silenced, I went for the cockpit, and made a series of head-on attacks to drive him away from home. When the ammo in the front gun was exhausted we tried beam attacks to give my rear gunner a chance. It was jolly good fun. Then we had to come back, regretfully, for the Cant, just above the waves, was still flying, though all his guns were silent. So we landed a little fed up.'

Before Pearson had actually got back to Paramythia, Air HQ had contacted the squadron and advised them that a Greek observer had witnessed the fight and had seen the Cant crash into the sea and sink. However this was incorrect; the damaged floatplane made it back to Brindisi.

Following receipt of Pearson's reconnaissance report, four Swordfish set off at 2230 to Durazzo. Thick cloud was met at 5000 feet for the last 30 miles to the target, and the first thing to be seen was some uncomfortably accurate AA. All pilots attacked independently, considerable shipping being seen and all torpedoes dropped. One crew reported seeing two explosions, but none stopped to view results as the AA was too heavy.

Meanwhile the Italians now reciprocated, three Z.1007bis from 47° Stormo raiding Larissa during the early hours, while close behind them came two BR20s of 37° Stormo to attack Yanina. Two hours later three CR42s of 160° Gruppo made a strafing attack on the latter airfield where AA fire hit Cap Luigi Corsini's fighter, causing him to bale out over Italian lines during the return flight. Next night – 17/18 March – six 37 Squadron Wellingtons led by Wg Cdr Collard, attacked Durazzo again, hits being reported on the dockyard; one Wellington was slightly damaged by AA.

Little was seen by day during the next few days, although formations of escorted Blenheims continued to attack targets in Albania. On 18 March an Anson crew of 13 Mira spotted and attacked a submarine close to St. George's Island, south of Athens. The sighting was radioed to the unit, and within five minutes all available aircraft were in the air. The submarine was believed badly damaged as great quantities of petrol were seen on the surface of the sea. A 230 Squadron Sunderland flown by Flt Lt A M G Lywood was about to take off from Scaramanga on patrol, and this searched for the submarine, but saw nothing. No record of an Axis submarine loss is recorded, however.

On Corfu on this date Andrew Stamatopoulos, then a 14-year old living in the village of Kondokali, recorded in his diary:
'It was midday – March 18th 1941. The drone of a rather high-flying aircraft made me search the sky. After a short while I saw a big, graceful aircraft coming in from the NW towards us and flying at a height of about 3000 metres. It was a Cant Z.1007bis Alcione (single fin and rudder version). At the same time another pitch of drone attracted our attention; three old-looking piplanes were crossing towards us from the east above the sea, flying in perfect formation, rather slowly at the height of about 2000 metres. These were Breguet XIXs and they must

116

have seen the Italian as they opened their throttles wide so that to climb higher and fly faster to catch the enemy. The Italian, seeing them, turned 360° to the right at the moment that it flew above Corfu Town, intending to return to its base. There ensued an exchange of fire for about 2–3 minutes, close to the village of Synarades, where a lot of empty cases fell from the sky. But the Alcione was so much faster and it easily fled. Shortly after, we heard bomb explosions at the NW part of the island; possibly that the bomber got rid of its bombs. Then the Breguet XIXs flew again over our heads and vanished towards the east – and their landing ground at Paramythia.'

The young Andrew was quite certain that the biplanes he had seen were Breguets – indeed he even sketched their wing plan in his diary at the time. Yet there were no aircraft of this type at Paramythia at the time, and on this date a trio of Gladiators from 112 Squadron which had taken off from Paramythia, engaged a Z.1007bis over Corfu which escaped them.

Bad weather during the night of 18/19 March prevented a further attack on Durazzo being made but a reconnaissance on 19 March again showed this port to be the most promising target, and a further strike was laid on. Because of the known shallowness of the water, it was decided to arm two aircraft with six 250 lb bombs each, plus flares, and only one with a torpedo. The trio set off at 0150, reaching the target area two hours later. Recalled Ken Sims, observer in the torpedo-equipped aircraft:

'It was a long slog up to Durazzo, about 100 miles past Valona. We took a line well out to sea in the hope that the latter place wouldn't notice what we were up to and give warning. After two hours we turned in, came over Durazzo at about 8000 feet and started dropping flares. The harbour seemed quite full. So was the air – full of anti-aircraft fire. the place was well defended.'

Lt Clifford bombed a ship of 3–4000 tons, but did not observe any hits, while L/Air Laurie Smith in Sub Lt Forde's 'F' saw two explosions after an attack was made on a ship in the north-east corner of the bay. Sub Lt Macaulay searched for a suitable target for his torpedo meantime; Ken Sims recalled:

'A largish ship which looked like an oil tanker stood out away from a jetty with a fair expanse of water on one side of it. I guessed that was what Mac had his eye on. We did a copy book attack such as often practised but seldom achieved. A vertical dive with a jink halfway to line up direction and check speed, then down again to pull out and level off on the water close to the target. We seemed terribly unmasked out there in the light of our own flares. But the vertical dive did the trick as far as return fire was concerned. I looked back to see the air full of gunfire above us but we got in close with little visible reaction at our level. By the time they started with the small arms and Breda we had dropped the fish and turned away. There were some moments of suspense before we crossed the harbour wall but much of the fire trailed behind us. I saw no balloons but I did see a hit on the target lit as it was by the flares. Nothing spectacular but nevertheless a hit. The display went on for some time behind us. I guessed the boys with the bombs had not dropped them all at once and pulled back for a second go. I wished them luck.'

Following this raid bad weather over Albania and Greece frustrated operations to an even greater degree. Not until 21/22 March was 815 Squadron again able to launch a raid, and then the single Swordfish sent out to Valona had to beat a hasty retreat when two fighters were seen, the bomber crashing on return. Several reconnaissances were flown over the Yugoslavian and Bulgarian borders by 113 Squadron's Blenheims at this time, seeking to check on developments here, since German forces were now known to be in Bulgaria in strength (see Chapter 5). On 21 March, 24° Gruppo CT G.50bis escorted S.79s carrying Benito Mussolini and his party from Devoli back to Italy, but an MC 200 of 371ª Squadriglia crashed while patrolling over Valona, the pilot (Sottoten Enrico Pani) being killed. A reconnaissance Z.506B was reported attacked by a Gladiator south of Cephalonia Island, the crew claiming to have shot down their tormentor; no Allied account of this interception has been found.

Macchi C 200 fighters of 373ª Squadriglia, 153° Gruppo CT prepare for take off. (*AMI via N Malizia*)

At last Italian reconnaissance discovered the airfields at Paramythia, and at 0635 on 22 March, 29 MC200s from the 153° Gruppo CT at Lecce and Brindisi took off to make a strafing attack. Eight Macchis swept in, claiming two Blenheims destroyed on the ground; one aircraft of 211 Squadron was actually hit and burnt out. As the other 21 patrolled overhead they reported engaging 12 Gladiators and claimed two shot down with a third as a probable. There were in fact only two of these aircraft from 112 Squadron in the air, Flt Lt Fraser and Plt Off Bowker having scrambled after the bombers reported over Corfu, where they encountered four Z.1007bis from 47° Stormo and the Macchis, reported as usual

as 'G 50s'; neither side actually suffered any casualties. Five BR20s from 37°
Stormo then attacked Paramythia in the face of intense AA which damaged two
of the bombers, but little damage was caused to the target.

Capitanos Mario Larker and Giuseppe Cenni of 239ª Squadriglia, 97° Gruppo Autonomo B a'T with
a member of the unit's groundcrew; Ju87Bs in the background. (*C Gari via N Malizia*)

In the afternoon 27 more Macchis repeated the strafe, while 15 more flew top
cover. This time two Wellingtons were claimed destroyed, one of them exploding,
whilst a fighter was also claimed. One unserviceable Wellington of 37 Squadron
went up in flames, as did one of the Gladiators left behind by 80 Squadron. Six
Ju87s of 239ª Squadriglia were also out from their Italian base, Cap Mario
Larker leading these to attack some small ships off Corfu, claiming one sunk and
a second damaged.

Gloster Gladiator of 80 Squadron destroyed during an Italian strafe of Paramythia on 22 March,
1941. (*E Bevington–Smith*)

Under the impression that the Macchis had been G.50bis from Berat, an attack on this airfield was laid on for 23 March, 13 Hurricanes of 33 Squadron from Larissa, led by Sqn Ldr Pattle, rendezvousing with 11 Gladiators of 112 Squadron to escort six Blenheims from 84 Squadron to attack this base. Approaching at low level due to heavy cloud, the Blenheims bombed from only 1500 feet, but only minor shrapnel damage was caused by the AA defences. Two Hurricanes were harder hit, and were forced to return to Larissa under escort by Flg Off Holman's section. The remaining Hurricanes regrouped close around the bombers, but near the border a 24° Gruppo G.50bis attacked Flg Off Dyson's V7415, hitting the glycol and fuel tanks, escaping fluid almost blinding the pilot. He managed almost to reach Larissa before baling out when the engine seized up; he was soon picked up by Greek troops and returned to the airfield. During this interception Ten Enrico Giordanino and Sottoten Giorgio Moretti of the 24° Gruppo claimed one Hurricane shot down and one probable.

Early in the afternoon Sqn Ldr Pattle was off again at the head of ten Hurricanes, briefed to strafe Fier airfield, some miles west of Berat. as the fighters approached the target they were attacked by an estimated 20 G.50s and MC200s, and a number of dogfights ensued, three G.50bis being claimed shot down, one each by Pattle, Flg Off Holman and Flg Off Woodward, who also claimed another damaged; Flg Off Newton claimed a probable and a damaged also. As a result the Hurricanes were scattered all over the sky, only Pattle and Woodward actually carrying out the strafe on the airfield, where the former claimed three aircraft destroyed. He then spotted a G.50bis at 200 feet, preparing to land, and gave this a burst; he saw it roll over, but did not witness it crash, so claimed only a probable. On return he was extremely angry with his pilots for not carrying out the full strafe as briefed. The result of the morning raid had seen two Ro.37bis and a G.50bis damaged on the ground, while now one further G.50bis went up in flames; despite the claims made, there is no record of any Italian fighters having been shot down in combat on this occasion. Italian pilots of 154° Gruppo claimed one British fighter shot down and one probable, while similar claims were put in by the CR42 pilots of 150° Gruppo; there were no RAF losses.

The moon having waned, opportunities for night attacks had now diminished, and the detachment of Wellingtons at Menidi were ordered to return to rejoin 37 Squadron in Egypt. Three of 815 Squadron's pilots led by Lt Lamb were also despatched in a 267 Squadron Lodestar, to collect new Swordfish. On 24 March, however the main body of 113 Squadron arrived an Menidi from Egypt, absorbing the detached photo-reconnaissance flight there. Commanded by Sqn Ldr R H Spencer, the unit was initially to attack shipping carrying supplies to the Italian Dodecanese Islands in the Aegean, and to maintain the reconnaissance sorties over Rumania and Bulgaria. The squadron was amazed to discover that Lufthansa civil Ju52/3m airliners were still regularly operating from Menidi, and at times shared the circuit with the Blenheim IVs.

In 33 Squadron Flt Lt Young was posted away, his place at the head of 'B' Flight being taken by Flg Off 'Dixie' Dean, who was promoted Acting Flt Lt. The squadron also learned of the award of a Bar to Flg Off Dyson's DFC for actions in North Africa. 80 Squadron gained two more decorations, a DFC for Plt Off

Bill Vale ($13\frac{1}{2}$ victories) and a DFM for Sgt Donald Gregory (seven victories). On 26 March however, Sqn Ldr Nedwill, 211 Squadron's new CO, who had only flown his first sortie two days earlier, borrowed a Gladiator from 112 Squadron to perform aerobatics. He lost control during one manouevre and crashed to his death. Flt Lt Jones, one of the flight commanders, took over command of the unit. On the other side of the lines during the day before, Magg Oscar Molinari, who had only recently returned to command the 160° Gruppo at Devoli on recovery from wounds, had also been killed while practising aerobatics in his CR 42!

Macchi C 200 fighters of 372ª Squadriglia, 153° Gruppo CT at Brindisi during the Balkans campaign. (*AMI via N Malizia*)

The 153° Gruppo CT Macchis were back over Paramythia for another strafe early in the afternoon of 26 March. As they approached they were met by four 112 Squadron Gladiators, which they again identified as 12 in number. One Gladiator was badly damaged, but the pilot managed to land safely, while Flt Lt Schwab pursued the MC200s to the coast, believing that he had possibly managed to shoot one down into the sea off Perdika. During the dogfight two Macchis broke away and strafed the airfield, claiming two Gladiators and a Wellington destroyed. In fact they managed to destroy one Gladiator, and hit the wreckage of the Wellington which they had already destroyed four days earlier.

121

Italian personnel pose with the wreckage of two Gladiators, apparently those destroyed during the late March strafes on Paramythia. (*Bruni via Lucchini/Malizia*)

113 Squadron undertook its first major raid on 27 March, Sqn Ldr Spencer leading 11 of the unit's Blenheims to attack Calato airfield on Rhodes. Nearly 12 000 lb of bombs were dropped, fuel dumps and buildings being left on fire, while it was believed that one aircraft had been destroyed. This action was associated with activity over Crete (see Chapter 4) and an 'Ultra' intercept which indicated an increased level of activity by Italian forces on Rhodes.

113 Squadron Blenheim IV at Menidi. (*S W Lee*)

At Yanina 112 Squadron was ordered to despatch all operational Gladiators to Paramythia, since it was intended to re-equip the unit with Hurricanes. Next day three pilots left in a Bombay to collect the first of these from Egypt. In the event these aircraft would go to 33 Squadron at Eleusis, rather than to 112.

During 27 March, six of 30 Squadron's Blenheim fighters were flown forward to Paramythia from where next morning at 0535 they set course for Lecce airfield in Italy, led by Flt Lt Tom Horgan. The attack was aimed to interfere with possible action against the Mediterranean Fleet which might be launched from this airfield. Arriving over the target an hour later, they dived from 10 000 feet to 1500 feet, an estimated 80–100 aircraft of all types being seen on the ground. The Blenheims undertook two strafing passes, taking the defences completely by surprise. One bomber, identified as a Ca135, was left in flames and another collapsed; at least 20 others were claimed to have been riddled with bullets. When at last the defences opened up four of the Blenheims were hit and slightly damaged. Sgt Ovens' aircraft subsequently force-landed at an advanced landing ground as a result. Two MC200s were scrambled from Lecce and three more from Brindisi, but they were unable to catch the attackers as they withdrew. The squadron's assessment of the damage they had caused was quite accurate; one S.81 was destroyed in flames and 25 other aircraft were damaged, while five airmen were wounded, one of them seriously, as was one civilian outside the base.

On 30 March at 1125, ten Blenheims of 84 Squadron were despatched without escort to raid a military camp at Elbasan, 20 miles south-east of Tirana. Sgt A Hutcheson's L1390 was hit by AA fire and he struggled back to force-land at Neapolis, near Koritza. The other nine bombers were intercepted by 154° Gruppo CT G.50bis which had scrambled from Devoli, and these took on the Blenheims as they made their attack. L1391 (Sgt GE Bailey) was badly shot-up, hit in the nose, fuselage and starboard wing, while T2427 (Flg Off I P C Goudge) was also hit – the Fiat pilots claimed two Blenheims probably shot down. Sgt Blackburn, the gunner in Flt Lt W T Russell's aircraft, believed that he had shot down one of the attackers which was seen diving vertically with smoke pouring from its engine; on this occasion crews identified two of their attackers as Re 2000s. That night five of 113 Squadron's Blenheims bombed an Italian supply convoy off Stampalia Island, but without obvious results.

At the end of the month 80 Squadron, having received its new Hurricanes, handed its last four Gladiators to 112 Squadron, where Flt Lt Schwab had just been promoted to take over the unit from Sqn Ldr Brown. Two of the unit's tired Gladiators (K7932 and 7984) were passed on to 21 Mira at Ptolemais. 80 Squadron's six new Hurricanes were P2927, V6629, 7344, 7718, 7748 and 7808; two had been flown to Greece by Free French pilots, F/Sgt Jacques Rivalant and F/Sgt Pierre Wintersdorff, who were now posted to the squadron. A Blenheim escorting the Hurricanes on their ferry flight carried Sqn Ldr Jones back from leave in Cairo. Three replacement Blenheim IFs were also received by 30 Squadron to re-equip its bomber flight, allowing the unit to become entirely fighter-equipped.

One of the two additional units intended for Greece, 208 Squadron, which was in Palestine, was ordered to prepare for the move. This tactical reconnaissance unit, commanded by Sqn Ldr J R Wilson, was equipped with two flights of very worn Westland Lysanders and just four Hurricanes; it was sadly deficient in fully-trained reconnaissance pilots and suitable aircraft. The second unit due to move, 73 Squadron, would never leave Egypt due to the commencement of the first offensive by the newly-arrived Deutches Afrika Korps under General Erwin Rommel in Libya.

On 1 April, 84 Squadron lost its senior flight commander when Flt Lt Boehm and his crew were killed in an accident in T2382 at Kiphissia, north-east of Athens, during a routine flight. 113 Squadron now moved its Blenheims from Menidi to Larissa, prior to moving again two days later to a newly-constructed landing ground at Niamata. This was situated in an area that was partially bog between Larissa and Volos. Menidi was required for the return of 37 Squadron's Wellingtons on a further detachment from Egypt.

Italian air raids resumed on 2 April, ten Z.1007bis from the 35° Stormo and 50° Gruppo bombing a heavily defended railway complex at Florina early in the morning, where hits on the target were claimed. A number of the bombers were damaged by AA fire, while others were attacked by seven Gladiators from 21 Mira at Ptolemais. The pilots claimed two of the Cants shot down, actual loss amounting to one 35° Stormo machine from which one member of the crew escaped by parachute.

At 1255 five more Z.1007bis, three from 260ª Squadriglia and two from 261ª Squadriglia of the 106° Gruppo, 47° Stormo BT, left Grottaglie to raid Volos. One turned back early with engine trouble, but the other four bombed their target at 1450, dropping eight 250 kg and 12 100 kg bombs from 22 000 feet. Four Hurricanes of 33 Squadron and six Gladiators of 112 Squadron were scrambled on warning of their approach. Flt Lt Littler and Flg Off Sir James Kirkpatrick, Bart, in two of the Hurricanes, intercepted and claimed one bomber shot down, while Flg Off Woodward, who had been delayed in taking off as his Hurricane was being re-armed at the time, pursued the bombers out towards the Gulf of Corinth. Even though only the four guns in the port wing had been loaded, he believed that he had shot down two of the bombers in flames on his first pass. Thinking that there had been four aircraft in the formation he was pursuing, he then attacked another of the bombers and the Cant flown by Ten Mario Bozzi was hit, ditching in the sea off Missolonghi in the Gulf of Patras, where the crew were later rescued from their dinghy. During the initial attacks by the Hurricanes one Cant of 260ª Squadriglia flown by Sottoten Maurizio Morandini had been shot down directly over Almyros airfield (home of 11 Squadron), falling a few miles away; one man had baled out, coming down near the base and being captured. This was believed to have been the aircraft shot down by Littler and Kirkpatrick, but it may also have been attacked by Woodward.

After the second bomber had gone down, Woodward had continued to pursue the survivors, claiming that the last Z.1007bis he attacked before his ammunition ran out was badly damaged. He recalled:

'I shot down three plus one probable of the "Green Mouse" squadron, sup-posedly commanded by Mussolini's son – he was believed to be the leader and the probable – I left him smoking and descending towards the western end of the Gulf of Corinth – I had no more ammunition.'

It seems that wartime propaganda had made a good story out of this engagement, which Woodward had been led to believe. The 'Green Mice' emblem was actually carried by S.79s of the 41° Gruppo BT, not by any of the 47° Stormo units. Bruno Mussolini was indeed commanding officer of 260ª Squadriglia, but on this occasion the formation had been led by Cap Pier Luigi Braga. It would seem probable that Woodward had attacked Ten Bozzi's aircraft twice, thinking that he had shot it down the first time, and claiming it as a probable on the second occasion, when he possibly found it alone after it had fallen away from the other two aircraft, leading to the belief that there was only one survivor from the Italian formation.

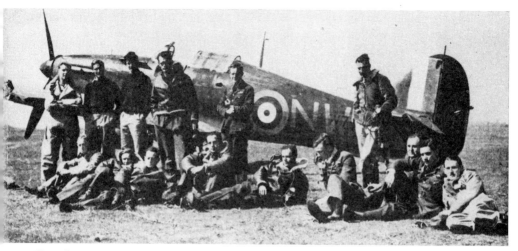

Pilots of 33 Squadron in front of Hurricane V7419 at Larissa in early April 1941. L to r: standing: Plt Off D S F Winsland, Plt Off R D Dunscombe, Plt Off C A C Chetham, Flg Off P R W Wickham, Flg Off D T Moir, Flg Off H J Starrett; sitting: Flg Off E J Woods, Flg Off F S Holman, Flt Lt A M Young, Flg Off V C Woodward, Sqn Ldr M T StJ Pattle, DFC, Flg Off E H Dean, Flt Lt J M Littler, Flt Lt G Rumsey (adjutant), Plt Off A R Butcher.

Early April continued much as late March, escorted Blenheims attacking Berat on the third day of the month, while on the fourth Ju87s from Lecce raided Greek shipping off Corfu three times. Off at 1050, six 239ª Squadriglia aircraft attacked vessels in Dafnila Bay without result. During the early afternoon four more of this unit's aircraft, plus two from 209ª Squadriglia, attacked the small freighter *Susanah* steaming off the coast of the island, and Cap Cenni sank this vessel with a direct hit. At about 1720 Cap Mario Larker led six 239ª Squadriglia machines back to Dafnila Bay where this time the destroyer *Proussa* was sunk.

Six more Hurricanes (V7730, 7765, 7838, 7854, 7860 and 7861) now reached Eleusis, three of them flown by the 112 Squadron pilots and three by pilots of 33 Squadron, to which unit they were all issued. They would urgently be needed, for next day British Intelligence had received sufficient 'Ultra' intercepts to be fully aware that the German invasion of Yugoslavia and Greece was imminent, although there was nothing that they could do other than to warn the Yugoslav Government.

With evening on 5 April, six Swordfish of 815 Squadron again arrived at Paramythia armed with torpedoes, but reconnaissance had shown that neither Valona nor Durazzo warranted a strike. At 1930 therefore the six set out for an offensive sweep over the sea lanes, one aircraft carrying 'W' Wing's Wg Cdr Coote as observer. Two flew up the Italian coast to Bari, two to San Giovanni, while two patrolled between Otranto and Valona. Nothing was seen, but as the last pair returned from Valona, Lt C S Lea's P4064 developed engine trouble and the propeller flew off. As the Swordfish was too low for the crew to bale out, Lea crash-landed in a dried-up river bed 20 miles short of Paramythia. Although the aircraft was badly damaged, Lea and his observer were unhurt. They had however come down in a very remote area, and they were forced to trek out on foot, which would take them three days to do. By the time they reached Paramythia again they found a very different war in progress!

Bassi

Cobolli Gigli

Graffer

Magaldi

De Salvia

Spallacci

Trevisi

Fusco

Eight of the Regia Aeronautica's fighter pilots received awards of the Medaglia d'Oro, their nation's highest award for valour, for actions over Greece – but all were made posthumously. They were, from the top clockwise: Ten Livio Bassi (395ª Sq, 154° Gr), shot down on 20 February 1941, dying of wounds sustained on 2 April; Cap Giorgio Graffer (365ª Sq, 150° Gr), killed 28 November 1940; Serg Marcello De Salvia (354ª Sq, 24° Gr), killed 4 March 1941; Sottoten Ernesto Trevisi (363ª Sq, 150° Gr), killed 14 November 1940; Ten Alfredo Fusco (361ª Sq, 154° Gr), killed 20 February 1941; Serg Luigi Spallacci (355ª Sq, 24° Gr), killed 11 March 1941; Cap Nicola Magaldi (364ª Sq, 150° Gr), killed 27 November 1940; Sottoten Nicolo Cobolli Gigli (355ª Sq, 24° Gr), killed 4 March 1941. (*Stato Maggiore via N Malizia*)

Chapter Four

CRETE AND THE SEA LANES,
OCTOBER 1940 – APRIL 1941

While the British were initially reluctant to become heavily involved in Greece, the waters around the mainland were of considerably more immediate interest to them – particularly the integrity of the island of Crete, Italian possession of which could offer a considerable threat to the Royal Navy's control of the Eastern Mediterranean, and of the bases on Cyprus and in Egypt and Palestine. Already Italian forces were present in the Aegean area, garrisoning islands in the Dodecanese group which had been ceded by Turkey following the Italo–Turkish War of 1912. Strength on these islands was not sufficient to represent any major threat when war broke out between Italy and the United Kingdom in June 1940, but any increase in Italian involvement in the area was to be resisted strongly. The main Italian Dodecanese islands (literally Twelve islands) were Rhodes, Scarpanto (Carpathos) and Stampalia (Astypalaia), and the smaller Castelorizzo 72 miles east of Rhodes. The main islands all featured airfields, four in the case of Rhodes, at Maritza, near Rhodes town; Kattavia, on the southern tip of the island; Gadurra, on the coast near Kalathos, and Kalathos itself, known to both British and Italians as Calato. A small air contingent was based on Rhodes.

Savoia S.79 believed to have force-landed on Crete about 13 August, 1940. (*A Stamatopoulos*)

127

As early as 19 July, 1940 the first engagement at sea had occurred in the area when the Italian cruisers *Giovanni delle Bande Nere* and *Bartolomeo Colleoni* were seen near Cape Spada by RAF air reconnaissance. Intercepted by the cruiser HMAS *Sydney* and four destroyers, *Bartolomeo Colleoni*, was hit by *Sydney*'s gunfire, then torpedoed and sunk by the destroyers *Ilex* and *Havock*, 525 members of her crew being rescued by the British warships. Nine days later *Sydney* and the British cruiser HMS *Neptune* sortied into the Gulf of Athens and sank a small Italian tanker *Ermioni*, carrying petrol to the Dodecanese.

On 26 August 1940 a Sunderland from 230 Squadron in Egypt, captained by Flt Lt W W Campbell, DFC, who had been credited with sinking two Italian submarines during June, was forced to alight on Greek waters and was interned by the Greeks, while two days later an Italian Z.506B floatplane which was shadowing the British Mediterranean Fleet, was intercepted just off the coast of Crete by a Sea Gladiator fighter from the carrier HMS *Eagle*. The floatplane was shot down by Cdr Charles Keighley-Peach and the crew observed to bale out within swimming distance of the coast, and were assumed to have also been interned by the Cretan authorities.

The biggest operation in the area began during the night of 3/4 September when the cruisers *Orion* and *Sydney* and two destroyers shelled Scarpanto as part of a Mediterranean Fleet sortie into the Aegean. When the Italian motor torpedo-boats MAS536 and 537 attempted to interfere, the latter was sunk by *Ilex* in the Kaso Strait. As dawn broke Swordfish torpedo-bombers from HMS *Illustrious*'s 815 and 819 Squadrons raided Calato and Gadurra airfields on Rhodes. They were followed by more such aircraft from *Eagle*'s 813 and 824 Squadrons, but these had been delayed in taking off, and as the thirteen bombers arrived over Maritza airfield, they were to find the defences fully alerted.

Fiat CR32s and CR42s of 163ª Squadriglia were scrambled, one of each type colliding during the take-off and being destroyed, while a second CR32, flown by Serg Aristodemo Morri, failed to return. The rest however shot down four of the Swordfish (E4C, E4H, E4K, E4M), one falling to the commanding officer, Cap D'Ajello. Two of the bombers came down in the sea, from where E4H was recovered with its crew by an Italian submarine; another (K8043 E4M) force-landed on Scarpanto island. Of the twelve Naval airmen lost, four were killed including Lt D R H Drummond and his crew, and the rest taken prisoners. On the ground at Gadurra considerable damage was done by the thirty high-explosive and twenty incendiary bombs dropped. Two S.79s of 39° Stormo were destroyed and three were damaged, together with two Cant Z.1007bis, an S.81 and an S.82 transport. Four men were badly wounded and twenty slightly hurt, while a quantity of fuel, oil and bombs were destroyed. A number of hangars at Maritza were lightly damaged while a lorry and its trailer were destroyed; one man was injured, as was the case at Calato, where damage was also negligible.

Off the island patrolling Fulmars from *Illustrious* enjoyed some success. At 1030 Lt W L Barnes and Sub Lt A J Sewell of Yellow Section/806 Squadron engaged four S.79s, these escaping after each pilot had inflicted damage on them. The same pair met two more of these aircraft at 1105, attacking Ten Nicola Dell'Olio's 201ª Squadriglia machine and shooting it down in flames, then

Swordfish E4H of 813 Squadron from HMS *Eagle* is recovered from the sea off Rhodes after being shot down by 163ª Squadriglia Autonomo CT Fiat fighters early on 4 September, 1940. (*AMI via N Malizia*)

damaging the other. Sub Lt I P Godfrey, flying Yellow 3 in N1871 (with L/Air Harry Phillips as TAG), hit another in its port engine. Three S.79s of 92° Gruppo were damaged during these attacks, two of them severely, and landed with two dead and five wounded aboard. Meanwhile at 1005 Lt Cdr R A Kilroy (newly-appointed commanding officer of RNAS Dekheila, Egypt, on passage to take up his new post but meanwhile giving 806 Squadron a helping hand) and Sub Lt S G Orr had been vectored onto an aircraft they identified as a Caproni Cal33 bomber-transport, as it was going into land, and this was shot down into the sea. Two occupants were seen to bale out. Their victim would seem in fact to have been an S.81 of 223ª Squadriglia flown by Sottoten Filippo Tedesco. During the early afternoon at 1345 Red Section met two S.79s at 7000 feet 50 miles south of Castello Point. Lt O J Nicolls leading the patrol closed to 100 yards and saw bits fly off the starboard engine of the one he attacked but the bombers escaped serious damage.

This attack was followed during the night of 18/19 September by a raid on Rhodes and Leros, a more northerly Italian island, by Egypt-based Wellingtons of 70 Squadron. *Orion* and *Sydney* returned to shell Stampalia island on 2 October, while four days later the Italian submarine *Tricheco* accidentally sank its sister submarine *Gemma* in the south-eastern approaches to the Aegean. Meanwhile British submarines had strayed up the west coast of Greece, to the seas off Albania, where Italian convoys were delivering troops prior to the attack on Greece. Here on 22 September HMS *Osiris* had sunk an escorting torpedo-boat *Palestro*, while during 4–9 October, HMS *Regent* sank two ships off Durazzo totalling 6088 tons. During the night of 13/14 Swordfish from *Illustrious* and *Eagle* raided Leros whilst returning from escorting a convoy from Alexandria to Malta, during which the Mediterranean Fleet had clashed with Italian warships in the Ionian Sea. Finally, on 19 October, Italian bombers from Rhodes flew a 2800-mile round trip to bomb the Standard Oil Company installation on Bahrein Island in the Persian Gulf, refuelling in Eritrea before returning to their base. En route they also bombed Dhahran in neutral Saudi Arabia.

The scene was well set therefore for swift British action towards Crete as soon as Greece became involved in the war. Consequently on 29 October, the day after the Italian invasion begun, the first reconnaissance patrols from Egypt reached the island, by agreement with the Greek authorities. That very afternoon the first convoy left Alexandria, arriving in Suda Bay on the north-west coast of Crete on 1 November, accompanied by the AA cruisers *Calcutta* and *Coventry*, and the cruiser *Ajax*, which carried the 2nd Battalion, Yorks and Lancaster Regiment as garrison. The Italians reacted at once, 14 S.79s of 34° Gruppo from Rhodes attacking at 1330, escorted by six CR42s of 162ª Squadriglia. A number of merchant vessels were bombed and strafed without effect, while the warships put up a screen of fire, claiming damage to one bomber, which reportedly left the target trailing smoke and flame; no Italian losses were recorded.

By 3 November anti-submarine defences had been laid, and convoys began arriving from the 6th onwards with stores and defence equipment, which would allow General Metaxas to move Greek troops from the island to the Epirus front. The only airfield available on Crete was at Heraklion, 70 miles east of Suda Bay, so work was at once put in hand to build a second at Maleme, 11 miles west of Suda for the defence of the new naval base.

Although the Regia Aeronautica ordered its 5ª Squadra Aerea in Libya to support Dodecanese garrisons in resisting the British intrusion into the Aegean, little effective work was done, and the rest of November passed quietly by as the British presence on Crete was consolidated. On 29 November two Swordfish from *Illustrious* were detached to Heraklion to undertake some limited bombing of selected targets in the Dodecanese. This action failed to bring forth any reaction apart from a surprise strike against Suda Bay on 3 December by two S.79s from Libya. Cap Massimiliano Erasi and Ten Carlo Emanuele Buscaglia, of 278ª Squadriglia from El Adem, managed to release their torpedoes beyond the anti-torpedo nets, both gaining hits on the cruiser HMS *Glasgow*, effectively putting her out of action for nine months.

Elements of the Mediterranean Fleet sortied into the Aegean again during the middle of the month and on the night of 16/17 December six Swordfish of 815 Squadron from *Illustrious* carried out an attack against targets on Rhodes. Bad weather prevented all but one aircraft from reaching the target; a few bombs were reported having fallen on Rhodes town, causing slight damage to a number of

Fairey Fulmar fighter of 806 Squadron from HMS *Illustrious* visiting Heraklion airfield, Crete, in November 1940. (*D J Tribe*)

buildings but no casualties. Meanwhile, five Swordfish of 819 Squadron headed for Stampalia, again meeting bad weather although four reached the target area, but their bombs fell wide and caused no damage; the fifth aircraft released its bombs over Condronisi island. All returned safely to the carrier.

With the arrival of the New Year plans were being prepared in Cairo for the invasion of the main Dodecanese islands of Rhodes and Scarpanto, preceded by a landing on Castelorizzo, which was only some 150 miles west of Cyprus. This island was required as a forward torpedo-boat base and was considered to be a relatively easy objective for the newly-formed and therefore inexperienced commando units which were to make the landings. However on the 20th of the month Rhodes was suddenly reinforced by the arrival of a contingent of the Luftwaffe, 17 He111s of II/KG 26, a few reconnaissance Ju88Ds from I(F) /121, and supporting Ju52/3m transports arriving from Sicily. The arrival of the Germans added a greater urgency to Operation 'Mandible', as it was called. Crete was to be the launching pad as soon as sufficient and suitable landing ships could be organized.

Coincidentally, it was two days after the arrival of the Germans that Italians aircraft from the Dodecanese were at last seen over Crete again. Perhaps spurred by the presence of their allies, a pair of 162ª Squadriglia CR42s carried out a reconnaissance of Suda Bay, where they reported a cruiser, two destroyers and three merchant vessels. Encountering very heavy AA fire, they also spotted a Walrus amphibian over the Bay, attacked, and claimed it shot down. This aircraft, detached from the damaged cruiser *Glasgow* and now operating from the Bay, was attacked four times by the Fiats, but Sub Lt John Phillips skilfully evaded each time, the Walrus sustaining only four hits in the upper mainplane, before AA fire from an armed trawler drove the attackers away.

131

A pair of Rhodes-based Fiat CR 42s from the 162ᵃ Squadriglia Autonomo CT in flight over the Aegean. Their unit emblem is a black cat arching its back, with the legend 'Varda ce te sbrego!' (Beware lest I claw you!) (*AMI̅ via N Malizia*)

A more major attack occurred on 29 December, when about two dozen aircraft bombed Heraklion airfield from altitude without causing any damage of note. Next day four Swordfish of 815 Squadron flew into the new airfield at Maleme from Dekheila, led by Lt Cdr J de F Jago. Six had left this base, landing at Sollum to refuel, but here one had broken its tail oleo, a second remaining behind to render assistance; this pair would follow a few days later. Some of the unit's ground personnel had arrived at Suda Bay with stores and equipment a few days earlier aboard a small coaster, while the other flight remained in the desert for several more weeks. One of the Telegraphist/Air Gunners (TAG), Leading Airman Ken Sims, arrived aboard HMS *Ajax*, and recalled:

'We sailed into Suda Bay and were to set up a new airfield at Maleme. At this time it was no more than a dirt strip which was being enlarged by removing small trees and bracken. Its position was on the northern coast of the island rather towards the western end. We would live in tents set amongst some trees on the side of a hill to the south and overlooking the airstrip. But first to shift the stores from the boat to the field. It was all-hands to the wheel and we split into groups, each with a lorry. Most of these were very ancient and evidently had been commandeered locally. The populace welcomed us – we'd come to defend the island against those Italians next door.'

Lt Cdr Jago had previously been sent to Suda Bay with the original party with orders to arrange construction of the airfield, and have it built within four days! With the aid of local labour, the task had been completed. He had then returned to Alexandria to take command of 815 Squadron, then aboard *Illustrious* which had then been seriously damaged near Malta on 10 January, leaving survivors of the unit free for other operations.

On four recent nights Wellingtons from Egypt had carried out limited raids on Rhodes but without causing very much damage. Now, on the night of 30/31 December, it was the turn of II/KG 26's He111s to undertake their first mining mission to the Suez Canal Zone. Only light AA fire was experienced and all returned safely. However, the Luftwaffe detachment suffered its first loss next day when a Ju52/3m of I(F)/121 crashed on Rhodes, killing three members of its crew.

815 Squadron suffered its first loss from Crete on 3 February, when one Swordfish piloted by Lt A W Burnaby Drayson ran out of fuel whilst on an anti-submarine patrol and was forced to come down on the island of Antikythera. The crew were unhurt, but the aircraft was damaged beyond repair. The night of 4/5 February saw six Wellingtons of 37 Squadron set out to raid Maritza airfield but three returned early with engine problems. The remaining three carried out a successful attack, Plt Off A de L Thomas taking his big bomber down to 600 feet after he had bombed, and machine-gunned hangars and buildings. One CR42 was destroyed on the ground during this raid, one S.79 and three CR32s badly damaged, and one each S.79 and S.81 less seriously damaged.

Four nights later two more Wellingtons from this unit again raided Rhodes, both crews bombing what they believed was Calato airfield but was apparently Gadurra. Sqn Ldr A Golding saw a large explosion following his low-level attack, his aircraft being slightly damaged by machine-gun fire, while earlier Flt Lt M J Baird-Smith went down to 200 feet and machine-gunned aircraft dispersed around the aerodrome. The crew believed they had destroyed at least two multi-engined aircraft and indeed an S.79 was destroyed and a second damaged, while 30 drums of fuel went up in flames. Baird-Smith's aircraft (T2812 'A') was hit sixteen times during the attack and both fuel tanks were punctured but it got back to Egypt safely. This mini raid was followed by that of eight Wellingtons of 38 Squadron, the crews also apparently mistaking Gadurra for Calato but probably bombing on the fires caused by the earlier raid.

On return the crews reported several buildings probably hit and about ten aircraft, three of which were identified as BR20s, believed destroyed. One S.79 was badly damaged, a further six being hit by bomb splinters. The next night seven aircraft of 37 Squadron again visited Gadurra, incendiaries being dropped amongst dispersed aircraft, at least one observed to be on fire. One S.79 was totally destroyed and another four damaged, two seriously, as well as 33 drums of fuel being set ablaze. AA fire was intense, Flt Lt Lemon's aircraft (R1095) taking hits in the fuel tank and having its starboard wheel punctured. This same night Lt L J Kiggell led four of 815 Squadron's Swordfish, equipped with 250 lb bombs and flares, to attack targets on Stampalia, these being successfully bombed.

During this period Bombay transports of 216 Squadron had been ferrying men, stores and equipment to Heraklion, but as Flt Lt D R Bagnall's aircraft was being unloaded on 13 February six CR42s from Rhodes arrived overhead and began strafing, the Bombay being set on fire. Bagnall managed to save a number of valuable items from the blazing aircraft whilst it was still under attack. On this same day S.79s of 34° Gruppo on Rhodes bombed Maleme, where crews claimed four aircraft destroyed on the ground, although no losses were actually suffered. L/Airman Sims recorded:

'We hadn't been at Maleme long before the Italians made an attack. About eight S.79s came over at 8,000 feet and dropped a pattern of bombs across the field. In terms of damage done it was pretty ineffective. Holes in the field we could fill up. They should have aimed round the edges where the aircraft were dispersed or even up the slope where the camp was in the trees. But it certainly wasn't good for morale.'

On the edge of the airfield, in a small clump of trees, a corrugated iron shed had been erected and this became the Ops Room. In it was placed a field telephone exchange of ten lines. Lines went to the Bofors guns, the HQ of the Black Watch, who provided airfield ground defence, one to the Naval Officer-in-Charge, Suda Bay and the most important of all to 252 AMES (radar) station at the top of the hill. Ken Sims continues:

'The Air Gunners were the operators and we manned it in shifts. Also in the hut we rigged our pack set. When our aircraft were on anti-submarine patrol an A/G also manned the pack set as a ground station. The local church bell was rigged on a tree outside this hut and formed the air raid warning. When we got the buzz from AMES we would rush out and ring the bell and then rush in again to man the phone and wait for the Duty Officer and standby A/G to come and give a hand.'

The Italian attacks of 13 February were responded to that night, four Wellingtons of 38 Squadron raiding Midi Bay airfield on Scarpanto, and Kattavia and Calato on Rhodes. At Midi Bay a CR42 was claimed destroyed and AA positions put out of action, while buildings were hit at Kattavia. However AA shot down T2742 'H', flown by Plt Off A B Loveridge, the aircraft crashing on Rhodes with the loss of all the crew. Next night, 14/15th, two 37 Squadron aircraft bombed Rhodes and Scarpanto harbours, but T2821 'T' (Flg Off A G Wright) failed to return. It was subsequently learned that the bomber had crashed at Koyceges in the mountains of Turkey, 50 miles on from Rhodes, with the loss of all the crew; probably it had been damaged by AA fire, as Italian gunners claimed two bombers shot down.

Following the recent raid on Maleme some form of fighter protection for the airfield and Suda Bay was deemed desirable, and three Fulmars were despatched from Dekheila for this purpose on 15 February. Recalled Ken Sims:

'... three Fulmars joined us. We cheered them in. They too brought a pack set which was also put in the Ops Room. As they were short of air gunners, we manned it. It operated on a different frequency to ours and was used to control the Fulmars and direct them towards enemy aircraft. There was no R/T and so the route of control was a bit tortuous. From AMES via telephone line. Then verbal to the pack set operator. He then sent off the morse in abbreviated self-evident code to the A/G in the Fulmar, who then relayed it by voice-pipe to the pilot. How clumsy it all sounds. Yet quite effective if all the links worked.'

Capt L A 'Skeets' Harris DSC, RM, (left) who led the first flight of Fairey Fulmar fighters to Crete. With him is Lt Cdr A F Black who subsequently commanded 805 Squadron on the island. (*IWM*)

In charge of the Fulmar Flight was a Royal Marine pilot, Capt L A 'Skeets' Harris, DSC, who had flown over N4000, with observer Sub Lt E J H Dixon in the back seat. The other two crews were Lt P F Scott/L/Air R Woodfine (N1938 '7M') and Lt AHM Ash/L/Air W J Newman (N2001). The Flight was attached to 815 Squadron for servicing and administration, and would share the tented accommodation and Mess. The crews were part of a small group of FAA aircrews who had arrived in Egypt a few days earlier, having ferried their Fulmars from Takoradi (West Africa) on a five-day journey over jungle and desert.

The newly-arrived fighters did not have to wait long for action, for on the day after their arrival (16 February) Lt Scott was ordered off in N1938 to intercept a lone reconnaissance S.79 of 92° Gruppo from Maritza. Attacked south of the island by what the Italian crew took to be a 'Spitfire', the bomber was damaged and one member of the crew slightly wounded.

That night a Wellington of 37 Squadron took off to attack Rhodes, but en route the port engine of N2757 gave trouble, and after jettisoning the bombload,

Plt Off L J Winbolt was forced to turn back. Suddenly the engine burst into flames and the airscrew broke loose, hitting the cockpit area and putting all the instruments out of action, while the hydraulic system failed. Fortunately they were now near the Egyptian coast, and were able to force-land at Syallia, but while doing so Plt Off Winbolt was killed in the crash, although all the rest of the crew were unhurt.

Operation 'Mandible'

The planned seizure of islands in the Dodecanese was well advanced by mid-February, and on the 17th 'Z' Wing was formed in Cairo. Primary objective was to take Rhodes (Operation 'Cordite'), but first objective would be the capture of Castelorizzo, planned for the following week, and of Scarpanto (Operation 'Armature'). It was not considered necessary to provide air cover for the Castelorizzo operation, but for the Scarpanto venture 'Z' Wing would supply two Blenheim and one Wellington squadrons for striking power, and air cover of 12 Fulmars of the newly-formed 805 Squadron, aided by six of 806 Squadron, ex-*Illustrious*. These units would operate from Crete, but would be joined by HMS *Formidable*, this carrier providing additional air support, including her own Fulmar squadron, 803. The Wellingtons and Blenheims would be withdrawn from the desert and would be based at Heraklion, joined by a flight of 6 Squadron Lysanders for reconnaissance, while local airfield defence would be in the hands of a trio of Hurricanes to be detached from 274 Squadron.

Senior Air Staff Officer was to be Wg Cdr G R Beamish, one of the three distinguished air force brothers (Victor Beamish, DSO, DFC, had commanded North Weald airfield in Fighter Command's 11 Group during the Battle of Britain, while Charles Beamish, DFC, was one of the night fighter pioneers of the early days of the war). 'Z' Wing's advanced HQ would be at Heraklion, where the airfield commander was to be Sqn Ldr A J Trumble, recently CO of 261 Squadron on Malta. On the HQ Staff was to be Flg Off P J Valachos, DFC, a Canadian of Greek ancestry, who had been a Wellington pilot in 148 Squadron. The actual landing force was to consist of two Glen ships carrying 14 assorted landing craft, accompanied by a cruiser, two destroyers and three submarines. To cover this force would be HMS *Formidable*, one cruiser, one AA cruiser and four destroyers.

To begin softening up the Italian defences, two Wellingtons of 70 Squadron from Kabrit and three from 38 Squadron at Shallufa, set out to attack Scarpanto during the night of 17/18 February, joined by three Swordfish from Maleme. One of the 70 Squadron bombers turned back with engine trouble. Next day Capt Harris led his trio of Fulmars on a strafing attack on Midi Bay airfield (Scarpanto), where one CR42 was damaged on the ground.

Meanwhile during late February HMS *Eagle* had left Alexandria to meet two fast merchantmen, *Clan Macauley* and *Breconshire*, which were en route for this port from the Western Mediterranean. *Eagle* had embarked six Fulmars, three each from 805 and 806 Squadrons, to augment her small Sea Gladiator Flight, and two days out, on 21 February, the convoy came under attack at 1625 by five

He111s from 4/KG 26 on Rhodes. Two of the 805 Squadron Fulmars were on patrol, flown by Lt Cdr A F Black, the commanding officer, and Lt A R Ramsay, and these engaged just as the Heinkels commenced their attack. Alan Black recalled:

'Before I was able to press home my attack I saw one of the Heinkels release its bombs, one of which appeared to go right through the funnel of one of the ships (in fact one bomb did indeed pass straight through *Clan Macaulay's* funnel and continued over the side into the sea without exploding!). After Ramsay had discontinued his attacks I concentrated on the starboard engine of one Heinkel and got so close that my aircraft was covered in oil from that engine, before it stopped. The Heinkel then force-landed in the sea. I flew around it for a few minutes and saw the crew in the water. On return to the *Eagle* I reported to the Captain. To attempt to rescue the crew was deemed to be inexpedient.'

Lt R MacDonald-Hall of 806 Squadron, who was engaged in combat with Heinkel He111s of KG 26 near Rhodes on 21 February, 1941.

While this was going on, two Fulmars of 806 Squadron had been scrambled and these also intercepted the Heinkels, Lt R MacDonald-Hall and Lt P S Touchbourne, a Canadian, sharing in shooting one down, which they reported crashed into the sea. Only one Heinkel was actually lost – IH + BM captained by

Ofw Josef Pretsch, although a second returned with an engine badly damaged and the rear-gunner dead.

Maleme was now being regularly visited by Italian reconnaissance aircraft, these going about their task unhindered except for usually inaccurate AA fire. However on 24 February Lt Scott managed to get off in good time on the approach of another 'snooper' and although it took the Fulmar some time to gain height, Scott did eventually make contact as the S.79 headed back towards Rhodes and claimed it probably shot down following a brief engagement.

At last the next day, Operation 'Mandible' began, destroyers *Decoy* and *Hereward* landing 200 commandos in their first action in the Middle East, and a number of Royal Navy personnel, on Castelorizzo, while the gunboat *Ladybird* landed a detachment of Royal Marines. Only slight resistance was met. At once S.81s of 56° Gruppo from Rhodes, escorted by 163ª Squadriglia CR42s, were sent out to bomb and strafe British positions, claiming a hit on a cruiser; in fact it was the gunboat *Ladybird* which was damaged, while AA fire from the destroyers shot down one S.81, which ditched near the island, the crew being rescued by a Z.506B floatplane. This aircraft was itself claimed damaged by the ships' gunners, while during the day gun crews added claims for a further S.81 and a reconnaissance 'Ro41'(sic) shot down. Late in the day the two destroyers returned together with the cruisers *Gloucester* and *Bonaventure*, carrying 'B' Company of the 1st Sherwood Foresters, who were to garrison the island. By now it was dark and *Hereward* signalled for lights to be positioned to enable the troops to be landed. However the vessel was advised from the shore that enemy ships had arrived in the vicinity, and in consequence Admiral Renouf ordered the vessels back to Alexandria until the position became clearer.

Indeed the commandos had suffered not only air attack, but also shelling from two Italian destroyers, including the *Crispi*, and two torpedo-boats *Liva* and *Libra*, which arrived from Rhodes with 100 Naval marines and other personnel, 50 commandos and 15 soldiers. Soon the British force began to give ground, with ammunition and food rapidly diminishing, and while some managed to slip away by night, the majority were forced to surrender. When Renouf's ships returned in the early hours of 27 February to land the Sherwood Foresters and their supplies, no sounds of gunfire were heard, so reconnaissance patrols were despatched. These found small groups of commandos and led them back to the harbour, but it was by now obvious that the operation had failed; again Renouf ordered his forces back to Alexandria. As they withdrew the destroyer *Jaguar* contacted an Italian ship in the inner harbour and fired torpedoes, four explosions being heard. An Italian destroyer was then engaged, and two hits were claimed before it escaped.

March – April 1941: Crete under Attack

The month of March saw a rapid escalation of the war over the seas around Greece, and over Crete. The island itself was becoming an ever-more important staging base, and was as a result to come under greatly increased attack. The defences were reinforced just in time for this however, for on 6 March six more

Fulmars (N1915, 1933, 1939, 1947, 2000 and 2015) and three Buffalos (AS419, 420 and AX814) from 805 Squadron, led by Lt Cdr Black, flew in to Maleme from Dekheila. Capt. Harris' Fulmar Flight was absorbed into the squadron.

Duties at Maleme would include convoy escorts and maritime reconnaissance as well as fighter defence, and with the absorbtion of the existing fighter flight, Lt Cdr Black had twelve pilots available, including himself. The others were: Lt R A Brabner, MP (who had been elected Member of Parliament for Hythe in 1939, and who was effectively in charge of the Buffalo flight); Lt T B Winstanley (a former Albacore pilot of 826 Squadron who had been shot down by a Bf109 during the Battle of Britain); Lt Ramsay (an Australian); Lt H J C Richardson (an Engineer Officer as well as a pilot); Sub Lt R C Kay; Sub Lt R F Bryant; Sub Lt R Griffin and Sub Lt J H C Sykes (who had been seconded to 64 Squadron, RAF, during the Battle of Britain, and had been shot down by British AA fire). There were two observers – Lt John Shuttleworth and Sub Lt D H Coates, plus Sub Lt Dixon of the original flight, and six TAGs. One other observer, Sub Lt R V Hinton, was currently in hospital in Cairo and would follow in due course.

Lt (A) Rupert Brabner, MP, 805 Squadron. (*Capt A F Black*)

139

Lt Alec Ramsay, 805 squadron (*Capt A F Black*)

Sub Lt Roy Hinton (observer), 805 Squadron. (*R V Hinton*)

The mixed force of groundcrew, two thirds Naval ratings and the balance on loan from the RAF, would arrive shortly, with their equipment, aboard the battleship HMS *Valiant*. However Lt Cdr Black had early problems, for the Buffalos proved troublesome. He recalls:

'The Buffalo was a delight to fly – very manoeuvrable (compared to the Fulmar). It would have been an excellent fighter but the guns could not be fired because the ends of the wires which were part of the interrupter gear, failed and 805 did not have the necessary spares. At no time did I request that the Buffalos be exchanged for Sea Gladiators but I do remember that in the light of the inadequacy of Fulmars against CR 42s I requested that the Sea Gladiators, if not required for other operations, should be sent to Maleme, to reinforce 805.'

The squadron was to suffer its first loss of a Fulmar on 10 March when Lt Brabner, with Lt Shuttleworth as observer, was forced to ditch 'L7-Z'. Recalled John Shuttleworth:

'Rupert and I took off in a panic to intercept an attack on Suda Bay (which apparently did not materialize) and, I think, without a full load of petrol. Anyhow, the engine cut after 85 minutes, over Suda Bay, and we force-landed in the entrance to the Bay with a dead engine, more or less alongside HMS *Hotspur*, who picked us up and took us back to harbour – no serious injury to either of us, but I gashed my knee badly on the IFF set when we hit the water.'

About this time the squadron received an additional pilot when Lt P R E Woods of the Suda Bay Walrus Flight, requested a transfer, although he had no fighter pilot training. Lt Cdr Black personally helped initiate him into air combat tactics and on one occasion narrowly avoided a collision – Black was acting as target for Woods in another Fulmar to carry out quarter attacks. Woods apparently lost sight of the CO's aircraft in the final stage of a practice attack and passed two or three feet above it. 'A near thing!' commented Black.

The forces on Crete and at sea were supported at this time by the Egyptian-based Wellington bombers of 257 Wing, which made frequent small-scale night attacks on the Italian airfields in the Dodecanese. Ten such bombers from 37 and 70 Squadrons attacked Gadurra (Rhodes) during the night of 10/11 March, six returning to repeat the attack two nights later, Maritza and Kattavia airfields also being bombed. During these raids one S.79 was destroyed and four others damaged at Gadurra, and one S.81 damaged at Maritza. However Crete's resident striking power – such as it was – was reduced when six of 815 Squadron's Swordfish were detached to Paramythia, in north-west Greece, as recounted in the previous chapter.

Crete came under air attack again during the night of 12/13 March when seven bombs fell on Heraklion, damaging the runway. Next day S.79s from 34° Gruppo BT raided shipping in Suda Bay, but inflicted no damage. Other bombers of this type attacked Mytilene, one of the largest Greek Aegean islands, but while the harbour was bombed, no damage was suffered here either. On the 17th two aircraft from 2 PRU from Heliopolis, Egypt, arrived at Heraklion to carry out sorties over Rhodes. One of the arrivals was the modified Hudson

(N7364), again captained by Flt Lt Walker, the other a Hurricane PR1 (V7423), which was painted Royal Blue matt overall, and carried two 8-inch cameras; it was flown by Flt Lt A M Brown. A deterioration in the weather soon after arrival postponed their mission, and the aircraft were ordered to remain at Heraklion until an improvement allowed them to proceed with their duties.

Next day three of 805 Squadron Fulmars (Lts Brabner, Ramsay and Richardson) had their first encounter when two Ju88s – probably aircraft of LG 1 from Sicily – were seen and pursued without success. At Aboukir (Egypt) five more Fulmars from 806 Squadron, recently arrived from Malta after the damaging of their carrier, HMS *Illustrious*, were ordered to prepare to reinforce 805 Squadron at Maleme, but at the last moment they were embarked instead on the newly-arrived HMS *Formidable* for a sortie to Malta in support of a convoy from Alexandria.

Brewster Buffalo AS419 of 805 Squadron which turned over during a force-landing after engine failure on 19 March 1941, Lt Brabner at the controls. (*D H Coates*)

The first major action occured early on 19 March when at 0630 ten S.79s from 34° and 92° Gruppo BT set out from Rhodes, escorted by five 162ª Squadriglia CR42s; their target was again shipping in Suda Bay. Weather closed in as they approached, frustrating their attacks, but they were intercepted by three Fulmars (Lt Richardson, Sub Lts Kay and Griffin) and Lt Brabner in Buffalo AS419. The Buffalo developed engine trouble however, and Brabner was forced to turn back, crash-landing short of the airfield, where the aircraft turned over onto its tail; Brabner was unhurt. Meanwhile Sub Lt Kay shot down Ten Mario Catalano's S.79, and was seen to inflict damage on two more bombers before colliding with a fourth and crashing into the sea. Both Kay and L/Air D R Stockman, his TAG, perished.

The S.79 with which he had collided struggled on as far as Scarpanto where it crashed while attempting to land and was destroyed, although only one member of the crew suffered any injury. Lt Richardson also claimed damage to one bomber, he and Griffin managing to evade attacks by the escorting CR 42s, and returned to Maleme. Nonetheless, the Italian fighter pilots claimed one 'Hurricane' shot down and two others probably so, while the bomber gunners claimed two more shot down, including the one which had collided. Following the action Lt Woods, with Sub Lt Coates in the rear seat, took off to search for the missing aircraft, but saw no sign of it, or of any survivors from the S.79.

S.79s and Z.1007bis bombers from Rhodes returned next day to again attack shipping, claiming damage to a destroyer and a merchantman. The crews reported being attacked by fighters – presumably 805 Squadron Fulmars – and claimed one shot down, but no defending fighters were actually lost or damaged.

After waiting for five days for the weather to improve, the photo-reconnaissance aircraft at Heraklion were at last able to get off on 22 March. However after 45 minutes in the air Flt Lt Brown was taken ill and both aircraft turned back. Within an hour of their return, six CR 42s from the 162ª Squadriglia swept in low at 1505, led by Cap Leopoldo Sartirana. Four strafed the airfield, where they claimed (according to one report) four Hurricanes destroyed or damaged, and one shot down! Another report claimed that their success was over six twin-engined aircraft and one Hurricane! Actual casualties were the Hudson badly damaged, and a single Blenheim slightly hit. The only Hurricane, the 2 PRU machine, suffered no damage, and was flown back to Mersa Matruh that evening.

Cap Sartirana returned at 0700 next morning at the head of seven CR 42s, three diving on the airfield where one aircraft was claimed destroyed by strafing. AA fire damaged two of the biplanes, the pilot of one of these also misjudging his pull-out, hitting the top of the Hudson's wing with one wheel, almost tearing off the undercarriage. He made it back to Scarpanto where he force-landed. Following this attack the Hudson was written off, but not before both engines, all instruments and other removable parts had been salvaged, and subsequently flown back to Egypt.

On 24 March an unserviceable Fulmar (N1947) was flown back to Aboukir by Sub Lt B Sinclair. Here 806 Squadron was reforming, and Sinclair became the first of several 805 Squadron pilots to be attached to this unit. From Maleme a day later a Sea Gladiator, one of three which had arrived via HMS *Formidable* two days earlier, provided the sole air cover for a convoy. AS-22, which came under attack by three Ju88s north of Gavdhos Island. The pilot attacked, claiming damage to one of the bombers, although his own aircraft was hit by return fire and suffered slight damage. Two Fulmars escorted Lt Winstanley in another Sea Gladiator (N5517) to carry out a photo-reconnaissance to Stampalia, Winstanley using a hand-held camera for this purpose; no opposition was encountered.

Five Blenheims from 30 Squadron flew into Maleme from the Athens area in preparation for strike on Calato airfield, and against Scarpanto. Sqn Ldr Milward in L8446 led three aircraft to Calato where many He111s were seen, he

Lockheed Hudson N7364 of No.2 Photo Reconnaissance Unit written off at Heraklion on 23 March after a damaged Italian fighter had collided with one wing. It is seen here, stripped of wings, engines and tail unit following the German occupation of the island in late May 1941. (*Bundesarchiv*)

personally claiming one badly damaged and hits on four others. Flg Off Smith (K7105) claimed another four damaged, while Flg Off Richardson (K7177) carried out a general strafe. On the return flight the crews spotted a 7000 ton merchant vessel close to Stampalia island and strafed this. After their return two Swordfish of 815 Squadron were sent out at 1830 to attack this ship, but failed to find it. Meanwhile the other two Blenheims, led by Flg Off Davidson, had made for Scarpanto, but Plt Off Jarvis had turned back with engine trouble; Davidson continued alone but saw no aircraft on the airfield here.

The Italians immediately retaliated for these attacks by despatching three 162ª Squadriglia CR42s to again strike at Heraklion, while four others flew top cover. The damaged Blenheim was hit again and set on fire, being completely burned out. AA fire hit one of the strafers, the gunners believing that it had crashed into the sea; in fact it struggled back to Rhodes where the pilot made a successful landing.

Next morning, at about 0800, three CR42s of this unit appeared over Suda Bay, but their role was reconnaissance on this occasion. Intense and accurate AA fire greeted them, one being damaged by shrapnel splinters. They had made their sortie to seek evidence of the results of a night attack on shipping in the harbour, as will be related later, and were able to report sighting the damaged cruiser *York* and three or four cargo vessels. That evening five 815 Squadron Swordfish left to attack Stampalia, but were forced back by bad weather. On return Lt E D J Whatley crashed on Maleme airfield; he and his crew escaped injury, but the landing of the rest of the formation was considerably delayed as a result.

On 27 March two more reinforcement Sea Gladiators (N5509 and 5538) arrived at Maleme, having been flown from Dekheila by Lt Lloyd Keith, a Canadian, and Sub Lt R W M Walsh; both pilots were retained by 805 Squadron on a brief attachment. Lt Keith had previously flown Sea Gladiators and Swordfish) with some success whilst serving with HMS *Eagle*; Walsh had flown Hurricanes with 111 Squadron, RAF, during the Battle of Britain. On this same day two Ju88s from 6/LG 1, based at Catania, Sicily, while on an armed reconnaissance south-west of Crete attacked a freighter. However a twin-engined fighter reportedly intercepted Uffz August Johannesmann's aircraft, putting out an engine and wounding the pilot, who, nevertheless, nursed the damaged aircraft back to Catania, but crashed on landing, all the crew being killed. No such combat has been found in British records. It is feasible that the attacker may have been a Bf110 flying a long-range sortie from Libya or Sicily; such mistakes of misidentification did happen all too often.

815 Squadron lost another Swordfish on the last day of the month when Lt Whatley again crashed, this time while on patrol off Kythera Island, when his aircraft, 'X' suffered an engine failure. The crew got aboard their dinghy and reached the island from where they were rescued next day. To make good these losses four more Swordfish were ferried over from Dekheila; these were ex-829 Squadron aircraft from *Formidable*. The island was to be further reinforced on 5 April with the arrival on detachment of six Blenheim IFs of 30 Squadron to undertake sea reconnaissances, convoy patrols and night fighting.

Meanwhile on 3 April Lt Ramsay of 805 Squadron was up in a Fulmar covering the approach of Convoy ANF-24 through the Antikythera Channel, when two Ju88s attacked the vessels. Ramsay intercepted one of the bombers, and while he did not observe the results of his attack, observers aboard ship reported that the Junkers was almost certainly shot down. The second bomber then reappeared and attacked the convoy but failed to gain any hits. Two hours later at 1857, nine Ju88s attacked, gaining two hits on *Northern Prince* (10 917 tons) which killed a number of the crew and started fires. The vessel was carrying several thousand tons of explosives, destined for the Greek ordnance factories; the surviving members of the crew were taken off, and soon afterwards the ship blew up. The previous evening the small freighter *Cyprian Prince*, also part of this convoy, had been hit and damaged during an attack by He111s of II/KG 26, but she managed to keep up with the convoy as it proceeded towards Piraeus.

Yet again Heraklion came under attack by CR42s on 4 April, seven refuelling at Scarpanto and then proceeding to Crete where five strafed the airfield. Only slight damage was caused, although 40 cases of ammunition were destroyed, but again the efficient airfield AA hit one of the fighters, and this time it did crash into the sea. Serg Domenico Chiappa was killed.

Lt Brabner of 805 Squadron was on patrol next day when radar picked up a suspicious plot. Vectored onto this, Brabner's Fulmar soon intercepted the intruder, but fortunately good visibility allowed him to recognize it as an unannounced Bombay transport of 216 Squadron. This aircraft would depart again next day, carrying Lt Keith and Sub Lt Walsh back to Dekheila at the end of their brief attachment to 805 Squadron.

805 Squadron Fulmar on patrol, flown by Sub Lt R F Bryant. (*D H Coates*)

Maleme was to be inundated with aircraft of all types on the 6th, as elements of 208 Squadron staged through on their way to Greece. Six 'almost new' Swordfish also arrived for 815 Squadron, led by Lt Lamb. These had been used by HMS *Formidable*'s Air Group during the recent naval operations off Cape Matapan (see later). On return, they were flown over to Crete by Pool pilots, but on arrival at Maleme were taken over by 815 Squadron pilots, who flew them on up to Paramythia for operations.

The remaining elements of this squadron at Maleme suffered a further loss on 9 April when Lt Burnaby Drayson and his crew (Sub Lt A Carroll and L/Air F Faulks) were forced to ditch ten miles north of the island due to engine failure while on anti-submarine patrol. On taking to their dinghy, they found that it carried no survival kit, leaving them with no food or water, while the distress flares did not work. Due to unserviceability, only one Swordfish was available at Maleme to search for them, but while they could see this taking-off and landing, they could not attract the crew's attention. After four days and three nights, Burnaby Drayson decided to try to swim for shore since a wind had sprung up which was beginning to blow the dinghy further out to sea. Against the advice of the other two, he entered the sea and swam off. Shortly after this, the wind direction changed and blew the dinghy ashore where Carroll and Faulks, weak and suffering from exposure, staggered to a nearby village. Here the locals gave them goats milk and eggs before contacting the military for assistance. Burnaby Drayson's body was washed ashore, and was buried on 14 April.

Action continued meanwhile, and on the 11th a Z.1007bis trimotor of the 172[a]

Squadriglia on Rhodes, set off on a reconnaissance over Alexandria, carrying Sottoten Alessandro Laurenzi of the Regia Marina as observer. At 1245, when 60 miles north of Alexandria, it was intercepted by two Hurricanes from 274 Squadron, which were on detachment at Ismailia, Flg Off A A P Weller and Plt Off D J Spence shooting the Cant down into the sea. Two survivors of Ten Giulio Gabella's crew were rescued by a Sunderland. That night Rhodes' Calato airfield came under attack by Wellingtons from 37 Squadron's Greek-based detachment, but after bombing these were ordered to fly direct to Egypt due to bad weather over the Athens area.

172ᵃ Squadriglia tried again next day, another Z.1007bis approaching Alexandria. Again two Hurricanes intercepted, and the aircraft was badly damaged, the pilot being wounded and one member of the crew mortally hit. Although the bomber regained Rhodes, it crash-landed short of its airfield and was destroyed. Three days later Heraklion was once more attacked by 162ᵃ Squadriglia CR42s, six aircraft strafing gun positions and dispersed Blenheims, two of these being claimed destroyed. AA was as fierce as ever, the Bofors hitting four of the Fiats, three of which were damaged, the fourth being shot down; the pilot, Ten Luciano Corsini, was taken prisoner. Next day 815 Squadron's unlucky Lt Whatley again came to grief, force-landing his Swordfish on Kythera island following engine failure while on an anti-submarine patrol. He and his observer were picked up by Walrus amphibian from Suda Bay.

South of Gavdhos island, off the southern coast of Crete, Convoy AN-27 en route for Suda Bay, was attacked by four Ju88s at 1930 on 17 April. The gunners on the escorting Australian destroyer *Vampire* engaged and claimed damage to the port engine of one bomber; the convoy suffered no damage. This same day Lt Ramsay of 805 Squadron attacked a reconnaissance Ju88 but the Fulmar had great trouble in effectively dealing with the fast Junkers and again it escaped without obvious damage. Meanwhile Lt Keith and Sub Lt Walsh were on their way back to Maleme, ferrying in two further Sea Gladiators (N5535 and 5568) for the squadron. On the way they sighted a lone He111 which they attempted to intercept without success. As a result they were dangerously low on fuel when they broke cloud over the airfield, where the defences at once opened fire – fortunately not with any accuracy. Lt Keith again remained on attachment, but Walsh was flown back via a departing Bombay to collect another Sea Gladiator – only to find that no more were available.

At 1305 on the 18th Flg Off Andy Smith set out from Maleme in his 30 Squadron Blenheim to patrol over Convoy AN-27 as it approached Suda Bay. After 30 minutes on station he saw two S.79s approaching from the south-west of Melos. These were torpedo-bombers of 281ᵃ Squadriglia, led by Cap Giuseppe Cimicchi, on which Smith closed from astern, opening fire on the leading aircraft. Black smoke poured from the starboard engine, the undercarriage dropped down, and he believed that the aircraft had fallen into the sea; it had indeed come down, Ten Barbani putting it down in the water near Camilloni Island, all the crew sustaining injuries; they were later rescued by a Cant floatplane. Meanwhile Smith attacked the second S.79, seeing sparks from the starboard engine, but the

Blenheim was then hit by return fire. As Smith returned to Maleme one of his engines began to burn as he went into his final approach, but the fire was swiftly extinguished by the observer, Plt Off J H Strong.

Savoia S.79sil torpedo-bomber of 279ª Squadriglia AS, based on Rhodes during April 1941 for anti-shipping duties. (*F Longhi via Lucchini/Malizia*)

As the torpedo-bombers had carried out their attack, one torpedo – that presumably released by Cap Cimicchi – hitting the oiler *British Science*, three S.79 bombers from 34° Gruppo attempted to bomb from higher level, claiming a hit on a cruiser. They were intercepted by an 805 Squadron Fulmar, Sub Lt Royston Griffin forcing the bombers to break off their attack, but in fact he may have damaged all three, although the crews reported that it was AA shrapnel which struck their aircraft, one airman being wounded. In return the gunners claimed to have shot down Griffin's fighter, which in fact suffered no damage. The torpedoed oiler was forced to reduce speed to six knots, proceeding along towards Suda Bay; she would be torpedoed again the following day, and was sunk.

A steady flow of aircraft were now coming in and out between Greece and Egypt. On 18 April a Sunderland flown by Flt Lt A M G Lywood alighted on Suda Bay from Greece en route for Alexandria, carrying King Peter of Yugoslavia, General Simonovitch, and other members of the Yugoslav Royal Family and of the political and military staffs. Two days later Flt Lt D K Bednall staged through on his way to Scaramanga, returning with 16 RAF passengers and the AOC's wife, Mrs D'Albiac, with – of all things – her pet canary!

During the 20th – the day of the big battle over Athens – Blenheims of 30 Squadron were again out on convoy patrols, as were 805 Squadron Fulmars. 35 miles south-east of Gavdhos Island 30 Squadron's Flg Off Smith spotted an S.79 approaching Convoy AS-26 and again carried out a stern attack. After one burst however, his guns jammed and he was forced to break away. He had nonetheless been successful in causing the bomber to break off its intended attack, and believed his short burst had killed the rear-gunner. 805 Squadron's Lt Ash encountered a Ju88 of 4/LG 1 from Sicily, and attacked this to the south of Crete, wounding the pilot, Uffz Berthold Bornschein, before the fast German aircraft escaped.

Next day Convoy AS-26 was again attacked, just south of Gavdhos Island, by two Ju88s from 7/KG 30, also operating from Sicily. One bomb near-missed *British Lord*, which was disabled at 1100, the crew being taken off by *Vampire*, while HMS *Auckland* took the ship in tow. Gunners on the sloop hit Lt Alfred Pich's 4D + DR, which the pilot was forced to ditch just off the coast of Crete, two of the crew being killed in the crash; Pich and one other were taken prisoner. On this day however, the Canea area of Crete was attacked for the first time by Luftwaffe bombers operating from bases on the Greek mainland – Ju88s of I/LG 1 and I/KG 51. AA fire struck one of the raiders, wounding a member of the crew, but the raid marked the end of Crete's independent little air war. The island was about to become enmeshed in the main fighting.

The War at Sea

At the start of March the first of a series of convoys began loading in Alexandria for Operation 'Lustre', the movement of 58 000 troops – British, Commonwealth, Cypriot and Palestinian, with assorted motor transport, tanks, guns, stores and equipment to Greece. These convoys were to carry coded numbers as follows:

AN–   Alexandria, Northbound
AS–   Alexandria, Southbound
ANF–   Alexandria, Northbound Fast Convoy
ASF–   Alexandria, Southbound Fast Convoy
AG–   Alexandria to Greece (special troop-carriers, including cruisers)
GA–   Greece to Alexandria (empty troop-carriers)

On 4 March Convoy AN-17 left Alexandria for Piraeus, but as it approached the Kaso Strait near Crete next day, Italian bombers from Rhodes commenced isolated attacks by two or three aircraft, the first appearing at 1126. The nearest they came to success occurred at 1710, when a single S.79 narrowly missed torpedoing the AA cruiser *Coventry*. The attack resumed at first light on 6 March, bombers and torpedo-bombers attacking, both S.79s and S.81s being employed; all were driven off by AA fire. At 0710 the escorting destroyer *Greyhound* depth-charged a submarine contact, forcing the *Anfilnite* to the surface. Here it was riddled with heavy gunfire, sinking after about half an hour, the crew having abandoned ship.

The Mediterranean Fleet, which had been without an aircraft carrier since *Illustrious* had been damaged in January, and *Ark Royal* had gone home for a refit, was greatly strengthened on 10 March by the arrival of the newly-commissioned, armoured-deck 23 000 ton HMS *Formidable* (Captain A W la T Bisset). This vessel came up through the Suez Canal in preparation for Operation 'Mandible' – the proposed Dodecanese invasions mentioned earlier in this chapter. Her Air Group consisted of Albacore biplane torpedo-bombers of 826 Squadron (Lt Cdr W H G Saunt) and 829 Squadron (Lt Cdr J Dalyell-Stead), this latter unit operating a mix of these aircraft and Swordfish; finally 803 Squadron had ten Fulmars, led by Lt J M 'Bill' Bruen.

Two Fulmars had already been lost en route from the UK to Freetown, West Africa, one disappearing during a patrol, the other force-landing in Vichy French Senegal, the crew being interned. The Air Group had attacked targets along the coast of Italian East Africa as the carrier approached the Red Sea, but here two Albacores had been lost to AA fire over Massawa harbour, Eritrea. On arrival at Port Sudan, the ship had been delayed while the Suez Canal had been swept for mines laid by Dodecanese-based He111s. While here two Fulmars, flown by Lt A J Wright, RM, and Sub Lt W C Simpson, intercepted an Italian 'mailplane' en route to Somaliland, claiming this probably shot down.

Before the carrier had sortied, two He111 torpedo-bombers of II/KG 26 from the Dodecanese came across elements of the Mediterranean Fleet whilst on an armed reconnaissance on 16 March, to the west of Crete. The battleships *Warspite* and *Barham* were identified, each pilot selecting one as his target and releasing their torpedoes from low-level and at relatively close range. As they turned away columns of water were seen where hits might have been expected and both crews believed that they had damaged their targets. This information was passed to the Italian Naval Command, and would prove to have serious consequences for the Italian Fleet. Spurred on by the German Naval Command, the battleship *Vittorio Veneto*, eight cruisers and 13 destroyers put to sea from bases at Naples, Taranto and Brindisi to interrupt, and hopefully intercept, the convoys transporting troops and supplies from Egypt to Greece. The problem for the Italians was to be that the British battleships had not in fact suffered any damage....

The Mediterranean was filling with ships, for on 18 March Convoy AN-21 comprising 13 ships left Alexandria for Greece, while two days later four fast merchantmen departed with vital supplies for Malta as MW-6. The latter was escorted by the AA cruisers *Calcutta*, *Coventry* and *Carlisle*, with attendent destroyers, and by *Formidable*. The carrier took aboard not only her own Air Group, but six additional Fulmars of 806 Squadron. Three Sea Gladiators also went aboard, but these were for 805 Squadron and were to be flown off to Maleme at the end of the operation.

Both convoys came under air attack on 21 March, two Ju88s bombing the cruiser *Bonaventure* which had joined MW-6 when near Gavdhos Island at 1225. Green Section of 803 Squadron were up on patrol and were vectored to attack, Lt Bruen, with Lt D J Godden in the rear seat of N1951 '6A', catching L1+DM of 5/LG 1 (Lt Friedrich-Wilhelm zur Nieden), and chasing it down to sea level in the direction of the Fleet, inflicting severe damage as they went. Here the warships' AA opened up, and the bomber crashed into the sea. Sub Lt D H Richards, Green 2, had become separated and lost in poor visibility, but he fortuitously encountered a patrolling Fulmar of 805 Squadron, flown by Lt Ramsay and followed him back to Maleme. Somewhat later Capt Harris and Lt Scott of 805 took off and landed their Fulmars on *Formidable* to aid in the patrols over the convoy for the next two days.

At 1604, as Convoy AN-21 passed through the Kythera Channel, three Ju88s –

150

again from II/LG 1 suddenly appeared at 300 feet out of squally weather, and dropped bombs near the tanker *Havre*. A further Ju88 then arrived and attacked the Danish tanker *Marie Maersk* (8271 tons), one bomb hitting the bridge and causing a number of casualties; the tanker caught fire. The crew abandoned ship, 27 men being picked up from the sea by HMAS *Stuart*, which also recovered two bodies. HMAS *Waterhen* then put a salvage party aboard, the two destroyers withdrawing while the armed trawler *Amber* stood by. By midnight the fires were under control, engines were started, and under her own steam the vessel made for Suda Bay, arriving there at midday on the 22nd. The fires were finally extinguished six hours later, only 500 tons of the oil cargo being lost.

As the rest of the convoy reached a point south-east of Gavdhos Island on 22 March, He111 torpedo-bombers of II/KG 26 attacked, the 3798-ton Greek freighter *Embiricos Nicolaos* being badly damaged; she sank after the crew had been rescued. The Norwegian tanker *Solheim* was also badly damaged, and would later also be abandoned and left to sink.

At dusk Convoy ASF-21 entered the Kythera Strait, being joined off Kupho Island by the AA cruisers *Coventry* and *Carlisle* just as three S.79s from 34° Gruppo were positioning to release their torpedoes. Five more S.79s made bombing runs at higher level, but no hits were gained by any of the attackers, the combined fire power of the escort shooting down one of the bombers, which fell in flames through the darkening sky.

With the other convoy (MW-6), one of 803 Squadron's Fulmars (N1936), was obliged to force-land on Kythera Island with engine trouble. The crew were unhurt and were taken by boat to Suda Bay. A few days later Lt Cdr Black was flown out to the island in a Walrus to fly the repaired aircraft to Maleme, recalling:

'The local inhabitants at Kythera were very anxious to help and I well remember when taxying over the shingle beach being most concerned that I might decapitate one or two who got dangerously close to the propeller. On the take-off run I had some difficulty in countering a tendency of the Fulmar to swing down the beach and into the sea but, in an unloaded condition – with guns and ammunition and W/T set removed, and with little petrol – in the end all was well.'

Formidable's duty to MW-6 was completed on 23 March, and she now headed back east to Alexandria. At a comfortable distance from Crete the two 805 Squadron Fulmars and the three Sea Gladiators were flown off to Maleme. The latter were ex-*Eagle* aircraft (N5513, 5517 and 5567). Capt Harris had a frightening experience on his last patrol from the carrier when his Fulmar suffered a hydraulic failure while flying on, and landed on one wheel. During the day Sub Lt A C Wallace of 803 Squadron in N1918 came across a lone Ju88, but it escaped. Shortly afterwards he again met a Ju88 – possibly the same machine – and claimed to have destroyed it. Elsewhere a single S.79 of 281ª Squadriglia, a unit recently arrived on Rhodes, attempted a torpedo attack on Convoy AS-22. Engaged by heavy AA fire, Ten Giorgio Sacchetti's aircraft was damaged.

On 24 March the cruisers *Orion*, *York* and *Calcutta*, returning from various escort duties through the Kythera Strait, came under attack by small formations of Ju88s at 1257, and again at 1411, but these were driven off without damage. *Calcutta* entered Suda Bay that evening, the other warships remaining at sea to cover another Piraeus-bound convoy. The latter was bombed in the Salamis Strait by six Ju88s next day, but without damage.

Things were afoot however, for 'Ultra' intercepts had picked up several pieces of information. German twin-engined fighters (obviously Bf110s of ZG26) from Libya had been ordered to Palermo (Sicily) 'for special operations' – proposed support and protection for the Italian Fleet preparing to challenge a supposedly weakened and stretched Mediterranean Fleet, and possibly to intercept British supply ships to Greece. The German Naval Liaison Officer in Rome advised the Italian Naval Staff:

'The German Naval Staff considers that at the moment there is only one British battleship, *Valiant*, in the Eastern Mediterranean fully ready for action. It is not anticipated that heavy British units will be withdrawn from the Atlantic in the near future. Force "H" is also considered unlikely to appear in the Mediterranean. Thus the situation in the Mediterranean is at the moment more favourable for the Italian Fleet than ever before. Intensive traffic from Alexandria to the Greek ports, whereby the Greek forces are receiving constant reinforcements in men and equipment, presents a particularly worthwhile target for Italian Naval Forces. The German Naval Staff considers that the appearance of Italian units in the area south of Crete will seriously interfere with British shipping, and may even lead to the complete interruption of the transport of troops, especially as these transports are at the moment inadequately protected.'

It proved to be a most serious and inaccurate assessment by the Germans, which was to cost the Italians dear.

Other 'Ultra' intercepts established that 25 March was D-Day minus three for a major operation involving Rhodes Command. Next day intercepts confirmed that the German and Italian cyphers referred to the same operation. The Italian High Command also requested further information about British convoys between Alexandria and Greece, and ordered attacks on Maleme and Heraklion to neutralize British air strength. With this foreknowledge Admiral Sir Andrew Cunningham (Commander-in-Chief, Mediterranean Fleet) put his own plans into action. Late on the 26th he cancelled southbound Convoy GA-8 and ordered that a Piraeus-bound convoy, AG-9, should reverse course after dark. Vice-Admiral Pridham-Wippell's Force 'B' – the cruisers *Orion* (with early-type ASV radar), *Ajax* (with the more modern type, as yet untried in battle), *Perth*, *Gloucester* and four destroyers of the 2nd Flotilla, currently operating between Greece and Crete – was ordered to assemble 30 miles south of Gavdhos Island at dawn on 28 March. The First Battle Squadron would depart Alexandria after dark the day before.

During the late afternoon of 25 March meanwhile, the cruisers *York* and *Orion* entered Suda Bay, where just as dusk fell they were spotted by a reconnaissance S.79. The Italian crew reported the presence of one cruiser, two destroyers and 12 cargo vessels, but at 2230 hours *Coventry* arrived also, to refuel from the 8324 ton Norwegian tanker *Pericles*. A fourth cruiser, *Gloucester*, had also anchored nearby, having similarly refuelled, while *York* was berthed next to the tanker. Under cover of darkness two Italian destroyers, *Crispi* and *Sella*, had slipped out of Stampalia harbour carrying six one-man explosive motor-boats (known as MTMs – Motoscafo Turismo Modificato) of the X Flottiglia. Ten miles from the entrance to Suda Bay the MTMs were lowered into the sea just before midnight, and led by Ten Vascello Luigi Faggioni, headed for the Bay.

Just after 0500 on 26 March the attack commenced, each MTM aimed at selected targets by their pilots, who then evacuated the craft into their own small liferaft. Only three actually hit, two (those of Sottoten Vascello Angelo Cabrini and Sottoten Tullio Tedeschi) striking *York*, which had to be beached with her engine and boiler rooms flooded, and with no power to operate her guns. The third, Sottoten Lino Beccati's craft, hit the *Pericles* amidships, and badly damaged her, although she remained operational and continued to provide oiling facilities. During the height of the attack, gunners aboard *York* had opened fire at what they presumed to be unseen low-flying aircraft, and when Ten Faggione and his compatriots – Cabrini, Tedeschi, Beccati plus Sottoten Alessio De Vito and Sergente Emilio Barberi – were all found at dawn floating in their rafts, they were interrogated as to the locality of their crashed aircraft. Each of these brave men would be awarded the Medaglia D'Oro. Admiral Cunningham was to record:
'While the Italians as the whole displayed little enterprise and intiative at sea, it always amazed me how good they were at these sort of individual attacks. They certainly had men capable of the most gallant exploits.'

Next day *Coventry* and two destroyers sailed again to provide escort for a collection of 16 empty small British and Greek merchantmen returning to Port Said, guiding them through the Kaso Strait. During the morning three Ju88s attacked, but were driven off without causing any damage. A much heavier attack developed in the afternoon, 24 Ju88s, apparently from both III/KG30 and III/LG 1, approaching. *Coventry* and the destroyers were hard-pressed to provide adequate cover, but put up such a barrage that two of the bombers were claimed shot down. Certainly Oblt Walter Weller's 4D + GR of 7/KG30 was badly hit and crashed on the south coast of Crete, while an aircraft of 8/LG 1 struggled back to Catania, where it crash-landed. *Coventry*'s Captain Gilmour was advised that W/T intercepts and radars indicated that three more bombers had ditched and had been calling their bases for help, but it seems that these calls were from the two aircraft mentioned, for no other losses were suffered. Two of the merchant vessels were damaged by near-misses during the attack, but managed to stay with the convoy.

On the morning of 27 March the first sighting of elements of the Italian Fleet was made at 1220 by a patrolling Sunderland of 230 Squadron from Scaramanga, Flg Off R S Bohm's crew reporting a force of three cruisers and one destroyer 80 miles east of Cap Passero, the south-eastern tip of Sicily. These were steering south-east and were possibly en route to the Greek convoy lancs. The force sighted was the 3rd Cruiser Division (Vice-Admiral Sansonetti) comprising the three heavy cruisers *Trieste*, *Trento* and *Bolzano*, which was spearheading the Italian Fleet. Behind came the 1st Cruiser Division (Vice-Admiral Cattaneo) with three more heavy cruisers, and the 8th Cruiser Division (Vice-Admiral Legnani) with two light cruisers; accompanying these forces were nine destroyers. They would shortly be joined by Admiral Angelo Iachino, Commander-in-Chief of the Fleet, in his flagship, the battleship *Vittorio Veneto*, and four destroyers, which were steaming from Naples. Quite a formidable force but none of these warships had any radar.

This was the sighting Admiral Cunningham had been waiting for, and he ordered the First Battle Squadron to put to sea after dark. Meanwhile as a ruse for prying eyes, he appeared at the Alexandria Golf Club in sporting attire, with overnight case in hand. The local Japanese Consul was known to spend most afternoons at the golf course, and the sighting of Cunningham here was bound to reach him and be passed on to his Axis partners. The delusion was compounded when at 1400 a Z.1007bis reconnaissance aircraft from the 172ª Squadriglia on Rhodes, flew over Alexandria unopposed, the crew reporting the sighting of two aircraft carriers, three battleships and an undetermined number of cruisers still in harbour.

At 1600 *Formidable* got underway, flying on her Air Group from Dekheila an hour later. Due to the shortage of TSR (Torpedo-Spotter-Reconnaissance) aircraft, 826 and 829 Squadrons could muster only ten Albacores (five fitted with long-range tanks) and four Swordfish between them. Thirteen Fulmars were available, three 806 Squadron aircraft joining those of 803 Squadron. Admiral Cunningham returned to the harbour after dark and went aboard *Warspite*, the Battle Squadron departing harbour at 1900. Both *Formidable* and *Valiant* were equipped with the latest radar equipment. They were joined by *Warspite* and *Barham*, and by nine destroyers of the 10th and 14th Flotillas. It would be noon of the 28th before Iachino received infomation that the carrier and battleships had put to sea, and by then his force was already under attack from *Formidable*'s torpedo-bombers.

First light on 28 March found the Battle Squadron 150 miles south of eastern Crete, and here at 0550 five TSRs were launched to search for the Italian ships, while a Swordfish began an anti-submarine patrol, and two Fulmars provided Combat Air Patrol (CAP). At about the same time four of 815 Squadron's Swordfish from Maleme, all armed with torpedoes, began an offensive search to the west of the island. During this one aircraft suffered engine trouble, and the leader led all four back to base. A Fulmar was sent off by 805 Squadron to continue the search, but nothing was seen.

The first sighting of the Italian Fleet was made at 0720 by Albacore '5B', about 25 miles south-east of Gavdhos Island, the crew reporting four cruisers and four destroyers. Twenty minutes later Lt A S Whitworth in '5F' made a second sighting which he reported as four cruisers and six destroyers at a position 20 miles from the earlier sighting. '5B' signalled again at 0804, amending its earlier report to four cruisers and six destroyers. When these reports were first received it was suspected that the searchers might have seen Pridham-Whippell's Force 'B', which was in the general area waiting to rendezvous, and itself comprised four cruisers and four destroyers. However by now Force 'B' itself had sighted three unidentified ships 18 miles to the north, and signalled Cunningham accordingly. They had spotted 3rd Division cruisers, and these opened fire at 0812, concentrating their aim on *Gloucester* initially. Salvoes were exchanged, and *Gloucester* launched her Walrus amphibian ('Alice II', P5668), flown by Lt H J F Lane, to spot for the guns. By the time this aircraft had gained height and position the engagement had ceased, the Italians withdrawing westwards. Lt Lane commenced shadowing the cruisers, and quickly spotted a second force – the 1st Division, comprising the cruisers *Zara*, *Fiume* and *Pola*, with attendant light cruisers and destroyers. Admiral Iachino's element was also nearby, ten miles to the north, and indeed it had been *Vittorio Veneto*'s Ro43 reconnaissance-spotter biplane which had made the first sighting of Force 'B'.

Meridionali Ro.43 reconnaissance floatplane on the bows of an Italian cruiser. (*Luce via N Malizia*)

An Ro.43 is launched from the side of an Italian cruiser to search for the British Fleet. (*AMI via N Malizia*)

On learning of this engagement, Cunningham ordered *Formidable* to range a strike force. Six Albacores of 826 Squadron were readied, each armed with a torpedo, but these were not launched immediately due to the withdrawal of the Italian units. Instead Maleme was signalled to despatch its strike force, but the signal was not relayed to Ops Control until 1005, and it was 45 minutes later when three Swordfish set out, led by Lt M G W Clifford. Meanwhile *Formidable*'s strike was ordered off, led by Lt Cdr Saunt and escorted by Red Section of 803 Squadron (Lt D C E F Gibson in '6J' and Pty Off (A) A W Theobald in N1912), joined by a single Swordfish to observe the action. Their target was estimated to be about 80 miles away.

Force 'B' came under attack again at 1100, *Vittorio Veneto* opening fire at 12 miles range and expending 94 15-inch shells. Italian observers believed that several hits had been achieved as well as many near-misses. This was not so although near-misses caused some damage to the cruiser *Orion*. Aboard this ship was a young midshipman experiencing his first taste of action, one Philip Mountbatten, later Duke of Edinburgh. His father, Prince Andrew of Greece, was married to the sister of Capt Lord Louis Mountbatten, commander of the 5th Destroyer Flotilla, currently operating out of Malta, while his sister, Princess Sophie, was married to Prinz Christoph of Hesse, a Luftwaffe pilot and Nazi sympathiser!

As *Orion* came under attack cruisers of the 3rd Division closed on her starboard quarter, but at this critical moment the Albacores of the strike force arrived, only to be fired on by the British warships – fortunately without any hits being gained. Seeing the Italian ships ahead, the TSRs began to position for attack when two Ju88s dived on them out of the sun. Fortunately the Fulmars had spotted them, and attacked head-on. L/Air Freddy de Frias in the back seat of Pty Off Theobald's aircraft, recalled:

'The enemy fleet was just about in sight when Theobald spotted a Ju88 below us. The two Fulmars went into a diving attack (our only chance of getting an 88) and shot it down. At our speed of just over 200 knots you only got the one pass. I couldn't see much – there was practically no forward vision from the rear seat of a Fulmar, and in any case I was busy looking for other 88s. You didn't last long if you forgot to do that. The 88 must have got off a signal before he went down because we had no trouble finding the enemy fleet, which was firing everything into the air. But we made our dive without a scratch and as we pulled out I had the satisfaction of letting off a pan from the Thompson sub-machine gun I carried. I claim to be the only man to take on a battleship with a Tommy gun!'

Although the Fulmar crews did not see the Ju88 hit the sea, one Albacore observer (Lt M G Haworth) in Lt H M Ellis's '4F' apparently confirmed that it went in, and another observer (Lt F H E Hopkins in the CO's '4A') reported that it went down in flames. This is not confirmed from the Luftwaffe records, although a Ju88 of I/LG 1 flown by Uffz Georg Albrecht did crash-land on return to Krumovo, in damaged condition.

Meanwhile the first sub-flight of Albacores carried out an attack on *Vittorio Veneto* from the starboard bow, the Italians initially mistaking the aircraft for an expected CR42 escort from Rhodes. When it was realised that an attack was under way, Admiral Iachino was relieved to see the torpedoes miss their mark, but the other sub-flight was by then approaching from the beam as the ship manoeuvred. Although the crews believed they had gained at least one hit on the stern, and possibly a second, the vessel again escaped damage.

Not long after this first attack, the three 815 Squadron Swordfish spotted the 3rd Cruiser Division and attacked *Bolzano*. Under heavy AA fire, they completed their drop, but all three torpedoes failed to score. The gunners on the cruisers believed that they had shot down one Swordfish, but all returned to Maleme.

The First Battle Squadron was now closing on the Italian ships, and at 1215 *Warspite* launched both her Swordfish floatplanes from their catapults to make visual contact; it was estimated that the opposing fleet was two hours' sailing away. On *Formidable* a second strike was being prepared, but was pitifully weak – three Albacores and two Swordfish of 829 Squadron, to be led by Lt Cdr Dalyell-Stead. Again two Fulmars would provide escort, led by Lt Bruen, while a further Swordfish was to go as observer to report results. These aircraft flew off at 1222, following which the returning Albacores and Fulmars of the first strike landed on. Behind them came a pair of CAP Fulmars and *Gloucester*'s Walrus. This latter had been airborne for nearly four and a half hours, and was dangerously low on fuel, Lt Lane being ordered to land on the carrier to refuel. He had experienced much difficulty in finding the ship, and had almost diverted to Tobruk, the nearest landfall. During the flight he had seen a lone Ju88 and a small flight of S.79s, but both had passed without attacking.

Meantime the Italian cruisers had launched some of their Ro43s to search for the British Fleet, and at 1225 one reported sighting *Formidable*, one battleship, six cruisers and five destroyers some 80 miles east of the main Italian units. As the aircraft could not be recovered from the sea during action, it was ordered to fly to Rhodes, from where a signal of the sighting was despatched to Admiral Iachino, but as a result he did not receive this until two hours after the British ships had been sighted.

Formidable came under attack at 1254 by two torpedo-carrying S.79s from 281ª Squadriglia – possibly the aircraft seen by the Walrus crew. These carried out individual attacks, one releasing at close range, the other from 1500 yards. Both missed as the carrier took violent evasive action, her AA gunners gaining hits on one of the bombers, which nonetheless managed to get back to Gadurra airfield.

Following refuelling *Gloucester*'s Walrus was off again from the carrier at 1400, and was directed to land at Suda Bay, having first contacted the destroyer *Juno*, which was operating in the Kythera Channel. It was close to sunset when the little amphibian finally put down in the Bay.

During the early afternoon a Sunderland of 230 Squadron flown by Flt Lt Lywood had sighted a reported two battleships and three cruisers (actually the five cruisers of the 1st Division) and had signalled Air HQ, Athens. On receipt of this information three Blenheims from 84 Squadron were despatched and these attacked *Vittorio Veneto* at 1420. Although the bombs fell close, there were no hits and no damage was caused. Thirty minutes later six more Blenheims, this time from 113 Squadron, led by Sqn Ldr Spencer, made a high-level attack on the battleship, and once more only near-misses were achieved. Ironically, while waiting to take-off at Eleusis airfield, these aircraft had queued with a Lufthansa Ju52/3m!

Even as the Blenheims were attacking, Lt Cdr Dalyell-Stead's second strike, which had taken off at 1222, were approaching *Vittorio Veneto* for a head-on attack, while the two Fulmars machine-gunned the bridge and gun turrets to distract the gunners' aim. Leading the trio of Albacores in '5G', Dalyell-Stead closed to about 1000 yards before releasing his torpedo, but almost immediately the Albacore was hit repeatedly, dipped, and crashed into the sea. The pilot and his crew (Lt R H Cooke and Pty Off (A) G L Blenkhorn) all perished. The two following Albacores dropped their torpedoes, as did the two Swordfish which were coming in from the starboard side. While it was believed that three hits had been gained, in fact only one struck home (probably Dalyell-Stead's), hitting the battleship just above the outer port screw with a mighty explosion. The engines stopped as water flooded into the ship and she began to list to port. At this moment the last of the Blenheims attacked, one bomb also scoring a hit when it fell very close to the stern.

At about the same time as *Vittorio Veneto* was under attack, the 1st Cruiser Division was also being engaged by other Blenheims, six from 113 Squadron led by Flt Lt Rixson and five from 84 Squadron led by Sqn Ldr Jones making the attack. Jones recorded:
'The weather was hazy over the sea, but we soon found the Iti Navy – two groups of ships steaming like billy-ho for home. They started to zig-zag as soon as they saw us, and their AA opened up. We made a dive attack and fairly plastered them. Observers in my squadron registered hits on one big ship, and we think on a smaller one. They were difficult targets, but quite a number must have been damaged or delayed by near-misses.'

Both *Zara* and the smaller *Garibaldi* were near-missed, but not damaged.

Other Blenheims, three more from 84 Squadron led by the Australian commander of 'B' Flight, Flt Lt D G Boehm, and six from 211 Squadron led by Flt Lt Jones, found and attacked ships of the 3rd Division, both *Trento* and *Bolzano* being near-missed, but neither suffering any damage. One 84 Squadron crew believed that they had scored hits, F/Sgt Gordon later reporting:
'Though they changed formation and zig-zagged violently, and their AA was reasonably heavy, we were able to spend some time taking aim, and made a low-level attack. I saw two of my biggest bombs hit the largest ship amidships. Clouds of black and yellow smoke issued for a long time and the ship stopped.'

This was confirmed by the observer, who added:
'It was a hefty but agreeable surprise when I saw those bombs hit and just the place they were aimed at – right amidships. At first there was just the normal white smoke of the bomb burst, and then columns of black and yellow smoke shot up into the air to a height of 200 feet or so. For 50 minutes afterwards the rear-gunner had a good view of the ship, and gave us a running commentary over

the intercom and we proceeded home. She had stopped and was listing when we lost sight of her.'

Although reportedly part of the formation attacking the cruisers, the content of these comments tends to lead to the view that Gordon and his crew had actually made the final attack on *Vittorio Veneto*, just at the moment when 829 Squadron's torpedoes had also struck home. Certainly the battleship was in close proximity to the 3rd Cruiser Division at this time.

The Italian battleship *Vittorio Veneto* limps away from Matapan, her stern low in the water following the torpedo strike on her. One of her Ro.43 reconnaissance aircraft can be seen, damaged and tilting on the very stern. (*Marina Militaire via N Malizia*)

The crews from 211 Squadron were less sanguine as to their results, Flt Lt Jones, the acting CO, recalling:
'The enemy fleet appeared to be in great confusion and was zig-zagging violently, and now and then one would cross the course of another, or two would converge, and there were as a result many phenomenal avoidances. We bombed and added to the confusion. I saw no hits, but there were plenty of near-misses, which could have done them no good, and when we left the enemy was busy laying a smoke screen.'

Although *Vittorio Veneto* had slowed to a halt, her damage control party soon had two engines restarted, and before long the battleship was making 16 knots. By 1700 she was heading for Taranto, 420 miles away, by now making 19 knots. Admiral Iachino was bitter about the continued absence of any form of fighter protection, which had been promised by both Luftwaffe and Regia Aeronautica, but at this range very little other than the handful of CR42s on Rhodes could have reached the fleet.

Learning that *Vittorio Veneto* had been damaged, Cunningham ordered a further strike to be made at dusk with the intention of finishing off the battleship. All available TSRs were armed, and at 1730 six Albacores of 826 Squadron and two Swordfish of 829 Squadron began taking-off, Lt Cdr Saunt at their head. Owing to the imminence of darkness, they were ordered to land at Maleme on completion of their attack. Just before the strike force departed, two sections of Fulmars took-off to patrol overhead, but one aircraft suffered engine trouble and was obliged to land on again. The other three were vectored onto a hostile plot, one encountering an S.79 torpedo-bomber from the 34° Gruppo BT, which had just attacked an unidentified cruiser, claiming a possible hit. The Fulmar could only make a brief attack before the bomber disappeared, the Italian gunners believing they had driven off the 'Hurricane'. Three more Fulmars were boosted off in anticipation of further attacks, but none materialized.

Maleme had also launched its own further strike, but only two torpedoes remained available, having been ferried over from Eleusis during the afternoon. At 1655 therefore two Swordfish had set out, Lt Torrens-Spence in L9774 accompanied by Lt Kiggell. Just over an hour later they saw four cruisers and six destroyers, but came under immediate fire. Flying round, just out of range, they had positioned for a possible opening to attack when Lt Cdr Saunt's strike force was seen approaching from the east, flying in line astern at about 100 feet. Torrens-Spence decided to join the end of the line, but initially caused some confusion as his two Swordfish were thought to be CR42s, and avoiding action was taken. By 1925 however, Saunt had judged the light and circumstances to be right, and commenced the attack in line astern and at low-level. Intense fire met them, splitting up the formation at 3000 yards from the ships, individual attacks developing as the pilots seized opportunities to strike. Blinded by searchlights and dense smoke, they found sightings difficult to make, and several realised that they were releasing at a large cruiser, rather than at *Vittorio Veneto*. The two 815 Squadron aircraft followed the carrier planes into the murk, as Michael Torrens-Spence recalled:
'All the Italian ships made smoke. When I got into the smoke I could see nothing, and had no idea what formation the enemy was in, or where the principal targets were, and can't imagine how anybody else could either. I therefore climbed up to about 3000 feet, where I could see down into the formation and to find a bit of space to get down into the attack on one of the main targets.'

Sub Lt G P C Williams in '5A' of 826 Squadron was the last of *Formidable*'s pilots to attack, dropping his torpedo at 1945, his target evidently being the heavy cruiser *Pola* of the 1st Division, which reportedly was hit amidships on the starboard side at 1946. However, Lt Torrens-Spence again entered the arena:
'I selected a *Pola* class cruiser which had a bit of space on her bow, inside the screen and came down into it and slipped the kipper at her! The Albacores were credited with hitting the *Pola*, but I don't believe it! This was probably ten minutes after the Albacore attack, and the Italians probably thought it was all over.'

Torrens-Spence's aircraft received slight damage to its tail during the action, but

160

The ill-fated Italian cruiser *Pola*, sunk during the closing stages of the Cape Matapan battle during the night of 28/29 March 1941. (*Marina Militaire via N Malizia*)

this and the other Swordfish returned safely to Maleme, landing at 2120. Indeed only one of the strike aircraft failed to reach Crete, Sub Lt Williams ditching '5A' in Suda Bay when it ran out of fuel. Coming down near *Juno*, the crew were promptly picked up by the destroyer's boat.

A witness to the attack was Pty Off F C Rice DSM, and his observer, Lt Cdr A S Bolt, DSC, in one of *Warspite*'s Swordfish floatplanes ('Lorna', K 8863). The crew could take no part in the attack, to their chagrin, as they had been forced to jettison their bombs earlier in the day, prior to being hoisted back aboard their parent ship for the further launch.

With the arrival of the TSRs at Maleme, air action for this hectic day was at an end, although the Italian Fleet was to be 'shadowed' during the night by 826 Squadron's Albacores. One of these, short on fuel, was also forced to ditch in Suda Bay when returning from its duty; Lt D W Phillips and his crew were picked up safely. An assessment of results of the day's attacks revealed that 826 and 829 Squadrons had dropped 19 torpedoes, 815 Squadron adding five more, for five possible hits being claimed; *Vittorio Veneto* having been the main target. In fact only two of the 24 torpedoes had actually struck home, one on the battleship and one on the cruiser *Pola*.

The Blenheims had flown 29 sorties, dropping more than 13 tons of bombs, mainly from medium altitude. Although returning crews claimed two direct hits on a cruiser, one on a destroyer, and probably two more on another cruiser, as well as a number of near-misses, the only success had been the single hit on *Vittorio Veneto*. But this was not surprising – bombers very seldom scored successes against moving ships when bombing from altitude. However considering that there was no fighter opposition to the attacks, and that while at times heavy, the AA fire was generally inaccurate, the results for such a concerted effort seem meagre. Losses had been light however. Apart from Lt Cdr Dalyell-Stead and the two 826 Squadron Albacores that were forced to ditch, the only other loss, albeit temporary, was Albacore '5B' (the first aircraft to spot the Italian Fleet in the morning), which had become lost, the pilot making for the nearest

161

landfall on running short of fuel, and landing at Bardia, on the Libyan/Egyptian border.

Nevertheless the dusk strike had been instumental in allowing a considerable victory to be achieved. Although flying for the day had finished, apart from the 'shadowing' TSRs, Admiral Cunningham continued to pursue the Italians westward. The subsequent night action in which three cruisers and two destroyers were sunk by the British warships has been well documented ('The Battle of Matapan' by S W C Pack; Batsford 1961), and it will suffice here to summarize the events of this dramatic night.

Force 'B' regained contact with elements of the Italian Fleet after the final TSR strike, and eight destroyers were ordered to locate and attack, leaving just four to screen the larger vessels. At 2210 it was reported that an enemy vessel was lying damaged and stopped three miles to the east. This was at first thought to be *Vittorio Veneto*, but was found to be *Pola*. As the Battle Squadron approached the scene two more heavy cruisers were sighted – *Zara* and *Fiume* – together with the destroyer *Alfieri*, with four more destroyers astern. This force had been despatched to aid the crippled *Pola*, as the Italians were completely unaware of the proximity of the British Fleet. *Warspite* and *Valiant* opened fire, *Fiume* soon being hit and sinking about 2300. *Zara* was next hit and crippled, following which *Alfieri* went down at 2315, sunk by *Barham*. The latter then transferred her fire to *Zara*, which also subsequently sunk. The other Italian destroyers attempted a torpedo attack, but were engaged by *Stuart* and *Havock*, one of them (*Carducci*) promptly being hit and blowing up. Later two other British destroyers, *Jervis* and *Nubian*, were detached to torpedo and sink the abandoned *Pola*, after her crew had been taken off.

With dawn on 29 March *Formidable* launched three Albacores at 0430 on search duties, and another to Maleme with a message for Lt Cdr Saunt. The search aircraft returned after two hours having seen nothing but wreckage and many survivors clinging to debris. Three Swordfish sent out from Maleme by 815 Squadron, returned to report similar scenes. 230 Squadron also sent out Sunderlands, Flt Lt P R Woodward in L2160 landing amongst large patches of oil and wreckage when about 25 rafts were seen. He estimated that some 600 men were within sight, but when he had attempted to identify which ship they were from, he received only appeals for water. All he could do was inform Scaramanga of their position and continue his patrol.

By about 0800 the Battle Squadron's destroyers were on the scene to commence rescue operations, reporting many corpses, but picking up more than 900 Italian seamen, including 55 officers. Many of those who were rescued had been injured, and some died later. About an hour after the arrival of the ships, a reconnaissance Ju88 appeared overhead, and fearing an imminent attack, Admiral Cunningham ordered a cessation of rescue work, the Fleet withdrawing eastwards. A signal was sent to the Chief of the Italian Naval Staff advising that more than 350 survivors were believed to be on rafts, giving their position and recommending that a fast hospital ship be despatched. The Italians replied that the *Gradisca* was already on the way from Taranto. When she arrived, a further 160 seamen were picked up, while that evening the Greek destroyer *Ydra*, picked up another 112. With the 257 taken off *Pola* by *Jervis*, it was estimated that some 2400 Italian seamen had lost their lives.

At 1325, as Flt Lt Woodward was nearing the end of his patrol, a Bf110 suddenly appeared and attacked the Sunderland four times. However only a few hits were gained on the elevators and tailplane before it broke away, and no casualties were suffered. Woodward put down in Suda Bay for minor repairs.

The anticipated retaliation materialized somewhat belatedly at 1511, when *Formidable*'s radar detected a number of aircraft approaching from the north-west. Within three minutes three Fulmars were boosted off to join two already up on CAP, but the latter had been drawn off by an apparent decoy aircraft, the Fleet being left unprotected until the trio climbing up had reached height. Twenty minutes later a dozen Ju88s from II/LG 1 had come within range, all the guns opening up. It was believed that one received a direct hit and blew up before the rest commenced dive-bombing attacks, but there is no confirmation of this.

Formidable was narrowly missed by four bombs, but as the last flight of Ju88s began their attack, the Fulmars pounced on them, forcing them to jettison their bombs and turn away. Uffz Georg Kunz's L1+EP of 6 Staffel was attacked by Lt C W R Peever and Sub Lt Wallace, the bomber crashing into the sea. An eyewitness reported:

'We saw him, slowly it seemed, through the burst of grey smoke, come lower and lower, until with a great splash he crashed into the sea to port, and instantly disappeared.'

However, Kunz and his crew survived to take to their dinghy. Before falling, the rear-gunner (Gefr Josef Leitermann) had got in a good burst at Wallace's N1918, the Fulmar being hit many times. As it approached the carrier to land on, the engine cut and it spun into the sea; Wallace and his TAG, L/Air Dooley, managed to struggle free, suffering only superficial cuts, and within minutes were picked up by the destroyer *Hasty*. Somewhat surprisingly there were no further attacks on the Fleet as it headed back towards Alexandria.

At about the time of II/LG 1's raid, a reconnaissance Maryland from 69 Squadron had been despatched from Malta at the Navy's request in an effort to discover the results of the battle. This however reported being hit after flying near some unidentified warships, and attempted a force-landing on a beach at Zante Island. The aircraft (AR727) came down in the sea just short of the beach and flipped over, the pilot, Flg Off F R Ainley, being killed and the navigator, Sgt G Brown, injured. He and the air-gunner, Sgt A E White, got out of the wreck. Local Greeks helped them to reach Athens, from where they later evacuated, via southern Greece, to Crete and from there to Alexandria. Some weeks later they would arrive back in Malta to rejoin their squadron.

Later this same afternoon Flt Lt I F McCall of 230 Squadron on patrol in Sunderland L2161, spotted a dinghy containing four survivors. The crew believed that this was probably from an Italian aircraft shot down by the Navy, but it is likely that they had seen Uffz Kunz and his crew.

During the day the Regia Aeronautica in Italy had at last reacted, Macchi C.200 fighters from Grottaglie providing belated air cover as the Italian Fleet headed for Cap Colonne, near Crotone. Numbers of Z.1007bis were out searching for the British Fleet, first off being aircraft of the 47° Stormo BT, also from Grottaglie, which sent off the first sortie at 0635; by early afternoon this unit had despatched twenty-one aircraft. Another six machines from the 50° Gruppo BT at Brindisi were up in the afternoon, following sightings of a cruiser and three destroyers 24 miles south-west of Cephalonia by other Z.1007bis of 35° Stormo BT, also out from Brindisi. It is believed that these were Greek ships from Patras. Twelve Ju87s drawn equally from the 208ª and 239ª Squadriglia B a'T were despatched from Lecce after these warships, but failed to locate them after searching from Paxoi Island to the Preveza region.

On 30 March reconnaissance aircraft from Rhodes were also out looking for the British Fleet, but an S.79 of 92° Gruppo BT from Gadurra piloted by Sottoten Federico Curti, failed to return, no reason for its demise having been found. Search aircraft were out again from Southern Italy, looking for survivors. A 35° Stormo BR Cant Z.506B floatplane from Brindisi spotted Uffz Kunz and his crew in their dinghy and landed to rescue them.

By late afternoon the First Battle Squadron was almost home. As the capital ships approached the Great Pass into Alexandria harbour, a submarine contact was reported, escorting destroyers carrying out depth charge attacks without result. *Formidable* and the battleships entered harbour at 1645, their task well done. Submarines were about elsewhere however, and at 0300 next morning two of these, *Dagabur* and *Ambra*, gained some retribution for the Italian Navy's defeat when they intercepted Convoy GA-8 not far from the position where the Italian cruisers had been sunk. Working together, they each fired a torpedo at the British cruiser *Bonaventure*, which went down almost at once. Destroyers *Hereward* and *Stuart* raced to the scene, *Hereward* picking up 310 survivors whilst the Australian warship carried out a depth charge attack. *Dagabur* launched a torpedo at her, but apparently this exploded in her wake, causing no damage. Both submarines then escaped.

On 2 April Convoy ASF-22, consisting of seven empty troopships, left Piraeus and joined AS-22 – nine empty freighters – bound for Port Said. Escorted by *Calcutta* and three smaller warships, with Fulmars and Sea Gladiators in range at Maleme, the combined convoy headed for the Kythera Strait. At 1245 an attack developed when no air cover was present, two S.79s of 281ª Squadriglia and two from 34° Gruppo, all torpedo-carriers, swept in, while three more 34° Gruppo aircraft bombed from higher altitude in an effort to distract the gunners; all three were damaged by splinters, as was one of the torpedo-carriers. They claimed hits on two steamers, but none actually suffered any damage.

By 1700 the vessels had steamed round the western coast of Crete and were just north of Gavdhos Island. Suddenly six Ju88s appeared from over the mountains along the Cretan coast, and skilfully dive-bombed, four bombs striking the Greek *Koulouros Xenos*, while the *Homefield* (5000 tons) was also hit, casualties being suffered on both vessels. Both were abandoned by their crews, who were picked up by the escorts. The Australian destroyer *Voyager* put boarding parties onto both ships, but they were found to be damaged beyond salvage. *Homefield* was sent to the bottom by a torpedo fired from *Nubian*, while the Greek ship went down to gunfire and depth charges. A third ship, SS *Teti*, had also been damaged by a near-miss, causing her to list badly; her skipper was forced to seek anchorage near Lissmore on the Cretan coast.

Half an hour later came a third attack, three S.81s of 39° Stormo BT hitting the MV *Devis* (6054 tons) with several bombs, which set her afire, and caused seven fatalities, while 14 others were wounded. The fires were soon under control however, and the *Devis* rejoined the convoy. At twilight a lone 281ª Squadriglia S.79 flown by Cap Buscaglia made a final torpedo attack. The crew believed that they had hit a large freighter, but no strike had actually been made.

Most air/sea action during the next two weeks took place around the Greek coast, and not until 18 April was a major naval action to get underway again. On this date the Mediterranean Fleet sailed from Alexandria at 0650 preparatory to undertaking a bombardment of Tripoli, the main Axis supply port in Libya. This action was designed mainly to relieve pressure on the British Forces in the Western Desert, but would cause much action over the Eastern Mediterranean during the next few days. A screen of three battleships, three cruisers and eight destroyers surrounded HMS *Formidable*, joined during the day by two more destroyers that had been escorting an incoming convoy.

At 1820 the Fleet was sighted by two S.79s from 281ª Squadriglia on Rhodes, and although pursued by a Fulmar patrol from 803 Squadron, no success was seen. Indeed Lt Donald Gibson, pilot of '6J', the leading Fulmar, was wounded in an arm by return fire and almost completely blinded by hot oil; he recalled:
'I was shot down by three Cant bombers (sic) – I got too close in and a lot of explosive shells came into my cockpit. The aircraft was hit in the oil cleaner (I should think); the oil came into my cockpit. We were 40 miles from the Fleet. The engine finally stopped when I was about 2000 feet over *Formidable*. I knew I could catch a wire, she was into wind. I caught a wire very fast; this tore the bottom out of the aeroplane. I collided with the island and set fire to the petrol refilling station; the tail folded over my head. I skidded on, hit 'A' turret and somersaulted into the sea. I was run over by the whole length of the ship; had a great struggle to get out and was picked up in the wake by HMS *Hereward*. Alas Peter Ashbrooke (Sub Lt P C B Ashbrooke, the observer) was lost. I was very young and foolish, and should have ditched.'

Meanwhile, Red 2 (Pty Off (A) Theobald and L/Air de Frias in N1912) continued attacking Ten Rodolfo Guza's bomber, wounding three members of the crew before it escaped. The badly damaged aircraft struggled back to Gadurra where it force-landed with the torpedo still beneath the fuselage.

Because heavy losses of fighters were deemed possible, the carrier had aboard 15 Fulmars when she sailed, including six aircraft and crews of 806 Squadron, led by Lt Cdr Charles Evans. On 19 April the Fleet put into Suda Bay to allow the destroyers to top-up on fuel. As *Formidable* entered the Bay at 1225, radar picked up a hostile plot; a Fulmar was on the booster catapult, but not manned. L/Air de Frias happened to be on the Flight Deck with helmet and 'Mae West' when Lt Gibson, wounded arm in plaster, came rushing up and urged the TAG to join him in the Fulmar (N1912). 'I just had time to tighten my harness' recalled

Freddy de Frias, 'when we were sent off with the ship out of wind, hardly any way on, high ground in front of us... and with a pilot on the sick list. Why did I have to get tangled up with a hero? But we made it OK, though the attack did not develop.'

Next day the Fleet was on its way again, heading for Tripoli, but at 1043 an unidentified aircraft appeared on the radar. A section of Fulmars from 806 Squadron were on patrol, flown by Lt Cdr Evans and Sub Lt Jackie Sewell, two of the unit's most combat-experienced pilots, and they were vectored onto a lone Cant Z.1007bis, apparently on passage from Cyrenaica to Sicily. This aircraft was shot down by them at 1115. Some two hours later a small formation was reported at a distance of about 25 miles, two more sections of 806 Squadron Fulmars being scrambled to intercept. This proved not to be a bombing raid, but a formation of five Ju52/3m transports from I/KGzbV.9 on their way to Africa. Brown Section (Lt J H Shears and Sub Lt P D J Sparke, a former TSR pilot with the DSC and Bar) spotted them first, and were quickly joined by Grey Section, led by Lt R S Henley.

One of the trimotors escaped northwards, but the other four were all claimed shot down, two of them exploding in the air, suggesting that they were loaded with fuel. It appears that one of these fell to Lt Shears, but his aircraft was hit by return fire and spun into the sea; he and his observer, Sub Lt Dixon, ex-805 Squadron, were killed. Robert Henley recalled:

'... after I had made my first attack (on a lone Ju52) I pulled into the sun and watched Johnny Shears close from dead astern to within 50 yards or so when he was obviously hit and nosed vertically into the sea. I made another pass and claimed a possible, then returned to where Johnny had gone in, to search for him, in vain.'

As four Ju52/3ms were officially credited to the Fulmars, it would seem that Lt Henley received credit for one, as did Lt Shears, whilst it is believed that Sub Lt Sparke claimed the other two. In fact it seems that only two Junkers were actually lost, Ofw Josef Kastl and Fw Walter Heyer and their crews being reported missing.

As night fell the Fleet split, *Formidable*, *Ajax*, *Perth* and four destroyers drawing away to fly off air support, whilst the three battleships and *Gloucester*, covered by seven destroyers, headed inshore for the bombardment. During the early hours of 21 April, Wellingtons from Malta bombed the port, while flares were dropped by Swordfish of 830 Squadron, also from that island. Other Swordfish and Albacores from 826 and 829 Squadrons from the carrier followed to drop more flares for the Naval gunners, and at 0503 fire was opened from a range of 11 000 yards by the 15-inch and 6-inch guns. After twenty minutes the Fleet changed course to withdraw, firing for a further twenty minutes until the range had opened to 16 000 yards. Only during this latter phase was any return fire experienced from the shore, and that achieved no hits. One Swordfish crashed while landing-on, but the Fleet was soon well away.

Following this audacious enterprise, heavy air attack was expected, but none developed – a sure sign of the complete surprise that had been achieved. At 1110

166

a 'shadower' appeared, and was intercepted by Orange Section of 803 Squadron; it turned out to be another Z.1007bis. Half an hour after reporting interception, Orange 2 (Sub Lt Simpson) returned, reporting that the aircraft had been damaged, but the Orange 1, Lt Wright and his observer, Sub Lt F W Ponting, had lost contact. At last at 1340 contact was resumed, and White Section of 806 Squadron (Sub Lt Stan Orr and Sub Lt G A Hogg, two more of the unit's very experienced combat pilots) were directed to find Lt Wright and lead him back. After flying 20 miles, this pair spotted a Do24N flyingboat from Seenotstaffel 6, out from Syracruse (Sicily), heading south at 1000 feet, too low to be picked up on the ship's radar at that range. This was attacked at once and forced down onto the sea with its port engine on fire. It made two attempts to take-off again, but hit each time the Fulmars attacked it settled in the water, streaming a trail of petrol and oil; it was claimed destroyed. Meanwhile, Lt Wright had at last found his own way back to *Formidable*, landing on to report that the Z.1007bis he and Simpson had attacked had, in fact, been shot down.

During the assault on Tripoli about ten tons of bombs and 553 tons of shells had been expended, air reconnaissance later reporting that some destroyer berths had been hit and one destroyer badly damaged, while five merchant vessels were burnt out and at least four others had been set on fire. As the Fleet headed back towards Alexandria, it was about to enter a new phase of action with Greek-based units of the Luftwaffe, as will be related in Chapter 6.

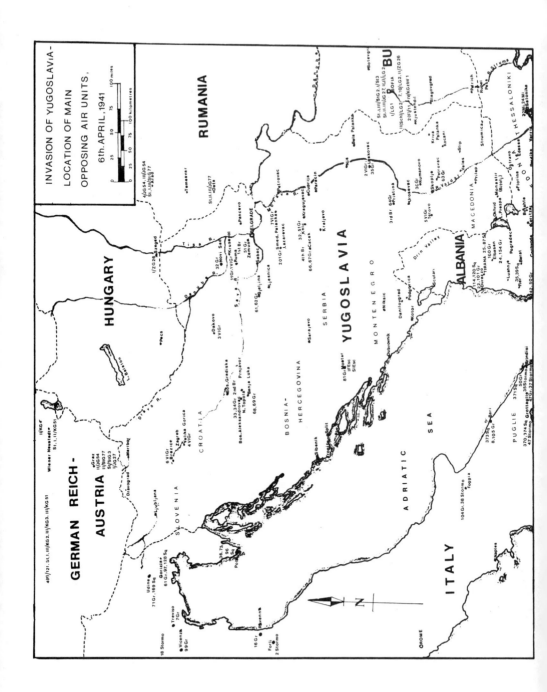

INVASION OF YUGOSLAVIA -
LOCATION OF MAIN
OPPOSING AIR UNITS,
6th. APRIL, 1941

GERMAN REICH-

AUSTRIA

HUNGARY

RUMANIA

YUGOSLAVIA

CROATIA

SLOVENIA

BOSNIA-

HERCEGOVINA

SERBIA

MONTENEGRO

MACEDONIA

ALBANIA

ITALY

ADRIATIC

SEA

PUGLIE

Chapter Five

THE GERMAN INVASION

Throughout the operations of the winter one thought had remained paramount in Allied minds – the possibility of German intervention. This threat had appeared a strong eventuality from the first days of British involvement. For the hard-pressed British, it was a question of when, rather than if. How should they meet such a situation? Stretched to the limit, it would be very difficult to deliver and supply a force of sufficient size to counter any serious German thrust into the country. The shortage of airfields made it almost impossible in any event realistically to provide a viable level of air support to whatever force could be assembled. Yet the cause was seen to be a just one; how could the gallant Greeks be deserted in their hour of need? How would home morale and neutral opinion respond to such a betrayal? Surely even a lost cause would be smiled upon by posterity, given the stakes?

For the Greeks the situation was even more straightforward. While the Italians were seen clearly as the enemy, there was much goodwill towards the Germans. While Italy might be held at bay, and with British help even beaten, logically war with Germany could end in only one way – overwhelming defeat. Therefore, while help for the Italian Front – particularly in the air – was of extreme importance, this should none the less only be accepted if it did not unduly antagonize the Germans. Perhaps Germany would stay out; it was a delicate balancing trick.

In the event the British appraisal was the more realistic one. They believed that the Germans would find it quite unacceptable to see their Italian allies face defeat in the Balkans. They were right; as early as 4 November 1940, Adolf Hitler had ordered a study to be made of the problems involved in sending German troops to Greece, and by the 18th of that month he was giving his views to the Italian Foreign Minister, Count Ciano, on his future Mediterranean policy. We know now, with the benefit of hindsight, that Hitler's mind was already full of the plans for Operation 'Barbarossa' – his great crusade against Communism in the East – and nothing would be allowed to stand in the way of this. By now German political and military domination of Rumania was almost complete, assuring supplies of oil for the forthcoming adventure, and now overtures were being made to Bulgaria. However, even if the latter proved amenable, the country was wild and little-developed, and it would be March 1941 at the earliest before any move against Greece could be made. The main delaying factors were the winter

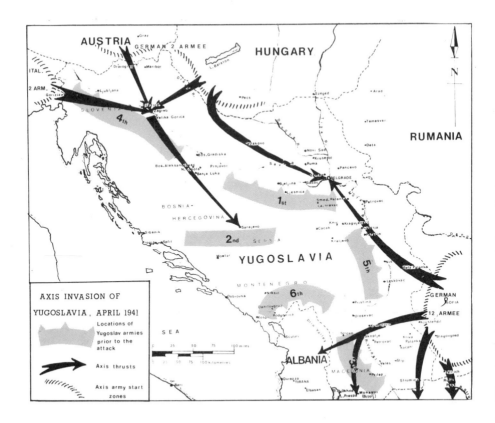

AXIS INVASION OF
YUGOSLAVIA, APRIL 1941

Locations of
Yugoslav armies
prior to the
attack

Axis thrusts

Axis army start
zones

weather and the need to get an army across the River Danube. Efforts would therefore be directed against the British Fleet during the winter of 1940–41, and to this purpose the relatively experienced anti-shipping units of Fliegerkorps X would be despatched from Norway to Sicily, and also to aid the Italians in the neutralization of the island of Malta.

For the British there was just one possibility which might stem disaster – to reach an understanding with the two most powerful Balkan states, Turkey and Yugoslavia. Yugoslavia was however rife with internal dissent, under political pressure from the Germans, and in no mood to make commitments to lost causes. Following the traumas of her virtual rebirth during the twenties, Turkey was not anxious to become embroiled in the war either. Her forces were woefully ill-equipped and unprepared, and only a massive injection of material aid from Britain might persuade her to throw in her lot with the Allies. It hardly needs saying that such aid was simply not available. Diplomatic negotiations progressed throughout the winter as the British tried to talk the Greeks into accepting an expeditionary force. It was on the other side however, that power politics were achieving more positive results.

On 13 December 1940, Hitler issued a directive for the planning of Operation 'Marita', a proposed move through Bulgaria to occupy Grecian Macedonia, and

170

possibly the whole of mainland Greece. The basic reason for this operation was to stabilize the Balkans, preventing the British establishing bases there from which both Italy and the Rumanian oilfields might be threatened by bomber aircraft. The first moves were made early in January 1941 when German troops were transported through Hungary into Rumania, ready for passage to Bulgaria. Chosen for this task was the 12th Armee under Feldmarschal Wilhelm List, which would be supported by General Freiherr Wolfram von Richthofen's 'crack' Fliegerkorps VIII – a specialized ground-support formation, strong in dive-bombers (Stuka) and ground-attack (Schlacht) aircraft.

The Fliegerkorps was initially to field 153 bombers (39 Junkers Ju88As and 114 Junkers Ju87Bs) and 121 fighters (83 Messerschmitt Bf109Es and 38 Bf110s), and was to be supported by liberal quantities of mobile Flak (anti-aircraft artillery). List's command included five Armee Korps Headquarters, a group of four armoured divisions (Panzers), one motorized, two mountain and 11 other general divisions – a most formidable force.

After some initial postponements, bridging of the Danube commenced, the first crossings being made on 28 February; next day Bulgaria formally joined the Axis, and on 2 March, Hitler announced that all operations preparatory to Operation 'Barbarossa' must be completed by 15 May. Well aware of what was afoot, the British now decided unilaterally that a force must be despatched to Greece – a decision which was subsequently acceded to by the Greek government. The first contingent was to comprise an armoured brigade and the newly-arrived New Zealand Division (less its 3rd Infantry Brigade), plus two medium artillery regiments and some anti-aircraft batteries.

Events were now beginning to accelerate. By Hitler's plan, the Greek operation should be little more than a swift formality. Only one matter remained outstanding for the complete subjugation of the Balkans – Yugoslavia must be brought into the fold. Indeed, Yugoslavian troops might even be allowed at a later date to occupy part of Thessalonica. Consequently on 17 March, the Yugoslav government was asked to sign the Tripartite Pact, and subject to certain conditions relating mainly to their desire that their country should not thereby be committed to any war operations, the ministers of Prince Paul's cabinet seemed about to do so. Here, however, the courage and independence of spirit of the Serbian majority suddenly and unexpectedly began to assert itself. In a wave of protest against the proposals, three Serbian cabinet ministers resigned on 22 March – it was time for Germany to wield the iron fist! Next day an ultimatum was issued, requiring signature by midnight that night. Negotiations followed, and on 25 March actual signing took place. All now seemed set, particularly as one day earlier Feldmarschal List had reported that the 12th Armee was in position in Western Bulgaria, and ready to invade Greece on 1 April.

But the best laid plans can go awry, and Yugoslavia remained the joker in the pack. Two days after signing the Pact and becoming a member of the Axis, the government was toppled in a 'coup d'etat', led by General Dusan Simonovitch, Chief of the Air Staff, who with other officers deposed the Regent and set the 17 year-old Prince Peter on the throne. The Pact was at once repudiated.

Hitler's fury at this upstart action can well be imagined. At a stroke his cherished plans for the undisturbed and secure start to 'Barbarossa' had been put at risk! He decided to act at once. The 12th Armee was to stay its hand for the moment; 'Barbarossa' was postponed for four weeks – four precious summer weeks which could well have seen the Panzers right into Moscow! Yugoslavia was to be ruthlessly and totally crushed and subjugated at once, at the same time as Greece was secured. On 2 April, Army Order No.4 was issued; 2nd Armee in Austria and Hungary, supported by Luftflotte 4, was to act simultaneously with 12th Armee in the invasion of the Balkans. Italy was to support her ally with an attack into Yugoslavia from Northern Albania, while Bulgarian and Hungarian units were to join the Germans in their venture. All efforts were to be given to a swift and crushing *Blitzkrieg*; the eastern frontiers of Rumania and Bulgaria were to be guarded by the forces of those nations only. No reaction by Turkey was anticipated. British and Greek diplomatic efforts were redoubled, but despite a flight into Yugoslavia by a joint military mission, no worthwhile agreements could be made in the chaos that then prevailed; the Turks remained cautious and ambivalent.

Initial moves were to be made by 12th Armee, which now had some 20 divisions in Bulgaria, six in the west ready for immediate action. XVIII Korps (one armoured, one infantry and two mountain divisions) had moved to the west of the River Struma, and on 4 April made preparation to cross the River Vardar. It was to advance through the Rupel Pass on Salonika, Verria and Edessa. Allied forces were warned of a possible attack next day, and stood to. Further east, XXX Korps was to capture the Northern Aegean ports, right up to the Turkish frontier, while XL Korps (one armoured, one infantry and one SS division) was to enter Southern Yugoslavia and head for Skoplje, and then the Albanian frontier to link with the Italians on the Epirus Front.

To support 12th Armee, Fliegerkorps VIII had now grown to 414 aircraft, while at airfields in Austria, Hungary and Rumania, Luftflotte 4 had a further 576 – ex-Sicily, France and Germany. One hundred and sixty-eight more were on call from Fliegerkorps X in Sicily, and several of this formation's units were to move to south-eastern Italy for operations over Western Yugoslavia (see page 180 for Luftwaffe Order of Battle). It will be seen that the whole of Fliegerkorps VIII was based around the Sofia area of Bulgaria, comprising, apart from a single reconnaissance Staffel with Dornier Do.17s, a transport Gruppe and a Gruppe of Ju88As, three Gruppen of Stukas, three Gruppen of single-engined fighters, together with one Gruppe and two additional Staffeln of ground-attack fighter-bombers and one Gruppe of Zerstörer, which would also operate in the ground attack role.

The main bomber strength of Generaloberst Alexander Löhr's Luftflotte 4 was based in central Austria, while the tactical elements were grouped in two task forces, one at Graz, near the point at which the borders of Austria, Hungary and Yugoslavia meet, the other at Arad in Rumania. III/JG 52 was based at Bucharest in reserve, and as immediate defence of the Rumanian oilfields. Apart from these forces, seven independent Staffeln of Henschel Hs 126 army co-operation aircraft were attached to 2nd Armee, and six more with 12th Armee in Bulgaria. Generally one such Staffel was attached to each Armee Korps, and one

172

specialized tank co-operation unit to each Panzer Division.

From Sicily 7/JG 26, a single Staffel of Bf109E fighters led by the great 'ace' Joachim Müncheberg, and III/ZG 26 with Bf110s had moved to Taranto and Grottaglie on 5 April, while Sicily-based bombers stood ready to operate from that island. The Regia Aeronautica too had been reinforced for the coming operations, and its Order of Battle available for use over Yugoslavia and Greece can be noted on pages 182–4.

In Greece efforts had been made to strengthen the RAF, but only a handful of Greek aircraft now remained serviceable. Available British units at the start of April are noted on pages 184–5, as can the EVA Order of Battle. A limited flow of reinforcements for the RAF were on their way.

The less-known factor was still Yugoslavia. German assessment of the Yugoslav army was that it was ill-equipped and its training out of date. Senior officers were elderly and regressive in their thinking. However the troops – particularly the Serbs – were known to be brave and hardy, likely to put up a tough fight in hand-to-hand conditions. They were not however, expected to last long when faced with the modern German army – a remarkably accurate assessment, as it was to turn out. The air force was also written off as small and equipped largely with out of date types, but this was not necessarily so. Until late 1937 the air forces had been completely obsolete, comprising only auxiliary arms to the army and navy, equipped with a miscellany of 1920s types, including Breguet XIXs, Potez Po 25s, Avia BH33Es, Ikarus 10s, Dornier Wals and Do Ds. Rising world tension had however brought forward a plan to form an independent air force, the JKRV (Jugoslovensko Kraljevsko Ratno Vazduhoplovstvo – Royal Yugoslav Air Force), from the nucleus provided by the Army Air Force. This was to have nine regiments by 1943, equipped with 1068 modern aircraft, partly purchased abroad and partly licence-built, backed by a reserve of 369. Each regiment was planned to have three squadrons (Grupa), each comprising three flights (Eskadrila).

By early 1938 it had become clear that, quite apart from the question of finance, most principal arms manufacturing nations considered the needs of Yugoslavia to be well down their lists of priorities, and in consequence such purchases and licences as could be negotiated, had to be grasped with both hands. Bristol Blenheim I and Hawker Hurricane I aircraft from Britain, Dornier Do17K bombers and Messerschmitt Bf109E fighters from Germany, and Savoia S.79 bombers from Italy were all purchased, the former three types also being the subject of licence production arrangements. The indigenous aircraft industry also produced a few IK-2 and IK-Z fighters, the latter being fully up to international standards, while other types were under development.

This situation of acquiring what could be obtained meant that by 1941 the JKRV was equipped with 11 different types of operational aircraft, 14 different types of trainers and five types of auxiliary aircraft, with 22 different engine models, four different machine guns and two models of aircraft cannon. The Do17K for example was a German aircraft with French engines, Belgian armament, Czech photo equipment and Yugoslav instrumentation! It was a Quartermaster's nightmare!

A JKRV Dornier Do.17K; this was the 20th German-built aircraft of this type to be delivered. (*Z Jerin*)

Because of the delays in obtaining equipment, the reorganisation of the air force had only commenced at the end of 1939, and was not completed until a few days before the outbreak of hostilities. By this time only about 340 aircraft were available to the bomber and fighter regiments, with 120 more totally obsolete types serving with the army reconnaissance squadrons. There were plenty of pilots – about 2000 of them, with commensurate numbers of other aircrew, all of whom had received an adequate training. All were lacking in operational-type experience, hardly any of the bomber crews having any experience in night or bad weather flying – a factor which would militate against them considerably during the poor climatic conditions which prevailed during April 1941. The fighter pilots had seldom practiced formation flying in numbers greater than two or three, or in co-operation with other units, and had little aerial gunnery practise due to shortage of tracer and incendiary ammunition. Most of their aircraft were without radio transmitters or receivers; flying time in the new Me109s (as they were known in Yugoslavia, and as the JKRV machines will be referred to herein to differentiate them from the basically similar Luftwaffe fighters) was particularly low.

Since the main airfields would be known to an enemy, about 100 auxiliary fields had been prepared during the 12 months prior to hostilities, but only some 50 of these were ready, most of them practically useless in wet weather to all but the lightest of aircraft.

174

Yugoslav pilot with a Wright Cyclone-powered Breguet XIX/8 of one of the Army Aviation Grupas of the JKRV. (*Z Jerin*).

Amongst the regiments, the 2nd Puk was the least ready; previously a reconnaissance regiment, its 48 Po25s, 52BrXIXs and 48 BrXIX/7s had been passed to the army reconnaissance squadrons early in 1941, the intention being that it should be re-equipped with heavy fighters such as the Potez 631 or Messerschmitt Bf110, or even the indigenous R313, for the defence of Belgrade and the war industries of Serbia. In the last month of peace a few Hurricanes and a squadron of Me109s were taken from the 4th and 6th Puk to provide some semblance of operational readiness, all further Hurricane production from the Zmaj factory in Zemun then being directed to this unit.

The navy's air component had also been re-organised into three hidroplanska komanda (floatplane commands) each equivalent to a JKRV regiment, but as only the 2nd and 3rd were fully equipped, the 1st HK was incorporated into the 2nd at late date.

Well-comouflaged Messerschmitt Me109Es of the JKRV's 32 Grupa, 6th Fighter Puk, seen during 'war games' in summer 1940. The aircraft in the centre background carries the code L-5 in black on the fuselage side. (*Z Jerin*)

Still in service in April 1941 was Dornier Wal No.200, which had been acquired in 1927. It served with 26HE of 3 HG, and survived the fighting, only to be scrapped by the Italians subsequently. (*Z Jerin*)

A look at the map shows the headache facing the Yugoslav Staff planners in early 1941, since their country was surrounded on nearly every border by unfriendly states. Only the small segment of southern border with Greece could be left out of a direct defence plan. Until autumn 1940 the south was considered to be unimportant, but Mussolini's attack on Greece had made it clear to all that Yugoslavia was likely soon to be involved in the war. Not until the end of February 1941 was a new defence directive, R-41 (Rat 1941 – War in 1941) issued to the armed forces, by which time there were no further doubts as to the intentions of the Germans, whose army was by then already established in Bulgaria.

From the start of Italy's attack on Greece, border incursions mainly by Italian aircraft had been frequent, the first on 5 November 1940, when southernmost Yugoslav Macedonia was twice bombed with much damage to property, the death of nine persons and injury to 21 more. Next day 18 Hurricanes from the 4th Puk were sent from Zagreb to Konjar, near Prilep in Macedonia, while ten Me109s of the 102 Eskadrila moved to Mostar from Zemun-Belgrade to patrol over the coastal region from Split to the Albanian border. Frequent attempts were made to intercept intruding bombers and reconnaissance aircraft during the next few months, in the course of one of which on 14 December, 1940 Sgt Vucevic in his Hurricane forced a Greek Hs126 from 3 Mira to force-land near Bitolj, the crew being interned.

During this period no Italian aircraft were shot down, but on 18 November 1940, an RAF Wellington crashed in the mountains of Veliki Garac, four bodies being recovered, including that of an American war correspondent (Ralph Barnes of the New York Herald Tribune in Sgt Palmer-Sambourne's aircraft of 70 Squadron – see page 38). On 23 February 1941, a Savoia S.79 lost in bad weather after an attack on Greece crashed while attempting a force-landing, the crew being interned, while on 1 March, a Luftwaffe Ju52/3m transport of IV/KGzbV 1 landed at Skoplje due to a navigational error with eight military personnel on board.

The JKRV was secretly mobilized on 6 March, and six days later dispersal to the auxiliary airfields began, being completed by 20 March. However on 3 April, Major Vladimir Kren defected to Graz in Austria in a Po 25, with information as to the location of many of these airfields, and of the codes and cipher used by the air force command, which had urgently to be changed as a result.

After the 'coup d'état' of 27 March, there had been so many violations of Yugoslav airspace as to keep the JKRV fighters constantly on alert. Two days later Milan Djordjevic was killed in a crash-landing of his Me109 after running out of fuel during a prolonged chase of a German reconnaissance aircraft. A few days later a Messerschmitt Bf110D landed at Kraljevo due to a navigational error during a deep penetration reconnaissance, and was at once seized and incorporated in the 51st Grupa at Zemun. An He111 was also believed to have been badly damaged by AA fire over Maribor, Slovenia, on 3 April. These incursions quickly highlighted the inadequacy of the ground observation post network, which was practically non-existent, and of the lack of adequate radio communications which were soon to bedevil the defences to a considerable degree. By now the 4th Puk's Hurricanes had returned to their allotted bases from Macedonia, followed on 5 April, by the 102 Eskadrila Me109s from Mostar, which were incorporated into the 51 Grupa of the 6th Puk. Their engines were much in need of overhaul after nearly five months patrol duties in the south. That same afternoon the British Col Macdonald visited General Borivoja Mirkovic, Chief of the JKRV at Zemun to confirm what the Yugoslavs already knew – that the German attack on Belgrade would commence at 0630 next morning. As can be seen, the JKRV was not well-placed to meet such an onslaught.

Ten pilots of the 102 Eskadrila, 51 Grupa, at Mostar with the Messerschmitt Me109E-3 fighters in late 1940 after Yugoslav airspace had been repeatedly violated by Italian aircraft flying from Albania. (*Z Jerin*)

The Order of Battle at dawn on 6 April 1941 for the JKRV is on page 187–191. It will be noted that on paper at any rate, this was a substantially stronger force of relatively modern aircraft than the combined British and Greek air forces to the douth!

The Assault on Yugoslavia

For the sake of clarity and continuity the actions during the opening days of the German invasion will be dealt with separately, those actions occurring over Yugoslavia being recounted first, followed by those connected with the thrusts into Greece.

The initial German attacks followed two distinctly separate routes. The first and principal push was launched by 12th Armee from Bulgaria from the lower Struma valley in three westward columns in typical *Blitzkrieg* fashion. The northernmost would follow the line Kjustendil-Kriva-Palanka-Kumanovo-Skoplje; the central thrust would be along the road Blagoevgrad-Delcevo-Kocani-Stip-Veles-Prilep-Bitolj, while the southernmost followed the River

178

Strumica to the town of the same name. These moves would be supported by the full might of Fliegerkorps VIII.

The Wehrmacht moved across the frontier at 0515 on 6 April, following some earlier attacks by infantry on border fortifications. Dr. Goebbels announced the declaration of war 45 minutes later at 0600. While Ju87s were at once active in support of the army's spearheads, the primary objective for the rest of von Richthofen's units was the neutralization of the local elements of the JKRV – notably the regiments of the 3rd Mixed Brigade which were responsible for the defence of the whole south-east. Following the moves of 12 March, the 35 and 36 Grupa of the 5th Fighter Puk were at Kosancic, near Leskovac and at Rezanovacka Kosa, near Kumanovo respectively. The 3rd Bomber Puk, which had only arrived in the area from Skoplje a month earlier, had three eskadrila of the 64 Grupa at Obilic, near Pristina (208 and 210 Esk) and at Stubol, near Urosevac (209 Esk), with a total strength of 30 Yugoslav-built Do17Ks. The 63 Grupa, which disposed a similar number of German-built Dorniers, was at Petrovac, since the regimental commander had found the field at Bojnik, near Leskovac, to be unsuitable for bombers.

5th Fighter Puk Hawker Fury No.43, seen later in April after capture by the Italians. Behind it is Breguet XIX No.77. (*via A Stamatopoulos*)

Before dawn the fighter pilots of 36 Grupa were awakened with news of the German attacks and were ordered to be prepared for imminent air raids. Two Furies went off at sunrise to patrol towards Kratovo, but as they departed 17 Bf109Es and a single Bf110 – mainly aircraft from Lehrgeschwader 2's Gruppen – swept in to attack Rezanovacka Kosa. Here other pilots were in the seats of their biplanes, the Kestrel engines already ticking over, and most were able to get into the air before the German fighters had opened fire; the initial assault destroyed on the ground only one Fury, one RWD 13 and three training aircraft. In the air however, the 111 Eskadrila was caught at a grave disadvantage at the point of take-off, although their fate did allow 112 Eskadrila pilots to gain

179

LUFTWAFFE ORDER OF BATTLE – BALKANS, 5 APRIL, 1941

Luftflotte 4

4(F)/121	Seyring, Austria	Ju88Ds
Stab, I and III/KG 2	Zwölfaxing, Austria	Do.17Zs
III/KG 3	Münchendorf, Austria	Do.17Zs
II/KG 4	Aspern, Austria	He111Ps
Stab, I and II/KG 51	Wiener Neustadt, Austria	Ju88As
III/KG 51	Schwechat, Austria	Ju88As

Fliegerführer Graz (under command Kommodore StG 3)

II/JG 54 (less 4 St.)	Graz, Austria	Bf109Es
II/StG 77	Graz, Austria	Ju87Bs
Stab/StG 3	Graz, Austria	Ju87Bs
I/JG 27	Graz, Austria	Bf109Es

Fliegerführer Arad (under command Kommodore StG 77)

III/JG 54	Arad, Rumania	Bf109Es
Stab, I and III/StG 77	Arad, Rumania	Ju87Bs
4/JG 54	Arad, Rumania	Bf109Es
I/ZG 26	Szeged, Hungary	Bf110s
Stab, II and III/JG 77	Deta, Rumania	Bf109Es

Attached 2 Armee, Austria/Hungary

2(H)/31 serving	XIV Korps	Hs126s
3(H)/13 serving	XLIX, LI and LII Korps	Hs126s
4(H)/13 serving	XLI Korps	Hs126s
3(H)/21 Pz serving	11th Panzer Division	Hs126s
3(H)/41 Pz serving	5th Panzer Division	Hs126s
3(H)/12 Pz serving	5th Panzer Division	Hs126s
2(H)/32 Pz serving	14th Panzer Division	Hs126s

Fliegerkorps VIII

2(F)/11	Sofia-Filiporci, Bulgaria	Do.17s
Stab, I and III/StG 2	Belica and Krainici, Bulgaria	Ju87Bs
I/StG 3	Belica, Bulgaria	Ju87Bs
Stab, II and III/JG 27	Belica and Sofia-Vrba, Bulgaria	Bf109Es
I(J)/LG 2	Sofia-Vrazdebna, Bulgaria	Bf109Es
I/LG 1	Krumovo, Bulgaria	Ju88As
II(Sch)/LG 2	Sofia-Vrazdebna, Bulgaria	Bf109Es (two Staffeln) Hs123 As (one Staffel)
7/LG 2	Sofia-Vrazdebna, Bulgaria	Bf110s
10/LG 2	Krainici, Bulgaria	Hs123As
II/ZG 26	Krainici and Vrazdebna, Bulgaria	Bf110s
7 Seenotdienstaffel	Varna, Bulgaria	Various floatplanes
IV/KGzbV 1	Krumovo, Bulgaria	Ju52/3ms

180

Attached 12 Armee, Bulgaria

5(H)/13	serving	XXX Korps	Hs126s
2(H)/10	serving	XVIII Korps	Hs126s
4(H)/22	serving	XL Korps	Hs126s
4(H)/32	serving	XI and L Korps	Hs126s
1(H)/14 Pz	serving	2nd Panzer Division	Hs126s
1(H)/23 Pz	serving	9th Panzer Division	Hs126s

some height before giving battle. In minutes 11 Furies (including the initial pair on patrol) were shot down, or had been destroyed in force-landings after suffering severe damage; seven of the pilots were killed and one wounded, the dead including both eskadrila commanders, Capts Vojislav Popovik (111 Esk) and Konstantin Jermakov (112 Esk). The latter was seen to ram the wing of a Bf110 – presumably deliberately – after his ammunition was exhausted. Eleven victories over the Furies were indeed claimed by the Bf109E pilots, and by Bf110 pilots of II/ZG26; three of these were credited to Oblt Erwin Clausen of I(J)/LG2 (his 6th–8th victories), while Lt Fritz Geisshardt of this unit claimed four more to bring his personal score to 17. In return the Yugoslavs claimed three Bf109Es and one Bf110 shot down. One aircraft of I(J)/LG2 was lost, Ofw Heinz Eckhardt being reported missing, while one morw of this unit's Messerschmitts and three others from II(Sch)/LG2 crashed on return to Vrba, Belica and Plovdiv, though whether as a direct result of damage sustained in combat is not known. However II/ZG26 lost two Bf110s, Fw Helmut Recker and Uffz Adolf Sondermann and their gunners all being lost. The Yugoslavs reported that the body of a Bulgarian officer was found in the wreckage of one Bf110, who it was presumed had directed the Germans to their target.

Following this attack only two 36 Grupa Furies remained flyable, both setting out later in the day to Stubol landing ground to be incorporated into 35 Grupa. One ran out of fuel on the way and crash-landed, only one surviving. A similar fate to that suffered by 36 Grupa had been planned for the sister unit at Kosancic, but when 20 low-flying Bf109Es appeared overhead they failed to spot the well-camouflaged Furies of 109 and 110 Eskadrila, attacking instead the 16 Breguet XIXs of the 2nd reconnaissance Grupa of 5th Army on nearby Sorlince; these were taken to be Furies by the Luftwaffe pilots, and claimed as such. Only about a third of the 35 Grupa pilots were present at the time of the attack, the regimental commander, Lt Col Bajdak, leading off some members of 110 Eskadrila in an attempt to follow the Messerschmitts back to their base. They were fired on by Yugoslav AA near Pirot, and unable to catch the German aircraft, gave up the chase. They were then moved to the reserve airfield at Bojnik, ten miles from Kosancic, as a precaution against further attack.

At much the same time as I(J)/LG2 was destroying 36 Grupa, 20 miles to the south four Ju87s attacked and silenced the AA defences around Petrovac airfield, Bf110s then diving in to bomb and strafe the 30 Do17Ks there, under cover of a Bf109E escort. In 20 minutes 14 of the bombers had been destroyed, as had some liaison and training aircraft. One Dornier attempted to take off, but stalled and crashed. At the end of this attack only three aircraft of 206 Eskadrila and the

REGIA AERONAUTICA ORDER OF BATTLE FOR ACTION OVER THE BALKANS – 5 APRIL, 1941

Comando Aeronautica Albania

Unit	A/C	Base	Comment
Fighters			
22° Gruppo Autonomo CT	(37 MC200)	Tirana	Two squadriglie only
24° Gruppo Autonomo CT	(26 G.50bis)	Devoli	Two squadriglie only
150° Gruppo Autonomo CT	(20 MC.200)	Valona	Two squadriglie only
154° Gruppo Autonomo CT	(27 G.50bis)	Devoli	Two squadriglie only
160° Gruppo Autonomo CT	(30 CR 42)	Tirana	Three squadriglie
Bombers			
101° Gruppo Autonomo B a'T (208ª, 238ª Squadriglia)	(20 Ju87B)	Tirana	
Reconnaissance			
25ª Squadriglia OA	(9 Ro.37bis)	Tirana	
31ª Squadriglia OA	(9 Ro.37bis)	Berat	
35ª Squadriglia OA	(8 Ro.37bis)	Peqini	
39ª Squadriglia OA	(9 Ro.37bis)	Berat	
42ª Squadriglia OA	(9 Ro.37bis)	Valona	
87ª Squadriglia OA	(7 Ca311)	Tirana	
114ª Squadriglia OA	(8 Ca311)	Tirana	
120ª Squadriglia OA	(9 Ca311)	Durazzo	

4ª Squadra Aerea – Bari

Unit	A/C	Base	Comment
Fighters			
8° Gruppo Autonomo CT (92ª, 93ª, 94ª Squadriglia)	(14 MC200)	Oria	Magg Vincenzo La Carrubba
153° Gruppo Autonomo CT	(38 MC200, 9 CR 42)		Magg Alberto Beneforti
(372ª Squadriglia		Brindisi	
373ª Squadriglia		Bari	
374ª Squadriglia)		Grottaglie	
370ª Squadriglia Autonomo CT	(12 MC200)	Grottaglie	
356ª Squadriglia Autonomo CT	(6 MC200)	Bari Palese*	Cap Vincenzo Sant'Andrea

(*arrived too late for sustained employment over Yugoslavia)

Unit	A/C	Base	Comment
Bombers			
13° Stormo BT	(24 BR20)	Gioia del Colle	Col Antonio Pirino
(11° Gruppo BT – 1ª, 4ª Squadriglia)			Magg Giuseppe Aini

182

(43° Gruppo BT – 3ª, 5ª Squadriglia)			Ten Col Roberto Pagliocchini
37° Stormo BT	(30 BR20)	Lecce	Col Giuseppe Scarlata
(55° Gruppo BT – 220ª, 221ª Squadriglia)			
(116° Gruppo BT – 276ª, 277ª Squadriglia)			
38° Stormo BT	(16 BR 20)	Foggia	
39° Gruppo BT – 51ª, 69ª Squadriglia)			Ten Col Giorgio Porta
(40° Gruppo BT – 202ª, 203ª Squadriglia)			
35° Stormo BT/BM	(15 Z.1007bis, 12 Z.506B)	Brindisi	Col Enrica Grande
(86° Gruppo BM – 190ª, 191ª Squadriglia)			
(95° Gruppo bT – 230ª, 231ª Squadriglia)			Magg Giovanni Morbidelli
47° Stormo BT	(26 Z.1007bis)	Grottaglie	
(106° Gruppo BT – 260ª, 261ª Squadriglia)			Ten Col Gori Castellani
(107° Gruppo BT – 262ª, 263ª Squadriglia)			Ten Col Amedeo Paradisi
50° Gruppo Autonomo BT	(8 Z.1007bis)	Brindisi	
(210ª, 211ª Squadriglia)			
104° Gruppo Autonomo BT	(15 S.79)	Foggia	
(252ª, 253ª Squadriglia)			
105° Gruppo Autonomo BT	(15 S.79)	Bari	
(254ª, 255ª Squadriglia)			
97° Gruppo Autonomo B a'T	(20 Ju87)	Lecce	Ten Col Antonio Moscatelli

2ª Squadra Aerea – Padua

Fighters			Gen D A Tullio Toccolini
4° Stormo CT			Ten Col C Magno Grandinetti
(9° Gruppo CT)	(23 MC200)	Gorizia	Ten Col Marco Minio Paullo
(73ª, 96ª Squadriglia)		Alture/Pola	
(97ª Squadriglia)		Gorizia	
(10° Gruppo CT)	(23 MC200)	Ronchi Leg	Ten Col Carlo Romagnoli
(84ª, 90ª, 91ª Squadriglia)			
54° Stormo CT		Treviso	Col Carlo Calosso
(7° Gruppo CT)	(22 MC200)	Treviso	Magg Marcello Fossetta
(76ª, 86ª, 98ª Squadriglia)			
(16° Gruppo CT)	(22 MC200)	Ravenna	Ten Col Francesco Beccaria
(167ª, 168ª Squadriglia)			
(169ª Squadriglia)		Udine	

Bombers

18° Stormo BT	(32 BR20)	Aviano	Col Paolo Aitan
(31° Gruppo BT –			Ten Col Giuseppe Bordin
65ª, 66ª Squadriglia			
(37° Gruppo BT –			Magg Pietro Lauri Filzi
47ª, 48ª Squadriglia)			
25° Gruppo Autonomo BT	(15 BR20)	Forli	Magg Gabriele Rivalta
(8ª, 9ª Squadriglia)			
99° Gruppo Autonomo BT	(14 BR20)	Vicenza	Magg Nello Brambilla
(242ª, 243ª Squadriglia)			

Reconnaissance

61° Gruppo Autonomo OA		Gorizia
(34ª Squadriglia)	(8 Ca311)	Gorizia
(36ª Squadriglia)	(8 Ro.37bis)	Alture
63° Gruppo Autonomo OA	(14 Ro.37bis)	Udine
(41ª, 113ª Squadriglia)		
71° Gruppo Autonomo OA		Udine
(38ª, 116ª Squadriglia)	(12 Ro.37bis)	Udine
(128ª Squadriglia)	(7 Ca311)	Gorizia

Total Strength	*Aeronautica Albania*	*2ª Squadra Aerea*	*4ª Squadra Aerea*	*Total*
Fighters	140	90	65	295
Bombers	—	61	149	210
Bomber Floatplanes	—	—	12	12
Dive Bombers	20	—	20	40
Reconnaissance	68	41	—	109
	228	192	246	666

BRITISH AIR FORCES ORDER OF BATTLE, BALKANS – 5 APRIL, 1941

Royal Air Force

Fighters

33 Squadron at Larissa and Eleusis	Sqn Ldr M T StJ Pattle	Hurricanes
80 Squadron at Eleusis	Sqn Ldr E G Jones	Hurricanes
112 Squadron at Yanina and Paramythia	Sqn Ldr L G Schwab	Gladiators
30 Squadron at Eleusis and Maleme	Sqn Ldr R A Milward	Blenheim IFs

Bombers

11 Squadron at Almyros	Sqn Ldr P Stevens	Blenheim Is
84 Squadron at Menidi	Sqn Ldr H D Jones	Blenheim Is
113 Squadron at Niamata	Sqn Ldr R T Spencer	Blenheim IVs

211 Squadron at Paramythia	Sqn Ldr A T Irvine	Blenheim Is
37 Squadron at Menidi	Wg Cdr R C M Collard	Wellington ICs

Reconnaissance

208 Squadron at Eleusis	Sqn Ldr J R Wilson	Lysanders & Hurricanes
230 Squadron detachment at Scaramanga	Sqn Ldr P H Alington	Sunderlands

Fleet Air Arm

Fighters

805 Squadron at Maleme:	Lt Cdr A F Black	Fulmars and Sea Gladiators

Bombers

815 Squadron at Paramythia and Maleme:	Lt F M A Torrens-Spence	Swordfish

Additionally, Wellingtons of 257 Wing (38, 70 and 148 Squadrons) from Egypt, flying from the advanced landing ground at Fuka, were available for limited operations.

ELLENIKI VASSILIKI AEROPORIA ORDER OF BATTLE – 5 APRIL, 1941

Fighters

21 Mira at Paramythia	Gladiators
22 Mira at Salonika/Sedes (would withdraw to Kalambaka/ Vissiliki on advance of German forces)	PZL P24s
23 Mira at Larissa	PZL P24s
24 Mira at Salonika/Sedes (would withdraw with 22 Mira)	Bloch MB151s

Bombers

31 Mira	The remnants of these units only remained; they were assembled at Menidi.	Potez 63s
32 Mira		Blenheim Is and IVs
33 Mira		Battles

Reconnaissance

13 Mira at bases in the Peloponnes	Ansons
11 and 12 Mira in the Athens area, barely operational	Do22s and Fairey IIIFs

185

Breguet XIXs of the 601 Eskadrila, 201 Training Grupa, after a strafing attack on Lazarevac by Luftwaffe Bf110s on 7 April 1941. (*Z Jerin*)

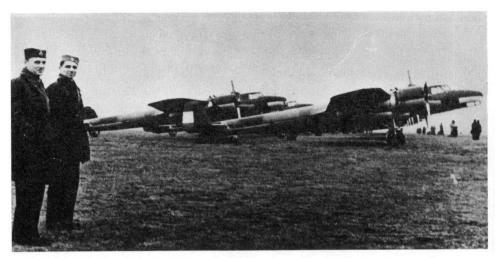

3rd Bomber Puk Do.17Ks. (*Z Jerin*)

JUGOSLOVENSKO KRALJEVSKO RATNO VAZDUHOPLOVSTVO (JKRV) – ORDER OF BATTLE, 6 APRIL 1941

Headquarters: Ljesnica   Commander-in-Chief: Brigadni General Borivoje Mirkovic
Chief of Staff: Ppk Miodrag Lozic

Units under Direct command:

701 Eskadrila VZ (Liaison unit) (Ljesnica)		Bf108 and Fi156
11 Ind (LR Recce) Grupa: (Veliki Radinci, near Ruma)	Mj Dragomir Lazarevic	
21 Eskadrila:	Kp Ranko Milovanovic ⎫ Kp Ljuba Jancic ⎭	9 Blenheim I, 2 Hind
22 Eskadrila:		
81 (Bomber) Grupa: (Mostar-Ortijes)	Mj Milutin Bostanic	
261 Eskadrila:	Kp Sergije Frantov ⎫ Kp Raja Nedeljkovic ⎭	14 S.79
262 Eskadrila:		
Ind Fighter Eskadrila: (Mostar-Kosor)	Kp Mihajlo Grbic	3 Hurricane I, 3 Me109, 3 Avia BH-33E (2 detached at Podgorica)

1st Lovacka Vazduhoplovna Brigada (Fighter Air Brigade);

Headquarters: Belgrade-Zemun   Commander: Pk Dragutin Rupcic

702 Eskadrila VZ (Liaison unit) Belgrade-Zemun)		Bf108, Fi156, 2Me109
2nd (Fighter) Puk: (Kraljevo*)	Ppk Franjo Pirc	
31 Grupa: (Knic)	Mj Ilija Milovanovic	
101 Eskadrila: (Susicko Polje)	Kp Kosta Lekic ⎫ Kp Franc Berginc ⎭	19 Me109
141 Eskadrila: (Susicko Polje)		
52 Grupa: (Knic)	Mj Miodrag Blagojevic	
163 Eskadrila: (knic)	Kp Milos Bajagic ⎫ Kp Ivo Ostric ⎭	15 Hurricane I
164 Eskadrila: (Knic)		

6th (*Fighter*) *Puk:* (Zemun-Belgrade*)	Ppk Bozidar Kostic	
32 Grupa: (Prnjavor)	Mj Danilo Djordjevic	
103 Eskadrila: (Prnjavor)	Kp Ilija Vlajic	
104 Eskadrila: (Prnjavor)	Kp Bora Markovic	27 Me109
142 Eskadrila: (Prnjavor)	Kp Milutin Grozdanovic	
51 Grupa: (Zemun-Belgrade)	Mj Adum Romeo	
102 Eskadrila: (Zemun-Belgrade)	Kp Milos Zunjic	10 Me109
161 Eskadrila: (Zemun-Belgrade)	Kp Savo Poljanec	3 IK-Z
162 Eskadrila: (Zemun-Belgrade)	Kp Todor Gogic	3 IK-Z

2nd Mesovita Vazduhoplovna Brigada (Mixed Air Brigade):

Headquarters: Nova Topola   Commander: Pk Jakov Djordjevic

703 Eskadrilla VZ (Liaison unit) (Nova Topola)		Bf108 and Fi156
4th (*Fighter*) *Puk:* (Zagreb*)	Ppk Radislav Djordjevic	
33 Grupa: (Bosanski Aleksandrovac)	Mj Nikola Nikolic	
105 Eskadrila: (Bosanski Aleksandrovac)	Kp Aleksandar Radicevic	7 Hurricane I
106 Eskadrila: (Bosanski Aleksandrovac)	Kp Dragisa Milijevic	6 Hurricane I
34 Grupa: (Bosanski Aleksandrovac)	Mj Arsenije Boljevic	
107 Eskadrila: (Bosanski Aleksandrovac)	Kp Zarko Vukajlovic	8 IK-2
108 Eskadrila: (Bosanski Aleksandrovac)	Kp Mladen Milovcic	7 Hurricane I
8th (*Bomber*) *Puk:* (Zagreb*)	Pk Stanko Diklic	
68 Grupa: (Rovine)	Mj Lazar Donovic	
215 Eskadrila: (Rovine)	Kp Vladimir Jovicic	6 Blenheim I
216 Eskadrila: (Rovine)	Kp Serije Vojinov	6 Blenheim I

188

69 Grupa: (Rovine)	Mj Dobrosa Tesic	
217 Eskadrila: (Rovine)	Kp Matija Petrovic	6 Blenheim I
218 Eskadrila:	Kp Vladimir Ferencina	6 Blenheim I

3rd Mesovita Vazduhoplovna Brigada (Mixed Air Brigade):

Headquarters: Stubol (Pristina) Commander: Pk Nikola Obuljen

704 Eskadrila VZ (Liaison unit) (Stubol Pristina)		Bf108 and Fi156
3rd (Bomber) Puk: (Skoplje*)	Pk Zdenko Gorjup	
63 Grupa: (Petrovac)	Mj Branislav Djordjevic	
205 Eskadrila: (Petrovac)	Pr Mato Culinovic	
206 Eskadrila: (Petrovac)	Kp Mihajlo Djonlic	30 Do17K
207 Eskadrila: (Petrovac)	Kp Miodrag Nikolic	
64 Grupa: (Petrovac)	Mj Branko Fanedl	
208 Eskadrila: (Obilic, near Pristina)	Kp Sima Mijuskovic	
209 Eskadrila: (Stubol)	Kp Dusan Milojevic	30 Do17K
210 Eskadrila: (Obilic)	Kp Vojislav Grujic	
5th (Fighter) Puk: (Nis*)	Ppk Leonid Bajdak	
35 Grupa: (Kosancic)	Mj Vasa Zivanovic	
109 Eskadrila: (Kosancic)	Kp Pavle Goldner	15 Hawker Fury
110 Eskadrila:	Kp Oyo Sep	
36 Grupa: (Rezanovacka Kosa)	Mj Drago Brezovsek	
111 Eskadrila: (Rezanovacka Kosa)	Kp Vojislav Popovic	15 Hawker Fury
112 Eskadrila: (Rezanovacka Kosa)	Kp Konstantin Jermakov	

4th Bombarderska Vazduhoplovna Brigada (Bomber Air Brigade):

Headquarters: Ljubic (Cacak) Commander: Pk Petar Vukcevic

705 Eskadrila VZ (Liaison unit) (Ljubic)		Bf108 and Fi156
1st (Bomber) Puk: (Novi Sad*)	Pk Ferdo Gradisnik	
61 Grupa: (Bjeljina)	Mj Branko Malojcic	
201 Eskadrila: (Davidovac)	Kp Dragisa Nikodijevic	6 Blenheim I
202 Eskadrila: (Davidovac)	Kp Stevan Filipovic	5 Blenheim I
62 Grupa: (Bjeljina)	Mj Krsta Lozic	
203 Eskadrila (Bjeljina)	Kp Todor Pavlovic	6 Blenheim I
204 Eskadrila: (Bjeljina)	Kp Nikola Ivancevic	6 Blenheim I
7th (Bomber) Puk: (Mostar*)	Ppk Hinko Dragic-Hauer	
66 Grupa: (Preljina, near Cacak)	Mj Dusan Sofilj	
211 Eskadrila: (Preljina)	Kp Kresimir Boras	
212 Eskadrila: (Preljina)	Kp Aleksandar Dobanovacki	} 13 S.79
67 Grupa: (Gorobilje, near Uzicka Pozega)	Mj Ranko Raskovic	
213 Eskadrila: (Gorobilje)	Kp Arsenije Ikanjikov	} 13 S.79
214 Eskadrila: (Gorobilje)	Kp Jefta Bosnjak	

Army Aviation:

**1 VIGrupa (Ruma)	I Army	15 aircraft
2 VIGrupa (Sorlince, near Leskovac)	V Army	16 aircraft
3 VIGrupa (Staro Topolje, near Djakovo)	II Army	19 aircraft
4 VIGrupa (Velika Gorica (Kurilovac), near Zagreb)	IV Army	18 aircraft
5 VIGrupa (Tetovo)	III Army	14 aircraft
6 VIGrupa (Cerklje and Brega, near Brezice)	VII Army	16 aircraft
7 VIGrupa (Smederevska Palanka)	VI Army	18 aircraft
Samostalna Izvidjacka Eskadrila (Jasenica-Mostar) (Coastal Army Commando)		4 aircraft

**VIGrupa — Vazduhoplovna Izvidjacko Grupa (Air Reconnaissance Group). All aircraft were obsolete; types included Breguet XIX, XIX/7, XIX/8 and Potez Po25

Navy Aviation:

Headquarters: Kastel Luksic, near Split   Commander: Kbb Nikola Nardeli

2 Hidroplanska Komanda: (Divulje*)	Kk Marjan Butkovic	
3 Hidrogrupa:	Pbb Avgust Groselj	
5 Hidroeskadrila: (Tijesno)	Pbb Jovan Mikolic	5 Sim XIV, 1 SM
25 Hidroeskadrila: (Zlarin and Visovac)	Pbb Igor Beran	6 Do22, 1 PVT-H
4 Hidrogrupa:	Pbb Tomislav Mihelic	
26 Hidroeskadrila: (Krapanj-Jadrtovac)	Pbb Albin Pavlinic	5 Do Wal, 1 SM, 1 PVT-H
15 Hidroeskadrila: (Vodice)	Pf Franjo Pavic	2 Sim XIV, 6-7 IO, 1 Sim/XII

3 Hidroplanska Komanda: (Boka Kotorska*)	Kk Eduard Pikl	
1 Hidrogrupa:	Pbb Pavle Zupan	
1 Hidroeskadrila: (S Krtole)	Pbb Albin Unger	5 Sim XIV, 1 SM
11 Hidroeskadrila: (S Rosa)	Pbb Stevan Rajter	2–3 Sim XIV, 1 He 8 (also had 8–10 elderly training aircraft on its inventory)
2 Hidrogrupa:	Pbb Vladeta Petrovic	
20 Hidroeskadrila: (Orahovac)	Pko Milan Malnaric	6 Do22
21 Hidroeskadrila: (Dobrota)	Pbb Oskar Bizjak	6 Do Wal, 1 Do D, 1 Fleet, 2 PVT-H
SHEskadrila (training unit for auxiliary tasks, based at Razetinovac, nr Trogir)	Pbb Ivan Konte	1 Sim XIV, 1 PVT-H, 2IO, 1–2 Sim XI, 1 Fleet, 1 DH Moth, few SM

Notes: (1) *The locations marked thus were the peacetime bases of the Puk or Komanda.
       (2) The JKRV also had ten training units (TE – Trenazna Eskadrila), some of which were incorporated in the operational regiments, and some were independent units. They were equipped with Breguet XIX, Potez 25 and Caproni 310 aircraft, and a large number of primary training aircraft mostly of Yugoslav origin, but including German Bücker Jungmann biplanes.

(3) Unit designations used are listed below with direct translations and the nearest RAF equivalent:

JKRV	RAF
Puk (Regiment)	Wing
Grupa (Group)	Squadron
Eskadrila	Flight

NB: Hidroplanska Komanda (Floatplane Commando) equivalent to a JKRV Puk

Rank abbreviations used here relate to the Yugoslav ranks set out below. In the text the English translation and its abbreviation is used for the sake of clarity.

JKRV			Naval Ranks		
PK	– Pukovnik	– Colonel	Kbb	– Kapetan Bojnogbroda	– Captain
Ppk	– Potpukovnik	– Lieutenant Colonel	Kf	– Kapetan Fregate	– No direct comparative rank
Mj	– Major	– Major	Kk	– Kapetan Korvete	– Commander
Kp	– Kapetan	– Captain	Pbb	– Porucnik Bojnogbroda	– Lieutenant Commander
Pr	– Porucnik	– 1st Lieutenant	Pf	– Porucnik Fregate	– Lieutenant
Ppr	– Potporucnik	– 2nd Lieutenant	Pko	– Porucnik Korvete	– Sub-Lieutenant

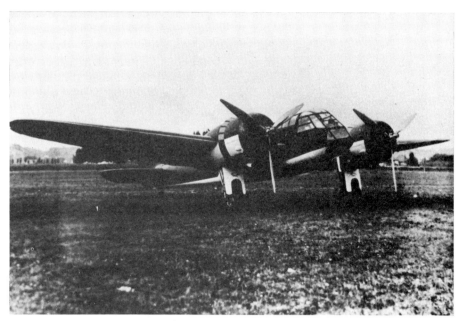

An Ikarus-built Blenheim I bomber of the JKRV on delivery. 62 of these aircraft had been received by April 1941, and 20 more were in various stages of production. (*Z Jerin*)

A Dornier Do17Z-2 bomber of III/KG3 as employed during the initial raids on Belgrade, and thereafter throughout the campaign. 5K+FR, seen here in flight, served with the gruppe's 7 Staffel. (*Bundesarchiv*)

193

regimental commander's aircraft at Skoplje airfield remained intact, these all flying to join 209 Eskadrila at Stubol. When at about 0700 news was received at 64 Grupa of the disaster which had befallen 63 Grupa at Petrovac, Maj Fanedl led off his whole unit of Dorniers to bomb the German armour between Kjustendil and Guesevo in Bulgaria. At Kjustendil they found the tail of a column some 17 miles long which they bombed with 100kg bombs and then strafed. Several aircraft were hit by return fire, but all safely reached their airfields.

As the Luftwaffe's first wave returned to its airfields, other aircraft were on the way to attack Veles, Stip, Stracin and Kriva Palanka, elements also strafing the railway up the Vardar Valley and the practically deserted Nis airfield. Here Hpt Herbert Ihlefeld, commander of I(J)/LG2, was hit by small arms fire and wounded slightly in the head. He crash-landed his damaged Messerschmitt on a nearby hill and became a prisoner. While the Dorniers at Petrovac were still burning, Skoplje, Stip and Veles were all heavily bombed by Ju87s and Ju88s, escorted by Bf110s which also strafed. One of the latter was claimed shot down by the AA defences at Skoplje – possibly one of the two aircraft lost by II/ZG26 on this date, which have already been mentioned.

Throughout the day Fliegerkorps VIII's Stukas were active against the Yugoslav defences, especially on the Kumanovo-Skoplje axis. The little town of Kriva Palanka, eight miles from the border, was occupied by 0800, the next objective for the Panzers being Stracin, 17 miles further up the road. Here the advance was held by strong defences, but without proper AA guns, the Yugoslavs soon fell victim to the Ju87s and Hs123s. One of the latter was the only casualty, shot down by a single lucky round from the rifle of a Yugoslav sergeant. Uffz Hannenberg crash-landed his little biplane which was destroyed by fire, and he was taken prisoner.

At 1020 Skoplje and Nis were again bombed, while at 1100 ten Bf109Es strafed Do17Ks of 64 Grupa at Stubol as these were awaiting orders for their next attack on the German columns. Fifteen of the bombers were destroyed or badly damaged, although three 208 Eskadrila machines managed to get into the air during the attack and followed the Messerschmitts back to their base at Vrba. Here they bombed lines of Luftwaffe aircraft on the ground, claiming at least four destroyed; they flew to Obilic airfield near Pristina to land. During the afternoon strong formations of Bf109Es and 110s again attacked Petrovac where ground crews of 63 Grupa were frantically trying to repair some of the damaged Dorniers. After 15 minutes all ten damaged aircraft had been destroyed or reduced to irreparable condition. This brought 3rd Puk losses during the day to 41 destroyed or badly damaged, with three more slightly damaged, to which must be added the 16 Breguets of the reconnaissance unit. Fliegerkorps VIII claimed a total of 60 aircraft destroyed during the day, including the 11 Furies and an unidentified aircraft shot down, plus 34 Do17s and 14 Furies (in fact mainly Breguet XIXs) destroyed on the ground. Losses included one Bf109E, two Do17s (of which more later) and a Ju87 missing (the latter Ofw Herbert Flor's aircraft of 3/StG2, lost over Popliwista), one Hs123, one Ju87, two Bf110s and six Bf109Es destroyed, plus two Ju87s and five Bf109Es damaged – although this total

194

includes losses and damage suffered in accidents also. An Hs126 of 1(H)/23, attached to 12th Armee, was also lost in the Kriva Palanka area, Fw Ewald Bruns and Hpt Hans Hoffman being reported missing in 6K + EH. A second Hs126 of 3(H)/21 was reported destroyed on the ground in this area during the day – possibly by the bombs of the trio of Yugoslav Do17Ks. Thereafter action in the south was devoted mainly to ground support, not only of the drive on Skoplje, but also for the southern thrust which pushed through the town of Strumica during the morning, before bearing south towards the Greek frontier.

Junkers Ju87B Stuka dive-bombers over the Balkans, April 1941. (*Bib für Zeit*)

While von Richthofen's units had been opening the attacks in the south, GenObst Löhr's Luftflotte 4 commenced the second most important role allocated to the German forces by Hitler in his Directive No.25 – punishment of the Belgrade government. While the Führer himself spent the night in his special train in a tunnel on the Wiener Neustadt-Fürstenfeld railway, and Göring followed operations from a headquarters at Semmering, Austria, the Luftwaffe prepared a massive strike on the capital which was to follow Fliegerkorps VIII's initial actions by about one hour. When the first alarms were sounded in the city at 0645, 74 Ju87s from StG77 were approaching between 8000–10 000 feet, with 160 He111s of II/KG 4 and Do17Zs from KG 2 and 3, with escorting Bf110s at 11 000–12 000 feet, 100 Bf109Es (including 56 aircraft from Stab, II and III/JG 77) providing top cover at 15 000 feet.

The Yugoslavs were in no way taken by surprise. Indeed the AA defences had already reported the approach of one raid from Rumania at 0300, leading to a false alarm, while listening posts on the frontier had heard the engines of Fliegerführer Arad's aircraft warming up well before take off. At Zemun 51 Grupa had been brought to alert well before daylight. By the time news of the attacks on Rezanovacka Kosa and Petrovac were received, and of German reconnaissance aircraft over areas near Belgrade, the first patrol was already in the air, although nothing was to be seen.

First off in defence of Belgrade on 6 April, 1941 were the Rogozarski IK-Z fighters of the 51 Grupa, 6th Fighter Puk, one of which is seen warming up on the city's Zemun airfield. (*Z Jerin*)

When the first big Luftwaffe raid approached, 51 Grupa had its third patrol of the morning in the air, while a second formation from 32 Grupa was also airborne. The German aircraft began to approach in Gruppe strength at intervals of 15 minutes, and as the first small dots appeared in the sky to the north, all 51 Grupa's fighters scrambled in two parallel columns from the grassy surface of Zemun airfield. Twenty-five miles to the north-west at Prnjavor the Me109s of 32 Grupa also took to the air in three flights. One of the 51 Grupa's IK-Zs was obliged to turn back with engine trouble, but 34 Yugoslav interceptors headed for the first intruders:

196

51 Grupa	161 Eskadrila	two IK-Zs
	162 Eskadrila	three IK-Zs
	102 Eskadrila	ten Me109s
32 Grupa	103 Eskadrila	seven Me109s
	104 Eskadrila	six Me109s
	142 Eskadrila	six Me109s

6th Fighter Puk pilots with one of their Me109Es. (*Z Jervin*)

The five IK-Zs made the first contact with the bombers, but within moments the Bf109Es of JG77 were upon them and a fierce series of fights commenced. Ten claims were to be made for the defenders, five by the Messerschmitts of 102 Eskadrila and five by the IK-Zs, but three of the Yugoslav fighters were shot down, six more being badly hit and subsequently destroyed or damaged in force-landings; two pilots were killed, while five more were wounded. The dead were Capt Milos Zunjic, commander of 102 Eskadrila, and 2/Lt Dusan Borcic of 161 Eskadrila, whose aircraft, carrying the number '10', crashed on the banks of the Danube, 12 miles north of the city. 2/Lt Eduard Banfic of 162 Esk baled out, wounded, while Capt. Mihailo Nikolic of 102 Eskadrila crash-landed after suffering wounds in an attack by a Bf109E, claiming to have first shot down a Ju87. Sgt Djordje Stojanovic of 102 Eskadrila force-landed his Me109 when it was hit and set on fire by the rear gunner of a doomed twin-engined bomber; he was badly burned as his aircraft was totally engulfed in flames. Capt Sava Poljanec, commander of 161 Eskadrila, claimed an He111 (or Do.17) and a

Bf109E shot down, returning with no ammunition and with his IK-Z badly damaged by another German Messerschmitt which he avoided in a spin. As he landed his aircraft was strafed by a Bf110, suffering severe damage while the pilot suffered wounds also.

Meanwhile Capt Milan Zunic and Sgt Vladimir Puzic of 102 Eskadrila claimed a further twin-engined bomber shot down between them, and Sgt Milisav Semiz a Ju87. Lt Dragoslav Krstic and Sgt Vukadin Jelic from the same unit dived out of the sun on a large formation of bombers, Jelic claiming one in flames while Krstic was hit by return fire and crash-landed on Zemun airfield. As 51 Grupa's survivors returned, the unit found it had only five Me109s and three IK-Zs still airworthy.

Following this initial attack came the Messerschmitts of 32 Grupa, the pilots of which claimed four more bombers shot down for the loss of two of their own number, 1/Lt Vasa Kolarov and F/Sgt Dragoljub Milosevic both baling out safely; several more Me109s were hit and damaged, one crash-landing. As the last formation of Ju87s withdrew at about 0800, Hurricanes of 52 Grupa from the 2nd Puk at Knic appeared on the scene, three NCO pilots of 163 Eskadrila engaging one of the Stukas which they believed they had shot down. During this initial attack the pilots of JG77 claimed ten victories, one pilot of the Stabsschwarm claiming a Bf109, unidentified pilots of II Gruppe making six more claims, while Oblt Armin Schmidt and Lt Emil Omert of III Gruppe each claimed Messerschmitts. Ofw Riehl of this unit claimed a fighter identified as a 'Dewoitine' – almost certainly one of the IK-Zs. Six more aircraft were claimed destroyed on the ground, two each by the Stab and the two Gruppen.

Yugoslav fighter pilots, one with his baby daughter, with a Messerschmitt Me109E of the 32 Grupa. (*Z Jerin*)

During this raid it had not been easy for the Yugoslavs to gain a clear account of what had in fact happened. Several 51 Grupa pilots, having lost their wingmen and run out of ammunition, had landed at Zemun to rearm, then taking off and returning to the fray. AA batteries had fired at all and sundry – not surprisingly finding that they could not distinguish between friendly and hostile Messerschmitts! When the first indication of the approach of the raiders had been received a training unit (201 Grupa) at Lazarevac, 25 miles to the south had put seven old Potez 25s into the air, led by Capt Ivanovic of 602 Eskadrila to see if they could help. Arriving over the city after the attack had ended, they were able only to take a few photos of the carnage below. Next day Ivanovic was removed from his post...

The next attack occurred at about 1000 and lasted about an hour, 57 Ju87s and 30 Messerschmitts appearing overhead. Nine Me109s of 32 Grupa, with six IK-Zs. and Me109s of 51 Grupa took off, the latter now commanded by Capt Gogic, since the previous commander, Maj Adum Romeo had at once been removed by the Brigade Commander due to his lack of activity during the first attack. This time the interceptors claimed two Ju87s forced to land and a Bf109E shot down, but Sgt Strbenk's Me109 was hit by another escorting Bf109E and he broke away to land. Shortly afterwards he was killed in a 102 Eskadrila Messerschmitt; two more 32 Grupa Messerschmitts were damaged, 2/Lt Lajh crash-landing one of these on the airfield. One patrol of 101 Eskadrila Messerschmitts from 31 Grupa at Kragujevac followed the Stukas as they departed, Capt Zivica Mitrovic reportedly shooting down two of them before he was shot down and killed by the escort; his wingman was also shot down, but managed to bale out. They had joined the fight over Belgrade without the orders of their grupa commander.

Two more attacks followed during the afternoon, one at 1400 by 94 twin-engined bombers from the airfields around Vienna, escorted by 60 fighters, and one at 1600 made by 90 Ju87s and 60 fighters. The first of these was met by six 51 Grupa and 12 32 Grupa fighters, these units claiming one and three victories respectively (one bomber was claimed by Capt Gogic and 1/Lt Vujicic of 162 Eskadrila jointly). Three 32 Grupa Messerschmitts were shot down; 1/Lt Bogdan Presecnik baled out with severe burns, while 1/Lt Dobrica Novakovic and Presecnik's wingman, F/Sgt Petrov, were both killed. During these afternoon raids JG77 made two more claims, one for an aircraft on the ground by III Gruppe, and one shot down by II Gruppe. III/JG 54 also claimed successes over three Yugoslav Messerschmitts, credited to Oblt. Hans-Ekkehard Bob, Kapitän of 9 Staffel for his 20th victory; to Lt Max-Hellmuth Ostermann for his ninth, and to Oblt Gerhard Koall as his first. During the day's actions a number of victories were also claimed by the Bf 110s of I/ZG 26, two Messerschmitts being credited to Uffz Stiegleder of this unit. Total Luftwaffe claims over Belgrade amounted to 19 Me109s and four unidentified types.

In one of the afternoon encounters Lt Keseljevic of 142 Eskadrila, 32 Grupa – regarded by his unit commander as something of an 'enfant terrible' – who had little experience flying the Me109, had taken off to chase German twin-engined aircraft without success, when he heard frantic calls from Maj Djordjevic, his

Grupa commander: 'All into the air! All into the air! 100 German aircraft over Novi Sad!' Seeing clouds of exploding AA shells in the distance, he headed for them, observing many small dots that gradually transformed themselves into aircraft. 'I never saw so many aircraft together in my life, not even in a photo or in the cinema...' he recalled. He had never flown at altitude in the Messerschmitt before, nor used the oxygen equipment; he longed for his old Fury, in which he would have felt more at home.

Alone in the sky, he picked the last formation of bombers, chose one and opened fire with all guns. The bomber evaded to the right, and he was soon out of ammunition for his 20mm FF wing guns, continuing the attack with the two nose-mounted 7.9mm guns, which were not loaded with tracer or incendiary bullets. He was so close that he could not miss, but the bomber would not go down; instead it began flying large circles far behind its compatriots. Convinced that it was totally armoured, he watched in frustration as something black separated from the lonely Ju88 — it was a man whose parachute swiftly opened. Still the Junkers circled over Prnjavor, close to 32 Grupa's airfield, and now regimental commander Kostic and 2/Lt Lajh arrived to attack. Then came 2/Lt Kapesic of 103 Eskadrila, but still the bomber circled, on and on, lower and lower, with no sign of serious damage or fire. At last it crashed east of Prnjavor. The dead pilot was found still in his seat, the automatic pilot switched on....

The fighting over Belgrade on 6 April had cost the 6th Puk five pilots killed and seven wounded; eight of its aircraft were shot down and 15 damaged. Additionally two fighters from the 2nd Puk had also been lost; they had between them claimed some 22 Luftwaffe aircraft shot down and two more forced to land. German losses had actually been substantially lower then this; during the first raid 8/KG 3 recorded the loss of two Do.17Zs, one of them 5K + DS flown by Uffz Heinz-Werner Neuwirth, while I/ZG 26 suffered the loss of no less than five Bf110s, some of which were probably amongst those claimed by the Yugoslavs as twin-engined bombers. Of these five, four were shot down (two reportedly lost to the AA defences) with the loss of three of the crews — Ofw Willi Messemer, Lt Reinhold Eymers and Oblt Kurt Krebitz and their gunners — whilst the fifth was destroyed in a crash-landing. One more crash-landed and it appears that a seventh may also have been damaged. During the later raids KG 51 was heavily attacked by fighters, one I Gruppe Ju88A being damaged 60%, one 35% and one 20%; no loss of one of these aircraft was recorded however, so the identity of the aircraft claimed by the four 32 Grupa pilots cannot be ascertained. During the day's raids II/StG 77 lost four Ju87s, including S2 + BM flown by Ofw Heinz Ritter and S2 + GN (Uffz Gottfried Lannewers); a Bf109E of Stab/JG 54 was also lost.

The Yugoslav 2nd Puk had seen relatively little combat, although its Hurricanes and Me109s had flown many patrols in their sector between Cacak-Kraljevo-Kragujevac and Paracin. Few aircraft had radio sets, and communications were extremely primitive, so they were generally informed too late to join the battles over Belgrade. During one patrol however, Nedeljko Pajic of 31 Grupa engaged an Hs 126 (5D + AK) of 2(H)/31 over the Velika Morava valley, near Paracin, as it was flying at some 8000 feet at a leisurely pace. Pajic dived at

Henschel Hs126A of Heeraufklarüngsgruppe 32; two Staffeln from this unit operated over the Balkans during April 1941. This example is seen later in the month at Athens airport. (*Bruni via Lucchini/Malizia*)

full speed on it, but overshot, his fire missing the reconnaissance aircraft. Turning after it, he had to drop his speed almost to the stall to have any chance of hitting it as Lt Hans Pichler threw the agile aircraft into a series of tight-turning evasive manoeuvres. After several attempts, during which the observer appeared to have been killed by his fire, Pajic got in some telling strikes and the doomed Henschel poured forth a trail of black smoke as it went into a gentle dive before crashing in flames; the jubilant fighter pilot then performed a number of victory spirals overhead.

While the attacks on Belgrade had continued, Stukas had started to bomb troops and artillery positions on the northern Yugoslavian-Bulgarian border from midday, but no invasion by ground forces followed. Other aircraft flew reconnaissances and made attacks on strategic railways, bridges, airfields, troop concentrations etc throughout the country. From the Luftflotte 4 area and Fliegerführer Graz, harrassing attacks were made on Yugoslav defences on the Austrian and Western Hungarian borders, penetrating deep into Western Bosnia. At 0600 reconnaissance aircraft strafed Banja Luka airfield in Bosnia, 180 miles from any frontier, while at 0700 Bf109Es of 3/JG 27 attacked Potez 25s and hangars at Ljubljana airfield. Here the Messerschmitt of a young unknown, Obfhr Hans-Joachim Marseille, was hit in the fuselage by an AA shell, but returned to Graz without further trouble – he would soon become one of the Luftwaffe's most famous fighter pilots. Later in the day Velika Gorica airfield near Zagreb was attacked, two eskadrila of the 4 reconnaissance Grupa of IV Army being totally annihilated with the loss of 18 Breguet XIX/8s and some Potez 25s. VII Army's 6 Grupa at Cerklje and Brege, ncar Brezice, 22 miles north-west of Zagreb suffered a similar fate. Both attacks were carried out by II/StG 77 Ju87s escorted by Bf109s. It seems that on at least one occasion these were aircraft of JG77, which claimed eight aircraft destroyed on the ground (five by II Gruppe and three by

201

III Gruppe) during a midday raid; one Bf109E was shot down by AA, Oblt Heinz Deuschle returning to his unit on 9 April.

Throughout the day Luftwaffe aircraft attacked positions at the rear of IV and VII Yugoslav Armies, which were responsible for the defence of about 100 miles of border with Austria and Hungary, along the River Drava between Dravograd and Gyekenyes. Hurricanes and IK-2s of the 4th Puk were unable to hinder them as they bombed and strafed, since the JKRV fighters were based too far away at Bosanski Aleksandrovac, 150 miles from the area.

Apart from the ill-fated Dorniers, the Yugoslav bombers also played little part on this first day. In the 1st Puk, the 23 Blenheims of 61 Grupa were transferred from Bijeljina, 60 miles west of Belgrade, to Davidovac in the Morava valley, only 45 miles from the Bulgarian border. The Puk's other Grupa, No.62, was ordered to send out two pairs of bombers on armed reconnaissances of the Rumanian frontier during the afternoon, but nothing was found to attack.

Sergeant Murko (left) of 216 Eskadrila, 68 Grupa of the 8th Bomber Puk with his groundcrew in front of his Blenheim I. Murko was the first Yugoslav pilot to bomb targets in Austria on 6 April 1941, attacking Graz railway station. (Z Jerin)

The 8th Puk's Blenheims at Rovine, in the Banja Luka area of Western Bosnia, spent most of the day on the ground and were lucky not to be spotted by Luftwaffe reconnaissance aircraft. During the afternoon some aircraft from 68 Grupa's 216 Eskadrila were sent out to attack targets in Austria, bombing railway stations at Fürstenfeld and Graz, and airfields at Graz and Wiener Neustadt with 100kg bombs. One became lost, crashing into a mountain in south-east Austria. Two 4th Puk Hurricanes were sent as escort, but lost their charges in cloud, where one fighter pilot attempted to intercept some Bf109Es. Sgt Karel Murko was the first of the few pilots to attack targets in the Steyr area of Austria during the afternoon. Loaded with four bombs, they were ordered to bomb Graz station from 1000 feet. Reported Murko:

'Because of the murky weather we didn't fly at the prescribed height of 2,500 metres, but pressed down to the ground and followed some river courses and rail tracks, which led us directly to Graz. There we must climb to about 500 metres for better orientation and when we discovered the railway junction I put my Blenheim in a gentle dive. Three bombs went down amid the tracks and there were only one or two trains, but the fourth one was a direct hit on a large two-storey building, obviously some sort of magazine. We were convinced that no air raid warning was given before our bombs exploded, as we could see people quietly walking in the streets. There was no enemy reaction over the town, although I climbed in a large circle to some 700 metres to observe the damage. In the low flight home I emerged over the aerodrome of Talerhof near Leibnitz crowded with Messerschmitts and Stukas. Some Me109s scrambled after me, but only one was persistent enough to catch me when I was already over our own territory. After one short burst of his guns, this adversary also turned for home, and I returned safely to Rovine, where my mechanics found only two small holes in the tail surfaces. ...'

Fiat BR20M bomber of 48ª Squadriglia, 37° Gruppo, 18° Stormo BT in action over south-western Yugoslavia. (*N Malizia*)

The remaining Yugoslav Blenheims in the 11th Independent Grupa were retained for long range reconnaissance under the direct command of the commander of the JKRV, Brigade Gen Borivoje Mirkovic. From the large airfield at Veliki Radinci, 45 miles north-west of Belgrade, they had already despatched one pair of aircraft to attack Arad in the morning, and another pair to attack Temisoara airfield in Rumania, where the Stukas and Messerschmitts of Fliegerführer Arad were based. Without fighter cover, these were real suicide missions, and sure

203

Italian-based Cant Z.1007bis bombers were also making raids on Yugoslavia from the first day, including these Brindisi-based aircraft from 210ª Squadriglia, 50° Gruppo Autonomo BT. (*AMI via N Malizia*)

enough only one aircraft from the Temisoara raid returned two hours later, reporting a successful attack on the railway station and tracks. The other Blenheim of this pair and both those attacking Arad were shot down, one of the latter by Hpt Arnold Lignitz, Gruppenkommandeur of III/JG54, for his 20th victory.

Italian bombers pass over a Yugoslav Navy seaplane base, where two Dornier Wal flying-boats are seen on the water. (*via A Stamatopoulos*)

The third area of activity during the day was in the west, where from 0630 onwards reconnaissance aircraft of the Regia Aeronautica's 4ª Squadra Aerea appeared overhead, followed half an hour later by bombers and by units of Fliergerkorps X. At 0700, 15 Cant Z.1007bis raided Mostar, and five Fiat BR20s bombed Split, the permanent bases of the Naval Air Force's 2 Hidrokomanda and Skolaska eskadrila; the arsenal at Tivat and Zelenika in Boka Kotorska were also attacked. After a further 30 minutes 22 Luftwaffe bombers, covered by 15 fighters, attacked Rajlovac and Sarajevo airfields, dropping 88 250kg and 220 50kg bombs, while 26 more bombers attacked Mostar and four hit Boka Kotorska. Meanwhile Bf109Es of 7/JG26 strafed Podgorica airfield.

Third bomber type employed by the JKRV was the Savoia S.79. This aircraft of the 7th Bomber Puk was based in the Mostar region. (*Z Jerin*)

Apart from some AA guns, the sole defence of this large area lay in the hands of nine fighters forming the Independent Flight of the 2nd Fighter School – three Me109s and three Hurricanes at Kosor airfield in the Mostar area, and three old Avia BH33Es, two of which were on detachment at Podgorica. Both these were shot down during the attack by 7/JG 26, one over the airfield at 1205 by Oblt Joachim Müncheberg (34th victory) and one five minutes later during a violent dogfight over the mountains by Lt Klaus Mietusch (6th victory); these fighters were claimed by the German pilots as Furies, 1/Lt Milenko Milivojevic and F/Sgt Djordje Cvetkovic both being killed – the latter on his 29th birthday. Müncheberg then went on to claim a Breguet XIX destroyed on the ground.

Twice more during the day Fliegerkorps X bombed Podgorica, while Mostar suffered from more air raid warnings during the day than any other town in Yugoslavia – nine in all, although most were concentrated on the three airfields. The last attack included a strafe of Ortijes airfield by escorting Bf110s. The Savoia S.79s of the 7th Puk had been hitting back, initially in support of Yugoslav troops who went onto the offensive against Italian defences around the Drin valley area of the Albanian frontier, near Scutari. 66 Grupa, led by 4 Bombarderska Brigada Col Petar Vukcevic, attacked Taraboshit airfield near Scutari, together with military camps and bridges on the Drin and Buene rivers, returning without loss. Other S.79s of the 81 Independent Grupa at Mostar-Ortijes were also given similar targets, one eskadrila bombing Taraboshit airfield also. Ordered to go out again in the afternoon, these bombers were being prepared when the III/ZG 26 Bf110s swept in to strafe as mentioned above. Four of the Messerschmitts spotted the bombers, two of which were destroyed and three damaged. The remainder, four in number, were sent to attack a column heading up to Zara-Benkovac road.

81 Independent Grupa Savoia S.79 destroyed at Mostar-Ortijes airfield on 6 April, 1941 by strafing Messerschmitt Bf110s of III/ZG26. Italian officers are inspecting bombs which had been laid out ready to arm the aircraft, following the cessation of hostilities. (*Z Jerin*)

Meanwhile soon after midday 4ª Squadra Aerea had returned in force, ten Z.1007bis from the 260ª, 261ª and 263ª Squadriglia attacking Mostar where they came under interception by the Me109s and Hurricanes, which split them up into two formations. One Messerschmitt pilot, Sgt Grujic, shot down a 206ª Squadriglia Cant flown by Sottoten Giovanni Della Costa, while two more were damaged; the Italian gunners claimed two Messerschmitts shot down in return.

206

Subsequently Capt Stipcic in another of the Me109s claimed a Luftwaffe twin-engined aircraft shot down during the day; two of the Messerschmitts were damaged during these skirmishes, one of them probably by Ofw Richard Heller of III/ZG 26, who claimed a Yugoslav Me109 shot down south of Sarajevo during the afternoon for his 5th victory; a second was also claimed by this unit.

Yugoslav Hawker Hurricane I of the Fighter School Independent Fighter Eskadrila at Mostar-Kosor airfield. (*via A Stamatopoulos*)

Kotar was also attacked by nine Italian Ju87s of the 239ª Squadriglia, 97° Gruppo Ba'T during the afternoon, one of these being shot down by AA and two damaged. Their attack damaged a single Dornier Wal flyingboat of 21HE at Dobrota. Soon after came ten more high-flying Z.1007bis of 35° Stormo BT, which attempted without success to hit the Tivat arsenal; three were damaged by AA. Finally a lone reconnaissance S.79 appeared over Mostar, 1/Lt Fasovic in one of the Hurricanes gaining several hits on it before it escaped.

2ª Squadra Aerea units in Northern Italy which were due to attack targets in Slovenia, Croatia and the Northern Adriatic coastal area were prevented by bad weather which was spreading steadily from the west, although some small German formations did encroach on these areas during the day. Yugoslav Navy units on the coast had also been relatively inactive. During an attack on the 2 HK base at Divulje, a Rogozarski PVT-H training seaplane with a speed of less than 150 mph tried in vain to intercept the five 37° Gruppo BT BR20s, while 3 HK Do.22s and SIM XIVs covered the minelayer *Jastreb* as it laid a minefield before the harbour of Budva.

As daylight ended, all activity in the air came to a halt until about 2300, when a small force of German bombers appeared over Belgrade, dropping bombs on the fires that were still burning. Such intrusions continued until 0400, causing considerable panic amongst the already shocked inhabitants. During the day the city had suffered attack by 484 bombers and Stukas, which had dropped 360 tons of bombs. Most of the estimated 4000 people killed in Belgrade during the campaign died on this first day; more than half the number were never found, since during the occupation which followed, no attempt was made to remove the debris. The Luftwaffe had dropped all categories of bombs from small incendiaries to 1000kg landmines, carried by He111P-4s of II/KG 4. Seven hundred and fourteen buildings were totally destroyed, 1888 heavily damaged and 6615 damaged to a lesser extent – 47% of the total building stock in the city. Only a small proportion of these were military targets of any sort. Some air raid shelters had also been hit, including one in the Church of Alexander Nevsky, where 70 people had died, and another where up to 200 were believed to have lost their lives.

Throughout the country on this first day the JKRV had flown 474 sorties, 377 by fighters, 93 by bombers and four by reconnaissance aircraft, apart from the efforts of the army reconnaissance and naval units. Forty-seven fighters, 45 bombers and three reconnaissance aircraft had been destroyed or damaged, together with about 50 army reconnaissance BrXIXs and Po.25s.

One of 20 Fieseler Fi156 Storch light aircraft employed by the JKRV for liaison duties. (Z Jerin)

The focus of activity on the ground remained in the south on 7 April, where Fliegerkorps VIII directed most of its activity in support of the northernmost of the columns penetrating Macedonia. During the afternoon these troops would reach the Vardar river and enter Skoplje. The central column also reached the Vardar at Veles, while the southern thrust crossed the same river to the south and reached points on the Yugoslav-Greek border. Attacks were also made on the towns of Stip, Veles and Gradsko, and on the 64 Grupa airfields at Obilic and Stubol.

Not a Yugoslav fighter remained available to counter the omnipresence of the Luftwaffe, but the JKRV sought to send out the bombers of the 1st and 3rd Puks against the armoured columns throughout the day, some 60 sorties being made. First off at 0600 were five Do.17Ks which hit troops in the open at Slaviste, near Stracin, attacking with complete surprise and escaping unscathed. Trios of Blenheims from 201 Eskadrila of the 1st Puk followed at hourly intervals, the first returning unmolested, but thereafter the German Flak crews then began to get their eyes in. The last trio despatched by 61 Grupa returned well shot-about, while at 1500 62 Grupa lost the commander of 204 Eskadrila, Capt Ivancevic, when his Blenheim was shot down in flames. One more Blenheim from 61 Grupa and two from 62 Grupa were obliged to crash-land on return from sorties, while a badly wounded pilot of the latter unit damaged his aircraft in a force-landing. These losses were caused in no small extent by the worsening weather, which forced pilots of the later flights to launch their attacks at an altitude of only some 600 feet, where they were extremely vulnerable to the German fire.

Müncheberg   Geisshardt   Bob   Ubben

Lignitz   Omert   Heller   Mütherich

Baagoe   Ihlefeld   Huy   Rödel

Noteable Luftwaffe fighter pilots active over the Balkans during April and May 1941 (the number of victories claimed by each man are indicated in brackets: Oblt Joachim Müncheberg, 7/JG 26 (1); Lt Fritz Geisshardt, I(J)/LG 2 (6); Oblt Hans-Ekkehard Bob, 9/JG 54 (2); Oblt Kurt Ubben, 8/JG 77 (1); Oblt Arnold Lignitz, III/JG 54 (1); Lt Emil Omert, 8/JG 77 (3); Fw Richard Heller, III/ZG 26 (1); Oblt Hubert Mütherich, 5/JG 54 (2); Oblt Sophus Baagoe, 5/ZG 26 (1), who was killed on 14 May 1941; Hpt Herbert Ihlefeld, I(J)/LG 2 (1); Oblt Wolf-Dietrich Huy, III/JG 77, who undertook two successful fighter-bomber attacks on British ships; Oblt Gustav Rödel, II/JG 27 (6). (E Obermaier)

The Dorniers were more fortunate, eight more from 64 Grupa and four from 63 Grupa attacking columns between Stracin and Kriva Palanka during the morning with only a single bomber suffering slight damage. No fighters were met throughout the day, though during attacks on the 64 Grupa airfields these managed to destroy three more Do.17Ks on the ground. The last attack was made during the early evening by four 63 Grupa aircraft, which were now incorporated in 208 Eskadrila. Six 35 Grupa Furies took off from Bojnik at one point to try and intercept some German bombers, but four suffered gun jams, and none were able to catch the faster Luftwaffe aircraft.

Luftflotte 4 was also active, particularly the units of Fliegerführer Arad, which penetrated further south on this date, to attack airfields in Central Serbia in the general area of Belgrade. Ju87s and Bf110s failed to find any operational bases of the JKRV's main units, but did discover 201 Training Grupa's field at Lazarevac, south of the city. Here the 36 aircraft of 601 and 602 Eskadrila were strafed, 12 being destroyed in flames and 17 more badly damaged. At Smederevska Palanka most of the 18 Breguet XIXs of the VI Army's 7 VIGrupa were dealt with in similar fashion, as were 3 VIGrupa's aircraft attached to II Army at Staro Topolje, near Djakovo.

No adequate fighter opposition could be offered, as the surviving elements of the 6th Puk were engaged over the capital itself throughout the day. Luftwaffe tactics here proved very different on 7 April, no repetition of the mass attacks of the previous day being forthcoming. Instead throughout the morning and early afternoon small formations of three or four aircraft approached high above the clouds, dived through them to bomb and retreated at once. 32 and 51 Grupa sent up aircraft to intercept every intrusion, some pilots making up to eight scrambles during the day as a result. Several victories were claimed without loss, although some fighters suffered damage. One of these (an IK-Z flown by 2/Lt Milisav Semiz) was hit by return fire from three bombers and landed having been hit 56 times, 20 bullets having lodged in the engine and airscrew.

At about 1600 however, larger formations appeared, including 24 twin-engined bombers, 26 Ju87s and an escort of about 45 Bf109Es and Bf110s. One claim for a Bf110 shot down was made by an IK-Z pilot near Novi Sad, but the fiercest clash occurred when nine Me109s of 32 Grupa engaged the dive-bombers further west as these were attacking railway installations at Indjija, ten miles from Krusedol (Prnjavor), where the Yugoslav unit was based. Three bombers were claimed shot down, but Bf109Es from 4/JG 54 then dived on the Yugoslav Messerschmitts, eight of which were either shot down or severely damaged. Four claims were submitted by the pilots of 4/JG 54, two by Oblt Hans Philipp (his 24th and 25th victories), one by Ofw Max Stotz for his 16th, and one by an unidentified pilot. Other claims during the day included three more Me109s, three Hurricanes, two IK-Zs and a 'PZL' by Luftwaffe units.

Five Yugoslav pilots were actually killed:

Capt Miha Klavova (104 Eskadrila)   Sgt Vladimir Gorup (103 Eskadrila)
2/Lt Jovan Kapesic (103 Eskadrila)   Sgt Milivoje Boskovic (104 Eskadrila)
Wt Off Branislav Todorovic (103 Eskadrila)

Sgt Gorup was believed to have shot down a Bf109E before he fell. Additionally, Sgt Stojanovic was wounded, Sgt Stelcer baled out unhurt, and 2/Lt Miodrag Aleksic (142 Eskadrila) claimed a Bf109E shot down, but was hit by two more and force-landed some way from Prnjavor.

There is a strong possibility that the three dive-bombers claimed by the 32 Grupa pilots before the unit's demise, were Ju88s rather than Ju87s. Luftwaffe records indicate no losses of Ju87s over Belgrade on this date, but I/KG 51 did lose three Ju88As to fighters, including 9K+GL(Lt Hans-Jurgen Krüger), 9K+MK(Ofw Johann Gerritzen) and 9K+KH(Uffz Schmitt). Other losses on this date included a Do.17Z of 3/KG 2 over the capital (possibly the aircraft claimed as a Bf110), while a second aircraft from the Gruppe's 2 Staffel (U5+HR; Maj Dreyer, the Gruppenkommandeur) crashed near Novska, near Zagreb, cause unknown. Losses to other causes were high, a II/KG 51 Ju88A crash-landing at Recita in Rumania and requiring writing-off, while a second such bomber, this time from III/KG 51, was also destroyed in a crash-landing at Arad due to engine failure. Two of I/StG 77's Ju87s collided over the same airfield during the day with the loss of both aircraft and pilots, while a third overturned whilst landing. Further south at Sofia, II/ZG 26 recorded severe damage to one Bf110 during a crash-landing.

Since Prnjavor had been spotted by the Germans during the main afternoon engagement, the decision was swiftly taken to move all remaining airworthy JKRV fighters to Veliki Radinci, an airfield from which the Blenheims of 11 Independent Reconnaissance Grupa had been transferred to Majur, near Sabac, 22 miles to the south. That evening therefore four Me109s left Prnjavor, although one crashed while landing at Veliki Radinci due to the fatigue of the pilot, Capt Grozdanovic, who was gravely injured. Three IK-Zs and three of the last Me109s of 51 Grupa also moved to this airfield, the last five 32 Grupa Messerschmitts following next morning.

2nd Puk fighters were also active on 7 April, patrolling over Central Serbia in expectation of Luftwaffe attacks on factories in Kragujevac and Kraljevo which in the event never materialized. However, when at 1000 two pairs of 31 Grupa Me109s took off on one such patrol, one pair spotted two Hs126As east of the Morava river, almost at the same position as that shot down by Pajic on the previous day. Pilots Kodra and Crnjanski opened fire and hit the first Henschel at once and it went down to crash near the monastery of St Petka; the pilot, Josef Ricklin, and his observer were killed. Meanwhile the second Hs126A made good its escape unharmed.

In the north too, the Blenheims were out in some strength, 8th Puk aircraft leaving Rovine airfield in the early hours to attack the railway junction at Feldbach, and other targets. In bad weather the trio became lost, only one actually arriving over Austria where the crew bombed a bridge and road in Upper Steyr through an opening in the cloud. Finally emerging into clear sky over Wiener Neustadt, they were fired on by Flak, one shell severing a fuel line which caused an emergency landing, the crew becoming prisoners.

At 1000 both Grupa were ordered to attack railway stations and airfields in Hungary, 68 Grupa heading for Szeged with eight aircraft while six from 69

Grupa made for Pecs. At around noon Bf109Es of 5/JG 54 intercepted Blenheims near Pecs – apparently the 68 Grupa formation – and claimed six shot down, two by the Staffelkapitän, Oblt Hubert Mütherick (9th and 10th victories), one each by Lt Wolfgang Späte and Lt Josef Pöhs (8th), and two by unidentified pilots. Two more Blenheims were claimed in the Szeged area by Hungarian AA gunners. Five 68 Grupa Blenheims were shot down by fighters, all the crews being killed including the Grupa commander, Maj Lazo Donovic, the 215 Eskadrila commander, Capt Vladimir Jovicic, and the 216 Eskadrila commander Capt Sergije Vojinov, together with Lts Andrija Pozder and Radomir Lazarevic, and all the navigators and gunners. The survivors reported that the airfield they had sought to attack was empty, so they had dropped most of their bombs on the railway network. Three Bf109Es were believed to have been shot down in return, but only one of these claims was considered certain.

The three surviving aircraft made for base, but one landed at Novi Sad when it ran out of fuel, the other two then being fired at by 'friendly' AA. One was hit and force-landed nearby, so that only one returned to Rovine, its nose plexiglass completely shattered – it was the aircraft that had made the initial attack on Austrian soil on the previous day. Meanwhile the 69 Grupa formation had also suffered casualties – probably to the Hungarian AA – the unit commander, Maj Dobrosav Tesic being shot down and killed over Pecs, while three more Blenheims were hit and damaged. Most bombs had hit airfields in the area where units of the Hungarian Air Force was based, but damage had not been ascertained. While the unescorted Blenheims had been suffering such fearful depredations, the Hurricanes and IK-2s of the 4th Puk had again been flying patrols over the same general area without event, other than occasionally to chase a high-flying reconnaissance aircraft over Bosnia and Croatia.

The Hurricane I of the Independent Fighter Eskadrila crash-landed by Sgt Delic following combat in the Mostar area on 7 April, 1941. (Z Jerin)

Small formations of bombers from Fliegerkorps X attacked many targets in the west during the day, although without escort, III/ZG 26 returning to Sicily on this date, followed on 8 April by 7/JG 26. There was only one encounter in this part of Yugoslavia during the day, when soon after midday a small formation of Ju88s headed over Mostar towards Sarajevo. Capt Danilo Grbic and Sgt Delic of the Independent Fighter Training Flight gave chase in two Hurricanes, but were both hit by return fire. Sgt Delic managed to reach the airfield and crash-land despite the wounds he had suffered, but Capt Grbic continued to pursue the bombers northwards. Suddenly he was bounced by Bf109Es, apparently from the north, and was forced to bale out of his crippled Hurricane, suffering severe wounds; he subsequently died from loss of blood. It seems possible that his victor was Lt Hans Beisswenger of 6/JG 54, who claimed one such victory on this date.

Due to the poor weather, most Italian attacks were made against shipping targets, rather than inland, except on the Albanian frontier where units of Aeronautica Albania were active against Yugoslav troops who had advanced 30 miles into that country in places. In return 81 Grupa sent seven S.79s to attack Durazzo and Tirana during the morning. A further trio became lost in cloud soon after take off, and were subsequently shot-up by Yugoslavian AA defences at Boka Kotorska on the coast, one of the bombers actually being shot down. With the 7th Puk, 66 Grupa was grounded due to the condition of the airfield at Preljina, but 67 Grupa sent out several flights to attack targets at the front, one crew claiming to have shot down a Fiat fighter which attempted to attack them.

Little activity was undertaken by the army reconnaissance Grupas or the naval units, only Breguet XIXs of 4 VIGrupa making a few attacks on a bridge over the Drava at Gyekenyes. By evening on 7 April the JKRV disposed 83 fighters, 86 bombers and eight twin-engined reconnaissance aircraft; the air force had lost nearly 60% of its operational aircraft in 48 hours!

The weather deteriorated further the next day as the southernmost of the 12th Armee columns crossed the frontier into Greece and advanced on Thessalonika. Of greater immediate danger to the Yugoslavs was the route taken by the northern thrust, which now swung north from Skoplje through the Kacanik Gorge towards Kosovo Polje, and up a parallel valley north of Kumanovo towards Bujanovac and the Morava river valley. While climatic conditions all-but grounded Fliegerkorps VIII, desperate efforts were made by the JKRV to delay this new direction of attack which now threatened many of that force's own airfields.

All targets previously notified to 4th Bomber Brigade were cancelled and a maximum effort was ordered against the forces in the Kacanik Gorge by 1st Puk and 11 Independent Grupa Blenheims, 3rd Puk Do.17Ks and 7th Puk S.79s, joined by the Hurricanes of the 2nd Puk's 52 Grupa – a total strength of about 70 aircraft. In the event the bombers would be sent out in widely-spaced trios to attack the eight miles of closely-packed German convoys. Only the Savoia crews were fortunate to find gaps in the cloud, allowing them to bomb relatively unscathed from 3000 feet; all other units were forced down to the cloud base at 300–500 feet, where they were very vulnerable to light automatic Flak and even infantry small-arms fire.

The Blenheims of 62 Grupa encountered the severest Flak, the first trio being led in to attack by the Puk commander, Col Ferdo Gradisnik. Lt Branko Glumac, observer in the second aircraft, later reported:

'Col Gradisnik at the sight of numerous tanks on the Skoplje-Kumanovo road pressed his Blenheim even lower in the drizzle, which obscured the visibility to about 500 metres (1700 feet). I saw one of his bombs going down and exploding, but at practically the same moment violent flames erupted from the starboard wing fuel tank of his Blenheim. A few seconds later also from the port wing flames erupted and the Blenheim crash-landed besides the road. In the next second we were over it, but our gunner Zecevic saw the Blenheim explode.'

It was later discovered that the pilot, Sgt Zivan Jovanovic, and the Colonel had been killed, but that the gunner, Sgt Terzic, had got out with his clothes on fire, rolling in the wet grass at the feet of some astonished German soldiers as he sought to extinguish the flames. Even as the first Blenheim struck the ground, so too was the third hit and fell, though Lt Glumac considered that this might possibly have been shot down by an Hs 126 which he spotted in the valley nearby; this was not so in fact, both bombers having fallen to Flak.

The next two sections from 62 Grupa failed to find the target in clouds and did not bomb, but aircraft of 61 Grupa were more successful, encountering slightly improved weather which allowed them to attack and escape without severe damage. They were followed by a further four Blenheims and a single Hawker Hind biplane from 11 Independent Grupa, which attacked one of the columns north of Kumanovo. The Blenheim flown by Capt Zivomir Petrovic was shot down, all on board being killed, while a second Blenheim became lost and landed at 61 Grupa's airfield at Davidovac. The Hind crashed into Mount Vlasic in heavy cloud when some 20 miles from base, Lt Rastislav Pesic and his observer, Sgt Gardasevic, both being killed.

Three Do.17Ks of 64 Grupa's 210 Eskadrila then attacked, two being shot-up by small arms fire. As they headed back for base, Sgt Josip Telar's bomber was attacked and shot down by two Bf110s, only the pilot surviving to bale out. The Hurricanes then swept in through a patch of very bad weather to strafe, headed by aircraft of 163 Eskadrila led by Lt Boris Cijan; they were followed by Capt Ivo Ostric and his 164 Eskadrila, but one of these fighters was hit and crash-landed by the road; Lt Pantelije Grandic leapt out and managed to run to safety, escaping capture.

The raids failed signally to slow down the Germans, who were meeting only limited resistance on the ground. At last Fliegerkorps VIII managed to send out some Bf110s to strafe the JKRV airfields at Stubol and Obilic, where 10–12 aircraft (including some Do.17Ks) were destroyed on the ground. The only claim against the Germans occurred when an infantry detachment claimed a reconnaissance aircraft shot down near Kosovska Mitrovica, this aircraft reportedly falling into the River Ibar. This may have been an Hs126A (5F + DH) of 1(H)/14, flown by Uffz Waldo Thaisen, the only loss of the day recorded by the Fliegerkorps, which was reported missing over Kalindra, Greece. During the day further Wehrmacht forces moved due west from Skoplje towards Tetovo to cut off all forces in southern Macedonia from the rest of the country. In this area Breguet XIXs of 5 Reconnaissance Grupa bombed a bridge over the Vardar in an effort to delay this latest thrust, but without success. This unit's 3 Eskadrila now moved to an airfield at Florina in northern Greece to continue operations. Meanwhile during the early hours other divisions from 12th Armee based in northern Bulgaria had crossed the frontier, advancing towards Nis and central Serbia with the objective of an advance through the Morava valley to Belgrade.

Fliegerkorps VIII provided some support, although this was less effective than in the past due to the weather. Ju87s operated over one column closing on Pirot and Bela Palanka, bombing both towns. Forty bombers raided Nis, Leskovac and other more distant targets. In return a dozen 3rd Puk Do.17Ks attacked at low level, bombing troops advancing up the River Nisara in the Pirot area. Before the day was out the 3rd Puk's airfield at Stubol had been occupied by the Germans, and they were dangerously close to Obilic, the Dorniers flying out to Kraljevo and Gorobilje, near Uzicka Pozega, where 66 Grupa's S.79s were based. When the town of Bela Palanka, 45 miles east of Nis, was assaulted during the afternoon, the 35 Grupa Furies flew out to strafe before preparing to evacuate to Kraljevo next morning.

When the German attack had commenced, 3rd Puk crews had collected two new Do.17Ks from the factory at Kraljevo, but one further bomber had remained there. Now a test pilot, Nikolai Jankovski, took off in this aircraft to bomb targets in the Nis area. Here two Messerschmitts gave chase, but Jankovski escaped. Bombed-up again, he then flew south to attack the convoys in the Kacanik Gorge where he dropped 90 small bombs. Small arms fire and Flak hit the Dornier, Jankovski being hit and wounded in the leg, but he managed to get his riddled bomber back to Kraljevo and to land safely.

In the far north elements of 2nd Armee crossed the Drava river in several places and occupied Maribor in preparation for drives into Slovenia and Croatia. Ju87s and Bf109Es provided close support, while Luftflotte 4 medium bombers raided targets in the area. One of the latter was claimed shot down by Yugoslav infantry fire at Banja Luka, crashing on military barracks in the town. Hurricanes patrolled over Slovenia and north Croatia, clashing several times with German fighters, but without result. Other 4th Puk Hurricanes escorted three 8th Puk Blenheims to attack a target in southern Austria, but most of the latter unit's bombers were grounded, awaiting orders, which were subsequently cancelled, to attack Croats of the 108th Infantry Regiment who were in rebellion at Bjelovar.

The remaining fighters of the 6th Puk were now all at Veliki Radinci, reinforced by five Hurricanes of 105 Eskadrila, 33 Grupa, 4th Puk, led by Capt Radicevic. The Me109s of the 2nd Puk's 31 Grupa at Kragujevac were grounded because rain had caused the airfield to become too soft and waterlogged for operations. News of the German advance on Nis resulted in plans being drawn up to burn the aircraft if they remained stuck in the mud; the meteorological forecast was poor, and rumours abounded of an imminent paratroop assault.

In the west meanwhile, S.79s of 81 Independent Grupa raided Italian positions at Zara in preparation for an assault by the Yugoslav Jadranska Division. Regia Aeronautica units from Albania and the 2ª Squadra Aerea bombed Yugoslav troops still advancing towards Scutari, while the base of the 2nd and 3rd Torpedo Boat Divisions at Sibenik was also raided. Two Fiat fighters then strafed moored Dornier Wal flyingboats of 26 HE, 2HK at Jagrtovac, three of the four aircraft there being destroyed. Lt Ratko Jovanovic again took off in his old PVT-H trainer to try and intercept. Elsewhere along the coast Do.22s and Sim XIVs flew reconnaissances.

Rogozarski Sim XIV floatplanes of 1 HE, 1 Hidrogrupa at Boka Kotorska. (*Z Jerin*)

The 12th Armee column threatening southern Macedonia advanced through Tetovo and Prilep towards Bitolj on 9 April, this thrust and that on Nis receiving most Fliegerkorps VIII support on this date. During the morning snow fell in Serbia and Macedonia, the Blenheims of 61 Grupa at Davidovac being grounded by a ten inch fall, while the 31 Grupa Messerschmitts at Kragujevac remained immobilized, joined now by 52 Grupa's Hurricanes at Knic. All these airfields were now threatened, particularly when Nis fell during the late morning. The only aircraft that could be moved at once were the Furies at Bojnik and Kosancic, where all damaged or unserviceable aircraft were first burned. Breaking through dense fog, the biplanes were then fired on by Yugoslav troops in the west Morava valley, Lt Pisarev carrying out an emergency landing when his Fury was hit by small arms fire. Worse followed when a PVT trainer, flown by Capt Oto Sep, commander of 110 Eskadrila, was hit by AA and crashed, the pilot being mortally injured. Breguet XIXs from 5 Grupa's eskadrila at Florina bombed the column advancing on Bitolj, but one of these elderly aircraft was shot down, Capt Stokic, the eskadrila commander, and his gunner being killed, while the observer, Lt Krasojevic, was badly wounded.

3rd, 6th and 7th Puk units also failed to operate due to the weather, but in the north elements of Luftflotte 4, including the aircraft of Fliegerführer Graz and Arad, were out attacking troops and communications throughout the area. Airfields were also attacked, including Cerklje where 6 VI Grupa was based, and

A factory-fresh example of the Ikarus IK-2 fighter, eight of which were still in service with 107 Eskadrila of the 4th Fighter Puk in April 1941, seeking combat on the 9th against Luftwaffe fighters. (*Z Jerin*)

Rovine, home of the 8th Bomber Puk. At about 1400 two Staffeln of Bf109Es from III/JG 54 approached Rovine just as two IK-2s of 107 Eskadrila from Bosanski Aleksandrovac were landing. One of these, flown by Sgt Branko Jovanovic, engaged the Messerschmitts in a seven-minute dogfight during which the pilot employed every ounce of his skill and the obsolescent fighter's extreme manoeuvreability to escape damage. This allowed five 108 Eskadrila Hurricanes to arrive and join the combat, followed by others from 106 Eskadrila and more IK-2s also, although a third Staffel of Bf109Es also appeared on the scene.

In a melee ranging from Rovine to Bosanski Aleksandrovac, the Yugoslav pilots claimed one or two Messerschmitts shot down, but lost three of their own number. One victory was claimed by Sgt Zivorad Tomic, and it was believed that a second German fighter had probably fallen to Capt Dragisa Milijevic, commander of 106 Eskadrila, who was then himself shot down and killed. A second Hurricane was also lost, F/Sgt Mitic baling out burned and bruised, while an IK-2 was also shot down, Sgt Stikic being badly wounded. The Germans then, obviously low on fuel, broke off and headed away north. Three victories were indeed claimed by III/JG 54, but the claims were for one Hurricane by Lt Erwin Leykauf (his 6th victory) and two IK-2s, one by Oblt Hans-Ekkehard Bob, the 9 Staffel commander, the other by Oblt Gerhard Koall – one of two victories he

217

was to claim over Yugoslavia. Gefr Fabian of this unit was reported missing, returning a few days later – possibly shot down during this combat.

Although clearly recorded in Yugoslav accounts as occurring on 9 April, this engagement was noted by the Germans as having taken place on 7 April. This difference over what evidently was the same combat has not been resolved, but on the evidence available 9 April has been accepted here as the likely date. Towards evening rumours that the Germans were nearing Kragujevac panicked 31 Grupa personnel into burning all their mired-in Me109s there, only to discover subsequently that the enemy were still 40 miles distant!

In the south-west the Italians now counter-attacked in Albania, 81 Independent Grupa S.79s attacking the Zara area again at 1100, gaining hits on the naval arsenal and on the main ammunition dump with devastating results. 2ª Squadra Aerea aircraft attacked Sibenik and Divulje once more, nine fighters strafing the seaplane base at the latter location where they hit a number of worn-out Ikarus SM and 10 aircraft that had been moored as decoys. Five more Fiats attacked the 5 HE base at Tijesno on Murter Island, and here three Sim XIVs were destroyed, two more being damaged. 3 HK at Boka Kotorska was more active, and one pilot, Ivan Korosa in a Do.22 No.307 of 20 HE, spotted a convoy of 12 transports and eight destroyers crossing the Adriatic during the day. He attacked twice in the face of intense AA, but without success. Three more Do.22s raided Durazzo harbour, but were driven off by the weight of defensive fire. Over the Albanian fron a Ro.37bis reconnaissance aircraft of 114ª Squadriglia OA was shot down by AA in the Okhrid-Struga area, Mar Francesco Lojacono crashing in Italian-held territory.

Yugoslav sailors with a Do.22Kj (known as the Do. H by the Navy). No.302 was the first of the type to be delivered and differed from those that followed in points of detail – notably the four-bladed propeller and a retractable radiator. (Z Jerin)

The next day, 10 April saw 12th Armee elements enter Bitolj and the fighting in Yugoslavian Macedonia neared its end. In the north-west 14th Panzer Division occupied Zagreb and a new independent Croat State was proclaimed. With weather universally bad over the country as a whole, all ground units facing the Germans were in full retreat, and no requests were even made for JKRV support. Flights were undertaken to seek more secure airfields in the west, but all were hidden beneath cloud in the valleys of this mountainous area.

As aircraft from Luftflotte 4's airfields in Austria, Rumania and Hungary swept over the northern areas, the 6th Puk's fighters remained grounded at Veliki Radinci; only the Hurricanes of the attached 105 Eskadrila were able to get into the air and engage in a few skirmishes. In these circumstances, in common with much of the Yugoslav armed forces, the JKRV now began to disintegrate fast. At Knic rumours of a German armoured column approaching caused the Hurricanes of 52 Grupa to try and get off in dreadful weather. Five 164 Eskadrila fighters got into the air, but two collided almost immediately, Capt Ostric and Lt Mato Momcinovic both being killed. A third flew into a mountainside in fog a few minutes later, Veljko Vujicic suffering mortal injuries; the two survivors then gave up and returned to Knic. Here the aircraft of 163 Eskadrila were rendered unserviceable, but when news then came through that the Germans were in fact still far away, feverish attempts were made to repair the least damaged.

The situation at Davidovac was genuinely much more serious as German forces entered Paracin, only three miles away. Despite fog and soft snow all Blenheims on the airfield took off. Of ten 61 Grupa aircraft, one crashed at the end of the runway, although fortunately the crew survived unhurt. Less fortunate were the crew of the 11 Independent Grupa Blenheim which had landed at Davidovac two days earlier; as the pilot pulled it off the ground, the bomber stalled and all four men aboard were killed in the crash which followed. The nine remaining 61 Grupa machines meanwhile successfully reached Bjeljina 150 miles away, undertaking the whole flight at an altitude of only 80 feet; here they joined 62 Grupa.

The Furies of 35 Grupa were also on the move from Kraljevo to Preljina near Cacak. From here they were off again to strafe a column near the town of Cuprija in the Morava valley, flying on to land at Sarajevo, Breguet XIXs of 7 VIGrupa were also out attacking armoured columns in this area, Vlado Jankovic's aircraft being hit by Flak. Wounded, he made for Smederevska Palanka, but on landing found that his observer, 1/Lt Slobodan Mihic had also been hit, and had died in the air from loss of blood.

Already at this stage some aircrews were beginning to consider escape from their obviously-doomed country. From Uzicka Pozega, Sgt Petko Milojevic of 64 Grupa's 210 Eskadrila took off in his Do.17K to fly to the Soviet Union, but crashed in the Carpathian mountains while passing over Rumania, all three members of the crew being killed. A second crew had intended to follow, but flew instead to Mostar where they sought to escape aboard an 81 Independent Grupa S.79 which was to fly out next day. All was chaos with this latter unit, since an uprising of the Croat Ustashi had caused virtual disintegration, leaving crews completely demoralized. One S.79 flown by 1/Lt Branko Prodanovic of 211

Eskadrila did get off for Russia during 10 April, but this also crashed near Mamaia as it attempted the flight; there was only one survivor.

Further demoralization occurred next day when to the shock of the Dornier crews, the Commander-in-Chief removed Col Gorjup from his position at the head of the 3rd Bomber Puk, holding him responsible for the disastrous losses suffered by 63 Grupa on the ground on 6 April; his place was to be taken by Maj Dragomir Zikic. The one bomber unit which had suffered few casualties was the 7th Puk with its Savoias, but the crews of these were also at low ebb since they were unable to operate due to their airfields being covered with snow. When the Germans were rumoured to have reached Kraljevo on 11 April, the crews of 66 Grupa, who were nearest the approaching enemy, decided either to set fire to their bombers, or to fly them out. A few got to Mostar, their peacetime base, where the last 12 S.79s of the Puk were then assembled. In the situation prevailing, the crews soon decided to follow the example of those of 81 Grupa, and to escape either to the Soviet Union, or to Niksic in Montenegro.

Sabotage was now added to their problems, for several of the waiting S.79s were found to have had the tyres of their undercarriages slashed, and there were no spares available. Finally, eight more Savoias set off for Russia during 11 April, four from each unit, but only four got through; 1/Lt Milos Jelic with seven passengers landed at Kisinev, 1/Lt Hinko Soic and five others came down at Staraya Farmosika, 1/Lt Uros Djeric at Savat with four on board, and 1/Lt Zivko Milojkovic at Prvomayskaya. Of the others which set off, Capt Jefta Bosnjak, commander of 214 Eskadrila, heavily-laden with ten men, crashed in mountains 30 miles after take off, while Sgt Branko Tomic's similarly-laden aircraft, carrying the crew of Sgt Milojevic's 64 Grupa Dornier amongst others, crashed into Mount Igman in the Sarajevo area; in both aircraft all those aboard were killed. The third Savoia landed in Hungarian Transylvania, where the crew were interned; in late 1942 the Italians exchanged this aircraft for two Fiat CR 42s with the Hungarian Air Force. This latter force also gained a Do.17K which was obliged to land in their territory, and a Blenheim, flown in by a JKRV defector of Hungarian extraction; this was later employed as a liaison aircraft. The fate of the fourth missing Savoia is not known. Meanwhile however, four more 81 Independent Grupa S.79s and at least four from the 7th Puk reached Niksic safely, where the crews prepared to fly on to Greece.

To return to 10 April however, while the bomber force had begun its ultimate disintegration, the Blenheims of the 8th Puk and 11 Independent Grupa had remained at Rovine and Majur, grounded by the weather. The units of the Naval Aviation were also beginning to fall apart, at least insofar as the 2nd Hidroplanska Komanda was concerned. Some of this unit's pilots decided to fly to Boka Kotorska to join 3 HK, which was still in good shape, and during the day two of 5 HE's damaged Sim XIVs were repaired and flown up to be incorporated in 1 HE. A Do.22 from another of 3 HK's units, 20 HE, made a spirited attack on an Italian tanker near Bari, claiming a near-miss which it was believed had caused some damage. The only other achievement of the day was recorded by fighters from the 4th Puk, this unit's Hurricanes claiming a single Messerschmitt shot down when chasing a number of reconnaissance aircraft over

Bosnia. The unit was similarly-engaged next day, this time claiming a Bf110 shot down over Nova Gradiska. During 11 April, more of 2 HK's aircraft reached Boka Kotorska, three Do.22s of 25 HE and a Wal flyingboat (No 258) from 26 HE arriving from Zlarin to be incorporated into 20 and 21 HEs.

The Navy's Dornier Do.22Kjs remained active until late in the fighting. (*Z Jerin*)

Weather had cleared somewhat in the west on this day, though it remained poor in the east where Fliegerkorps VIII continued to give support to 12th Armee units. In all sectors the Wehrmacht was punching deep into the hinterland, and on this date a bridgehead was gained over the Sava river at Sabac in Serbia. In the north-west and in Bosnia Yugoslav forces were in full retreat, Luftwaffe aircraft flying overhead to reconnoitre and attack unscathed. Nine Ju87s from II/StG 77 raided three of the remaining airfields at Banja Luka, Bihac and Prijedor. Small formations also appeared over the capital for the first time in three days. They met no interception, the 6th Puk not even being advised of the raids. Few orders to operate were received by the JKRV, and throughout the day only 31 sorties were made by fighters and 14 by bombers as most remaining units prepared to withdraw deep into the country.

Bjeljina had become the favoured haven, aircraft flying in all day from Srem, Majur, Klemak, and even Topolje, from which base the Breguets of 3 VIGrupa arrived. They were not secure here however, for the Luftwaffe now launched attacks on airfields in the north-east, Bf110s destroying a few 1 VIGrupa Breguets at Novi Sad, while at 1530 two Schwarme of these Zerstörer swept in below cloud over Bjeljina itself, destroying a 7th Puk S.79, two Blenheims, a few Breguets and some Bücker Jungmanns. On the River Danube the 1st and 2nd Squadrons of river monitors, which had been operating near the Hungarian border, now began withdrawing towards Novi Sad, coming under repeated attack by Stukas, while in the south-west the Italian 2nd and 9th Armies in Albania attacked Yugoslav troops near Scutari, supported by fighters. Near Sibenik three Italian Ju87s attacked 2nd Division torpedo boats, the crews claiming to have hit two of the attackers with return fire. These would seem to have been aircraft of 238ᵃ Squadriglia, 101° Gruppo BaᵀT; the Regia Aeronautica recorded on 12 April that one of these aircraft was shot down by AA and a second was forced to ditch in the Adriatic, Ten Carlo Bongiovanni and his gunner being lost in the former aircraft – it seems likely that these losses actually occurred the day before.

With the Yugoslavs now 'in extremis', Hungarian forces joined the attack, crossing the border in several places in the northern sector. Junkers Ju86 and Caproni Ca135bis twin-engined bombers of the 4th and 3rd Regiments respectively, were despatched to bomb Novi Sad, but were recalled when it was learned that the Luftwaffe had already attacked this airfield. Instead they bombed frontier forts, while Heinkel He170A aircraft from the 5th Reconnaissance Regiment undertook reconnaissance sorties. Fiat biplane fighters from the 1st and 2nd Regiments were also committed to the venture, but in the event were called on only to make additional reconnaissance sorties. During the evening a battalion of 120 Hungarian paratroops had been ordered to secure bridges over a canal joining the rivers Tisa and Danube in the Srbobran and Vrbas area. Four Savoia S.75 transports took off, each carrying 30 men, but one crashed as it departed Veszprem, 23 of those aboard being killed. The mission was then postponed, but was later sent off after darkness had fallen. In bad weather the troops were dropped 15–20 miles short of their objective and were unable to complete their task.

The weather of 12 April was much as it had been on the previous day; indeed in the east Fliegerkorps VIII was grounded by the conditions, and failed to operate at all. To the north and west Fliegerführer Arad was particularly active over Belgrade and Sarajevo, and over the remaining airfields at Bjeljina, Sokolac, Mostar and Banja Luka. This command would despatch 64 bombing and 28 dive-bombing sorties during the day, backed up by 50 Zerstörer and 23 fighter flights. The JKRV at the start of the day still possessed 41 fighters, 37 bombers and nine long-range reconnaissance Blenheims, but once again few sorties were undertaken – 14 by fighters, 11 by bombers and seven by the reconnaissance unit – and the strength available was on the point of further significant reduction.

At Veliki Radinci, 6th Puk had suffered the loss of two of its remaining Me109s during a strafing attack by Luftwaffe fighters on 11 April. Now early the next day the unit's ground crews burned the last 11 aircraft – eight Me109s and three IK-Zs, together with two or three Hurricanes of 105 Eskadrila. Two or three more of the latter unit's Hurricanes flew over to Bjeljina, and one more reached Sarajevo with a few 6th Puk trainers – mainly Jungmanns. At around the same time 11 Independent Grupa burned two unserviceable Blenheims at Majur, the other seven aircraft flying to Bjeljina also.

No sooner had these moves been completed then at 0730 three Staffeln of Bf110s swept in low over Bjeljina, undertaking three strafing passes. It proved to be one of the most effective attacks of the campaign. About ten 1st Puk Blenheims and the seven 11 Grupa aircraft were destroyed, as were the 105 Eskadrila Hurricanes, the Breguet xIXs of 1 and 3 VIGrupas, and a considerable number of trainers. When the Zerstörer departed, Bjeljina had just two 1st Puk Blenheims, one Hurricane, a few Bücker trainers and some other biplane trainers left flyable. The two Blenheims were at once ordered off to make good their escape, but one was then shot down over Bosnia by Yugoslav AA, and the other was destroyed on the ground by strafing Italian fighters as soon as it landed at Niksic. The JKRV was down to five or six Blenheims still airworthy, all of the 8th Puk on the soft airfield at Rovine.

At Knic meanwhile the last two Hurricanes of the 2nd Puk's 163 Eskadrila took off to escape approaching German vehicles, flying to Zemun. Here 1/Lt Boris Cijan went in and landed but was at once taken prisoner by German civilians. Aware that all was not well, the pilot of the second Hurricane, the unit commander, Capt Milos Bajagic, broke off his landing run and headed for Bjeljina. Before he could reach this destination however, his fuel ran out and he attempted to crash-land near Valjevo, 40 miles short of the airfield; he was mortally wounded in the crash, which destroyed his aircraft.

Still the least hard-hit of the fighter units was the 4th Puk, which still had airworthy five or six Hurricanes and four or five IK-2s. The unit continued to chase reconnaissance aircraft during the day, but all escaped, except one Ju88 of II/KG 51 (9K+LP, flown by Oblt Helmut Westen) which was shot down by a Hurricane pilot in the Banja Luka area (Luftwaffe records indicate this loss as occurring on 11 April, together with the following combat). Other bombers from this unit attacked Mostar airfield where they were intercepted by one of the last two fighters available to the Independent Fighter Eskadrila – a Hurricane and an Me109, both of which were in the air patrolling to the north and west of the city. Franjo Godec in the Hurricane attacked Fw Gügel's Ju88, using up all his ammunition, but his fighter was hit by fire from the rear gunner, and he baled out at 10 000 feet, suffering a broken leg. The Me109 failed to make contact, and would be destroyed on the ground by strafing fighters next day.

There were still 10–11 Do.17Ks of 64 Grupa serviceable at Gorobilje, these taking off during the day to attack columns in the Morava valley, led by Maj Branko Fanedl. Spotting an important undamaged bridge over the Morava at Cuprija, he personally attacked this, gaining two direct hits with 100kg bombs, which nonetheless failed to demolish the target. His bomber was then hit by Flak and crashed ten miles to the north, all on board being killed. One more Dornier was damaged, but got back to base. The remaining eight serviceable aircraft left late for Butmir, near Sarajevo.

Early in the morning the Stukas of Fliegerführer Arad had again gone out looking for the Yugoslav monitors on the Danube, finding these at 0730 at Ciba, 20 miles from Novi Sad. Even as the attack on Bjeljina was underway by the Bf110s, the Ju87s dived on these vessels again, concentrating their attack on the 1st Squadron's *Drava*. This vessel had shelled the Hungarian frontier airfield at Mohacz on 6 April, and again two days later. Since then she had evaded repeated Stuka attacks, but now nine of the dive-bombers gained hits on her. These generally proved quite ineffective against the foot thick deck armour, but by chance one went straight down the funnel and exploded in the engine room. Fifty-four members of the crew were killed, only 13 escaping from their stricken vessel. During the attack gunners on the monitors claimed three Ju87s shot down.

In the course of the night of 12/13 April German forces entered Belgrade, while next morning further crossings were made of the Sava river, the advance progressing into Bosnia. The Yugoslav High Command was forced to admit that there was now no more fighting in Macedonia and Slovenia, and that the Wehrmacht had advanced deep into Croatia. An urgent appeal to the British Foreign Minister seeking an answer to a request made on 6 April for massive military aid, elicited the reply that none could presently be given. A Greek representative also arrived to advise of the very serious situation which had now developed in that country, as will be recounted later in this chapter. While this envoy was flown back to his own country from Niksic by Maj Dusan Milojevic, commander of 209 Eskadrila, in a Do.17K, Gen Danilo Kalafatovic was ordered to seek a cease-fire with the Germans.

Luftwaffe bombers were very active during the day, attacking troop concentrations and airfields, while KG 51 Ju88s attacked the health resort of Ilidza on specific orders from Adolf Hitler, since he had been advised that the Yugoslav government had taken refuge in hotels there. Few sorties were flown by the JKRV's remaining aircraft – eight fighter and four bomber sorties only. All the former were undertaken by the 4th Puk, one Hurricane pilot claiming a Bf110 shot down north of Banja Luka, while another Hurricane was destroyed during the day, the pilot, Voja Grbic, being badly wounded.

Around noon the weather again deteriorated as the evacuation of Butmir was being prepared. At this the commander of the 2nd Air Brigade ordered all remaining aircraft of the 4th and 8th Puks to be destroyed and all personnel to withdraw by road to Sarajevo. In the latter area there were already 15 000 airmen who it was planned to employ as infantry as the Germans approached from three directions. At the last moment the order was cancelled, and all surviving aircraft at Rajlovac and Butmir were flown to Niksic. The Furies of 35 Grupa also made for this base, but on the way met 12 Italian fighters. Details of this engagement are not available, but apparently losses were suffered on both sides.

The Regia Aeronautica was quite active at this time, and it was reported that Italian fighters had again strafed the Yugoslavian floatplane base at Trogir on 12 April, claiming six more aircraft destroyed here. This is not recorded by the Yugoslavs, but on 13 April it was noted that Divulje was attacked by strafing fighters, one floatplane being destroyed here, while the SHE Training Eskadrila's

35 Grupa Fury, No.53, lined up with a Rogozarski Fizir and a PVT, both trainers, together with other aircraft at the cessation of hostilities. (*via A Stamatopoulos*)

base near Trogir was also attacked. These attacks were probably those noted by the Italians. Of more import, seven Ju87s of 208ª Squadriglia, 101° Gruppo Ba'T, accompanied by CR42s of 160° Gruppo Aut CT and Macchi C.200s of 150° Gruppo Aut CT, attacked Mostar's airfields. Over the target, where two hangars were hit during the raid, Magg Giuseppe Donadio's Ju87 was hit and the Gruppo commander force-landed. He and his gunner were captured and rather roughly handled by some Yugoslav soldiers before being imprisoned with some Luftwaffe Stuka pilots; they would be liberated a few days later. Meanwhile the escorting fighters strafed, the CR42 pilots claiming 11 aircraft destroyed and the Macchi pilots 22 more.

Yugoslav records indicate that the latter fighters destroyed all the remaining S.79s which had been abandoned after their tyres had been slashed, and many other aircraft, including the Independent Fighter Eskadrila's last Me109. Italian aircraft were also active over Albania, bombing and strafing Yugoslav forces who still retained the initiative here, and were unaware of the disasters which had befallen their comrades everywhere else. Indeed they would not be advised of this until some days after the fighting with the Germans had ended.

Next day – 14 April – 15 German bombers attacked Mostar-Ortijes airfield as a follow-up to the Italian attack. When the Italians subsequently occupied the city they counted more than 100 aircraft destroyed or badly damaged on the airfields there. The Luftwaffe also launched a daring coup at Bjeljina. Here a reconnaissance Bf110 from Fliegerführer Arad passed over the airfield, followed by 11 Ju87s, 23 Bf110s and 18 Bf109Es. While the Stukas and Zerstörer attacked and pinned down the defence, 17 troop-carrying Ju52/3m transports swept in to land, the soldiers leaping out and swiftly overwhelming the defenders to take possession of the airfield; they captured 210 of the defenders at a cost of three dead and four wounded.

During the day Gen Mirkovic, the Commander-in-Chief, handed over control of the remaining operational elements of the JKRV to Col Petar Vukcevic, commander of 4th Bomber Brigade. The latter had his surviving aircraft concentrated at three locations; at Mostar were about 100 aircraft, nearly all of which were damaged; at Trebinje a quantity of trainers were assembled, whilst at Niksic were all types including eight Do.17Ks, seven or eight S.79s, at least seven Furies, one Hurricane, three Lockheed 10A Electras, some Caproni Ca310s, a few Bf108s, some Bücker Jungmanns and many other types, about 60 Breguet XIXs and Potez 25s amongst them – approximately 130 aircraft altogether at the airfield here (Kapino Polje). There were also 30–40 000 airmen assembled around these bases.

Damaged Bücker Bu131 Jungmann at Mostar. (*via A Stamatopoulos*)

Italian troops examine a Bücker Bu131 at Mostar. (*via A Stamatopoulos*)

War booty from Yugoslavia for the Italians. In the foreground are two Rogozarski Fizir trainers, while in the background are a number of Bücker Bu131 Jungmanns, already repainted in Italian national marking for service with Regia Aeronautica training units. (*A Stamatopoulos*)

The government now left Pale, near Sarajevo, for Niksic from where they were to be evacuated. Late in the afternoon two RAF Sunderland flyingboats arrived at Boka Kotorska to take out diplomats and British personnel. Meanwhile King Peter also arrived in Niksic just as four Italian S.79s were bombing the town. An hour later he left in a 7th Puk S.79 flown by Maj Dusan Sofilj, commander of 66 Grupa, making for Greece. Fired on by AA along the Adriatic coast, the crew shot off flares, following which RAF fighters arrived to escort the Savoia and an accompanying Do.17K into Paramythia. Its arrival will be detailed later.

Italian aircraft remained active, Ju87s, BR 20s and S.79s attacking along the Albanian frontier; one Ju87 of 101° Gruppo Ba'T was hit and force-landed and two more were damaged, all by AA, while attacking a bridge at Podgorica. Italian fighters claimed one Yugoslav bomber shot down, but no details of such an engagement have been discovered, unless the aircraft was in fact one of the surviving Hurricanes, of which more later. The attacks on bridges at Podgorica and Dolojani were repeated next day, and again the Italian Stukas suffered to the effective Yugoslav AA batteries here, one 238[a] Squadriglia Ju87 being shot down and a second damaged.

Finding no more resistance on 15 April, the Germans pushed on through Bosnia to enter Sarajevo, while most Luftwaffe activity was directed against ports in the southern coastal areas to prevent withdrawals, or any British attempt at reinforcement. German aircraft joined Italian bombers in raiding shipping in Boka Kotorska and Dubrovnik, whilst an Italian motorized column now advanced up the Dalmatian coast to occupy Split and threaten Mostar. This city was reached on 16 April, but meantime the German advance had slowed everywhere in anticipation of imminent unconditional surrender. On 15 April, the Yugoslav Commander-in-Chief ordered no further firing on Axis aircraft, while at noon on this day the evacuation commenced, an 'air bridge' to northern Greece being established which was to be maintained for two days.

The Do.17Ks and S.79s undertook most of the flights, joined by the five remaining Lockheed 10As (two had been shot down, one in Greece on 7 April, and one near Belgrade on an unrecorded date). Each aircraft made its sorties loaded not only with evacuees, but also with 50kg of gold bars from the State Treasury. Two or three of these aircraft were destroyed in landing accidents in Greece, but most reached either Paramythia or Yanina. Many of the smaller training and liaison types also reached Paramythia including Br XIXs, Po.25s, a Bf108 and a Sim X. They were joined here by the remaining Br XIXs of 5 VIGrupa from Florina, which had lost several of its aircraft during a strafe on this Greek airfield by German fighters.

One of the S.79s which did not make it was carrying Gen Mirkovic to Greece on 16 April when it was fired on by Greek AA near Preveza, and was hit. The aircraft crashed, the fuselage breaking into two parts, and Mirkovic was badly injured, a government minister who was travelling with him losing his life. Vojislav Rakic tried in vain to reach Greece in the sole surviving Hurricane, but was forced by bad weather to return to Niksic, where the fighter was abandoned. On an earlier date – believed to be 15 April, but possibly one day earlier – it had been engaged in a clash with Italian fighters and had been hit 37 times, but was still flyable. While the 'air bridge' aircraft escaped interception throughout the three days of the evacuation, not all aircraft were so fortunate. During 16 April Macchi C.200s of 150° Gruppo scrambled from Valona to intercept aircraft identified as 'Yugoslav Blenheims', two of these being claimed shot down and a third probably so between Cap Linguetta and Saseno. There is little doubt that these were the very similar-looking Caproni Ca.310s of 603 Training Eskadrila attempting to escape to Greece via Corfu, at least one of these aircraft being lost in such circumstances during the day, all six people aboard being killed in the crash.

The surrender was signed on 17 April, but while all flights were supposed to cease at once, still some aircraft continued to leave the country, the last off at 1600 being a 209 Eskadrila Do.17K flown by Maj Milojevic, who had already undertaken two round trips during the two preceding days. His aircraft would later be one of those to reach Egypt and join the RAF. Milojevic himself would be killed on 19 December, 1943 when flying in a B-24 Liberator bomber of the US 15th Air Force during a raid on Augsburg.

In their brief fight, the JKRV had suffered the loss of 49 aircraft to Axis fighters and Flak, with many more damaged beyond repair; another six had been shot down by Yugoslav AA defences in error. These losses had cost the lives of 27 fighter pilots and 76 bomber aircrew. Eighty-five more aircraft had been destroyed on the ground by air attack, while many others had been destroyed or disabled by their own crews, or had crashed during operations, or in evacuation flights. Between 40 and 50 aircraft reached Greece, the fates of which will be recorded later; at least two Hurricanes, two Furies, one Do.17K and one S.79 were captured intact by the invading forces, as were a number of trainers and 28 various floatplanes of the Naval Aviation. Amongst naval vessels captured was the floatplane tender *Zmaj*, capable of carrying ten aircraft, which was to become the German-manned minelayer *Drache*. The surrender also resulted in 375 000

Yugoslav troops becoming prisoners of the Germans, with 30 000 more in Italian hands. The only items not to end up in hostile hands were ten Curtiss P-40B Tomahawk fighters from the United States, earmarked for delivery in May and diverted instead to the RAF.

While the surviving aircraft of the JKRV and Army Aviation made their way to freedom further south, so too had a number of the operational types of the Naval units. On 13 April a further three Do.22s from 25 HE of the 2 HK at Zlarin had flown to Boka Kotorska for incorporation in 3 HK's 20 HE. When the news of the approaching cease-fire became known to the crews of this Komanda on 15 April, most determined to escape. Early the next day therefore, seven Do.22s from 20 and 25 HE left Orahovac, five of them reaching Corfu at 0700. One returned early to base, while a second suffered engine trouble and was then hit by AA and landed at Santa Quaranta, Albania. The crew undertook repairs offshore, and remained uninterfered with; the aircraft took off again, reaching Corfu two hours later.

At 1400 three more Do.22s took off, two of which reached Corfu, although the third became lost and returned to Orahovac. Two Sim XIVs of 1 HE then set out, one reaching Corfu, but one suffering damage from AA fire from the Albanian mainland. This aircraft came down on the sea, but was taken in tow by a Greek fishing boat, which put into Pakios. The floatplane was found not to be airworthy however, and was abandoned. A third Sim XIV and the sole He 8 of 11 HE then followed, but the Sim caught fire in the air and had to alight on the sea. The elderly Heinkel (No. 192) returned to base to raise the alarm, and the crew of the stricken aircraft were subsequently rescued, although all suffered burns. Next day eight of the Do.22s and the one surviving Sim XIV reached Patras, where in the afternoon to the surprise of all, the He 8 also arrived. It had set out again in the company of another Sim XIV, but this too had been forced to turn back. During the evening the ten escapee floatplanes flew on together to Salamis, and from there to Suda Bay, Crete. The campaign in Yugoslavia was at an end.

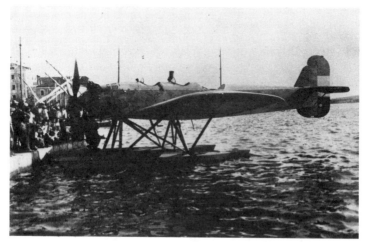

The sole Heinkel He8, No.192, of 11 HE which escaped with other Naval floatplanes to Greece, and then Crete. (*Z Jerin*)

Greece – The First Round

While the Yugoslavs were staggering under the initial German blows on 6 April, the first moves against Greece were also underway. There had at least been a declaration of war, the German Ambassador in Athens, Prinz Erbach-Schönberg presenting an appropriate note to the Hellenic government at 0530 that morning, at which time the first troops crossed the Bulgarian borders to begin the assault on Salonika and north-east Greece generally.

Plt off Bill Winsland of 33 Squadron, seen in the North African Desert later in 1941. (*DSF Winsland*)

As German forces streamed through the Rupel Pass, the Royal Air Force waited tensely for news. Plt Off Winsland of 33 Squadron at Larissa later recorded:
'We heard the news before dawn, got up, washed in freezing water and dressed. Everyone was tense; our feelings and thoughts were confused – what was going to happen now? Our army was on the retreat in Egypt; the Greeks were only just managing to hold the Italians back in Albania; had we sufficient British troops to hold the Germans in Greece? What was going to happen in the air? While we had sufficient to cope with the Italians, surely we were going to be hopelessly outnumbered by the Germans? For weeks past we had heard of colossal German air forces forming up in Bulgaria. What were we in for? Little did we know! In the afternoon (having been on instant readiness all morning, with all available Hurricanes parked at the end of the runway, facing into wind, ready for take off) all available Hurricanes (12) took off for an offensive patrol over Bulgaria. I had the good fortune to be flying next to Sqn Ldr Pattle. Suddenly we spotted eight Me109s and dived to attack. This was my first really good look at a Hun from close quarters. I saw the CO beside me shoot down two of them in a few seconds.

What a sight. I shall never forget it. What shooting too. A two second burst from his eight guns at the first enemy machine caused a large piece to break off in mid air, while the machine turned over vertically onto one wingtip as the pilot baled out – his parachute opened while his feet were still in the cockpit but he got clear in spite of the chute opening so soon. A similar fate awaited the second enemy machine which went spiralling down in flames. I did not have time to see what happened to its pilot.'

One of the first RAF pilots to achieve success against the Luftwaffe over Greece was 33 Squadron's F/Sgt Len Cottingham.

The Bf109Es were aircraft of 8/JG 27, led on patrol over the Rupel Pass area by Oblt Arno Becker; Becker was one of those shot down and killed, his aircraft – Black 2 – crashing in flames. He was possibly Sqn Ldr Pattle's second victim; the first was undoubtedly Lt Klaus Faber, who baled out to become a prisoner. F/Sgt Len Cottingham claimed a third Bf109 shot down, from which he saw the pilot bale out. As the German pilot floated down, another Messerschmitt circled round to give protection, and Cottingham promptly attacked this aircraft. It would seem that this was the fighter under attack by Winsland, who added:
'While all this was in full swing and machines were twisting and turning in all directions I found myself directly on the tail of another Hun at whom I let off burst after burst, but either he was made of cast iron or possibly my shooting wasn't so hot! I fear it was the latter as I have had cause to discover several times since. However, I do know the cause – excitement – which is something. I start firing with the centre of the gunsight dead on target, then find myself a few seconds later aiming purely by my tracer – looking round the edge of the sight instead of through it! On this occasion the enemy plane merely "vibrated" all

over and started a diving turn to the left. I continued to chase it but still could not get it down. Luckily another Hurricane (F/Sgt Cottingham) suddenly came diving at it as well as myself and at last the enemy "bought his packet".'

The two pilots claimed a half share each, whilst Flg Off Peter Wickham claimed one more shot down out of a trio he engaged. Apart from the loss of Becker and Faber, Ofw Gerhard Fromming was wounded and crash-landed his badly damaged 'Black 8', while a fourth pilot baled out of 'Black 6' and returned to his unit on foot, unharmed.

Meanwhile further south Flg Off Dowding of 80 Squadron had been scrambled at 1500 as a reconnaissance Ju88D from 2(F)/123 (4U + EK) approached Athens. Sighting the intruder, he chased it out over the Gulf of Corinth, exchanging fire with the gunners. The Hurricane received a few minor hits before he delivered the mortal blow, the German machine falling into the sea off Patras, with the loss of Uffz Fritz Dreyer and two of his crew. A Blenheim was sent out by 113 Squadron on a reconnaissance to Zante Island at 1515 – possibly to look for the crew of the downed Junkers.

The Greek air force was also active during the day. The PZLs of 22 Mira and the few serviceable Bloch 151s of 24 Mira now moved to Kalambaka/Vassiliki airfield, where they were soon to be joined by the Gladiators of 21 Mira. During the day Capt Andoniou, commander of 22 Mira, intercepted a reconnaissance aircraft thought to be Bulgarian, over Kilkis, 20 miles north of Salonika, and claimed this shot down. It seems much more likely that this was one of the Hs 126s reported lost operating in support of 12th Armee. During another sortie 1/Lt P Ikonomopoulos, flying one of the Bloch 151s, claimed a reconnaissance Do.17 shot down over the estuary of the River Strymon – probably one of the aircraft recorded as missing by Fliegerkorps VIII, and almost certainly from 2(F)/11.

As night fell both sides' air forces were active against communications. Six Wellingtons of 37 Squadron raided an ammunition train and various installations in Bulgaria at Sofia, Gorna Djunmaya and Simitly, while Blenheims from 84 Squadron attacked a railway station 50 miles further south, and others from 113 Squadron raided Petrich. Two of the latter, L9338 and T2168, crash-landed on return, while one Wellington was damaged by Flak.

The Luftwaffe activity in the opposite direction achieved quite extraordinary success out of all proportion to the effort expended. As evening fell a force of about 20 Ju88s from III/KG 30 in Sicily took off to attack the major Greek supply port of Piraeus which was heavily congested with merchant vessels, including three ships loaded with ammunition and explosives, amongst other stores. The German intention was to make a low level combined bombing and mining attack. They were followed some time later by 11 He 111s from 2/KG 4 led by Hpt Kühl, which were to mine the bay outside the port. 7 Staffel of KG 30, led by Hpt Hajo Herrmann, was flying the low position as the Ju88s approached their target. Those aircraft flying higher carried mines only, but Herrmann's flight were more heavily laden with both mines and bombs. Weather at higher levels was atrocious, and several of the other crews were forced to jettison their mines

232

and return early. 7 Staffel pressed on however, Herrmann and his crew marking the route with flares.

In Piraeus at 2035 the air raid alarm was sounded – not for the first time that evening – and within half an hour Herrmann's Staffel swooped on the harbour, approaching from the direction of Corinth. Diving from 10 000 feet to 3000 feet, he concentrated on a large freighter by the quayside which was accurately hit. Over the next two hours bombers continued to appear overhead and many ships sustained hits, several quayside buildings also being destroyed. Fires raged and at the height of the attack the 7529 ton *Clan Fraser*, which had been partially unloaded, but still had 250 tons of TNT aboard, was hit three times, some of her crew being killed. Other bombs fell alongside the burning freighter, destroying buildings, stores and equipment, including a number of crated Hurricane fighters, the blast from which lifted the ship out of the water and snapped its mooring lines. This was probably the explosion reported by Herrmann and his crew, the shockwave from which apparently hurled their Ju88 around like a leaf. By now one of the other explosive-carrying ships, the 7100 ton *City of Roubaix* was also on fire.

At about this time the British Naval Attache (Athens), Rear-Admiral C E Turle, arrived on the scene and immediately ordered that tugs should tow the blazing ships from the harbour. He was however overruled by the port authorities who feared that, as the harbour had been mined, a sunken ship might block the channel and deny any shipping movements. Apart from a few large fires the situation appeared to be almost under control, although there was a horrified awareness of the danger of explosion posed by *Clan Fraser*, her sides glowing with the heat of the fires raging through her.

Two lighters, loaded with 50 tons of TNT, were still secured alongside the doomed ship and volunteers were called to salvage these. Admiral Turle's aide, Cdr John Buckler, took over command of one tug and set out to secure one lighter when, suddenly at 0315, *Clan Frazer* blew up with a vast explosion and resultant fireball, which engulfed not only the two lighters, but Buckler's tug and other vessels nearby. Minutes later *City of Roubaix* also went up, her cargo of ammunition (destined for Turkey) demolishing further buildings, other ships and lighters. The series of explosions were so severe that windows in Athens, seven miles away, were shattered, and the blasts were reportedly heard up to 150 miles away. The port was devastated and a total of 11 merchant vessels were destroyed, amounting to 41 789 tons, together with two tugs, 60 lighters and 25 caiques; other vessels were damaged, some seriously.*

*NB Merchant vessels destroyed at Piraeus, night of 6/7 April 1941:-

British:	*Clan Fraser*	(7529 tons)	Greek:	*Petalli*	(6564 tons)
	City of Roubaix	(7108 tons)		*Evoikos*	(4792 tons)
	Cyprian Prince	(1988 tons)		*C Louloudis*	(4697 tons)
Maltese	*Patris*	(1706 tons)		*Styliani*	(3256 tons)
				Agalliani	(1656 tons)
				Acropolis	(1393 tons)
				Hakyon	(1100 tons)

Three British cruisers had been present in port – HMAS *Perth*, HMS *Ajax* and *Calcutta*. All fortuitously avoided serious damage and evaded the many mines in the harbour to reach the open sea safely. Here they saw the convoy ANF 25 (the last of the 'Lustre' convoys – see Chapter 6) approaching, the vessels being diverted to Salamis and Volos. Piraeus would be closed to all shipping for ten days, some 20 merchant vessels being stranded outside the harbour, devoid of fuel and water; a number of these would subsequently fall victim to air attack as a result. Even when the port was re-opened, the damage had been so severe that it was unable to function efficiently.

Meanwhile the small force of bombers responsible for this calamity to the Allied cause, returned to Sicily minus one of their number. Herrmann's 4D + AR had been hit in the port engine by AA fire, and rather than risk the long flight back on one engine, Herrmann headed instead for Rhodes. On arrival here however, he was advised to hold off landing as an RAF air raid was in progress. Only two Wellingtons of 38 Squadron from Shallufa, Egypt, were over the island, Plt Off C S Davis attacking Maritza airfield where he believed that six aircraft had been set on fire. At least one S.79 had succumbed, for when Herrmann finally received permission to land, with his fuel practically exhausted, his aircraft ran off the runway and almost collided with the wreckage of the Italian bomber. (Herrmann would subsequently gain fame and the coveted Ritterkreuz as originator of the 'Wilde Sau' (Wild Boar) form of single-engined night fighter defence of the Reich in 1943).

On the first day of the German offensive two of 113 Squadron's Blenheim IVs came to grief at Niamata. The nearest, which straddled a ditch, broke its back. (*S W Lee*)

6 April had also seen the arrival of some further reinforcements for the Allied side when the first elements of 208 (Army Co-operation) Squadron reached Eleusis, via Crete; the unit flew in three Hurricanes and eight Westland Lysanders. Activity over Greece was more limited on 7 April, as the Luftwaffe continued to concentrate its main efforts over Yugoslavia, but the RAF was busy, formations of Blenheims going out to attack German columns inside Yugoslavia, often bombing with telling effect. One such attack by nine aircraft from 11 Squadron was escorted by a dozen of 33 Squadron's Hurricanes early in the afternoon, three more of the unit's Blenheims returning to attack similar targets east of Strumica later in the day, this time with an escort of two Hurricanes. As the little formation turned for home, Sqn Ldr Pattle spotted a single aircraft several thousand feet below which he identified as a Dornier Do.215, and diving on this, he claimed to have shot it down in flames.

This may have been a Do.17 from the Stabstaffel of Stukageschwader 2, which suffered 15% damage from enemy action during the day in the Theodaristi area; other losses of Do.17s on this date were over northern areas of Yugoslavia. A Ju87 of 3/StG 1 flown by Oblt Bruno Dilley, was lost while attacking Greek concentrations in the Verria area of Macedonia, although Dilley and his gunner survived to return to their unit later. A Yugoslav Lockheed 10A (YU-SBD) from the JKRV's transport Grupa had delivered official mail from Valjevo, west of Belgrade, to Athens on this date. While returning from Athens, it refuelled at Thessalonika, but soon after take off from here it was hit by British AA fire and was forced to land near the village of Khalkidon, where it was abandoned.

During the morning of 8 April, eight Blenheims of the RAF's 11 Squadron again took off to attack targets in the Strumica region, but one crashed on take-off and the others were forced to return by bad visibility. Eight more from 211 Squadron with an escort of nine 33 Squadron Hurricanes, attacked Petrich airfield in the south-west corner of Bulgaria, which had been occupied by the Luftwaffe. After the bombing, the Hurricanes strafed and several aircraft were reportedly left in flames, two of them by Sqn Ldr Pattle.

During the day the Lysanders and Hurricanes of 208 Squadron were transferred from Eleusis to Kazaklar, 15 miles south of Larissa, to begin operations. Amongst other units, notification of more decoration awards were received at this time, 211 Squadron being advised of the gazetting of DFCs for Flg Offs Buchanan and Dundas, and for Plt Off Pearson. A communique issued by the Greek forces stated that on this date small forces of German paratroops had been dropped behind their positions in the Fort Rupel and Fort Ussita areas. Seventy had been captured and the remainder annihilated. During the day 'Ultra' intercepts indicated to the British command that XL Korps would threaten to outflank the Commonwealth forces in their initial defensive positions by attacking from the direction of Bitolj. As a result of this information the GOC decided to begin withdrawing his troops to new positions in the Mount Olympus area.

Bad weather again prevented any worthwhile bomber operations and restricted fighter activity on 9 April. 80 Squadron sent out a six-Hurricane patrol, but these became lost in the mountains in conditions of heavy cloud, and were obliged to land at Larissa. From this airfield a pair of 33 Squadron's fighters were

33 Squadron pilots at the time of the German invasion of Greece. L to r: Flt Lt 'Dixie' Dean, Flg Off Peter Wickham, Flg Off Vernon Woodward, Flg Off David Moir and plt Off Charles Chetham. (*E C R Baker*)

scrambled. Sqn Ldr Pattle spotting a twin-engined aircraft by chance as it was disappearing into the murk. Believing it to be a Ju88, he got in one good burst into its starboard engine before losing it to sight, and returned to claim it damaged with flame gushing from the stricken engine. After lunch he was informed that a bomber had crashed in the vicinity of his engagement, and with Flg Off Holman he drove to the site to inspect the remains. His victim would in fact appear to have been another Do.17Z (U5+BT) of 9/KG 2 which had been flown by Uffz Ulrich Sonnemann.

A Blenheim IV leads replacement Hurricanes to Greece, the latter fitted with long-range tanks for the journey. V7795 is being flown by ex-Malta fighter pilot, Sgt J K 'Jock' Norwell. (*J K Norwell*)

236

During the day 33 Squadron was joined by 'C' Flight of 208 Squadron on detachment, Flt Lt L G Burnard leading in two Hurricanes (one an unarmed photo-reconnaissance machine) and a Lysander; Flg Off R J Hardiman and Flg Off R R Stephenson were the other pilots. At Eleusis meanwhile a Blenheim IV arrived from Egypt via Crete, together with six new Hurricanes, for which it had been navigating. One of these was flown by Flg Off h starrett, who then returned to 33 Squadron, and one by Flg Off F J Aldridge, who was attached to 80 Squadron on arrival. The other four pilots were all veterans of 261 Squadron on Malta, who had been rested from operations; these four – Sgts Jim Pickering, Harry Ayre, 'Jock' Norwell and O R Bowerman – were to make their own way back to Egypt, hitching a lift on a returning Bombay next day. The new Hurricanes were V7732, 7745, 7747, 7795, 7823 and 7852.

Ferry pilots waiting to return to Egypt in the 216 Squadron Bombay behind them. L to r: Sgt Harry Ayre, Sgt 'Jock' Norwell, Sgt 'Drac' Bowerman and Sgt Jim Pickering. (*J Pickering*)

By night 30 Squadron Blenheim IFs stood at readiness at Eleusis, one being ordered off at 0520 on 10 April to intercept an aircraft held in the searchlights at 8000 feet over Athens. Identifying it as a Ju88, F/Sgt Innes-Smith attacked, but his opponent dived away rapidly, the rear gunner returning fire and obtaining a single hit on the Blenheim. An unconfirmed report was subsequently received that an aircraft had crashed near Scaramanga Bay.

On the ground all was far from well for the Allies. While the Greeks had again attacked on the Epirus Front on 9 April, that same day armoured units of the German XVII Armee Gruppe had entered Salonika despite sustained resistance by three Greek divisions under General Bacopoulos, and next day all fighting in Eastern Macedonia would come to an end. In Yugoslavia the Panzers were slicing through the defences everywhere; with no news forthcoming of events within that unhappy country, a Blenheim from 84 Squadron had been flown to Sarajevo during 9 April, carrying a Greek general to try and ascertain the position and see if any concerted action might be possible. It was not.

Weather yet again prevented much activity on 10 April; during the early

GERMAN ADVANCE
THROUGH GREECE,
APRIL 1941
▬ ▬ ▬ Initial Greek
defence line

Subsequent British
▬·▬·▬·defence lines

afternoon nine Blenheims from 84 Squadron got through to attack columns on
the Prilep-Bitolj road, but one observer was badly wounded and his pilot slightly
hit by ground fire. At 1530 five Blenheim IFs of 30 Squadron took off to strafe
the same road, while ten bomber Blenheims from 11 Squadron escorted by a
number of 33 Squadron Hurricanes headed for this same target, and four more
Hurricanes from 80 Squadron made for Bitolj itself. Sqn Ldr Milward led his
fighter-Blenheims in a successful attack which was believed to have caused much
damage, but the main formation was attacked by a number of Bf109Es and
Bf110s. Cloud provided cover which prevented losses being suffered, while Sqn
Ldr Pattle of 33 Squadron got a burst into a Bf110 which he reported crashed in
flames; he then attacked a Bf109, seeing the pilot bale out before the aircraft
spun down.

Two Bf110s from 7/LG 2 were lost during the day, as was a Bf109E of Stab/JG
27, but all apparently as a result of accidents. One Bf110 flown by Oblt Peters
was damaged in a crash-landing near Botevgrad, the gunner dying of the injuries
he received, while a second crashed near the airfield of Krainici in Bulgaria, far
from the Prilep-Bitolj area, Oblt Gravinghoff and his gunner being killed. Oblt
Herbert Mardaas of JG 27 was also killed when he crashed into a mountain near
Bogomila in bad weather.

Meanwhile the 80 Squadron quartette strafed vehicles and troops, and a small ammunition dump south of Bitolj. Heavy return fire was encountered and the engine of Flt Lt 'Timber' Woods' Hurricane was hit, seizing up immediately. Woods was able to locate a level field and put his aircraft down on its belly at once, recalling:

'As I clambered out the aircraft went on fire. One of the others – Ginger (Plt Off Still) – circled round with his wheels down as if about to land. I realised he would never make it and waved him away. The field was much too rough for a Hurricane landing, though I would have liked to have ridden back with him. The Jerries were about a mile away and a patrol was after me, so I sprinted away as hard as I could go in the direction of our lines. I should think that I ran for about a quarter of an hour when a patrol of Aussies picked me up. I was just about dead beat. They quickly got into position and put a few shots in the direction of the advancing Jerries, who at once pushed off. The Aussies said they had seen me land and had come out at once, for they could also see the Germans making towards the aircraft. We continued back to their position in some hills, where they fed me and then sent me back in a car.'

While raiding targets in Greece a Ju87 of III/StG 77 flown by Fw Willi Holtgreve (FH + KP) was reported missing in the Lamia area. Further west a Z506B floatplane of the 86° Gruppo BM bombed a railway bridge over the River Arkadeika, north of Kyparissia. Other raids and reconnaissances were flown by the Regia Aeronautica, while Italian fighters strafed various targets. One Italian aircraft was claimed shot down during the day when 1/Lt Ikonomopoulos of 24 Mira intercepted a reconnaissance Z1007bis. By night the Swordfish detachment at Paramythia – reinforced by six new aircraft from HMS *Formidable* – resumed operations. Over the next few nights the Italians would be stopped from using Valona harbour, four more ships being claimed sunk here.

The collapse of Greek resistance in Eastern Macedonia now allowed the Germans to begin moving southwards, and over the next five days the British forces facing them began withdrawing to the partly-prepared Servia line. Early in the morning of 11 April, Fliegerkorps X bombers from Sicily again approached the Greek coast. Sqn Ldr Pattle of 33 Squadron who had taken off after breakfast to fly to a satellite airfield, was vectored onto a number of unidentified low-flying aircraft near Volos. He identified these as Ju88s and He111s which were attempting to lay mines in the sea at the entrance to Volos harbour. Attacking at once, he claimed one of each shot down. It would seem that both his victims were Ju88s however, III/KG 30 losing Oblt Hans Schaible's 4D + JR of 7 staffel and Lt Wimmer's 4D + FS of 8 Staffel, with their respective crews.

A little later six 84 Squadron Blenheims set out to bomb the Prilep-Bitolj road, where tanks and lorries were reported hit, as was a nearby train. The Germans were ready for them this time however, and a hail of ground fire hit all six aircraft, F/Sgt L Nuthall's Blenheim being shot down and all the crew killed. Bad weather prevented further sorties by Blenheims of 11, 30 and 113 Squadrons, all of which were scheduled to operate. However a new detachment of Wellingtons from 38 Squadron in Egypt arrived during the day, and were in action that night against Sofia and Veles. 'C' Flight of 208 Squadron was also operating during 11 April, moving forward again to Kazaklar, joined now by a further Hurricane and two more pilots. Fliegerkorps VIII aircraft were active over Greece during the day, 4 New Zealand Brigade reporting being attacked by German aircraft in the Servia area, casualties being suffered. Other Luftwaffe attacks were made on transport vehicles in the Kozani region. During the day Stab/StG 2 again lost a Do.17 when T6+FA was reported missing near Xanthe. The crew of Oblt Gerhard Krieger later returned, suffering from various wounds, to report that they had been shot down by AA.

After dark Sqn Ldr Milward of 30 Squadron, up on patrol in Blenheim IF K7095, engaged a Ju88 in searchlights at 8000 feet north-west of Athens. As he attacked, his aircraft was hit by return fire and burst into flames, and while he was able to bale out, his gunner, Sgt John Crooks, was killed. Believed by troops on the ground to be a German, he was shot at in his parachute; he then narrowly avoided high tension cables and crashed into a glasshouse, escaping this whole catalogue of misfortunes with no more than a severe shaking. Many ground observers reported that a Ju88 was seen to spin down and crash with an explosion, but this may well have been the falling Blenheim, or bombs. No Ju88 was reported lost and the only identification of Milward's possible opponent may have been a Ju88A of 9/LG1 which crash-landed on return from a sortie over Crete, 60% damaged.

RAF Blenheims and Hurricanes were out over the Bitolj-Veles road during the morning of 12 April, while in the afternoon Sqn Ldr Pattle led a formation of 33 Squadron Hurricanes on a sweep up the Struma valley. East of Salonika a lone aircraft identified as a Do215 was intercepted and this was at once claimed shot down by Pattle. As the squadron returned towards Larissa they were warned of hostile aircraft in the vicinity and almost at once encountered a reported three S.79s 3000 feet below, apparently escorted by Bf109s. Ordering three sections to take on the fighters, Pattle led Flg Offs Holman and Starrett down on the bombers, reportedly sending one down in flames, while the other pair claimed a second. Pattle then engaged the Bf109s, reporting hits on one which caused a panel to fly off the starboard wing and the wheels were seen to drop down. Fliegerkorps VIII reported the loss of a Ju88 on this date – possibly an aircraft of I/LG1 – but the details of this casualty are not included in the Quartermaster's Loss Returns.

Luftwaffe bombing sank the 674 ton ship *Retriever* off Phleves on this date, 11 of the crew losing their lives. Due to bombing and aerial minelaying activities around Scaramanga, 230 Squadron's detachment of Sunderland flyingboats here had to be withdrawn to Suda Bay, Crete. With darkness, six of 815 Squadron's Swordfish at Paramythia were serviceable and available for renewed attacks on harbours in Albania and Italy. Five Swordfish flew down to Eleusis to exchange torpedoes for mines, preparatory to a mission to Durazzo. However rumour that the Yugoslavs had possibly captured this port from the Italians led to a last minute cancellation, and the attack was directed on Brindisi instead.

At 0130 Lt Torrens-Spence led off six aircraft, five with mines and one with a torpedo, the formation climbing up to 10000 feet and approaching within 25 miles of the target. Heavy cloud covered the Italian coast at 6000 feet, but a break was found and the harbour was located by its flashing lighthouse. Gliding down, the pilots saw before them a large number of ships in the roadstead; it was assumed that these were preparing for a dash across to Durazzo. L/Airman Ken Sims flying in Sub Lt Rudorf's L9743 'R' recalled:

'With torpedoes we would have had a bonanza. But what to do with mines? There was no point in putting them in the inner harbour entrance as planned. Instead we selected a largish ship, turned over the harbour entrance and came back at her. As we did so the shore batteries woke up to our presence and opened up.... Our ship looked big as we flew over her at about 100 feet. She was anchored and we dropped the mine right alongside. We hoped they would take long enough to get underway that the mine would activate as she swung in the current. We were not to know the result at the time though later I gathered it had not been effective.'

However Sub Lt Macaulay, flying the single torpedo-armed aircraft, launched at a tanker which was claimed as hit, one crew reporting seeing a large flash down on the water as they departed. All Swordfish landed safely at Paramythia at dawn.

Junkers Ju88A-4 over Greece, April 1941. (*Bib für Zeit*)

An improvement in the weather allowed the air forces out in greater strength on 13 April. From Bulgaria and Eastern Yugoslavia, the Luftwaffe now began to intrude more forcefully into Greek airspace, and during the morning some 70 bombers attacked Volos, the port being devastated. Amongst the ships lost was the 7140 ton *City of Karachi*, while the 5000 ton Norwegian tanker *Brattdal* was severely damaged and was considered a total loss. One raid by 20 Ju88s of I/LG 1 was intercepted by seven 33 Squadron Hurricanes, the German unit reporting the loss of Ju88A Ll + UH flown by Lt Gert Blanke. Flg Off Peter Wickham caught a reconnaissance Bf110 from 7(F)/LG2 over Mount Olympus and shot it down in flames (L2 + HR, flown by Lt Georg Lange). It is possible that the bomber was shot down by Sqn Ldr Pattle, since a diary lists five victories for him next day, two of these being Ju88s. A second Ju88 was lost on 13 April when an aircraft of II/LG 1 from Sicily (LI + EN, flown by Fw Hans Garz of 5 Staffel) ditched in the sea off Crete, many miles to the south. However LG 1 were also in action against Piraeus, harbour on 14 April, where Lt Georg Sattler attacked a 6000 ton merchant vessel in the wrecked harbour, seeing the blast of his bombs throw the vessel against the quay. Unfortunately, there is a distinct lack of documentary evidence concerning Pattle's sorties in mid April.

Over the Albanian front action occurred on 13 for the first time since the German invasion had begun. Here Sqn Ldr Schwab led the 112 Squadron Gladiators on an offensive patrol over Koritza, seeing eight 104° Gruppo BT S.79s escorted by a recorded 'three Me109s and one G-50' (almost certainly all MC200s of 153° Gruppo CT). Schwab claimed the 'G-50' shot down, but Plt Off Brunton was forced to bale out when the propeller flew off his aircraft; he returned on muleback with the aid of local peasants. Gunners in the S.79s claimed one Gladiator shot down and two probables.

RAF Blenheims were very active throughout the day, but at last their apparent virtual immunity was to come to an end as the Luftwaffe finally managed to intercept one unescorted raid. 211 Squadron had already undertaken two raids during the morning on vehicles and troop concentrations in the Florina region, both under Hurricane escort; no opposition had been encountered. At 1500 the unit was briefed to send six more bombers to the area, but this time no Hurricanes were available. Only seven serviceable Blenheims could be mustered for this operation to Prilep but as they were being made ready a signal arrived from AHQ, calling for one aircraft to carry out a photo-reconnaissance sortie over Valona and Durazzo. Plt Off Jack Hooper was the obvious choice for this task, his aircraft being the only one not already 'bombed-up', so off he went. Wg Cdr 'Paddy' Coote, O/C Western Wing, decided to go along with the raid as an observer to assess the progress of the German advance, while his deputy, Sqn Ldr L E Cryer, DFC, would accompany another crew. The formation would be led by Sqn Ldr Irvine, the commanding officer.

As the bombers approached Lake Prespa, some 40 miles short of the target zone, three Bf109Es from 6/JG 27 were seen closing rapidly on the rear 'vic' of three Blenheims, the gunners at once opening fire. Hpt Hans–Joachim Gerlach, leading the German formation attacked L8449 (Flg Off AC Godfrey), which caught fire almost at once. Only Godfrey managed to bale out, and he later

242

recalled:

'We were ordered to dive. Next thing the cockpit was a mass of flames. As they blazed up in my face I tore the hatch back and jumped. I noticed that there were three aircraft in the air – all in flames. My crew was dead.'

His aircraft crashed near the village of Karia where it was joined almost immediately by a second Blenheim. This was L8604, shot down by Uffz Fritz Gromotka; Flg Off C E V Thompson, DFC, and his crew did not survive. Less than a minute later L1539 was falling in flames, hit by Fw Herbert Krenz, and again only the pilot, F/Sgt A G James, was able to bale out, breaking his ankle on landing near the village of Mikrolimni; this aircraft crashed near the south-west shore of the lake.

The leading 'vic' now came under attack, and first to fall was L1434 in which Sqn Ldr Cryer was flying as passenger to Flt Lt L B Buchanan, DFC. Hit by Hpt Gerlach, Buchanan was critically injured, but managed a controlled ditching in the south-eastern corner of Lake Prespa. An unconfirmed report stated that Cryer and Buchanan both died of their injuries in an Albanian hospital. Meanwhile Uffz Gromotka had his second victory when Flg Off R V Herbert's L4819, in which Wg Cdr Coote was flying, crashed near the village of Trigonon; one parachute was seen, partially open, but all the crew died. Sqn Ldr Irvine was now alone, but L8478 did not last long. Fw Krenz speedily overhauled the Blenheim and sent it down to crash near Vigla, again with the loss of all the crew. The two survivors, Godfrey and James, made contact and buried those of their dead comrades that they could find before making their way by foot, mule and Greek lorry to Larissa, 150 miles distant!

Even as this slaughter was taking place, nine more Blenheims from 113 Squadron had set off 15 minutes later at 1515, heading for the same target, but with an escort of six Hurricanes. The Blenheims were led by Flt Lt D F Rixson, who recalled:

'We were going up the line to bomb the enemy forward troops. In the valley as we went north, we suddenly saw far more aircraft than we had ever seen in the air before, and going down the other side of the valley to attack our forward troops – later confirmed as a Luftwaffe bomber formation. I remember our Hurricanes fussing around us like bees, but obviously both formations had the same instructions "do not leave your bombers" because although only a few miles apart none interfered with the other.'

During the afternoon Flg Off Vernon Woodward of 33 Squadron carried out a lone reconnaissance to Bitolj and Vire. He was intercepted by three Bf109s, one of which he claimed to have shot down, believing that he had seen the pilot bale out. He then finished his reconnaissance and returned unscathed. That night five Wellingtons of 38 Squadron attacked Sofia again, but one failed to return. Sofia came under attack again during the night of 13/14 April, six Wellingtons from 37 Squadron's detachment at Menidi raiding the city's marshalling yards. Light Flak was encountered and Sgt D D Strickland's T2875 was slightly damaged. During the return flight Plt Off W D Costello's crew spotted a convoy of about 30 vehicles, the pilot taking the big aircraft down to strafe, the gunners causing much apparent confusion. Eight more Wellingtons were despatched by 38 Squadron at Shallufa, briefed to attack the same target. Two failed to locate their destination in bad weather, but the rest bombed, one crew reporting seeing a Bf110 with a searchlight installed in its nose. However no interceptions were reported.

It was on 14 April, as the British army completed its withdrawal to the Olympus-Servia line, that improving weather and reduction of effort over Yugoslavia, allowed aerial activity over Greece to show a marked increase. Early in the day six Blenheims from 84 Squadron, escorted by four Hurricanes, attacked vehicles and troops north of Ptolemais. Intense Flak was experienced and two Bf109s also attacked the bombers, four Blenheims being damaged, one of which was believed to have crash-landed in Yugoslavia. Some five hours later at 0930, eight more 113 Squadron Blenheims were off with an escort of ten Hurricanes, seven from 33 Squadron and three from 80 Squadron. Returning from attacking targets north of Ptolemais, Ju87s were seen dive-bombing Allied troops near Servia and one of these was claimed shot down by Plt Off Bill Vale of 80 Squadron; a Blenheim gunner fired at one of the dive-bombers, reporting seeing smoke and flame pouring from this aircraft, but this is believed to have been the machine attacked by Vale.

An hour later over the Epirus Front, ten Z.1007bis bombers of 35° Stormo BT were attacked by nine Gladiators of 21 Mira near Yanina. One of the latter was claimed shot down by the gunners in one bomber, and one by an escorting 153° Gruppo CT MC200; no losses of any Gladiators have been recorded. During the day a further claim for a Gladiator was submitted by Uffz Gromotka of II/JG 27 south of Florina.

Over Athens three Hurricanes of 80 Squadron and four Blenheim fighters of 30 Squadron scrambled to intercept Ju88s and Bf110s attacking Piraeus early in the afternoon. The Blenheims failed to make contact, but it seems that one Hurricane was hit and force-landed. An hour later pairs of Hurricanes were despatched by 33 Squadron to patrol over troops in the Servia area who were now under constant Stuka attack. Flg Offs Woodward and Dean came across six of the dive-bombers as they were peeling off to attack motor transport, and three were claimed shot down with three others damaged, Woodward claiming two destroyed and one damaged, and 'Dixie' Dean the remainder. Greek PZL pilots of 22 Mira also intercepted Ju87s during the day, one being claimed shot down by Sgt Argyropoulos near Trikkala.

Several Ju87s were indeed lost over the area during the day, and it is believed that one of these was probably that shot down by Vale earlier in the morning. It seems that I/StG3 lost Ofw Rudolf Schnurawa and his gunner over Servia, while 9/StG 2 lost Oblt Christian Banke and Fw Georg Hoser in T6+KT south-west of Mount Olympus. A second 9 Staffel aircraft was badly damaged and crash-landed on its return to Prilep-West, Ofw Paul Lachmann and his gunner both having been wounded. 2/StG1, recently arrived from Libya, lost A5+EK to fighters near Trikkala (obviously the victim of the Greek PZL); Fhr Walter Seeliger and Gefr Kurt Friedrich were taken prisoner, and were taken to the

Headquarters of Colonel Stanley Casson, who wrote:

'A couple of young dive-bomber airmen were brought in to me in the late afternoon. The subaltern was young (Seeliger was 19 at the time) and dark, his companion, a sergeant, was bullet-headed, morose and sullen ... the subaltern was a Viennese dandy. He wore elegant riding breeches and field boots, an odd costume for an airman. I thrust him and his surly friend into a cowshed, our only available prison. After an hour there he asked to see me and complained, after many salutes and heel-clickings, that it was very cold there. I told him that he had visited Thessaly of his own volition – that no one had invited him, and reminded him that Greece in Spring is very chilly in the evenings; he should have brought his overcoat. Later we sent him to Athens.'

(Seeliger did not remain in captivity long, being released when Athens fell; Friedrich was not so fortunate however, for he had already been moved to Egypt, and remained in Allied hands for the duration.)

German records actually list the losses suffered by 2/StG 3 and 2/StG 1 as occurring one day later, but the British report of the capture of Seeliger and Friedrich shows this undoubtedly to be an administrative error in the case of the StG 1 aircraft. No claims were made for any Ju87s on 15 April, and it therefore seems likely that the StG 3 loss was similarly entered a day late.

Late that evening another pair of 33 Squadron's Hurricanes were returning to Larissa from a fruitless one and a half hour patrol when they became separated in heavy cloud. Recalled Plt Off Winsland:

'I sighted what I thought to be a friendly Greek or British fighter. However, after circling round it I identified it as a German Henschel 126. What a gift – or so I thought. But again I had the old trouble – excitement! To make things more difficult the enemy put down his flaps and cruised at about 70 mph so that I had to shoot past him after each attack. He also used his camouflage to his best advantage by flying low – 500 feet – thereby giving me no room to dive away downwards after attacking. All this was, of course, very much to his credit and courage. However, all that was no excuse for my not having blasted him out of the sky with the first attack. After my last burst at him I could no longer see him flying, yet neither could I find the machine smashed up on the ground. However, I can at least say that a report came in next day from Field HQ that a Henschel 126 had been found wrecked near Katerine and that it crashed at the very time and place I claimed to have been attacking it – but with this difference – the Greeks claimed having got it by Acc-Acc!'

Nonetheless the Hs 126 – believed to have been a machine from 2(H)/10 – was credited to Winsland; the crew survived, although Oblt Hans Wiedemann, the observer, was wounded.

A second Hs126 (5F +AH) from 1(H)/14 was shot down in the Larissa area, the pilot – Lt Hans Wendler – being killed; his victor was a PZL pilot of 23 Mira, Col Casson recording of this busy day:

'In the early afternoon a German Henschel, an ancient type of craft used for reconnaissance and photography, as obsolete for fighting purposes as a Lysander, came popping along over us all by itself at the ridiculous height of about 3000 feet. This looked like our afternoon off, and everybody with any kind of machine gun loosed off at it from all over the plain. This pilot of that Henschel must surely have been drunk. However, none of us hit him, and over he went across the ridge between us and Larissa. The other side a Greek in an ancient Potez machine (sic) chugged up into the air and shot him down; and that was that. I rather think that about now the Germans were beginning to get a little above themselves and were reckless.'

PZL P-24 fighters of the EVA remained active during April, and were involved in several successful engagements with Luftwaffe aircraft. German personnel examine a damaged example on a captured airfield. A second can be seen in the background, completely burnt out. (*A Stamatopoulos*)

By this date the Luftwaffe had been reinforced by the arrival of three transport Gruppen, KGzbV 1, 2 and 3 in Bulgaria, with quantities of Ju52/3ms. These made their presence felt on 14 April, when troops of the 19th Australian and 4th New Zealand Brigades holding positions around Servia and Portas Pass, reported seeing numerous aircraft of this type air-lifting infantry to the Kozani Plain.

A Blenheim attempted to deliver unfused bombs (by airdrop) to troops at Grevena during the day, who were to use these for demolition purposes. However the bomber was intercepted by an unidentified Bf109, and was damaged, being forced to return to base, its mission uncompleted. The day also saw the arrival at Paramythia of Wg Cdr Dudley Lewis from AHQ, who had instructions to disband Western Wing and arrange the evacuation of both Paramythia and Yanina. The Gladiators of 112 Squadron and the last five Blenheims of 211 Squadron were to move to Agrinion to continue operations, the Blenheims beginning ferrying down the ground personnel – nine to an aircraft – next morning; this operation would take three days to complete. Fliegerkorps VIII

246

aircrew claimed to have shot down a Fairey IIIF floatplane of 11 Mira over Athens; the claimants were probably a bomber crew, but no Greek crew casualties are recorded, although the aircraft may have force-landed without casualties to personnel.

As already mentioned, one source has credited Sqn Ldr 'Pat' Pattle of 33 Squadron with five victories during five different sorties on this date – a Bf109 at 0710, Ju88s at 0843 and 1740, a Bf110 at 1004 and an S.79 at 1308. II/KG 51 lost two Ju88s on this date, one shot down during a raid on Illidza, the crew baling out unhurt, while the second crash-landed at Pecs airfield on return, after suffering battle damage. These would thus seem to have been the opponents of 33 Squadron either during the morning or evening raids. With regard to the other victories mentioned, few possibilities exist. The only Bf109 lost on this day was that flown by Hpt Gerlach, Staffelkapitän of 6/JG 27, who was taken prisoner when his aircraft was hit in the engine during a strafing attack. The only possible identity of the Bf110 is a Do.17Z of 10/KG 2 which crash-landed in Rumania 60% damaged – a highly unlikely candidate, while no Italian trimotor bombers are recorded lost in combat with fighters on this date, although one Z.1007bis of the 262ª Squadriglia, flown by Ten Mario di Angelis, was reported shot down by AA fire over Preveza harbour during an attack by five of these bombers. It is very unlikely that this was involved however, as its loss was reported far from the area over which 33 Squadron was operating.

As recorded earlier, it was on this date that King Peter of Yugoslavia was flown out from Niksic in a 7th Puk S.79, heading for Greece. At Paramythia during the afternoon a Do.17K flew in, followed by the Savoia which was flying a white flag and was escorted by six 112 Squadron Gladiators. The young monarch and his Prime Minister were at once provided with a Guard of Honour composed of airmen of 211 Squadron. The King commented that it was the smartest guard he had seen, and most certainly the first on a battlefield. One of those involved was Corporal Tom Henderson, who recalled:
'What His Majesty didn't know was that 90% of the gear we were wearing was borrowed from our comrades, there was a dire shortage of decent uniforms and equipment at the time. One piece of luggage unloaded off the S.79 was reported to contain the Yugoslav Crown Jewels! It may have been true, but true or not it brightened up our lives at a time when our luck appeared to be running out.'

(It probably was true, for a week later the Jewels were taken aboard HMS *Defender* at Kalamata and carried to Egypt.)
Later that evening the King left for Menidi in the S.79, escorted by a Blenheim, but now as already described, Yugoslav aircraft began arriving in numbers – mainly S.79s, Do.17Ks and Lockheed Electras, but also including the large number of smaller biplanes of many types. Tom Henderson remembers:
'As far as I can recollect the Yugoslav boys (S.79s and Do.17s mostly) began arriving on 12th or 13th and over a period of about three days kept trickling in – I saw no Furies or Hurricanes but an odd Lockheed twin-engined aircraft was present. I have never seen such magnificent uniforms as some of the Yugoslav chaps wore – and such marvellous moustaches!'

By the end of this day the number of Yugoslav machines present at Paramythia had reportedly reached 44, but others were landing elsewhere. Two multi-engined aircraft, believed to have been Caproni 310s from 603 Training Eskadrila, came down on the island of Corfu. One of these landed on Garitsa airfield but nosed over in muddy conditions. No one on board was hurt but the aircraft was damaged; the passengers were taken from the island by boat to the south. The second aircraft landed about 20 minutes later at Lefkimi, on the south-east tip of Corfu, in a field unsuitable for a take-off, and was abandoned. Both aircraft were later burned by the Corfiots to prevent them falling into Italian hands.

By night British bombers were again out in some force. Nine of 38 Squadron's Wellingtons from Egypt were briefed to attack a bridge spanning the Vardar at Veles. Led by Wg Cdr W P J Thomson, they attacked through heavy Flak, two crews believing that their bombs had hit the target; Plt Off H W E Lane reported seeing the west end of the bridge collapse. However Flg Off H W Adams' Wellington (R1099), was seen to be shot down, all the crew being lost. Blenheims from 11 Squadron attacked vehicles, armour and troops in the Mount Olympus area.

Meanwhile seven Swordfish from 815 Squadron staged through Paramythia, heading for Valona at 2350, led by Lt Torrens-Spence; all were armed with torpedoes on this occasion. In poor, hazy visibility, the formation climbed to about 8000 feet before gliding in to attack independently. Only six made the attack, for Lt C S Lea had been forced to turn back early due to technical problems. Targets were not found where they had been expected, and all aircraft had to fly round the harbour looking for ships. Torrens-Spence found and attacked one vessel – 'there was a big bang and no mistake about it' – which was apparently a 7000 ton ammunition ship. Sub Lt Macaulay reported having got a strike on a merchant vessel of some 6000 tons after Lt H A Swayne had missed it from astern. In the darkness the attacking crews overestimated the sizes of their respective targets but not the results – the steamer 'Luciano', a 3329-ton freighter, was sunk, as was the smaller 'Stampalia' (1228 tons). Two crews failed to find targets after a 45-minute search and returned with their torpedoes, but P4137 crewed by Sub Lts W C Sarra and J Bowker hit the water and crashed; they survived to become prisoners. After landing at Paramythia to refuel, the six remaining aircraft left for Eleusis at dawn on 15 April.

Immediately they had left, before the mass of Yugoslav aircraft at Paramythia could be refuelled and got away, MC200s of the 22° Gruppo CT swept in to strafe, claiming six bombers and one fighter destroyed, plus ten aircraft damaged. Some sources have stated that all 44 aircraft were destroyed or damaged, but this is not so, as nine would be flown out to Egypt on 19 April. At least one airman was killed during the attack. Meanwhile nin G.50bis from the 24° Gruppo CT were attacking Yanina, while 15 more flew top cover. Six of 112 Squadron's Gladiators managed to get off and a sharp dogfight began. Plt Off Brunton got on the tail of one Fiat, but his guns jammed and he was attacked by another, his aircraft being badly shot-up, while he was wounded. As he came in to land several G.50s followed, but the airfield defences drove them off. Two G.50s were claimed damaged during this fracas, whilst the Italian pilots claimed three

Gladiators shot down and three probables, six further aircraft being claimed destroyed on the ground. No RAF losses or casualties were suffered other than to Brunton's aircraft, but the Yugoslav S.79 at this airfield was destroyed, and other Yugoslav machines may also have fallen victim to the strafing.

At about 1100 another Yugoslav Do.17K flew in, carrying the RAF liaison officer to Yugoslavia, Sqn Ldr T G Mappleback, who advised the commanding officer at Paramythia that further Yugoslav aircraft were due to arrive that afternoon. Since the airfield was in the process of evacuation, it was requested that an RAF officer remain behind to direct the incoming aircraft to fly on to Agrinion, where the Greeks had agreed they might be based. After flying on to Yanina to advise Wg Cdr Lewis of these arrangements, Mappleback returned to Montenegro in the Dornier to confirm them. Four S.79s and six Do.17Ks arrived at 1400, and were met by 211 Squadron's Medical Officer, Flt Lt W P Griffin, who advised them of the new destination. The four Savoias and two of the Dorniers left promptly, but the pilots of the remaining four ignored Griffin's pleas to leave at once. Within minutes an estimated 40 Bf109Es swooped down on the airfield, and all four bombers were destroyed.

Over Eastern Greece the Allied airfields also suffered a bad day. Bill Winsland of 33 Squadron recorded:

'What a day. Reveille 5 AM. Cold, dark morning. Rough, bumpy journey with a dozen other pilots in the back of a lorry through the almost deserted and ruined town (Larissa) over broken roads, over hill and dale to our satellite airfield (Churton's Bottom) – well away from the main aerodrome (Larissa) and safer from bombing. An hour or two later we were in our cockpits, engines warming up and ready to take to the air at a moment's notice when the orders came through on our radios. At about 7 AM the first alarm was sounded.... A few seconds later (we were already lined up into wind and engines running) six Hurricanes roared into the air. We had reached some 10 000 feet in cloud, when suddenly my machine shook violently and tremendous vibration set up. I thought at first that I had been jumped and hit by an enemy fighter and so took evasive action by half rolling onto my back and diving. However, there was no response from my throttle – and nothing behind me either. What had actually happened was that my crankcase had fractured causing oil to stream out and so seize up the engine. The speed of the machine forced the propeller to keep turning much against the will of the engine, so causing friction and tremendous vibration.... I was lucky considering the situation – the main aerodrome was in sight and it looked as though it might be possible to reach it in a long glide from about 7000 feet. I had to use hand-pumping emergency devices to lower flaps and the undercarriage – but judged everything OK, thank God, and reached the main aerodrome (Larissa) without any further damage to the aircraft. I was lucky again that I came across no enemy fighters on that glide! On stepping out of my aircraft I learnt that nine Messerschmitt 109s had only 20 minutes previously shot down two of our machines on their take-offs and afterwards strafed all our other machines on the ground – two were still burning after I had landed – I had seen the flames and smoke during my forced landing.'

A 33 Squadron pilot inspects Lt Jacob Arnoldy's Messerschmitt Bf109E of II/JG 77 after its crash-landing at Larissa on 15 April, 1941.

Close-up of the tail of Arnoldy's Bf109E showing victory bars indicating his six previous victories, mainly achieved over Norway in 1940.

This attack on Larissa had occurred at 0650, when the stand-by flight of Hurricanes flown by Flt Lt Mackie, Plt Off Chetham and Sgt Genders, were scrambled just as Bf109Es of II/JG 77 – an estimated 15 in number, but actually only eight strong – swept over the airfield in threes. The first trio narrowly missed the barely-airborne Hurricanes, but the next three caught them at 1500 feet, Lt

250

Jacob Arnoldy obtaining hits on Charles Chetham's aircraft. Onlookers saw the latter come down in a seemingly controlled glide and disappear behind some trees outside the airfield boundary; he was in fact killed. Arnoldy now overshot the other pair of Hurricanes and John Mackie immediately latched onto his tail and managed to put a few shots into the Messerschmitt before Fw Otto Köhler engaged him from astern. The Hurricane flipped over, caught fire and exploded on crashing, killing the Canadian pilot.

Meanwhile Arnoldy – an 'Experte' of the Norwegian Campaign of the previous Spring – had been hit in the chest by Mackie's quick burst and struggled to bale out at 1000 feet. As he floated down over the airfield Greek soldiers fired on him. It is not known whether he was hit again, but he died within a short time, in the Medical Officer's tent. His aircraft – 'White 5'; Werk Nr 5277 – made an almost perfect belly-landing and was virtually undamaged; just two bullet holes below the cockpit hood, in line with the pilot's chest.

Sgt George Genders, 33 Squadron.

The one remaining Hurricane, piloted by Sgt George Genders, participating in his first combat, managed to evade the Messerschmitts and to get on Fw Köhler's tail; Köhler, like Arnoldy a member of 4 Staffel, was shot down and crash-landed not far from the airfield. However, when a party arrived to capture the pilot, he was nowhere to be seen – the cockpit contained his parachute only. Köhler evaded capture and eventually rejoined his unit. On the airfield several aircraft had been destroyed, including one more Hurricane, a Gladiator (N5783) which was still on the strength of 33 Squadron, and several Greek aircraft including a captured S.79, some Avro Tutors, Potez 63s and an unserviceable Bloch 151. During the day, 26 Bf109Es from Stab, II and III/JG 77 claimed a total of 19 aircraft destroyed on the ground in the Larissa area; it is possible that their claims included the Yugoslav Dorniers at Paramythia.

At about the same time as the attack on Larissa was taking place, other Bf109Es from II/JG27 approached the Greek airfield at Kalambaka/Vassiliki where the remnants of the EVA fighters had assembled, apart from the eight PZLs of 23 Mira, which were still at Larissa. Here some 15 fighters – Bloch 151s, Gladiators and PZLs – had just scrambled on report of the approach of an estimated 18 bombers with fighter escort. At the last moment the formation turned away towards Trikkala, but just as the first Greek fighters reached the bombers, they were met by the Messerschmitts, some 20 strong.

One of the Bloch pilots, Cpl George Mokkas, was reported to have shot down two of the bombers, but he was then shot down and killed by Oblt Gustav Rödel, who identified the unfamiliar Bloch as a Hurricane, for his 15th victory. A few minutes later Rödel claimed one of the Gladiators shot down, while at the same time Ofw Otto Schulz claimed a PZL (his 5th victory). Another Gladiator was then claimed by Lt Ernst Börngen, while at 0705, 15 minutes after the opening of the action, Rödel claimed a PZL and Oblt Wilhelm Wiesinger a Gladiator (his 9th victory). One Gladiator, flown by Capt Kellas, commander of 21 Mira, was hard hit and the slightly-wounded pilot at once crash-landed, his aircraft bursting into flames. Sgt A Katsarelles of 22 Mira was shot down in his PZL, but survived with severe wounds, while another of this unit's pilots, 1/Lt B Kontogiorgos, received slight wounds.

Immediately these airfield attacks were over, two Lysanders from 208 Squadron took off from Larissa, to carry the two 211 Squadron pilots, sole survivors of the Blenheim massacre of two days' earlier, to Athens. Flg Off Godfrey was passenger in Flg Off D B Waymark's L4719, while Sgt James was with Plt Off J W Stewart in L4690. Almost at once fighters were seen which were thought to be Hurricanes, but they were soon recognised as hostile; both Lysanders dived for the ground and attempted to carry out evasive tactics at an altitude of a few feet. The Messerschmitts were upon them swiftly, L4690 going down almost at once; the Lysander hit the ground at about 200 mph disintegrating and catching fire. Stewart survived the crash with only minor injuries, but James was killed. Meanwhile the other Lysander was being pursued by another Messerschmitt, at which Godfrey discharged a pan of ammunition from the single Vickers machine gun without success. It was only a matter of minutes before they too were hit and crashed into the ground at speed. Godfrey, who had already been hit in one hand, losing two fingers, suffered severe leg injuries in the crash, but Waymark walked away with scratches only.

Round about this time another PZL from 23 Mira at Larissa had given chase to a Luftwaffe reconnaissance aircraft, which Sgt Pericles Koutroubas was credited with having shot down in the Litochoro area, near Mount Olympus. Shortly after this combat, he too was intercepted by German fighters, and was shot down and killed. Fliegerkorps VIII claims during the day included the Hurricane, two PZLs and three Gladiators by II/JG 27, three Hurricanes by II/JG 77 over Larissa during the morning – the third slightly after the initial pair – while I(J)/LG 2 was apparently credited with one or two Lysanders and the third PZL.

At Larissa following the JG 77 attack, Plt Off Winsland was asked to carry out a flight and gun test in a Hurricane which had just undergone a routine inspection.

'I was asked to test this machine immediately – when a poor bloody lowest of the low Pilot Officer is "asked" to do anything its really a bloody order! – I had started the machine and was taxying along the edge of the aerodrome to the take-off point when suddenly the surface of the drome to my right became a mass of exploding cannon shells and incendiary fire from a low level ground attack – there were no less than 12 or more 109s diving in formation across the drome, strafing everything they saw yet again. How they did not see me I just don't know. Not only was I in a perfectly good aeroplane – the others – most of them anyway, were already damaged – but I was bumping along the surface, the sun flickering on my cockpit hood and shiny wings and my prop was, of course, revolving – enough to have attracted every Hun's attention one would have thought. God! Was I scared. I lowered my seat and crouched up double inside the cockpit in an effort to get some protection from the engine in front and the small bit of armour plating behind. The situation looked so awful that I felt like undoing my straps, jumping out of the cockpit and running to the nearest slit trench, but since that would have looked very bad in front of all the Greek and British ground airmen in the trenches, I seemed to have no real alternative but to take off right through the middle of it all. It was not a pleasant prospect especially after hearing of the fate of my two friends under the same circumstances. However, in the heat of the moment I soon found myself in the air. In those particular moments I did a little thing which again I will never forget. I behaved like an ostrich, my action only making my existence more precarious than ever and giving me no possible additional protection – I took off by instruments with my head and shoulders in a crouched position below the sides of the cockpit, believing for some amazing and unexplained reason or other that if my head was not visible the enemy would not shoot at me! Just one of those peculiar things one does in a really terrifying moment, I suppose. I kept my machine low and flew away at full throttle hoping to evade such hopeless odds. Having left the aerodrome well behind me I climbed up into the sun. Fires repeatedly appeared here, there and everywhere (on the drome). There must have been far more than just those 12 Messerschmitts on the job (afterwards I learnt that a second wave of 20 attacked the aerodrome, while I was gaining height). During that climb I suddenly heard a terrific yell over my radio from someone on the ground who was apparently watching the aircraft though they did not know who was the pilot. An agitated voice shouted "Hullo Hurricane, look out, beat it, there are five 109s just above and behind you." Few Hurricanes have ever dived more quickly and vertically! I had just got over that fright and was again climbing when I spotted 12 109s below me, flying south near my aerodrome.

Having the advantage of height I decided that I should at least make one attack on them, even if I did beat it afterwards! Accordingly I positioned myself between them and the sun and dived vertically down on top of the enemy formation, firing all the time (grossly out of range at first) and flattened out just above their heads and pointing in the opposite direction. I had come and gone too quickly for them to do much about me. Gone so quickly in fact that I didn't have time to observe the results of my attack!'

One source stated that 14 Hurricanes were destroyed during these two attacks on Larissa.

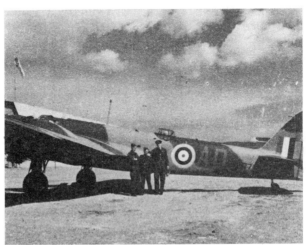

Top: on arrival in Greece in March 1941 Plt Off L A S Grumbley and his crew (Sgt J T Latimer and Sgt S W Lee) of 113 Squadron's trategic reconnaissance flight pose proudly with their pristine Blenheim IV, T2177, AD-V. A month later the same aircraft is inspected at Niamata by Luftwaffe aircrew (above); the bomber had been disabled with most of the unit's other aircraft, during the strafe of 15 April. Note the Dornier Do.17Z bombers in the far background of this photo. (*S W Lee and Bib Für Zeit*)

Larissa, Kalambaki/Vassiliki and Paramythia were not the only targets how-ever, for at 0750 waves of Bf109Es attacked Niamata, home of 113 Squadron, where crews were breakfasting prior to taking off on a raid. This first attack by eight Messerschmitts destroyed six of the unit's Blenheims and wounded four airmen. Two hours later three Bf109s from II/JG27 swept over the airfield and several more Blenheims were rendered unserviceable, two more airmen being wounded. Bofors fire was fairly accurate and two of the attackers were hit, but both got back to Bitolj where one crash-landed. At 1100 four more Bf109s appeared over Niamata and proceeded to destroy four more Blenheims; they were followed by another quartette 45 minutes later, these damaging one more Blenheim and the station Magister communications aircraft. An hour later came the final attack of the day on this field, all remaining Blenheims being shot up and rendered unserviceable.

During these attacks all motor vehicles on the airfield were also destroyed, as was much tented accommodation. 113 Squadron had ceased to exist as an operational unit; ten Blenheims had been destroyed or damaged beyond repair. Flt Lt Rixon recalled:

'There was very little, if any, early warning. I have a vivid recollection of my air gunner crouching under a little bridge firing off a .38 revolver at the Iron Crosses!'

By the end of the day Fliegerkorps VIII's claims for aircraft destroyed on the ground totalled 22, including four Hurricanes, two Blenheims, two Potez 63s and 13 unidentified types.

Further south at 0845, 25 Ju88s from I/LG 1 and I/KG 51 had appeared over Athens where they were intercepted by six Hurricanes of 80 Squadron and four Blenheim 1Fs of 30 Squadron. Plt Off Bill Vale claimed two bombers shot down, Sgt Ted Hewett one and one probable, while one each were claimed by Plt Off Still and F/Sgt Rivalant, one of the French pilots. A sixth was claimed by a new pilot, Plt Off Roald Dahl, who had only arrived at Eleusis the previous evening, having flown a replacement Hurricane from Egypt. On this, his first operational sortie, and with only seven hours' experience on Hurricanes, Dahl came across six bombers. Attacking from astern he was greeted by a hail of fire from the rear gunners but succeeded in getting on the tail of one and, after a short burst, saw pieces fly off its starboard engine; the crippled Junkers slowly tumbled down, three crew being seen to bale out. In spite of the intense return fire only one bullet hit Dahl's V7826, this piercing the propeller. One of these claims was adjudged to be the unit's 100th victory of the war. Another of the squadron's recent replacement pilots, Flg Off The Hon David Coke, a former Battle of Britain pilot, ranged further north and encountered a number of Bf109s – probably aircraft of I(J)/LG 2 – and claimed one shot down. Some time later, at 0930, one of the Blenheims, piloted by Plt Off T H C Alison, came across ten Ju88s at 12 000 feet over the capital, but these dived to attack shipping in the harbour. The Blenheim caught up with one of the raiders and Alison made a starboard quarter attack, but broke away as the bomber was diving too steeply. Sgt Connors, the air gunner, sighted another Junkers and they closed to 75 yards; the crew believed that this aircraft was shot down after Connors had fired 1250 rounds at it.

One of the LG 1 aircraft, L1+JK, was flown by Lt Sattler, who reported seeing his bombs hit an 18 000 ton transport; on the return flight he believed that he saw his target sinking. This was possibly the *Clan Cumming* which had been temporarily repaired after being seriously damaged during the raid on Piraeus during the night of 6/7 April, and had been towed into the Bay of Athens; she now struck a mine and sank. Two other large merchant vessels, the *Goalpara* (5314 tons) and 'Quilloa' (7765 tons) were both severely damaged by air attack in Eleusis Bay, and both beached. As the Ju 88s overflew Eleusis airfield on their return to Krumovo, air gunners sprayed Hurricanes seen about to take off, but no damage was recorded.

It is believed that 80 Squadron's opponents were the I/KG 51 aircraft, two of which were lost in crash-landings at Krumovo as a result of severe damage. Two more of this unit's bombers landed at Salonika with minor AA damage. 30 Squadron probably engaged the I/LG 1 aircraft, this unit losing Uffz Karl Stütz and his crew in L1+SK; a second aircraft crash-landed at Kozani with engine trouble and was completely destroyed (although the crew survived), while a third crash-landed at Salonika with AA damage and was written off.

During the morning there were several other actions reported. At 1000 Sgt V G Hudson, RAAF, an 11 Squadron Blenheim pilot, was flying the unit's Magister from Almyros to Larissa to collect operational orders from Wing HQ, when several Bf109s appeared and attacked him. Although not hit, he was forced down short of Larissa – almost certainly by I(J)/LG 2. Ten minutes later he took off and made for the airfield, arriving just before another of the heavy attacks which rendered most aircraft unserviceable, although the Magister escaped with a few holes in the port wing. Shortly thereafter Hudson flew safely back to Almyros. At Kazaklar during the day Flt Lt Lewis Burnard of 208 Squadron was briefed to carry out a tactical reconnaissance, but on take off the Hurricane struck the wing of a poorly-dispersed Greek PZL. On his return the undercarriage collapsed on landing, the Hurricane suffering further damage.

With the German advance now approaching the Olympus–Servia line, and threatening to outflank the defenders, the decision had been taken to begin withdrawal of the Imperial force to Thermopylae. The reason for this latest move was again an 'Ultra' intercept, which indicated that German armour would be operating to the south of the Olympus line by this date. Following the morning attacks on the Allied airfields, AVM D'Albiac was flown up to Larissa in a Lysander to see for himself the extent of the damage and losses. As a result of the ground forces' planned withdrawal and the day's air attacks, the airfields at Yanina, Kazaklar, Paramythia, Larissa, Niamata and Almyros were to be evacuated. 33 Squadron's remaining Hurricanes would join 30 and 80 Squadrons at Eleusis, while 112 Squadron's Gladiators would share Hassani with 208 Squadron. The remaining Blenheims of 11 and 84 Squadrons would go to Menidi, from where the Wellington detachments of 37 and 38 Squadrons would leave for Shallufa. The few remaining Blenheims of 211 Squadron would withdraw to Eleusis. That evening a Hurricane was despatched by 80 Squadron to drop a message bag to 11 Squadron at Almyros, containing instructions for the move. Unfortunately the drop was made in the wrong area on an airstrip still under construction. As a result the cannister was not located until next morning, the withdrawal not taking place until the evening of 16 April as a result.

When stock could be taken late on 15 April, the strength of the RAF had been seriously reduced, as had the remaining elements of the EVA. RAF operational numbers were now as follows:

Bombers		Fighters	
11 Squadron	8 Blenheims	30 Squadron	14 Blenheim IFs
84 Squadron	9 Blenheims	33 Squadron	5 Hurricanes
113 Squadron	0 Blenheims	80 Squadron	11 Hurricanes
211 Squadron	5 Blenheims	112 Squadron	12 Gladiators
	208 Squadron	2 Hurricanes,	5 Lysanders

By 16 April all was going badly for the Allies. Whilst the Imperial forces were still managing to withdraw in good order across the Plain of Thessaly, improved weather now brought them under constant and heavy air attack just at the point at which the cover afforded by the mountains ran out. To the west, the advance of the German XL Korps units from Skoplje threatened to outflank the gallant but nearly exhausted Army of the Epirus. The offensive against the Italians had already been broken off, whilst the evacuation of the airfields close behind the front – particularly that at Paramythia – denuded the Greek soldiers of the residue of air cover that they had been enjoying.

To ensure the security of these forces, a rapid withdrawal southwards was required, but to give up the territory captured with such sacrifice from the Italians would be quite unacceptable to the troops on morale grounds. All looked hopeless, and during the day general Papagos would explain to General Maitland-Wilson the plight of his army and suggest a British withdrawal to save the country from the full devastation of war.

For the RAF 16 April proved somewhat quieter as the reorganization associated with the general withdrawal south was put into effect. During the morning two of 80 Squadron's Hurricanes were successful in intercepting a raid on Khalkis harbour by some 20 Ju88s from I(K)/LG 1 and I/KG 51. Flg Off Graham caught one – probably 9K+FM of KG 51, flown by Uffz Johannes Uhlick – and shot it down north-east of Poltika. A second bomber – L1+HL of LG 1 flown by Oblt Horst Beeger – was shot down by AA fire into the sea off Khalkis. This was probably the same aircraft pursued by Plt Off Dahl as it lined up to bomb an ammunition ship in the harbour. He only had time to get off a short burst before overtaking it in a steep dive, and was amazed to see it plunge straight into the sea not far from its intended target. Two other Ju88s were lost in crash-landings subsequent to this sortie, possibly both having suffered damage from AA fire. One came down near Salonika with 40% damage, whilst the other crashed at Krumovo while trying to land; the latter was a complete write-off, although all crew members survived in both aircraft.

During the day Hurricanes of 33 Squadron were sent out either singly or in pairs to provide cover for the convoys crossing the Thessaly Plain. During one such sortie Flg Off Dyson was ordered to drop a message bag to one convoy north of Lamia, but while attempting to do so, flying low and slow with full flaps down, a bomb exploded just ahead of him, the blast flipping his aircraft over on its back; he just managed to regain control, and returned to Eleusis badly shaken – a bomb splinter had even ripped the oxygen mask off his face! On another sortie F/Sgt Len Cottingham spotted an Hs 126 observation aircraft of 1(H)/14 'snooping around' and claimed to have shot this down. The Germans reported that this aircraft was 40% damaged by AA over Tirnavas, rather than by fighters, Fw Richter, the observer, being killed, although the pilot survived unhurt. It seems likely that he failed to spot his attacker, and incorrectly identified the cause of the damage suffered.

Two of 208 Squadron's reconnaissance Hurricanes were ordered forward to operate from an advanced landing ground at Pharsala during the day, but next day they would be withdrawn to Eleusis, where they were to be attached to 80 Squadron. At this base Sqn Ldr 'Pat' Pattle, 33 Squadron's illustrious commander, was now both combat fatigued and ill. Although feverish, he would barely accept medication, let alone consider hospitalization, and insisted on continuing to fly. He did however allow his adjutant, Flt Lt Rumsey, to take over the more mundane duties of squadron administration.

Eleusis noted the arrival of two Yugoslav S.79s and two Lockheed 10As from Paramythia during the day, all carrying government personnel. That evening a Do.17K came in to land at Menidi from the same location, but met an unexpected reception, as Marcel Comeau (a 33 Squadron airman) recorded:
'Its occupants, surviving the blitz upon Paramythia on April 15th and the two more heavy bombing and strafing attacks while their aircraft underwent repairs, did not take kindly to the volume of small-arms fire which now greeted them from trigger-happy erks at Menidi. The aircraft circled the aerodrome for a full half hour, kept aloft by airmen pot-shooters. When it eventually landed and discharged its voluble cargo of irate, fist-brandishing Yugoslavs, the erks made themselves scarce....'

In the opposite direction, two Sunderlands of 230 Squadron were flown up to Kotor harbour on the Yugoslav coast by Sqn Ldr P R Woodward and Flg Off E Brand, ostensibly to evacuate the British Legation party which was supposed to have made its way there from Belgrade. On arrival there was no sign of the British party, but a number of foreign diplomats and their staff were present, all anxiously awaiting some form of transport. Rather than return empty-handed, the two flyingboats flew back with 44 such persons aboard, plus four British subjects, one of whom was a wounded Blenheim pilot.

Towards evening six 80 Squadron Hurricanes were again scrambled, this time intercepting bombers – again reported as Ju88s – which were attacking a munitions factory half a mile from Eleusis. Plt Off Vale and Plt Off Still each claimed one destroyed near the target, whilst Sgt Ted Hewett chased another to the north and claimed this shot down as well. These would appear to have been Do.17Zs of Stabstaffel/KG 2, which lost three such aircraft – reportedly in the Larissa area. These were U5+GA(Lt Ludwig Rohr); U5+BA (Lt Heinrich Hunger) and U5+DA (Hpt Konrad Ebsen); all the crews failed to return.

During the day the remaining Greek fighters at Kalambaka/Vassiliki were withdrawn to Amphiklia/Lodi, at the foot of Mount Parnassus, to avoid the danger of their being caught on the ground by Luftwaffe fighters now that the whereabouts of their existing base was known. Twenty-one fighters – 11 PZLs, eight Gladiators and two Bloch 151s – flew down to their new airfield. Meanwhile Paramythia and nearby Katsika were again strafed by Bf109s, the pilots of which claimed three aircraft destroyed at the former airfield and two at the latter. The three remaining 815 Squadron Swordfish at Agrinion returned to Eleusis where they joined the other three aircraft of the Greek detachment in evacuating torpedoes and mines to Crete. Fliegerkorps VIII recorded its own losses for the day as three Ju88s destroyed, one Do.17 and two Ju88s missing, five Ju88s, one Bf109, four Do.17s and one Ju87 damaged. One Hurricane was claimed shot down and five unidentified aircraft destroyed on the ground.

Next day Kampfgeschwader 2 again reported the loss of a Do.17Z, this time from I Gruppe (U5 + NH), in the same area as on 16 April, but this was to be the only Luftwaffe loss that day. Only one RAF claim was made when Sgt Barker of 80 Squadron set off to drop a message to the 19th Australian Brigade at Katerine. Having completed his task he was intercepted by three Bf109s, apparently from III/JG 77, which he managed to evade, claiming one shot down; this was confirmed by the Australian troops. Twenty-seven Bf109s (eight of them Jabos) from Stab, II and III/JG 77 were out attacking shipping and airfields near Volos, claiming a direct hit on a freighter and two aircraft destroyed on the ground. One aircraft of III/JG 77 was hit by AA and 60% damaged, the pilot crash-landing at Dojransko on return, but no aerial combats were reported!

At Eleusis 30 Squadron was ordered to despatch half its Blenheim fighters to Crete for convoy patrols and sea reconnaissances, seven aircraft leaving for Maleme next day in consequence. The last of the 16 Wellingtons detached to Eleusis also departed on 17 April, although two were forced to return temporarily with minor technical problems. A further Luftwaffe bombing attack on Piraeus sank the Greek vessel *Petrakis Nomikos* (7020 tons).

Following the capitulation of the Yugoslav armies, rumours were rife in Greece that surrender was imminent. The King of the Hellenes was determined that his country should fight on, and resolved to stay in Athens until the last possible moment, although others counselled that he and his government should evacuate to Crete forthwith. At 1245 on 18 April, 16 Hurricanes from 33 and 80 Squadrons flew low over Athens to strengthen morale amongst the population, but in the city martial law was declared. The president, Alexander Korizis, was against a retirement to Crete, since he considered that pro-German elements would then seize power on the mainland and seek an armistice. Following an emergency cabinet meeting at which no decision was reached, this unhappy man shot himself, having learned that the commander of the Army of the Epirus, Lt Gen George Tsolakaglou, had initiated negotiations with the German 12th Armee for its surrender. Mr K Kodzias, the Governor of Athens, took over as temporary Premier until relieved by the King two days later; Emmanuel Tsouderos was then appointed.

Once of his first actions was to replace Gen Tsolakaglou, and order the Army of the Epirus to fight on. It was by then too late however, the Army's officers deposing the new commander and continuing their negotiations with the Germans; a surrender would take place on 21 April. At this point a British withdrawal from the mainland was agreed between General Wavell, the Supreme Commander, and the Greek King, one of the main reasons being the strength of the opposing air forces, and the inability to counter them with the resources and airfields available.

Meanwhile during the afternoon of 18 April the 16 Hurricanes were again in the air at 1315 on a defensive patrol, but nothing was seen. During the day the fighter force was reinforced by the arrival of five more Hurricanes from Egypt, together with new pilots for the two squadrons; these were Flg Off G D Noel-Johnson (V7800); Sgt M W Bennett (V7773); Sgt F H Leveridge (V7760); Sgt A F Butterick (W9243) and Sgt R T Ware (W9297).

With all the Blenheims now concentrated at Menidi, it was decided that all crews would operate under the control of 11 Squadron. Consequently 14 Blenheims – six each from 11 and 84 Squadrons, and two from 211 Squadron – were off individually during the afternoon to make bombing and strafing attacks on German columns in the Kozani, Katerine, and Lake Kastoria area. During one such sortie Sqn Ldr H D Jones, 84 Squadron commanding officer, was attacked by two Bf110s in the Larissa area, and was chased to the coast near Mount Mavrovouni, where he was obliged to ditch L1391 in the sea.

Local villagers saw the crew climb into their dinghy and start paddling towards the shore, a local motor boat starting out to meet them. At this juncture the Bf110s dived on the dinghy and strafed it – Sqn Ldr Jones, F/Sgt J Webb and Sgt H Keen were all killed, their bodies being recovered and buried in the nearby village of Keramidi. A second Blenheim – T2348 of 11 Squadron – was caught in the Kozani area by a Bf109E of 9/JG 77 flown by oblt Armin Schmidt, and was shot down after it had attacked a German troop column in which eight soldiers were killed and 15 wounded; Plt Off Patrick Montague–Bates and his crew were all lost.

During the day Ju88s of I/LG 1 were briefed to attack roads leading towards Larissa which were now congested with retreating British and Greek troops and refugees. Elements of 4 New Zealand Brigade were caught by the low-flying aircraft, and the Brigade Intelligence Officer, an elderly Major named Ted Dawson, was seen firing a Bren LMG at the strafers; his courage was not rewarded, for moments later the gallant soldier fell to the ground mortally wounded. The steady evacuation of all but first-line aircraft from Greece continued early on 19 April when three 81st Independent Grupa S.79s (Nos 3712–4), two 3rd Bomber Puk Do.17Ks (3348, 3363) and three Lockheed 10As (YU-SAV, -SBA and SBB of Aeroput) all flew off from Eleusis and Menidi for Egypt. They were soon followed by a further S.79 (3702) and by the nine Yugoslav seaplanes which had reached Suda Bay late on 17 April.

Initially seven of the Do.22Kjs and the single Sim XIV (No.157) set off, with an RAF liaison officer aboard No.309, for the flight to Aboukir. En route apparently they passed over a Greek freighter evacuating personnel, and terrified all aboard, who identified the aircraft as hostile! All arrived safely, but No.302 suffered damage when it hit the beach during its landing. One further Do.22Kj which had been left behind at Salamis due to engine trouble, reached Suda Bay next day, flying on to Aboukir on 27 April. The ancient He8 was left behind in Suda Bay due to lack of range, and it was subsequently sunk here. The Dorniers (302, 6–7–8–9–11–12 and 313) later served with 2 (Yugoslav) Squadron under RAF command in Egypt. Altogether about 40 JKRV and Naval Aviation pilots flew out of Yugoslavia to join the Allied forces, while about 200 more airmen made good their escape by ship or on foot.

Yugoslav Naval airmen with Dornier Do.22Kj No.308 after arrival in Egypt. (*Z Jerin*)

The two RAF Wings had by now been abolished and Air Vice-Marshal D'Albiac took personal command of the remaining units from his headquarters in Athens. 19 April was to prove a busy day for the RAF, beginning at 0635 when Sqn Ldr Pattle was reported to have intercepted bombers approaching Athens – the first of an almost continuous chain of raids throughout the day – and apparently claimed two Ju88s shot down and a third probable. There is no confirmation of such losses from the German records on this occasion.

At daybreak Luftwaffe reconnaissance aircraft spotted the Australian, New Zealand and Greek troops retreating across the Thessaly Plain when they were near Pmokos. Soon some 40 Ju87s arrived, bombing and strafing, and causing much damage and confusion, and many casualties. On this occasion seven Hurricanes of 80 Squadron, led by Flt Lt Woods, arrived in the area and

The Yugoslav He8, No.192, partially submerged after being abandoned in Suda Bay, Crete, is inspected by newly-arrived German troops after the fall of the island late in May 1941. (*A Stamatopoulos*)

promptly claimed four of the Stukas shot down before escorting Bf109Es of II/JG27 could intervene. Cheering troops reported seeing at least three of these crash; two were claimed by Plt Off Bill Vale, flying V7134, and one each by Flg Off Dowding and F/Sgt Rivalant. Apparently two Ju87s were lost, one from Stab/StG2, crewed by Oblt Sebastian Ulitz/Ofw Emil Kuklau, which crashed southwest of Elasson with the death of the crew (recorded by the Germans as having been on 18 April), and one of I/StG3 which crash-landed near Kozani, Lt Herbert Wingelmayer being killed and his gunner wounded. The escorting Messerschmitts then attacked, two Hurricanes being claimed shot down, one each by Oblt Wilhelm Wiesinger and one by Uffz Alfred Heidel; in fact only Sgt Casbolt's aircraft was hit, and he was able to return to Eleusis without undue trouble. Casbolt claimed to have damaged one of the attackers, and Flg Off Trollip to have shot one down, but no Messerschmitts were hit on this occasion. The next time Oblt Wiesinger operated however, he was to be shot down by ground fire while strafing, and became a prisoner – but only until the fall of Greece a few days later.

Further defensive patrols were made by the Hurricanes, one at 0758 seeing nothing, while at 0920 seven 33 Squadron aircraft were led off by Pattle to cover the Lamia area, where the army was still hard-pressed as it approached the end of its current withdrawal. Here a lone Hs 126 from 1(H)/23 was seen – 6K+AH, flown by Fw Herman Wilhus. Although the slow reconnaissance machine was flying very low, Pattle led his section down onto its tail and fired a brief burst into it. His attack was followed by Flg Off Woodward, and then by Flt Lt Littler, after which the Henschel caught fire, tipped forward and crashed in flames. The Hurricanes regrouped and continued their patrol for another half an hour when an estimated nine Bf109Es (actually five aircraft from III/JG77) were encountered head-on.

Pattle's quick reactions allowed him to get on the tail of one Messerschmitt, and he reported that following his attack it went down in a glide, flipped over and crashed into the ground inverted. The sky was now full of dogfighting aircraft, but Pattle managed to get on the tail of another Bf109 which he spotted flying low down in a valley towards Lamia. He believed that he had killed the pilot with his first burst, as this aircraft went into a dive and crashed. Meanwhile Flg Off Woodward had claimed a further Messerschmitt, as had Flg Off Moir, whilst Flt Lts Littler and Mitchell both claimed damage to others. In return Moir's aircraft was badly hit and he was forced down at Amphiklia, where P2643 was later destroyed as there were no spares available to repair it. Flt Lt Mitchell's aircraft was also hard hit, but he was able to get back and force-land at Eleusis.

Three Hurricanes were claimed shot down by the German pilots, one each by Oblt Kurt Ubben, Uffz Johann Pichler and Ofw Erwin Riehl. However Ubben's Bf109 was badly damaged and he force-landed in Allied lines, while the Staffelkapitän of 9/JG77, Oblt Armin Schmidt, was shot down and killed northeast of Lamia. A third Messerschmitt flown by Oblt Werner Patz, was also hit and crash-landed at Larissa during the day, but there is no definite confirmation that he had been involved in the fight with 33 Squadron. Subsequently Stabsarzt Dr Stormer of this Gruppe flew down in a Fieseler Storch and landed to pick up Ubben and fly him out; so sudden had been the combat that Ubben believed his aircraft had been hit by ground fire.

By now Pattle's condition had worsened to a point where Sqn Ldr 'Tap' Jones, now acting as Wing Commander, Eleusis, ordered him to reduce his flying and to take off only when the air raid alarm sounded. Pattle took him at his word, and was in the air again with Sgt Casbolt when the alarm went off at 1450. The two flew around for some time without seeing anything, and became separated before Pattle at last saw two aircraft over Khalkis harbour – Casbolt had found the raiders, and as Pattle watched, the Ju88 he was attacking went down trailing black smoke. Pattle then spotted another bomber heading north and diving for its lines. Giving chase, he soon caught up and attacked, reporting that it dived into the sea after its crew had baled out. One Ju88 was indeed reported lost in this area, 9K + EK of I/KG51 being lost, although the Gruppenkommandeur, Hpt Heinrich Hahn, who was abroad, survived to return to his unit. A second Ju88 from I/LG 1 flown by Hpt Siegfried von Eickhorn crash-landed at Salonika due to icing-up, the pilot being injured.

Amphiklia/Lodi, the landing ground at which Flg Off Moir had come down, was to be the target of the Luftwaffe's latest surprise attack on 19 April. Due to the disruption of the warning system, none of the Greek fighters now based there were able to get airborne as Bf109s swept overhead, strafing with great efficiency and skill. All but three of the 21 PZLs, Gladiators and Blochs were destroyed. The German pilots claimed ten 'Glosters' and nine unidentified aircraft destroyed,

263

plus one Spitfire (sic) shot down over the airfield – presumably a Bloch 151 attempting to join the combat. The three surviving fighters were ordered to fly to Eleusis; only 23 Mira's few PZLs, now based at Argos in the Peloponnese remained to offer any Greek aerial resistance.

From Menidi the last remaining Wellington of the 37 Squadron detachment took off to fly back to Shallufa. North-west of Crete the aircraft was attacked by unidentified fighters – probably CR 42s – but was not hit despite several passes. The rear gunner believed that he might have hit one of the attackers, the bomber reaching its destination safely.

Apparently Pattle was again involved in an interception at 1820, when according to his fitter's diary he engaged a number of Bf109s, claiming one shot down and possibly a second, but no further losses were recorded by the Luftwaffe in such circumstances. Two Do.17Zs were lost by I/KG 2 during the day, both apparently to small-arms fire from Imperial infantry, one crew being lost and one surviving, whilst another Dornier from III/KG 2 suffered severe AA damage, and a Hs123 ground-attack aircraft of II(Sch)/LG 2 was hit to a lesser degree. Italian aircraft now turned their attention from the Yugoslav coastal area to the Army of the Epirus, Ju87s attacking Greek columns throughout the day, while 150° Gruppo CT Macchi fighters strafed the airfields at Katsika and Yanina, claiming four Gladiators destroyed on the ground, with a fifth probable. As no serviceable aircraft were based at these fields any longer, these were probably either derelict wrecks, or dummies.

Aircraft burn at Menidi following II/ZG 26's strafe on 20 April, 1941. Blenheims and other aircraft can be seen on the airfield. (*S W Lee*)

Despite its losses, the RAF continued to operate. The two 208 Squadron Hurricanes were out on reconnaissance sorties during the day in the hands of Flt Lt Burnard and Plt Off Attwood, while by night 15 of the remaining Blenheims undertook individual attacks in the Katerine area, all returning with the dawn on 20 April. If 15 April had been the worst day so far for the Royal Air Force in Greece, the 20th was to be its ultimate nemesis. Faced by the continued successful resistance of the British air units, the Luftwaffe now launched a sustained attack on the Athens area. At dawn two Hurricanes from 80 Squadron were up on patrol, but although hostile aircraft were reported approaching, none were seen. Soon 12 more Hurricanes were airborne from Eleusis, six drawn from each of the squadrons, and these began to patrol to the south of Domokos. Again no Luftwaffe aircraft were seen, but as the formation headed for home a lone Do.17Z of III/KG 2 was encountered near Larissa – probably U5+ES, flown by Lt Gert Lauriant. It was at once engaged by several Hurricanes and shot down into the sea, but Flg Off Frank Holman's fighter, V7860, appeared to be hit by return fire and he broke away to make a belly-landing in a field near Megara. Striking an obstruction, the Hurricane flipped over on its back, the pilot's neck being broken in the crash.

Between 0550 and 0650, 36 Bf109Es of Stab, II and III/JG 77, five of them carrying bombs, attacked shipping targets around Athens, claiming a direct hit on a 3000 ton steamer and a near miss on a 1500 ton vessel. A Schwarm from III Gruppe broke off to attack Menidi airfield, where they claimed five Blenheims destroyed on the ground, including one by Oblt Kurt Lasse. Several were indeed badly hit, and an ancient Valentia biplane transport of 216 Squadron (JR9764) went up in flames. About an hour later a formation of Bf110s from II/ZG 26, led by Oblt Ralph von Rettburg, made a second strafe of the airfield, their arrival coinciding with that of a Blenheim flown by Sgt Vernon Hudson, which the latter managed to get down and taxi to safety seconds before the Messerschmitts hit the target.

For his second lucky escape in four days he received the nickname – 'Lucky'! Marcel Comeau graphically described the second strafe:
'Preceded by a terrified assortment of stray dogs racing across the landing ground, the 110 destroyers hit Menidi. Bellies scraping the grass, they flashed past as if propelled by the rhythmic thumping of their cannons. Suddenly the aerodrome was alight with Bofors and small-arms fire. A Greek Junkers burst into flames on the hangar apron. A Blenheim collapsed suddenly on a broken oleo. The noise was terrific. So low were the Messerschmitts flying that a nearby Bofors sent a burst into another Bofors across the aerodrome, killing the officer in charge. Then they were diving back for a second run in.... Out in the open a bunch of eight Aussie soldiers having a late breakfast alternated between taking mouthfuls of tinned sausage and rifle-potting the passing aircraft. A dozen columns of smoke arose among the Blenheims.'

LAC 'Paddy' Duff, an 11 Squadron mechanic, was seen to grab a Lewis gun from an unserviceable 84 Squadron Blenheim and walk up the centre of the airfield, blazing away from the hip at the oncoming Zerstörer. Miraculously he was not hit! During the two raids four Blenheims had been totally destroyed, two each from 11 and 211 Squadrons, one more from 84 Squadron had been seriously damaged, and another five from all three units had been less seriously hit. A Yugoslav S.79 had also gone up in flames, as had the Greek Junkers and the Valentia.

Valentia JR9764 of 216 Squadron burnt out at Menidi following the 20 April strafe. (*E Bevington-Smith*)

Two hours later at 0945, two 80 Squadron Hurricanes were despatched to intercept German aircraft reported to be attacking Khalkis harbour, where the Greek *Moscha L. Goulandri* (5199 tons) was bombed and sunk. As the British fighters approached, they were attacked by three Bf109Es from Stab/JG 27, Plt Off Still (V7748) promptly being shot down and killed near Tanagra by Maj Wolfgang Schellmann, while Sgt Bennett's V7356 was badly damaged, although he managed to return to Eleusis.

By midday formations of Luftwaffe bombers and fighters were roaming over the plains of Southern Greece at will, bombing and strafing almost with impunity, although the few Hurricanes at Eleusis were constantly going out on patrol. Bill Winsland of 33 Squadron recalled:

'Somehow or other during that hectic day though I went up a number of times I never made contact with the enemy. There was a good deal of cloud about, amongst which their bombers and fighters sneaked in and out. Every time we spotted any machines they hopped into the clouds so that we were often unable to get any "duck-shooting" at all. Others however had very different stories to tell. Every time they went up they ran into absolutely hordes of the bastards! Though I never fired my guns that day I honestly think it made me an older man. I was on edge every second. Every speck on my windscreen was an enemy, every bird behind me was a Hun; my head was all but twisted off my neck with continuously looking round behind my tail. In and around every cloud I expected to come up against one of those hordes. I honestly thought I was bound to "catch my packet" that day. We all thought the same deep down somewhere.'

At last at about 1400, 29 Bf109Es from II and III/JG 77 appeared over Eleusis and Tanagra airfields, Sqn Ldr Pattle engaging one formation from III Gruppe and claiming two shot down during a brief combat. One of these is believed to have been the aircraft flown by Uffz Fritz Borchert, which failed to return, whilst the second was damaged and crash-landed at Larissa. The German pilots claimed a further 13 aircraft destroyed on the ground.

Messerschmitt Bf109E of III/JG 77 crash-landed on Larissa airfield on 20 April 1941, the pilot being captured. It is possible that this aircraft had been damaged in combat by Sqn Ldr 'Pat' Pattle of 33 Squadron. (*IWM and E G Jones*)

At 1535 Eleusis itself came under attack by II/JG 27 Bf109Es, their fire destroying several aircraft including two 33 Squadron Hurricanes and two of the three surviving Greek fighters here. A petrol bowser was hit and set on fire, AC Cyril Banks of 33 Squadron promptly jumping into the blazing vehicle and driving it clear of the other Hurricanes. Six RAF personnel were also slightly wounded during the attack. Flt Lt Davidson of 30 Squadron had a narrow escape; at the controls of a Blenheim, he had just arrived in the circuit as the Messerschmitts appeared, but believing these to be Hurricanes, he continued his approach, waiting his opportunity to land.

Suddenly to his horror he realised that the fighters were hostile, and seeing a cloud of smoke over the corner of the airfield rising from some burning aircraft or motor vehicles, he hurriedly put down and 'hid' in this Plt Off Roald Dahl later wrote of the attack:

'There were many 109s circling the aerodrome, and one by one they straightened out and dived past the hangars, spraying the ground with their guns. But they did something else. They slid back their cockpit hoods and as they came past they threw out small bombs which exploded when they hit the ground and fiercely flung quantities of large lead balls in every direction .... then I saw the men, the ground crews, standing up in their slit trenches firing at the Messerschmitts with their rifles, reloading and firing as fast as they could, cursing and shouting as they shot, aiming ludicrously, hopelessly, aiming at an aeroplane with just a rifle. At Eleusis there were no other defences. Suddenly the Messerschmitts all turned and headed for home, all except one, which glided down and made a smooth belly-landing on the aerodrome.'

This was Ofw Fritz Rockel in Werk Nr.4952, whose shin had been shattered by a bullet. Dahl continues:

'Then there was chaos. The Greeks around us raised a shout and jumped on to the fire tender and headed out towards the crashed German aeroplane. At the same time more Greeks streamed out from every corner of the field, shouting and yelling and crying for the blood of the pilot. It was a mob intent upon vengeance and one could not blame them.'

Fortunately for Rockel, RAF personnel reached him first and he was lifted from the cockpit and driven to the Medical Officer for emergency treatment.

Bill Winsland had a narrow escape during this attack:

'I was enjoying the luxury of a hot bath, when suddenly all hell was let loose on the building; two cannon shells smashed through the window over the bath and exploded against the tiled wall three feet to my right, and just below the level of the top of the good old-fashioned cast iron bath. Bits of concrete and shell hit the outside of the bath without penetrating it, and the window glass spent its force against the inside top edge before falling quite gently onto the water and settling down all over me without actually cutting me or damaging the "family jewels" at all!'

'Pat' Pattle was airborne at the time the attack developed, and came upon a Ju88 which he claimed shot down at 1541. He then returned to Eleusis to replenish his ammunition ready for the next attack. However, following the assault on the airfield, there had been a pause in activity which allowed a little time for the ground crews to bring the maximum possible number of Hurricanes up to readiness state. Sqn Ldr 'Tap' Jones decided that if no further attack had developed by 1800, all available Hurricanes would undertake an offensive sweep in an effort to raise morale amongst the civilian population of Athens and the surrounding areas, and as a boost to the defenders of Eleusis as well as to the pilots themselves.

However at about 1645 a formation of 100 plus Ju88s and Do.17s, escorted by Bf109s and 110s was reported approaching Athens. The Junkers – aircraft of I/LG 1 – peeled off to make low-flying attacks on shipping at Piraeus, while individual Bf110s of II/ZG 26 scoured the area, shooting up likely targets. One appeared over Eleusis just as the Hurricanes – nine of 33 Squadron and six of 80 Squadron – were preparing to take off. Fortunately, none were hit, and all took to the air individually, climbed to 20 000 feet and headed for Piraeus, forming sections of two or three en route.

The first trio to arrive over the port, flown by Flg Offs Wickham, Starrett and 'Ping' Newton, caught 15 Ju88s dive-bombing ships in the harbour; indeed, the Greek hospital ship *Ellenis* was sunk during the attack. The three Hurricanes followed them down and attacked as they pulled out of their dives; Wickham claimed one shot down, whilst the Rhodesian Newton claimed two more. Just then Plt Off Vale arrived on the scene, reporting seeing some 30 Ju88s:
'I carried out eight attacks on the Ju88s. One caught fire and started going down, so I left him and attacked another. Big chunks broke away from his wings and fuselage, and smoke poured from his engines. He went down vertically. I was then attacked by a 109, but I easily outmanoeuvred him, had a crack at some more, and came home when my ammo was exhausted.'

One Ju88 flown by Uffz Helmut Benke (L1+ZH) was lost near Athens with all the crew; a second, L1+UK, piloted by Obfhr Werner Ziegler, was hit by a Hurricane's fire and the navigator, Gefr Heinrich Baumgartner, received three bullets in the head and neck, dying almost at once. The gunners believed that they had shot down the attacking fighter, reporting seeing it fall into the sea near Kalamaki (it was probably the crash of Renke's Ju88 they had seen, or the explosion of bombs). A second Hurricane then attacked, putting the starboard engine out of action. This was also claimed hit by Gefr Hans Baumann, the radio operator/air gunner, and was seen making for land. However the Ju88 was rapidly losing height and although the crew threw out all removable equipment to reduce weight, it ditched in shallow water near Karies, at the foot of mount Athos. The remaining members of the crew survived the crash. A third Ju88 suffered engine trouble, but struggled back to Krumovo, where it crash-landed.

The Hurricane hit by Baumann was probably that flown by Harry Starrett (V7804), which caught fire as a result. Starrett decided to fly back to Eleusis to attempt to save his aircraft, and Bill Winsland witnessed his approach, wheels-up:
'A Hurricane came in, in flames from end to end, to try and land at Eleusis. He

was holding off, going up and down between 50–100 feet, being terribly burnt no doubt, and "feeling" for the ground, almost certainly being unable to see it, except possibly at right angles sideways. He soon hit the ground very hard.'

The Hurricane had almost slid to a halt when the glycol tank blew up and the aircraft was enveloped in flames. Starrett managed to get out, but had been very severely burned; he was rushed to hospital but died two days later.

Four more 80 Squadron Hurricanes now joined the battle, Flt Lt Woods leading Sgt Casbolt, and the Frenchman F/Sgt Pierre Wintersdorff, to attack a formation identified as Bf110s, but probably composed of Do.17Zs from I and III/KG 2, escorted by the twin-engined Messerschmitts. Woods carried out two or three separate attacks, believing that he had probably shot down two before breaking off to return to Eleusis to rearm. Wintersdorff claimed one aircraft shot down in flames, which he identified as an 'FW 187', but he was then attacked by a Bf110 and wounded in one leg; his Hurricane was hard hit and he baled out into the sea from where he was soon rescued. Sgt Casbolt claimed two aircraft as Bf110s, but was also then attacked from astern and had his rudder shot away. Breaking away, he encountered a Bf109 which he reported he had shot down in flames.

Meanwhile the fourth pilot, Sgt Ted Hewett, found himself above six Bf109s and later reported:
'I dived on the rear one, and he rolled on his back, and crashed to the ground with smoke pouring out. I made a similar attack on a second, and the pilot baled out. Then I had a go at a third, but didn't see what happened this time.'

These Messerschmitts were possibly from III/JG 77, two aircraft from this unit crash-landing, badly damaged. Three Do.17Zs also failed to return; U5+AL (Uffz Helmut Riem), U5+HL (Lt Joachim Brüdern) and U5+AR(Oblt Ludger Holtkampe) were all lost with their crews. Apparently Bf109Es from 4/JG 27 were also involved in combat at this time, possibly with the 80 Squadron aircraft. Oblt Rödel claimed three Hurricanes shot down in just over ten minutes, 1657–1708, while Ofw Schulz claimed another at 1710.

At Eleusis the returning Hurricanes were being refuelled and rearmed as swiftly as possible, before climbing back into the fray. Sqn Ldr Pattle was by now very ill with influenza, his temperature having been recorded as 103°. Nonetheless he took off with Flg Off Vernon Woodward, following Flt Lt Woods, who was now off for the second time. Pattle and Woodward had not taken off before, as their aircraft had not been ready. Woodward recalled:
'I took off late with Sqn Ldr Pattle – we climbed into a swarm of Ju88s protected by masses of Messerschmitt 110s. We were overwhelmed. In sun I recall shooting a 110 off Pattle's tail, in flames, then probably a Ju88. Shortly afterwards Pattle got a confirmed Ju88 (or Bf110). Subsequently I lost contact with him, then damaged three more 110s, then, being out of ammunition returned tentatively to Eleusis. It was all over – for that day.'

Ahead of Woodward, Pattle was seen going to the aid of the Hurricane flown by

Flt Lt 'Timber' Woods, which was being attacked by a Bf110. He opened fire at this aircraft and it was seen to burst into flames (presumably the aircraft Woodward had seen him destroy), just as Woods' Hurricane also caught fire and dived into Eleusis Bay. Two more Bf110s latched onto the tail of Pattle's AS988, and it quickly began to blaze – there was an explosion, and the wreckage fell into the sea. Flt Lt Jimmie Kettlewell arrived on the scene just in time to see the demise of his gallant leader and attacked one of the two Messerschmitts responsible, shooting this down into the Bay also. He too was then attacked by yet another Bf110, and was forced to bale out when V7807 was badly hit. He landed heavily, cracking two vertebrae in his spine.

Yet another Hurricane was falling to the 110s at this time; F/Sgt Cottingham had claimed three of the big Zerstörer in flames, but he was hit by a fourth and wounded, baling out of his stricken aircraft. The pilots of II/ZG 26's 5 Staffel, led by Hpt Theodor Rossiwall, claimed five Hurricanes shot down in this engagement, one each by Rossiwall himself (his 12th victory), Oblt Sophus Baagoe (for his 14th), Ofw Hermann Schönthier, Uffz Fritz Muller and Ofw Theodor Pietschmann. However two of the Gruppe's aircraft were lost in return – 3U+EN (Oblt Kurt Specka) and 3U+FN (Fw Georg Leinfelder), while a third crash-landed with severe damage.

Probably one of the last pilots in the air was Plt Off Dahl, who saw numbers of aircraft before attacking a Ju88 which was already going down to ditch in the sea. He was shot at by the gunners even as the aircraft started to settle in the water! Dahl managed to get his badly damaged Hurricane – the result of earlier tussles with Messerschmitts – back to Eleusis.

Junkers Ju88A-4, believed to be from KG 51, seen at Athens in April 1941, following the capture of the capital. (*Bruni via Lucchini/Malizia*)

During this day of incessant combat, the Luftwaffe claimed 14 Hurricanes and one Spitfire (sic) shot down, whereas eight Hurricanes had actually been lost, and a ninth badly damaged; four pilots had been killed, one died subsequently, two were wounded and one injured. The Germans also claimed three aircraft destroyed on the ground at Agrinion airfield (possibly Yugoslav S.79s and Do.17Ks), six at Tanagra (where the last of the EVA bombers – Blenheims, Battles and Potez 63s – were all destroyed), five at Menidi (RAF Blenheims) and seven (four Blenheims and three Hurricanes) at Eleusis. The aerial victories had been credited four to II/JG 27 and five to 5/ZG 26, the claimants for the remaining five being uncertain, but probably pilots of 4 and 6/ZG 26. Total Luftwaffe losses amounted to four Do.17Zs, two Ju88As, three Bf110s and five Bf109Es (one of which crashed into a hillside in bad visibility).

The Hurricane pilots were credited with 20 shot down, the breakdown of types differing in various reports; this account considers the claims to have been for five Ju88s, eight Bf110s, one 'FW 187', one Do.17 and five Bf109s. Eight were also listed as probables, including seven twin-engined types and a Bf109. Fourteen of the 20 'confirmed' were claimed during the final battle, as were the eight probables; ground defences claimed two more Bf109s shot down. For the RAF, the greatest loss had to be that of Sqn Ldr Pattle, who in his last battle had accounted for what may well have been his 50th victory (by far the top-scoring RAF pilot of the war). Twenty-six year-old Marmaduke Thomas St John Pattle, a first generation South African of English parentage, would never be forgotten by the small band of survivors. Christopher Buckley in the official history ('Greece and Crete'; HMSO) stated:

'In terms of heroism in the face of odds, the pilots of these 15 fighters deserve to rank with the heroes of the Battle of Britain. They destroyed 22 enemy aircraft, perhaps eight more, but in the action they lost a third of their number. And that indeed constituted a Pyrrhic victory.'

(The quoted 22 victories seems to have been made up of an addition of the 14 'confirmed' and eight 'probables', or alternatively the total claimed by the defences for the whole day, including the two claimed by the gunners; both these equations add up to 22.)

The 15 Hurricanes which took part in the final battle over Athens had been flown by:-

80 Squadron
Flt Lt W J Woods, DFC   (V7852) Killed in action
Flt Lt G F Graham
Flt Lt G W V Kettlewell   (V7807) Injured in action
Flg Off The Hon D A Coke
Plt Off R Dahl
Plt Off W Vale, DFC
Sgt E W F Hewett, DFM
Sgt C E Casbolt
F/Sgt P Wintersdorff   (V7718) Wounded in action

33 Squadron
Sqn Ldr M T StJ Pattle, DFC and Bar (AS988) Killed in action
Flg Off H Starrett   (V7804) Died of burns
Flg Off V C Woodward
Flg Off P R W Wickham
Plt Off P A Newton
F/Sgt L Cottingham   (V7765) Wounded in action

Even as the battle raged over Athens, the last two reconnaissance Hurricanes of 208 Squadron had managed to carry out three sorties from Eleusis, flying over the battle areas to the south of Elasson, Larissa, Almyros and Lamia, Ju52s being seen landing troops and guns near this last location. All sorties were completed without interception, but on this date the unit's last three Lysanders at Hassani were ordered to fly to Argos in the Peloponnese. That night the RAF attempted to hit back, all available remaining Blenheims at Menidi going off at ten minute intervals from 0300 onwards to bomb Kozani and Katarine airfields, and any motor vehicles which might be seen.

The Germans pressed their advantage next morning, starting at Eleusis which was attacked between 0700 and 0730 by 20 Fliegerkorps Ju87s and escorting Bf109Es, which strafed. It had become apparent from previous attacks that the Luftwaffe hoped to take Eleusis for their own early use, and whilst strafing attacks had been made, no bombs had been dropped. Although several Hurricanes had been damaged in these attacks, few had been destroyed, and with the realization that bombers would probably not appear, the damaged aircraft had been moved into one of the hangars where they could be repaired reasonably free from attack.

On this morning however, the Stukas proved the reading of the situation wrong, splitting up to attack the hangars. The others contained only training and non-combatant machines, but seven Ju87s attacked that containing the Hurricanes, gaining four hits. Light AA fire seemed to have no effect, and a breakdown in the raid warning organization had prevented any fighters being scrambled in time; two Hurricanes in the hangar were destroyed and several others suffered further damage. When the Bf109s came down to strafe, the AA gunners had more success, claiming two shot down; it would appear that one at least was hit, Bf109E 5599 of I(J)/LG 2 crash-landing near Larissa after the attack.

Menidi was next to be attacked, 12 Bf109Es strafing at 1100, followed by Bf110s. Several Blenheims were damaged, one of them beyond repair. The fighters also attacked Agrinion, claiming two aircraft destroyed here – presumably abandoned Yugoslav machines. At 1445 it was Eleusis's turn for a repeat visit, but between the two raids the last two Swordfish of 815 Squadron still there had departed for Crete, flown by Lts Oxley and Clifford. It appears that 31 Bf109s from II and III/JG77 were also involved in this attack, and in strafing Menidi airfield, eight aircraft being claimed destroyed on the ground by these units. Between 1340 and 1440 the two JG 77 Gruppen sent out 36 more aircraft to Piraeus, where six Jabos claimed a direct hit on a ship in harbour. One II Gruppe aircraft was hit by AA, Uffz Pfeifer crash-landing his damaged fighter and returned on foot that evening.

Over the same area two Bf110s of 5/ZG 26 collided, Fw Helmut Recker and Ogfr Heinz Nagel and their crews surviving unhurt. In the Larissa area a Do.17Z of Stab/StG 2 (T6+GA) was shot down, Ofw Josef Engler and his crew all being injured and taken prisoner. A Hs 126 of 2(H)/10 flew low over Australian lines in the Thermopyle area and was shot down by a Bren gunner of 2/1st Field Company. Fw Hans Kaisch was unable to control the aircraft (T1+KK) which nosed over, hit the ground and exploded, killing the crew. Elsewhere a Ju88 of I/KG 51 sustained damage and crash-landed on return to Krumovo.

During the day the Luftwaffe had been involved in an incident of rather different character. A Ju52/3m of II/KGzbV 172 flown by Fw Werner, was carrying a dozen paratroops of FallschirmjägerRegiment 1 to the Balkans, when it strayed across the Bulgarian frontier into Turkish airspace near Edirne. Turkish AA guns at once opened fire and the aircraft fell in flames on Bulgarian soil at Otopeni, all on board being killed. Alarmed that some form of invasion might be threatening, the Turkish armed forces were put on immediate alert, two squadrons of Vultee V 11GB attack-bombers and one of PZL P 24 fighters at once being moved to forward airfields in the area. Nothing further transpired, however.

That evening Greek forces defending the Larissa area surrendered to Feldmarschal List, while on the Albanian Front the Army of the Epirus capitulated to the Germans also, Yanina airfield and town falling to the Adolf Hitler SS Motorised Division. It was time for the RAF to get out of Greece – quick!

Cant Z.1007bis bombers of 47º Stormo BT move over from Italy to a Greek airfield for further operations. In the foreground is a burnt out RAF Blenheim; behind are bombers from 261ª Squadriglia, 106º Gruppo (left) and 263ª Squadriglia, 107º Gruppo (right) (*via A Stamatopoulos*)

274

Chapter Six

EVACUATION

Junkers Ju87Bs of the Luftwaffe on a Greek airfield. In the left foreground is the burnt-out wreck of an EVA Potez 25. (*Bib für Zeit*)

Following the surrender of the Army of the Epirus and the damaging air attacks of 20 and 21 April on the Athens area, the British forces prepared to leave Greece as quickly but in as good order as was possible. Only Menidi suffered further heavy attack on 22 April, 31 Bf109s of II and III/JG77 again sweeping in to strafe. Recorded Marcel Comeau:

'Messerschmitt fighters over Menidi put on an aerobatic display which would have drawn a crowd in times of peace. Yellow-nosed 109s skimmed around the perimeter, making daisy-cutting turns, chasing stray airmen down the trenches, and firing at everything and everybody. Twice forming line-astern they roared flat-out across the grass towards the hangars, stood on one wing, and sped like letters through a letter-box through the gap between the sheds. Messerschmitts appeared suddenly from below hedges, among tents, and round hangar corners. Airmen in tree-tops and trenches, firing at them, stood in admiration of their flying skill.'

Eight British aircraft were claimed destroyed by the German pilots, and indeed a number of Blenheims were destroyed (some of them aircraft which had been damaged in earlier raids), whilst others were damaged. By now 11 Squadron had only four left still serviceable, and two of these were Mark Is which had recently been returned by the Repair and Salvage Unit after previous damage had been made good. Between raids these, together with those remaining in 84 and 211 Squadrons, began evacuating personnel to Crete. Each aircraft carried nine passengers at a time. On landing at Heraklion, 11 Squadron's N3560 burst a tyre, swung violently and suffered the collapse of an oleo leg; the pilot broke an arm, but there were no other casualties.

While flying back to Menidi from Heraklion for another load of passengers, the lucky Australian, Sgt Hudson, experienced a further miraculous escape. His Blenheim (L1481) was intercepted by five CR42s from Rhodes and was badly shot-up; he just managed to make a force-landing on the surface of the sea near a small ship, and was soon rescued. Hudson's ordeal was far from over however, for as the vessel and another which was accompanying it approached Nauplia harbour, they were attacked by Ju87s. Since both were carrying munitions, this was more than usually dangerous. Both caught fire, one blowing up on reaching port, while that on which Hudson was present, was abandoned. As he and the crew swam for shore they were machine-gunned by the Stukas, which swept low over the burning ships. Nonetheless, Hudson managed to get ashore safely, and subsequently hitched a lift on another Blenheim for Crete. Soon after take-off, this was attacked by a Bf110 and badly damaged, but managed to reach Heraklion.

He would receive a DFM for his service in Greece, but after returning to Africa his bombed-up Blenheim collided with another while he was preparing to take off for a night sortie during June. On this occasion the aircraft blew up, but yet again he survived – uninjured, but understandably shaken!

At the other airfields the RAF was also now in the process of withdrawal. From Hassani the 14 Gladiators of 112 Squadron (only six of which were operationally serviceable) and four remaining Lysanders of 208 Squadron left for Crete's Heraklion airfield. 112's ground party had only just reached Athens from the Epirus Front, but they were ordered now to move to Argos in the Peloponnese, from where they were to be evacuated. They would reach their destination next day after negotiating scores of overturned vehicles on the Corinth-Argos road, but only to find that some 11 000 RAF and Army personnel had got there before them, and that the two ships on which they were to leave had been sunk! During the night of 23/24 April they moved on again towards

Nauplia, coming under constant air attack when daylight returned, but here at last they were to be ferried out to waiting warships by a number of loading barges.

Meanwhile on 22 April Sqn Ldr P R Woodward had flown in to Scaramanga in a 230 Squadron Sunderland, evacuating 18 RAF passengers and members of the Greek Royal Family to Suda Bay, Crete. From Eleusis soon after dawn six Hurricanes were flown down to Megara landing ground, ten miles south – no more than a field on the coast, surrounded by olive groves. Here as soon as it was light, several hundred local villagers – old men, women and children – appeared and scattered armfuls of heather and bracken over the flattened grass in an attempt to camouflage the new strip. The fighters were hidden amongst the gnarled olive trees, not being called upon for action throughout the day. That evening they were ordered to move on to Argos where the other 12 flyable Hurricanes from Eleusis had arrived a few hours earlier in various states of repair. Argos was another smallish field amongst the olive groves, the pilots finding that the closeness of the trees gave them some problems when landing. A Greek training field, Argos was to be shared with large numbers of Avro 626s and Tutors, all the surviving Potez 25As of 1 Mira, eight PZLs of 23 Mira, and a miscellany of other elderly aircraft; all machines were dispersed amongst the groves. Ground defence was provided by local Greek troops with two Bofors guns and two Hotchkiss machine guns; in the confusion the British AA unit allocated to defend the airfield had gone to the wrong location. Nervy Greek gunners had opened fire as the first of the Hurricanes arrived, and one had been badly damaged. Command of the RAF forces in the area was assumed by Air Cdr J W B Grigson, DSO, DFC, who sought to provide rearguard protection and cover for the retreating troops and ships evacuating them.

The shipping was continuing to suffer severely from the weight of Luftwaffe attacks, particularly in the shattered remnants of the port of Piraeus. Here 23 vessels had been sunk in two days, including the hospital ship *Ellenis*. Nearby, at Megara, the old Greek destroyer *Psara* was attacked by Ju87s whilst at anchor. She put up a fierce barrage in a vain attempt to protect herself but was soon hit by a heavy bomb which shattered her from bow to bridge – 40 crewmen were killed by this one bomb; *Psara* slowly sank, leaving 118 survivors. A second Greek destroyer was lost later this same day when *Ydra* was caught escorting a convoy of ships leaving Piraeus during the evening. An estimated 35 Ju87s arrived and *Ydra* was hit almost straight away, all her guns being put out of action, and about 50 of her crew killed – the destroyer was abandoned, and later sank. Many survivors reached the shore; others were picked up from the sea.

Merchant vessels were hunted down and attacked wherever they could be found, and there were many such targets. Ju87s from I/StG2 found choice pickings in the Gulf of Corinth where, at Antikyra, the 1300-ton tanker *Theodora*, loaded with petrol, was caught by 2 Staffel, Fw Horst Hermann being amongst those who claimed hits on the defenceless vessel; the skipper and 12 crew were killed. Nearby the small coastal tanker *Theodol 2* (657 tons) was also hit and started to burn fiercely. Remaining crewmen on the larger tanker tried to move their vessel to safer waters, but it went aground and the cargo began to leak out.

Soon petrol on the sea started to burn; *Theodol 2* exploded and sank, whilst *Theodora* was completely burnt out. A third vessel, the small freighter *Thraki*, also succumbed to the Stukas. However the attackers did not escape unscathed during this day of intense action against shipping and ground targets – a Ju87 of III/StG 77 (F1+AN; Oblt Wilde) was lost in the Eleusis area, while two Bf109Es, one from Stab/JG 27 (Uffz Caplan missing) and one from II/JG 27 (Uffz Rohlfs wounded) were lost over Molos and Larissa.

'Ultra' intercepts had by now indicated to the British command that Crete was likely to be the next German objective, although Cyprus also seemed to be at risk to provide a 'stepping-stone' to Syria and Iraq if the situation in those countries warranted further involvement. Even as the RAF elements were arriving in Crete therefore, Air Chief Marshal Longmore and Air Vice-Marshal D'Albiac flew in on a short visit to assess the requirements of a fighter defence. Their conclusions: 'No intention of reforming RAF Greece HQ. Left Wg Cdr (promoted Acting Gp Capt) Beamish as Wing HQ, Sqn Ldr Trumble effective o/c Heraklion. 112 Squadron to remain until relieved by flight of 33 Squadron. Other flight at Maleme – with 100% reserve pilots at both aerodromes as they will be on 'stand-by' during daylight hours. Maleme congested so will request C-in-C Med to move 815 Squadron out, enabling Hurricanes and remaining FAA fighters to be dispersed, including in olive groves. At Heraklion no natural cover but aircraft pens built.' (signal to Air Ministry).

Lt Sutton, Senior Observer and FAA Liaison Officer in Greece, now arrived at Maleme with orders to direct construction of an underground operations room, but already the first three Swordfish of 815 Squadron were ordered to leave for Egypt. This was a 300-mile flight to Mersa Matruh, Lt Kiggell taking off to lead Lt Lamb and Sub Lt Rudorf. After about an hour's flight Rudorf's engine began to play up, and sighting a convoy through a gap in the clouds, he headed down, intending to ditch near one of the ships. On emerging into clear air directly over the vessels, he spotted a section of Fulmars climbing towards him, and fearing that these might consider his aircraft to be hostile, he climbed back into cloud, thereby losing sight of the convoy. As a result he decided to head on for Mersa Matruh, landing there safely after some four hours, ten minutes over the sea, despite his faulty engine. Kiggell and Lamb had already arrived, though both had experienced engine misfires.

The Fulmars seen by Rudorf had come from HMS *Formidable*, now well on her way back to Alexandria after the actions over Tripoli (see Chapter Four). Fighter patrols had been maintained all day as the presence of 'shadowers' had constantly been reported, but it was 1724 hours before a raid was finally detected approaching. Two sections of Fulmars intercepted two Ju88s 30 miles out, as more groups appeared on the radar screens. All available interceptors were scrambled, and by the time the attackers got near, 14 Fulmars were in the air. The first pair of bombers (aircraft of 8/LG 1) were attacked by Green Section of 803 Squadron (Lt Bruen and Sub Lt Richards) and Grey Section of 806 Squadron (Lt Henley and Sub Lt Sparke). Green Section forced one Junkers to jettison its bombs and make off into clouds, possibly damaged, while the second raider, flown by Uffz Gerhard Pfeil, was also seen to jettison its bombs before it was shot down into the sea by Julian Sparke; Henley's guns had failed to operate. Lt Jasper Godden, Bruen's observer in '6A', N1951, recalled:

'We saw nothing until the Fleet was well on its way back to Alexandria – at about 1700 hours we spent 30 minutes in combat with two Ju88s. One was shot down – not by us – all I had was a Thompson sub-machine gun – you could see the 0.45in. bullets trickling out of the muzzle – the muzzle velocity was so low!'

Black and White Sections of 806 Squadron also intercepted a lone Ju88, reported to be a 'shadower', and this was claimed probably destroyed by Lt Cdr Evans, Sub Lt Sewell and Sub Lt Orr. No damage was caused to the Fleet, but it had certainly not been 'all action' for the fighters; Godden continues:

'During the Tripoli operation Bill (Bruen) and I flew ten sorties totalling 23 hours – fighter patrols over the Fleet. Very monotonous indeed – especially for the non-driver. The average sortie was two and a half hours, spent scanning the (mostly blue) skies with binoculars and supping oxygen.'

Interceptions next day all proved to be patrolling Sunderlands, and at 1100 on 23 April, the Fleet entered Alexandria safely.

Dornier Do.17Zs off the coast of Greece, seeking Allied shipping. (*Bibliotech für Zeitung*)

At Argos on the morning of the 23rd, ground crews were working hard in very primitive conditions to get as many Hurricanes as possible serviceable, but many tools and spare parts had been lost during the retreat, and only sufficient aircraft would be readied for limited patrols and reconnaissance sorties. During one reconnaissance during the late morning Plt Off Vale (in V7134) encountered a Do.17 near the airfield and chased it away, claiming damage; it is possible that this was 5K+DS of III/KG 3, reported shot down by AA near Corinth; Uffz Wiesmüller and his crew were lost. Two more Hurricanes had been despatched on a defensive patrol to the north, these encountering three Ju88s of I/LG 1 in the process of bombing the road between Athens and Corinth. They had been out on armed reconnaissance looking for ships between the mainland and Crete, but failing to find any, had decided to attack a secondary target rather than carry their bombs back to base. Flg Off Newton attacked L1+LK, causing considerable damage and wounding both the navigator and radio operator/gunner. With the starboard engine knocked out, Uffz Alt crash-landed the bomber amongst olive groves near Almyros. The trio of Junkers had previously attacked a lone Bf109E of Stab/JG 77 in error; Ofw Sawallisch had returned fire and hit one of the bombers, one member of the crew being killed. The pilot managed to regain his base at Krumovo before force-landing.

A further section of Hurricanes was sent to give some protection to hard-pressed Piraeus, where the pilots saw many Ju87s dive-bombing shipping. Sgt Genders made a spirited attack on these, claiming three shot down; on this occasion no definite confirmation of any German losses has been found. However it is possible that this engagement may have actually occurred on 24 April, when three Stukas were reported missing, but no Allied fighter claims for such aircraft have been found.

Meanwhile five replacement Hurricanes had arrived at Argos from Maleme, flown by 80 Squadron pilots. No sooner were these down however, when hordes of Luftwaffe aircraft appeared overhead, the Germans having discovered the whereabouts of the RAF fighters. An estimated 20–25 Do.17s made a level bombing attack from altitude, followed by a similar number of Ju88s which dive-bombed, escorting Bf109s from II and III/JG 77 then sweeping down to strafe. Marcel Comeau recorded:

'Spitting fire, the 109s hit the strip at 400 mph – cutting down the Bofors crews almost before they had a chance to fire. A Hurricane, hit by a cannon shell, roared across the landing field, caught in a ditch and flipped over on its back. Four more Hurricanes, quickly airborne, disappeared from view, but most of the remaining fighters were destroyed on the ground before pilots could reach them. Nearby a handful of Greek Avro trainers folded up in flames.'

The Hurricane which had been hit attempting to take off was piloted by Sgt George Barker – he was slightly wounded and burned. Other pilots hauled him out of the cockpit and helped him to a nearby slit trench. It seems from the records of Fliegerkorps VIII that he had been shot down by a Bf110. Eyewitness Comeau continued:

'There was a 208 Squadron Lysander airborne, skimming the trees with its wheels

Camouflaged Hurricane of 80 Squadron at Argos. (*E G Jones*)

barely 50 yards away with a diving 109 on its tail. Hugging the ground the 'Lizzie' flew past us, its parasol wing and squat body already ripped by the strings of tracers hacking into the aircraft like golden chisels. Neither fire from our machine guns nor the desparate bursts of .303 from the rear gunner could alter the course of events. As the pilot threw his machine towards the protection of a tree-lined gulley, a burst at point-blank range from the fighter sent it crashing into the hillside.'

The crew, Flg Off R H C Burwell and Sgt Feldon, survived the crash, the pilot shaken and the gunner slightly injured. They had been shot down by a pilot of III/JG 77, who claimed the Lysander as a PZL.

During an earlier attack on airfields around Athens by Bf109Es of II and III/JG77 and I(J)/LG2, Hpt Franz Lange, Kommandeur of II/JG77, had reportedly been shot down and killed near Karopi, south of Athens, by a direct AA hit. It is possible that he was shot down by Sgt Genders, who claimed one Bf109 during the morning, either while returning from the sortie to Piraeus, or when scrambled from Argos.

Numbers of German aircraft continued to attack the airfield during the afternoon, but it was not until shortly before sunset that a further major attack developed. Three Hurricanes were up on patrol, one of them flown by Plt Off Winsland, who recalled:

'Three of us were up together on a dusk patrol over our retreating army when suddenly one fire after another blazed up below us, particularly along the road and round our own landing field. We were as nervous as hell already, and the sight of the fires did not improve matters, as it meant enemy fighters were strafing our troops from treetop height and we could not see them. The fading light

281

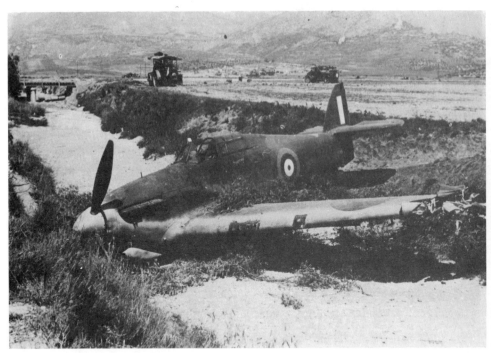

V 7773, an 80 Squadron Hurricane carrying the name 'Surrey' below the cockpit, lies in a dry river bed on the edge of Argos airfield following a crash-landing. It was inspected here by German war photographer, Benno Wundshammer. (*B Wundshammer*)

Hurricane V3732 stands abandoned amongst the olive trees at Argos, surrounded by the shattered wrecks of EVA Avro Tutor trainers. (*B Wundshammer*)

Wrecked Hurricanes at Argos. These machines give the impression of having been rendered unserviceable by the groundcrews, rather than destroyed by strafing. (*Bundesarchiv*)

Smashed Avro Tutors at Argos. (*Bundersarchiv*)

Tanmina

Saturday 1st March. 80 Squadron Hurricanes operating from Paramythia escorted bombers of 30 and 211 squadrons on three raids on Paraboar (north of Buzi), Berat and Valona harbour.

Sunday 2nd March. Tanmina. *weather good* Orders were received for the squadron to proceed to Elevsis with all possible speed, where refitting with Hurricanes would be completed. From Paramythia Hurricanes escorted Blenheims on a raid on Berat aerodrome.

One Hurricane had to return owing to trouble with the undercarriage. The pilot Sgt. Hewett took off as soon as possible to overtake, but on the way ran into 5 C.R.42's which attacked him. He shot three of them down, the other two making off.

A signal was received to the effect that on the recommendation of the A.O.C in C. His Majesty the King had been graciously pleased to award the D.F.C. to S/Ldr. Jones and F/O Cullen for courageous determination and devotion to duty.

Monday 3rd March. Tanmina. *weather good. no cloud* The advance party left at dawn and reached Amphissa by road. Two Hurricanes of 80 Squadron, piloted by F/O Cullen and F/O Ackworth (112) while on patrol S.W. of Corfu intercepted 2 formations of 5 Cant 1007's, the former shooting down 4 and the latter one. Hurricanes also escorted Blenheims on a reco and bombing raid on the road between Tomba and Memalin. Hits were registered on M.T. concentrations near the bridge at Tepelene.

Tuesday 4th March. Tanmina. *weather fair - cloud 5/10 @ 10,000 ft.* Six enemy warships bombarding Himare were attacked by a force of 14 Blenheims escorted by 10 Hurricanes (4 of 80 Sqdn) operating from Paramythia. The fighters engaged an enemy force of 24 G.50's and C.R.42's, and destroyed 80 Squadron Hurricanes destroyed 4 G.50's and 3 C.R.42's and 1 C.R.42 (unconfirmed), 3 G.50's being shot down by F/Lt/Lt. Pattle and 1 G.50 and 3 C.R.42's by Sgt. Hewett. Unfortunately 1 Hurricane *is missing* piloted by F/O Cullen who had only recently had such amazing success. It is hoped that he is safe but no news was obtained and it is feared that he is killed.

Four pages of 80 Squadron's Operational Diary were discovered, written in draft, in the cockpit of an abandoned Hurricane at Argos by the German war photographer Benno Wundshammer. One such page is displayed here. (*B Wundshammer*) together with their excellent camouflage made it virtually impossible to distinguish anything below from the shadows of fields and woods and innumerable fires. It was obvious that there were swarms of enemy machines somewhere below us, but I am damned if I could see them. During that patrol I was on edge from start to finish. My head never stopped turning up and down, round and round for fear of being surprised by the enemy's covering fighters somewhere high above us. The failing light, the fires, the dense columns of black smoke, all those enemy machines, the knowledge that sometime shortly through lack of fuel we would have to go down to land with the enemy ruling the air – all those thoughts did not put me at my ease. Eventually we could keep in the air no longer and went down to land. The wood in which we had hidden all our grounded machines was in flames. Thirty twin-engined German fighters had raked it with cannon-shell and machine gun fire a few minutes before we landed – and once again we never saw them. When I say "we" I only refer to two of us who were following our leader, for, strangely enough, our leader had seen them as he afterwards admitted. His action therefore of not attacking them may seem bad in the eyes of many. His defense however for not doing so was quite reasonable, and I admit I would have done the same had I been leader. Supposing we had attacked and shot down four each (almost impossible and extremely unlikely anyway) the enemy would never have noticed the difference, and we would certainly have suffered very heavily in the process. He maintained that in this case it would not have been clever or anything else to have attacked – it would have been sheer stupidity, especially as the remaining two of us were comparatively inexperienced pilots at the time. Thank God, anyway, for what he eventually did!'

On the airfield all available Hurricanes had been preparing to take off at 1800 to carry out an urgently-ordered shipping protection patrol, but when an estimated 40 Bf110s of I/ZG 26 – led by Maj Wilhelm Makrocki – arrived, only two (Flg Off Coke and Plt Off Dahl) had departed. All the remaining Hurricanes were hit, but the pilots managed to scramble clear and reach the safety of nearby slit-trenches, although Sgt Ted Hewett received a shrapnel wound in the back while sheltering. The Zerstörer remained over the airfield for some 40 minutes, blasting every wreck again and again. Airmen on the ground, hiding amongst the olive groves and in trenches, fired at the low-flying aircraft with machine guns and rifles; Cpl Kimber of 33 Squadron was seen to hit one in its starboard engine and it flew off trailing smoke. Air Commodore Grigson stood in the centre of the field with a rifle, calmly pot-shooting at the many targets while an airman acted as his loader.

By the end of the attack some 13 Hurricanes had been wrecked, including the last reconnaissance aircraft of 208 Squadron. Almost all the Greek aircraft had been destroyed, the Luftwaffe claiming 53 destroyed at Argos during the day. Only two Hurricanes were found still to be flyable following this latest attack, plus the five aircraft which had been airborne. Two of these, those flown by Coke and Dahl, returned to the scene of devastation shortly after the Messerschmitts had departed, the pilots having been unaware of the attack. As they approached Argos, Dahl sighted a small twin-engined aircraft, which he assumed to be a German reconnaissance machine, and dived to get on the tail of this. As he lined up to attack, Flg Off Coke flew up alongside and waggled his wings. It was only then that Dahl realised this his intended victim was an RAF Rapide, which was making for Argos as part of the evacuation force.

The Luftwaffe had also attacked Menidi, Megara and Hassani during the day, Bf110s of II/ZG 26 claiming two twin-engined aircraft destroyed at Menidi, where one 6 Staffel aircraft was shot down by the ground defences; the pilot survived but his gunner, Uffz Kurt Schwan, was killed. At Megara six aircraft were claimed and at Hassani four more. Amongst those destroyed were the six Do.22s of 2 Mira which had been converted into landplanes by the substitution of wheeled undercarriages for their normal floats. One Bf109E of III/JG 77 crash-landed at Almyros during the day.

The Stukas move to Southern Greece to continue the pursuit of the retreating Commonwealth forces. Armourers prepare to rearm these Ju87Bs with recently de-crated bombs.

At the entrance to Suda Bay, Crete, the 300-ton former whaler, HMS *Syvern*, was attacked by Ju87s, the captain and some of the crew being killed and others wounded, although the vessel herself survived. It may have been while returning from this raid that the Stuka crews spotted a Sunderland of 230 Squadron, which was moored at Scaramanga. This aircraft, 'P', L2161, had attempted without success to take off on three engines, so Flt Lt I F McCall had returned to moorings. Seven Ju87s then strafed, the 'boat being repeatedly hit and the inner fuel tanks catching fire; the aircraft rapidly became a mass of flames and a refuelling lighter alongside was also engulfed. While the attack was in progress the two midships gunners, Sgts V C Cordery and G C Starkey, remained at their posts, keeping up a steady fire. They claimed one Ju87 shot down in flames and others hit – although it was possibly during this engagement that Sgt Genders and his wingman appeared overhead and attacked the dive-bombers. Both gunners finally abandoned the sinking and blazing Sunderland, but on jumping into the sea one admitted that he could not swim and had to be aided to safety by the other. Both were subsequently awarded the Military Medal. This attack brought Fliegerkorps VIII's claims for aircraft destroyed during the day to one flyingboat, six twin-engined aircraft, 50 unidentified types, together with one Hurricane and one 'PZL' shot down.

Damaged PZL P-24 of 23 Mira, EVA, abandoned on Argos airfield. Note the unit emblem on the fuselage side ahead of the roundel – a long-legged crab. (*Bundesarchiv*)

During another attack on Suda Bay that morning, a patrolling Blenheim IF fighter of 30 Squadron, flown by Flg Off R E M Blakeway, intercepted and attacked two Ju88s without obvious results. Seven other Blenheims from this unit flew up to Eleusis to pick up a group of stranded personnel from 33 and 80 Squadrons, but whilst there Flg Off Richardson inspected an abandoned Blenheim fighter which had a smashed tailwheel. With the help of several others, the aircraft's tail was raised onto a trolley and pushed onto the runway. Richardson then set off down the runway and got airborne, flying safely back to Maleme where the aircraft was soon repaired.

Five large twin-engined tank landing craft – known as 'A' Lighters for security purposes – each capable of carrying 900 troops, had arrived in Suda Bay during the previous few days to assist in the evacuation of troops from Greece (to be organized as Operation 'Demon', and due to commence during the evening of 24 April). Two of these vessels, A1 (Sub Lt D Peters) and A19 (Lt Cdr P C Hutton – in command of the Lighter Squadron) now sailed up to Megara at 1700 hours, intending to find seclusion under rocky cliffs in nearby inlets or coves until required. While they were seeking suitable hiding places, six Ju87s suddenly appeared and dive-bombed both craft. Neither was hit, but A1 had her light AA guns put out of action before shelter was found under a cliff at Paki Island. Further east, at Lavrion Bay, near Raphtis, a third 'A' Lighter, A6 (Sub Lt J D Sutton), arrived just as Ju88s came in to attack a small Greek steamer in the bay. A6 opened fire with her two pom-poms and as one Ju88 – apparently 9K +CK of I/KG 51 flown by Lt Dietrich Sachweh, swept by, black smoke was seen pouring from the aircraft before it was reported to have crashed into the sea. A second aircraft from this unit flown by Ofw Ernst Mundlein, was also hit by AA fire, the pilot and two members of the crew being wounded. Following this attack, Ju87s arrived on the scene and whilst A6 survived many near misses, the craft was riddled by machine gun fire; she went into hiding until required.

Evacuation of non-essential key personnel from Crete was now underway, some 20 flyable Blenheim bombers from 11, 84 and 211 Squadrons, in varying stages of repair, flying out to Heliopolis via Fuka, while two more of 815 Squadron's Swordfish also left, flown by Lt Torrens-Spence, the commanding officer, and Lt Clifford. They carried Sqn Ldr Tom Wisdom's puppy, 'Wimpey', amongst their passengers. Two unarmed BOAC Empire flyingboats, G-AEUI 'Coorong' (Capt J L M Davys) and G-ADUV 'Cambria' (Capt F V W Foy) arrived at Suda Bay during the day with a 230 Squadron Sunderland to aid in the evacuation. Both 'boats had been partially camouflaged, but time had only allowed the upper surface of the mainplanes and fuselage to be painted. It was 'Coorong's' second trip – she had carried 35 troops to Alexandria during the previous evening. Another arrival was Sunderland L2160 of 230 Squadron, which landed in the bay with 11 passengers evacuated from Scaramanga, including King George and Crown Prince Paul of Greece, Sir Michael Palairet, the British Minister in Athens, and his wife and daughter. They were followed in by a 228 Squadron Sunderland with 50 RAF personnel aboard.

At Argos, following the day's disastrous attacks, Air Commodore Grigson ordered that the seven remaining Hurricanes should fly out to Maleme at dawn; the nine pilots left without aircraft to fly were to be evacuated in the Rapide, which had arrived safely despite Dahl's attentions. After dark three Lodestar transports of 267 Squadron flew in to collect key personnel, the aircrafts' crews reporting seeing the burning hulks of 18 aircraft and much motor transport on fire, as well as two blazing oil tankers in the nearby harbour. At 0430 the Hurricanes and Lodestars set out for Crete, followed by four Greek Avro Tutors and the sole remaining PZL fighter, and five Ansons of 13 Mira (N51, 52, 55, 56 and 61), the latter loaded with personnel. One more of these, flown by Wg Cdr Lord Forbes from the RAF's Air HQ, flew up to Eleusis to collect the wife of a Greek Government official, but as light crept over the airfield, Messerschmitts appeared overhead and swooped down to strafe the helpless Anson, setting it afire. None of those aboard were hurt, but Forbes' adventures were only just beginning! No airworthy Allied aircraft were now left on the mainland; only a handful of seaplanes remained at some of the coastal harbours.

Throughout 24 April the Luftwaffe was to continue its assault on Allied shipping in particular. Three vessels had arrived in Nauplia Bay before dawn, the Greek *Nicolaou Georgios* (4108 tons) and the British *Cavallo* (2269 tons) and *Santa Clara Valley* (4665 tons). All were loaded with ammunition and explosive, while the latter also carried 500 mules and some horses – the Greek Army had used some 20 000 mules for transportation of supplies in the mountains during the war to date. It was immediately clear that there were no facilities for unloading the explosives, but the Veterinary Officer sought to have as many animals released into the sea as possible before air attacks commenced. At about 1100 the first wave of Ju87s arrived overhead, four direct hits killing four members of the crew and causing the vessel to sink with the loss of many of the animals still tethered below. An hour later the *Cavallo* went down, while at about 1500 the Greek vessel, which had been repeatedly hit and set on fire, blew up with a mighty blast which caused damage to many buildings ashore.

Elsewhere two hospital ships, the 2068-ton *Andros* and 875-ton *Policos*, were sunk at Loutraki and Methana respectively, while the defenceless A-1 lighter at Paki Island was attacked at evening by four Ju87s and sent to the bottom by five direct hits; her crew had already evacuated the vessel and gone ashore. The worst disaster occurred at Piraeus at 1800, where the Greek luxury yacht *Hellas* had arrived to help with the evacuation. Capable of carrying over 1000 passengers, 500 members of the British community, mainly Maltese and Cypriots, had come aboard together with many of the Australian walking wounded and their nurses. At this point Ju88s appeared and dive-bombed the harbour, the yacht and a nearby jetty being set on fire; hard-hit, the *Hellas* soon sank with the loss of many lives, only a few of those on board surviving. One of those was Wg Cdr Lord Forbes, pilot of the ill-fated Anson earlier in the day; he managed to swim ashore and later reached Crete aboard a caique. At Piraeus two more small Greek merchantmen were also sunk – *Teti Nomikou* (1882 tons) and *Dimitrios Nomicos* (1171 tons).

These attacks had not been made entirely without cost to the Luftwaffe, although no fighter defence of any sort could be offered. Two of I/StG 2's Ju87s (T6+JH, Uffz Wartmann/Gefr Zapletal; T6+LK, Gefr Hermann/Gefr Lange) were lost in the Athens area, as was a Ju88 of I/KG 51; another Ju87 from I/StG 3 (S7+LL, Lt Edmund Reichardt/Uffz Riegel) was reported missing near Khalkis. The three Stukas may have been the aircraft claimed shot down by Sgt Genders of 33 Squadron on the previous day. A Bf109E of II/JG 77 also came down near Athens, the pilot – future 'Experte' Lt Siegfried Freytag – being wounded.

During the day a 228 Squadron Sunderland flew 40 personnel from Scaramanga to Suda Bay, including Air Vice Marshal D'Albiac and General Sir Thomas Blamey, commander of the Australian forces. This island was coming under increasing attack now however, Ju88s attacking a Greek vessel, the 5524-ton *Kyriaki* in Suda Bay and sinking her. Lt Winstanley of 805 Squadron was up on patrol in a Sea Gladiator and made two attacks on the bombers, but without

Short Sunderland I flyingboats of 228 Squadron off Scaramanga with typical Greek terrain in the background. (*IWM*)

observed results. However Blenheim fighters of 30 Squadron were out around the island on shipping patrol, and at 1775 Plt Off L W Basan spotted a Ju88 dead ahead – L1+KH of I/LG 1, flown by Fw Walter Zucker. Approaching apparently unseen, Basan put four bursts into the aircraft, which made off to the north-east, pouring·black smoke. Another pilot subsequently saw this aircraft dive into the sea. Zucker however, subsequently claimed that he had been shot down by Gladiators, his crew claiming to have shot down one of the attackers.

More Blenheim fighters – this time Mark IVFs of 203 Squadron, which had seen considerable action over East Africa, flying from Aden – now arrived on Crete, five of these aircraft flying in led by Sqn Ldr J M N Pike; another four would arrive next day led by Sqn Ldr J P D Gethin. Each aircraft carried a number of ground crew and a supply of spares, including tail wheels – frequent victims of Heraklion's rutted landing ground! In the opposite direction went 208 Squadron's six Lysanders and the last PZL, all Egypt-bound.

During 24 April the full evacuation of troops from Greece commenced under the codename Operation 'Demon'. This was made easier by the availability of the vessels of Force Z, which had originally assembled for the invasion of Rhodes. This included three assault ships – *Glenearn*, *Glengyle* and *Glenroy*, six of the 18 'A' Lighters, and support transport. *Glenroy* unfortunately went aground in

As 208 Squadron's remaining Lysanders evacuated Greece for Egypt, one came to grief on Crete's Heraklion airfield, losing a wheel. (*E Bevington-Smith*)

Alexandria harbour and would play no part. Six beaches were selected for the main embarkations and were designated as follows:

Beach C	Raphina	Beach S	Nauplia
Beach D	Raphtis	Beach X	Monemvasia
Beach P	Megara	Beach Z	Kalamata

(see Map on page 292 for locations)

Many thousands of troops were now gathering at these points, and all roads leading to them were becoming heavily congested with British, Australian and New Zealand motor transport, Greek ox-drawn waggons and thousands of fleeing refugees. The first evacuations were scheduled for the night of 24/25 April from Nauplia and Raphtis, and during the late afternoon vessels began approaching these sites. As they did so, two He111s attacked, hitting *Glenearn*, which began to burn, four casualties being suffered. However the fires were extinguished and she continued to her destination. On arrival at 2200 off Nauplia the transport *Ulster Prince*, which was accompanying her, ran hard aground, and could take no further part in the operation. All else went well, 6685 personnel (including Marianne, a beautiful blonde dancing girl from Maxim's in Athens) were ferried out to the waiting vessels by lighter A-5, ten smaller 'B' lighters launched by *Glenearn*, each capable of carrying 70 passengers, and the ships' boats. *Glenearn* alone embarked 5100, the rest going aboard the escorting warships.

Amongst those at Nauplia were a party from 113 Squadron, who had made their way from Niamata, led by Flt Lt Rixson. He recalled:

'It was particularly galling and humbling to see the very poorly equipped Greek peasants going north to war, armed perhaps with old fashioned rifles, when we were running away. After crossing the Corinth Canal, we found a railway train which we fired and drove to, or near the port, which was a gathering place for

291

SEA

Agrinion
Missolonghi

Mt.
Parnassus -Dadion
Lepanto
Patras
Gulf of Corinth

EUBOEA
Molos
Thermopylae
ATTICA
Topolia
Khalkis
Tanagra
Menidi
Eleusis Tatoi
Megara
Corinth Canal
Piraeus
ATHENS
Raphina
Raphtis
Laurion
'D' 'C'
Khios

PELOPONNESE

Argos
Nauplia
Mylol
'S'
'P'

Sparta
Kalamata
Moladi
Monemvasia
Neopolis
'X'
'Z'
C.Matapan
Kythera

Kythos

CYCLADES

MIRTOAN
SEA

Melos

Melos

N

Kythera Channel

Antikythera
Antikythera Channel
Kissamos Bay
C.Spada
Kastelli
Maleme Suda Bay
Galatos Canea
Selinos
Sphakia
Plaka Bay
Retimo
Heraklion
CRETE
Tymbaki

SEA OF CRETE

Gavdhos

SOUTHERN GREECE
EVACUATION BEACHES

'C' Raphina   'P' Megara
'D' Raphtis   'X' Monemvasia
'S' Nauplia   'Z' Kalamata

0   25   50   75   100 miles

0   25   50   75   100 kilometres

292

people like ourselves, and other military support units who were hoping to get away. There was a fair amount of general disorder, but the Squadron was extremely well disciplined and received praise from an Irish Guards staff major who was endeavouring to co-ordinate the evacuation as there was considerable unruliness amongst the various nationalities and arms being evacuated. We were evacuated with many others, getting to a variety of Naval ships, using landing type barges. The Navy looked after us very well, although the RAF was not all that popular as naturally the German air force had control of the air, and there was very little protection for the Naval ships.'

At Raphtis 5750 more troops – mainly New Zealanders – were ferried out to *Glengyle* and the AA cruiser *Calcutta* by A-6, the corvette *Salvia*, and other smaller vessels. A-6 then carried 500 more men down the coast to Zea Island for later evacuation. The vessels from the two beach areas rendezvoused at 0800 and set course for Suda Bay, arriving safely late in the afternoon of the 15th despite attack by three Ju88s, one of which was claimed probably shot down by the AA guns of the escorting warships. At dawn six Blenheim IFs from 30 Squadron from Maleme and three Mark IVFs of the newly-arrived 203 Squadron from Heraklion had been sent off to cover the vessels, but had not been advised of each other's involvement, and consequently Blenheim pursued Blenheim! However at 0800, as the two sets of shipping rendezvoused, Flg Off Smith of 30 Squadron spotted two Ju88s at about 4000 feet and attacked both, claiming hits on one which dived away pouring black smoke; the other was believed to have been hit by the ships' AA, but in neither case has any record of damage been found in German documents.

The day was to see the virtual end of the main fighting, when the Thermopylae Pass was taken after a heroic defence by ANZAC troops – on ANZAC Day! Under constant assault by Fliegerkorps VIII Stukas, the Allied troops had been unable to halt the two Panzer Divisions and the infantry of 141 Mountain Division, although at least 15 tanks were claimed destroyed and as many more temporarily out of action. Withdrawal to the next line of defence was ordered. Meanwhile other German troops occupied Lemnos and other Aegean islands.

Aircraft of Fliegerkorps VIII again strafed Argos airfield, claiming 19 aircraft destroyed – but these were obviously some of the damaged and wrecked aircraft left here. While escorting three Ju87s at midday, one of two Bf109Es of III/JG 77 was shot down by AA near Nauplia, Fw Otto Unertl of 9 Staffel being killed. The anti-shipping forces were again out in strength; bomb-carrying Bf109Es from III/JG 77 were led off from Tanagra by Maj Alexander von Winterfeldt (an ex-World War I pilot), to hunt for shipping engaged in the evacuation. In Nauplia Bay the stranded *Ulster Prince* was soon spotted, and while von Winterfeldt and his adjutant, Lt Diethelm von Eichel-Streiber, carried out distracting mock attacks to draw off the AA fire, Oblt Wolf-Dietrich Huy gained a direct hit on the transport from low level. The Messerschmitt pilots subsequently reported that the ship poured forth heavy smoke and at once capsized. It appears however that Ju87s attacked at the same time, as did Ju88s of I/LG 1. Lt Gerd Stamp of the latter unit reported seeing his bomb strike the vessel which soon became a blazing wreck. All three attacking units believed that they had been responsible for the sinking! By now Huy's Rotte were very low on fuel and were forced to land at Corinth airfield, still behind British lines. Here they discovered cans of fuel on the abandoned base, and after refuelling, started their engines again with hand cranks, returning to Tanagra where it had been assumed that they had all been shot down.

Other bombers sank the Greek *George A Dracoulis* (1570 tons) off Piraeus. Two of I/LG 1's bombers then spotted a convoy approaching during the afternoon – this was the next phase of the evacuation underway, the 16 082-ton Dutch vessel *Pennland* and the *Thurland Castle*, with an escort provided by the AA cruiser *Coventry* and three destroyers, on their way from Suda Bay to Megara – Beach P. The Ju88s attacked at about 1500 hours, one bomb shattering *Pennland*'s bridge and wheelhouse, putting her compasses and stearing gear out of action. The destroyer HMS *Griffin* went to her aid, and for a while she headed on towards Megara, but the damage was too great, and she turned south for Crete, accompanied by *Griffin*. At 1650 the bombers returned, one gliding out of the sun to place two bombs directly onto the ship, one of which pierced the deck and exploded in the engine room, killing three of the crew. Capt van Dalken gave the order to abandon, and before she sank 300 survivors were rescued by the attendant destroyer. Two more destroyers were ordered to join the Megara force, followed later by another three.

Despite the loss of the *Pennland*, 5900 persons – mainly Australians – were evacuated from Megara that night, including 1500 sick and wounded and 80 nurses. Lighter A-19 suffered engine failure and was abandoned, some 300 troops being left behind at Megara as a result.

228 Squadron's Sunderland T9048, DQ-N, evacuating RAF personnel just prior to its loss in a night landing accident on 25 April, 1941. (*IWM*)

Another of 228 Squadron's ubiquitous Sunderlands – T9048 – had flown up to the Githeon area in search of an RAF party, but on landing Flt Lt H W Lamond was met by a Greek air force officer who directed him to fly further up the coast. Here flashes from a hand-held mirror were spotted and the 'boat alighted to find the missing group of 101 officers and men of 112 Squadron, 52 were flown out, Lamond promising to return that evening, orders permitting. True to his word, he returned after dusk, but as he attempted to land the Sunderland struck an obstruction and crashed. Lamond and three of the crew survived, but two of these were seriously injured. They drifted for several hours on an upturned wing until picked up, but Lamond then elected to stay with the injured, the three of them subsequently becoming prisoners when the Germans overran the area.

On Crete three more of 815 Squadron's Swordfish returned to Egypt during the day, while efforts were redoubled to form a viable fighter defence for the island. Due to shortage of Hurricanes 80 Squadron was required to leave only four pilots on the island, the remainder being evacuated to Egypt in a 267 Squadron Lodestar. These four, Flg Off Wanklyn Flower, Plt Off Vale, F/Sgt Rivalant and Sgt Bennett, joined others of 33 Squadron to form a composite unit with seven Hurricanes (V7181, 7461, 7761, 7795, 7800, 7826 and W9297). One of these had an irreparable hole some ten inches in diameter through the main spar of one wing, but was still to be used due to the small numbers available; the pilots agreed to take turns in flying it, although it was feared that any tight turning would probably result in the wing breaking off!

From Egypt Convoy AG14 headed out towards Crete to aid in the evacuation; *Glenearn*, on her second trip, was joined by the *Khedive Ismail* and the Dutch *Slamat*, escorted by three warships. Towards evening the vessels were twice attacked in the Kaso Strait by three S.79s, but no damage was done. On arrival in Suda Bay that night increasing congestion was found. Two more 'A' Lighters – A-15 and 20 – had arrived, as had a Yugoslav submarine, *Nebojsa*, and two torpedo-boats which had been at sea for eight days since leaving Cattaro Bay. An unusual craft to arrive was a refuelling barge which had been used by 230 Squadron's detachment at Scaramanga. This carried 600 gallons of aviation fuel and was fitted with four salvaged Vickers machine guns, manned by Sqn Ldr Alington, three other RAF men, a Colonel and a private soldier of the Greek Army and three nursing sisters! The barge had reached Suda Bay without being attacked.

As these various vessels reached Crete, the convoy loaded with troops from the Megara beaches was also now on its way southwards towards the island, but with daylight on 26 April it came under attack by a constant procession of small formations of aircraft. First came two Ju87s, then a pair of bomb-carrying Bf109Es, then a few Do.17Zs. At midday a dozen Ju87s attempted to attack, but their formation was broken up by fire from *Coventry* and the destroyers, while three 203 Squadron Blenheim fighters which were in the vicinity on patrol, attempted to engage. Sqn Ldr Gethin attacked eight of the Stukas, hits being observed on several from both front and rear guns. Observers on the ships reported that at least one was seen to be shot down, but no German losses are recorded. Gethin continued his pursuit for ten minutes, but could not gain on the fleeing aircraft. Flg Off E W Lane-Sansom was attacked by a reported five Bf109s and one Ju87, his aircraft receiving some hits in the wings, but he escaped by diving away and leading his pursuers over the naval barrage.

A Junkers Ju88A leaves on a sortie from its new Greek airfield, passing over the remains of one of the previous residents – a Greek Blenheim IV which exhibits evidence of a fighter strafe, both 7.9mm bullets and 20mm cannon shells having passed through the fuselage. (*Bundesarchiv*)

At 1150 three Ju88s from I/LG 1 attacked, but gained no hits, while a further attack by three more at 1315 achieved no more success. As the vessels approached Suda Bay, Hurricanes, Fulmars and Sea Gladiators from Maleme and 30 Squadron Blenheims appeared overhead. At 1800 the convoy put into Suda Bay; *Thurland Castle* had six feet of water in her hold due to damage to her plates caused by near misses, but there were no casualties amongst the 3500 troops she carried.

Meanwhile *Glenearn*, *Khedive Ismail* and *Slamat*, escorted by *Calcutta* and four destroyers had set out for Greece, during the afternoon coming under increasingly heavy attack by formations of Ju87s and 88s. The most determined attack came at 1820 as the vessels entered the Gulf of Nauplia, one Stuka narrowly missing *Glenearn*, shock wave damage so loosening her plates that the engine-room flooded and the engines were put out of action. The destroyer *Griffin* again gave assistance, towing the crippled ship safely back to Suda Bay. *Slamat* was also slightly damaged by one small bomb, while *Khedive Ismail* suffered six casualties from a near miss.

During the day the 6303 ton Greek *Maria Stathatou* was bombed and sunk off Piraeus, while during the late afternoon the *Sprapas* – loaded with British troops – was attacked off Melos and some casualties were suffered. Off the north coast of Crete another convoy, AG-15, heading for Suda Bay from Egypt, was bombed, the transport *Scottish Prince* being hit and abandoned. The Australian destroyer *Vampire* and the trawler *Grimsby* went to her aid, put some of the crew back on board, and the vessel reached her destination under her own steam.

A major evacuation attempt was again programmed for the hours of darkness, but meanwhile dramatic events were occurring on the mainland. For some time prior to the German advance, the British Admiralty and the Commander-in-Chief Mediterranean, Admiral Cunningham, had been considering the blocking of the Corinth Canal, separating mainland Greece from the Peloponnese in the event of evacuation. Blocking with a sunken ship was considered, but opposed by the Greeks. At last, after no action had been agreed, on 24 April Lt C M B Cumberledge, RNR, was given the task. Obtaining eight depth charges and a magnetic mine, he had these lashed together and lowered into the water with a seven-day delay detonator attached. Reports suggest that this devise exploded on 1 or 2 May, sinking a ship. Whatever the truth, Italian engineers were called in and by 10 May the canal was open again, although fouled by the structure of the bridge, which as will be seen later, was demolished; this would not be cleared until 17 May (see Chapter 8).

Meanwhile however the Germans sought to seize the bridge over the canal to cut the Allied retreat from Thermopylae. Available for this task was Fallschirmjäger Regiment 2(FJR2) of the Luftwaffe under the command of Oberst Alfred Sturm, which had arrived in Bulgaria during March. The paratroops had originally been intended to land on the island of Lemnos in the event of a British occupation of the island, but this had not been necessary, ordinary infantry landing unopposed. To carry the airborne force was KGzbV 2, a transport Gruppe of four Staffeln with some 53 Junkers Ju52/3ms, plus a number of DFS 230 gliders (and their Ju52/3m tugs of I/Luftlandesgeschwader 1) which would carry a back-up force of sappers.

Shortly before 0600 on 26 April, Ju88s of 1/KG51 carried out a high-level bombing attack on Allied positions around the Canal, apparently to locate and pinpoint the sites of the AA defences. On the hour a force of 20–30 Ju87s, escorted by an estimated 80–100 Bf110s (including aircraft of 1/ZG 26) attacked all ten such gun positions, while the escorting Zerstörer strafed the gun pits as well as transport on the nearby roads. Within 30 minutes all the guns were out of action, although apparently they had hit one Bf110 – U8+AL of 3/ZG 26, which later crashed with the loss of Uffz Wilhelm Rödel and his gunner; a Ju87 from I/StG3 was also lost near Larissa.

As suddenly as they started, the attacks ceased, but before the defenders could react, the Ju52/3ms appeared, flying in vics of three at 200 feet, and began to disgorge two battalions of FJR 2. The defending force comprised three companies of 2/6th Australian Battalion and a detachment of sappers, plus a company from

297

Junkers Ju52/3m transports operate from a Greek airfield, the remnants of a burnt-out PZL P-24 still present nearby. Note that unusually, this P-24 still had its wheel-spats fitted. (*Bib für Zeit*)

19th New Zealand Battalion, aided by a squadron of armoured cars of the NZ cavalry and four tanks from HQ Squadron, 4th Hussars. FJR 2's 1st Battalion under Hpt Hans Kroh was dropped north of the bridge while Hpt Pietzonka's 2nd Battalion fell to the south, the paratroops engaging the defenders in battle while 12 DFS 230s led by Lt Wilhelm Fulda were released to land near the bridge, carrying 52 Fallschirmpionere under Lt Häffner. The Ju52/3m tugs, led by Oblt Schweitzer, put their charges in an ideal position for an accurate landing, Lt Häffner and his group of sappers swiftly capturing the bridge intact. While this was happening Bf109Es of II(Sch)/LG 2 shot up the approach roads to north and south to seal off the area.

While many paratroops were lost during the drop, not a single Ju52/3m was shot down, although one tug was damaged by AA, and one member of the crew was killed. By 0800 the fighting around the bridge was virtually at an end – but not before the defenders had managed to blow it, despite its capture. Charges had been attached to the bridge supports, and as German sappers endeavoured to dismantle these, two British officers set off the detonators with carefully-aimed rifle fire; it was to little avail, for a temporary structure was soon installed to replace it.

Casualties amongst the battle-weary and dispirited defenders were relatively light, although four armoured vehicles had been knocked out before they could even get into action. However over 900 British, Australian and New Zealand troops were taken prisoners, as were some 1450 Greek soldiers who had played no part in the fighting. The cost to FJR 2 was 63 killed and 174 wounded from a force of about 800. The loss of the bridge did mean that 4th New Zealand Brigade under Brigadier E Puttick, which was holding the area north of Athens, was now cut off from the evacuation beaches in the Peloponnese. On receipt of this news, the New Zealanders prepared plans for a counter attack and if necessary, a swim across the Canal, but orders were received for them to make instead for Raphina and Port Raphtis, where they and 1st Armoured Brigade would be evacuated during the following night.

RAF personnel in retreat through Southern Greece. (*IWM*)

Despite this setback the evacuation planned for the night of 26/27 April proceeded as planned, Beaches C, D, S, T and Z all featuring in the night's activities, while the destroyer *Nubian* called at Myli in the Gulf of Nauplia to embark HQ personnel including General Maitland-Wilson (GOC Greece) and Prince Peter of Greece, and their staffs – only to find that a Sunderland had already flown them out. Totals brought out were:

Beach C – Raphina   3503 from nearly 4500, in *Glengyle* and the destroyers.
Beach D – Port Raphtis 4720 in *Salween* and HMS *Carlisle*. 4000 remained.

Beach S – Nauplia	2968, mainly in HMS *Orion*. No troops reached *Khedive Ismail* and the Captain of *Slamat* delayed sailing, hoping to embark more than the estimated 500 that had got aboard. Despite repeated signals, it was well past 0400, more than an hour behind schedule, when this vessel left.
Beach T – Tolon	1550 in HMAS *Perth*, *Isis* and *Stuart*. 570 more were lifted to Saundy Bay in A-5 for later evacuation.
Beach Z – Kalamata	8650 of 15 000 in *Dilwara*, *City of London* and *Costa Rica*; the troops here were disorganized and in a poor state of morale, having discarded much of their equipment and arms. This delayed loading and resulted in the large number left behind.

As a result of the delays at Nauplia, dawn on the 27th found the convoy from this beach well behind schedule. The AA cruiser *Calcutta* was positioned between the two transports ready for the impending assault, but when the first attack came at 0715, the Ju87s dived on *Slamat* with precision, gaining several near-misses before two large bombs struck her, killing many aboard, including Capt Lundinga. The destroyer *Diamond* went to the aid of the blazing vessel, taking off more than 500 troops and crewmen. A second destroyer, *Wryneck*, was sent to assist, recovering some 50 soldiers and some more members of the crew from boats and rafts. After sinking the hulk with a number of torpedoes, the two warships set off after the convoy, *Wryneck* calling for fighter support at 1025.

At 1115 a fighter approached *Diamond* which the crews of both destroyers initially took to be a Hurricane, as it appeared to be painted black and white below in the current RAF style. It proved to be a Bf109 however, which suddenly swooped down and strafed *Diamond*'s crowded deck, causing many casualties amongst the troops and gun crews there. Almost immediately a Ju88 followed, this releasing two bombs, one of which split open the hull with a near miss, the other exploding in the engineroom. Minutes later *Wryneck* suffered a similar attack by a Bf109 and a Ju88, three bombs striking the ship, one of which penetrated the engineroom of this vessel also. Both destroyers sank swiftly, and within 15 minutes of each other. Some 63 survivors would get ashore to safety next day, but around 1000 men lost their lives in this disastrous attack.

Meanwhile the Kalamata convoy had also come under attack, initially by a single Do.17 at about 0800; this was claimed probably shot down by the gunners on the destroyer *Defender*, but unfortunately their fire also hit a pursuing Blenheim of 30 Squadron (K7177; VT-N), which was found to be damaged beyond repair when F/Sgt Innes-Smith got back to Crete. Twenty minutes later 12 Ju87s appeared, six taking *Defender* as their target; shrapnel from a near miss killed one soldier on deck, but gunners believed that they had shot down one Stuka and damaged a second. Three Blenheim IVFs of 203 Squadron, which had just overflown the burning *Slamat*, arrived on the scene and attacked, reporting that the formation comprised 20 dive-bombers, six Bf110s and some Bf109s.

Sqn Ldr Pike in T1821 fired three bursts into one Ju87, but was attacked by several other aircraft, his own machine suffering severe damage. Flt Lt J C Whittall (L9237) and Plt Off J K Wilson (L9215) chased a Bf110 of I/ZG 26, but after being seen to close in and fire a burst from the starboard quarter, Whittall's Blenheim disappeared in a steep dive and was not seen again. It was presumed that the Australian and his crew had been shot down by the Messerschmitt they had been chasing, or another. While Pike returned to Heraklion, Wilson maintained a lone patrol over the ships.

Observers aboard the destroyer *Hero* reported seeing a Blenheim shoot down a Ju87, and this may have been a Stuka of III/StG 77 (F1+MN), flown by Oblt Harry Lachmann, shot down by Pike; this was the only Luftwaffe casualty however, and was reported lost to AA near Nauplia. Further sections of Blenheims continued to patrol over the various small convoys throughout the day, but there were no other engagements, although attacks on the vessels continued. High level raids were made by single Dorniers at 0840 and 1101, a dozen Ju88s making a more determined attack at 1215 – without result. The convoy from Raphina/Raphtis was also attacked by three Ju88s at 1205, the assault ship *Glengyle* being near-missed and strafed, machine gun fire killing one soldier and wounding two others. As the various vessels neared the northern coast of Crete two more Ju88s attempted to dive-bomb, but were driven off by intense AA fire, but at 1445 three more of these bombers caught the transport *Costa Rica*, laden with 2400 troops 20 miles north of Maleme. A 500-kg bomb exploded close alongside, splitting the hull, but fortunately the ship began to settle only slowly, allowing three destroyers to come alongside and rescue all aboard. The vessel sank at 1600.

Lighter A-20 had been damaged by an air attack in Suda Bay and was unable to take any part in the evacuation as a result, but during the day A-15 set out for Monemvasia, with Lt Cdr Hutton, the commander of the squadron, aboard, following his recent adventures with A-19. About eight miles short of the destination the craft was caught by the Luftwaffe and sunk with the loss of all on board. Suda Bay was also attacked by Ju88s during the day, one of these being intercepted by a pair of 805 Squadron Fulmars, Lt Scott and Sub Lt Bryant claiming to have damaged it. Lt Cdr Black in Sea Gladiator N5568 also patrolled over the Bay, while a 33 Squadron Hurricane flown by Flg Off Kirkpatrick intercepted a reconnaissance Ju88, 7A+AM of 4(F)/121, and shot this down into the sea with the loss of Lt Hans Michaelis and his crew. A number of Greek vessels were also bombed and sunk around the coasts of Greece during the day, including *Danapris* (2113 tons) off Piraeus, *Ypanis* (1459 tons) and *Maiotis* (1712 tons).

On the mainland Luftwaffe attacks on the retreating Allied troops had also continued. On the approaches to Markopoulon, en route to Port Raphtis, elements of 19th and 20th Australian Brigades and 4th New Zealand Brigade had just immobilized their transport before heading for the beaches, and were breakfasting in nearby olive groves when about 20 Bf110s from I/ZG 26 swept in, followed by Ju87s. Attacks continued throughout the day and many casualties were suffered by the almost defenceless troops, although their small arms fire brought down two of the Bf110s, one crashing near Sparta with the death of the gunner, while the other crash-landed with severe damage, the crew surviving unhurt. A further Bf110 of II/ZG 26 was brought down near Athens while strafing – again without injury to the crew – while a Do.17 of III/KG 2 (U5+DT) was lost during a sortie to Tripolis, north of Sparta.

It was on this date however that Athens fell to the invaders. Young Andrew Stamatopoulos recorded:

'I happened to be in Athens when the Germans entered the city... the night of 26/27th was a nightmarish one..... We well knew the Germans were at the door of Athens. I was living in City Palace hotel, Stadiou Street. At 0010 hours of 27th there was a continuous noise of traffic along the Stadiou Street. We thought it was the Germans entering. Nay! These were the rearguards of the British and Commonwealth Expeditionary Force in Greece. They were mostly lorries of all sorts in an endless column, going one after another, very close, like an endless snake. They had their curfew lights lit. They moved from Omonoia Square to Syndagma Square towards Phaleron. This movement lasted until 0100. Then it was all quiet but the traffic began again at 0230 until about 0400. Then quiet again. Shutters closed. No people in the streets – a deathly silence. At 0800 a motor-cycle, with a German flag wrapped so the swastika could be well seen fixed at the back seat, passed very fast directed from Omonoia Square to Syndagma Square. We felt an impact on our lungs – it was occupation, it was tyranny.'

'The big Victory Parade began about 0830 and lasted for an hour – until 0930. German Generals, including the commander of the Luftwaffe units in Greece, General Wolfram von Richthofen, stood in front of Grande Bretagne Hotel (Panepistemiou Street) while the motorized troops and Panzers passed in front of them, coming from Omonoia Square. The tanks were painted nearly black and so were clad their drivers. There were many very big tanks that caused awe but the granite faces of their seasoned servants were still worse, and a bad omen of what was still to come. There were also many lorries (Opel-Blitz) full of troops carrying their rifles and Spandau machine guns. The air was full of roar. At 0900 hours there appeared a Do.17 from the direction of Piraeus and flew in circles above Athens for about 20 minutes. Shortly after there appeared from the direction of the Acropolis a flight of three Hs123, at the height of about 1000 metres. Five minutes later there began the flypast from south-west towards north-east at the height of about 1000 metres. There came the following types and numbers of aircraft in the order that they are written: 25 Hs123; 25 Ju87; 25 Me110; 25 Ju88; 25 Me109E; 25 Do.17; 25 He111 and again 25 Me109E. Lastly 25 Savoia Marchetti S.79 – these last over despised by the Germans and ashamed of the Greeks. Later during the day there flew nearly constantly over Athens one or two Hs126 and Fi156, all too often flying in circles over the sacred rock of the Acropolis where the Germans had hoisted the swastika.'

Late in the evening, due to the congestion in Suda Bay and the increasing level of Luftwaffe attack on Crete, five of the transports used in Operation 'Demon' sailed for Alexandria in Convoy GA-14, carrying many thousands of evacuated troops. These vessels – *Glengyle, Salween, Khedive Ismail, Dilwara* and *City of London* reached their destination without further attack. The evacuation was continuing however, and at 2200 the cruiser *Ajax* and three attendant destroyers arrived off Raphtis, where A-6, three caiques and the ships' boats commenced ferrying out the waiting troops. By 0330 on 28 April 4640 had been embarked, including 2500 in *Ajax* alone. The destroyer *Havock* was despatched to nearby Raphina where 800 troops – mainly New Zealanders – were rescued from imminent capture. This small force had been left behind and were surrounded by German troops, some of whom had advanced within a quarter of a mile of the beach.

With dawn on 28 April three Blenheim fighters from 203 Squadron approached to escort the vessels, but while lowering their undercarriages and flashing the letter of the day, they were nonetheless fired on by one of the destroyers. No damage was initially reported, but a few minutes later Plt Off P J Gordon-Hall in L9044 reported to the formation leader that his starboard engine had caught fire and he was returning to Crete. A mile and a half short of Retimo the aircraft, having lost height steadily, came down in the sea, where Gordon-Hall was trapped in his seat. Sgt Poole, the navigator, just managed to free him as the Blenheim slipped beneath the waves, both then climbing into the dinghy which the gunner had released. The trio then began paddling for the shore, but while still a mile out, they were surprised to be met by a Greek soldier who had swum out to aid them. Passing a rope aboard the dinghy, he proceeded to tow them to shore! Subsequently a signal of protest was despatched to the Navy by AHQ Crete, three Blenheims having recently been fired on in this manner after making proper recognition signals!

Actions over the whole area of Southern Greece and the sea lanes between there and Crete, continued throughout the day. From Suda Bay a Seagull amphibian (A2-17), normally the catapult aircraft aboard the Australian cruiser HMAS *Perth*, took off for a reconnaissance patrol to the evacuation beaches. Off Monemvasia at around 0900, it was attacked by a lone Ju88, fire from this bomber causing sufficient damage to require a force-landing; Flt Lt E V Beamont and his naval crew took to their dinghy before the amphibian sank. Luftwaffe aircraft were very active in this area, crews also reporting discovering a number of seaplanes on the water at Monemvasia, four of which were claimed as destroyed. These would appear to have been Do.22G floatplanes of the Greek 12 Mira, only one of which was later to escape to Egypt. The Germans also at last caught up with one of the two remaining 'A' Lighters, nine Ju87s attacking A-5 off Monemvasia just after it had landed 480 soldiers, including many wounded, a little to the north of the harbour. The first Stuka strafed, then dropped two bombs, both of which struck the craft just as the gunners shot down the attacker, which was seen to crash with a mighty splash as it began pulling out of its dive. The remaining eight dive-bombers completed their attacks, but only one further bomb struck the lighter as the gunners claimed a second attacker shot down. Despite the ferocity of the attack, no members of the crew suffered injury, but all were forced to abandon the very badly damaged A-5, all reaching shore safely. Subsequently further waves of Ju87s and 88s bombed the stranded vessel again, and she eventually went down in shallow water with her bow blown completely away.

A particularly heavy attack on Kalamata sank all caiques in harbour here, while an estimated six mines or delayed-action bombs effectively closed the port to any further rescue ships. Another Luftwaffe aircraft landed on Melos Island, 65 miles north of Suda Bay, the crew demanding the immediate surrender of the island under dire threat of intensive bombing. The islanders refused categorically to capitulate in this way, and several severe attacks followed, many small vessels being sunk in the harbour, while a large number of magnetic mines were dropped.

From Crete a single Blenheim IF of 30 Squadron, flown by Flt Lt Walker, and carrying the war correspondent, Sqn Ldr 'Tommy' Wisdom as observer, undertook a reconnaissance for 'strays' on the beaches of Southern Greece. None were seen in the area Gulf of Kolokythia to Githeon, but off Cape Matapan fishing boats were seen and inspected to identify any loaded with evacuees. Off Karavi island a small ship was spotted under attack by two Bf110s, and approaching unseen, Walker opened fire on one, seeing strikes. The two Messerschmitts dived away, the gunners returning fire, and when Walker returned to Crete, it was to find that his aircraft had been hit in the port wing and engine nacelle. Nearer to Crete, Flg Off Kirkpatrick of 33 Squadron encountered an observation-type aircraft, which he tentatively identified as an Hs 126 or Italian Ro.44, claiming to have shot this down. It is believed to have been an Aegean-based aircraft of the Regia Aeronautica, but further details have not been discovered.

On Crete preparations for the continued air defence of the island were being pressed, but a new airfield at Pediada Kastelli, west of Maleme, was rendered completely unserviceable as it was by now clear that it could not be ready in time. 112 Squadron was now established at Heraklion, but only six of its 14 Gladiators were serviceable. It was decided to send one flight back to Egypt therefore, and on the toss of a coin the eight pilots of 'A' Flight flew out in a Bombay, the flight's ground crew following by sea next day. Ten pilots remained under Flt Lt Fry, hoping to receive early reinforcements of Hurricanes; their strength was rapidly augmented by the arrival of six new pilots from 1430 Flight, recently arrived from East Africa, under Flt Lt J E Dennant. 805 Squadron at Maleme also despatched some of its less-essential ground personnel to Egypt at this time, 23 Naval ratings and borrowed RAF other ranks leaving by ship. Four non-combatworthy Fulmars had already flown back to Aboukir, leaving only five Fulmars and the seven Sea Gladiators operational, although in need of proper servicing. The two remaining Buffalos were also totally unserviceable now. At the same airfield 30 Squadron could boast seven operational Blenheim IFs, but all were suffering constant wear and tear from the long convoy patrols and sea reconnaissances. Reinforcements generally were urgently needed!

When the plans for Operation 'Demon' had been drawn up, it had been intended that the night of 28/29 April should see evacuations only from Monemvasia. However with an estimated 7000 men still at Kalamata, an urgent change of plan was required. Two cruisers – *Perth* and *Phoebe* – and six destroyers, to be known as 'B' Force, were assembled and set out from Suda Bay to carry out the evacuation of all possible troops from Kalamata; their departure was shadowed by German aircraft. By 1930 the force had arrived at a point 20 miles south-west of the port, and from here the destroyer *Hero* was sent into harbour to make contact. As she approached, it was obvious that a battle was raging, many fires and streams of tracer bullets being observed. At about 1800 a German motorized unit consisting of 300 troops in trucks, two armoured cars and two tractors hauling 60 pounder guns had swept down the main road into Kalamata, running into a unit of the 4th Hussars. In an engagement lasting 15 minutes, the British force had put one armoured car out of action before running out of ammunition. The Germans then entered the town, capturing a number of small units, including the Naval Sea Transport Officer, who had been in charge of the evacuation.

Groups of New Zealanders, Australians and RASC troops promptly counter-attacked, one group being led by Sgt J D Hinton of the NZ Reinforcement Battalion, and these groups routed the Germans. By 0100 the town had been cleared at a cost to the intruders of all their guns and motor transport, and about 150 men taken prisoner. However during the fighting Sgt Hinton, who would later receive the award of the Victoria Cross for his part in this action, had been wounded and taken prisoner.

Junkers Ju87R dive-bombers on a Greek airfield – apparently Argos – prepare for another attack on British shipping. The Hurricane in the foreground is believed to be V7773, illustrated earlier, after any worthwhile painting on the fabric covering of the rear fuselage has been stripped by souvenir hunters. Note the orange gas-warning diamond on the top of the rear fuselage, ahead of the tail fin, also visible on the previous photograph of this aircraft. (*Bundesarchiv*)

Meanwhile at 2045 when *Hero* was still some three miles offshore, a signal lamp from the land flashed the news that the Germans were in the harbour. A motor launch was sent ashore to ascertain the situation, while Capt Sir Philip Bowyer-Smith, captain of *Perth*, and officer in charge of the operation, was radioed for instructions. He promptly decided to call off the evacuation, fearing that his force would provide easy targets to any hostile warships at sea, since the British vessels would be silhouetted against the fires ashore. The possible presence of submarines had also been reported. In fact no submarines or other warships were in the area, as *Hero* was ordered to rejoin 'B' Force to head for Suda Bay. However *Hero*'s motor launch crew were advised that a number of troops had assembled on a beach two miles south-east of the port, and other boats were sent to start ferrying them out. At 0110 three more destroyers arrived to help, and when these warships departed at 0230, 332 troops had been embarked. Unfortunately about 3000 more troops had reached Kalamata during 28 April, bringing the total here to the vicinity of 10 000, of whom about 4000 were British, Australian and New Zealanders, nearly 4000 were Palestinian and Cypriot pioneers, 1500 were Yugoslav soldiers, and the remainder mainly Greek and Yugoslav civilian women and children. When the main force arrived next morning, a surrender of these mainly unarmed and non-combatant troops was arranged for 0530. Those who wished to effect their own escapes were given permission to do so, and many parties set out down the coastline to seek any vessels to get away in. Some officers were assembling their surrendering troops on the beach at daylight, when a force of Ju87s arrived. Unaware of the surrender, these attacked at once, 200 men being killed or wounded.

More successful operations had continued at Monemvasia, where *Ajax* and four destroyers had been detailed to continue the evacuation. Delayed by a search for a suspected submarine, the cause of the alarm proved to be the crew of the Seagull shot down during the day, who had fired a distress flare. They were picked up by *Havock* just north of Kythera Island. The four destroyers finally arrived off Monemvasia just before midnight, but with the aid of six 'B' Lighters (ex-*Glenearn* craft, despatched to aid the evacuation after their parent vessel was damaged) and two caiques, all those waiting ashore were brought out, totalling 4320, mainly New Zealanders of 6 Brigade, including General Freyberg. It had been intended that on completion, the 'B' Lighters should all be destroyed, but in the rush to leave before dawn only one or two were actually sunk. This proved just as well, for several of these craft were taken over by escaping troops and Greeks left behind in the Peloponnese, bringing them to safety.

Almost 700 RAF personnel from Argos had reached Kythera Island during the previous day on an old Greek freighter, and were now waiting at Kapsali Bay with 60 British and 60 Greek soldiers. During the night the sloop *Auckland* and two corvettes arrived, with a single 'B' Lighter dropped off by *Ajax* on her way to Monemvasia, and all were picked up safely.

Amongst the many small vessels which would reach Suda Bay, was A-6, the last of the five 'A' Lighters despatched to Greek waters. The evacuation was now nearing an end, and at 1100 on 29 April a convoy of six transports coded GA-15, sailed for Alexandria, carrying 10 931 evacuees, including many wounded and sick troops, merchant seamen rescued from sunken vessels, nurses, women and children, and even Italian prisoners of war. Soon after departing harbour, a single Ju88 appeared and attacked one of the escorting destroyers, HMS *Nubian*, causing some damage with a near miss; the crew believed that they had shot their attacker down. From Alexandria the First Battle Squadron set out to rendezvous with the convoy, commanded by Rear Admiral Rawlings in HMS *Barham*; this force included a second battleship, *Valiant*, and a destroyer escort comprising those vessels which had recently brought convoy GA-14 safely into Alexandria. Air cover was provided by Fulmars of 803 Squadron, reinforced by a detachment from 806 Squadron, aboard HMS *Formidable*.

Crete had suffered its first air raid alarm of the day at 1015, just before the convoy departed, when a number of Hurricanes were scrambled from Maleme. Over Suda Bay Flg Off Vale in V7781 spotted a Do.17 heading out to sea and pursued it to within 400 yards, firing all his ammunition, while the rear gunner maintained a constant return fire, which gained several hits on the Hurricane, none of them serious. He last saw the bomber losing height, with black smoke pouring from its port engine. On this date Sqn Ldr Jones and Flg Off Wanklyn Flower were to depart Crete, leaving the small Maleme detachment under Vale's command.

The alarm sounded again at 1615 as some 20 Ju88s approached Suda Bay. This time all available Hurricanes were scrambled, as well as 805 Squadron's Fulmars and Sea Gladiator N5509 in the hands of Lt Cdr Black. Again it was Vale, this time in V7795, who made contact, seeing nine bombers at 6000 feet, two of which he attacked. He reported that following a short burst, the first fell away with flames pouring from the starboard engine and crashed just north of Maleme. Giving chase to two more which were heading out to sea, he got close enough to fire after five minutes, his victim this time apparently diving into the sea. Circling above, he spotted two survivors in the water, reporting this to control. As he returned to Maleme, he encountered another Ju88, carrying out a head-on attack, but after a short burst, he ran out of ammunition. The bombers had attacked shipping in the bay, the Greek freighter *Konistra* (3537 tons) being badly hit and beached. Two Bofors guns sited to protect the anchorage, were also knocked out, but without any casualties to the gun crews. On this occasion no Luftwaffe bomber losses appear to have been recorded.

Following the attack on Melos the previous day, a report was received that four Ju52s had landed there. Two Blenheims were despatched by 30 Squadron on an offensive reconnaissance, but no aircraft or troops were to be seen.

After dark three destroyers – *Hero*, *Isis* and *Kimberley* – were despatched to Kalamata to discover the situation and rescue any troops seen. On arrival their motor launches were sent ashore to the beach used during the night of 28/29, but only a small party of 16 officers and 17 men were found and taken off. These reported that small isolated groups were still fighting in and around the town, but that the situation was very confused. These three vessels would return next night (30 April/1 May), with a little more success, rescuing 202 more men. Gunfire could be heard, but the rescued advised that this was the last mopping up of a few gallant bands of men who preferred to fight on, rather than surrender. That same night two more destroyers, *Havock* and *Hotspur*, were sent to Melos to evacuate a reported 3500 troops, although it was still not clear whether the Germans had landed or not. Boats went ashore to find only 692 men, including about 400 Palestinians, the rest being mainly Cypriots and a few Indians. These were all taken aboard, together with a number of Greek soldiers and fishermen. On arrival at Suda Bay one of the 'soldiers' turned out to be a Greek girl, wearing helmet and greatcoat.

At sea on 30 April the First Battle Squadron had been joined by *Perth* and *Phoebe* with three destroyers, when 80 miles south of the Kaso Strait, this powerful force escorting convoy GA-15 for the next 12 hours. *Perth* and *Nubian* were then despatched to see the vessels safely into harbour, the rest of the squadron returning to the vicinity of Greece. The only alarm had come at 0924 when radar reported enemy activity. White Section of 806 Squadron had encountered five Fiat CR42s, obviously from Rhodes, but after a brief engagement without any damage to either side, the Italians had departed. Despite the approach of several aircraft towards the island, Crete suffered no actual incursions until the evening. Just after 1700 hours, six Ju88s were seen low over Suda Bay, and were intercepted by Flg Off Vale, who chased them northwards. He reported:

'I attacked one after a very long chase, firing nearly all my ammunition into it from very close range and it hit the sea. (Ed: Again no Luftwaffe losses were recorded over Crete on this date). I was then fired upon by another Ju88 which came up in line abreast, so I carried out a quarter attack which finished off my ammo. No apparent damage. While returning to base I saw four aircraft in line astern, very low down. I went very close and recognised them as Blenheims with what appeared to be English markings. ... I reported this and was informed that no Blenheims were airborne.'

Obviously the Operations Room at Maleme was unaware of what was going on at Heraklion, for the four Blenheims were 203 Squadron aircraft, the vanguard of the detachment now ordered back to Egypt. Each carrying three ground crew, the aircraft had just taken off from Heraklion, and were heading off for Egypt. En route they approached the Battle Squadron and were intercepted by two sections of Fulmars. Orders – which had not been conveyed to Sqn Ldr Gethin of 203 Squadron – required aircraft approaching the Fleet to do so in line astern with the leader firing the colours of the day. Leading Airman de Frias was in the rear seat of Petty Officer Theobald's Fulmar (N1912) and recalled:

'With our Ju88 complex, they were fair game ... fortunately we only damaged them on the first run and realised as we turned in for another go that they couldn't be 88s if we could have two goes at them!'

The Blenheim attacked, but Plt Off Wilson's L9215 was only slightly damaged. The other Fulmars pulled away when Very lights were fired and the Blenheims continued on their way. On return to *Formidable* both Theobald and de Frias were grounded pending a possible court martial, but this was apparently soon forgotten when action intensified in the weeks to follow. Meanwhile another departure on this date was the flight from Maleme of the last serviceable Swordfish of 815 Squadron, flown by Sub Lt I J Evans; the ground party left on the SS *Destro*.

Amongst the small vessels still arriving at Suda Bay from Greece was a little caique carrying Gp Capt A G Lee with a party of 12 RAF personnel, a mixed party of 20 British troops, Palestinians, Greeks and Cretans. They had reached Kythera during the previous night, rested, and then sailed for Crete at dawn. Another arrival was a Lodestar which landed at Maleme, bringing General Wavell to the island. Driven to the Army Headquarters at Platanias, he relieved General Maitland-Wilson of his brief command of 'Creforce', passing this to the just-arrived General Freyberg. He brought with him the enlightening, if disturbing, news that the plans for the German invasion of Crete had been deciphered (by 'Ultra' intercepts – a fact which he did not disclose to Freyberg). Sufficient Ju52s were now dispersed in Southern Greece to land an estimated 3–4000 paratroops in one sortie, while the Luftwaffe had been ordered not to destroy the airfields at Maleme and Heraklion, nor the landing ground at Retimo. An airborne invasion was thus highly probable. The Luftwaffe had also been ordered not to mine Suda Bay. This intelligence now allowed Freyberg to plan his defence accordingly, and he requested permission to reposition his forces which were deployed mainly for a seaborne invasion. Wavell was unable to explain to Freyberg the reason behind his refusal of this entirely reasonable request – the need to refrain from any action which might lead German Intelligence to suspect the security of their Enigma cipher traffic. Crete's security had to bow to the greater benefits likely to spring from the maintenance of 'Ultra's' secrecy in the future.

In the early hours of 1 May, Sunderland T9050 of 230 Squadron left Suda Bay for Alexandria in the hands of Wg Cdr Francis. Aboard were Air Vice-Marshal D'Albiac, Gen Maitland-Wilson and several members of the Greek Royal Family, including Prince Paul and his wife and two children. Operation 'Demon' was at an end, and with it the campaign in Greece. British forces had departed their last foothold on mainland Europe. 'Demon' had been an undoubted success in itself. An estimated 50 732 troops, including 60 Greek soldiers, had been evacuated by the Royal Navy, and by transports under their protection. This was from a total of 62 564 British and Commonwealth personnel sent to Greece. Many hundreds more, including 800 air and ground personnel of the EVA, escaped by other means – in small Greek merchant vessels, caiques, fishing boats, etc. More were rescued from isolated beaches in the Peloponnese by destroyers of the Royal Hellenic Navy (seven of which, with the cruiser *Averoff*, two torpedo-boats and five submarines, would reach Alexandria and later serve alongside the Royal Navy). It was believed that some 3000 British and Commonwealth troops were killed or presumed killed during the campaign, and about 9000 taken prisoner, including British non-combatant troops. Contemporary German figures for losses suffered during the invasion of Greece included 70 officers and 1414 men killed, 181 officers and 3571 men wounded, plus 192 Luftwaffe aircrew killed or wounded.

It was believed that additionally about 500 Allied soldiers, mainly Australians, were lost at sea during the evacuation, together with about 600 seamen, Royal Navy and Merchant Marine. Finally more than 1700 personnel had been evacuated by air from Greece, Crete and Yugoslavia by the end of April. The number of sorties together with passengers carried are shown on the table below:

	Greece–Crete	Greece–Egypt	Crete–Egypt	Yugo–Greece
230 Squadron; Sunderland	12/385	1/15	7/268	2/48
228 Squadron; Sunderland	5/227	—	1/40	—
BOAC; Empire flyingboat	—	—	13/550	—
216 Squadron; Bombay	—	2/25	11/158	—
267 Squadron; Lodestar	—	3/31	6/52	—
Totals:	17/612	6/71	38/1028	2/48

Within the next two days 216 Squadron would increase the numbers evacuated by its Bombays to more than 350, mainly surplus aircrew and other key personnel. Sgt G E Ford, who had joined the squadron in 1927, ferried more than 100 passengers to Egypt personally. Blenheims had also been used to ferry a limited number of aircrew from Greece to Crete, and later from Crete to Egypt. Further personnel had been ferried to Crete by the four Junkers G-24s and three Ju52/3ms of EEES; these civil airliners had been fired on by British warships on more than one occasion for obvious reasons, and one had sustained slight damage. Due to the confusion existing at the end of the fighting in Greece orders failed to arrive in time for them to be evacuated to Crete, and only one G-24 made good its escape, the others being captured by German troops.

During five months' service in Greece, the Royal Air Force had claimed 231 aircraft shot down, of which 150 were Italian; 94 probables had also been claimed in air combat, while 28 aircraft were claimed destroyed on the ground, with five more probables. In the same period the EVA had claimed the destruction of 58 Italian and five German aircraft, plus 23 probables, the JKRV adding claims for at least another 30 Luftwaffe machines. Against these claims, the RAF had lost 72 aircraft in combat, 55 destroyed on the ground and 82 abandoned. 148 aircrew were reported killed and 15 as prisoners. Additionally, 815 Squadron, Fleet Air Arm, lost two aircraft on operations, plus three ditched and two force-landed due to operational accidents, resulting in one killed and five prisoners. Greek losses included 32 aircraft in combat (seven reportedly to AA fire), which cost at least 55 killed and 18 badly wounded, and approximately 130 operational aircraft, together with numerous training types, destroyed on the ground. More than 500 operational Yugoslav aircraft are known to have been destroyed or captured.

Italian losses for the period 28 October 1940–30 April 1941 were recorded as 65 in combat or to AA, plus 495 damaged, 371 of them to AA. A further 14 were destroyed on the ground, where 71 more were damaged, ten of them seriously. Five additional aircraft were shot down over Yugoslavia, and 22 damaged there. These operations cost 240 aircrew dead or missing and 70 wounded. Claims over Greece totalled 218 British and Greek aircraft shot down, plus 55 probables, while a further five and one probable were claimed against the Yugoslavs. During April the Luftwaffe recorded the loss of 182 aircraft (60%–100% damaged) to all causes, of which about 164 are believed to have been lost in combat, including about 50 in operations over Yugoslavia. Aircrew losses amounted to 150 officers and 42 NCOs killed or missing. Claims totalled 110 aircraft shot down, 30–40 of them Yugoslavian, and 246 destroyed on the ground, of which around 140 were British and Greek machines. Luftwaffe losses included 54 Bf109Es, 34 Ju88s, 29 Ju87s, 29 Do.17s, 23 Bf110s, six Hs126s, two Hs123s, one He111 and four 'hack' aircraft.

A Blenheim I of 84 Squadron, L1388, VA-W, photographed at Athens on 2 May, 1941 by Italian personnel. (*Bruni via Lucchini/Malizia*)

Chapter Seven

THE DEFENCE OF CRETE – PHASE I

The start of May 1941 found a tense air of expectant calm pervading the skies around Crete following the conclusion of the evacuation. That Crete would soon be invaded was already known. What could be done to stiffen the island's defences in the lull while the Germans pressed forward their preparations for the next round was a greater problem. In North Africa the victorious British army which had conquered all Cyrenaica with such dash and elan four months earlier, had been driven back in ignominious defeat by advanced elements of General Rommel's newly arrived Afrika Korps. Malta was still suffering desperately from the air attacks of the Sicily-based Luftwaffe, and was barely holding on. Trouble was brewing in Iraq and Syria, hostility by pro-Axis elements in the former and aggrieved Vichy French authorities in the latter, threatening imminent military action.

Only in East Africa was there some light on the horizon, for here the main Italian colonial forces in Eritrea and Ethiopia had been totally defeated, allowing reinforcements already experienced and battle-hardened, to be released for service further north. At home in the United Kingdom too the crisis of 1940 was now passed, and although the night 'Blitz' was at its height, the immediate threat of invasion seemed much reduced now that Intelligence could point to the movement of large parts of the German forces to the East. At last worthwhile supplies of tanks and aircraft could be released for the war in the Middle East, and indeed were already at sea. "Tiger" Convoy was on its way to Alexandria, comprising five heavily-escorted large freighters carrying 295 tanks and 53 crated Hurricane fighters, on the safe arrival of which depended any future plans for the area.

Until this convoy arrived, Air Chief Marshal Longmore had available to him just 90 twin-engined aircraft (Wellingtons, Blenheims – both bombers and fighters – a few Beaufighters and Marylands) and 43 Hurricane fighters to cover all his responsibilities in Egypt, Libya, Iraq, Cyprus and Crete. Twenty-five Hurricanes and their pilots aboard the old training carrier *Argus*, intended for Greece, had been diverted to Malta, whevw there was also a desperate need for fighters. Unbeknown to the British however a bonus awaited them with which they were to supplement the still meagre fighter force. Just prior to the German invasion a Greek Purchasing Mission, having been unsuccessful in securing supplies of modern fighter aircraft from Britain, visited the United States intent on fulfilling their requirements. However the only aircraft made available for immediate delivery were thirty Grumman F4F-3A Wildcats, originally destined for the US Navy; these were snapped up with the promise of a further fifteen to follow, and arrangements made for them to be shipped to Greece.

By the time the American freighter carrying these crated aircraft reached Port Suez, having sailed via the Cape and Suez Canal, Greece had already fallen. The story goes that the US Navy test pilot in charge of the small team who were to erect and test these aircraft, Lt Cdr Henry Cooper, drew the attention of the Royal Navy to the crates (an unneutral act!) and machinery was put in action for the British to take over these aircraft. (Named Martlet III by the Royal Navy – a few Martlets were already in service with the Fleet Air Arm – the aircraft retained their standard non-specular light grey finish and US serial numbers: BuAer 3875 to 3904, although surviving aircraft would later be renumbered in the British AX serial range). The US had also agreed to the sale of 30 Curtiss P-40Bs to Greece, while the RAF proposed to supply 30 Curtiss H-75A Mohawks (ex-French contract), but events overtook deliveries of either type. Freedom of passage up the Red Sea and through the Suez Canal had also brought urgent supplies of fuel for beseiged Malta to the eastern end of the Mediterranean. Thus the main area of activity during early May looked set to occur over the vital sea lanes.

On Crete activity would tend to centre around the two main airfields, Maleme and Heraklion, where not only the fighter and anti-aircraft defences but also the early-warning radar service was being improved. 252 AMES at Maleme was already fully operational at the start of May, but 220 AMES at Heraklion was still being installed, the speed of events having overtaken the construction programme. From the former field Hurricanes, Fulmars, Sea Gladiators and Blenheim fighters maintained continuous patrols over Suda Bay on the first day of the new month, although no contact was made with reported intruding reconnaissance aircraft. Other Gladiators of 112 Squadron patrolled over the Heraklion area, but all was quiet, despite the closeness of Italian units in this area, which were now being strengthened by the arrival of He111s of II/KG 4, which were flying in to Gadurra airfield on Rhodes. Heraklion noted the arrival of a single photo-reconnaissance Hurricane from 2 PRU in Egypt. V7428, which was flown by Flt Lt A C Pearson, was fitted with three 14-inch cameras; the unarmed aircraft was to carry out a sortie over Rhodes, but on arrival in the target area, it encountered a number of patrolling CR 42s, Pearson being obliged to abandon his mission and return to Egypt.

The only other engagement this day occurred over the sea where the First Battle Squadron was patrolling southern waters. In the course of the day one section of Fulmars from *Formidable*, which were providing cover, were vectored onto a hostile plot, Lt Peever and Pty Off (A) W T Chatfield encountering a lone Ju88 – obviously a reconnaissance aircraft – which both attacked. Withering return fire hit Peever's aircraft, which suffered damage to the rear fuselage and to the observer's compartment, although Pty Off (A) F Coston, the TAG, escaped injury. Chatfield then got in a good burst as the Junkers broke away, but no damage was actually caused.

Strong winds which whipped up dust storms over Crete reduced flying on 2

May, only a few uneventful patrols being undertaken. The plan for the employment of the Hurricanes was to maintain aircraft at readiness. On early warning of enemy aircraft being plotted one aircraft would come to standby; if enemy aircraft approached the island, and were positively identified as hostile, the standby aircraft would take-off. During periods of congestion at Suda Bay, when unloading ships, standing patrols were maintained. The periods of readiness were a great strain on the pilots, and it was deemed desirable to pool pilots of the units at Maleme to relieve the burden. Lt Cdr Black offered 33 Squadron the services of a number of his more experienced pilots, and over the next few days half a dozen of the Navy pilots familiarized themselves with the Hurricane.

The stormy conditions this day allowed urgently needed servicing to be carried out, while from Maleme one unserviceable Fulmar was flown back to Egypt, leaving just six of these fighters on the island, none of them in the best of condition. Another Fulmar, this one from 803 Squadron on *Formidable*, was forced to ditch while on patrol, the crew being rescued by escorting destroyer HMS *Waterhen*. The carrier and the Battle Squadron would return to Alexandria next day.

Next morning Luftwaffe intrusions over Crete resumed, sporadic attacks being made on Suda Bay throughout the day. Most of these intrusions were by small groups of aircraft, but at 1440 an estimated 24 bombers – Ju88s of I/KG51 and I/LG1 – arrived overhead to bomb and damage a supply vessel. Four Hurricanes and a Sea Gladiator (N5567) were scrambled, Capt Harris in the latter aircraft intercepting three of the bombers but finding to his chagrin that only one of his guns would fire. The Hurricane pilots enjoyed more success; Sgt Genders in V7800 claimed two Junkers shot down and two others damaged, Flg Off Woods (V7461) claimed one and one damaged, Flg Off Moir a probable and Flg Off Newton one more damaged. AA gun teams around Suda Bay submitted two further claims for bombers destroyed but the aircraft seen falling were probably those downed by the Hurricanes. In the event two aircraft from 1 Staffel of KG 51 were lost, Fw Fanderl's 9K+LH crashing on the island, whilst Lt Rudolf Ortner's 9K+GH went into the sea off Suda Bay, the pilot at least being rescued. Interrogation of prisoners established that 1/KG 51 had only arrived at Krumovo on 18 April with eight aircraft, only three of which had survived to participate in this raid.

Another attempt to reconnoitre Rhodes was made by a 2 PRU Hurricane, this time V7823 in the hands of Flt Lt Brown, but again the mission was aborted owing to heavy cloud. Next morning a Blenheim from 30 Squadron reconnoitred Piraeus harbour to check on the number of ships present, but no movements were observed. The aircraft overflew Hassani airfield where a number of aircraft were seen which had been well-dispersed.

With weather more sultry than had been the case over recent days, the intrusions over Suda Bay continued on 4 May, 16 Ju88s appearing at about 1800 hours. The supply ship damaged during the previous day's raid was now sunk, while one of the AA gun positions was also hit and two members of the gun crew were wounded. Four Hurricanes and a Fulmar were scrambled, Lt Brabner in the Naval fighter claiming one bomber shot down over the Bay, while the

314

Hurricanes chased the others off to the north. Flg Off Newton claimed one probable, Flg Off Woods (V7461) and Flg Off Noel-Johnson (V7826) each claiming two damaged, only breaking off and returning when the southern extremities of the Greek mainland appeared below. Two more bombers were claimed damaged by the guns. During this attack one Ju88 from I/KG 51 was badly damaged – possibly by Brabner – and crashed at Krumovo on return and was destroyed. One more bomber from I/LG 1 was also hit, landing at Eleusis with a dead engine.

A new arrival with 33 Squadron late in the campaign was Flg Off George Noel-Johnson. (*Mrs K Noel-Johnson*)

From Heraklion the PRU Hurricane at last accomplished its reconnaissance of Rhodes and returned to Egypt with its photographs. At sea Luftwaffe bombers attacked and sank a merchant vessel between Piraeus and Istanbul (Turkey).'This turned out to be a neutral Turkish ship, the 2485-ton *Trabzon*. For the first time in some days the RAF Wellingtons were over the area by night, two bombers from 148 Squadron out of Fuka raiding Kattavia and Gadurra airfields on Rhodes, a S.79 being damaged at the latter location. The Germans also operated by night 24 hours later (5/6 May), He111s of II/KG 4 from Gadurra dropping mines in Alexandria harbour and the Suez Canal.

Meanwhile on 5 May Ju88s again appeared over Suda Bay in small numbers, but now also approached the Heraklion area. Hurricanes were up from Maleme, Flg Off Noel-Johnson making contact with a lone aircraft but unable to get

315

within firing range. Amongst the patrols flown, one Hurricane was piloted by Capt Harris of 805 Squadron but no enemy aircraft were seen. It was not until the early evening that an effective interception was made, Flg Off Vale (V7181) catching a Ju88 over the Bay and claiming it shot down; he also claimed a second as damaged, but no bombers of this type were recorded as lost on this date.

Over the Heraklion sector Ju88s were intercepted by two 112 Squadron Gladiators flown by Canadian Plt Off L L Bartley and Plt Off Jerry Westenra, the New Zealander, each pilot claiming a bomber damaged. On a solo patrol Sgt Ralph Ware, recently attached to the unit, intercepted a reconnaissance S.79 high over the airfield and claimed it probably shot down, this action apparently being confirmed by army witnesses. Patrols continued over the approaches to the island next day, but without any engagements occurring. On this date a 230 Squadron Sunderland flew out six members of the Greek Royal Family and nineteen other personnel to Egypt. The King however declined to leave.

The 'Tiger' Convoy Operation

On 6 May *Formidable* and the five cruisers of the First Battle Squadron put to sea from Alexandria for their part in the 'Tiger' Convoy operation. Due to the previous night's aerial mining, the ships had to be led out of harbour individually by minesweepers, although DWI Wellingtons (fitted with de-gaussing ringsO from 1 GRU were being employed to explode the magnetic mines which the German bombers had laid. Having joined the destroyer escort outside harbour, *Formidable* flew on her Air Group, which included Fulmars of both 803 and 806 Squadrons. The initial task of the Squadron was to escort four large merchant vessels and two tankers, carrying 24 000 tons of fuel, to Malta. 'Tiger' Convoy was approaching from the west meanwhile, escorted by Force 'H' from Gibraltar. Rendezvous was to be made near Malta, and the five big freighters escorted to Alexandria. Halfway to the island rendezvous, *Ajax* and three destroyers were detached to bombard Benghazi by night (7/8 May), harbour installations and shipping being successfully shot-up. While returning to rejoin the main force, these warships encountered two Axis transports, one of which blew up violently when attacked, the second running ashore and being left in flames.

Very poor visibility and occasional rain frustrated many efforts by the Luftwaffe's reconnaissance aircraft to find the fleet on the 8th. Frequent radar plots indicated the presence of the searchers, radio intercepts indicating the occasional fleeting sightings which were achieved. During the early part of the morning Blue Section of 803 Squadron was vectored onto two Italian bombers, identified as Cant Z.1007s. Both were engaged and both believed shot down. Recorded L/Air Tim Dooley, TAG in Sub Lt Wallace's N1913:

'We circled round and watched our target dive into the sea; there was no sign of our leader (Lt Peever/Pty Off (A) Coston) – the last I saw of them they were following their target down, still knocking pieces off it.'

The Fulmar failed to return and was assumed shot down by return fire from its victim.

Early in the afternoon radar indicated that a number of enemy aircraft were approaching and two sections of Fulmars were scrambled to join 806 Squadron's White Section (Lt MacDonald-Hall and his TAG, L/Air Harry Phillips, in N1990, with Lt Touchbourne flying as White 2 in N1865) which was already airborne. MacDonald-Hall recalls:

'We came across two He111s. The first of which I rather stupidly flew in formation with some 50 yards behind, but managed to blow-up the Heinkel's starboard engine, the debris of which being glycol and fuel, smothered my cockpit and I watched it cartwheel down and hit the sea. I then rejoined Touchbourne and we harrassed, attacked and shot down the other Heinkel prior to returning to *Formidable*. My hydraulics had been damaged and the starboard wheel would not come down, and the port wing was badly damaged by the rear-gunner's fire, as was the port tyre. I landed with one leg down, the other retracted and the wheel deflated.'

Meanwhile Green Section of 803 Squadron (Lt Bruen and Lt Godden in N1951, with Sub Lt Richards flying Green 2) intercepted another He111 which Bruen shot down. A fourth Heinkel was claimed by another 806 Squadron section, shot down into the sea by Lt L S Hill; his No.2, Lt G B Davie (late of 805 Squadron) crashed into the sea on returning to the carrier, only the TAG surviving. The claims made were very accurate, and it appears that White Section's victims were probably both aircraft of 6 Staffel, KG26 – 1H+AP flown by Ofw Willi Kleinknecht and 1H+FB (Oblt Hermann Pfeil). There were no survivors. One of the other Heinkels was from 4 Staffel (Oblt Eberhard Stüwe's 1H+BC), the other from 5 Staffel, 1H+FN flown by Oblt Max Voigt; the crews perished. These bombers had been despatched to attack the Suez area.

Later in the afternoon two sections from 806 Squadron encountered Ju88 'snoopers', Lts Henley and Sparke believing they had shot down an aircraft of 2(F)/123 off Cap Passero. In fact they had damaged it, wounding two members of the crew, but it regained its base at Catania, Sicily. Lts MacDonald-Hall and Touchbourne were up again towards the end of the day and they too engaged a lone Ju88, reporting that it had crashed into the sea with no survivors following their attack.

The bad weather which had saved the fleet from sustained air attack also had tragic consequences for a number of *Formidable*'s aircraft. Two Albacores on anti-submarine and reconnaissance patrols were lost, only one crew being rescued, while a Fulmar crewed by Pty Off (A) Chatfield and L/Air C F Norman crashed into the sea with the loss of both men. During the day Marylands of 39 Squadron at Fuka undertook a number of maritime reconnaissance sorties to the south and north of the fleet, but two were lost. AH296, flown by Lt A U M Campbell, SAAF, was intercepted by a Bf109E of 3/JG 27 from Gazala (piloted by Hpt Gerhard Homuth) while flying near the North African coast between Bardia and Tobruk, and was shot down into the sea off Derna with the loss of all aboard. Plt Off J W Best had instructions to land AH281 at Malta on completion of his sortie to the north of the ships, but due to technical difficulties, he was forced to come down at Methone on the southern tip of the Peloponnese, near Cape Akritas, where the crew was captured. (One gunner, Sgt J A Quitzow, later escaped from the POW camp at Salonika and got back to Egypt.)

Far to the west 'Tiger' Convoy and Force 'H' also came under intense attack by German and Italian aircraft from Sardinia and Sicily. During these actions, five Axis aircraft were claimed shot down by Fulmars from HMS *Ark Royal* for the loss of two fighters and one crew. That night however one of the freighters was badly damaged by a mine and blew up some hours later. The crew were taken off, but 57 tanks and ten crated Hurricanes went down with the ship. A second vessel was slightly damaged by the explosion of a mine caught by her mine-sweeping paravane. By 0800 on 9 May the First Battle Squadron was 120 miles to the south of Malta, while 'Tiger' Convoy was 90 miles to the west. The weather remained uncertain, with many fog patches and visibility less than two miles. By early afternoon the fuel convoy from Alexandria had safely reached the island, and at 1515 'Tiger' Convoy and escorting destroyers joined forces with the Battle Squadron some 40 miles off Malta. Axis aircraft searched all day, but the only contact came when Lts Henley and Sparke of 806 Squadron again caught a reconnaissance Ju88, this time a machine from 1(F)/121, which they attacked and badly damaged; the Junkers crashed on return to Catania and was totally destroyed, although the crew survived. At 1600 one of the searchers at last located the ships, but no attack developed before darkness fell.

The 'snoopers' were out in force next morning, but in variable visibility they experienced trouble in maintaining contact when sightings were made. Similarly patrolling Fulmars were unable to achieve any effective interceptions. A He111 sighted and pursued by Lts MacDonald-Hall and Touchbourne disappeared into the murk before they could get within range. A little later the approach of another hostile caused a scramble to be ordered, but as Lt Touchbourne's N1865 was boosted off by catapult the aircraft crashed over the starboard side, both the pilot and his TAG, L/Air C H Thompson, perishing. As a result of this fatal accident the remaining crews were not keen to make use of the booster in spite of assurances from engineers. In an effort to raise morale and restore confidence, the Commander (Flying), Cdr C J N Atkinson, allowed himself to be boosted off even though he had not flown a Fulmar before.

Not long after this there was warning of enemy aircraft in the area and three sections of Fulmars were ranged for take-off, the booster being used. In the last aircraft was newly-attached Sub Lt Basil Sinclair (ex 805 Squadron) and his TAG, L/Air Freddy de Frias, who recalled:

'I asked him (Sinclair) if we were to be boosted – "Shouldn't think so. I've only got eight hours on Fulmars and I've never done a booster. They'll probably shoot off the others and then we'll do a normal take-off." I relaxed but was soon shaken when we were waved up to the loading position. Sinclair must have made some frantic signals because he throttled back and the Flight Deck Officer hopped up on to the stub plane. I heard everything through the intercom which Sinclair had left on. "What's the snag?" (enquired the FDO) "None except I've never been boosted or even had a briefing" (replied Sinclair) "No time to argue, there's a gaggle (of enemy aircraft) on the plot. Listen, when you are on the trolley I'll wind you up. Get your straps as tight as you can. Normal take-off flaps and course pitch. Let the stick centre itself, put your hand behind it and tuck your elbow into your guts. Open the throttle to full take-off power and tighten up the screw. Then lift your left hand and put your head back against the pad. When you drop your hand I'll give you a moment to put it at the back of the throttle so it won't close, then off you go!" I sat there horrified. In my mind I still had the picture of the Fulmar which had pranged off the booster floating down the starboard side with the TAG strapped in the rear seat, which had come adrift, with his head at an odd angle and obviously dead. The pilot had slumped forward but appeared to be moving a bit. Then it sank as it reached the stern and the planeguard hadn't picked up anything. We were now mounted on the booster carriage and the engine roared. I saw the operator push the lever and felt the usual rush of blood to my face. There was a yell from up front and my hand flew to the canopy-jettison handle. But it was only Sinclair yelling "It works! It works!"'

Still bad visibility continued to protect the fleet, and only one further engagement was to occur as the vessels neared Alexandria on 11 May. Once again Lts Henley and Sparke were involved, this intrepid pair attacking a formation of Ju88s from II and III/LG 1. Each selected a target, Henley attacking an aircraft from 5 Staffel, his fire wounding the gunner, Ogfr Horst Goldner. Sparke meanwhile closed to very short range on Ofw Otto Engel's L1+IR from 7 Staffel, but either collided with, or was simultaneously shot down by, the bomber, the two aircraft falling together into the sea. Only one parachute was seen by Henley who then failed to locate its occupant in the sea.

According to reports, Lt Cdr Evans, volatile commander of 806 Squadron, demanded that a search be made as sea conditions were very slight and oily calm. He considered that if Julian Sparke or his TAG, L/Air Arthur Rush, had baled out, or if their aircraft had force-landed, there was a very good chance that they would be found. Captain Bisset however refused to allow such a search as it was already late afternoon, and the dangers inherent in allowing the carrier to slow down while a search was made required him to put the safety of the ship, its escorts and the convoy first. The morale of the aircrew aboard was badly affected by this ruling Late on the morning of 12 May therefore, 'Tiger' Convoy and the First Battle Squadron steamed into Alexandria, carrying 238 tanks and 43 Hurricanes for Wavell's forces. Ten of the fighters would be flown to Crete during the following week for issue to 33 and 112 Squadrons.

The relatively heavy attrition suffered by the Fulmars during this operation left only a few serviceable aboard the carrier, and until others could be rendered so, *Formidable* would be unable to put to sea to escort warships and convoys between Egypt and Crete. On arrival in port Charles Evans was rested from his long spell as commanding officer of 806 Squadron, this unit being taken over by Lt Cdr J N Garnett, a former Swordfish pilot with 830 Squadron on Malta, who had recently commanded the Sea Gladiator Flight aboard HMS *Eagle*.

Continued Defence of Crete

While these actions over the sea had been underway, operations around Crete had continued in a desultory fashion, daily patrols netting no engagements between 7 and 10 May. During this period five unserviceable Blenheims were flown out to Egypt for complete overhaul, while 805 Squadron was further depleted in like manner, three Fulmars and two Sea Gladiators leaving on the 8th, one more Fulmar on the 10th, and another Sea Gladiator next day. This left the unit with just two Fulmars and four Sea Gladiators; of the three Buffalos two were unserviceable, the other badly damaged. On 8 May meanwhile Convoy AN-30, four merchantmen en route to Crete – were subjected to an evening attack south of the Kaso Strait by He111s of KG26. A torpedo struck the 4998-ton *Rawnsley*, leaving her badly damaged and capable only of eight knots. Taken in tow by the armed trawler *Grimsby* and escorted by the destroyer *Waterhen*, she reached Hierapetra Bay in south-east Crete, where she was anchored. She was heavily bombed next evening and sank during the morning of 12 May.

Finally, during the evening of the 11th five Bf110s of II/ZG 76, which had arrived at Argos from North Germany four days earlier, swept in over Heraklion airfield to strafe. Insufficient warning allowed only a single 112 Squadron Gladiator to get into the air, but Bofors and Lewis gunners opened fire as the Zerstörer swept round the airfield. As they completed their circuit, Plt Off Bowker attacked one and a low level dogfight commenced, during which the lone Gladiator pilot attempted to lead his opponents over the gun positions. After a few minutes the Bf110s made off to the north-west, Bowker landing to claim one probably shot down. Next day one of 2 PRU's Hurricanes again arrived at this airfield prior to making a reconnaissance of the Greek airfields at Hassani, Eleusis, Menidi and Argos, and of the Corinth Canal, where no sign of any obstruction was noted.

At Maleme the composition of the fighter defence now underwent a complete change when Wg Cdr Francis landed his 230 Squadron Sunderland in Suda Bay, bringing with him Sqn Ldr E A Howell to take over command of 33 Squadron, together with three relatively inexperienced pilots, Flg Off A R Butcher, a former 112 Squadron pilot, and Sgts Butterick and Leveridge, who had joined the unit in Greece but had been evacuated back to Egypt. The majority of the unit's pilots were now about to leave, as it was intended that more replacements would soon fly in with new Hurricanes. Of the originals, only Flt Lt Woodward and Plt Off Dunscombe would remain, together with the ex-1430 Flight pilot, Flt Lt Mitchell. The new commanding officer, Sqn Ldr Howell, was a highly experienced fighter pilot and former instructor, who had not however flown on operations, nor even flown a Hurricane.

Next day Wg Cdr Francis embarked as many passengers as it was possible to cram into the Sunderland (T9050), every space being occupied until 74 were aboard as well as the ten-man crew; this even included six standing in the lavatory! Most of these evacuees were aircrew, including the seven departing 33 Squadron pilots, a number of Blenheim crews, including Flt Lt Rixson of 113 Squadron, and Capt James Roosevelt, son of the US President, who had been in Greece and Crete as a 'Military observer and adviser!'. It is interesting to note that due to the shortage of trained and experienced aircrew in Egypt, orders had been issued re priorities for evacuation, indicating orders of preference beginning with Blenheim pilots, then Wellington pilots, followed by Hurricane pilots.

Amongst the crew members, radio operators were to be given priority over air gunners, then observers. After aircrew, engineer officers were the next most important category, followed by cypher and signals officers and airmen. Accounts officers, carpenters and metal workers were bottom of the list! Thus laden, Wg Cdr Francis had trouble getting the Sunderland into the air, the big flyingboat, having the largest number of persons ever to be carried in such an aircraft, requiring some three miles run before it finally lifted from the water.

At Maleme patrols continued, but high-flying reconnaissance aircraft were not to be intercepted on 13 May. At 1100 on this date Plt Off Dunscombe overshot the runway while coming in to land from a practice flight, crash-landing Hurricane V7800 and damaging it. This serious loss was somewhat offset by the arrival of two replacement aircraft (V7714 and W9298) in the hands of Sgts C D Ripsher, a Scot, and Welshman Glawil Reynish, who were led to the island by a 30 Squadron Blenheim; both men remained to strengthen 33 Squadron.

A number of aircraft pens had by now been constructed from sandbags and earth-filled petrol drums, while to provide some defence for the grounded Hurricanes, one airman had constructed a small gunpit and installed a Lewis gun. A number of Bofors were sited on either side of the runway.

While 33 Squadron was being rebuilt, Flg Off Bill Vale was operating virtually as a 'one-man air force' so far as 80 Squadron was concerned, with his personal Hurricane, V7795. The only other member of the unit still present was Sgt Bennett, while Hurricane V7181 was on the unit's strength, although shared with the Naval pilots of 805 Squadron. That same evening at 2000 Vale scrambled in the latter aircraft after an unidentified plot reported flying off the coast. Within 30 minutes he had been vectored onto a Ju52 and had landed again, claiming to have shot this down into the sea.

At Heraklion a number of aircraft, identified as Bf110s, attacked the airfield in a desultory fashion which caused little damage and a few minor casualties to army personnel. Five Gladiators got off, two flown by 1430 Flight pilots, but only Plt Off Westenra was able to attack, fighting with six of the intruders and getting in several good bursts, though his own fighter was badly shot about, landing with four mainspars shot through, large areas of fabric missing and numerous bullet holes. This action, witnessed by many of the defenders on the ground, had proved quite a tonic to morale. Airfield defence Bofors and Lewis guns kept up an intense fire, as did a convoy offshore. This included the Dutch transport *Nieu Zeeland*, carrying the Royal Marines of the 23rd Light AA, who put up such a barrage that they were able to report one of the low-flying aircraft shot down into the sea. This would seem to have been a reconnaissance Bf110 of Aufklärungsstaffel XI Fliegerkorps, crewed by Uffz Scharlow and Oblt Holthöfer. It would seem that yet again some of the reports of Bf110s related to Do.17s, for on this date U5+DK (Lt Katers) of I/KG 2 failed to return from an attack on Heraklion, while three more of the unit's aircraft returned to Menidi suffering AA damage.

During the nights of 12/13 and 13/14 May, Wellingtons from 257 Wing (37, 38, 70 and 148 Squadrons) from Egypt were over airfields in Greece and the Dodecanese Islands but results were negligible. Crete had not been left free from night raids either, frequent small-scale forays by He111s being made from time to time. A new airstrip came into use by the Luftwaffe, constructed on the recently-occupied island of Melos.

The first really serious attacks on the RAF in Crete were launched on 14 May, beginning at first light when a number of Ju88s bombed Suda Bay and Maleme airfield, six bombs falling on the latter target, damaging one of 30 Squadron's unserviceable Blenheims; the unit's operational aircraft had already been despatched to Heraklion to undertake convoy escort sorties. The three Hurricanes at readiness were not ordered off, but at 0600 60 Bf109s of II and III/JG 77 swept over the airfield and beach. This time the two fighters piloted by Sgts Ripsher and Reynish were scrambled at once, turning and twisting to gain altitude as they came under attack. They were quickly followed by Sqn Ldr Howell, who was attacked head-on by a group of five Messerschmitts just as he became airborne. These flashed past, but others then attacked as he gained height, but already two aircraft were falling in flames. Sgt Reynish had shot down one Bf109 (believed to be that flown by Gefr Hans Gabler of 6/JG 77) which fell inverted into the hills, but he was then shot down by another, the Hurricane (V7714) falling blazing into the sea. Reynish, on his first operational sortie, was able to bale out, but was presumed lost. In fact he managed to swim towards the shore and after two hours was picked up by a Cretan fishing boat. He finally got back to Maleme to find that he had been given up for dead.

Sqn Ldr E A Howell, 33 Squadron's commanding officer on Crete during May 1941. He is seen here following his escape from captivity and return to England in 1942. (*Wg Cdr E A Howell*)

Meanwhile Sqn Ldr Howell, having evaded his attackers, spotted two more Bf109s flying low over the sea:

'I went right on the tail of the second 109 till I was in close formation on him,' he later recorded. 'I could have lifted my nose and touched his tail with my prop ... the Hurricane shook and shuddered as rounds poured into him, bits broke away and a white trail burst from his radiator as coolant came pouring out. He turned slowly, to the right in a gentle dive. I was determined to see my first victory confirmed and made the mistake of following him down. I had no difficulty as he was past taking evasive action and I continued pouring ammunition into him (this was probably Uffz Willi Hagel of 4 Staffel, who failed to return) till I noticed tracer coming past me. The other 109 was on my tail. I realised my mistake and pulled quickly up into a turn to port, then flick rolled over into a steep turn the other way and found myself coming in on the enemy's quarter and gave him a burst. ... We screamed down together to water level ... I kept him dodging in a cloud of bullets and spray till I ran out of ammo ... he was certainly full of holes.'

The third Hurricane, W9297 flown by Sgt Ripsher, was seen by those at Maleme to attack Bf109s flying out to sea and was believed to have shot one down, which hit the sea with a mighty splash (this was probably in fact Howell's victim, Uffz Hagel's aircraft). Two Messerschmitts then latched onto Ripsher's Hurricane, which took desperate evasive action before heading for Maleme as the aircraft was repeatedly hit – it is believed by Lt Emil Omert of 8 Staffel. Ripsher had lowered his undercarriage and flaps in an attempt to land, but tragically the Hurricane was hit by Bofors fire and crashed on the edge of the airfield, killing the pilot. Out of fuel and ammunition, Howell landed w9298 at Retimo landing ground, his non-arrival at Maleme being assumed to indicate his loss also. Those Messerschmitts not engaged with the trio of defenders strafed Maleme airfield, one unserviceable Hurricane and the unserviceable Fulmar going up in flames, while down on the beach the three Buffalos were all hit. In Suda Bay a tanker was hit and set on fire, while further up the coast the island's principal town of Canea was bombed. Later in the morning a further small formation of Bf109s repeated the attack, but caused little damage – there were not many targets left.

Four Hurricanes were claimed shot down, one by II/JG 77 and three by III Gruppe (one by Lt von Eichel-Streiber), this unit claiming five more destroyed on the ground.

It was then the turn of Heraklion, where about a dozen II/ZG26 Bf110s appeared overhead. Two Gladiators were off, Flg Off Stan Reeves of 1430 Flight and Plt Off Westenra getting airborne. The New Zealander bounced one of the low-flying Zerstörer, that flown by Oblt Sophus Baagoe, a 14-victory 'Experte' from 5 Staffel, the aircraft falling into the sea just offshore, the pilot and his gunner, Ofw Daniel Becker, being killed; this aircraft was also claimed by the Bofors gunners whose accurate fire brought down a second Messerschmitt, 3U+EM of 4 Staffel. The latter crash-landed half a mile from the airfield with the port airscrew, fin and rudder all shot away. Gefr Adolf Ketterer and his gunner, Gefr Hans Bromba, were both captured. Returning Bf110 pilots claimed four victories; Flg Off Reeves' Gladiator was badly damaged and force-landed. Two

Messerschmitt Bf110C Zerstörer of ZG 26 pass over Greek caiques while on patrol around the Aegean islands. (*Bib für Zeit*)

more Gladiators were damaged on the ground. Several of the Bf110s had carried bombs, whilst others were seen to jettison long-range tanks over the coastline. Little serious damage resulted from this attack.

Just before dusk Maleme was again alerted when aircraft were heard approaching, and on this occasion one of the Bofors gun crews obtained a direct hit on a Messerschmitt, which reportedly blew up and fell into the sea. This was probably Lt von Eichel-Streiber's Bf109E from III/JG 77 which returned heavily damaged from an evening attack, during which three more aircraft were claimed destroyed on the ground. Von Eichel-Steiber crashed at Molaoi on return, his aircraft being written-off.

These attacks on Maleme by Bf109s made it apparent to Grp Capt Beamish and his staff that the Luftwaffe was now operating from bases in the Peloponnese, which meant that further bomber raids would enjoy full fighter protection. Thus the few defending Hurricanes were likely to become entangled with the Messerschmitts while the bombers operated undisputed. Beamish and Sqn Ldr Howell discussed the possibility of operating Hurricanes from Egypt, using Maleme and Heraklion as advanced bases. This was considered impractical in view of the distances involved and the small number of fighters available. Howell suggested as an alternative that his small force attempt to intercept the incoming bombers over the Greek islands before they met their escorts. This was an idea which recommended itself to Beamish, once sufficient reinforcing Hurricanes became available.

When darkness at last closed in over Maleme it brought only temporary respite, for three He111s soon appeared to attempt a low level attack with 50kg bombs and machine-gun fire. Those on the ground replied with small-arms fire, and one bomber was obviously hit, a large piece of engine cowling clattering down onto the airfield where it was retrieved as a trophy. Five Wellingtons from 257 Wing flew the other way to attack the Luftwaffe's airfields in southern Greece again. Little damage resulted although a number of fires were seen following the raid on Menidi, while at Hassani six aircraft were believed destroyed and as many as eighteen fires seen burning. However there is no record of any Axis aircraft being destroyed or damaged this night.

The assault resumed at 0500 on 15 May when a single bomber approached unobserved and dropped a stick of bombs on Maleme, damaging a Blenheim and wounding three airmen in a lorry. The airfield was now becoming too dangerous for these aircraft, and an hour later the last three serviceable Blenheims departed for Egypt, one of them accompanied by an 805 Squadron Sea Gladiator. Half way to Mersa Matruh the Gladiator's engine failed and Lt Peter Scott was obliged to ditch. The Blenheim circled the position, but could see no sign of the pilot, who was not found by a 228 Squadron Sunderland sent out to pick him up.

Dornier Do.17Z bombers from KG 2 and 3 were to play a considerable part in the attack on Crete during May 1941. (*Bib für Zeit*)

No sooner had the Blenheims gone than an estimated nine Bf109s swooped on the airfield, shooting up dispersed aircraft and gun positions, while a second Staffel circled above at 3–4000 feet, and another at 10 000 feet as top cover. Flt Lt Vernon Woodward, whose DFC had just been announced, was at readiness, and recalled:

'I started my aircraft and seconds later whilst commencing to taxi the engine stopped and burst into flames. I jumped out and dashed to a standby aircraft (partially u/s I recall). No time to fasten parachute or harness – again attempted to get airborne, but as I gained ground speed there were two 109s firing at me from 600–800 yards – I almost made it, but flames again, so up undercarriage and skid to a stop and exit very smartly to cover in a ditch off the edge of the airstrip. Frankly I'd had enough for one day – it had to be the most uncomfortable few minutes of my life – if there is such a thing as a "guardian angel" – he was working overtime that day on my behalf!'

A Sea Gladiator also attempted to take-off, but tipped over, trapping the pilot. At once a New Zealand soldier rushed to his aid and freed him, but the Messerschmitts then promptly shot up this aircraft and a second Sea Gladiator nearby; the wrecked Buffalos also received a further strafing.

During a lull in the attacks four further replacement Hurricanes arrived from Mersa Matruh, flown by 30 Squadron pilots, guided and escorted to the island by a 24 SAAF Squadron Maryland. Two of the fighters (N2610 and V7827) landed at Maleme for 33 Squadron, while the other two went to Heraklion for 112 Squadron. The ferry pilots would not remain and would return to Egypt on a departing Sunderland. A further raid on Maleme and Suda Bay at midday by Do.17s of III/KG2 brought a scramble for several Hurricanes, but no contact was made, although one Dornier was hit by AA shrapnel. Following this attack more aircraft evacuated the airfield; the last remaining Swordfish of 815 Squadron (P4272 'H'), which had almost been abandoned, had been made flyable by the armament Officer, Lt Denis Lough, and the servicing party. Lough, who was also a pilot, decided to fly the aircraft out himself, taking Sub Lt Donald Coates of 805 Squadron with him as navigator. It was agreed that they would act as guide for four Greek Avro Tutors, each carrying three Greek military personnel, to Egypt. First however, the little formation had to fly to Heraklion, where, Donald Coates recalled:

'We were fired upon by all the defences along the north coast – no one believed there were any Allied aircraft left in Crete, let alone a formation of five! – and had the greatest difficulty in landing.'

Next morning they set out for Mersa Matruh, all arriving safely.

Just before dusk Maleme was subjected to another strafing attack by a dozen Bf109s, but little further damage was caused. By night two supply ships left Suda Bay for Port Said, the *Lossiemouth* carrying 2000 non-combatant troops from the island. A number of warships provided escort, including the cruiser *Dido*, which itself carried £7 000 000 of Greek bullion to safety. Just before daybreak on 16 May, at the northern end of the Kaso Strait, *Lossiemouth* suffered an engine failure, thereby presenting an ideal target to any marauding bomber or submarine. Fortunately the engines were soon restarted, and the convoy got underway again. At 1145 five S.79s appeared and subjected the vessel to a sustained attack, but while straddled by bombs, she was not hit.

Again dawn on 16 May brought a resumption of attacks on Maleme. At 0615 Hurricanes were scrambled and Flg Off Vale in V7795 encountered a number of Bf109s, one of which he claimed to have shot down. A midday scramble brought no further combat, but at about 1600 Sqn Ldr Howell set off in N2610 to carry out a reconnaissance over the island of Melos at Grp Capt Beamish's request. Seeing nothing hostile on the island after the 20-minute flight from Maleme, he was heading back towards Crete when he spotted a lone Ju52 (IZ + GX of IV/KGzbV 1, flown by Fw Walter Steinbach), flying low over the sea in the opposite direction. Three separate attacks were required to set the port engine and wing on fire, following which the trimotor transport turned on its back and fell into the sea, no survivors being seen. Continuing on towards Crete, Howell then saw more aircraft below, again flying in the opposite direction. These were Ju87s of I/StG 2, escorted by Bf110s of II/ZG 26, which had just attacked Maleme and Suda Bay. Closing on the Stukas and coming under fire from many rear-gunners, he selected one and attacked it, whereupon it flicked over on its back and headed towards the sea in a vertical dive – probably an evasive tactic. A number of Bf109s now took shots at the Hurricane as they sped past on their way back to Greece, but no damage was sustained.

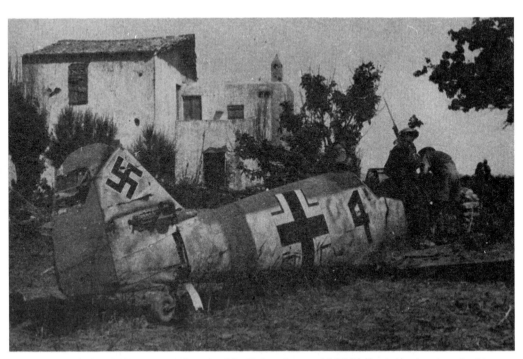

Messerschmitt Bf109E 'Black 4', flown by Ofw Herbert Perrey of 8/JG77 after being shot down by Lt A R Ramsay of 805 Squadron, Fleet Air Arm, near Maleme on 16 May, 1941. (*via D H Coates*)

Meanwhile all the other serviceable 33 Squadron Hurricanes had been scrambled from Maleme, this time flown by the Naval pilots of 805 Squadron who had been on readiness. They soon ran into Bf109s, from both I(J)/LG 2 and III/JG 77, Lt Ash being shot down into the sea almost at once and was killed. Lt Richardson's Hurricane was also seen to be under attack, and he baled out not far from the airfield, his parachute apparently failing to open. His body was found by local peasants, who laid him in their village church. The third pilot, Lt Ramsay in V7461, encountered Bf109s of 8/JG 77 and shot down two of them, Ofw Herbert Perrey's 'Black 4' force-landing on its belly near a village, while Lt Harald Mann baled out, wounded, but managed to evade capture, Ramsay's Hurricane was badly damaged in the fight, and he put down at Retimo, causing those at Maleme to believe that all three 805 Squadron pilots had been lost.

Bill Vale had been on patrol over Suda Bay in his 80 Squadron aircraft when the raid approached, and he was soon in the thick of the fight. Unable to prevent the Ju87s attacking the shipping in the Bay on his own, he was able to attack one which he claimed to have shot down, before being attacked by Bf109s which he evaded without damage. This latest victim raised his personal score to 28 and three shared, seven of them claimed whilst flying from Maleme. The two Luftwaffe fighter units involved in this raid each claimed two victories, one of those by I(J)/LG 2 being credited to Lt Geisshardt.

The dive-bombers had caused considerable damage during their attack. Two tankers were hit, the 10 694-ton Danish *Eleanora Maersk* being set alight before she could discharge her cargo, and with several of her crew killed, she was beached near Kalami Point, where she burned for five days. The British chartered *Logician* (5993 tons) and *Araybank* (7258 tons) were both set on fire, the former being a total loss, while three Greek ships were sunk – *Nicolaou Ourania* (6397 tons), *Thermoni* (5719 tons) and *Kythera* (1070 tons). Since the start of May fifteen supply ships had reached Suda Bay, but eight of these had been sunk or damaged in harbour, and only 15 000 tons of stores had actually been offloaded, including just 3000 tons of munitions from the anticipated total of 27 000 tons.

At Heraklion meanwhile, 112 Squadron was preparing to put its two new Hurricanes into use, but only three pilots had previously flown the type, and only Flt Lt Fry had any real experience. Crete was hardly the ideal place to undertake operational training, but most pilots managed to get at least one flight between raids. When yet another strafing attack by Bf110s approached – this time undertaken by thirty aircraft of I and II/ZG 26 – both Hurricanes and three Gladiators were ordered off. Fry in Hurricane V7857 managed to bounce one of eight Messerschmitts at 6000 feet and got some telling hits on Uffz Erhard Witzke's 3U+SM of 4 Staffel. Unfortunately for him, as he broke away Witzke's gunner, Fw Karl Reinhardt, got an accurate burst of fire into the Hurricane's engine and as it streamed glycol, Fry was forced to bale out. Struck a glancing blow by the tailplane as he did so, he landed three miles from the airfield with a badly bruised chest. Meanwhile Witzke's Messerschmitt was forced to ditch as he struggled to get back to Argos, when the damaged port engine failed. Rescued from the sea by a Cretan fishing boat, the crew were brought back to Crete where they were hospitalized.

The second Hurricane had come under attack by other Bf110s, and force-landed after sustaining damage, but Bofors gunners of 7th Australian Light AA Battery hit U8 + MK of 2 Staffel, this aircraft crashing into the sea with the loss of Uffz Erwin Bauer and Gfr Karl-Heinz Heldmann.

At Retimo during the day a low-flying Henschel Hs126, probably from 4(H)/22, appeared, obviously on reconnaissance. Australian troops were entrenched in the hills on either side of the airfield, and two Greek battalions around Adhele village, their joint small-arms fire bringing down this aircraft. On board were found photographs of the area which indicated that their positions were so well-concealed that only one trench could be seen from the air.

During the afternoon nine Beaufighters of 252 Squadron, newly arrived in the Middle East from the UK, and led by Sqn Ldr R G Yaxley, MC, flew from Malta to Heraklion. This followed an appeal by Grp Capt Beamish to Middle East HQ for a strike to be made on southern Peloponnese airfields where the deadly Bf109s were assumed to be located. While they were being prepared for a dawn strike on 17 May, Wellingtons also attacked these targets by night, four aircraft from 37 Squadron and one from 70 Squadron raiding Argos, while eight from 38 Squadron were briefed to attack Molaoi. The latter proved difficult to find, but was attacked successfully, four aircraft being claimed destroyed here.

Five more Wellingtons from 148 Squadron attacked Menidi in southern Greece, where violent explosions were seen, and it was believed that at least two aircraft had been destroyed. In fact the giant Junkers G38 GF + GG of KGrzbV 172 was destroyed; this four-engined 'flying-wing' machine had been pressed into service with the Luftwaffe ex-Lufthansa, where it had been registered D-APIS, and carried the name 'Generalfeldmarschal von Hindenburg'. A Hs126 was also destroyed during the raid. Finally, two more 38 Squadron Wellingtons attacked Maritza airfield on Rhodes, where two Z.1007s, an S.81 and a CR42 were damaged, together with various buildings, a power station and hangar, several vehicles and 21 drums of fuel.

Before dawn on 17 May the Beaufighters of 252 Squadron left Heraklion in three sub flights of three aircraft each, to attack Hassani, Argos and Molaoi airfields. Sqn Ldr Yaxley led Flg Off P S Hirst and Sub Lt K Holme, FAA, to Hassani, where it was believed some twenty Ju52s were hit; actually one of these transports from the Transportstaffel VIII Fliegerkorps was destroyed and four others of Sanitäts-Flug-Bereitschaft 7 quite badly damaged, but Hirst's aircraft (T3228) was hit by Flak and crashed, he and Sgt E R Payton losing their lives. Flt Lt R E Jay's sub flight of Flg Off J C Davidson and Sub Lt I F Fraser, FAA, went to Argos where Bf 110s of I and II/ZG 26 were reported lined up wingtip to wingtip. 13 of these Zerstörer were hit, three being destroyed and the other ten damaged, as was one more of II/ZG 76. The final trio – Flg Off J W Blennerhassett, Flg Off G J Lemar and Flg Off J B Holgate – hit the coastal strip at Molaoi where a number of Bf109s and He111s were believed to have been damaged. After refuelling at Heraklion the eight surviving Beaufighters returned to Malta.

While this attack was underway Maleme was submitted to further intense ground strafing, the last Fulmar (N1932 'B') and last Sea Gladiator being destroyed. During the many such attacks being endured, personnel not required immediately on the airfield retreated to slit trenches prepared in the surrounding hills; hence casualties were kept to a minimum. Early in the afternoon the three remaining serviceable Hurricanes were scrambled – V7795 (Flg Off Vale), V7761 (Lt Cdr Black) and N2610 (flown by a pilot of 33 Squadron) – as Ju88s approached. Bill Vale claimed damage to one aircraft on this occasion, but later in the day he and Black were unable to make an interception when ordered off again. At Heraklion, during a lull in attacks, three more Hurricanes flew in from Egypt, led by a South African Maryland. The ferry pilots, also from 30 Squadron, were to return to collect further aircraft ready for another reinforcement flight.

Several Ju87s from I/StG 2 at Scarpanto spotted a large vessel in the Kaso Strait and dived to attack. The white-painted 7938-ton craft was the hospital ship *Aba*, which escaped damage but sent out an urgent SOS. A patrolling Sunderland of 228 Squadron was ordered to the area, but when Flt Lt J C O Grunert arrived the dive-bombers had already gone. However an aircraft believed to be a Ju88 was sighted, and this attempted to bomb the low-flying Sunderland. The cruisers *Phoebe*, *Dido* and *Coventry* were also ordered to investigate, and shortly after their arrival, their radar indicated an incoming raid. More Stukas appeared overhead and proceeded to both dive-bomb and strafe *Aba* and *Coventry*, both of which were near-missed. Machine-gunning of the cruiser's deck wounded several members of the crew, including Pty Off A E Sephton, a gun director. Although seriously hurt, Sephton refused medical aid and continued to direct the fire of his battery until the Ju87s departed. He succumbed to his wounds next day, subsequently being awarded a posthumous Victoria Cross.

During the day the Luftwaffe lost one of its elderly air-sea rescue He60 floatplanes when D1+EK of 2/126 crashed into the sea when out from Scaramanga, believed due to an accident rather than hostile action. The pilot, Fw Karl Wottge was killed in the crash. A further accidental crash occurred when a Ju52 of KGzbV 1 came to grief when landing at the newly-constructed airstrip on Melos.

During this period He111s of II/KG 4 from Gadurra (Rhodes) were maintaining a limited but regular night assault on Alexandria and the Suez Canal Zone, mainly mines being dropped in the harbour and canal. On this night eleven Heinkels set out to mine but Fw. Hans Borcher's aircraft (5J+KM) was shot down in flames by a Hurricane of 94 Squadron, flown by South African Lt A H M Moolman, the bomber having been illuminated by searchlights. Tragically the blazing aircraft crashed onto a house killing six Egyptians as well as the crew.

At Maleme the morning of 18 May was spent by 805 Squadron burying Lt Richardson in Canea cemetery following his death two days previously. As the truck carrying the funeral party returned to Maleme, it was attacked by a Bf109, although all aboard escaped injury. Almost continuous strafing attacks were made during the morning by Bf109s and 110s, without interception. At 1200 however, a Royal Marine Bren-gun crew (Sgt T H Hawksworth and Marine R G Kimber) shot down a Bf110, believed to have been an aircraft of 6/ZG 26 flown by Lt Heinz Knecht and Fw Georg Schultz, which came down in the sea southeast of Spetsai island while trying to get back to Argos after suffering damage; the crew were rescued from the water.

Sgt Vernon Hill flew in the last replacement Hurricane to Crete on 18 May, 1941 – his first operational flight. He never landed, being shot down and killed as he approached the airfield by Fw Otto Niemeyer of 4/JG 77. (*G Hill*)

Ju87s of I/StG 2 dive-bombed Maleme and Suda Bay, where the RFA oiler *Olna* was seriously damaged and beached, while Bf109s also strafed Maleme in support of the Stukas. In the midst of this attack a lone replacement Hurricane arrived from Egypt, piloted by 21 year-old Welshman, Sgt Vernon Hill, on his first operational flight. Probably short of fuel and unaware that the attack was in progress, since he was not in radio contact, Sgt Hill lowered his undercarriage and prepared to land just as eight Messerschmitts swept in behind him. Obviously suddenly aware of his predicament, he was seen to pull away out to sea as the 109s vied to get on his tail. As one overshot, watchers believed that he may have shot this down, but by then Fw Otto Niemeyer of 4/JG 77 had got in a telling burst of fire and the Hurricane crashed into the sea with a mighty splash, Hill being killed.

The only German loss recorded during this raid was for a Ju87 (T6+JH) flown by Uffz Ernst Tauscher, which was hit by AA fire and crash-landed; the pilot was killed, but the gunner (Uffz Düring) survived and evaded capture. Meanwhile a number of He111s appeared overhead, one bomb scoring a direct hit on the pen sheltering Sqn Ldr Howell's Hurricane, N2610, which went up in flames. On the other side of the airfield Flg Off Vale's faithful V7795, and V7761, were both put out of action. LAC Eaton and AC1 Marcel Comeau were buried in their gunpit by one bomb burst, but were quickly dug out by others, before suffering any serious effects. With the attack still in progress, Comeau headed for the shelter of a nearby slit trench just as two elderly Cretan civilians reached it, and just as another bomb landed close by, causing the walls of the trench to collapse, and again burying Comeau. This time he managed to free himself, but could no longer see the Cretans. Digging frantically with his bare hands, he managed to locate and free them, although one died soon afterwards. He would later receive the Military Medal for this action.

Following this attack only one Hurricane remained serviceable at Maleme, W9298, which was flown off by Lt Cdr Black on a reconnaissance of Kalamata and the surrounding area. On his return Grp Capt Beamish ordered that the minimum operational formation was to be a pair, and no-one, including Black and Howell, were to fly the Hurricane again unaccompanied.

Heraklion was also attacked repeatedly, and the airfield was rendered unserviceable. Two Hurricanes and two Gladiators were airborne at the time, and were ordered to land instead at Retimo. The remaining Hurricane and Gladiators at Heraklion were no longer flyable. On arrival at Retimo the four pilots were ordered to evacuate to Egypt, and after refuelling, all took off. Flg Off A R Costello and Sgt W Bain flew the two Hurricanes, Flt Lt Dennant and Plt Off Westenra the Gladiators; all arrived safely. During the day a Bf110 of 4/ZG 26 on a very low-level reconnaissance over Retimo was hit by Lewis-gun fire and crash-landed. Reportedly, the pilot was wounded and on capture was found to have amazingly detailed maps of the landing ground with him, these showing all gun positions, and even slit trenches were prominently shown. Strangely, German records indicate that the aircraft did not fall, but landed back at base in a damaged condition!

That evening at 1800 Flt Lt Lywood brought Sunderland N9020 down on the waters of Suda Bay to deliver a few passengers and some freight, but primarily to take back to Egypt a full load of personnel, including Flg Off Vale and Lt Cdr Black, the latter ordered by Cdr G H Beale, officer commanding Maleme, to make representations to Rear Admiral Boyd that more fighter aircraft should be sent. Black's unit, 805 Squadron, was now represented by just Lt Ramsay and Sub Lt Hinton, two TAGs, L/Air Tom Jarvis and L/Air Bill Jary, about 55 ground personnel, and no aircraft. This party was to return by sea should no further aircraft become available. Additionally, Lt Keith of this unit was still in hospital on the island, suffering from dysentry.

33 Squadron still expected the arrival of further Hurricanes, and new aircraft pens were in the course of construction. No additional reinforcements were earmarked for Crete however, other than seven Fulmars of 800X Squadron. These aircraft were currently at sea and were due to guide a delivery of Hurricanes from the carrier *Furious* to Malta, and then after refuelling, fly on to Maleme. They were not however, due until 21 May, by which time the order had

been rescinded due to the start of the German invasion of Crete, and they remained instead on Malta.

Under cover of darkness twelve Wellingtons, drawn equally from 38 and 70 Squadrons, headed for airfields in southern Greece. Three were unable to locate their specified target area, others returned with reports of many fires as a result of the bombing. One Wellington was attacked by a twin-engined night fighter but was not hit.

Early on 19 May some 40 bomb-carrying Bf109s attacked Maleme without prior warning having been received. After scattering 50kg fragmentation bombs over the area, they flew out to sea before returning to strafe. When this attack ended all the airfield's Bofors guns had been silenced and a number of casualties suffered by the gun crews. Cpl F E Pacey's crew and gun were buried by the earth thrown up by a near-miss, but were dug out, shaken but unhurt. Sgt H Yates' gun continued firing despite several strafes, the crew claiming hits on a number of Messerschmitts before their gun was put out of action.

The last serviceable Hurricane on Crete, W9298 'X', which was to be flown out to Egypt by Sgt Maurice Bennett on 19 May, 1941. (*Wg Cdr E A Howell*)

During the afternoon the Messerschmitts returned and resumed shooting-up the airfield and surrounding area. Close to the aircraft pens, the redoubtable Comeau had found an intact Vickers 'K' machine-gun in a sandbagged pit, while fellow 33 Squadron airman LAC R G 'Ginger' Stone installed a Browning salvaged from a Hurricane. One very low-flying Bf109 came within range and both opened fire, reporting hits which knocked off a piece of the aircraft, this falling onto the airfield. Subsequently the surrounding area was heavily bombed by two Staffeln of He111s. In between these attacks Grp Capt Beamish ordered

Sqn Ldr Howell to despatch all airworthy Hurricanes at Maleme to Egypt, but by now only W9298 remained flyable. From the many hopefuls eager to make this flight, Howell selected the sole remaining 80 Squadron pilot, the seemingly forgotten Sgt Maurice Bennett, who took off forthwith. At Heraklion three more Gladiators had been made airworthy, and these too left for Egypt, flown by Flg Off D H V Smith and Sgts P O Bates and Ware. There were no more operational aircraft left on Crete – the first phase of the island's defence was at an end.

Chapter Eight

THE INVASION OF CRETE

As the German armies had swept through Yugoslavia and Greece, Generalleutnant Kurt Student, commander of XI Fliegerkorps which comprised the Luftwaffe's paratroop and air landing divisions and their associated air transport units, having recovered from the wounds he suffered in Belgium during the May 1940 operations, had approached Hermann Göring with a proposal for the capture of Crete. The elite paratroops were great favourites of Adolf Hitler's and Göring had referred Student to him. The plan was opposed by Feldmarschal Keitel, the Chief of Staff, who favoured the use of the Fliegerkorps against Malta, which he considered to be a priority target for such action. Student's ideas appealed to the Führer however; he saw them as the 'crowning glory' of the Balkans campaign, closing the Eastern Mediterranean to the British Navy, and offering a springboard for further adventures in North Africa, the Suez Canal and the oil-rich territories to the east.

However Operation 'Barbarossa' had already been delayed a month from May to June as a result of the Balkan operations, and nothing, Hitler decreed, must be allowed to postpone this further. Already he had ordered the withdrawal of most units from Greece, control of which was to be left to the Italians so far as possible. He was prepared to issue Directive No.28 for Operation 'Merkur' ('Mercury') for the invasion of Crete, but, he advised Student, it must be accomplished by the troops of XI Fliegerkorps alone, supported by the air power of Fliegerkorps VIII, and it must be undertaken by mid May.

Generalleutnant Student began at once, ordering the paratroop and air landing divisions from their bases in Germany to make with all speed for Southern Greece. Travelling by road and rail, these forces became delayed in the Macedonian mountains by the movement northwards of 2nd Panzer Division for 'Barbarossa', the latter enjoying priority on the roads. As a consequence 22nd (Airborne) Division was held in Rumania, Generalleutnant Ringel's 5th Mountain Division of Austrian mountain troops who had already taken a prominent part in the fighting in Greece, being substituted. Unfortunately, although in themselves an elite force also, the Alpenjäger were not trained for airlanding operations – particularly in the face of determined opposition. All units had reached Greece by 14 May, the last to arrive being the 1st and 2nd Companies of the Assault Regiment, but other delays were resulting in the proposed date for the commencement of the operation, originally fixed for 17 May, to be deferred.

General Gerhard's air contingent of XI Fliegerkorps had withdrawn all their transport aircraft from the Balkans to Germany for overhaul after their considerable transport activities during the invasion, but by 15 May almost 500 aircraft were back at airstrips in Southern Greece. These were not the hard-surfaced permanent airfields around Athens however, but earth strips where the operation of heavy aircraft raised dense clouds of dust which choked air-intakes and blinded pilots, reducing the rate at which formations could be operated and greatly increasing the risk of accident. Coupled with this, some 9000 tons (650 000 gallons) of aviation fuel would be required for the transport aircraft to allow three waves – an estimated 1500 sorties – to be launched on the first day. The tanker *Rondine* carrying much of this fuel to Piraeus, from where it would be pumped into 45-gallon drums and despatched by road to the airfields, was delayed by the fallen bridge in the Corinth Canal, the result of the earlier airborne operation detailed in Chapter 6. Another vessel was due to arrive from Italy very shortly carrying 8000 40-gallon drums of fuel, while four more vessels, one a tanker, were not far behind. As a bonus 1500 tons of British aviation fuel was discovered at Drapetzona, near Athens, abandoned unburned due to a disagreement with the Greek authorities over plans for large-scale demolitions.

While the Corinth Canal was being cleared the plans for the proposed Operation 'Merkur' were being finalized. The forces available were to be divided into three components: Group West under Generalmajor Eugen Meindl; Group Centre under Generalmajor Wilhelm Süssmann; Group East under Generalleutnant Julius Ringel. Actual landings were to be preceded by continuous bombing and strafing of troop concentrations and known AA gun positions, first by medium bombers and then by Stukas, supported by fighters and Zerstörer. Initially two companies of the 1st Assault Regiment were to land via 27 DFS 230 gliders south of Maleme airfield, to nullify any surviving AA positions and to attack the camp; nine more gliders carrying the Headquarters battle group would have the capture of the bridge over the Tavronitis river as their objective.

Within minutes the main body of 1st Assault Regiment – three battalions with over 1850 troops – would be dropped by Ju52/3ms to capture the airfield. Simultaneously detachments from Group Centre comprising two more companies of 1st Assault Regiment would land south and west of Canea, the island's capital, and Suda Bay in 30 more gliders, with a similar AA suppression role. Five more DFS 230 carrying Generalmajor Süssmann and his Staff would follow, together with the paratroops of FallschirmjägerRegiment 3 (FJR 3), who were later to be reinforced by 100th Mountain Regiment, to capture Canea, Suda town and Galatas.

During the afternoon of this first day the second wave of transports would carry 1500 more paratroops of FJR 2 to Group Centre's second set of objectives in the Retimo area, while Group East – the paratroops of FJR 1 reinforced by 2nd Battalion of FJR 2 – would drop near Heraklion. 5th Mountain Division (less 100th Mountain Regiment) would follow later, one battalion by sea direct, while a second was detailed to disembark in the Maleme area. Tanks, vehicles, AA weapons, anti-tank guns and engineer troops would also follow by sea. As soon as the airfields at Maleme and Heraklion had been captured, Ju52/3ms would fly in reinforcements and supplies, priority being given to the capture of Maleme. 15 750 airborne and 7000 seaborne troops were to participate.

To carry these forces the air component of XI Fliegerkorps comprised 520 Ju52/3m transports in ten Gruppen and 72 DFS 230 gliders. They were commanded and based as follows:

Group	Commander	Base
Kampfgeschwader zbV 1	Oberst Wilke	Dadion,
I/Kampfgeschwader zbV 1	Maj Förster	Megara and Corinth
II/Kampfgeschwader zbV 1	Hpt Arnold Willerding	
I/Kampfgeschwader zbV 172	Maj Krause	
II/Kampfgeschwader zbV 172	Maj Bodekuhl	
Kampfgeschwader zbV 2	Oberst Büdinger von Heyking	Topolia
Kampfgruppe zbV 60	Maj Walter Hammer	
Kampfgruppe zbV 101	Oberstlt Ernst Mundt	
Kampfgruppe zbV 102	Maj Walter Erdmann	
Kampfgeschwader zbV 3	Oberst Buchholz	Tanagra
Kampfgruppe zbV 40	Maj Deutsch	
Kampfgruppe zbV 105	Maj Reinhold Wenning	
Kampfgruppe zbV 106		
I/Luftlandesgeschwader I	Maj Stein	
(DFS 230 glider tugs)		

In support of the invasion Generalmajor Wolfram Freiherr von Richthofen's VIII Fliegerkorps comprised:

228 medium bombers, 205 Stukas, 114 Zerstörer, 119 fighters and 50 reconnaissance aircraft. 514 of these 716 aircraft were serviceable at this time. The units were:

Stab, I and III/KG 2 under Oberst Herbert Rieckhoff	Do.17Z at Menidi
III/KG 3	Do.17Z at Menidi
I, II/LG 1	Ju88A at Eleusis
II/KG 26	He111 at Eleusis
Stab, II/StG1 under Oberst Walter Hagen	Ju87B at Argos
Stab, I/StG2 under Oberst Oskar Dinort	Ju87B at Molaoi and Mycene
III/StG2 under Hpt Heinrich Brücker	Ju87B at Scarpanto
I/StG3	Ju87B at Argos
I, II, III/StG77	Ju87B at Argos
under Maj Clemens Graf von Schonborn-Wiesentheid	
Stab, I, II/ZG 26 under Maj Johann Schalk	Bf110 at Argos

II/ZG 76	Bf110 at Argos
II, III/JG 77 under Maj Bernhard Woldenga	Bf109 at Molaoi
I(J)/LG 2 under Hpt Herbert Ihlefeld	Bf109 at Molaoi
2(F)/11	Do.17P, Hs126A
2/Seeaufkl Gr 126	He60 at Scaramanga
Seenotdienststaffel 7	Do.24 at Scaramanga
7(F)/LG2	Bf110
Aufkl Staffel XI Fliegerkorps (detached)	Bf110

Additionally II/KG 4 was based at Gadurra (Rhodes) but concerned mainly with mining operations against Alexandria and Suez Canal.

The paratroops themselves were all Luftwaffe personnel. Part of their advantage in the forthcoming conflict lay in that the British authorities did not know how many divisions of these troops were available, or what their organization, equipment and operating methods were. They were kitted out with weatherproof padded overalls, topped with leather jerkins and round, padded crash helmets. During the actual drop most carried only Luger 08 pistols, platoon commanders alone carrying their MP38 machine-pistols. The mens' MP38s and MG34 light machine-guns were carried in special five-foot containers, four to each aircraft, these being fitted to specially-adapted racks in the bomb bays of the transports and dropped at the same time as the paratroops jumped. A number of trained marksmen were included in each section, and for them the containers carried Mauser rifles fitted with telescopic sniper sights. There were also detachments from anti-tank units with anti-tank rifles, four flame-thrower sections and mortar-equipped detachments.

A Rhodes-based Fiat CR 42 fighter of the 163ª Squadriglia Autonomo CT at the time of the invasion of Crete. (*N Malizia*)

Each man was issued with two day's rations; special Wittler bread; processed chocolate; rusks; tartaric acid; sugar; thirst quenchers. Each company was equipped with portable water sterilising equipment, although it was intended to fly in 1500 gallons of fresh water daily to Group West once Maleme airfield was captured. Medical officers and orderlies would also be dropped, equipped with comprehensive medical supplies including tubes of blood for transfusions in the field. They would also carry supplies of a caffein-sodium solicylate solution to inject into those suffering from extreme fatigue, while all troops were issued with benzedrine tablets to combat tiredness.

The Germans could also look to their Italian allies for help at sea from destroyers and motor torpedo boats, if not from the Italian Fleet as a whole, as well as such support as might be offered by the Comando Aeronautica Egeo which now had serviceable 21 bombers, four torpedo-bombers, 20 fighters, four fighter-reconnaissance floatplanes and two reconnaissance floatplanes. These were:

39° Stormo:

92° Gruppo BT	S.79	Gadurra, Rhodes
(200ª, 201ª Squadriglia)		
41° Gruppo AS	S.84	Gadurra, Rhodes
(204ª, 205ª Squadriglia)		
281ª Squadriglia Autonomo AS	S.79sil	Gadurra, Rhodes
50° Gruppo Autonomo BT	Z.1007bis	Maritza, Rhodes
(210ª, 211ª Squadriglia)		
172ª Squadriglia RT	Z.1007bis	Maritza, Rhodes
161ª Squadriglia Autonomo CM	Ro.43/Ro.44	Leros
162ª Squadriglia Autonomo CT	CR 42	Scarpanto
163ª Squadriglia Autonomo CT	CR 32/CR 42	Gadurra, Rhodes
Sezzione Soccorso	Z.506B	Rhodes

On 25 May, 231ª Squadriglia from the 95° Gruppo BT at Brindisi would fly to Rhodes with six Z.1007bis for operations over Crete, remaining until 1 June, when the aircraft were passed to the 50° Gruppo and the unit returned to Italy.

While these preparations had been under way, supply ships had continued to arrive in Crete's harbours, while fast warships came in by night to drop off vital supplies and personnel. Fresh arrivals included 2000 Royal Marines at Suda Bay, 2/Leicesters at Heraklion, 1/Argyll and Sutherland Highlanders at Tymbaki, together with small armoured elements comprising 16 Mark VI light tanks of 3rd Hussars and nine 'Matilda' tanks of 7th Royal Tank Regiment, all war-weary machines. Artillery included eight 3.7-inch howitzers and 49 elderly field guns, mainly French and Italian 75 mm and 100 mm pieces, with varying quantities of ammunition. Fuel supplies had increased, and while no aircraft remained on the island, Maleme and Retimo had 5000 gallons and Heraklion 10 000 gallons for any units which might employ the airfields as forward bases. 180 000 weekly rations had been amassed, sufficient to keep 'Creforce' fed for six weeks. At nearly

42 000 men, the garrison was now far stronger than the Germans estimated. The numbers included 17 247 British, including the 2000 Marines, over 600 RAF and 425 Royal Navy personnel, and about 1000 Palestinian and Cypriot pioneers. However only about 6400 of these were deemed combatants. There were also however 6540 New Zealanders and 7702 Australians, mainly infantry, plus about 10 250 Greeks, including 2800 well-armed and motivated Cretan police. Most of the Greeks however were poorly-trained and ill-equipped and included 800 EVA cadets and 300 military cadets.

Dispositions were as follows:- around Maleme and Canea were the 5th and 10th Brigades of the New Zealand Division and two Greek battalions, all commanded by Brigadier-General Puttick, while Suda Bay was defended by most of the Marines under Lt General E C Weston, plus four Australian and one Greek battalions. At Maleme the Marines and the Royal Australian Artillery each maintained ten Bofors guns and crews, the Marines also providing two pairs of 3-inch AA guns at Canea, and five more two-gun sections of these weapons at Suda Bay, together with two 3.7-inch batteries, 16 Bofors and two four-barrelled machine-guns, plus 24 searchlights in three clusters. Artillery support for the infantry in the Canea-Suda Bay area came from 'Z' Battery of 15th Coast Regiment with four 6-inch, two 4-inch and two 12-pounder guns. Seven light tanks and two 'Matildas' were also allocated to the area.

Further along the coast at Retimo, the landing ground was protected by four Australian and two Greek battalions, and two 'Matilda' tanks, under the command of Brigadier G A Vasey, whilst in the Heraklion Sector Brigadier B H Chappel had three British, two Australian and three Greek battalions, with six light and four 'Matilda' tanks. 'X' Battery of 15th Coast Regiment had ten 4-inch guns here, while AA cover was provided by ten Bofors of 156th LAA Battery, Royal Artillery, ten Royal Marine Bofors, four 3-inch two-gun sections and two pom-poms, also manned by the Marines.

In reserve General Freyberg had 4th New Zealand Brigade in the Karatsos area, 1/Welsh in the Akrotiri area, and 1/Argyll and Sutherland Highlanders at Tymbaki. To guard against seaborne invasion Admiral Cunningham had assembled a very substantial fleet; four battleships, 19 cruisers and 43 destroyers, divided into two large formations which were cruising to the west of Crete to keep the Italian Fleet at bay, and seven light forces, each capable of dealing with any invasion convoy encountered. Although 'Ultra' intercepts had indicated the new invasion date as 20 May, it would be only one day prior to this that Middle East Command would be informed, although interrogation of airman prisoners had already divulged not only the date but the likely time of the commencement of the assault.

Thus it was that at 0530 on the morning of 20 May the first of almost 500 heavily-laden Ju52/3m transports began taking off, hampered by the billowing clouds of dust which rose to 3000 feet, and required a 20-minute interval between the take-off of each Staffel to allow visibility to clear. As a result it took over an hour for the various Gruppen to assemble into formation over Kythera Island before heading south to approach Crete from the west, over the Antikythera Strait.

Junkers Ju52/3m transports at a Southern Greek airfield. Drums of urgently-awaited gasoline have been dumped in the foreground, ready for use. (*Bib für Zeit*)

Already disaster had struck however; first off had been the glider tugs of I/LLG 1, with their DFS 230 charges trailing behind, each glider carrying ten fully-equipped assault troops including the pilot, who was expected to participate in the fighting on landing. The glider carrying Generalmajor Süssmann, commander of Luft Division 7, and six members of his Staff, was buffeted by the slipstream of a low-flying He111 of II/KG26 which passed close by, causing the towing cable to snap. Oblt Kruppe, the pilot, was unable to retain control and the wings broke off under the stress, the fuselage spiralling down to crash on the little island of Aegina in Athens Bay; all aboard perished.

The He111s, joined by KG 2 Do.17s from Menidi, were first over Crete just after 0700, approaching the Maleme-Canea area and subjecting the defenders to intensive and concentrated bombing, many bombs falling around the airfield and on the slopes of Kavkazia Hill (known as Hill 107), which overlooked the airfield, and where 22nd New Zealand Battalion were entrenched. Due to the effective slit trenches which had been dug by the soldiers and airmen here in recent weeks, casualties were relatively light. At the airfield the rear parties from 30 and 33 Squadrons numbered 229 officers and men, together with three officers and 50 ratings of 805 Squadron.

Following the bombers, StG 2's Ju87s arrived including 1 Staffel led by Oblt Frank Neubert who, during the Polish Campaign of September 1939, had gained

341

the first aerial victory of the war. Staffel upon Staffel of Bf109s and Bf110s accompanied the Stukas, strafing from low-level. The Luftwaffe's attack seemed well co-ordinated for whenever the marauding fighters came under fire from any well-concealed AA guns, be they Bofors, Lewis, Vickers or Brens, the Stukas appeared to be called in to deal with them; the intensity and accuracy of the resultant attacks invariably silenced the particular target. On the airfield the empty pens, remaining gun positions, and the wrecks of the Hurricanes and Buffalos were repeatedly strafed by fighters which appeared suddenly from behind surrounding hills, or along the beach at very low-level.

Intermittently the defenders scored successes against the low-flying strafers, as when six Bf109s were seen circling over Theodhoroi Island, just east of Maleme, prior to sweeping across the beach towards the airfield – every gun that could fire put up such a terrific barrage that almost at once the leading aircraft, Black 3 of 5/JG 77, flown by Oblt Berthold Jung, was hit and he broke away back out to sea, trailing black smoke. The following pair both took hits in the engine, Oblt Gerhard Rahm and Ofw Werner Petermann crash-landing White ≪ and Black 1 on the beach. Meanwhile Jung, obviously fearing that his damaged fighter would not get back to Greece, turned back again and crash-landed near Maleme, while the three remaining fighters gave up their attempt to attack and fled out to sea. The defenders believed these had been hit also, for all were observed trailing black smoke, but this was obviously caused by the DB601 engine's exhaust. All three pilots who had been shot down survived, but one of the wingmen was assaulted by local peasants, who pulled him out of his cockpit, a Cretan woman hacking off his ring finger, complete with engagement ring, with a carving knife before troops could get to them and take them into custody.

The tugs and gliders of I/LLG 1 arrived at 0805, releasing the tows over the sea to allow Maj Koch's I Battalion of the Assault Regiment to land on target. Misty conditions and smoke caused a number of the glider pilots to misjudge their landing area, which was in the valley of the Tavronitis, just behind Hill 107. As a result several crashed on the rocky slopes nearby, killing or injuring the occupants. Others came down in isolated areas, where they were swiftly dealt with by the defenders. AC Comeau of 33 Squadron was again in the thick of the action, two gliders crash-landing close to the trench in which he was sheltering. Approaching the nearest with some trepidation, armed only with a rifle, he was nonetheless sufficiently composed to shoot the first two dazed soldiers who came staggering out. As more men followed from both gliders, Comeau beat a hasty retreat to cover.

Maj Koch gathered as many men of 4 Company as he could find and advanced on the camp areas of 22nd NZ Battalion at the base of Hill 107, where it had been hoped to catch the New Zealanders off guard and unprepared. The camp was nearly empty however, so the Germans turned to their main objective, the capture of the hill. Since Hill 107 dominated the airfield, whoever controlled it, controlled Maleme – and the prompt seizure of one of the airfields was vital to the success of the whole operation. As the men advanced up the slopes they were suddenly met by a hail of fire from well dug-in defenders; amongst those who fell dead or seriously wounded was Maj Koch; the survivors were pinned down, unable to move.

A crumpled DFS 230 glider, its duty done, lies in a Cretan field. (*Bib für Zeit*)

Just a mile away to the west 12 more gliders carrying 3 Company under Lt von Plessen, approached the dried-up river-bed, only to come under heavy fire from the fully alerted defenders. The vulnerable DFS 230s, constructed as they were of tubular steel, canvas and wood, made easy targets during their slow descents, and many occupants were killed or wounded in flight. One glider went down in flames and another was hit by a heavy burst as it touched down. Others broke up on landing, but von Plessen and sufficient numbers of his men survived to attack the New Zealanders on each bank of the river at its mouth, and to capture their positions, thereby silencing their AA guns. This extemely important if brief action was to ensure the ultimate success of the whole venture, for now at 0820 the first elements of the main paratroop force appeared overhead, the slow Ju52/3ms flying a steady course at under 400 feet to drop 1800 men, very little anti-aircraft gunfire being experienced.

Within minutes hundreds of parachutists were disgorged over the Maleme area, I Battalion coming down to the east and west of the airfield, while II and IV Battalions landed amidst very little resistance to the west of the river. Accompanying them were two heavy-weapons companies with 20 mm anti-tank rifles and small pack-howitzers. III Battalion was less fortunate however. Because the 600 paratroops were due to land on or near the beach to approach Maleme village and the airfield from that direction, the 50 Ju52/3ms of KGrzbV 102 came in over Canea Bay and were forced to fly inland to prevent the parachutists being blown out to sea by the wind prevailing. This brought them over Bofors gun positions at Pirgos and near Modhion, several being shot down. One was seen to fall out of control into a batch of parachutists, while a second fell in flames as the men attempted to jump out, a third splashing into the sea. One more force-landed near Canea with one member of the crew dead, and a fifth aircraft was badly damaged, crash-landing on return to Topolia.

Most of the unfortunate III Battalion jumped over the slopes of surrounding hills, coming down on heavily-defended New Zealand positions where they were greeted by intense small-arms fire. Many were killed or wounded as they floated down; others were caught in trees and shot before they were able to free themselves, while yet more were injured landing on the rocky terrain. Many of the survivors were never able to get to their weapons containers, whilst those of 10 Company came down amongst dwellings in the Modhion valley, where a number were cut down by machine-gunners attached to the New Zealand Engineers as they attempted to free themselves from their harnesses. Local villagers attacked others, men, women and children armed with knives, axes and even ancient flintlock rifles, killing several. Within an hour all the Battalion officers, including the commander – Maj Scherber – were dead or seriously wounded; over two thirds of this unit, nearly 400 men, would die in the fighting.

Meanwhile nine more gliders carrying Maj Braun's detachment, which brought with it anti-tank guns, motor-cycles, mortars and flame-throwers, came down in the Tavronitis valley with the objective of seizing the old iron bridge over the river. Although Braun was killed when a burst of machine-gunfire raked the DFS 230 in which he was travelling, the objective was quickly achieved, demolition charges removed and the crossing secured.

With many units of paratroops now down and armed, fierce fighting was developing at the eastern end of the RAF camp where groups of airmen were being cut off as the Germans infiltrated. One small party of six airmen from 33 Squadron held out in their trench until their ammunition ran out, and then attempted to retreat as paratroopers approached over the iron bridge. Only three made it, ACs Banks, Eaton and Dixon all being killed. An urgent call went out for medical aid on the airfield and 30 Squadron's ambulance, driven by LAC H F Betts, with LAC N J Darch as medical orderly, ventured out across the open area under fire. Although wounded in the back by two bullets, Darch helped rescue a number of wounded and got them to comparative safety.

The RAF men were congregating mainly on the lower slopes of Hill 107 in small parties, trying to reorganize and formulate some plans for defence and survival. It had been proposed that in the event of invasion, officers and NCOs of the two units would defend allocated sections, and would each be responsible for small groups of airmen. Following the initial landings, Sqn Ldr Howell made his way to 22nd NZ Battalion HQ where he discussed events with Cdr Beale and Colonel Andrew, VC. Coming under sniper fire, the three carried out a recon-naissance of the forward area to inspect troop disposition, Col Andrew expressing his satisfaction with these before returning to his command post. Beale and Howell, accompanied by a handful of airmen, continued to the area where gliders had landed when suddenly a shot rang out and Beale fell, a bullet in his stomach. At about the same instant Howell was hit by machine-gunfire, one bullet smashing his left shoulder, a second striking his right forearm; an airman was also hit in the ribs.

Now under continuous fire, the wounded Cdr Beale, aided by an airman, managed to apply a tourniquet to Howell's right arm and dragged him to his feet to get him under cover. They placed him in a hollow dug into a hillside, Beale promising to send a rescue party for him. Two airmen volunteered to remain with their CO, but one of these was sent to gain safety (he was subsequently captured). So severe was the pain and loss of blood suffered by Howell that he begged the remaining airman to shoot him. When the plea was refused Howell ordered him to escape, but he too was captured while trying to regain British-held ground. When a rescue party eventually arrived they found the Sqn Ldr unconscious, soaked in blood and covered in flies. Believing him dead, they left him where he lay.

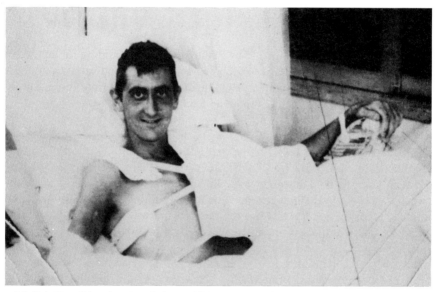

Sqn Ldr E A Howell in prison hospital at Kokinia, recovering from the wounds he suffered during the fighting at Maleme. (*Wg Cdr E A Howell*)

Ill-armed and in a hopeless position the various groups of airmen were now led away from the vicinity of the airfield by their officers or NCOs, some aided by New Zealand officers; most headed inland for safety. Fighting side by side with them had been the FAA personnel, remnants of 805 and 815 Squadrons. Lt Alf Sutton, who had been acting as Cdr Beale's principal assistant, had dug a hole near a Royal Marine gun position with his bayonet, taking pot-shots at paratroops from here until Ju87s attacked the Marines and put the guns out of action. Under constant sniper fire they managed to get one gun working again. At the bottom of the hill LAC Denton, an RAF mechanic attached to 815 Squadron, manned a Lewis gun until the barrel burned out, then retreated up the hill. Lt Ramsay, now in charge of 805 Squadron, mustered his party on high ground overlooking the camp, and although inadequately armed and under constant attack both by aircraft and paratroops, they held onto their position, inflicting many casualties. A second group from this unit were led to high ground by Sub

Lt Hinton, arming themselves from a German weapons container. Concealed in olive groves, without food or water, they consoled themselves from a gallon container of rum, liberated from the Mess.

When the attack on Maleme commenced, a number of airmen were in Sick Quarters suffering from Dysentry, including Lt Keith of 805 Squadron and 30 Squadron Medical Officer, Flt Lt T H Cullen. Although feeling very groggy, Lloyd Keith vacated his sick bed and spent most of the day stalking German snipers, armed only with his revolver; reputedly, he accounted for more than one. Although too weak to walk properly, Flt Lt Cullen attended to wounded throughout the fighting, continuing to do so until his post was overrun and he was taken prisoner. Even then he carried on alone in a nearby village, without sleep for three days, until captured New Zealand medical officers were sent to assist him. Over 1000 wounded passed through his hands before further aid was made available.

Some of the airmen had joined New Zealand troops in hunting the paratroops, among them a party from 33 Squadron led by Flt Lt Woodward, including the indomitable AC Comeau, and AC Hess, a middle-aged German-born Jew who had served in the Wehrmacht during the First War.

Still the flights of Junkers appeared overhead, and at 1000 hours Gen Maj Meindl, commander of Group West, was parachuted in with his Staff. Unaware of Maj Koch's death on Hill 107, he made for this location to join I Battalion. Revealing himself from cover, he raised a signal flag directed at where he supposed Koch to be. He was at once hit in the hand by a bullet, and then cut down by a burst of machine-gun fire. Although painfully wounded, the General continued to direct operations however. An hour later another flight of transports dropped large quantities of urgently needed ammunition, some heavy machine-guns, hand grenades and mortar bombs. Most of this fell into New Zealand hands, where the ammunition proved particularly welcome as many machine pistols had been retrieved from fallen or captured paratroops and put to use.

Further to the west a detachment of 74 men under Lt Maurbe had been dropped to reconnoitre the village of Pediada Kastelli, the site of the uncompleted airfield near Kissamos Bay; they were also to seize the little port. The area was defended by 1 Greek Battalion, an ill-trained and under-armed force of about 800 men, together with a detachment of Cretan police and a number of New Zealand officers and NCOs, all commanded by Maj T G Bedding. The Germans had the misfortune to land amongst the Greeks, many parachutists being killed in the air on the way down. Those who landed were stalked and killed with knives or clubs due to the lack of weapons. By 1100 the 28 survivors of Maurbe's force, 15 of whom were wounded, had been rounded up and taken prisoner. When the area was eventually overrun several days later stories of Greek 'atrocities', evidenced by the mutilated bodies of paratroops knifed or clubbed to death, outraged the Germans into taking reprisals against the local civilian population, believing them to have been responsible. Over 200 male civilians were rounded up and shot – the start of a long and bloody vendetta between the island's inhabitants and the occupation forces.

Meanwhile at the same time as the initial glider landings had taken place around Maleme, Group Centre had commenced its assault on Canea and Suda Bay. Following the untimely death of Gen Maj Süssmann in the air crash, command of Luft Division 7 had passed to Oberst Richard Heidrich, commander of FJR 3. First to touch down here were two companies of I Battalion of the Assault Regiment under Hpt Gustav Altmann, who were to capture AA positions on the Akrotiri peninsula. The DFS 230s came under heavy fire from their proposed objectives, three or four being hard hit and caused to crash, whilst the survivors were widely dispersed. More than half the force became casualties, while most others were swiftly rounded up and captured.

Eight more gliders came down near the gun battery they were to put out of action south of Canea, but one landed near a Royal Marine section whose fire raked the glider, killing three of the occupants. As the remaining troops clambered out, all were shot down. However the rest of Lt Alfred Genz's 1st Company assembled for their attack and swiftly overwhelmed the gun battery. They then attempted to take a nearby radio station, but were halted by the determined efforts of the defending Marines. Only 27 of Genz's force survived, later joining forces with the paratroops of FJR 3. Lt Rodulf Toschka's small unit of three gliders which had come down in the middle of Canea, also awaited the aid of the parachute forces after capturing their target gun position.

To support the valiant assault units, some 1800 men of FJR 3 were to be dropped west of Canea, I and II Battalions to land in Prison Valley on either side of the Canea-Alikianou road, whilst III Battalion was to land near Karatsos and along the coast road. These areas were heavily strafed by Bf109s just before the landings commenced, the first wave of over 150 Ju52/3ms then approaching. Although several gun sites had been put out of action by the glider troops, others put up a sustained fire, causing the transports to veer away and break formation. The result was that the parachutists fell over a wide area in scattered groups. Only two or three Junkers were actually shot down (believed to have been aircraft of KGrzbV 102 and 105), but included amongst them was an aircraft of Training Staffel, Fliegerkorps VIII, flown by Fw Joachim Meyer, and still bearing the civil registration D-ATRN. One transport was claimed shot down by Marine B V Jones armed with a Bren gun, while the Bofors gun manned by L/Cpl Tom Neill and his Marine crew was seen to obtain hits on several aircraft.

Due to the scattering which had occurred many elements of FJR 3 were too weak to be effective, while much of Maj Heilmann's III Battalion had fallen amongst their comrades of I and II Battalions. Those who had the misfortune to fall near Galatas were immediately routed by the New Zealanders of 19th Battalion, the majority being killed. Upon landing near the Canea-Alikianou road, Hpt von der Heydte's I Battalion was strafed by a low-flying Bf109, but without suffering casualties. By dint of fierce fighting the paratroops finally succeeded in capturing two vitally important hills a mile or so south of Galatas. Two companies of 19th Battalion at once counter-attacked, supported by two light tanks, but they were driven back, one of the tanks being knocked out by a 37 mm anti-tank gun, its two-man crew being killed. However these actions had already cost FJR 3 nearly a third of its strength in casualties, and the remaining men were fighting desperately to hold onto the ground taken.

With a pair of escorting Messerschmitt Bf110s waiting in the foreground, large numbers of Junkers Ju52/3ms are prepared for take off on a dusty Peloponnese airfield. (*Bib für Zeit*).

As the first wave of Ju52/3ms returned to Greece, they had lost no more than seven of their number over Maleme, Canea and Suda Bay, but as they reached their airfields most were forced to circle to allow the clouds of dust thrown up by the first down to subside. Several aircraft collided on the ground after landing, or were damaged in other accidents. Anxiously awaiting news from the invading forces, Headquarters of XI Fliegerkorps in Athens were ignorant of the catastrophies that had befallen much of both Groups, many of the radio transmitters carried in the DFS 230s having been damaged or destroyed in the landings.

During the early afternoon a single Ju52/3m arrived over Maleme airfield carrying Maj Snowatzki and an airfield servicing unit. Spotting a German flag on the western perimeter, Snowatzki believed this to indicate that the airfield had been captured, and ordered the pilot to land. As the Junkers approached however, it came under heavy fire and was badly damaged though the pilot managed to pull out to sea and return to Athens, where Snowatzki reported on the dire position at Maleme. At about the same time a radio message came through from FJR 3, advising of the failure to capture Canea and Suda Bay, and in the light of this unfavourable news General Student delayed the second wave attack on Retimo and Heraklion.

Over Maleme strafing fighters continued to mill around, Bf109s seeking to

348

winkle out defiant gun sites. During one such attack Lt R Parry-Lewis, the local Marine commander, was wounded, while Marine Kimber, already credited with at least one success, was mortally wounded whilst manning a Lewis gun. Members of 30 Squadron not occupied in defending the lower slopes of Hill 107 gave support to the New Zealanders. Plt Off R K Crowther, in charge of the detachment, led a handful of men to mop up a band of paratroops on the far side of the hill, where some 30 or so RAF and FAA personnel had been captured. So desperate was one German officer to seize the hill that he employed these prisoners as a human shield in an attempt to gain a footing. Some of prisoners were shot by New Zealanders who mistook them for Germans as they approached, but Pty Off Wheaton of 805 Squadron and a 30 Squadron airman, LAC Holland, were then ordered to approach the New Zealand lines and tell them to surrender.

As they reached shouting distance, the pair called out that they were going to make a dash for cover, but at that moment Plt Off Crowther's 30 Squadron party, and men of 33 Squadron led by Cpl Harrison, suddenly attacked the Germans from both flanks. The remaining prisoners attempted to reach safety during the confused fighting, but about half of them were killed before the Germans were shot down or dispersed. LAC Holland was one of the casualties, badly wounded in the back, but was rescued by the New Zealanders. Plt Off Crowther then led his band in a counter-attack on some Germans who had gained control of the eastern side of the RAF camp.

Despite constant strafing by Bf109s and fierce close-combat with the paratroops, the RAF camp area was regained, and with the failure to capture the hill, the paratroops called in Ju87s and Bf110s to attack the defenders again. Late in the afternoon a pair of Ju52/3ms again tried to land on the airfield, but were driven off by a hail of small-arms fire from the troops on the beach. Finally however, during the evening two detachments from the Assault Regiment managed to take Hill 107 despite fierce New Zealand resistance. Their victory found them almost out of ammunition, but no counter-attack came. They had secured ultimate control of the airfield by this coup, and from this point the battle was lost for the defenders.

At Canea meantime both sides had sought to consolidate their positions while Messerschmitt fighters cruised above, obviously uncertain of the locations of their own troops. During one sortie Hpt Paul Kleiner's Bf110 of 4/ZG 26 (3U+HM) was shot down near Canea with the loss of the crew, whilst JG77's low-flying Bf109Es continued to take regular losses. Fw Niemeyer of 4 Staffel was shot down and killed in Yellow 9, while Oblt Otto Grobe, from the same Staffel survived being shot down in Black 5 and managed to evade capture, later returning to his unit. A third Bf109, this from 7 Staffel, was lost when Fw Dietrich Saake was similarly brought down in White 6, he becoming a prisoner.

When the attack on Canea had begun King George of the Hellenes, his cousin Prince Peter, and the Greek Prime Minister, Mr Tsouderos (himself a Cretan), were at the King's villa south-west of the town. One glider landed just 300 yards away but its occupants were swiftly dealt with, while a number of paratroops dropped less than half a mile away, although they made off in a different direction. Led by the British Military Attache, Colonel J S Blunt, with an escort of 40 New Zealand and Greek soldiers, the Royal Party was guided to the nearby mountainous region, heading south. It would take them three days and nights to trek south to Ayia Roumeli, where their further adventures will be related later.

In Suda Bay, while fighting went on ashore, the Bay Patrol, comprising minesweepers, former whalers and motor launches, came under increasing air attack. The minesweeper *Widnes* and the South African whaler *Kos 23* were both bombed, and consequently beached, as was the 6200-ton freighter *Dalesman*, which had arrived a few days earlier with convoy AN-30; fortunately casualties were light.

The defenders at Retimo and Heraklion had been spared the morning assaults by the air landing forces, although a reconnaissance Do.17P of 2(F)/11 had appeared over the latter airfield at 0800, a high-level bombing attack then following; from then until midday aircraft were constantly overhead, bombing and strafing, but causing few casualties. At Retimo defence was provided by two Australian battalions, 2/11th and 2/1st, and by two Greek battalions, with two Mark VI tanks in support. There were no heavy AA guns, the Australians relying on tripod-mounted Brens and a few Vickers machine-guns. Here the German plan called for Oberst Sturm, commander of FJR 2, to drop with his Headquarters and one and a half companies very near to the airfield, from where he was to direct operations. Maj Kroh, one of the leaders of the successful Corinth Canal attack, was to land with I Battalion to the east of the airfield, which he was to capture, while Hpt Weidmann's III Battalion was to land in and around the village of Perivolia, from where an advance on the town of Retimo was to be made.

At 1600 several Staffeln of Bf110s commenced strafing the area while Ju87s went after specific targets and Do.17s bombed and strafed from low level. The Australian gunners put up an intense barrage which shot down two of I/KG 2's Dorniers and severely damaged a third. Both Oblt Heinz Schmidt's U5+EH and Lt Max Graf von Dürkheim's U5+BH fell in flames; two more of these bombers from III/KG 2 also suffered damage.

Fifteen minutes later two dozen Ju52/3ms were counted approaching from out to sea, these crossing the coast to the east of the Australian positions, but then turning to fly parallel with the coast, where advanced units of FJR 2 began dropping. More and more transports followed until an estimated 160 were over the target zone. Despite the lack of any opposition in the air, the drop was highly-disorganized, troops coming down in the wrong sequence, and as a result being scattered over a wide area. Partly this was due to the confusion by then reigning on the despatch landing grounds in Greece where Staffeln were being ordered off as soon as they were refuelled. It was also to an extent occasioned by the intense fire put up by the Australian gunners.

Groups of aircraft were broken up as bullets and shell fragments riddled the fuselages of the slow-moving Junkers, killing and wounding many of the men inside. At least seven aircraft were seen to fall in flames, two or three crashing near Perivolia, whilst others headed out to sea trailing tails of fire; two more collided. Amongst those lost were two from I/KGzbV 172 (one of these being

4V + IW flown by Fw Rudolf Krause); two more were lost by I/LLG 1, while Uffz Karl Kohnle's 1Z + FR of I/KGrzbV 1 also failed to return.

As with the earlier drops, many paratroops were killed even before reaching the ground; large numbers of I Battalion troops actually fell within the Australian positions where Bren and Vickers gunners took a heavy toll. Intended to support III Battalion, this force had fallen completely in the wrong area, but despite the losses and tribulations, Maj Kroh eventually managed to assemble quite a strong force, reinforced by a heavy weapons detachment with mortars, anti-tank guns, light howitzers and heavy machine-guns.

At much the same time Heraklion had also come under renewed attack. Following a lull in the air bombardment, a continuous stream of attackers appeared from 1600 onwards, attacking the airfield and gun sites here. At one point an estimated 50 Stukas were overhead, these being aircraft of Hpt Brucker's III Gruppe of StG 2 from Scarpanto, but courageously the defenders continued to hit back. When He111s of II/KG 26 came in at low-level two were hit, 1H + ZP (Oblt Kurt von Stetten) and 1H + MP both crash-landing on the airfield where von Stetten's crew were taken prisoner, the other crew evading capture. Strafing Bf109s were joined by Rhodes-based CR42s, and these were followed in by Bf110s of II/ZG 26. The latter were hunting for surviving gun sites, but accurate fire shot two 4 Staffel aircraft down into the sea. The Staffelkapitän, Oblt Reinhold Heubel (3U + AM) and his gunner were killed, but Uffz Otto Stein and Gefr Dietrich Hermann managed to ditch 3U + CN and reached the shore where they were captured; they would be released later.

Shortly after 1800 the first of some 240 Ju52/3ms came in, flying at about 100 feet over the sea, but climbing up to 250 feet to drop their charges. The results were close to disaster for the Germans; gunfire enveloped the formation, hitting many aircraft and killing numbers of paratroops before they could even jump. Several transports fell away trailing flame and parachutes as men aboard tried desperately to get clear. One unfortunate was seen to catch his parachute on the tail of one aircraft as it headed out to sea. The big trimotors crashed, or glided down to force-land all round the area, 15 burnt-out wrecks subsequently being found in the immediate Heraklion sector alone, while others fell in the sea KGrzbV 101 bore the brunt of the losses, at least eight of this unit's aircraft being shot down including G6 + KL (Oblt Hans Rehrmann), G6 + GK (Ofw Heinz Otto) and G6 + EK (Uffz Helmut Biewendt).

As with the landings at Retimo, the drop had been unco-ordinated, reserve and back-up troops often landing ahead of the main units. Second wave transports which arrived over the dropping zone in sections were easy targets for the defenders, the final troops being dropped some three and a half hours after the initial landings. II Battalion suffered worst, being almost wiped out immediately on arrival. Half the force landed amongst units of the Black Watch, only one officer and a few dozen men surviving the initial minutes. These men were then found to be very vulnerable when a bayonet charge was launched at the west end of the airfield by the Scots, during which large numbers of Germans were killed. One small group succeeded in establishing themselves in some Greek barracks to the west of the airfield, where they were to hold out for 24 hours. Of the other half of the battalion, which came down in the positions of 2/4th Australians, only five men survived; these later escaped by swimming along the coast to safety. The other three battalions came down more safely to the east and west, but too far from their objectives to be able to influence the fighting; indeed they saw only sporadic action before night fell at the end of this most violent day.

Owing to the lack of information coming from the Retimo area but believing the landing ground to have been captured, Air Headquarters in Athens ordered a Fi156 communications aircraft (presumably from 2(H)/31) to be despatched to this sector to obtain an up-to-the-minute situation report. Arriving during the early evening the pilot landed at Retimo, only for he and his observer to be taken prisoner by the Australians, thus leaving Air HQ none the wiser.

With the arrival of night, nine Wellingtons from 257 Wing in Egypt were despatched from Fuka to raid the mainland airfields in Greece, but they attacked the permanent bases, rather than the landing grounds where ground crews were performing Herculean tasks to bring back some semblance of order and serviceability amongst the transport fleet. At Eleusis a lone Ju88 of Wekusta 76 was damaged by 70 Squadron bombs, while attacks on Menidi and Topolia achieved nothing. At least one Wellington bombed Argos, where a single Ju87 of StabSt/StG 2 was destroyed and a second damaged.

The Royal Navy was also out, Capt Mack's Force 'E', comprising the destroyers *Jervis*, *Nizam* and *Ilex*, passing through the Kaso Strait to bombard Scarpanto. Fire was opened at 0245 against the airfield, where it was hoped to catch the dive-bombers of StG 2. In the event, the only damage was caused to two of the Stab Staffel's Do.17 'hacks', two groundcrew airmen being wounded. Meanwhile Admiral King's Force 'C' (the cruisers *Naiad* and *Perth*, and four destroyers) had also passed through the Strait during the evening, where it came under attack by Italian torpedo-bombers from Rhodes, but these failed to inflict any damage.

Six Italian MTBs then attacked, again without success, the destroyer *Juno* engaging these and claiming that four were damaged by machine-gunfire before being driven off. What none of the British warships had spotted was the flotilla of 25 small ships which had sailed from Piraeus to the island of Mélos during the day, carrying 2330 reinforcement troops from III/100 Mountain Regiment (III/GJR 100), and supporting units with anti-aircraft guns, ammunition and supplies. It was intended that this convoy would sail for Maleme next day.

Morning on 21 May found the Germans most favourably placed at Maleme, where daybreak attacks by Bf109s and Ju87s prevented the New Zealanders launching any organized counter-attack against the critical Hill 107. Apart from the constant strafing however, it was relatively quiet here and around Canea, with only skirmish activity occurring. The various RAF and FAA parties, mainly without arms, were gradually being led away from the forward areas. The two largest groups had congregated to the east of Hill 107, the 30 Squadron party with 23rd Battalion near the village of Dhaskaliana, while the main 33 Squadron party was along Vineyard Ridge with 21st Battalion. Everyone was keeping their heads well down, as Hs 126 spotter aircraft were meandering overhead, looking for targets for the Stukas and Messerschmitts. To the south of the hill was 252

AMES, the radar station, and this came under air attack by Bf109s and Bf110s during the morning, 17 of the 56 RAF personnel becoming casualties, or subsequently being captured.

Many of the FAA personnel had gathered in the same area, including Sub Lt Hinton's small party. Roy Hinton recalls:

'Dawn found myself and about four of my troops in a trench covered in bracken. We had a field of observation downhill and due east. After some time I got out to have a pee and lo and behold, some Germans were coming over the top of the hill. This was an occasion when I was thankful I was the open champion sprinter at school. We made it to the hollow of the valley, scrambled up the opposite side and fortunately came across a motley crowd of our own troops. We lay along the ridge taking pot-shots at the Germans on the other side of the valley. To my horror I found I was receiving some 20 shots in return to every one fired by me and realised I was firing tracer bullets!'

As the majority of the RAF and FAA were unarmed, Lt Sutton requested permission for them to be withdrawn. It was agreed that they could make for Canea, but would have to defend their present positions first until the return of the New Zealanders from their attempted counter-attack. Lt Ramsay and the armed FAA party took the right flank, while Lt Sutton and the RAF group covered the left; the unarmed men were ordered to remain under cover; the group was now about 160 strong.

Soon after the initial strafing attacks had been made, a section of Ju52/3ms appeared, carrying desperately needed ammunition for the Assault Regiment. Intense gunfire made it impossible for them to land on the airfield, but the formation leader, Uffz Grünert, decided to try and land on the rock-strewn beach. His gallant attempt was successful, but a second aircraft which tried to follow was raked with machine-gunfire as it landed, and then blew up as it received a direct hit from a mortar. In a desperate bid to aid his men in the assault on Maleme, General Student decided to commit most of his remaining paratroops (about 550 men) to the battle here, and at about 0900 more Ju52/3ms arrived carrying just over half this force, led by Oberst Bernhard Ramcke. They were dropped successfully as there was now virtually no anti-aircraft fire away from the environs of the airfield. Ramcke at once took over command of all the troops in the area, except the wounded General Meindl, who would be flown out to Athens later in the day.

With this success in hand, Student felt justified in despatching a battalion of 5th Mountain Division, originally intended for Heraklion, together with the remaining two companies of paratroops. Hence at about 1300 hours troop carrying Ju52/3ms arrived over Maleme with the mountain infantry, whilst others commenced dropping the final batch of parachutists. One of the first transports to touch down on the airfield burst into flames as it received a direct hit, while others careered along on smashed undercarriages. The transports were now being deliberately sacrificed to get the troops down, aircraft after aircraft going up in flames or sliding along on their bellies, shedding wings and engines, while troops evacuated the still-moving aircraft as rapidly as possible and raced for cover. Yet others crash-landed on the beach, many riddled with bullets and full of dead or dying men. Of six that came down near one Maori unit, only 20 men emerged alive, and these at once became prisoners. The two companies of paratroops had also come down in Maori lines between Pirgos and Platanias, where they were slaughtered before they could regroup.

On the airfield Maj Snowatzki's servicing unit had now safely arrived and was immediately down to business clearing the runway of wrecks, making good use of a captured Bren carrier to shunt shattered fuselages and wings to the perimeters. By 1600 some 60 aircraft had landed, and by nightfall more than 80 wrecks were piled up along the sides of the runway, but all the mountain troops had arrived. Maj Deutsch's KGrzbV 40, specially formed for the operation had been practically wiped out, more than 20 of the unit's aircraft being wrecked.

During the landings a number of Ju52/3ms had ventured over the Canea area while waiting to land, and here several had been shot down or damaged. Still manning his mobile Bofors gun here, L/Cpl Neill and his Marine team had been unofficially credited with shooting-down, or at least damaging, some nine aircraft during the two days. Each time low-flying aircraft appeared, he would wait for the last one to come within range before opening fire; when conditions got sticky, he would hitch the gun to a light lorry and move to a new position.

By the evening of 21 May, 1941 the north coast of Crete was becoming littered with crash-landed Ju52/3m transports as these aircraft were literally flown into the ground to get reinforcements onto the island. (*H Schliepacke via A Price*)

To the north of Crete a Maryland of 39 Squadron, flown by the Australian CO, Wg Cdr A McD Bowman, on a reconnaissance from Egypt, encountered a single Ju52/3m making for the island, believed to have been Fw Alfred Timme's 9P+FK of KGrzbV 40, which was promptly despatched into the sea. An important discovery by another reconnaissance aircraft, this time a Blenheim of 45 Squadron, was made when Flt Lt J M Dennis and his crew spotted a number of small craft escorted by destroyers, making for Crete from Melos. It was the reinforcement convoy with heavy equipment, arrival of which was critical to the success of the German invasion.

Meanwhile elsewhere on the island action had continued. At 1345 a small 300-ton coastal patrol vessel, Syvern, which had escaped the Luftwaffe's attention in Suda Bay up to this point, was suddenly strafed by an aircraft identified as a Ju88, but almost certainly was Hpt Wilhelm Makrocki's Bf110 (U8+AB) from Stab I/ZG 26. During the first pass every gunner of Syvern fell wounded, one of them mortally, but others took their places at the small automatic weapons as the attacker returned again and again. On the sixth pass, so close did the Messerschmitt come that when an ammunition locker on the coaster's deck blew up, pieces of debris hit the fighter's port engine, and the stricken machine smashed into the vessel's mast, then plunged into the sea. Makrocki, a nine-victory 'Experte', was killed, as was his 47 year-old observer/gunner, Hpt Heinrich Eisgruber. Fires aboard Syvern were extinguished and she limped back into harbour with only two members of her crew unwounded.

Heraklion had again suffered heavy bombing and strafing attacks during the morning, delivered by Ju87s and do.17s, supported by II/ZG26 Bf110s. Australian Bofors gunners and Royal Marines manning 3-inch Naval AA guns and pom-poms, put up a spirited defence, shooting down a 5 Staffel Bf110 (3U+LN flown by Lt Dietrich Oldenburg) and III/KG 2 Do.17 (U5+OR) captained by Lt Hugo Schilling; both crews were lost. It is possible that these guns also brought down a reconnaissance Bf110 from Fliegerkorps XI's Aufklärungsstaffel – 40+DH flown by Fw Richard Pielchen was lost during a sortie to the island.

Following this latest aerial bombardment, Maj Schulz's III/FJR 1 attacked Heraklion town from the west, hoping to capture the harbour. Fierce fighting ensued, and the western end of the harbour actually fell to the Germans, but British and Greek forces counter-attacked, forcing the surviving paratroops out of town by the evening. By this time FJR 1 had lost more than 1000 men. During the fighting the Australians of 2/4th Battalion had captured a number of German Very signal pistols and signal codes, and were able to use these to cause supply-dropping Ju52/3ms to release their cargoes of supplies and ammunition onto the Australian positions.

Air-Sea Actions

Well aware that a seaborne force had to get through soon, the Royal Navy was out in force throughout the next 48 hours, but the Luftwaffe was ready to challenge the warships and one of the biggest air-sea battles of the war to date developed. After making an uneventful sweep around Maleme, Canea and Kissamos Bay during the night of 20/21 May, Force 'D' (the cruisers *Dido*, *Orion*, *Ajax* and four destroyers) was retiring westwards through the Antikythera Strait during the morning of the 21st, when Ju88s of I/LG 1 attacked, *Ajax* being damaged by near misses. One of the attackers was Lt Sattler's L1 + BK, which failed to release its 2800kg SC1400 bomb on pulling out of its attack dive. Unwieldly with the heavy bomb still aboard, the bomber was hit many times in the port wing and fuselage before escaping. Sattler was soon back in the air, joining a force from I and II/LG 1, and Ju87s of Stab, I and III/StG 2, which attacked a substantial naval force during the afternoon and evening. Force 'D' had rendezvoused with Admiral Rawlings' Force 'A1' (the battleships *Warspite* and *Valiant* and six destroyers).

No vessels were hit during these raids, although there were some narrow escapes, and Sattler believed that he had gained a direct hit on a cruiser. The gunfire from this stronger fleet proved deadly however, three bombers being claimed shot down and two more damaged. Two Ju87s were actually lost, T6 + LR (Uffz Heinz Rauser) of 7 Staffel and T6 + HS (Lt Dieter Schilling) of 8 Staffel, both crews being reported killed, a Stab machine returning to Scarpanto badly damaged with both Lt Elmar Goblet and his gunner mortally wounded, while an aircraft of 2 Staffel returned with a badly wounded gunner. A Ju88 of II/LG 1 was also hit and damaged.

Further east Force 'C' came under severe attack from mid morning until early afternoon from Aegean-based units, including both Regia Aeronautica aircraft and Ju87s from III/StG 2 from Scarpanto. Just before 1300 the destroyer *Juno* was hit by three bombs, two of which exploded in the boiler and engine rooms, while the third detonated the magazine. Broken in two by the explosions, she sank in two minutes, 128 members of her crew perishing; 97 were plucked from the sea. When hit she had been under attack from Ju87s from III/StG 2 as well as by Z1007bis bombers of 50° Gruppo BT. During the various attacks on Force 'C' and Force 'D' the Axis believed that they had also severely damaged two cruisers and a destroyer and hit at least four more warships, but in fact *Juno* was the only casualty.

Just before dusk on 21 May Force 'D' again entered the Antikythera Strait to repeat the previous night's sweep along the Maleme-Canea coastline. Again Stukas of Hpt Brückner's III/StG 2 from Scarpanto attacked, but were met by intense and accurate AA gunfire, the gunners believing that they had shot down two or three of the Stukas, one of which was seen to break into two and plunge into the sea. This was clearly Fw Franz Kohl's T6 + GS from 8 Staffel, which failed to return, while a second Ju87, flown by Oblt Heinz Rutkowski, ditched near Kythos Island, only the gunner, Fw Otto Schupp, surviving.

Just before midnight Force 'D' encountered the reinforcement convoy of caiques and coasters heading for Maleme, and Admiral Glennie's destroyers at once attacked, causing great destruction during the next two and a half hours. At the start of the action two caiques were seen to burst into flames, and a steamer – believed to have been the 1601-ton Rumanian *Carmen Sylva* – obviously carrying ammunition, blew up. Some were sunk by pom-pom fire, others raked by machine-guns. German soldiers could be seen leaping into the sea, their cries for help being audible above the sounds of battle. The escorting Italian destroyer *Lupo* gallantly tried to defend her charges. Although hit by no less than 18 shells, she managed to stay afloat and even launched two torpedoes at the British ships. Four Italian MTBs aided her, but to little avail. More than half the convoy was sunk, just ten caiques managing to evade attack in the darkness, these turning back towards Melos.

The British force had prevented the first sea invasion taking place, and much heavy equipment – tanks, lorries, heavy weapons and ammunition went to the bottom. It was estimated by the jubilant Admiral Glennie and his staff that some 4000 troops must have perished, but in fact losses were only a little over 300. A further 1650 had been rescued from the sea by the damaged *Lupo*, by a second Italian destroyer (*Lira*), which came out to help, and by German and Italian air-sea rescue aircraft.

One single caique did get through however, landing its troops near Canea. Here they had orders to attack British gun positions on the slopes of Akrotiri, but most became casualties as they landed, and all the others bar one were killed, wounded or captured as they battled through the suburbs of Canea. The sole survivor managed to reach the positions held by elements of I/FJR 3.

A second convoy of 38 caiques and steamers intended for Heraklion was ordered back to Piraeus on receipt of the news of the fate of the Maleme-bound flotilla, but this collection of vessels was now being hunted by Admiral King's Force 'C', which was sweeping in from the east. It would be 0830 before the convoy was sighted as it headed away northwards, and only one troop-filled caique was sunk by *Perth*'s gunfire before German bombers located Force 'C' and attacks commenced. Admiral King ordered his force to retire and head west towards the Antikythera Channel. Harried by Ju88s from I and II/LG 1, and by Do.17s of KG 2 which bombed from higher level, the force soon began to sustain casualties, the cruisers *Naiad* and *Carlisle* both being hit, the former suffering serious damage. In return two Ju88s were shot down, Lt Wolfgang Schweickhardt's L1 + IK failing to return, while Ofw Heinrich Böcker's L1 + LL ditched the sea just off Monemvasia, after struggling back to the Greek coast; he and his crew were rescued. Ju87s were also out, but erroneously attacked the Italian destroyer *Sagittario* which had gone out to escort the returning caiques; others damaged another Italian destroyer, the *Sella*.

At 1312 Force 'C', which was still under heavy air attack, called for assistance from the Battle Squadron, which was on station to the west of Crete. As the two forces converged, *Warspite* was attacked by Ju87s and received a direct hit on her starboard side. Two bomb-carrying Bf109Es from 8/JG 77 then swept in, flown by Oblt Huy and Oblt Ubben, each of whom also scored direct hits on the battleship's starboard gun positions. The ships were also under attack by Bf110s from Stab and I/ZG 26, Oblt Fritz von Wuthenau's 3U + CC of Stab Staffel being shot down. The cruisers *Gloucester* and *Fiji* were both hit by 250 kg bombs dropped by Ju87s from I and III/StG 2, but neither vessel was seriously damaged. However the destroyer *Greyhound* sank a few minutes after being hit by three bombs just before 1400.

Two destroyers were at once ordered to rescue survivors, whilst *Gloucester* and *Fiji* stood by to provide cover; it was the prelude to disaster. Sections of Ju87s and Ju88s at once pounced on the isolated ships and within minutes *Gloucester* had succumbed to a welter of bombs rained upon her by Oblt Dr Ernst Kupfer's Staffel of Stukas; she sank following an external explosion. Some 500 survivors were later rescued by Italian ships and German air-sea rescue aircraft, although the crews of both the cruiser's Walrus 'spotters' were amongst those lost.

Meanwhile the other warships continued to fight back, one Ju88 of 5/LG 1 being hit and severely damaged. Fw Hans Richter struggled to regain his base but the aircraft crashed in flames just north of Eleusis, the crew perishing. Two other bombers from II/LGI were also damaged, both crash-landing on return. Following the sinking of *Gloucester*, *Fiji* and the two destroyers attempted to vacate the area with all speed, but at 1745 they were spotted by a lone Bf109 Jabo of I/LG 2. The unidentified pilot carried out a single-handed attack on *Fiji* with his single 1000kg bomb, scoring a near-miss which tore a hole in the cruiser's plates. A second aircraft from this unit then arrived, gaining a direct hit on the forward boiler room. At 1915 *Fiji* capsized with the loss of 276 of her crew.

As dusk fell three destroyers of Capt Lord Louis Mountbatten's 5th Flotilla arrived in the area from Malta, and were ordered to assist the destroyer *Kandahar* in rescue operations to the *Fiji* survivors. Before reaching the position of this vessel's demise however, a signal ordered the ships to divert to Crete, where they were to move inshore to bombard Maleme airfield, and intercept a suspected seaborne invasion. As one destroyer was suffering a steering fault, Lord Louis headed into Canea Bay with only his *Kelly* and *Kashmir*. Here they discovered a troop-laden caique, which was soon badly damaged by their gunfire; a short bombardment of Maleme airfield was then undertaken before they departed from the target area. On leaving the bay another caique was spotted and left in flames, but at daylight the ships were still well within range of Luftwaffe attack.

At 0755 they were seen by about two dozen Ju87s of I/StG 2, led by Hpt Hubertus Hitschhold, which attacked at once. The initial bombs were avoided, but *Kashmir* was then hit amidships and sank within two minutes. Even as she went down one of her Oerlikon gunners continued firing, and was believed to have shot down one of the attackers. As *Kelly* manoeuvred violently to avoid a similar fate her gunners thought that they saw at least two more Stukas fall into the sea. *Kelly* then took a hit in her engine room and rolled over at once, half the ship's company losing their lives. Survivors, including Lord Louis, were strafed in the sea before the destroyer *Kipling* arrived on the scene to pick them up, also rescuing survivors from *Kashmir*. Ju88s then attacked, and whilst undertaking desperate avoiding action, *Kipling* scraped the upturned hull of *Kelly*, tearing a hole in her own side. Although attacked several times more, she escaped further damage and arrived safely at Alexandria.

The survivors of the two sunken destroyers had somewhat over-estimated their successes against the highly manoeuvreable Stukas. Only one aircraft from 2 Staffel had been shot down, the wounded Oblt Wilhelm Kaiser being rescued from the sea, his gunner (Ofw Paul Golla) losing his life, while a second aircraft was badly damaged and crashed on its return to base.

The Luftwaffe had effectively won this round however, and the Royal Navy would not again venture into the waters north of Crete by day; the way was now open for the seaborne elements of the invasion. By night the ships still appeared, mainly to carry supplies and assist with evacuation. It will be recalled that the Greek Royal Party had begun a journey across the island on foot on 20 May. By now they had reached an isolated, desolate spot at Ayia Roumeli on the south coast, where after midnight on the night of 22/23 May they were taken out to the destroyer *Decoy* in a small local motor boat; the Greek bodyguard and Cretan guides remained behind to continue the fight. *Decoy* rejoined Force 'A1' and would be subjected to air attack and a possible submarine encounter before reaching Alexandria six nights later.

While the naval/air battles of 22 and 23 May had been underway, on the land the fighting continued. At last at 0330 on the night of 21/22, the 20th New Zealand and 28th Maori Battalions launched a counter-attack on the airfield at Maleme, supported by three light tanks of 3rd Hussars. Despite fierce opposition, the New Zealanders were nearing their objective at dawn, threatening both the airfield and the important high ground to the south, but one tank had been knocked out by an anti-tank gun, the other two suffering gun stoppages. While being withdrawn, they came under air attack, and one more tank was destroyed. By mid morning the whole of Brigadier Hargest's 5th Brigade had been committed to the battle, but the ground gained could not be held, and all units began withdrawing. With the airfield still in their hands, the Germans continued flying in men and supplies at an increasing tempo, Ju52/3ms landing at the rate of one every five minutes. Aircraft from I and II/KGzbV 1 predominated, some bringing in heavy equipment, including Kubelwagen utilities.

Aircraft continued to pile up on the airfield, at least 20 more crashing, crash-landing, or suffering less-severe damage, while three KGrzbV 105 aircraft were shot down. A further dozen either returned to Topolia or Tangara in a damaged condition, or crash-landed on arrival due to the state of the runways there. Perhaps because of the profligate wastage of transports, Brigadier Hargest gained the impression that the Germans were evacuating, and signalled Division HQ accordingly. What had actually been seen was probably the air evacuation of wounded back to the mainland.

Around midday on 22 May the Luftwaffe again made heavy attacks on the Suda Bay area, but in doing so lost a Ju87 of Stab/StG 77 and a Bf110 of II/ZG 76 (MB+FN: Lt Werner Hoffmann); a further Bf110 from II/ZG 26 crash-landed at Maleme. During the preparation for these attacks disaster had struck I/StG 3 at Argos when two Stukas collided on take-off, one crashing in flames. Its 500 kg bomb exploded and brought down a third aircraft just getting airborne. The pilots of the two aircraft which collided, Oblt Wilhelm Ebner and Uffz Herbert Marquardt, were both injured, while their gunners were killed. Additionally ten ground personnel were either killed or seriously injured. Perhaps as a consequence of the loss of these three machines and two experienced crews, added to the operational losses of the previous two days, reinforcements would soon arrive. 7 and 8 Staffeln of III/StG 1, led by Hpt Helmut Mahlke, would arrive from North Africa next day, and immediately go into action.

By now 5th New Zealand Brigade had begun pulling out of the Maleme area, taking up reserve positions behind 10th Brigade in the Canea area. All the time elements of the newly-arrived mountain troops of GJR 100 were pushing the retreating Kiwis, while GJR 85 skirted the defences and made towards Suda Bay, approaching from inland. During the evening II/FJR 3 began a series of heavy attacks on 10th Brigade positions along Prison Road towards Galatas Heights, where the defenders were just about able to hold on. The advance was temporarily halted by a charge carried out by 6th Greek Battalion. With evening Generalleutnant Ringel arrived at Maleme to take over command of all ground forces, his orders from Luftflotte 4 including: (1) to secure Maleme airfield (2) to clear Suda Bay (3) to relieve the paratroops at Retimo (4) to make contact with the forces at Heraklion, and thereafter, (5) to occupy the whole island.

At Heraklion early morning air reconnaissance was followed by supply-dropping Ju52/3ms, while Bf110s from I and II/ZG 26 strafed and dropped bombs on the airfield and its defences. Some bombing of Heraklion town and areas to the west also took place, intensified at 1800 when Do.17s and Bf110s carried out a heavy attack as a preliminary to a further paratroop drop. At least two of the troop-carriers were shot down – both aircraft of KGzbV 172, including Fw Wilhelm Friedrich's 4V + DT. Some 500 men landed to the east of the airfield and 300 more to the west of the town. Some of the latter got into the built-up area under cover of darkness, but were soon mopped up next day, even civilians and priests taking an active part.

The remainder dug themselves in two miles west of the town, cutting road communications with Retimo and Canea. Those who had come down near the airfield occupied a ridge overlooking both the field and the nearby radar site of 220 AMES. Armed with mortars and heavy machine-guns, they were able to sweep the airfield with fire. Local army units were only partly successful in ousting them, although a number of 15–17 year-olds were included amongst the prisoners taken. Apart from the Junkers shot down over the Heraklion sector, another reconnaissance Bf110 was also lost in the area, L2 + PR of 7(F)/LG 2, piloted by Oblt Erich Kissel, failing to return.

The small south coast port of Hierapeta was also attacked during the day

German personnel inspect an abandoned fighter-Blenheim IF of 30 Squadron (K7177, VT-N) on Maleme airfield. (*J-L Roba*)

when the Regia Aeronautica made a further brief appearance. CR 42s from Rhodes and Scarpanto, carrying pairs of 50 kg bombs underwing – the first use of the aircraft as a fighter-bomber – bombed and strafed; very little damage resulted from this attack.

With nightfall came the RAF's bombers from Egypt again, but this time three 70 Squadron Wellingtons carried urgently-needed supplies of ammunition and medical equipment, which were dropped from 200 feet to the defenders of Canea, Heraklion and Retimo; at the latter location the stores fell into the sea. Blenheims and Marylands were also to operate, the latter being prevented from take-off by extremely bad weather conditions. However at 0300 Sqn Ldr J O Willis of 45 Squadron led off five Blenheims from Fuka, briefed to bomb Maleme. Becoming separated in the darkness and in a storm, two failed to reach the target. The other three bombed individually, Lt E Jones, SAAF, seeing his bombs straddle the airfield. It seems that a Ju52/3m of KGrzbV 60 was destroyed by bombing during this attack.

German troops pile up ammunition boxes in front of the engineless abandoned 30 Squadron Blenheim, K 7177,VT-N. Note the wing of a Ju52/3m immediately behind that of the British aircraft, and another of these transports in the background. (*Bib für Zeit*)

With Maleme firmly in their hands, the Germans now began gathering in the wounded – both their own and British – from the various medical posts and from the field. By now 33 Squadron's badly wounded commander, Sqn Ldr Howell, had been found by passing paratroops after lying unattended in the open for three days. Realizing that he was still alive, they gave him some water, and a little later a German rescue party carried him to a nearby village where he received some rudimentary treatment from Flt Lt Cullen, the 30 Squadron doctor.

Other 33 Squadron groups had also fared badly; Plt Off Ray Dunscombe had been killed in the fighting, while Sgt Alec Butterick had been seriously wounded. His group had engaged in hand-to-hand fighting with the paratroops during which he was shot through the left knee by a burst of machine-gunfire. Taken prisoner, he would be held in a barn for several days without care and food, with a group of other prisoners, including some civilians; the civilians were then taken outside and shot. Three other pilots from the unit were captured – Flg Off Butcher and Sgts Reynish and Leveridge – as was the Admin Officer, Plt Off W E Myhill. Amongst the airmen killed was A C Hess, the German-born Jew. Those seriously wounded were soon to be flown to Athens in Ju52/3ms, including Cdr Beale, the CO of Maleme. Here Sgt Butterick would have his shattered leg amputated, while Sqn Ldr Howell would make a remarkable recovery from his wounds.

Sgt Alec Butterick of 33 Squadron, one of those pilots left on the island at the time of the invasion. He was wounded during the fighting and subsequently became a prisoner. (*Mrs J Hubbold*)

At Maleme the transports continued to stream in, bringing reinforcements; on this date these included 95 Mountain Artillery Regiment; 95 Anti-Tank Battalion and 55 Motor-Cycle Battalion, plus advanced elements of GJR 141. It was now considered safe for Bf109s to operate from the airfield, and a number of aircraft from III/JG 77 flew in at once, one crashing on arrival. It would now be possible to maintain standing patrols over the battle zones, none of which was more than about five minutes flying time away.

'Graveyard' of British aircraft at Maleme including, in the foreground, the engineless remains of Brewster Buffalo 'Z' of 805 Squadron. (*F Lankeman via J-L Roba*)

It was just at the point of the arrival of direct fighter support that RAF Egypt began to become more fully involved in the fighting. There was little enough available at this time in the Desert in any event. Air Commodore Raymond Collishaw's 204 Group, with its HQ at Ma'atan Bagush, was to be responsible for operations over Crete – it had already had the job of despatching replacement Hurricanes from 102 Maintenance Unit at Aboukir to the island. Available to Collishaw was 258 (Fighter) Wing of Hurricanes (1 SAAF, 3 RAAF, 73 and 274 Squadrons) under Grp Capt C B S Spackman; 3 RAAF and 73 were in the process of reforming after sustained and costly fighting at Tobruk.

The medium-bomber force comprised the Blenheim Wing with 14, 45 and 55 Squadrons (Blenheim IVs) plus the newly-arrived and untried 24 SAAF Squadron with Marylands; 257 Wing under Wg Cdr W H Merton was already active over the area by night; it comprised three squadrons of Wellingtons – 37, 38 and 70 – together with a number of crews from the currently reforming 148 Squadron, recently withdrawn from Malta. Finally there was 6 Squadron with Lysanders and a few tactical-reconnaissance Hurricanes, and a detachment of maritime-reconnaissance Marylands from 39 Squadron.

Further to the east, in the Alexandria–Cairo–Suez area, was 252 (Fighter) Wing, part of 202 Group, with responsibilities for the defence of this area. The Wing currently comprised 250 Squadron, still forming with Tomahawks; 94 Squadron with Hurricanes but with the majority of its pilots inexperienced South Africans just learning their trade, and mainly responsible for night defence of the area; a few Fulmars of 806 Squadron at Aboukir, and the Gladiators of 2 and 5 Squadrons, Royal Egyptian Air Force.

Air Commodore Collishaw was anxious to strike at Maleme by day on 23 May, five Blenheims of 14 Squadron and three Hurricanes of 274 Squadron, the latter fitted with non-jettisonable long-range fuel tanks normally used for ferrying duties, being detailed to make the attack. The leading Blenheim developed a fault just after take-off, all turned back and the raid was aborted. At 1300 seven of the SAAF Marylands set off, but two of these were also forced to return early. On arrival over Maleme the other five bombed and strafed from low-level. Lt C S Kearney reported shooting a motor-cyclist 'who foolishly tried to ride across the aerodrome during the strafing', as he later recalled. Three others pattern-bombed in formation, believing that they had caused considerable damage. They also reported seeing German dive-bombers in action over Suda Bay as they were bombing.

This attack was followed by the arrival of four Blenheims from 45 Squadron, which dropped 20 lb and 40 lb fragmentation bombs: the leader, Plt Off P J Vincent in V5624, was assumed shot down, as his aircraft failed to return, he and his crew later being reported killed; the Luftwaffe claimed two Blenheims shot down during this attack. Finally two Beaufighters of 252 Squadron, the only such available, which had just arrived in Egypt from Malta, swept in to strafe Ju52/3ms which were seen disembarking troops, Sqn Ldr Yaxley and Sub Lt Fraser claiming four destroyed. The sum total of these attacks was estimated to amount to ten Ju52/3ms destroyed: German records indicate that six were actually lost, mainly aircraft of KGrzbV 106 and I/LLG 1.

The aircraft spotted attacking targets in Suda Bay by the South Africans may well have been fighters, for during this day Bf109s and Bf110s hunted down the five Thorneycraft MTBs (MTB67, 213, 214, 216 and 217) of 10th Flotilla, which had been doing invaluable work here recently, and all were destroyed. Two were claimed by Uffz Rudolf Schmidt of 5/JG 77 and one by Fw Franz Schulte of 6 Staffel, while Lt Johannes Kiel of I/ZG 26 claimed several MTBs and small craft sunk or damaged. However Ju87s of I/StG 77 were also hunting for seaborne targets in this area, Uffz Werner Weihrauch of 2 Staffel claiming the sinking of a submarine, possibly a Greek craft, and a minesweeper during these attacks. The attacks on the Bay had by now so damaged the harbour installations that the Naval Officer-in-Charge began making plans to move his HQ to Sphakia, on the south coast.

Heraklion town, which again came under heavy air attack by large formations of Do.17s, escorted by Bf110s, had by now largely been evacuated except for the hospitals. Paratroops to the west of the town attempted to filter across to join those to the east of the airfield, many skirmishes developing. An ultimatum to surrender the town was flatly refused by the defenders. The airfield was still secure, and was now due for some renewed use as a forward base. From Sidi Haneish airfield, on the Egyptian coast, 73 Squadron was ordered to despatch six Hurricanes to land at Heraklion, from where they were to operate against the unescorted transport aircraft flying in to Maleme, and to strafe the troops there and those around Heraklion.

At departure time, 1135, a Blenheim arrived to undertake the navigating, the formation setting out over the sea, Flg Off G E Goodman leading the fighters. Two hours later five Hurricanes returned; Goodman reported that they had flown over a number of British naval vessels which had put up such a tremendous barrage that the formation had been scattered. He feared that the Blenheim and one of the Hurricanes – V7424 flown by Sgt Bob Laing, a Tasmanian in the RNZAF, might have been shot into the sea. In the circumstances, he had decided to return with the surviving aircraft of his flight.

73 Squadron was ordered to try again, and at 1520 the same five pilots, plus one replacement, set off again, led this time by a 24 SAAF Maryland. Soon after their departure the "missing" Blenheim appeared and landed at Sidi Haneish, the pilot reporting that after becoming separated during the barrage he met up with Sgt Laing's Hurricane, and that the pair had continued towards Crete, where he presumed Laing had landed at Heraklion. And indeed he had, as he later recalled: 'Having passed over the bleak looking slopes of the mountain range I soon sighted the crossed runways of Heraklion, close by the township of Canea. Having circled the landing strip I noticed some good sized bomb craters in the runway but as the place seemed deserted I decided to land. I made a good landing, running down to the south-east towards the beach. The propeller clanked to a standstill and there was not a sound, which to say the least was most eerie! I stepped out of the aircraft and decided to walk to the nearest building, a stone hut some 300 yards away. Having gone a few yards a machine-gun opened up on the aircraft and myself, with some degree of accuracy, and I realised I was not alone. To return to the Hurricane would have been of little use as it was merely a sitting duck and I decided to run for it. Bullets began to whistle round and I dived for a small depression in the ground, which gave me a little cover. I remained there lying with my head towards the direction of the machine-gunfire to make a smaller target; also my dark blue tunic against the runway was quite fair camouflage. They gave the Hurricane and myself the works for quite a time and I tried to pluck up courage to make a bolt for it – luckily my mind was made up for me by the approach of a British "Matilda" tank, which rumbled up and shielded me from the fire of the machine-gun. The tank commander, an Army major, lifted up the trap door of the tank, greeted me with a smile and apologised for the reception I got. Having exchanged views on the situation and the Bosch in particular, he suggested I taxi the aircraft down to the revetment area, about half a mile down the runway, where I would find some shelter. Apparently he wanted to save the aircraft, as in those days pilots were more easily replaced than aircraft. Fortunately the engine was not damaged and I was able to taxi down at high speed, helped along with bursts of fire from the Bosch machine-guns, who were very active at this time.'

Within half an hour six Bf110s arrived and commenced strafing the gun positions. The Hurricane was soon sighted and was reduced to a blazing wreck. Bob Laing sheltered with others as the airfield was constantly bombed and strafed, and he adds:
'We could do nothing about it, except the Aussie-manned guns accounted for

Sgt Bob Laing of 73 Squadron after his eventful lone landing at Heraklion. (*R I Laing*)

several aircraft but at a very heavy cost to themselves. Without my plane I was a mere spectator of the operation in progress, and one experienced a terrible feeling of frustration to witness Heraklion being reduced to a shambles.'

Just about dusk in the midst of yet another raid by about a dozen Ju88s, 73 Squadron's six Hurricanes arrived. Despite being low on fuel, the fighters attempted to intercept, both Flg Off Goodman and Plt Off J H Ward claiming bombers damaged during a brief skirmish as they pursued them over Canea and out to sea, before they were obliged to break away and headed back to Heraklion. The airfield had been heavily pitted with craters, two Hurricanes breaking their tailwheels on landing as a result. The airfield was still under small-arms fire from the paratroops positioned on the ridge and behind rocks on the perimeter, and as the pilots headed for shelter, they had constantly to throw themselves flat for cover. Two Hurricanes were rapidly refuelled and were sent up to patrol until dusk, but nothing more was seen. After a hurried consultation with the OC Land Forces, Goodman learned that there was no stock of .303 ammunition for the Hurricanes and only limited fuel available. It was decided that as the Hurricanes could offer little assistance they should return to Egypt in the morning.

Following a night's desultory sleep, the six Hurricanes prepared to depart, Laing and Goodman squeezing into the cockpit of W9198, Goodman using his companion's knees as a seat, the parachute pack having been discarded and stowed into the fuselage. Before heading for Egypt all pilots were to use up their remaining ammunition by strafing enemy positions around the airfield, which they did. Bob Laing continues:

'Our journey back across the Mediterranean was uneventful from enemy point of view but we struck a head wind during the last hundred miles and with petrol low, we were feeling anything but comfortable. We finally landed at Sidi Haneish in a sandstorm with our petrol gauges registering zero. Surely Allah had been with us and my only complaint was that I was so stiff and numbed after sitting for three hours in a cramped cockpit and used as a cushion for the pilot. However, I gave the flight commander a big hand and said: "Thanks Benny – a lot."'

They were the first to arrive, landing at 0830 but were followed shortly by Plt Off Ward; no others returned to base. It was later learned that Flg Off R F Donati had run out of fuel and force-landed V7802 at Fuka, Plt Off F M Moss coming down just inside Ras el Kanazis with V7879 also out of fuel. Of the other two – Plt Off R L Goord (V7736) and Plt Off R H Likeman (V7764) nothing was ever heard. It was assumed that both had come down in the water, the severe sandstorm over the coast and out to sea probably contributing to their loss.

The wreckage of Wellington L7866 'R' of 37 Squadron which crash-landed at Heraklion during the night of 23/24 May, 1941. Sgt W R Faulkner and his crew later became prisoners. (*Bundesarchiv*)

During the previous night of 23/24 May, the Wellingtons had again been out, five of six 37 Squadron aircraft bombing Maleme, one having returned early with technical problems. Only two of these returned from the raid: Sgt W R Faulkner belly-landed L7866 at Heraklion safely in the dark, he and his crew all surviving the crash, while Sgt G E Harris ditched T2875 in the sea 140 miles north of Ma'atan Bagush near to a cruiser, which rescued all the crew; of Sgt H J Mew's T2895 nothing more was heard, and it was assumed that it had either been shot down by Flak or had come down in the sea on the return journey. Another four of these bombers were despatched by 38 Squadron, three bombing Maleme, where at least one Ju52/3m of KGrzbV 102 was destroyed, the crews seeing this on fire after their bombing; Ofw Kurt Schulz and two members of his crew were apparently aboard at the time, and were killed.

RAF reconnaissance shows Maleme airfield littered with Ju52/3ms, most of them wrecked.

At Suda Bay during the hours of darkness the destroyers *Jaguar* and *Defender* arrived carrying 200 Commandos of Colonel R E Laycock's 'Layforce'. 750 more of these elite troops were due next night, and were to land at Selinos Kastelli on the south-western tip of the island. In the event when the three destroyers carrying them – *Isis*, *Hero* and *Nizam* – arrived, the weather proved too bad and the ships were recalled to Alexandria. Meantime when *Jaguar* and *Defender* departed Suda Bay well before dawn on 24 May, they carried with them 250 naval personnel no longer required on Crete, including the FAA party commanded by Lt Keith and Sub Lt Hinton of 805 Squadron. Next night, as the second party of 'Layforce' were trying without success to get ashore at Selinos Kastelli, the minelayer *Abdiel* slipped into Suda Bay with a consignment of ammunition, leaving again with 60 wounded and four Greek Cabinet Ministers aboard.

Selinos Kastelli was already a location which was beginning to gain the Luftwaffe's attention, for early on 24 May the crew of a Royal Navy motor launch, ML1011, which had sheltered just off shore during the night, spotted two Ju88s and seven Bf110s passing overhead soon after 0630, as they prepared to sail. At first the crew thought they had escaped attention, but suddenly the two Ju88s broke formation and dived on the launch, followed by the Messerschmitts. Lt A H Blake ordered the Lewis gunner to open fire, and so close did Lt Franz Reiner of II/ZG 76 approach in M8+AC, that the gunner was able to shoot the

368

Bf110 down into the sea. Despite this success, the launch was riddled and one member of the crew killed. The rest swam to shore where they met up with Lt Sutton's mixed FAA/RAF party making for Sphakia. After walking some distance with great difficulty, well aware that paratroops were in the vicinity, the party found a caique and sailed the rest of the way in this after dark. At about the time ML1011 was being attacked, a motorized barge left Selinos Kastelli for Egypt, loaded with wounded. This was also attacked just off the coast and sank with great loss of life; a few survivors managed to swim ashore.

Operations on the north coast continued. After the departure of 73 Squadron from Heraklion, Luftwaffe air attacks continued, seven Bf110s and a number of Do.17s and Ju87s bombed and strafed the airfield at 0800. Sgt S Wilson's Marine Bofors crew were seen to shoot down one twin-engined aircraft, believed to have been a Bf110 but probably Lt Johann Schweigl's Do.17 (T6+EA) of Stabst 1/StG 2, before his gun site came under attack. Of the crew of six one was killed and four others seriously wounded. A Ju88 (L1+DN) of II/LG 1, flown by Fw Herbert Schelm, also failed to return from an operational sortie. Ju52/3ms continued to fly into Maleme with men and supplies, taking out wounded on their return flights, but such was the chaos here that some 20 more aircraft would be written-off during the day, mainly in landing accidents; KGrzbV 1 recorded the loss of ten aircraft alone, I/LLG 1 losing seven more, and KGrzbV 102 a further six.

A Junkers Ju52/3m comes in to land at Maleme over the wreckage of one of 805 Squadron's Brewster Buffalo fighters. (*via A Stamatopoulos*)

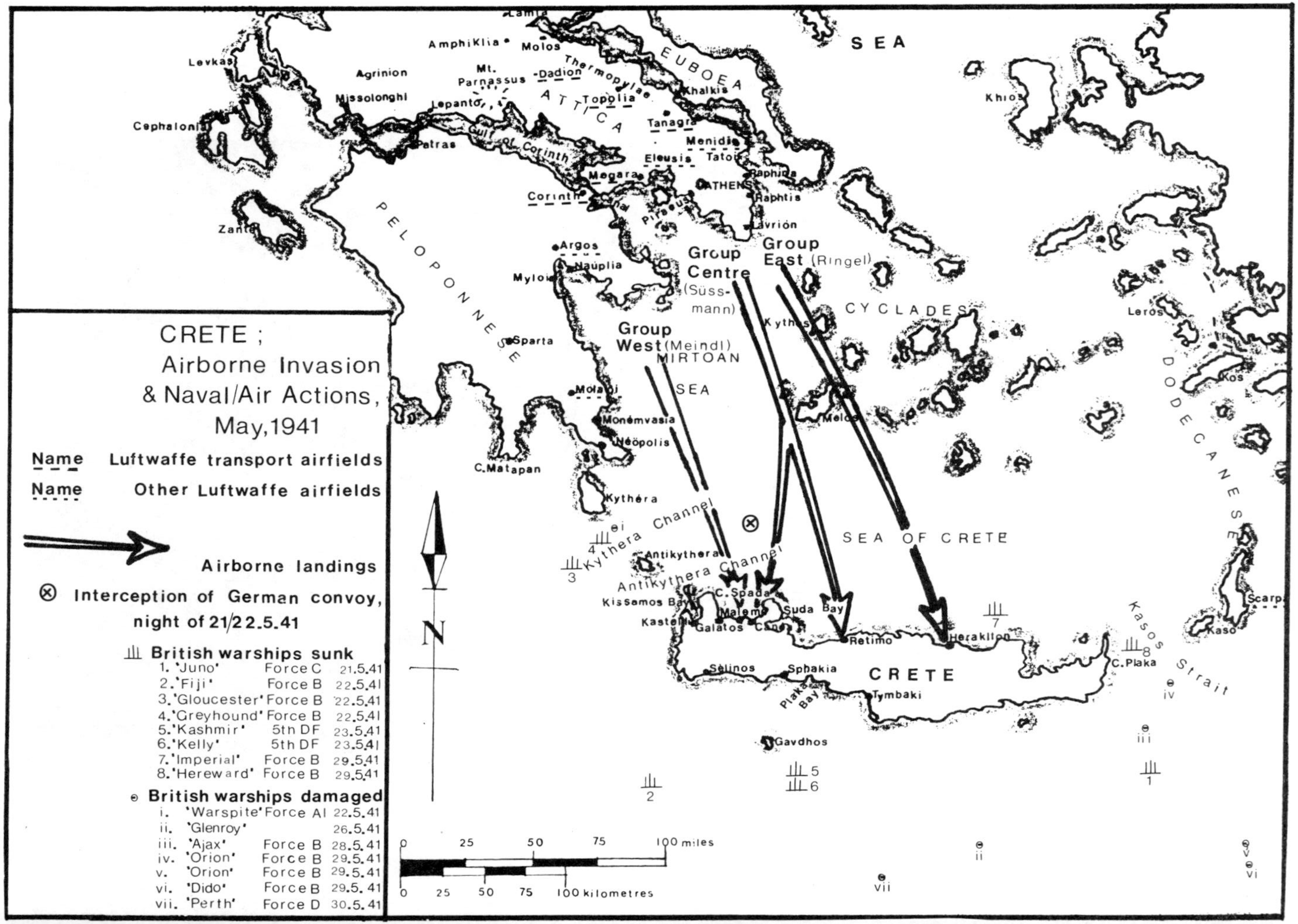
CRETE ;
Airborne Invasion
& Naval/Air Actions,
May,1941
Name Luftwaffe transport airfields
Name Other Luftwaffe airfields
Airborne landings
⊗ Interception of German convoy, night of 21/22.5.41
British warships sunk
1. 'Juno' Force C 21.5.41
2. 'Fiji' Force B 22.5.41
3. 'Gloucester' Force B 22.5.41
4. 'Greyhound' Force B 22.5.41
5. 'Kashmir' 5th DF 23.5.41
6. 'Kelly' 5th DF 23.5.41
7. 'Imperial' Force B 29.5.41
8. 'Hereward' Force B 29.5.41
British warships damaged
i. 'Warspite' Force Al 22.5.41
ii. 'Glenroy' 26.5.41
iii. 'Ajax' Force B 28.5.41
iv. 'Orion' Force B 29.5.41
v. 'Orion' Force B 29.5.41
vi. 'Dido' Force B 29.5.41
vii. 'Perth' Force D 30.5.41
SEA
EUBOEA
ATTICA
PELOPONNESE
CYCLADES
DODECANESE
MIRTOAN SEA
SEA OF CRETE
CRETE
Group East (Ringel)
Group Centre (Süss-mann)
Group West (Meindl)
Kythera Channel
Antikythera Channel
Kasos Strait
Lamia
Amphiklia
Molos
Levkas
Agrinion
Mt. Parnassus
Dadion
Thermopylae
Khalkis
Missolonghi
Lepanto
Topolia
Cephalonia
Tanagra
Patras
Gulf of Corinth
Menidi
Eleusis
Tatoi
Megara
ATHENS
Corinth
Raphina
Raphtis
Piraeus
Zante
Lavrión
Argos
Nauplia
Mylos
Kythnos
Sparta
Molaoi
Monémvasia
Néopolis
Melos
C. Matapan
Kythéra
Antikythera
Kissamos Bay
C. Spada
Maleme
Suda Bay
Kastelli
Galatos
Canea
Retimo
Heraklion
Sélinos
Sphakia
Plaka Bay
Tymbaki
Gavdhos
C. Plaka
Khios
Leros
Kos
Kaso
Scarpanto
N
0 25 50 75 100 miles
0 25 50 75 100 kilometres

Canea experienced such an intensity of air attack during the 24th that the British Headquarters was withdrawn to Suda Bay, although the AA defences of this area were seriously reduced, and all small craft in the harbour had been sunk or damaged. To the west of Canea a fierce battle for the Galatas Heights was now in progress, heavy bombing by Ju87s at 1630 preceding a determined assault on the town by II/GJR 100, who had taken their objectives by evening. The Stukas of StG 1 were forced to pay a heavy price for their involvement, II Gruppe losing Fw Klotzer in the Galatas area, while a second aircraft from this unit crash-landed at Maleme and was totally destroyed, one more force-landing on Dokos Island while trying to regain its base at Argos. The engine of a I/StG 1 aircraft flown by Fw Wilhelm Joswig was hit, the pilot being forced to ditch in the sea; he and his gunner were rescued by a Do.24 flying boat 26 hours later. An eyewitness saw Klotzer's aircraft come down:

'I saw a plane come down suddenly at a very steep angle and hit the curving slope of the hill behind Suda Bay. It bounced several times along the ground in great bounds, raising clouds of dust and shedding bits of itself as it went. Then it disappeared behind a ridge and a few moments later a column of black smoke and an echoing explosion announced its complete destruction'.

According to German records the three II Gruppe Stukas all fell victim to causes other than hostile fire; one suffered engine trouble, one ran out of fuel, and one was obliged to force-land due to technical problems. A Bf110 of 2/ZG 26 was also hit whilst strafing Retimo, Uffz Heinz Grychtol, the pilot, being wounded, but managed to regain his base.

During the night of 24/25 May the New Zealanders of 23rd Battalion counter-attacked, driving the German mountain troops out of Galatas again. The pressure was on however, and again the New Zealanders were driven back, being forced to evacuate the town again later in the afternoon of the 25th – this time permanently. By now General Freyberg was starting to have grave doubts of his ability to hold Crete. Without air support, and with his troops under constant air attack, the situation was becoming impossible. Next evening (26 May) he would cable General Wavell requesting permission to commence evacuation of Suda Bay, followed by Retimo and Heraklion. Wavell would not accede to his plea, urging him instead to continue the fight, but advising that if it proved impossible to hold Suda Bay, he was to withdraw on Retimo and continue to block the German move eastwards from there. Further troops and tanks were promised, although in the event these would not be forthcoming. Already in fact some troops were retreating southwards towards Sphakia, General Weston having instigated the initial stages of evacuation.

On learning of the latest situation, Winston Churchill cabled encouragement to Freyberg, while urging Wavell that all possible aid be sent. He suggested to the Chiefs of Staff that long-range Beaufighters be used to support the army and protect ships (although only a handful of 252 Squadron aircraft were available, Beaufighters of 272 Squadron were arriving from the UK), and that further troops be sent to the south coast ports. Air Chief Marshal Sir Charles Portal, Chief of the Air Staff, was discouraging: the few Beaufighters available would

British prisoners of war march past the remains of a Hurricane on Maleme airfield; note Ju52/3m transport in the background. (*via J-L Roba*)

need to have their secret ASV sets removed first, he advised the Prime Minister, and could not be readied until the last day of May at the earliest. Even then they would carry only sufficient fuel to operate over Crete for an hour at a time, numbers available would only allow one squadron to be operated initially, and lack of spares would make keeping them serviceable a problem. The scheme was abandoned. By 27 May, Freyberg would again cable Wavell requesting permission to start evacuating, and after consultation with Mr Churchill, Wavell finally agreed.

On 25 May meanwhile, 204 Group's involvement in the battle over Crete was much increased. Already during the night 37 Squadron Wellingtons had again set out to raid Maleme, although only two actually reached and bombed the target. At dawn however, four Marylands of 24 SAAF Squadron appeared overhead, bombing and machine-gunning the airfield and surrounding troop positions. They were followed by six 14 Squadron Blenheims, led by Sqn Ldr D C Stapleton, the crews of which saw a number of Ju52/3ms already on fire as a result of the South African's attack, and added their light bombs to the carnage. An estimated 24 aircraft were considered to have been destroyed or badly damaged, although many of those hit were almost certainly already wrecked. One Blenheim was slightly damaged by Flak splinters in return, the gunner of which was wounded in one foot.

At Gerawla 274 Squadron had by now received four Hurricanes fitted with long-range tanks. The pilots were not happy however, for not only did the tanks slow the Hurricanes down and make them less manoeuvreable, but also the armour plating behind the seats had to be removed and ammunition reduced to compensate for the weight of the extra fuel. Stated one:

'The additional tanks gave the Hurricane a range of 900 miles compared with the normal range of 600 miles. There were two additional tanks – one port, one

British prisoners of war prepare to board a Ju 52/3m for transport to the mainland. In the background (left) is another of these aircraft, while to the right is a Do.17Z bomber. (*F Lankeman via J-L Roba*)

starboard. The port tank emptied first, then the starboard tank. Air locks were liable to develop owing to bad refuelling or severe bumps in the air and throw the system out of commission. You never knew when the port tank emptied if the starboard tank was going to feed through. If your starboard tank refused to work over the sea, that was the end.'

Nonetheless, the four Hurricanes prepared to leave for Maleme at 0530 accompanying two Blenheims of 45 Squadron. One fighter burst its tailwheel on take-off and aborted, but the other three rendezvoused with one of the Blenheims, the other having crashed on take-off from Sidi Barrani. Near Crete the little formation entered dense, low-lying cloud and became separated, all but one Hurricane abandoning the strike and returning separately to Egypt. Only Plt Off A J C Hamilton continued alone in V 7562 towards Maleme. Over Suda Bay he encountered an aircraft identified as a Ju88, claiming this shot down in the sea. The only Luftwaffe loss recorded was Bf110 3U +CP of II/ZG 26, which reportedly ditched 30 kilometres west of Melos due to engine trouble, Gefr Heinz Nagel and his gunner being posted as missing. However, Hamilton's aircraft now developed the feared fuel problems, and he landed at Heraklion where the undercarriage suffered severe damage on the cratered runway.

The next strike was carried out by six more Blenheims from 45 Squadron, which dropped 20 lb and 40 lb bombs from 14 000 feet, seeing them fall amongst the clutter of transports, causing two explosions and three fires; the crews believed that about 12 Junkers had been hit. Three 55 Squadron Blenheims then attacked, all bombers returning to report only light Flak, and apparently no fighters. Just after midday three further Blenheims set out, again from 14 Squadron, but these did encounter Bf109s of II/JG 77 on patrol and ready for them over Suda Bay, and within minutes Flt Lt R A Green's T2065 had been shot down into the sea, followed by V5510 (Lt S R E Forrester, SAAF) and Sgt H P Jeudwine's T2003, all nine men aboard perishing. Two of the Blenheims fell to Uffz Rudolf Schmidt of 5 Staffel, the other being shot down by Uffz Herbert Horstmann of 6 Staffel. It would appear that fire from the gunners struck the Messerschmitt flown by the Gruppe's long-serving Kommandeur, Hpt Helmut Henz, who was killed when his aircraft crashed into the sea off Antikythera Island during this combat. Three 55 Squadron Blenheims which arrived shortly afterwards escaped interception and returned unscathed. They were followed during the afternoon by yet another four Blenheims from 45 Squadron, but three turned back with minor defects, Lt Jones, SAAF, attacking alone, reporting near-misses with his 44 20 lb bombs.

During lulls in between these raids on Maleme Junkers transports continued to fly in from the mainland, while others were engaged in flying out the wounded. One arrival during the day was the commander of Fliegerkorps XI, Generalleutnant Student, to see for himself the encouraging progress made by his gallant troops.

The final strike of the day against Maleme was to be made by three South African Marylands and two Hurricanes from 274 Squadron. Off at 1530, one Maryland soon developed a fault, turned back, and force-landed at Sidi Barrani. The two remaining bombers went in first, bombing and strafing the area. As they headed away over the mountains, Lt E G Ford's aircraft was seen trailing smoke from one engine; clearing the peaks, he crash-landed the stricken bomber near Tymbaki on the south coast. The crew were unhurt, but pursuing German fighters strafed the damaged aircraft and set it on fire.

Meanwhile the two Hurricanes, W9266 flown by Flt Lt Dudley Honor and P3469 flown by Flt Lt Hubert Down, had followed the Marylands in, as Honor later recalled:

'As we crossed over the mountains there were so many enemy aircraft in the sky that I was undecided whether to have a crack at the ones in the air or carry out my original orders and attack the aerodrome. I decided that I had better carry out my original orders. Down and I dived along the river valley. As we approached, we saw two transport aircraft circling to land. There were so many aircraft on Maleme that it was just a congested mess. Some were on their noses, some obviously burnt out. It was difficult to decide in that mass which of the aircraft on the ground to attack. I decided to have a crack at the two which were landing. I thought they were probably full of troops and equipment. They came in too fast for us. We were still about 2000 yards away as the second one started to touch down. I opened fire at this range and continued firing as I approached the aerodrome. I passed over at about 50 feet, spraying everything I could see. Down's aircraft was about 300 yards astern of me.'

'I saw three 109Fs taking-off from the aerodrome, going in an easterly direction. I thought they were going after the Marylands. I got to the north boundary, still at about 50 feet and noticed some troop-carriers, German and Italian (however, there is no evidence to suggest that Italian transport aircraft were involved in these ferrying operations – Ed), coming into the aerodrome along the line of the Cape Spada peninsula; they were at about 1000 feet. As I passed over the northern boundary the AA guns opened up; the sky was black around me with ack-ack bursts. I pulled up to the line of troop-carriers, head on. They stretched right along the peninsula, with about half a mile between each. There was an endless line of them, away to sea. I managed to get up to the same height as the leading aircraft – it was an Italian S.79 (sic) – and gave it a very short burst at dead range. It made no attempt at evasion and burst into flames and went straight down into the sea. I carried straight on and had a crack at a second, a Ju52 loaded with troops. He half turned away from me and went down. I saw him as he turned over on his back and hit the water.'

The two transports attacked were probably Ju52/3ms of KGrzbV 106.

Meantime, Flt Lt Down was being pursued out to sea by Bf109s of II/JG 77 – possibly those seen taking off by Honor; he did not return. The other German pilots gave chase to Honor, apparently joined by at least one Bf110, as he recalled: 'Suddenly there was a series of explosions and my control was gone. A 110 had attacked me from underneath and behind. I did not observe it before the attack. I started to take what evasive action I could. My controls were very badly damaged. I could only try to dodge him. The chase lasted about 15 minutes and I got closer and closer to the sea. I worked in as close to the cliffs as possible, watching him in the mirror. Each time I was a white puff coming from the front of him I did a skidding turn.'

'I saw the cannon shells bursting in the sea alongside. He must have used up all his ammunition without hitting me again because he sheered off. A 109F then took up the fight. He employed the usual tactics on me, diving and then climbing. I was unable to turn with him but managed to get him round the north of the peninsula, out of sight of the aerodrome. There was cloud at 2500 feet but I could not climb to get up there. After about five minutes a burst of fire hit my engine; there was a horrible bang and an awful smell of cordite in the cockpit. I was about 20 feet from the sea when I was hit. I could not pull out so I steered straight ahead to make a landing on the water at high speed, at about 220 mph. I reduced speed in order not to hit the water too hard and touched down at about 120 mph. After about 15 seconds the aircraft began to sink. I still had the cockpit hood closed and my safety harness was still fastened. I went down 40 feet before I realised what was happening. I noticed the sea turning from blue to dark green ... I opened the hood, which luckily had not jammed ... and turned the knob of my Mae West. I was wearing a German Mae West (taken from a Ju87 gunner who had been shot down during the Battle of Britain, during which time Honor had served with 145 Squadron) which inflates automatically, whereas the RAF type had to be blown up by mouth. I drifted to the surface slowly, noticing the water grow lighter and lighter. It seemed a long time. I broke surface to find the 109F still circling overhead at about 50 feet. Fortunately the pilot did not appear to see me and after a couple of circuits made off round the peninsula towards Maleme.'

In this engagement the II/JG 77 pilots claimed a total of three Hurricanes shot down, one by Uffz Schmidt, who had earlier shot down two of 14 Squadron's Blenheims, one by Fw Otto Köhler of 4 Staffel, and one by FjGefr Günther Marschhausen of 5 Staffel.

Dudley Honor meanwhile continued to float in the water:
'The sea was very rough; I was about half a mile from the cliff and after swimming for about a couple of minutes, I realised I was floating stern upwards. I still had my parachute on ... I jettisoned it and my trousers, which were hampering me. I carried on swimming for about three hours until I was just about 20 yards from the cliffs, which were about 100 feet high, not only sheer but overhanging. Each time I tried to get a handhold I was dragged away again by the suction of the retreating wave. My nails and flesh were torn by the rocks ... I found it impossible to get to the shore so I relaxed and allowed myself to drift round into a small cave. By this time it was nearly nightfall. I saw a German seaplane fly along the cliffs very near me ... I thought he might be searching for me. Eventually I was washed into another cave and although smashed up against the end by the drive of the sea, managed to hang on by grabbing a rock stalagmite and crawled up onto a little ledge.'

Luftwaffe transport pilot F Lankeman with his crew and Ju52/3m on Crete, May 1941. (*F Lankeman via J-L Roba*)

Further north during the day, a patrolling reconnaissance Maryland from 39 Squadron encountered a number of Ju52/3ms between Crete and Greece, which are believed to have been aircraft of KGrzbV 60. Flt Lt R A 'Butch' Lewis and his crew claimed to have shot down one and to have damaged two others; their victim would seem to have been Lt Ralf Billerbeck's aircraft, which crashed near Corinth, killing him and injuring three of his crew. Returning from their sortie, the Maryland crew reported seeing transports in formations of ten crossing the sea, each formation escorted by a single Bf109 or Bf110.

In Egypt, ready for the morrow, 274 Squadron received a further six long-range Hurricanes, flown up to Gerawla by newly-arrived pilots of 229 Squadron. At Sidi Haneish 73 Squadron received six reinforcement pilots from 213 Squadron, which had also just arrived, together with six non-tropicalised Hurricanes, attached 'for special duties over Crete.'

Of greater impact, the First Battle Squadron departed Alexandria at midday for operations around Crete. On this occasion the battleships *Queen Elizabeth* and *Barham* were accompanied by the carrier *Formidable* as well as eight destroyers. The carrier had aboard 12 Fulmars, crewed equally by 803 and 806 Squadrons, some of the aircraft being of doubtful serviceability but all that could be made available, plus 15 Albacores and Swordfish of a composite 826/829 Squadron. The Air Group's first task was to be a dawn raid on Scarpanto, since it was obvious that the airfield there was being extensively used for operations against Heraklion and the south coast ports.

As the fleet approached the area by night, two Wellingtons from 38 Squadron raided Scarpanto with unobserved results, while eight more from this and 37 Squadron attacked Maleme. At 0330 six Albacores took off, led by Lt Cdr Saunt, and while two were forced to return early, the other four gained complete surprise at dawn, finding rows of closely-parked CR42s and Ju87s; two were claimed destroyed and several damaged. The bombers were followed in by four 803 Squadron Fulmars, led by Lt Bruen in N1951 '6A'. Their strafing attack was considered to be very successful, and it was believed that at least 12 aircraft had been put out of action, and others damaged. Commented Jasper Godden, Bruen's observer: 'We shot up a number of Ju87s and CR42s. This was a very economical way of destroying enemy aircraft.' In fact there is no record of any Ju87s being damaged, although one Ju88 was recorded as destroyed and two more damaged, damage also being caused to one S.81 and six CR42s. One Luftwaffe airman was killed, the only casualty. All the Naval aircraft returned safely to the carrier.

Now reprisal raids could be anticipated, and the four Fulmars were refuelled and rearmed as quickly as possible, taking off at 0710 with two other sections as plots appeared on the ships' radars. Odd reconnaissance aircraft were seen, but interceptions proved abortive, and the Fulmars returned to refuel. Four sections were again launched at 0905, and once more at 1148, as intruders became more aggressive. One section comprising 806 Squadron's new commander, Lt Cdr Garnett, with Sub Lt Sewell as his No.2, encountered a pair of II/KG26 He111s the experienced Sewell swiftly shooting down Oblt Oskar Klapproth's 1H+CN into the sea. Within minutes two Ju88s of II/LG 1 were spotted and Garnett at once attacked, observing hits. Sewell joined the attack and soon the bomber was in trouble, but at that moment Garnett's Fulmar was hit by return fire. Recalls his observer, Lt Desmond Vincent-Jones:

'We were hit in the engine by the rear-gunner (Gefr Günther Peschke) and ditched. Jackie Sewell remained in company and orbitted over us until the destroyer *Hereward* saw us. The Ju88 ditched about 200 yards away – their dinghy worked, ours didn't!'.

Uffz Heinrich Geisenhoff and his crew from L1+CV were rescued with their victors.

Meanwhile another section of 806 Squadron Fulmars, flown by Lt MacDonald-Hall (N1957) and Sub Lt Hogg, also reported intercepting a pair of Ju88s from II/LG 1 (possibly the same pair as attacked by Garnett and Sewell). They attacked together, reporting that the first bomber – in all probability Oblt Wolfgang Meissner's L1+QV – burst into flames at about 7000 feet, and that the second was followed down until it hit the water with an almighty splash. No survivors were seen from either aircraft, but since LG 1 reported the loss of only two Ju88s it seems likely that the second aircraft was that flown by Uffz Geisenhoff.

Green Section of 803 Squadron (Lt Bruen and Sub Lt Richards) skirmished with another Ju88, Richards' N1951 collecting one bullet in the header tank. With the engine misfiring badly, he reached *Formidable* and crash-landed on the deck. His TAG, L/Air Stan Melling, recalled:

'This was not surprising as the carrier was still turning into wind. Fortunately we caught a wire although we did go half over the side, but managed to scramble back onto the flight deck.'

During this forenoon period the fighters had flown 23 sorties, engaging in 20 combats and skirmishes, during which four aircraft had been claimed shot down and one damaged.

Early in the afternoon the Battle Squadron suffered a most unfortunate stroke of luck. At 1310, by which time the force was 150 miles from the Kaso Strait, a formation of Ju87s was detected approaching from the North African coast. These were from II/StG 2, sister Gruppe of the units on Scarpanto (where I Gruppe from Greece had now joined III Gruppe), but Libyan-based. Led by Maj Walter Enneccerus, who had led the attack on the carrier *Illustrious* off Malta four months previously, the dive-bombers were not taking part in the Cretan operations, nor were they hunting for the carrier; they were searching for supply shipping making for Tobruk. Thus it was pure chance that Oblt Bernhard Hamester's 5 Staffel crews spotted *Formidable* and took advantage of this chance encounter to attack at once, followed by 4 Staffel (Oblt Eberhard Jakob) and Oblt Fritz Eyer's 6 Staffel. Two direct hits were scored on the flight deck, fore and aft, as well as several near-misses, one of which created a gaping hole in the carrier's starboard side underwater. Fires broke out, 12 men were killed and ten wounded – a relatively low number of casualties, given the very severe damage inflicted.

Two Fulmars flown by ex-805 Squadron pilots Sub Lts Sykes and Sinclair, had just landed when the attack commenced, and the two TAGs – L/Airmen Freddy de Frias and R E Northfield – had just entered their Mess, where they were moaning that no lunch had been saved for them. Suddenly, recalled de Frias 'The bomb penetrated the flight deck aft of our Mess and blew out part of the bows underneath us. We were both dazed by the explosion but unhurt; even the Mess was undamaged apart from a bulge in the deck and lockers and other furniture strewn all over the place. We gathered ourselves up and left. A damage control party was squirting hoses into the hole the bomb had passed through. Really we had a miraculous escape because had the bomb exploded a fraction of a second earlier it would have blown out the Mess. As it was, it exploded (as far as I recall) almost on the waterline, right in the stern, which was why our casualties were so light.'

Two relieving Fulmars had been launched as the Stukas approached, but these had not gained sufficient altitude to intervene. Now, as the dive-bombers retired, they attacked. Believed flown by Lt Pat Massy (previously a Sea Gladiator pilot aboard HMS *Eagle*, but now with 806 Squadron), and Sub Lt K L Wood, each pilot claimed one Ju87 shot down and a further two damaged. Only one Ju87, an aircraft of 5 Staffel, was actually lost, the gunner, Ofw Ewald Krüger, being wounded. One Fulmar, believed to have been Massy's aircraft, was hit by return fire, L/Air Colin Hearnshaw, the TAG, receiving four bullet wounds in one leg. Despite the damage to the carrier, both Fulmars were able to land on, and Hearnshaw was soon receiving attention to his wounds.

Formidable was not the only ship hit, for the escorting destroyer *Nubian* also had her bows blown off and her aft guns put out of action, 15 of her crew being killed and six others seriously wounded. As soon as the attack had developed, the carrier had sent out urgent signals requesting air cover, the initial response being the arrival of a solitary Blenheim IVF 'strafer' from 45 Squadron at Fuka, which remained on station for ten minutes. Three Hurricanes of 1 SAAF Squadron from Sidi Barrani then arrived, but were treated as hostile and met initially by a barrage of AA fire. These were relieved by three more Hurricanes from 274 Squadron at Gerawla, and then by three more from 73 Squadron at Sidi Haneish. Another three of this unit's aircraft appeared an hour later, these engaging a Ju88 which Sqn Ldr P G Wykeham-Barnes managed to hit before his reflector sight failed at the crucial moment, allowing the reconnaissance aircraft to escape.

By 1800 Cdr Atkinson considered that launches of Fulmars could recommence, although the catapult was out of action. Two aircraft were ordered off to patrol, bouncing over the battered, bumpy deck before becoming airborne, followed by two more 25 minutes later. No further attacks transpired, and when Lt Bruen and Sub Lt Richards landed after two hours *Formidable* had recorded the last operational flights by her Air Group in the Eastern Mediterranean. She would arrive in Alexandria next day, departing via the Suez Canal two months later for more permanent and extensive repairs. It would be many long months before a British carrier again ventured into the waters near Crete.

While the Battle Squadron had been so beset, the assault ship *Glenroy*, which had sailed for Suda Bay on 23 May carrying 900 men of 2/Queen's Royals, but had been ordered back to Alexandria due to the increased incidence of air attack, again sailed. This time her destination was Tymbaki on the south coast. At 1820 she too came under heavy dive-bombing attack as she neared the island. Her escorts, the AA cruiser *Coventry*, and two destroyers, put up a fierce barrage, claiming one attacker shot down and one damaged. While none of the ships were hit, *Glenroy* was damaged by several near-misses, which punctured her hull and damaged three of her special 'B' lighters; 11 men were wounded. At 2100 a number of torpedo-bombers attacked, and while all torpedoes launched were avoided, it was now decided to abandon the operation, since too much time had been lost, and it was considered impossible, and too risky, to land the troops by day. Again *Glenroy* returned to Alexandria with her cohorts.

Cmdt Georges Goumin, the 36 year-old Free French pilot killed on 26 May, 1941 when his 24 SAAF Squadron Martin Maryland was shot down while strafing Maleme airfield after dropping urgent supplies to the defenders. (*A Marteau*)

Throughout 26 May aircraft of 204 Group had once more been very active over Crete, the first strike of the day again being made by six 24 SAAF Squadron Marylands. Four of these were to bomb and strafe Maleme, while two dropped medical supplies and ammunition to the garrison at Retimo. Three of the bombers returned with Flak damage, but the two supply-droppers met stiffer opposition. One was crewed by volunteer Free Frenchmen under Cmdt Georges Goumin. The plan called for the pair to skim the waves on approach, climb to

2000 feet when about ten miles out, then dive to sea level and break through any defending fighters at high speed. The objective was reached without either aircraft being hit, and Capt K S P Jones, SAAF, flying the leading Maryland, reported: '... the German fighter screen was like a swarm of bees overhead. About half way across the island we saw them get the French Maryland. The pity was no effort could really help.' Apparently Cmdt Goumin, having completed his supply dropping task, had decided to strafe Maleme, as one of his crew – Adj Chef Albert Marteau, the WOP/AG – recalls:

'We noticed Canea on the way in and then arrived at Maleme; there was a crowd on the beach. The pilot sprayed the Ju52s with his machine-guns and I joined in with my two machine-guns in turn. The reaction soon came – tracers arrived from all sides – above, below, right, left. Sgt Roger Lefevre, the other gunner, stated later that a German fighter had been attacking us. (This was a Bf109 of III/JG 77, flown by Lt Emil Omert, who claimed his third victory against the Maryland – Ed). Brutally the plane sideslipped. I fell and Lefevre fell from his turret, landing on me with his knees in my back. In falling he pulled out his intercom wire; there was total silence and we became entangled in our parachute harnesses. The plane flew on but through the machine-gun holes I saw the ground rapidly approaching. I waited for the crash and I braced myself, then ... a void. On touching the ground the barrels of my machine-guns had pivoted on their axis and the sight had hit me on the head. When I regained my senses I saw that the plane was resting on its belly along a ditch, broken by the banking – an incredible chance. The engines were on fire and the heat revived me. No question of escaping from below so I detached my parachute and Lefevre struggled to free the hatch near the turret. I helped pull him out but the moment we reached the ground, a patrol of Austrian mountain troops appeared and captured us. I tried to indicate by gestures that there had been four of us in the burning plane.'

Capt James Roosevelt, son of the US President, discusses the Martin Maryland bomber with Adj Chef Albert Marteau (left), one of several Free French aircrew attached to 24 SAAF Squadron for operations over Crete. (*A Marteau*)

Cmdt Goumin however, was dead, having been hit in the chest by a bullet whilst still at the controls of the Maryland (1607, ex AH307). The observer, Lt Pierre Courcot, had not had time to take over before the crash; he was seriously injured, but would survive as a prisoner of war, as would the two gunners.

For their actions over Crete while attached to 24 SAAF Squadron, President Tsaldaris of Greece presents Sous Lt Albert Marteau (left) and Adj Robert Lefevre with the Order of George 1st of Greece in Egypt after the war. (*A Marteau*)

At Gerawla 274 Squadron also had a number of French airmen attached, all of whom had absconded from Syria when France capitulated. Initially they had been formed into 2 Free French Flight under Flt Lt Paul Jacquier (1 Free French Flight had formed about the same time in England, with escapees from France and Algeria), and operated the various aircraft in which they had fled – Morane Ms 406s and Potez 63.11s – until re-equipped with Hurricanes and attached to 274 Squadron. Having not so far seen any action, they were now about to be well and truly 'blooded'.

Six long-range Hurricanes were to go after the transports flying into Maleme, three setting out at 15-minute intervals commencing 1310, followed by the other three at 1415. New Zealander Flg Off Owen Tracey, a former Battle of Britain pilot with three victories to his credit, was first to arrive over Maleme. Here he promptly claimed a Ju52/3m shot down, but a Bf109 then fastened onto his tail, and he dived towards the steep cliffs, his Hurricane (Z4511) taking several hits in the fuselage, in the fuel tanks and in the propeller. Reaching sea-level, Tracey pulled clear at the last moment, believing that the pursuing Bf109 had plunged straight into the sea behind him. Having nursed his damaged aircraft back across

Flt Lt Paul Jacquier (Free French) of 274 Squadron in the cockpit of a Morane 406, with a Potez 63-11 in the background at Haifa, Palestine, in September 1940. (*Gen P J Jacquier*)

the sea to Sidi Barrani, he force-landed; he claimed both the Ju52 and the Bf109 as destroyed.

Whilst Tracey was fighting for his life, a second Hurricane (Z4312), flown by Sgt George Kerr, had arrived off Maleme, and he too at once claimed a Ju52 shot down in flames into the sea. Like Tracey, he was also pounced upon by a Messerschmitt, and soon followed his victim into the sea. Kerr survived the crash and managed to get ashore; next day he would by chance meet his flight commander, Flt Lt Honor, shot down the previous day. In fact Honor had witnessed the fight in which Kerr had sent the Junkers into the sea. It seems probable that the German pilots involved in these engagements were Hpt Herbert Ihlefeld and his wingman, Lt Fritz Geisshardt of Stab I(J)/LG 2, both of whom claimed Hurricanes on this day over Crete, Ihlefeld as his 36th victory of the war, and Geisshardt as his 19th.

The next lone Hurricane, Z4250 flown by Frenchman F/Sgt Marcel Lebois, evaded the now-alerted Messerschmitts but did encounter the Junkers transports, one of which he claimed shot down. He arrived safely back at Gerawla at 1800, where he awaited news of two of his fellow countrymen flying in the final section to Maleme. On nearing the island the three Hurricanes separated and hunted for the transports individually, Flt Lt Jacquier soon encountering one making for Maleme. He recalls:

'I was flying at approximately 10 000 feet about 20 kilometres north of Maleme when I noticed a single Ju52 flying very low (100–200 metres) heading for Crete. I

383

attacked from the rear, made a single pass, disengaged above and banked upwards to the right. I saw it disappear into the sea. Some minutes later I saw a second lone Ju52, at the same altitude. Again I attacked from the rear and broke away upwards and this also went into the sea. In both attacks the Ju52s only returned fire at the last moment. I regained altitude and continued to Maleme to strafe. While I was attacking, five Bf109s and two Bf110s on aerial defence were circling at about 500–1000 metres, at slow speeds – with undercarriages down – no doubt for identification by German airfield defence. I dived at great speed from 3000 metres, going west to east (sun behind me). I shot a Ju52, which blew up, and levelled out some metres above the ground. On the eastern edge of the airfield I received a shock – the engine was hit – it cut and petrol flooded the cockpit. Using my speed I glided along the beach between Maleme and La Canee (Canea) and landed (Z4632) wheels up amongst the German forward positions. I was captured immediately. Apart from rough handling by Austrian mountain troops on capture, I was treated well in accordance with the Geneva Convention. I was wearing the badges of my rank in the RAF and at my first interrogation by the Germans at Maleme, I indicated that I was French-Canadian. Some time later I met, in the PoW camp, Lt Courcot and two others (Marteau and Lefevre) in French uniform – surviving crew of the Glenn Martin – and I decided that I would share the same fate as my compatriots. Thus, at my second interrogation, in Athens, I stated that I was French.'

Free French pilots serving with 274 Squadron and operating over Crete in May 1941, seen here some months earlier after absconding to Egypt from Syria. In the background is one of the Morane 406 fighters from GC II/7 that remained in Egypt with them. L to r: Flt Lt (Capt) Paul Jacquier, Flg Off (Lt) Antoine Peronne, Wt Off (Adj Chef) Charles Coudray. (*Gen P J Jacquier*)

From this second trio of Hurricanes, only Flg Off Antoine Peronne (the other Frenchman) was to return, landing Z4538 back at Gerawla at 1915. During his five-hour sortie he too had met a Ju52/3m and claimed this shot down. The third pilot, Sgt Colin Glover, had been killed when his Z4606 was intercepted by Oblt Walter Höckner of 6/JG 77 and shot down into the sea; whether he encountered any transports before his demise is not known. At least six of the Junkers had been claimed by the Hurricane pilots; records indicate that three aircraft from I/KGrzbV 172 were shot down – those flown by Fw Gerhard'Kraus (4V + DW) and Ofw Hans Möckel – and one from KGrzbV 105. One each of KGrzbV 60, 106 and Stab XI FlK were damaged, and all obliged to crash-land at Maleme.

Six Blenheims drawn equally from 45 and 55 Squadrons were then briefed to make a dusk attack on Maleme, but just prior to their take-off at 1700, two more 274 Squadron Hurricanes flown by Sgt P B Nicolson and Wt Off Charles Coudray, another of the French pilots, were sent off to strafe, both carrying out their missions and returning safely. The Blenheims arrived however, to find the defences alerted, and while the three 55 Squadron aircraft again escaped interception, those of 45 Squadron were caught by patrolling JG 77 Bf109s of 6 Staffel, led by Oblt Höckner. This pilot first attacked Sgt N H Thomas' T2339 and shot it down in flames with the loss of all the crew. He then attacked the leader, T2350, and severely damaged it. Flg Off T F Churcher and his crew all baled out, he and the observer, Plt Off R D May, being captured at once. The gunner, Sgt H G Langrish, was more fortunate in that he evaded capture and wandered for two days and three nights until he reached the south coast, where he was picked up by a destroyer. The third Blenheim (V5592) meanwhile escaped the slaughter and returned across the sea, but became lost over the desert. When fuel ran out Plt Off J Robinson ordered a bale out. The three men gathered on the ground, but the observer, Sgt W B Longstaff, then wandered off on his own and was never seen again. Robinson and his gunner (Sgt A F Crosby) walked for four days and five nights without food or water before they were spotted and picked up.

On Crete by now Flt Lt Woodward's 33 Squadron party had arrived at Suda Bay with many tales of frightening experiences, as Woodward recalls:
'We crawled, at one point, through part of a New Zealand anti-personnel minefield in a vineyard, much to the consternation of the New Zealand troops who were watching our progress through binoculars.'

He was now informed that he would be flown out in a Sunderland that evening, and was told to stand by. At the last moment however, he was directed to take charge of a party of walking wounded and to lead them to a rendezvous with the Australian destroyer *Nizam* in Suda Bay. This warship, with *Abdiel* and *Hero*, took aboard some 930 wounded and surplus personnel, including merchant seamen from the many sunken vessels, and naval personnel including Lt Ramsay's 805 Squadron contingent. Amongst those missing were the two TAGs, L/Airmen Jary and Jarvis, both of whom had been killed in the fighting. *Abdiel* had earlier landed the remaining Commandos of 'Layforce' – those who had not been able to land two days previously – while the two other destroyers had delivered 150 tons of stores and ammunition.

With the departure of Flt Lt Woodward, command of the 33 Squadron party was assumed by Flt Lt Mitchell. His group now numbered just 41 out of an original 102 airmen, and they were ordered to make for Sphakia, two trucks being provided for their transport. Just before they departed, a Do.17 flew over the area dropping leaflets, printed in English and Greek, threatening reprisals against anyone, man or woman, found guilty of ill-treatment of German prisoners. In the Sphakia area to which this group was now heading, was the 50-strong 30 Squadron party, who had also lost more than half their original number.

The three warships with the wounded aboard left Suda Bay during the night and were met by Force 'A'. Three hours out, the escorts came under attack by an estimated 15–20 Ju88s of II/LG 1 and He111s of II/KG 26. HMS *Barham* was hit on one gun turret, and her bilges were flooded by near-misses. It took two hours to extinguish the fires that had broken out, by which time the force had been ordered to Alexandria to avoid further losses. During the attack two of the bombers were claimed shot down by the ships' gunners and a third damaged.

It was now decided that the handful of remaining small coastal patrol craft should withdraw to Alexandria, to prevent their certain destruction, so the South African whalers *Syvern* and *Kos 22* had put into Suda Bay to shelter until dusk, before making a dash for safety under cover of darkness. However, at 2000 on the evening of 27 May, just before setting out, two Ju87s suddenly dived on them, bombs scoring hits on both vessels and causing fires; the surviving crews scrambled ashore. A third vessel, *Kos 21*, was also attempting to get to Alexandria when attacked south of the island on two occasions during the early morning by Ju88s. Although the bombs missed, strafing caused two casualties. At 0830 four He111s came in at low-level, causing two fatalities, but the crew fought back, believing that they had shot down one Heinkel into the sea. Four hours later two more He111s attacked, causing further damage with near-misses, but still *Kos 21* survived, eventually reaching Alexandria two days later. One of the few surviving 'A' lighters – *A16* – had been undertaking valuable work in Suda Bay, and had endured 37 direct attacks. She was now ordered to be scuttled, her crew embarking on one of the departing destroyers.

By this day – 27 May – there were almost 27 000 Axis troops in Crete, including 4000 Italians. The Germans had even managed to land two tanks, towed across in an open barge. The German High Command was now as convinced of victory as was Wavell of defeat. Early on this day Wavell signalled the Prime Minister that Crete was no longer tenable and that troops must be withdrawn. He acknowledged the enemy's overwhelming air superiority, which made reinforcement impossible. The Chiefs of Staff reluctantly signalled their agreement. The RAF would largely be blamed for the loss of Crete, but lack of secure air bases was the prime reason, combined with the numerical strength of the Luftwaffe and the costly but daring use of their airborne forces.

The Heraklion area remained under constant attack, six Do.17s of III/KG 2 opening the daily bombing during the morning. The Bofors gunners somehow continued to survive and to resist, on this occasion shooting down one of the bombers, U5+ET, flown by Lt Rudolf Haberland, which crashed near Canea. 37

Ju88s then came over in three waves to pound the town and airfield. Amongst those who had been captured here during the early fighting had been Plt Off Neville Bowker of 112 Squadron. On this day he escaped by simply walking out of a German field hospital and succeeded in joining up with a party of British troops. He would be amongst those evacuated from Heraklion the following night.

Despite the approaching evacuation, Air Commodore Collishaw considered 204 Group should continue to do what it could to frustrate the German advance – but the next 24 hours were to prove more costly than effective. During the night of 26/27 May Wellingtons had again raided Maleme, six 148 Squadron aircraft starting a spectacular fire with resultant explosions. At 0300 three Blenheims of 45 Squadron prepared to take-off from Fuka to repeat the attack, but the leading aircraft – Z5896 – crashed on take-off and burst into flames, Flg Off N W Pinnington and his observer being killed; the gunner was thrown clear, though badly burned. He would succumb to his injuries three weeks later. The operation, during which spikes and small bombs were to have been dropped on the airfield, was cancelled.

Early on the morning of the 27th while two 39 Squadron Marylands were out making reconnaissances along the coastline of Crete, a photo-reconnaissance Hurricane (V7423) and 2 PRU made a sortie over Rhodes in the hands of an ex-30 Squadron pilot, Flg Off S N Pearce (this was claimed probably shot down by Italian fighters; it returned undamaged). In Egypt further Blenheims were readied for an afternoon attack on Maleme. 14 Squadron made available just three aircraft at Quotaifia landing ground (seven miles south-west of El Daba), while at Ma'aten Bagush six of 55 Squadron were prepared. Just after 1430 the first Blenheims began lifting off at the latter base.

The first pair collided as they became airborne, Flg Off Harris managing to belly-land T2051 without casualties, but Sgt W L Martin's aircraft spun in with the loss of all aboard. The other four got off and raided Maleme successfully, believing that several of the estimated 100 Ju52/3ms seen on the ground were probably destroyed by their bombing. In rapidly failing light the bombers became separated during the return flight, and only two landed at their base. The other two had become lost over the desert, both crashing. The wreck of Sgt J H Chesman's T2175 and the bodies of the crew were found by a 6 Squadron Lysander. The skipper of the other missing Blenheim, Sgt Bale, had ordered his crew to bale out when their fuel was exhausted; all three arrived back at their base two days later.

The 14 Squadron section fared no better. One aircraft returned early with engine trouble, while the other two, which were to bomb troop concentrations between Maleme and Suda Bay, could not find their target, so attacked the airfield instead. On return, in darkness, they became separated, both becoming lost and also crashing in the desert. Z5593 came down 30 miles south-west of Mersa Matruh; the French-Canadian pilot, Flg Off Jean Le Cavalier, was killed, while the other two managed to bale out, although only the gunner was found alive. The other Blenheim (T2338) crashed 60 miles south of El Daba, the all-New Zealand crew having baled out. Three days of air searches were necessary before the wreck was located, and three more before the observer, Sgt M B Fearn, and the gunner, Sgt J N McConnel, were found; of the pilot, Flg Off M Mackenzie, no sign was ever discovered.

The Blenheim strike had achieved little. Six of the nine participating bombers had been totally lost – none due to enemy action – while nine crew members had perished. 204 Group's Blenheim Wing could ill-afford such a rate of attrition.

The final operation of the day was launched at 1530 when two Hurricanes of 274 Squadron rendezvoused with a Blenheim IVF of 45 Squadron, directed to attempt further interception of the Ju52/3m air convoy, still streaming into Maleme. As the trio headed towards the south coast of Crete however, they encountered six Ju88s of II/LG 1 and attacked at once. The Blenheim pilot, South African Lt D Thorne, made a port beam attack on one low-flying bomber, the crew claiming that considerable damage had been inflicted and that the Junkers had probably been destroyed, although they did not see it crash. Both Hurricane pilots, Flg Off Weller (Z4250) and Sgt Nicolson (Z4536) also engaged, each believing that they had shot one down, and indeed the Blenheim crew reported seeing one Ju88 falling in flames and two others hit the sea. In fact only one was lost, Lt George Freysoldt and his crew perishing in L1 + EW; presumably all three fighters had attacked the same aircraft, each unaware of the others' involvement. Following the fight the Hurricanes became separated from the Blenheim, and after an uneventful patrol hunting for transport aircraft, both landed at Heraklion, from where they returned next day, at daybreak. Meanwhile the Blenheim had returned direct to its base.

With darkness two Wellingtons of 37 Squadron were off to bomb Maleme once again, also bombing the beach where many aircraft were seen, and six fires started. One Ju52/3m of KGrzbV 106 and one Bf109 of III/JG 77 were destroyed. Two more Wellingtons bombed Canea, while seven from 148 Squadron had Scarpanto as their target; here one more III/JG 77 Bf109 was damaged. Luftwaffe records indicate that three Scarpanto-based Messerschmitts had been lost on this date, either to AA or in combat, but no details are available, and no pilot casualties appear to have been suffered.

Following the losses on 27 May, few sorties were made by 204 Group aircraft next day, only two Blenheims of 55 Squadron making a strike on Maleme, and returning without incident. With the onset of evening two South African Marylands were scrambled from Fuka to cover returning warships, but saw nothing. Patrols were carried out by two 45 Squadron Blenheims, each escorted by a 274 Squadron Hurricane but saw no enemy activity. At Gerawla 274 Squadron was reinforced by five pilots on attachment from 73 Squadron, for operations over Crete, while at Abu Sueir three more Beaufighters arrived from Malta. Two of these were from 272 Squadron, including that flown by the commanding officer, Sqn Ldr A W Fletcher, while the third was flown by Flt Lt Bill Riley of 252 Squadron, who had just been released from brief hospitalization following an incident over Malta when his Beaufighter had been shot down in error by a Hurricane. He was a most experienced pilot, having flown Gladiators in Norway and Hurricanes during the Battle of Britain; he was credited with four and two shared air victories.

At Heraklion on the morning of 28 May events were reaching their climax. At about 1000 the defences were again subjected to a heavy raid by Do.17s of KG 2 and Bf110s of II/ZG 26 and II/ZG 76. One of the former unit's Zerstörer was hit by Bofors fire and crash-landed, heavily damaged. Shortly after this attack, 50 Ju52/3ms droned in at low level, disgorging 900 fresh troops two–three miles east of the airfield and near to the radio station at Gouines, their task to aid the survivors of FJR 1 to take the town. One of the transports was seen to land on high ground three miles north of the airfield, from where it subsequently took off again. However four Ju52/3m from I/LLG 1 and three from KGrzbV 172 were badly damaged in crash-landings at Maleme, while one from KGrzbV 40 crashed here and was destroyed; a ninth Ju52/3m from Stab/KGrzbV 2 crashed on return to Topolia and was also destroyed.

At about 1630 a heavy dive-bombing and strafing attack was made on the valley which housed the Brigade and RAF HQ, this lasting one and a half hours, while during the day a small force of Italian troops were landed by sea on the eastern extremity of the island, advancing towards Heraklion but arriving too late to influence the battle. Indeed not even the fresh paratroops were to encounter the defenders in any strength, for that very night the garrison was to be evacuated.

The wreck of a 112 Squadron Gladiator lies on the edge of Heraklion airfield, amidst a clutter of empty fuel barrels. (*F Lankeman via J-L Roba*)

The plans for the evacuation were now in the process of implementation, and would involve a number of phases, some concurrent, others to follow military actions. On the north coast, the troops in the Heraklion area were to be taken off from the harbour there, whilst those of Retimo were to be picked up in Plaka Bay. A small number of the men in the former location were cut off to the south of the town, and would be unable to make their way to the harbour at Heraklion. These were therefore to make their way to Tymbaki. Obviously there was no question of being able to get out the main forces around Maleme–Suda Bay area other than from the south coast, and these units were to make their way over the mountains to Sphakia. At all locations evacuations were to be carried out at night, usually between the hours of midnight and 0300, thus allowing ships to be well away to the south before hostile air attack began with the daylight hours. The withdrawal to Sphakia and other southern harbours was to be covered by a rearguard action fought by forces commanded by Maj Gen Weston, RM. These troops were to make a slow fighting withdrawal from Suda Bay to the south coast.

Wreckage of British biplanes on Heraklion airfield, a Gladiator of 112 Squadron in the foreground. (*F Lankeman via J-L Roba*)

Early in the day (28 May) Admiral Rawlings' Force 'B' (*Orion, Dido, Ajax* and six destroyers) had sailed from Alexandria to begin the evacuation from Heraklion, the force being subjected to ten air attacks en route. At 1920, when 90 miles from Scarpanto, the destroyer *Imperial* was damaged by a near-miss, while 90 minutes later *Ajax* was damaged by another, her hull being punctured and 20 members of her crew seriously wounded; she was ordered back to Alexandria. S.84s from 41° Gruppo BT claimed hits on both these vessels, but Ju87s from Scarpanto, where the various Stuka Gruppen were now massing in anticipation of plentiful shipping targets, and Do.17s were also involved.

The remainder of Force 'B' arrived safely off Heraklion at 2330, and an orderly evacuation began. Men were ferried out to the waiting cruisers on the decks of the destroyers until 0255, when the last stragglers of the rearguard boarded

Kimberley. Over 4000 men had been taken off under the very noses of the surrounding paratroops, and without interference from the Luftwaffe. The only men left behind were the sick and wounded in hospital at Knossos, this area having been cut off by infiltrators. However the RAF contingent at the airfield was amongst those so caught, only 64 of the original 140 being evacuated; similarly only 23 of the 37 airmen of the radar unit, 220 AMES, managed to get away; a few of those left behind would reach Tymbaki.

Amongst those taken prisoner were Sqn Ldr Trumble, officer commanding Heraklion, and Flg Off Valachos of his staff. Flt Lt Fry, the injured commander of 112 Squadron detachment, was also captured, as were two pilots of the 1430 Flight attachment, Flg Offs Hutton and Garside. With them 'into the bag' went Plt Off Hamilton, the 274 Squadron Hurricane pilot who had force-landed on the airfield on 25 May, and Sgt Faulkner's Wellington crew of 37 Squadron. Two more 112 Squadron pilots, Flg Off Bennett and Plt Off Bartley, did reach the south coast, but more of their adventures later.

As Force 'B' departed the Heraklion area, the blast-damaged *Imperial* suddenly developed steering gear failure. Admiral Rawlings despatched *Hotspur* to investigate, but the situation of the destroyer proved hopeless, and orders were given for the crew and troops aboard to be transferred to *Hotspur*, which was then to sink the crippled ship. As a result, when the first Ju87s from Scarpanto appeared overhead at 0600, *Hotspur* was still on her own, steaming after the main force at all speed. So skilfully did her captain manoeuvre the destroyer however, that all attacks were evaded and the dive-bomber crews shifted their attention to the main body of Force 'B'. Just after 0625 they obtained a hit on the destroyer *Hereward*, striking her just forward of her foremost funnel.

Her decks crammed with 450 soldiers, she reduced speed and swung out of line, heading for the coast of Crete, which was still only five miles distant. Seeing her direction, and mindful of the large numbers of helpless troops aboard his other ships, Rawlings had little option but to leave her to her fate and press on towards Alexandria. Concentrating momentarily on this 'sitting duck', the Luftwaffe crews soon sank her, but the majority of her crew and evacuees aboard survived, being rescued by Italian MAS boats, which took them to captivity on Scarpanto. While these rescue operations were underway, an Italian Red Cross Z506B floatplane arrived overhead, and circled low to keep the Stukas from strafing the men in the sea.

Meanwhile a further destroyer, *Decoy*, had also come under attack, suffering a near-miss which damaged her engine room, and caused nine casualties. Speed was reduced, but she managed to keep going. Admiral Rawlings had arranged with 204 Group for fighter cover to be available from 0630 onwards, at the point at which Force 'B' entered the Kaso Strait. Unfortunately, although five Hurricanes from 274 Squadron had been despatched, these were unable to locate the ships, apparently due to some confusion as to the times. In consequence the attacks on the departing vessels continued without respite, and at 0730 *Orion* also suffered damage from a near-miss which caused a reduction in her speed. A Ju87 then swooped down and raked the bridge with machine-gunfire, mortally wounding Capt G R B Back and slightly wounding Admiral Rawlings himself.

The Stukas were back at 0815, one bomb hitting *Dido* and putting her forward guns out of action; 46 men were killed and 38 seriously wounded in this attack. *Orion* was then hit again, fires breaking out and many casualties being sustained. Witnesses reported that one of the dive-bombers responsible was also apparently hit, failed to pull out of its dive and crashed into the sea just off *Dido*'s bows. A final attack commenced at 1045 and caught the ships just before they would pass out of range of the Stukas. 11 aircraft peeled off to bomb *Orion* in succession, one bomb passing through her bridge and exploding in the stoker's Mess, which was crowded with troops. The carnage was indescribable, and during these attacks 262 men were killed on *Orion*, including 155 soldiers – mainly men of the Black Watch; 300 more were wounded. Despite these conditions, the fires were contained, the wounded tended, and the cruiser continued her way at much reduced speed towards Alexandria.

On receipt of signals informing him of the air attacks, and continued lack of fighter cover, Admiral Sir Andrew Cunningham ordered that the standby Fulmar flight at Aboukir be despatched immediately. Two Fulmars of 806 Squadron scrambled, led by Lt MacDonald-Hall who recalls:

'We received a signal from the C-in-C to the effect that because of the evacuation and the heavy losses of ships, we were to provide the maximum air cover until relieved, and if not relieved, to ditch. As we were flying from shore the air gunner was strictly not necessary for navigational purposes, and in view of the signal we thought it prudent to discard with all air gunners.'

It seems that the Fulmars arrived at the tail-end of the Stuka attack, as he continues:

'On two occasions I engaged a Ju87. The first time it was considered a probable – smoke issuing from the engine and it pulled away from its bombing dive. On the second occasion it was very much a doubtful – it broke off its bombing run and beetled off towards Crete.'

The series of attacks cost the Stuka force just one aircraft, 2/StG 3's Uffz Martin Kretschmar and his gunner, Uffz Erwin Moritsch, being killed when their Ju87 crashed into the sea – probably the aircraft seen to crash near *Dido*, and possibly the same machine attacked by the Fulmar pilot, Lt MacDonald-Hall. The two Fulmars finally arrived over the ships at about noon, the first friendly aircraft actually seen by the sailors since their departure from Alexandria on the previous day.

Force 'B' was not attacked again until 1300, when Do.17s carried out a high-level attack, which was repeated at 1330, and again at 1500. No further damage was inflicted however, and at 2000 the ships entered Alexandria harbour. Here 3486 troops were disembarked; more than 600 had been lost, either killed during the attacks on various ships, or captured when *Hereward* went down.

While Force 'B' had been so involved, the four destroyers of Force 'C' (*Napier, Nizam, Kelvin* and *Kandahar*) had arrived at Sphakia to begin taking out the survivors of the Maleme and Suda Bay fighting. As the long columns headed across Crete to this port, the rearguard actions were being successfully fought by

5th (NZ) Brigade at Stilos, seven miles south of Suda Bay, while 2/8th Australian Battalion and the Commandos of 'Layforce' held off two assaults by GJR 85 at Babali Khani.

Between 5000 and 6000 troops were now crossing the mountains of central Crete, many on foot and many wounded. Some of the latter had received only very rudimentary treatment, but still staggered on the 30 miles to the embarkation area, many of them in considerable pain. There were men with amputated arms, severe leg wounds, and even one with a bullet-punctured chest, who nonetheless completed the trek with the aid of his comrades. All came under frequent air attack, which continued at night, amber flares being dropped to illuminate the packed single road to the south. On this occasion the Luftwaffe behaved impeccably however, and parties of wounded who displayed large Red Cross flags were not attacked. Indeed one instance was reported when a Bf109 pilot, having aborted his attack when he obviously spotted the flag, flew round above the group until they reached the coast, apparently protecting them from assault by other aircraft. He was even seen to lean out of the side of his cockpit and wave before departing.

The first departure from Sphakia was made at 0300, the destroyers having first offloaded urgently-needed stores and rations. They took away with them 744 persons, including the 33 Squadron party under Flt Lt Mitchell, and Lt Sutton, the FAA Liaison Officer; also aboard were two children and their pet dog!

With daylight on 29 May came the threat of air attack, and just after 0900 four Ju88s appeared, their bombs near-missing *Nizam* and causing slight damage. Apart from this single attack, the passage to Alexandria remained unhindered however, although a solitary aircraft identified as another Ju88 was seen approaching at 6000 feet just after 1300. This was at once engaged by an escorting Blenheim IVF (T2252) of 45 Squadron, Sgt R H McLelland making a quick frontal attack which he claimed had caused severe damage, possibly bringing the aircraft down.

While preparations for the initial phases of the evacuation had been underway on Crete during 28 May, two motor launches which had departed Suda Bay during the previous night – the last craft to get away – had set course for Alexandria. ML 1032 reached this destination without damage or casualty, despite one attack from the air, but ML 1030 was caught by a Ju88, suffering serious damage by strafing and then being sunk by a near-miss from a bomb. The nine man crew managed to reach shore after 21 hours in choppy seas, hanging on to a small raft; they eventually reached Sphakia, from where they were evacuated. With Suda Bay at last in their hands, the Germans and Italians began ferrying in more troops here in a variety of waterborne aircraft, including Do.24s of Seenotst 7, He60s of 2/126, Cant Z501s and Z506Bs.

Despite the fiasco over Force 'B' on 29 May, the RAF continued to do what it could. During the night of the 28th/29th two Wellingtons from 70 Squadron attacked Scarpanto again, where another of III/JG 77's recently arrived Bf109s suffered severe splinter damage. Two of the bombers returned again next night, while two more went to Rhodes, but all bombs missed their targets on both islands. During this latter night, eight other Wellingtons, from 37 and 148

Squadrons, were briefed to attack Scarpanto (five aircraft) and Maleme (three aircraft). As they taxied out at Shallufa, Sgt J W Kenner's W5685 turned across the flare path just as Sgt H N Goodall's W5622 began its take-off run. They collided and burst into flames, Kenner and four of his crew being killed instantly, while Goodall and his observer died of their injuries. The attack on Maleme gained no observable results, but that on Scarpanto met fierce and accurate AA fire, which shot down Sgt Strickland's aircraft, L7800 falling in a ball of flame to crash on Efialti airfield with the loss of all the crew. Sum total gain for the loss of three of the precious bombers seems to have been splinter damage to a single CR42 on the ground at Scarpanto.

Rather more success had been gained during the daylight hours of 29 May when despite the failure to protect Force 'B', 21 protective sorties were undertaken over various returning warships during the morning and early afternoon by Hurricanes of 274 Squadron. These patrols consisted of two or three aircraft at a time, usually accompanied by a single South African Maryland or a Blenheim IV of 45 Squadron. At 1200 a Maryland flown by Lt Miles Barnby was circling over the ships of Force 'B' when the crew spotted a lone aircraft at 13 000 feet. Barnby turned in behind to investigate and saw that it was a Ju88 – a reconnaissance aircraft of 2(F)/123, which at once dived away. Barnby followed, firing several times with his front guns, but breaking off at 6000 feet when an explosive bullet struck the Maryland and filled the cockpit with smoke. As the Junkers disappeared from the South African's view, pouring black smoke from its damaged starboard engine, it was attacked by one of the escorting Hurricanes, Flg Off Tracey in V7830 shooting 4U + EK down into the sea with the loss of Fw Ernst Chlebowitz and his crew. Meanwhile another of the Hurricane pilots, Plt Off Arthur Sumner (V7855), reported engaging an aircraft he believed to be a Do.17, which he claimed to have damaged before it evaded his attack and disappeared. The Luftwaffe also lost a Bf110 from II/ZG 76, Ofw Egger being reported shot down south of Suda Bay by AA.

During one of the earlier escort sorties, Sgt Peter Nicolson was detailed to break away and make a dash over central Crete to the Retimo area, where he was to drop a message bag to the besieged garrison. This contained orders for a withdrawal to Plaka for evacuation, "phrased in slang so as to make it unintelligible if picked up by the Germans." As Nicolson attempted to carry out this duty, his Hurricane (Z4634) was intercepted at about 0900 by Oblt Erich Friedrich of Stab/JG 77, and was shot down into the sea with the loss of the pilot. Whether or not he ever got to drop the message bag is not known, but it certainly never reached Lt Col I R Campbell at Retimo.

Further to the east during the early morning, the daily-visiting reconnaissance aircraft had been spotted on the radar screens, approaching Alexandria. On this occasion it was decided to attempt an interception of the high-flying 'snooper' with two of the new Tomahawk fighters of 250 Squadron. Climbing to 25 000 feet, the Tomahawks succeeded in making an interception and identified the intruder as a Z.1007bis, the leader opening fire and observing hits before his guns jammed. Plt Off A Wilson then closed in but suddenly lost consciousness due to an oxygen supply failure. He recovered just in time to bale out of AK425 before it crashed into the sea, from where he was subsequently rescued by a Sunderland flyingboat sent out to look for him.

A measure of the attrition being suffered by the Luftwaffe also, was the arrival at Molaoi landing ground in Greece of the Bf109s of III/JG 52 from Rumania. These had been sent south to reinforce JG 77 due to the heavy losses recently suffered both during strafing attacks and in landing accidents.

With evening on the 29th the evacuation continued, Force 'D' (the cruisers *Phoebe* and *Perth*, the assault ship *Glengyle*, the AA cruisers *Calcutta* and *Coventry* and three destroyers) under the command of Admiral King, arriving off Sphakia at 2330. Fears for the safety of *Glengyle*, should she be attacked when loaded with evacuating troops, had raised consideration of her recall, but instead three further destroyers were despatched to assist in personnel recovery should such a disaster occur. During the trip to the island a single Ju88 bombed *Perth*, but the stick of bombs fell wide. When the ships departed Sphakia at 0320, they had embarked no less than 6029 troops, including amongst them the intrepid Royal Marine Bofors gunner, L/Cpl Neill, and the two survivors of his crew. Neill's little team were believed to have accounted for, or certainly hit, some 20 German aircraft during the last two weeks on the island!

L/Cpl Tom Neill, the Royal Marine Bofors gunner, whose gun team is reputed to have shot down, or at least damaged, around 20 German aircraft.

Not until 0930 were the ships found, Ju88s of II/LG 1 then attacking and again singling out *Perth* as their target. One bomb hit near the bridge and exploded in her foremost boiler room; four members of the crew and nine troops were killed. Between midday and 1300 both *Perth* and the destroyer *Jaguar* were near-missed, but thereafter the handful of Hurricanes, Fulmars, Beaufighters and Blenheim fighters managed to keep the attackers at bay, on one occasion driving off a force of some 20 Ju87s and Ju88s before they could attack. Force 'D' reached Alexandria just after midnight.

Meanwhile the four destroyers of Force 'C' had sailed again for Sphakia, leaving Alexandria at 0915 on 30 May to undertake the night's evacuation. Three and a half hours later *Kandahar* experienced mechanical trouble and was forced to turn back, while at 1530 three of II/LG 1's Ju88s near-missed *Kelvin*, and she was also ordered back when her speed dropped due to damage suffered. The two remaining destroyers arrived off Sphakia just after midnight.

Throughout 30 May 274 Squadron's Hurricanes flew 30 sorties over the two naval forces, sometimes accompanied by a single Blenheim IVF or Beaufighter. Their first contact with the opposition was made just after 0800 when Sqn Ldr G E Hawkin's section of three Hurricanes encountered three bombers which were identified as He111s. Despite the identification – at this stage of the war all German aircraft were relatively new and uncommon to RAF pilots in Africa – these would seem to have been Do.17s of I/KG 2. Flg Off Peronne, one of the French pilots, gave the nearest bomber a quick burst and saw it fall into the sea; Uffz Heinz Hoevel's U5+GL was lost.

Late in the afternoon Plt Off G A Tovey (in W9329) was accompanying a Beaufighter flown by Flt Lt Riley of 252 Squadron when they came across Lt Walter Fischer's He111 (1H+KN) of II/KG26, which was on a ferry flight to Cyrenaica. Bill Riley attacked first, but closed so rapidly that his Beaufighter collided with the bomber, although both aircraft seemed to escape serious damage. This did however allow Tovey the opportunity to nip in and shoot the Heinkel down into the sea.

One of the most successful Free French fighter pilots with the RAF, Sous Lt Albert Littolff flew with 274 Squadron during the operations off Crete in late May 1941.

As dusk approached the final sorties were being flown by three Hurricanes and a Beaufighter, the latter flown by Sub Lt Fraser, FAA. In the fading light a reconnaissance Ju88 (7A+HM) of 4(F)/121 was seen, and was apparently attacked by both Fraser and Plt Off Sumner (Z7855) although each was ignorant of the other's presence. Fraser claimed a probable, Sumner a definite victory; whoever fired the telling burst, the Junkers crashed into the sea with the loss of Oblt Franz Schwarz-Tramper and his crew. On return to Fuka in darkness, the Beaufighter pilot had difficulty in finding his airfield, and after circling a couple of times crash-landed T3230 two miles south of his base, without seriously injuring himself or his observer.

Ready for the morrow, and whatever action it might bring, 274 Squadron at Gerawla now received a further influx of pilots to aid in the long patrol sorties. Three South Africans from 1 SAAF Squadron included the highly experienced pair of Capt K W Driver, DFC, with a score of 11 victories, and Lt R H Talbot, DFC, with eight. 73 Squadron also sent over three pilots, all Frenchmen and these included another highly skilled pilot, Sous Lt Albert Littolff. A veteran of the fighting in France the previous year, he had been credited with two victories and a third shared while flying with the Armeé de l'Air, then escaped to join the RAF and had been posted to join 73 Squadron in the Desert. In the past month, during the squadron's heroic defence of the Tobruk garrison, Littolff had claimed a further five victories.

While the troops at Sphakia waited for their third night of evacuation, the ridges above the harbour, the village itself, and the areas to the east and west of the beaches were repeatedly bombed and strafed. Yet strangely, the embarkation beach itself was not to be attacked during the hours of darkness on any night during the evacuation, at a time when great columns of troops were moving down to the ferries. As many as 60 aircraft at a time blitzed the village, but none of the warships offshore came under attack throughout this period – a most strange oversight on the part of the Luftwaffe, and one which played no small part in allowing the evacuation to achieve the success it did. Similarly, although Wellingtons from Egypt were over Maleme, or Scarpanto or Rhodes almost every night, the Luftwaffe failed to respond by posting into the area a night-fighter unit to deal with what would have been relatively simple targets. Nor is there any record of Bf110s from either ZG26 or ZG76 flying any nocturnal sorties in this respect.

Amongst those sheltering in the Sphakia area awaiting embarkation were General Freyberg and Grp Capt Beamish, both of whom were now ordered to depart with their staffs. A Sunderland was due to take them and their key personnel to safety, and just before 1800 two of these big flyingboats arrived. Flt Lt Brand in a 230 Squadron aircraft took on board Freyberg's party, totalling about 45 Army and RAF, while Flt Lt Frame in a 228 Squadron 'boat was due to pick up his passengers from Sphaki Bay. Some difficulty was experienced in finding the actual spot, so two members of the crew rowed ashore in a dinghy, but found no trace of anyone. On returning to the aircraft, they spotted a light flickering on Gavdhos Island and realised that their position was six miles to the south-west of their destination. Frame at once taxied to the correct position where a boat with the passengers aboard was located.

Although all had gone well with the evacuation from Heraklion, and was proceeding satisfactorily at Sphakia, this was not the case at Retimo. Here Lt Col Campbell had not received his orders to withdraw, he and his men continuing the fight against the survivors of Oberst Sturm's Group Centre. German reinforcements were now arriving however, and with ammunition and supplies rapidly running out, Campbell realised he would be forced to surrender to save his troops from being slaughtered. Those who could, escaped to the south – about 140 men, but 700 were obliged to surrender, amongst them Flg Off Reeves of the 1430 Flight attachment who had been left in charge of the Airfield Detachment. During their gallant defence, 160 Australian and British troops had been killed, here, but the garrison had accounted for some 700 paratroops killed and a further 500 captured, including Oberst Sturm, who was now released with his men.

At Sphakia the two destroyers (*Napier* and *Nizam*) had taken aboard 1510 more troops by 0230 on 31 May, when they set off on their return journey. At first light Oblt Mahlke led off his Ju87s of III/StG 1 from their new base at Heraklion, to hunt down the ships. At first nothing was sighted, but finally, at the extremity of their range, the Stuka crews spotted a single large vessel, Mahlke leading them down towards this, only to see a Red Cross flag being displayed; the attack was at once broken off. This vessel would appear to have been a hospital ship evacuating wounded from Crete. In the event the two destroyers suffered only one attack, when 12 Ju88s from II/LG 1 dived on them without warning at 0850, the action continuing for some 25 minutes during which *Napier* was near-missed. Although suffering damage to both engine and boiler rooms, she managed to go on at reduced speed. One bomber was believed to have been shot down by the ships' guns, and a second damaged.

Overhead a Maryland of 24 SAAF Squadron and three 274 Squadron Hurricanes, flown by the attached South African pilots, arrived on the scene and promptly gave chase to two Ju88s. Lt Talbot (Z4510) fired two bursts at one bomber, but it evaded him, then Capt Driver (Z4614) and Lt A J B Bester (P2646) made beam and stern attacks on the other, which then dived for the sea. Talbot and the Maryland pilot, Lt Kearney, gave chase for some 70 miles before Talbot succeeded in getting in a burst which hit an engine. Kearney, with his engines at full boost, overhauled the Hurricane, closed in on the damaged Junkers and poured all his remaining ammunition into it. The same engine appeared to have been hit again, for it now stopped and the bomber was last seen flying just ten feet above the sea.

It was assumed to have crashed, Kearney and Talbot being credited with its destruction, but in fact the pilot managed to nurse it back to Heraklion, where he crash-landed the badly damaged bomber. It was subsequently written-off, reportedly due to severe AA damage. Meanwhile Capt Driver reported meeting three or four other Ju88s and claimed to have shot one of these down into the sea; no other Ju88s were reported lost.

It would seem that the relieving section of Hurricanes from 274 Squadron which arrived to take over from the South Africans also met the Ju88s reported by Driver. Flown by three of the attached French pilots, these engaged the bombers, Sous Lt Littolff in W9329 claiming one shot down. He then reported meeting a lone Cant Z.1007bis, apparently a reconnaissance machine out from Libya, claiming this damaged before it escaped. However, one of the Hurricanes, W9273 flown by Sgt Auguste Guillou, failed to return; it may either have been hit by return fire from the Ju88s, or shot down by an escorting Bf110, for during the day the Germans were to claim four Hurricanes shot down south of Crete.

Early in the afternoon the three South Africans were up again on patrol when an intruder was seen. While Capt Driver and Lt Bester stayed with the ships, Lt Talbot set off in pursuit, identifying another Z.1007bis, presumably also a Libyan-based reconnaissance aircraft. After chasing his quarry for 100 miles westward he finally got into a position for an attack, reporting that he shot it down into the sea 50 miles off Tobruk.

While these actions were underway Force 'D', this time comprising *Phoebe* and four destroyers, had left Alexandria to make the last run to Sphakia. No opposition was met until the ships were nearing the Cretan coast. Here between 1825 and 1905 three attacks were made by Ju88s, but all bombs fell wide and it was believed that one bomber was hit by AA fire. By now the vessels were out of effective range of protecting Hurricanes, but some cover was still being provided by a few Marylands and Blenheim IVFs. On arrival over the British force, Lt Jim Williams of 24 SAAF Squadron saw two aircraft circling nearby, one another Maryland, the other a Bf110 which was apparently too involved in stalking this other Maryland to notice the approach of the new arrival. Closing to 150 yards range, Williams fired two bursts into the Zerstörer with his front guns, reporting that it burst into flames and spiralled down into the sea. This may have been Hpt Karl Heindorf's aircraft from 2/ZG 26, the loss of which was recorded next day – again reportedly to AA fire.

During the day Hurricanes of 274, 73 and 1 SAAF Squadrons had flown 44 sorties, Fulmars of 806 Squadron, Blenheims of 45 and 55 Squadrons, and Marylands of 24 SAAF Squadron each contributing another six, while Beaufighters, strengthened by the arrival of six more of these powerful aircraft, added another eight. The Marylands of 39 Squadron also continued their daily maritime reconnaissance duties, joined on this day by another such aircraft from 69 Squadron, out from Malta, flown by the commanding officer of that unit, Sqn Ldr R D Welland. This aircraft flew to Zante Island and Patras to check on shipping in the harbours; only one cruiser and two merchant vessels were seen.

Two Sunderlands again flew to Sphakia at dusk to pick up more key personnel, including Maj Gen Weston and his staff. Flt Lt Frame, back again in 228 Squadron's T9046, flew low and slowly along the coastline, flashing pre-arranged signals at places likely to conceal parties of evacuees. No response was seen, so after ten minutes he alighted. An SOS was then seen flashing from the shore. This signal came from Flt Lt Dudley Honor, the 274 Squadron flight commander shot down six days previously. He and fellow pilot Sgt Kerr had made their way south, aided by Cretans and Greeks, but so lacerated were Kerr's feet that he had temporarily been left behind as Honor scrambled over the rocks down to the shoreline.

Using his flashlight, Honor signalled a Morse message and eventually a one-man rubber dinghy arrived, paddled by Plt Off J C Pare, the Sunderland's second pilot. Just managing to squeeze in, Honor was rowed out to the 'boat, but while six Greeks were also taken aboard it was decided with regret that there was no time to go back for Kerr, who as a result subsequently became a prisoner. Frame then taxied the Sunderland down the coast where 230 Squadron's N9029 was embarking Maj Gen Weston's party, but on arrival here found that no more evacuees were available. Both aircraft then took off and flew back to Alexandria. They were followed at 0300 by the ships of Force 'D', which carried 3710 more troops from Sphakia; all those remaining would now have to be abandoned to their fate.

The RAF had continued its attempts to damage the Luftwaffe at its bases at night, but still without undue success. During the night of 30/31 May Sqn Ldr Wells had led seven of 148 Squadron's Wellingtons off with Heraklion as their target. Six attacked, reporting large fires and explosions, and claiming a number of Ju52/3ms damaged; at least one aircraft of I/KGrzbV 1 was indeed hit. At Maleme four 38 Squadron bombers attacked, claiming a further three aircraft destroyed, together with more fires and explosions; here three of KGrzbV 172's Junkers transports were badly damaged, one becoming a total loss. Other Wellingtons raided the Greek mainland, Piraeus harbour in particular, where some retribution for the Luftwaffe's devastating raid on this same port at the start of the invasion (when eleven Allied merchantmen were sunk), was gained. The Bulgarian steamer *Knyaguinya Maria Luisa* (3821 tons), at the entrance to Piraeus, was hit; her deck cargo of benzine in drums caught fire and detonated her cargo of ammunition. She blew up and sank two other ships, the German *Alicante* (2140 tons) and the Rumanian 3127-ton *Jiul*, causing some 200 casualties. Next night five Wellingtons from 37 Squadron again raided Maleme, while four of 70 Squadron went to Heraklion. Again it was believed aircraft were destroyed at Maleme, at least ten being claimed probably destroyed. Obviously many of these claims referred to already severely damaged wrecks.

As Force 'D' headed back to Alexandria for the last time early on 1 June, three of the newly-arrived Beaufighters were despatched at 0545, to meet and escort the ships during the potentially dangerous dawn and early morning period. At 0715 three Ju88s of I/LG 1 were seen and the Beaufighters engaged at once. Plt Off D Clark saw his target jettison its bombs, but he was then hit and slightly wounded by return fire, turning away. The leader, Flt Lt G L Campbell, and the third pilot, Sgt W M Deakin, simultaneously attacked another of the bombers, Deakin silencing the rear-gunner, but not before his own aircraft had been hit in the port engine, which ceased to function. Meanwhile Campbell continued the attack, getting in two or three accurate bursts which caused the bomber's starboard engine to catch fire, but at this crucial stage his guns jammed. The Junkers may have been hit, but crash-landed on Rhodes apparently due to engine trouble, while Sgt Deakin managed to fly his badly damaged aircraft back to Ma'atan Bagush on one engine.

In order to support Force 'D', the AA cruisers *Coventry* and *Calcutta* were sent out from Alexandria to rendezvous with the returning warships, and to provide their additional awesome fire power. At 0900, when 100 miles out, the radars on these vessels detected hostile aircraft approaching. Twenty minutes later two

Ju88s dived out of the sun, the stick of bombs from one aircraft narrowly missing *Coventry*, while two bombs from the other hit *Calcutta* with deadly effect; she sank within a few minutes with the loss of 117 of her crew; 255 survivors being picked up by her sister ship. This was to be the last Naval loss of the campaign.

At about this time a He111 of II/KG 4 had been briefed to fly a reconnaissance sortie to Alexandria. It failed to return, and two members of the crew who were subsequently picked up were under the impression that they had been shot down by AA fire. The aircraft may possibly have fallen to 806 Squadron Fulmars however, for Lt MacDonald-Hall and Sub Lt Hogg had been sent out from Aboukir about this time, encountering a lone bomber which they took to be a reconnaissance Ju88.

'We came across an 88 which appeared to be a reconnaissance machine and on that occasion we had considerable height advantage,' recalls Robert MacDonald-Hall, 'and although it turned towards Crete we both attacked it and watched it spiral down and hit the water.'

As the evacuation ended some 12 500 troops had been left behind, of whom 226 were RAF personnel. Many of these had already been captured, but to those still free General Wavell gave discretion to surrender, fight on, or escape if they might. The majority did surrender, but many attempted to evade and escape. Indeed, by the end of 1941 over 1000 escapees from Crete – as well as from the Greek mainland and the Aegean islands – had arrived back in Egypt by various means and routes. Some of the first got away quickly, before the German occupation was complete, and among these were a party of about 200 Australians of the 2/11th from Retimo, Black Watch and Argyll and Sutherland Highlanders from Heraklion, and a handful of RAF, all of whom made their way to Tymbaki on 1 June. In this group were Flg Off Bennett, Plt Off Bartley and their airmen from 112 Squadron. During the day a Blenheim swooped low over the latter party and dropped a quantity of most welcome rations. On arrival in the Tymbaki area they met up with Lt Ford and his 24 SAAF Squadron Maryland crew who had been shot down on 25 May, and together hatched a plan for escape.

An abandoned landing craft, holed beneath the waterline and with a twisted propeller, was made serviceable by members of the group, while others scoured the area for fuel and food. Six officers, including Bennett, Bartley, Ford, and his observer, 2/Lt G L W Gill, and 66 men opted to try their luck and put to sea on one engine. Three days out they were intercepted by an Italian submarine and ordered to stop. The officers were then ordered to swim to the submarine, but whilst attempting to do so, Gill was tragically drowned. A wounded Australian officer who had been left aboard was now ordered to return the craft to Crete, but Sgt D D McWilliam, one of the Maryland crew, assumed command, decided to ignore the order, and continued towards the North African coast.

The Italians did not intervene and four days later the craft reached Mersa Matruh safely. Heading in the same direction was another repaired landing craft that had also been abandoned earlier. This carried a mixed party of 142 Marines, Australians, New Zealanders and Commandos, who had set out from Sphakia, and although two of their number died of exposure and exhaustion during the eight days they were at sea, the rest survived to come ashore 12 miles west of Sidi Barrani.

Others later escaped via Greece or Turkey, some absconding from prison camps first. The submarines *Thrasher* and *Torbay* alone were to pick up nearly 200 of these men. Others were helped to get away by 'N' Section of MI 9 (the department of the British Secret Service to assist escapers and evaders from Greece and the islands), operatives of which established a clandestine base near Cesmo, on the Turkish west coast, opposite the Aegean island of Khios. From here caiques and other small craft would rescue groups or individuals over the next three years. One of those eventually to escape and return to Egypt would be 33 Squadron's commanding officer, Sqn Ldr Howell.

While basically the campaigns in Greece and Crete cannot be seen as anything other than unmitigated disasters for the British Commonwealth (and would prove tragically so for the Greek population), which weakened the British position in the Mediterranean and Middle East as a whole, and ensured the loss of all that had been gained against the Italians in Libya and Cyrenaica earlier in the year, the cost to the Axis powers had also been high – some might say inestimably so. Italian prestige had taken a fearful battering; Adolf Hitler had been so taken aback by the losses inflicted on his elite airborne force that never again would he allow their employment in their designed role in any major way. The Balkans had been turned into a theatre of war which would need constant and quite costly occupation and pacification over the coming years, with little advantage to show for it, while who knows what might have been gained had Operation 'Barbarossa' been launched against the Soviet Union that critical month earlier.

In tactical terms the British losses had been heavier, and at this stage of the war were harder to bear. Most damaging of all were the losses inflicted – entirely by air power be it noted – on the Royal Navy. Three cruisers and six destroyers had been sunk during the battle for Crete, and three battleships, an aircraft carrier, six cruisers and seven destroyers had been damaged, some of them grievously so. In these ships 1828 men had been lost and 128 more seriously wounded. The loss to the Allied Merchant Marine, at a time when attrition to U-Boats in the Atlantic was also severe, was very serious indeed. (Appendix 1 provides a detailed summary of Allied shipping losses, Naval and merchant).

On land, apart from the relatively bearable losses already suffered in Greece, 1751 troops had been killed and 1737 wounded; of these, 71 of the fatalities and nine of the serious wounded related to members of the RAF fighting alongside the army. While about 16 500 men had been evacuated from Crete, as already noted, 12 500 more had been left behind. In addition the Greeks had suffered severe, but undocumented losses, the Germans only reporting 5255 Greek prisoners on the island.

22 000 German troops had been involved in Operation 'Merkur', of which a shattering 6543 were recorded as dead, missing or seriously wounded, 3764 of them from amongst the airborne forces of Fliegerkorps XI, who lost many experienced officers and NCOs. In addition 311 Luftwaffe aircrew had been killed or posted as missing. Detailed losses were:

	Killed	_Missing_	_Wounded_
Luft Division 7	1520	1502	1500+
Gebirgsjäger Division	395	257	504
Fliegerkorps XI	56	129	90
Fliegerkorps VIII	19	107	37
	1990	1995	2131+

British Intelligence estimated that in the 12-day battle for Crete the Luftwaffe had lost 60 aircraft in the air (plus 14 probables) and 34 destroyed on the ground, with a further six probables, of which 61 of the destroyed aircraft were known to be Ju52/3ms. Although claims were not always very accurate, the overall figures were a considerable underestimate. During the period 13 May–1 June, the Luftwaffe recorded the loss of 220 aircraft, although only 147 of these were attributable directly to enemy action (80 Ju52/3ms, 55 Bf109s and Bf110s, 23 Ju88s, He111s and Do.17s, nine Ju87s). A further 64 were subsequently written off as a result of serious damage. Between 20 May and 1 June the Transport gruppen suffered the loss of 117 Ju52/3ms as total wrecks, with 125 more damaged but repairable (see Page 404 for breakdown of losses by date and cause). The true impact of this loss would not be felt until 1942 when the need to provide air supply to forces cut off on the Russian front came to a head at Stalingrad. Even by then the hard-pressed German aircraft industry had not been able to make good this catastrophic wastage.

The cost of these operations to 204 Group of the RAF during the same period had been seven Wellingtons, 16 medium bombers and 23 fighters. Compared to the Luftwaffe's losses the total looks modest in the extreme, but at this stage of the war in the Middle East it was a painful and dangerous cost to have paid. Air Marshal Arthur Tedder, who had recently taken over command of the RAF in the Middle East, vice Air Chief Marshal Sir Arthur Longmore, was well aware where the finger of blame would soon be pointed by the generals and admirals. On 30 May he had telegraphed the Chief of the Air Staff in London a long cable, the relevant paragraphs from which read:

Paragraph 1 'Have held stocktaking on Crete. Sorry to say that though effort has had some valuable results the cost has been heavy in relation to strength. Especially in Blenheims – Blenheim dawn and dusk raids in particular have been expensive both in Crete and on return to the Desert. No doubt I am to blame in not keeping tighter rein on Collishaw (A reflection on Air Commodore Collishaw's aggressive use of his resources – Ed). Total aircraft losses in Crete up to date have been 47 of which 30 between 20th to 27th. Stopped all day action over Crete other than recco on 28th. Except an attempt to drop message Retimo yesterday which failed.'

Paragraph 4 'There is and undoubtedly will be more loose talk about lack of air support Greece and Crete. I am taking line that root of situation is secure air bases. We failed to clean up Dodecanese and failed to secure our air bases in Larissa Plain. As result enemy air ops based on increasingly wide front, whereas ours increasingly cramped, till finally two remaining a/d (aerodromes) untenable and out of range of effective support from Africa. This campaign is primarily a battle for aerodromes.'

And that, really, said it all!

Losses of Junkers Ju52/3m Transport Aircraft

Aerial Combat or AA fire			Bombing Attacks			Accidents		
Destroyed	Written off	Damaged	Destroyed	Written off	Damaged	Destroyed	Written off	Damaged
20.5.	20	1	14	—	—	1	2	3	13
21.5.	19	2	5	2	—	—	6	1	2
22.5.	3	3	8	1	—	2	3	5	7
23.5.	2	1	5	2	1	—	—	2	6
24.5.	3	1	10	—	1	—	2	7	10
25.5.	2	—	3	2	—	5	1	2	1
26.5.	3	2	4	1	—	1	1	9	
27.5.	—	—	—	—	1	—	1	2	4
28.5.	—	—	—	—	—	—	2	1	6
29.5.	—	—	—	—	—	—	1	—	3
30.5.	—	—	—	—	—	—	—	1	3
31.5.	—	—	—	—	—	—	—	3	
1.6.	—	—	—	—	—	—	—	—	—
Total	52	10	49	8	3	9	19	25	67

Appendix

Known Losses of Principal (1000 + ton) Allied Merchant Shipping to Air Attack

Date	Identity of vessel	Tonnage	Nationality	Location
22.3.41	Emriricos Nicolaos	3798	Greek	off Gavdhos Island
22.3.41	Solheim (tanker)	8070	Norwegian	off Gavdhos Island
26.3.41	Pericles (tanker) (1)	8324	Norwegian	Suda Bay
2.4.41	Homefield	5324	British	off Gavdhos Island
2.4.41	Koulouros Xenos	4914	Greek	off Gavdhos Island
3.4.41	Northern Prince	10 917	British	Antikythera Channel
5.4.41	Sifnos	2290	Greek	Adamas Bay, Melos
5.4.41	Sona	1105	Panamanian	Adamas Bay, Melos
6/7.4.41	Clan Fraser	7529	British	Piraeus
6/7.4.41	City of Roubaix	7108	British	Piraeus
6/7.4.41	Cyprian Prince	1988	British	Piraeus
6/7.4.41	Petalli	6564	Greek	Piraeus
6/7.4.41	Evoikos	4792	Greek	Piraeus
6/7.4.41	C. Louloudis	4697	Greek	Piraeus
6/7.4.41	Styliani	3256	Greek	Piraeus
6/7.4.41	Patris	1706	Maltese	Piraeus
6/7.4.41	Agalliani	1656	Greek	Piraeus
6/7.4.41	Acropolis	1393	Greek	Piraeus
6/7.4.41	Hakyon	1100	Greek	Piraeus
11.4.41	Attiki (hospital ship)	1134	Greek	Piraeus
12.4.41	Marie Maersk (tanker)	8271	Danish	Piraeus
13.4.41	City of Karachi (2)	7140	British	Volos
13.4.41	Brattdal (tanker) (3)	4961	Norwegian	Volos
14.4.41	Clan Cumming	7264	British	Gulf of Athens
15.4.41	Goalpara (4)	5314	British	Eleusis
15.4.41	Quilloa	7765	British	Eleusis
16.4.41	Memas	4359	Greek	Khalkis
17.4.41	Petrakis Nomikos (5)	7020	Greek	Piraeus
18.4.41	Chios	1121	Greek	Khalkis
18.4.41	Fokion	1158	Greek	Nea Psara
19.4.41	British Science (oiler)	7138	British	Suda Bay
20.4.41	Moscha L Goulandris	5199	Greek	Khalkis
20.4.41	Ellenis (hospital ship)	1013	Greek	Piraeus
20.4.41	Damaskini	1013	Greek	north of Euboea
20.4.41	Assimina Baika	1334	Greek	north of Khalkis
21.4.41	Hesperos (hospital ship)	1070	Greek	off Missolonghi
21.4.41	Archon	1364	Greek	Euboea
21.4.41	Ioanna	1192	Greek	Patras
22.4.41	Frinton	1361	Greek	Megara
22.4.41	Pancration	2171	Greek	Melos

22.4.41	Sokratis (hospital ship)	1134	Greek	Gulf of Corinth
22.4.41	Theodora (tanker)	1300	Greek	Gulf of Corinth
22.4.41	Thraki	1532	Greek	Gulf of Corinth
22.4.41	Thassos	1565	Greek	Megara
23.4.41	Alberta	1193	Greek	Salamis
23.4.41	Katerina (tanker)	2398	Greek	Piraeus
23.4.41	Kerkyra	1461	Greek	off Salamis
23.4.41	Macedonia	1839	Greek	Gulf of Corinth
24.4.41	Teti Nomicou	1882	Greek	Piraeus
24.4.41	Dimitrios Nomicos	1172	Greek	Piraeus
24.4.41	Andros (hospital ship)	2068	Greek	Loutraki
24.4.41	Cavallo	2268	British	Nauplia
24.4.41	Santa Clara Valley	4665	British	Nauplia
24.4.41	Nicolaos Georgios	4108	Greek	Nauplia
24.4.41	Hellas (large motor yacht)	2295	Greek	Piraeus
24.4.41	Kyriaki	5528	Greek	Suda Bay
24.4.41	Prodromos	1070	Greek	Piraeus
24.4.41	Artemis Pitta	1433	Greek	Piraeus
24.4.41	Darmas	1593	Greek	Gulf of Patras
24.4.41	Kehrea	1968	Greek	Bay of Frangolimano
24.4.41	Kyrapanagia II	1012	Greek	Piraeus
24.4.41	Popi S	2083	Greek	off Melos
25.4.41	Ulster Prince	3791	British	Piraeus
25.4.41	George A Dracoulis	1570	Greek	Piraeus
25.4.41	Aghios Markos	4514	Greek	Piraeus
25.4.41	Pennland	16 381	Dutch	off Bela Pouli
25.4.41	Sofia	1722	Greek	San Giorgio
26.4.41	Maria Stathatos	6303	Greek	Mylos
26.4.41	Point Judith	4810	Greek	Kythos
27.4.41	Costa Rica	8672	Dutch	off Suda Bay
27.4.41	Slamat	11 636	Dutch	Gulf of Nauplia
27.4.41	Scottish Prince	3791	British	Suda Bay
27.4.41	Danapris	2113	Greek	Piraeus
27.4.41	Ypanis	1459	Greek	Piraeus
27.4.41	Maiotis	1712	Greek	Piraeus
27.4.41	Hollandia	1759	Greek	Piraeus
27.4.41	Astir	1335	Greek	Kapsalion
29.4.41	Konistra	3537	Greek	Suda Bay
4.5.41	Trabzon	2485	Turkish	Aegean
7.5.41	Katina P	1216	Greek	off Crete
11.5.41	Rawnsley	4998	British	Hierapetra
16.5.41	Eleonora Maersk (tanker)	10 694	Danish	Suda Bay
16.5.41	Kythera	1070	Greek	Suda Bay
16.5.41	Araybank	7258	British	Suda Bay

16.5.41	Nicolaos Ourania (6)	6397	Greek	Suda Bay
16.5.41	Thermoni	5719	Greek	Suda Bay
18.5.41	RFA Olna (oiler)	7073	British	Suda Bay
20.5.41	Dalesman	6200	British	Suda Bay
25.5.41	Logician (7)	5993	British	Suda Bay
26.5.41	Rokos	6426	Greek	Suda Bay

NB 90 vessels, each exceeding 1000+ tons, totalling 351 094 tons recorded herewith. However, it was reported that no less than 43 vessels, totalling 63 975 tons, were lost to air attack in Greek waters during the four days, April 21–24. Total Allied merchant shipping losses to air attack exceeded 360 000 tons.

Notes:
(1) Although *Pericles* was severely damaged by the MTM attack on night of 25/26.3.41, she subsequently sank due to continuous air attack.
(2, 3 and 4) These three vessels – *City of Karachi, Goalpara* and *Brattdal* – were considered by the Royal Navy to have been abandoned by their crews whilst still seaworthy, and that their subsequent loss was avoidable. Royal Navy boarding parties attempted to save the vessels.
(5) Although *Petrakis Nomikos* was severely damaged and beached at Piraeus, she was later repaired by the Germans and renamed *Wilhemsburg* (she was sunk by a British submarine in july 1943).
(6) The *Nicolaos Ourania* was also later repaired by the Germans, being renamed *Nikolaus.*
(7) *Logician* was initially damaged by bomb attacks on 16.5.41 whilst in Suda Bay, and was hit again on 23 May, and finished off two days later.

Principal Royal Navy Ships Lost as a Result of Air Attack Whilst Supporting the Greece and Crete Operations, 1940–41

	Date lost	Killed/missing	Wounded
Cruisers			
Calcutta	1.6.41	117	40
Fiji	22.5.41	276	24
Gloucester	22.5.41	725	?
Destroyers			
Diamond	27.4.41	155	1
Greyhound	22.5.41	84	23
Hereward	29.5.41	170	?
Imperial (1)	29.5.41	0	1
Juno	21.5.41	128	21
Kashmir	23.5.41	82	14
Kelly	23.5.41	130	17
Wryneck	27.4.41	108	5
		1975	146 at least

NB Additionally the cruiser *York*, which had been severely damaged by Italian MTM attack on the night of 25/26.3.41, was subsequently sunk by air attack.

(1) *Imperial* was damaged by air attack on 28.5.41, abandoned, and sunk by HMS *Hotspur* next day.

Royal Hellenic Navy Losses as a Result of Air Attack

Destroyers

Kilkis	21.4.41	
Leon	21.4.41	(severely damaged – towed to Suda Bay, repeatedly bombed and sunk)
Proussa	4.4.41	
Psara	22.4.41	
Ydra	22.4.41	

Additionally the destroyer *Vasilevs Georgios I*, trapped in Piraeus harbour due to air attack, was scuttled by her crew on 20.4.41, but was later salvaged by the Germans, repaired and became ZG 3.

Principal Royal Navy Ships Damaged as a Result of Air Attack, 1940–41

	Date damaged	Killed/missing	Wounded
Battleships			
Barham	26.5.41	7	6
Valiant	22.5.41	0	0
Warspite	22.5.41	43	69
Carrier			
Formidable	26.5.41	12	10
Cruisers			
Ajax	28.4.41	5	19
	28.5.41	6	19
Carlisle	22.5.41	14	25
Coventry	17.5.41	2	7
Dido	29.5.41	27	10
Glasgow	3.12.40	0	0
Naiad	22.5.41	7	31
Orion	26.4.41	6	1
	29.5.41	115	76
Perth, RAN	24.5.41	4	3
	29.5.41	4	0
Destroyers			
Decoy	29.5.41	1	8
Griffin	24.5.41	0	1
Havock	23.5.41	15	10
Jaguar	26.5.41	0	2
Jervis	30.5.41	0	4
Kelvin	29.5.41	1	4
Kingston	21.5.41	1	2
Kipling	23.5.41	5	1
Nubian	26.5.41	15	6
Assault ships			
Glenearn	26.4.41	0	4
Glenroy	26.5.41	0	1
		290	319

Royal Yugoslav Navy

Apparently no principal warships lost to enemy action – the light cruiser *Znaim*, the seaplane tender *Zmaj* and destroyers *Beograd*, *Dubrovnik* and *Ljubljana* were all captured, whilst the destroyer *Zagreb* was blown up by her crew on 17.4.41 to avoid a similar fate.

Known Losses of Axis Shipping to Air Attack

Date	Identity of Vessel	Tonnage	Location	Attacker
12/13.3.41	Po (hospital ship)	7289	Valona	815 Sqn
12/13.3.41	Santa Maria	3539	Valona	815 Sqn
14/15.9.41	Luciano	3329	Valona	815 Sqn
14/15.4.41	Stampalia	1228	Valona	815 Sqn
	German			
30/31.5.41	Alicante	2140	Piraeus	Wellingtons
	Rumanian			
30/31.5.41	Jiul	3127	Piraeus	Wellingtons
	Bulgarian			
30/31.5.41	Knyaguinya Maria Luisa	3821	Piraeus	Wellingtons

Leading Fighter Pilots of the Campaigns in Yugoslavia, Greece and Crete – Claims

Name	Squadrons	Air Combat Claims Greece	Crete	Total	Claims on Types Glads	Hurri	Total for War
Royal Air Force							
Sqn Ldr M T StJ Pattle, DFC+	80, 33	$46\frac{2}{3}$	0	$46\frac{2}{3}$	$11\frac{1}{3}$	$36\frac{1}{3}$	$50\frac{2}{3}$
Flg Off W Vale, DFC+	80, Hurri Flt Crete	$21\frac{1}{2}$ +2 sh	7	$28\frac{1}{2}$ +2 sh	$10\frac{1}{2}$ +1 sh	18 +1 sh	$31\frac{1}{2}$ +3 sh
Flt Lt R N Cullen, DFC	80	16	0	16	6	10	16
Sgt E W F Hewett, DFM	80	16	0	16	3	13	16
Sgt C E Casbolt, DFM	80	$10\frac{1}{3}$	0	$10\frac{1}{3}$	$4\frac{1}{3}$	6	$12\frac{1}{3}$
Flt Lt J F Fraser, DFC	112	$10\frac{1}{4}$	0	$10\frac{1}{4}$	$10\frac{1}{4}$	0	$10\frac{1}{4}$
Flt Lt V C Woodward, DFC	33	$9\frac{1}{3}$	0	$9\frac{1}{3}$	0	$9\frac{1}{3}$	$18\frac{5}{6}$
F/Sgt L Cottingham, DFM	33	$7\frac{1}{2}$	0	$7\frac{1}{2}$	0	$7\frac{1}{2}$	$13\frac{1}{2}$
Sgt D S Gregory, DFM	80	7	0	7	7	0	7
Sgt G E C Genders, DFM	33, Hurri Flt Crete	5	2	7	0	7	9
Sqn Ldr E G Jones, DSO, DFC	80	6	0	6	6	0	6
Flg Off H P Cochrane, DFC	112	6	0	6	6	0	6
Sgt G M Donaldson	112	5	0	5	5	0	6
Flg Off R A Aackworth, DFC	112, 80	5	0	5	2	3	$7\frac{1}{2}$
Flt Lt C H Fry, DFC	112	4	1	5	4	1	5
Fleet Air Arm							
Lt P D J Sparke, DSC++*	806	5	(6 combats, including 2 shared)				
Lt R MacDonald Hall*	806	4 or 5	(8 combats, including 6 shared)				
Regia Aeronautica							
Ten Livio Bassi	395ª Sq	7					
Cap Giorgio Graffer	365ª Sq	5					
Luftwaffe							
Oblt Gustav Rödel	II/JG 27	6 (3 Greek, 3 RAF)					
Lt Fritz Geisshardt	I(J)/LG 2	6 (4 Yugoslav, 2 RAF)					

*Further mention of these two pilots will be found in 'Malta: The Hurricane Years, 1940–41' by the same authors, also published by Grub Street in 1987.

Bibliography

T H Wisdom, *Wings over Olympus*, (Allen & Unwin)

E C R Baker, *Pattle*, (Kimber)

E A Howell, *Escape to Live*, (Grosvenor)

M G Comeau, *Operation Mercury*, (Kimber)

S W C Pack, *Battle of Matapan*, (Batsford)

M Apps, *The Four Ark Royals*, (Kimber)

A Hendrie, *Seek and Strike*, (Kimber)

R Sturtivant, *Fleet Air Arm at War*, (Ian Allan)

C F Shores & H Ring, *Fighters over the Desert*, (Spearman)

Viscount Cunningham, *A Sailor's Odyssey*, (Hutchinson)

P Singleton-Gates, *General Lord Freyberg VC*, (Michael Joseph)

J A Brown, *Eagles Strike*, (Purnell)

G Bowman, *Jump for It*, (Evans)

J Hetherington, *Airborne Invasion*, (Allen & Unwin)

D A Thomas, *Crete 1941*, (André Deutsch)

C Lamb, *War in a Stringbag*, (Cassell)

C Becker, *The Luftwaffe War Diaries*, (Macdonald)

Sir H Kippenberger, *Infantry Brigadier*, (Oxford U P)

G Stitt, *Under Cunningham's Command*, (Allen & Unwin)

A Clarke, *The Fall of Crete*, (Anthony Blond)

C Buckley, *Greece & Crete 1941*, (HMSO)

Baron von der Heydte, *Daedalus Returns*, (Hutchinson)

C Mackenzie, *Wind of Freedom*, (Chatto & Windus)

R Dahl, *Over to You*, (Mayflower)

R Dahl, *Going Solo*, (Jonathan Cape)

R Edwards, *German Airborne Troops 1939–45*, (Macdonald & Janes)

R P Bateson, *Stuka*, (Ducimus)

D M Gavin, *Crete: official history of NZ in 2nd World War*, (War History Branch, NZ)

D Richards, *Royal Air Force 1939–45: The Fight at Odds*, (HMSO)

G Long *Australians in the War 1939–45: Vol 2*, (Canberra)

C Hocking, *Dictionary of Disasters at Sea, 1824–1962* (Lloyds)

INDEX

Personnel

413

414

415

416

Toubakaris, 1/Lt Nickolaous, 13 Mira 78

Tsaldaris, President *382*

Tsitsas, 2/Lt Constantine, 23 Mira *30*, 39, 48

Tsolakaglou, Lt Gen George, Army of the Epirus 259

Tsouderos, Emmanuel, Premier 259, 349

Valcanas, Sgt Gregory, 23 Mira 38, 39

Yiakas, 1/Lt Demetrius, 4 Mira 35

Yianikostas, 1/Lt Constantinos, 22 Mira 19, *30*, 38

Yiannaris, 1/Lt Evangelos, 3 Mira 11

Yugoslavs:

Aleksic, 2/Lt Miodrag, 142 Esk, 32 Gr, 6th Ftr Puk 211

Bajagic, Capt Milos, 163 Esk, 52 Gr, 2nd Ftr Puk 187, 223

Bajdak, Lt Col Leonid, 5th Ftr Puk 181, 189

Banfic, 2/Lt Eduard, 162, Esk, 51 Gr, 6th Ftr Puk 197

Beran, Lt Cdr Igor, 25 HE, 3 HG, 2 HK 190

Berginc, Capt Franc, 141 Esk, 31 Gr, 2nd Ftr Puk 187

Bizjak, Lt Cdr Oskar, 21 HE, 2 HG, 3 HK 191

Blagojevic, Maj Miodrag, 52 Gr, 2nd Ftr Puk 187

Boljevic, Maj Arsenije, 34 Gr, 4th Ftr Puk 188

Boras, Capt Kresimir, 211 Esk, 66 Gr, 7th Bmr Puk 190

Borcic, 2/Lt Dusan, 161 Esk, 51 Gr, 6th Ftr Puk 197

Boskovic, Sgt Milivoje, 104 Esk, 32 Gr, 6th Ftr Puk 210

Bosnjak, Capt Jefta, 214 Esk, 67 Gr, 7th Bmr Puk 190, 220

Bostanic, Maj Milutin, 81 Ind Bmr Gr 187

Brezovsek, Maj Drago, 36 Gr, 5th Ftr Puk 189

Butkovic, Capt Marjan, 2 HK 190

Cijan, Lt Boris, 163 Esk, 52 Gr, 2nd Ftr Puk 214, 223

Crnjanski, 2/Lt Pavle, 31 Gr, 2nd Ftr Puk 211

Culinovic, 1/Lt Mato, 205 Esk, 63 Gr, 3rd Bmr Puk 189

Cvetkovic, Sgt Djordje, Ind Ftr Esk 205

Delic, Sgt Ind Ftr Esk *212*, 213

Diklic, Col Stanko, 8th Bmr Puk 188

Djeric, 1/Lt Uros, S 79 pilot 220

Djonlic, Capt Mihajlo, 206 Esk, 63 Gr, 3rd Bmr Puk 189

Djordjevic, Maj Branislav, 63 Gr, 3rd Bmr Puk 189

Djordjevic, Maj Danilo, 32 Gr, 6th Ftr Puk 187, 199

Djordjevic, Col Jakov, 2nd Mixed Air Brigade 188

Djordjevic, Milan, Me 109 pilot 177

Djordjevic, Lt Col Radislav, 4th Ftr Puk 188

Djuric, Lt Dragan, attached EVA 21

Dobanovacki, Capt Aleksandar, 212 Esk, 66 Gr, 7th Bmr Puk 190

Donovic, Maj Lazar, 68 Gr, 8th Bmr Puk 188, 212

Dragic-Hauer, Lt Col Hinko, 7th Bmr Puk, 190

Fanedl, Maj Branko, 64 Gr, 3rd Bmr Puk 189 194, 223

Ferencina, Capt Vladimir, 218 Esk, 69 Gr, 8th Bmr Puk 188

Filipovic, Capt Stevan, 202 Esk, 61 Gr, 1st Bmr Puk 190

Frantov, Capt Sergije, 261 Esk, 81 Ind Bmr Gr 187

Gardasevic, Sgt, 11 Ind (LRR) Gr 214

Glumac, Lt Branko, 62 Gr, 1st Bmr Puk 214

Godec, Franjo, Ind Ftr Esk 223

Gogic, Capt Todor, 162 Esk, 51 Gr, 6th Ftr Puk 188, 199

Goldner, Capt Pavle, 109 Esk, 35 Gr, 5th Ftr Puk 189

Gorjup, Col Zdenko, 3rd Bmr Puk 189, 220

Gorup, Sgt Vladimir, 103 Esk, 32 Gr, 6th Ftr Puk 210, 211

Gradisnik, Col Ferdo, 1st Bmr Puk 189, 214

Grandic, Lt Pantelije, 164 Esk, 52 Gr, 2nd Ftr Puk 214

Grbic, Capt Mihajlo, Ind Ftr Esk 187, 213

Grbic, Voja, 2nd Ftr Puk 224

Groselj, Lt Col Avgust, 3 HG, 2 HK 190

Grozdanovic, Capt Milutin, 142 Esk, 32 Gr, 6th Ftr Puk 188, 211

Grujic, Capt Vojislav, 210 Esk, 64 Gr, 3rd Bmr Puk 189

Grujic, Sgt, Ind Ftr Esk 206

Ikanjikov, Capt Arsenije, 212 Esk, 66 Gr, 7th Bmr Puk 190

Ivancevic, Capt Nikola, 204 Esk, 62 Gr, 1st Bmr Puk 190, 209

Ivanovic, Capt, 602 Esk, 201 Tr Gr 199

Jancic, Capt Ljuba, 22 Esk, 11 Ind (LRR) Gr 187

Jankovic, Vlado, 7 VIGr 219

Jankovski, Nikolai, Production test pilot 215

Jelic, 1/Lt Milos, S 79 pilot 220

Jelic, Sgt Vukadin, 102 Esk, 31 Gr, 6th Ftr Puk 198

Jermakov, Capt Konstantin, 112 Esk, 36 Gr, 5th Ftr Puk 181, 189

Jovanovic, Sgt Branko, 107 Esk, 34 Gr, 4th Ftr Puk 217

Jovanovic, Capt Ratko, SHEsk 216

Jovanovic, Sgt Zivan, 62 Gr, 1st Bmr Puk 214

Jovicic, Capt Vladimir, 215 Esk, 68 Gr, 8th Bmr Puk 188, 212

Kalafatovic, Gen Danilo 224

Kapesic, 2/Lt Jovan, 103 Esk, 32 Gr, 6th Ftr Puk 200, 210

Keseljevic, Lt, 142 Esk, 32 Gr, 6th Ftr Puk 199

Klavova, Capt Miha, 104 Esk, 32 Gr, 6th Ftr Puk 210

Kodra, Stanislav, 31 Gr, 2nd Ftr Puk 211

Kolarov, 1/Lt Vasa, 32 Gr, 6th Ftr Puk 198

Konte, Lt Cdr Ivan, SHEsk 191

Korosa, Ivan, 20 HE, 2 HG, 3 HK 218

Kostic, Lt Col Bozidar, 6th Ftr Puk 187, 200

Krasojecic, Lt Kaica, 3 Esk, 3 VIGr 216

Kren, Maj Vladimir, JKRV defector 177

Krstic, Lt Dragoslav, 102 Esk, 51 Gr, 6th Ftr Puk 198

Lahj, 2/Lt, 32 Gr, 6th Ftr Puk 199, 200

Lazarevic, Maj Dragomir, 11 Ind (LRR) Gr 187

Lazarevic, Lt Radomir, 68 Gr, 8th Bmr Puk 212

Lekic, Capt Kosta, 101 Esk, 31 Gr, 2nd Ftr Puk 187

Lozic, Maj Krsta, 62 Gr, 1st Bmr Puk 190

Lozic, Lt Col Miodrag, JKRV Chief of Staff 187

Malnaric, Lt Milan, 20 HE, 2 HG, 3 HK 191

Malojcic, Maj Branko, 61 Gr, 1st Bmr Puk 190

Markovic, Capt Bora, 104 Esk, 32 Gr, 6th Ftr Puk 188

Mihelic, Lt Cdr Tomislav, 4 HG, 2 HK 191

Mihic, 1/Lt Slobodan, 7 VIGr 219

Mijuskovic, Capt Sima, 208 Esk, 64 Gr, 3rd Bmr Puk 189

Mikolic, Lt Cdr Jovan, 5 HE, 3 HG, 2 HK 190

Milijevic, Capt Dragisa, 106 Esk, 33 Gr, 4th Ftr Puk 188, 217

Milivojevic, 1/Lt Milenko, Ind Ftr Esk 205

Milojevic, Maj Dusan, 209 Esk, 64 Gr, 3rd Bmr Puk 189, 224, 228

Milojevic, Sgt Petko, 210 Esk, 64 Gr, 3rd Bmr Puk 219, 220

Milojkovic, 1/Lt Zivko, S 79 pilot 220

Milosevic, Sgt Dragoljub, 104 Esk, 32 Gr, 6th Ftr Puk 198

Milovanovic, Maj Ilija, 31 Gr, 2nd Ftr Puk 187

Milovanovic, Capt Ranko, 21 Esk, 11 Ind (LRR) Gr 187

Milovcic, Capt Mladen, 108 Esk, 34 Gr, 4th Ftr Puk 187

Mirkovic, Brig Gen Borivoje, JKRV Commander-in-Chief 178, 187, 203, 226, 228

Mitic, Sgt, 4th Ftr Puk 217

Mitrovic, Capt Zivica, 101 Esk, 31 Gr, 2nd Ftr Puk 199

Momcinovic, Lt Mato, 164 Esk, 52 Gr, 2nd Ftr Puk 219

Murko, Sgt Karel, 216 Esk, 68 Gr, 8th Bmr Puk *202*, 203

Nardeli, Capt Nikola, Commander, Naval Aviation 190

Nedelikovic, 1/Lt Raja, 262 Esk, 81 Ind Bmr Gr 187

Nikodijevic, Capt Dragise, 201 Esk, 61 Gr, 1st Bmr Puk 190

Nikolic, Capt Mihailo, 102 Esk, 51 Gr. 6th Ftr Puk 197

Nikolic, Capt Miodrag, 207 Esk, 63 Gr, 3rd Bmr Puk 189

Nikolic, Maj Nikola, 33 Gr, 4th Ftr Puk 188

Novakovic, 1/Lt Dobrica, 103 Esk, 32 Gr, 6th Ftr Puk 199

Obuljen, Col Nikola, 3rd Mixed Air Brigade 189

Ostric, Capt Ivo, 164 Esk, 42 Gr, 2nd Ftr Puk 188, 214, 219

Pajic, Nedeljko, 31 Gr, 2nd Ftr Puk 200, 201, 211

Paul, Prince, Regent 171

Pavic, Lt Franjo, 15 HE, 4 HG, 2 HK 191

Pavlinic, Lt Cdr Albin, 26 HE, 4 HG, 2 HK 191

Pavlovic, Capt Todor, 203 Esk, 62 Gr, 1st Bmr Puk 190

Pesic, Lt Rastislav, 11 Ind (LRR) Gr 214

Peter, King, King of Yugoslavia 148, 171, 247

Petrov, Sgt Milutin, 32 Gr, 6th Ftr Puk 199

Petrovic, Capt Matija, 217 Esk, 69 Gr, 8th Bmr Puk 189

Petrovic, Lt Cdr Vladeta, 2 HG, 3 HK 191

Petrovic, Capt Zivomir, 11 Ind (LRR) Gr 214

Pikl, Cdr Eduard, 3 HK 191

Bassi, Ten Livio, 395ª Sq, 154º Gr Aut CT   34, 56, 65, 88, *88*, *126*

Baylon, Magg Giuseppe, 2º Gr Aut CT   24

Bazzi, Ten Domenico, 190ª Sq, 86º Gr, 35º St BM/BT   60

Beccaria, Ten Col Francesco, 16º Gr, 54º St CT   183

Beccati, Sottot Vasc Lino, X Flottiglia MAS   153

Beccia, Cap Giulio, 69ª Sq, 39º Gr, 38º St BT   22, 54

Bellagambi, Ten Mario, 355ª Sq, 24º Gr Aut CT   94, 96

Bellucci, Serg Dorva, 154º Gr Aut CT   40

Beneforti, Magg Alberto, 153º Gr Aut CT   182

Berlingieri, Ten Andrea, 253ª Sq, 104º Gr, 46º St BT   53

Bianchi, Serg Manfredo, 154º Gr Aut CT   57

Bincelli, 1º Av Arm Stefano, 238º Sq, 97º Gr Aut B a't   80

Biolcati, Serg Teofila, 160º Gr Aut CT   38

Bonato, Serg Magg Arturo, 393ª Sq, 160º Gr Aut CT   38, 39

Bongiovanni, Ten Carlo, 239ª Sq, 97º Gr Aut B a'T · 222

Bonola, Gen S A Augusto, 4ª ZAT (4ª Squadra Aerea)   23

Bordin, Ten Col Giuseppe, 31º Gr, 38º St BT   184

Bozzi, Ten Mario, 261ª Sq, 106º Gr, 47º St BT   124, 125

Braga, Cap Pier Luigi, 106º Gr, 47º St BT   125

Brambilla, Magg Nello, 99º Gr, 43º St BT   184

Brezzi, Ten Andrea, 236ª Sq, 96º Gr Aut B a'T   56

Buscaglia, Cap Carlo Emanuele, 278ª/281ª Sq, 132º Gr Aut AS   130, 165

Cabrini, Sottot Vasc Angelo, X Flottiglia MAS   153

Calosso, Col Carlo, 54º St CT   183

Campinoti, Ten Ettore, 160º Gr Aut CT   114

Carancini, Ten Mario Gaetano, 393ª Sq, 160º Gr Aut CT   2, 35, 38, 56

Carboni, Cap Ernesto, 253ª Sq, 104º Gr, 46º St BT   23

Carnicelli, Cap Giacomo, 221ª Sq, 55º Gr, 37º St BT   23

Caselli, Sottot Alessandro, 255ª Sq, 105º Gr, 46º St BT   38

Casini, Cap Gabriele, 252ª Sq, 104º Gr, 46º St BT   23

Castellani, Ten Col Gori, 106º Gr, 47º St BT   23, 183

Catalano, Ten Mario, 34º Gr Aut BT   142

Catamaro, 1º Av RT Gino, 236ª Sq, 96º Gr Aut B a'T   56

Cattaneo, Vice Adm Carlo, 1st Cruiser Division   153

Ceccacci, Cap Dario, 191ª Sq, 86º Gr, 35º St BM/BT   23

Cenni, Cap Giuseppe, 239ª Sq, 97º Gr Aut B a'T   *119*, 125

Chiappa, Serg Domenico, 162ª Sq Aut CT   145

Ciano, Ten Col Count Galeazzo, 105º Gr, 46º St BT and Foreign Minister   12, 22, 169

Ciano, Countess   111

Ciarlo, Ten Dino, 394ª Sq, 160º Gr Aut Ct   12

Cimicchi, Cap Giuseppe, 281ª Sq, 132º Gr Aut AS   147, 148

Clerici, Sottot Lorenzo, 365ª Sq, 150º Gr Aut CT   20

Cobolli, Gigli, Sottot Nicolo, 355ª Sq, 24º Gr Aut CT   101, 102, *126*

Corsini, Ten Luciano, 162ª Sq Aut CT   147

Corsini, Cap Luigi, 364ª Sq. 150º Gr Aut CT   59, 116

Cozzi, Ten Col Renzo, 72º Gr Aut OA   22

Crabbia, Serg Antonio, 160º Gr Aut CT   77

Crainz, Ten Edoardo, 160º Gr Aut CT   56, 77

Criscioni, Cap Francesco, 120ª Sq, 72º Gr Aut OA   22

Crotti, Cap Mario, 39ª Sq, 72º Gr OA   *19*

Cuomo, Cap Ubaldo, 210ª Sq, 50º Gr Aut BT   23

Curti, Sottot Federico, 92º Gr, 39º St BT   164

D'Ajello, Cap Giovanni, 163ª Sq Aut CT   128

Della Costa, Sottot Giovanni, 260ª Sq, 106º Gr, 47º St BT   206

Della Costanza, Sottot Romeo, 393ª Sq, 160º Gr Aut CT   35

Dell'Olio, Ten Nicola, 201ª Sq, 92º Gr, 39º St BT   128

Del Manno, Serg Luigi, 42ª Sq, 72º Gr Aut OA   46

De Prato, Cap Tullio, 150ª Sq, 2º Gr Aut CT   24

De Regis, Sottot Luigi, 238ª Sq, 96º Gr Aut B a'T   78

De Salvia, Serg Marcello, 354ª Sq, 24º Gr Aut CT   101, 102, *126*

De Vito, Sottot Vasc Alessio, X Flottiglia MAS   153

Di Angelis, Ten Mario, 262ª Sq, 107º Gr, 47º St BT   247

Di Carlo, Serg Magg Nicola, 238ª Sq, 97º Gr Aut B a'T   80

Di Robilant, Sottot Maurizio Nicolis, 393ª Sq, 160º Gr Aut CT   37, 61

424

Donadio, Magg Giuseppe, 101° Gr Aut B a'T 225

Drago, Sottot Ugo, 393ª Sq, 160° Gr Aut CT 35, 83

Erasi, Cap Massimiliano, 278ª Sq, 132° Gr Aut AS 130

Ercolani, Cap Ercolano, 96° Gr Aut B a'T 24

Ermo, Ten Col Erminio, 55° Gr, 37° St BT 23

Facchini, Serg Domenico, 365ª Sq, 150° Gr Aut CT 20

Faggioni, Ten Vasc Luigi, X Flottiglia MAS 153

Falcone, Cap Guglielmo, 51ª Sq, 39° Gr, 38° St BT 22

Faltoni, Sottot Egidio, 150° Gr Aut CT 92

Faltoni, Sottot Pasquale, 150° Gr Aut CT 65

Farina, Magg Armando, 372ª Sq Aut CT 24

Fava, Serg Bruno, 24° Gr Aut CT 106

Fiacchino, Cap Elio, 151ª Sq. 2° Gr Aut CT 24

Fissore, Sottot Giuliano, 154° Gr Aut CT 62

Foschini, Cap Ettore, 355ª Sq, 24° Gr Aut CT 22, 37, 96

Fossetta, Magg Marcello, 7° Gr, 54° St CT 183

Franchino, Ten Walter, 154° Gr Aut CT 32

Francinetti, Sottot Raoul, 160° Gr Aut CT 77, 95, *96*

Frascadore, Ten Mario, 394ª Sq, 160° Gr Aut CT 11, 12, 56

Fuchs, Cap 72° Gr Aut OA 46

Fusco, Ten Alfredo 361ª Sq, 154° Gr Aut CT 88, *126*

Gabella, Ten Giulio, 172ª Sq RST 147

Gambetta, Serg, 154° Gr Aut CT 88

Gardella, Cap, 72° Gr Aut OA 46

Gatti, Ten Francesco, 365ª Sq, 150° Gr Aut CT 67

Gioia, Cap Pietro, 277ª Sq, 116° Gr, 37° St BT 23

Giordanino, Ten Enrico, 24° Gr Aut CT 120

Giordano, Cap Francesco, 203ª Sq, 40° Gr, 38° St BT 22

Gismondi, Serg Magg Adrio, 154° Gr Aut CT 32

Giudici, Ten Eber, 160° Gr Aut CT 56

Graffer, Cap Giorgio, 365ª Sq, 150° Gr Aut CT 18, 22, 44, 45, *126*

Grande, Col Enrico, 35° St BM/BT 23, 183

Grandinetti, Ten Col Carlo Magno, 4° St CT 183

Grassini, Mar Attilio, 254ª Sq, 105° Gr, 46° St BT 36

Graziani, Gen, GOC Libya 4, 70

Guza, Ten Rodolfo, 281ª Sq, 132° Gr Aut AS 165

Iachino, Adm Angelo, CinC Italian Fleet 154, 155

Jannello, Sottot Pietro, 363ª Sq, 160° Gr Aut CT 34

La Carrubba, Magg Vincenzo, 8° Gr Aut CT 182

La Cava, Cap Giuseppe, 211ª Sq, 50° Gr Aut BT 23

La Ferla, Mar Guido, 22° Gr Aut CT 106

Larker, Cap Mario, 239ª Sq, 97° Gr Aut B a'T *119*, 119, 125

Laurenzi, Sottot Alessandro, 172ª Sq RST 147

Lauri Filzi, Magg Pietro, 37° Gr, 18° St BT 184

Legnani, Vice Adm Antonio, 8th Cruiser Division 154

Leoni, Serg, 72° Gr Aut OA 46

Leotta, Ten Col Eugenio, 24° Gr Aut CT 22, 77, 79

Lojacono, Mar Francesco, 114ª Sq OA 218

Locatelli, Ten Luigi, 22° Gr Aut CT 113

Loddo, Sottot Ernani, 365ª Sa, 150° Gr Aut CT 70

Longo, Sottot Mario, 211ª Sq, 50° Gr Aut BT 38

Longo, Gen D A Ulisse, Aeronautica dell'Egeo 24

Lucchetta, Serg Magg Ermes, 24° Gr Aut CT 106

Ludovico, Col Domenico, 38° St BT 11, 22, 54

Lui, Mar Marcello, 394ª Sq, 160° Gr Aut CT 12

Magaldi, Cap Nicola, 364ª Sq, 150° Gr Aut CT 22, 32, 43, *126*

Maggi, Cap Aldo, 261ª Sq, 106° Gr, 47° St BT 23

Maionica, Serg Romano, 150° Gr Aut CT 76

Malvezzi, Ten Ferdinando, 236ª Sq, 96° Gr Aut B a'T 24

Mandolesi, Ser Magg Maurizio, 160° Gr Aut CT 114

Manetti, Serg Augusto,393ª Sq, 160° Gr Aut CT 35

Marini, Magg Luigi, 86° Gr, 35° St BM/BT 23

Mariotti, Cap Luigi, 363ª Sq, 150° Gr Aut CT 18, 22, 79

Martinelli, Sottot Francesco, 606ª Sq 40

Mastragostino, Magg Angelo, 393ª Sq, 160° Gr Aut CT/154° Gr Aut CT 12, 18, 23, 53, 86

Matteuzzi, Ten Omero, 50° Gr Aut BT 17, *17*

Mazza, Ten Calogero, 254ª Sq, 105° Gr, 46° St BT 36

Mencarelli, Serg Magg Giovanni, 72° Gr Aut OA 98

Mencaraglia, Cap Renzo, 42ª Sq, 72° Gr Aut OA 22

Meneghel, Ten Attilio, 355ª Sq, 24° Gr Aut CT 39

Miazzo, Serg Ferruccio, 22° Gr Aut CT 113

Micheli, Serg Enrico, 363ª Sq, 150° Gr Aut CT 61

Mignani, Serg Corrado, 365ª Sq, 150° Gr Aut CT 44

Milano, Ten Michele, 42ª Sq, 72° Gr Aut OA 46

Minella, Serg Luca, 160° Gr Aut CT 38

Minio Paullo, Ten Col Marco 9° Gr, 4° St CT 183

Molinari, Magg Oscar, 160° Gr Aut CT 43, 48 55, 56, 121

Morandini, Sottot Maurizio, 260ª Sq, 106° Gr, 47° St BT 124

Morbidelli, Magg Giovanni, 95° Gr 35° St BM/BT 23, 183

Morelli, Cap Luigi, 394ª Sq, 160° Gr Aut CT 22

Moretti, Sottot Giorgio, 24° Gr Aut CT 48, 120

Morri, Serg Aristodemo, 163ª Sq Aut CT 128

Mosca, Magg, 38° St BT 20

Moscatelli, Ten Col Antonio, 97ª Gr Aut Ba'T 183

Munich, Serg Magg Aurelio, 160° Gr Aut CT 77

Mussolini, Cav Benito, Dictator 2, 3, 4, 5, 12, 51, *81*, 103, 111, 118, 177

Mussolini, Cap Bruno, 260ª Sq, 106° Gr, 47° St BT 13, 23, 125

Mussolini, Ten Vittorio, 47° St BT 13

Muti, Ten Col Ettore, 41° Gr Aut BT 24

Negri, Serg, 364ª Sq, 150° Gr Aut CT 43

Ortolan, Ten Col Raffaele, 50° Gr Aut BT 23

Pacini, Serg Achille, 364ª Sq, 150° Gr Aut CT 44

Pacini, Serg Tommaso, 355ª Sq, 24° Gr Aut CT 74

Pagliocchini, Ten Col Roberto, 43° Gr, 13° St BT 183

Pallara, Sottot Vincenzo, 262ª Sq, 107° Gr, 47° St BT 19

Pancera, Ten Domenico, 24° Gr Aut CT 41

Pani, Sottot Enrico, 371ª Sq, 150° Gr Aut CT 118

Panunzi, Ten Col Amato, 40° Gr, 38° St BT 22

Paradisi, Ten Col Amedeo, 107° Gr, 47° St BT 23, 183

Pasqualotto, Sottot Beniamino, 50° Gr Aut BT 17

Pecile, Serg Guido, 154° Gr Aut CT 56

Penna, Serg Magg Francesco, 160° Gr Aut CT 56

Penna, Sottot Paolo, 150° Gr Aut CT 49

Pirchio, Serg Vittorio, 393ª Sq, 160° Gr Aut CT 35

Pirino, Col Antonio, 13° St BT 182

Piva, Serg Emilio, 154° Gr Aut CT 56

Porta, Ten Col Giorgio, 39° Gr, 38° St BT/104° Gr, 46° St BT 23, 183

Prasca, Gen Visconti, GOC Albania 21

Pratesi, Cap G Piero, 25ª Sq, 72° Gr Aut OA 22

Pratelli, Ten Col Rolando, 150° Gr Aut CT 14, 22, 49

Pritoni, Cap Severo, 231ª Sq, 95° Gr, 35° St BM/BT 24

Quattrociocchi, Cap Bernardo, 263ª Sq, 107° Gr, 47° St BT 23

Ranza, Gen S A Ferruccio, Comando Aeronautica dell' Albania 22

Ratticchieri, Serg Walter, 393ª Sq, 160° Gr Aut CT 11, 35, 37, 39

Rignani, Cap Ezio, 230ª Sq, 95° St BM/BT 23

Ritegni, Serg Italo, 150° Gr Aut CT 34

Rivalta, Magg Gabriele, 25° Gr Aut BT 184

Rocca, Ten Francesco, 354ª Sq, 24° Gr Aut CT 101

Romagnoli, Ten Col Carlo, 10° Gr, 4° St CT 183

Rovetta, Ten, 150° Gr Aut CT 76

Ruggero, Sottot Francesco, 202ª Sq, 39° Gr, 38° St BT 16

Sacchetti, Ten Giorgio, 281ª Sq, 132° Gr Aut AS 151

Salvadori, Mar Giuseppe, 363ª Sq, 150° Gr Aut CT 39

Sandon, Cap Carlo, 276ª Sq, 116° Gr, 37° St BT 23

Sansonetti, Vice Adm Luigi, 3rd Cruiser Division 153

Sant'Andrea, Cap Vincenzo, 356ª Sq, 21° Gr Aut CT 182

Santinoni, Ten Giovanni, 237ª Sq, 96° Gr Aut Ba'T 24

Sartirana, Cap Leopoldo, 162ª Sq Aut CT 143

Savino, Serg Pasquale, 24° Gr Aut CT 45

Scagliari, Serg Mario, 160° Gr Aut CT   34

Scarlata, Ten Col Giuseppe, 116° Gr, 37° St BT   23, 183

Scaroni, Cap Ferruccio, 220ᵃ Sq, 55° Gr, 37° St BT   24

Scarpetta, Cap Giuseppe, 395ᵃ Sq, 154° Gr Aut CT   22, 34, 82

Scarpini, Mar Elio, 236ᵃ Sq, 96° Gr Aut Ba'T   20, 56

Senatore, Cap Domenico, 190ᵃ Sq, 86° Gr, 35° St BM/BT   23

Simini, Magg Guido, 39° Gr, 38° St BT   22

Soddu, Gen, GOC Albania   21

Spallacci, Serg Luigi, 355ᵃ Sq, 24° Gr Aut CT   106, *126*

Stevanato, 1° Av Mot Luigi, 236ᵃ Sq, 96° Gr Aut Ba'T   56

Susinno, Cap Carlo, 255ᵃ Sq, 105° Gr, 46° St BT   22

Tade, Col Scipione, 47° St BT   23

Tarantini, Serg Magg Luciano, 160° Gr Aut CT   39, 48, 77

Tedeschi, Sottot Vasc Tullio, X Flottiglia MAS   153

Tedesco, Sottot Filippo, 223ᵃ Sq, 56° Gr, 39° St BT   129

Tellini, Gen, President of International Commission   3, 4

Tessari, Col Arrigo, Cdr Fighters in Greece   14

Testerini, Cap Torquato, 393ᵃ Sq, 160° Gr Aut CT   22, 35, 38, 56

Toccolini, Gen D A Tullio, Cdr 2ᵃ Squadra Aerea   183

Torroni, Sottot Enzo, 22° Gr Aut CT   112

Traini, Sottot Italo, 160° Gr aut CT   95

Travaglini, Cap Edmondo, 152ᵃ Sq, 2° Gr CT/150° Gr Aut CT   24, 76

Trevisi, Sottot Ernesto, 393ᵃ Sq, 160° Gr Aut CT   34, 35, *126*

Triolo, Ten Alberto, 150° Gr Aut CT   49

Tufano, Serg Domenico, 393ᵃ Sq, 160° Gr Aut CT   37, 56

Vaghi, Sottot Edgardo, 22° Gr Aut CT   113

Valente, Magg Cesare, 24° Gr Aut CT   106

Valenti, Cap Ettore, 202ᵃ Sq, 40° Gr, 38° St BT   22

Vannini, Serg Magg Marino, 22° Gr Aut CT   106

Vescia, Serg, 72° Gr Aut OA   46

Victor Emmanuel, King, King of Italy   4

Viola, Serg Magg Natale, 363ᵃ Sq, 160° Gr Aut CT   39

Vitali, Cap Aldo, 254ᵃ Sq. 105° Gr, 46° St BT   22

Vivarelli, Ten Giovanni, 104° Gr, 46° St BT   53

Zanni, Ten Col Fernando, 160° Gr Aut CT   11, 22

Zoli, Serg Arrigo, 154° Gr Aut CT   52, 57, 60

Zotti, Serg Arrigo, 150° Gr Aut CT   45

Germans:

Albrecht, Uffz Georg, I/LG 1   156

Alt, Uffz, I/LG 1   280

Altmann, Hpt Gustav, I/Assault Regt, XI Flgkps   347

Arnoldy, Lt Jacob, 4/JG 77   *250*, 251

Baagoe, Oblt Sophus, 5/ZG 26   *209*, 271, 323

Banke, Oblt Christian, 9/StG 2   244

Bauer, Uffz Erwin, 2/ZG 26   329

Baumann, Gefr Hans, I/LG 1   269

Baumgartner, Gefr Heinrich, I/LG 1   269

Becker, Oblt Arno, 8/JG 27   231, 232

Becker, Ofw Daniel, 5/ZG 26   323

Beeger, Oblt Horst, I/LG 1   257

Beisswenger, Lt Hans, 6/JG 54   213

Benke, Uffz Helmut, I/LG 1   269

Biewendt, Uffz Helmut, KGrzbV 101   351

Billerbeck, Lt Ralf, KGrzbV 60   377

Blanke, Lt Gert, I/LG 1   242

Bob, Oblt Hans-Ekkehard, 9/JG 54   199, *209*, 217

Böcker, Ofw Heinrich, II/LG 1   357

Bodekuhl, Maj, II/KGzbV 172   337

Borcher, Fw Hans, II/KG 4   330

Borchert, Uffz Fritz, III/JG 77   267

Börngen, Lt Ernst, II/JG 27   252

Bornschein, Uffz Berthold, 4/LG 1   149

Braun, Maj, III/FJR 1   344

Bromba, Gefr Hans, 4/ZG 26   323

Brücker, Hpt Heinrich, III/StG 2   337, 351, 356

Brüdern, Lt Joachim, KG 2   270

Bruns, Fw Ewald, I(H)/23   195

Buchholz, Oberst, KGzbV 3   337

Caplan, Uffz, Stab/JG 27   278

Chlebowitz, Fw Ernst, 2(F)/123   394

Christoph, Prinz of Hesse   156

Clausen, Oblt Erwin, I(J)/LG 2   181

Deuschle, Oblt Heinz, II/JG 77   202

Deutsch, Maj, KGrzbV 40   337, 354

Dilley, Oblt Bruno, 3/StG 1   235

Dinort, Oberst Oskar, StG 2   337

Dreyer, Uffz Fritz, 2(F)/123   232

Dreyer, Maj, 2/KG 2   211

Düring, Uffz, I/StG 2   331

Dürkheim, Lt Max Graf von, I/KG 2   350

428

431

434

2 PRU   49, 141, 143, *144*, 313, 314, 320, 387
1 (Free French) Flight   382
2 (Free French) Flight   382
1430 Flight (Formerly 430 Flight)   114, 304, 320, 321, 323, 391, 398
102 Maintenance Unit   363
70 OTU   114
220 AMES, Heraklion   313, 360, 391
252 AMES, Maleme   134, 135, 313, 353
BOAC (National Airline)   288, 310

Fleet Air Arm

800 X Squadron   332
803 Squadron   136, 150, 151, 154, 156, 165, 167, 278, 307, 314, 316, 317, 377, 378
805 Squadron   *135*, 136, 137, 139–143, 145–148, 150, 151, 154, 166, 185, 301, 304, 307, 316, 317, 318, 320, 321, 325–328, 330, 332, 341, 345, 346, 349, *363*, 368, *369*, 378
806 Squadron   128, 129, *131*, 136, *137*, 137, 142, 143, 150, 154, 165, 166, 167, 278, 279, 307, 308,

316–319, 363, 377, 378, 379, 392, 399, 401, 411
813 Squadron   128, *129*
815 Squadron   109–115, 118, 120, 126, 128, 130, 132–135, 141, 144, 145, 146, 154, 157, 160, 161, 162, 185, 240, 248, 259, 273, 278, 288, 295, 309, 326, 345
819 Squadron   128, 131
824 Squadron   128
826 Squadron   139, 149, 154, 156, 160, 161, 166, 377
829 Squadron   145, 149, 154, 157, 159, 160, 161, 166, 377
830 Squadron   166, 319
HMS Eagle Fighter Flight   136, 319, 379
Suda Bay Fulmar Flight   *135*, 135, 139
Suda Bay Walrus Flight   131, 141

Royal Egyptian Air Force: 99, 363
2 Squadron   363
5 Squadron   363

Elleniki Vassiliki Aeroporia (EVA) – Royal Hellenic Air Force

Mire Dioxes (Fighter Squadrons)   27
  21 Mira   13, 16, 18, 20, 27, *29*, 36, 38, 40, 48, 56, 60, 67, *68*, 68, 72, 77, 79, 84, 91, 107, 123, 124, 185, 232, 244, 252
  22 Mira   *13*, 13, 17, *17*, 19, 27, *29*, 36, 38, 48, 60, 63, 66, 67, 68, 72, 76, 77, 86, 185, 232, 244, 252
  23 Mira   20, 27, 29, 35, 38, 48, 60, 63, 68, 72, 76, 77, 79, 84, 91, 185, 245, 252, 264, *287*
  24 Mira   27, 29, 68, *69*, 78, 186, 232, 239
Mire Vomvardismon (Bomber Squadrons)   27
  31 Mira   *15*, 27, 56, 60, 79, 107, 186
  32 Mira   13, *14*, *18*, 27, 35, 41, 61, 78, 107, 185

  33 Mira   *16*, 27, 37, *37*, 107, 185
Mire Stratiotkis Synergassias (Ground Support Squadrons)   2, 27
  1 Mira   27
  2 Mira   12, 18, 20, 27, 43, 286
  3 Mira   2, *8*, 11, 27, 40, 66, 177
  4 Mira   27, 35, 61
Mire Naftikis Synergassias (Naval Co-operation Squadrons)   27
  11 Mira   27, 186, 247
  12 Mira   *3*, *20*, 27, *45*, 186, 303
  13 Mira   *5*, 27, 78, 99, 116, 185, 288
EEES (National Airline)   310

Jugoslovensko Kraljevsko Ratno Vazduhoplovsto (JKRV) – Royal Yugoslav Air Force:

  11 Independent (LR Recce) Grupa: 187, 203, 211, 213, 214, 219, 220, 223
    701 Eskadrila VZ   187
    21 Eskadrila   187
    22 Eskadrila   187
    81 Independent (Bomber) Grupa: 187, 206, *206*, 213, 215, 218, 219, 220, 260
      261 Eskadrila   187
      262 Eskadrila   187
      Independent Fighter Eskadrila   187, 205, *207*, *212*, 213, 223, 225
1st Lovacka Vazduhoplovna Brigada: 187
(1st Fighter Air Brigade)
    702 Eskadrila VZ   187
  2nd Fighter Puk   175, 187, 198, 200, 211, 213,

215, 223
  31 Grupa: 187, 199, 200, 211, 215, 216, 218
    101 Eskadrila   187, 199
    141 Eskadrila   187
  52 Grupa: 187, 198, 213, 216, 219
    163 Eskadrila   187, 198, 214, 219, 223
    164 Eskadrila   187, 214, 219
  6th Fighter Puk   175, 178, 188, 196, 200, 210, 215, 216, 219, 221, 222, 223
  32 Grupa: 188, 196–200, 210, 211
    103 Eskadrila   188, 197
    104 Eskadrila   188, 197
    142 Eskadrila   188, 197, 199
  51 Grupa: 177, 178, *178*, 188, 196–199, 210, 211

439

202ª Squadriglia 16, 22, 183
203ª Squadriglia 22, 183
46° Stormo BT 23, 38, 52
105° Gruppo Aut BT 11, 12, 13, *15*, 22, 23, 37, 38, 41, 68, 92, 106, 183
   254ª Squadriglia 22, 36, *41*, 183
   255ª Squadriglia 22, 38, 183
104° Gruppo Aut BT *10*, 23, 41, 53, 77, 78, 79, 95, 112, 183, 242
   252ª Squadriglia 23, 53, 183
   253ª Squadriglia *10*, 23, 53, *53*, 183

5° Gruppo OA 68
   31ª Squadriglia 68, 182
   39ª Squadriglia *19*, *47*, 68, 182
22° Gruppo Aut CT 104, 106, 112, 113, 182, 248
   359ª Squadriglia 104
   362ª Squadriglia 104
   369ª Squadriglia 104, 106
24° Gruppo CT 15, 19, 22, 36, *36*, 38, 39, 41, 43, 45, 48, 54, 77, 81, 94, 95, 100, 101, *102*, 106, 118, 120
   354ª Squadriglia 22, 101, *102*
   355ª Squadriglia 22, *36*, 39, 74, 101
   361ª Squadriglia 22, 86, 88
72° Gruppo Aut OA 22, 37, 39, 46, 67, 97, 114, 115
   25ª Squadriglia 22, 41, 182
   42ª Squadriglia 22, 46, 182
120ª Squadriglia 22, 41, 182
101° Gruppo Aut B a'T 104, 108, 182, 222, 225, 227
   208ª Squadriglia 108, 164, 182, 225
   238ª Squadriglia 77, 80, 104, 182, 222, 227
150° Gruppo Aut CT *6*, 14, 22, 34, 38, 41, 43–46, 49, 50, 52, 55, 56, 59, 64, 67, 70, 76, 79, 80, 83, 91, 104, 120, 182, 225, 228, 264
   363ª Squadriglia *6*, 14, 18, 22, 34, 39, 41, 61
   364ª Squadriglia 14, 22, 41, 43, 50, 92, 114
   365ª Squadriglia 14, 18, 20, 22, 41, 44, 411
   371ª Squadriglia 104, 118
154° Gruppo Aut CT 23, 32, 38, 40, 41, 42, 49, 52, 56, 57, 60, 62, 64, 67, 68, 70, *71*, 79, 82, 86, *88*, 91, 120, 123, 182
160° Gruppo Aut CT 2, 7, 7, 11, 12, 18, 22, 23, 34, 38, 39, 40, 41, 43, 48, 55, 56, 67, 77, 94,

95, 96, 98, 112, 113, 115, 116, 121, 182, 225
   393ª Squadriglia 2, 7, 11, 18, 22, 35, 37, 39, 41
   394ª squadriglia 7, 7, 11, 12, 22, 32, 41, 68, *96*
   395ª Squadriglia 7, 22, 23, 86, 88, *88*, 114, 411

   35ª Squadriglia 182
   87ª Squadriglia 182
   114ª Squadriglia 104, 182, 218
   606ª Squadriglia 40
Comando 4ª Zona Aerea Territoriale (4ª ZAT) 9, 10, 11, 16, 19, 20, 23, 24, 51, 68
35° Stormo BM/BT 16, 23, 32, 38, 60, 70, *73*, 73, 81, *81*, 124, 164, 183, 207, 244
   86° Gruppo BM/BT 24, 38, 60, 70, *73*, 89, 115, 183, 239
   190ª Squadriglia 23, 60, 183
   191ª Squadriglia 23, *73*, *90*, 183
95° Gruppo BM/BT 23, 70, *81*, 183, 339
   230ª Squadriglia 23, 183
   231ª Squadriglia 23, *81*, 183, 339
37° Stormo BT 11, 16, 23, 61, *61*, 72, 73, 76, 79, 82, 92, 106, 116, 119, 183
   55° Gruppo BT 23, 183
   220ª Squadriglia 23, 183
   221ª Squadriglia 23, 183
116° Gruppo BT 23, *61*, 183
   276ª Squadriglia 23, *61*, 183
   277ª Squadriglia 23, 183
47° Stormo BT 11, 12, 16, 19, 23, 38, 45, 55, 56, 60, 70, 78, 79, 81, 83, 89, 98, 99, 113, 114 116, 118, 124, 125, 164, 183, *274*
   106° Gruppo BT 23, 124, 193, *274*
   260ª Squadriglia 13, 23, 124, 183, 206
   261ª Squadriglia 23, 124, 183, 206, *274*
107° Gruppo BT 24, 183, *274*
   262ª Squadriglia 19, 23, 183, 247
   263ª Squadriglia 13, 23, 183, 206, *274*

2° Gruppo Aut CT 24, 51
   150ª Squadriglia 24
   151ª Squadriglia 24
   152ª Squadriglia 24
41° Gruppo BT 4, 24, 68, 125, 339, 390
   204ª Squadriglia 24, 339
   205ª Squadriglia 24, 339
42° Gruppo BT 51
50° Gruppo Aut BT 17, *17*, 20, 24, 72, 78,

98, 99, 106, 124, 164, 183, *204*, 339, 356
    210ª Squadriglia *17*, 23, 183, *204*, 339
211ª Squadriglia 17, 23, 38, 183, 339
  96º Gruppo B a'T 16, 20, 24, 36, 51, 52, 56, *56*, 70
    236ª Squadriglia 24
    237ª Squadriglia 24
4ª Squadra Aerea (formerly 4ª ZAT) 68, 72, 103, 104, 182, 185, 205, 206
  13º Stormo BT *58*, 183
    11º Gruppo BT 183
      1ª Squadriglia 183
      4ª Squadriglia 183
    43º Gruppo BT *58*, 183
      3ª Squadriglia *58*, 183
      5ª Squadriglia 183
  35º Stormo BM/BT (see 4ª ZAT)
    86º Gruppo BM/BT
      190ª Squadriglia
      191ª Squadriglia
    95º Gruppo BM
      230ª Squadriglia
      231ª Squadriglia
  37º Stormo BT
    55º Gruppo BT
      220ª Squadriglia
      221ª Squadriglia
  38º Stormo BT
    39º Gruppo BT
      51ª Squadriglia
      69ª Squadriglia
    40º Gruppo BT
      202ª Squadriglia
      203ª Squadriglia
  47º Stormo BT
    106º Gruppo BT
      260ª Squadriglia
      261ª Squadriglia
    107ª Gruppo BT
      262ª Squadriglia
      263ª Squadriglia

  8º Gruppo Aut CT 182
    92ª Squadriglia 182
    93ª Squadriglia 182
    94ª Squadriglia 182
  50º Gruppo Aut BT (see 4ª ZAT)
    210ª Squadriglia
    211ª Squadriglia
  97º Gruppo B a'T 51, *80*, 80, 81, *119*, 183, 207
    209ª Squadriglia *80*, 125
    239ª Squadriglia 80, *119*, 119, 125, 164, 207

153º Gruppo Aut CT *118*, 118, *121*, 121, 183, 242, 244
  372ª Squadriglia Aut CT 24, *121*, 183
  373ª Squadriglia 51, *118*, 118, 183
  374ª Squadriglia 51, 183
  370ª Squadriglia Aut CT 51, 183
  356ª Squadriglia 183
104º Gruppo Aut BT (see Comando Aeronautica Albania)
  252ª Squadriglia
  253ª Squadriglia
105º Gruppo Aut BT
  254ª Squadriglia
  255ª Squadriglia

Aeronautica Dell'Egeo: 9, 25, 339
  30º Stormo BT 24, 128, 165, 339
    56º Gruppo BT 138
    222ª Squadriglia 24
    223ª Squadriglia 24, 129
  92º Gruppo BT 25, 129, 135, 142, 164, 339
    200ª Squadriglia 25, 339
    201ª Squadriglia 25, 339
  34º Gruppo Aut BT 25, 130, 134, 141, 142, 148, 151, 160, 164
    67ª Squadriglia 25
    68ª Squadriglia 25

    172ª Squadriglia RT 146, 147, 154, 339
    279ª Squadriglia AS *148*
    147ª Squadriglia RM 25
    185ª Squadriglia RM 25
    Sezione Soccorso 25, 339
    161ª Squadriglia Aut CM 25, 339
    162ª Squadriglia Aut CT 25, 130, 131, *132*, 142, 143, 144, 147, 339
    163ª Squadriglia Aut CT 25, 128, *129*, 138, *338*, 339
2ª Squadra Aerea: 184, 185, 207, 215, 218
  4º Stormo CT 184
    9º Gruppo CT 184
      73ª Squadriglia 104, 184
      96ª Squadriglia 184
      97ª Squadriglia 184
    10º Gruppo CT 184
      84ª Squadriglia 184
      90ª Squadriglia 184
      91ª Squadriglia 184
  54º Stormo CT 184
    7º Gruppo CT 184
      76ª Squadriglia 184
      86ª Squadriglia 184
      98ª Squadriglia 184

16° Gruppo CT 184
  167ª Squadriglia 184
  169ª Squadriglia 184
18° Stormo BT 184, *203*
31° Gruppo BT 184
  65ª Squadriglia 184
  66ª Squadriglia 184
37° Gruppo BT *203*, 207
  47ª Squadriglia 184
  48ª Squadriglia 184, 203

25° Gruppo Aut BT 184
  8ª Squadriglia 184
  9ª Squadriglia 184
99° Gruppo Aut BT 184
  242ª Squadriglia 184

243ª Squadriglia 184
61° Gruppo Aut OA 184
  34ª Squadriglia 184
  36ª Squadriglia 184
63° Gruppo Aut OA 184
  41ª Squadriglia 184
  113ª Squadriglia 184
71° Gruppo Aut oA 185
  38ª Squadriglia 185
  116ª Squadriglia 185
  128ª Squadriglia 185
5ª Squadra Aerea: 9, 130
281ª Squadriglia Aut AS 147, 151, 157, 164, 165, 339
16° Stormo BT 24, 38
53° Stormo CT 15
146ª Squadriglia RM *33*

Luftwaffe:

Luftflotte 4 172, 180, 195, 201, 210, 215, 216, 219
Fliegerkorps VIII 171, 172, 179, 180, 194, 195, 208, 213–216, 221, 222, 232, 240, 246, 253, 255, 259, 280, 287, 293, 335, 337, 403
Fliegerkorps X 169, 172, 205, 206, 213, 239
Fliegerkorps XI 321, 335, 336, 337, 348, 374, 402, 403
Fliegerführer Arad 180, 196, 203, 210, 216, 222, 224, 225
Fliegerführer Graz 180, 201, 216
Jagdgeschwader 26:
7/JG 26 173, 205, 213
Jagdgeschwader 27:
Stab/JG 27 180, 238, 266, 278
I/JG 27 180
3/JG 27 201, 317
II/JG 27 180, 244, 252, 253, 255, 262, 268, 272, 278, 411
4/JG 27 270
6/JG 27 242, 247
III/JG 27 180
8/JG 27 231
Jagdgeschwader 52:
III/JG 52, 173, 395
Jagdgeschwader 54:
Stab/JG 54 200
II/JG 54 180
4/JG 54 180, 210
5/JG 54 212
6/JG 54 213
III/JG 54 180, 199, 204, 217
9/JG 54 217

Jagdgeschwader 77: 197, 198, 199, 201, 253, 273, 349, 385, 395
Stab/JG 77 180, 195, 198, 252, 259, 265, 280, 394
II/JG 77 180, 195, 198, 199, 201, *250*, 250, 250, 252, 253, 259, 265, 267, 273, 275, 280, 281, 289, 322, 323, 338, 374, 375, 376
4/JG 77 251, 323, *331*, 331, 349, 376
5/JG 77 342, 364, 374, 376
6/JG 77 322, 364, 374, 385
III/JG 77 180, 195, 198, 199, 202, 252, 259, 262, 265, 267, *267*, 270, 273, 275, 280, 281, 286, 293, 322, 323, 324, 328, 338, 362, 381, 388, 393
7/JG 77 349
8/JG 77 323, *327*, 328, 357
9/JG 77 260, 263, 293
Zerstörergeschwader 26: *324*, 397
Stab/ZG 26 355, 357
I/ZG 26 180, 199, 200, 285, 297, 301, 328, 329, 337, 357, 360, 364
2/ZG 26 329, 371, 399
3/ZG 26 297
II/ZG 26 180, 181, 194, 211, *264*, 265, 269, 271, 286, 302, 320, 323, 327, 328, 329, 337, 351, 355, 360, 373, 389
4/ZG 26 272, 323, 328, 332, 349, 351
5/ZG 26 271, 272, 274, 323, 355
6/ZG 26 272, 286, 330
III/ZG 26 173, 206, *206*, 207, 213
Zerstörergeschwader 76: 397
II/ZG 76 329, 338, 359, 368, 389, 394
Lehrgeschwader 2: 179
Stab(J)/LG 2 383